Distance Education Environments and Emerging Software Systems:

New Technologies

Qun Jin
Waseda University, Japan

Information Science
REFERENCE

Senior Editorial Director:	Kristin Klinger
Director of Book Publications:	Julia Mosemann
Editorial Director:	Lindsay Johnston
Acquisitions Editor:	Erika Carter
Development Editor:	Myla Harty
Production Editor:	Sean Woznicki
Typesetters:	Mike Brehm, Keith Glazewski, Natalie Pronio, Jennifer Romanchak
Print Coordinator:	Jamie Snavely
Cover Design:	Nick Newcomer

Published in the United States of America by
Information Science Reference (an imprint of IGI Global)
701 E. Chocolate Avenue
Hershey PA 17033
Tel: 717-533-8845
Fax: 717-533-8661
E-mail: cust@igi-global.com
Web site: http://www.igi-global.com/reference

Library of Congress Cataloging-in-Publication Data

Distance education environments and emerging software systems: new
technologies / Qun Jin, editor.
      p. cm.
  Includes bibliographical references and index.
  Summary: "This book focuses on the discussions of computational methods,
algorithms implemented prototype systems, and applications of open and
distance learning"--Provided by publisher.
  ISBN 978-1-60960-539-1 (hardcover) -- ISBN 978-1-60960-540-7 (ebook) 1.
Distance education--Computer-assisted instruction. 2. Distance education--
Technological innovations. I. Jin, Q. (Qun), 1962-
  LC5803.C65D543 2011
  378.1'734--dc22
                        2011008157

British Cataloguing in Publication Data
A Cataloguing in Publication record for this book is available from the British Library.

All work contributed to this book is new, previously-unpublished material. The views expressed in this book are those of the authors, but not necessarily of the publisher.

Table of Contents

Section 1
New Frameworks and Architectures

Section 3
Development of Practical Systems

Section 4
Empirical Study: Evaluation and Assessment

Detailed Table of Contents

Section 1
New Frameworks and Architectures

Chapter 1

This chapter is dedicated to Computer-Supported Collaborative Learning (CSCL) employing dynamic groups, where at different stages students work independently, interact with each other in pairs, and conduct joint work in larger groups with varying numbers of participants. A novel Dynamic Group Environment for Collaborative Learning (DGE/CL) that supports students in making informed and intelligent choices about how, when, and with whom to collaborate is introduced. A face-to-face collaborative scenario, where all students are in the same room and can move freely around and interact with each other while using digitally enhanced printed materials with direct point-and-click functionality is considered. Flexible and efficient support for dynamic group management is ensured through the adopted Cluster Pattern Interface (CLUSPI) technology, which, while preserving the original touch-and-feel of printed educational materials, supports additional affordances and allows employment of new, non-traditional paper-based interactions. Possibilities for DGE/CL enhancements with specialized surface code readers and laser-based digital surface encoding being developed by the authors are outlined and references to recent projects are given.

Innovations in network and information technology have transformed traditional classroom lectures into new approaches that have given universities the opportunity to create a virtual laboratory. However, there is no systematic framework in existing approaches for the development of virtual laboratories. Further, developing a virtual laboratory from scratch is time consuming and costly. This paper proposes a systematic framework to classify the activities between learners and instructors in the laboratory and to design the mobile agent-based virtual laboratory by wrapping the existing CAI tools without knowing the source code. Using the existing CAI tools can reduce the time and cost in constructing a virtual laboratory. The framework consists of three parts: mobile agent execution environment, mobile agent and learning platform. Moreover, various mobile agent design patterns are provided for users to design and implement virtual laboratories. This framework of patterns could make mobile agent based virtual laboratories easier to design and understand. The authors' framework has the following merits: adaptability, cost-effectiveness and collaboration. Their framework has demonstrated its feasibility in several applications, including digital circuit, language learning and digital signal processing laboratories.

Chapter 3

    Hui-Chun Chu, National University of Tainan, Taiwan
    Gwo-Jen Hwang, National University of Tainan, Taiwan
    Pei-Jin Tsai, National Chiao Tung University, Taiwan
    Tzu-Chi Yang, National Chi-Nan University, Taiwan

The growing popularity of computer and network technologies has attracted researchers to investigate the strategies and the effects of information technology applied instructions. Previous research has not only demonstrated the benefits of applying information technologies to the learning process, but has also revealed the difficulty of applying them effectively. One of the major difficulties is due to the lack of an easy-to-follow procedure for inexperienced teachers to design course content with proper use of suitable information technologies. In this paper, a model for conducting information technology applied instructions is proposed. The novel approach can assist teachers in designing information technology applied course content based on the features of subject materials and the learning status of the students. An experiment on a Chemistry course in a junior high school was conducted to evaluate the performance of our novel approach. The results of the experiment show that the proposed approach is able to associate subject materials with proper information technologies, which is helpful to teachers who have limited experience in applying information technologies in their classes.

Chapter 4

    Krzysztof Gierłowski, Gdansk University of Technology, Poland
    Krzysztof Nowicki, Gdansk University of Technology, Poland

In this paper we propose a novel e-learning system, dedicated strictly to knowledge assessment tasks. In its functioning it utilizes web-based technologies, but its design differs radically from currently popular e-learning solutions which rely mostly on thin-client architecture. Our research proved that such architecture, while well suited for didactic content distribution systems is ill-suited for knowledge assessment products. In our design we employed loosely-tied distributed system architecture, strict modularity, test and simulation-based knowledge and skill assessment and an our original communications package called Communication Abstraction Layer (ComAL), specifically designed to support communication functions of e-learning systems in diverse network conditions (including offline environment and content aware networks).The system was tested in production environment on Faculty of Electronics, Telecommunications and Informatics, Technical University of Gdansk with great success, reducing staff workload and increasing efficiency of didactic process. The tests also showed system's versatility in classroom, remote and blended learning environments.

Chapter 5

Sotirios Botsios, Democritus University of Thrace, Greece
Dimitrios A. Georgiou, Democritus University of Thrace, Greece

Adaptation and personalization services in e-learning environments are considered the turning point of recent research efforts, as the "one-size-fits-all" approach has some important drawbacks, from the educational point of view. Adaptive Educational Hypermedia Systems in World Wide Web became a very active research field and the need of standardization arose, as the continually augmenting research efforts lacked interoperability capabilities. This article concentrates and classifies recent research work and notices important points that can lead to an open, modular and generic architecture of a Learning Management System based on widely accepted standards.

Section 2
Promising Support Mechanisms and Technologies

Chapter 6

Qing Li, Zhejiang Normal University, China
Jianmin Zhao, Zhejiang Normal University, China
Xinzhong Zhu, Zhejiang Normal University, China

Supporting efficient data access in the mobile learning environment is becoming a hot research problem in recent years, and the problem becomes tougher when the clients are using light-weight mobile devices such as cell phones whose limited storage space prevents the clients from holding a large cache. A practical solution is to store the cache data at some proxies nearby, so that mobile devices can access the data from these proxies instead of data servers in order to reduce the latency time. However, when mobile devices move freely, the cache data may not enhance the overall performance because it may become too far away for the clients to access. In this article, we propose a statistical caching mechanism which makes use of prior knowledge (statistical data) to predict the pattern of user movement and then replicates/migrates the cache objects among different proxies. We propose a statistical inference based heuristic search algorithm to accommodate dynamic mobile data access in the mobile learning environment. Experimental studies show that, with an acceptable complexity, our algorithm can obtain good performance on caching mobile data.

Gary K. L. Tam, Durham University, UK & Zhejiang Normal University, China

Rynson W. H. Lau, Zhejiang Normal University, China & City University of Hong Kong,
*   Hong Kong*

Jianmin Zhao, Zhejiang Normal University, China

Due to the increasing popularity of 3D graphics in animation and games, applications of 3D geometry models increase dramatically. Despite their growing importance, geometry models are in fact difficult and time consuming to build. A distance learning system for the construction of such models could greatly facilitate students at different time and geographical locations to learn and practice. In such a system, one of the main components is the search engine, which serves as both the data source of teaching materials and also a platform for sharing resources. Though there are many search engines developed for text and for multimedia data, such as images and videos, search engines for geometry models are still in its infant stage. To design a search engine for a distance learning platform, there are still challenges to face. In this paper, we investigate two important issues, namely, feature analysis that affects the general usage of a system and the speed that affects the number of concurrent users. Our focus in this work is on deformable models, i.e., similar models that may have different poses. Our method offers a mechanism to extract, index, match and fast retrieval of stable features from these models.

Stefan Dietze, Open University, UK

Alessio Gugliotta, Open University, UK

John Domingue, Open University, UK

Current E-Learning technologies primarily follow a data and metadata-centric paradigm by providing the learner with composite content containing the learning resources and the learning process description, usually based on specific metadata standards such as ADL SCORM or IMS Learning Design. Due to the design-time binding of learning resources, the actual learning context cannot be considered appropriately at runtime, what limits the reusability and interoperability of learning resources. This paper proposes Situation-driven Learning Processes (SDLP) which describe learning processes semantically from two perspectives: the user perspective considers a learning process as a course of learning goals which lead from an initial situation to a desired situation, whereas the system perspective utilizes Semantic Web Services (SWS) technology to semantically describe necessary resources for each learning goal within a specific learning situation. Consequently, a learning process is composed dynamically and accomplished in terms of SWS goal achievements by automatically allocating learning resources at runtime. Moreover, metadata standard-independent SDLP are mapped to established standards such as ADL SCORM and IMS LD. As a result, dynamic adaptation to specific learning contexts as well as interoperability across different metadata standards and application environments is achieved. To prove the feasibility, a prototypical application is described finally.

    Pi-Shan Hsu, Ching Kuo Institute of Management and Health, Taiwan
    Te-Jeng Chang, National Taiwan Normal University, Taiwan

By improving the imperfections of previous diagnostic techniques the new process phase real-time diagnostic technique is developed to be suitable for an adaptive e-learning instructional process. This new diagnostic technique combines measures of a learner's learning effort with associated performance in order to compare the efficiency of learning condition in a process phase, real-time, and non-interfering instructional process. The learning effort is represented as a visualized learning effort curve which is a user-friendly interface to enhance the decision making of learning path through the effective interaction between instructors and learners in an adaptive e-learning instructional process. The situated experiment was designed based on the new diagnostic technique and applied on 165 university students. In-depth group interview was conducted right after accomplishing the experiment. Results indicate that the learning effort curve is a capable real-time and non-interfering tool to diagnose learning progress in adaptive e-learning process.

    Yang Shuqun, Fujian Normal University, China
    Ding Shuliang, Jiangxi Normal University, China

There is little room for doubt about that cognitive diagnosis has received much attention recently. Computerized adaptive testing (CAT) is adaptive, fair, and efficient, which is suitable to large-scale examination. Traditional cognitive diagnostic test needs quite large number of items, the efficient and tailored CAT could be a remedy for it, so the CAT with cognitive diagnosis (CD-CAT) is prospective. It is more beneficial to the students who live in the developing area without rich source of teaching, and distance education is adopted there. CD is still in its infancy (Leighton at el.2007), and some flaws exist, one of which is that the rows/columns could form a Boolean lattice in Tatsuoka's Q-matrix theory. Formal Concept Analysis (FCA) is proved to be a useful tool for cognitive science. Based on Rule Space Model (RSM) and the Attribute Hierarchy Method (AHM), FCA is applied into CD-CAT and concept lattices are served as the models of CD. The algorithms of constructing Qr matrice and concept lattices for CAT, and the theory and methods of diagnosing examinees and offering the best remedial measure to examinees are discussed in detail. The technology of item bank construction, item selection strategies in CD-CAT and estimation method are considered to design a systemic CD-CAT, which diagnoses examinees on-line and offers remedial measure for examinees in time. The result of Monte Carlo study shows that examinees' knowledge states are well diagnosed and the precision in examinees' abilities estimation is satisfied.

Section 3
Development of Practical Systems

Chapter 11

Ioannis Kazanidis, University of Macedonia, Greece
Maya Satratzemi, University of Macedonia, Greece

Adaptive Educational Hypermedia Systems provide personalized educational content to learners. However most of them do not support the functionality of Learning Management Systems (LMS) and the reusability of their courses is hard work. One the other hand some LMS support SCORM specifications but do not provide adaptive features. This paper presents ProPer, a LMS that conforms to SCORM specifications and provides adaptive hypermedia courses. ProPer manages and delivers SCORM compliant courses and personalizes them according to learner's knowledge, goals and personal characteristics. In addition learner's progress and behavior is monitored and useful feedback is returned to tutors. ProPer will be used for an adaptive Java Programming course distribution to CS1 students. Statistical feedback will be gathered by tutors in order to improve course effectiveness. The technology background is briefly given and the system's architecture and functionality are analyzed.

Chapter 12

Ching-Jung Liao, Chung Yuan Christian University, Taiwan
Chien-Chih Chou, Chung Yuan Christian University, Taiwan
Jin-Tan David Yang, Ming Chuan University, Taiwan

The purpose of this study is to incorporate adaptive ontology into ubiquitous learning grid to achieve seamless learning environment. Ubiquitous learning grid uses ubiquitous computing environment to infer and determine the most adaptive learning contents and procedures in anytime, any place and with any device. To achieve the goal, an ontology-based ubiquitous learning grid (OULG) was proposed to resolve the difficulties concerning how to adapt learning environment for different learners, devices, places. OULG through ontology identifying and adapting in the aspects of domain, task, devices, and background information awareness, so that the adaptive learning content could be delivered. A total of 42 freshmen participate in this study for four months to learn Java programming. Both of pretesting and posttesting are performed to ensure that the OULG is useful. Experimental results demonstrate that OULG is feasibile and effective in facilitating learning.

Chapter 13

Gennaro Costagliola, University of Salerno, Italy
Vittorio Fuccella, University of Salerno, Italy

To correctly evaluate learners' knowledge, it is important to administer tests composed of good quality question items. By the term "quality" we intend the potential of an item in effectively discriminating between skilled and untrained students and in obtaining tutor's desired difficulty level. This paper presents a rule-based e-testing system which assists tutors in obtaining better question items through subsequent test sessions. After each test session, the system automatically detects items' quality and provides the tutors with advice about what to do with each of them: good items can be re-used for future tests; among items with lower performances, instead, some should be discarded, while some can be modified and then re-used. The proposed system has been experimented in a course at the University of Salerno.

A real-time interactive distance lecture is a joint work that should be accomplished by the effort of the lecturer and his students in remote sites. It is important for the lecturer to get understanding information from the students which cannot be efficiently collected by only using video/audio channels between the lecturer and the students. This paper proposes RIDEEUIM (Understanding Information Management system for Real-time Interactive Distance Education Environment) for collecting understanding information from each participant to the lecturer during real time distance education activities. The usefulness of RIDEE-UIM has been confirmed by experiments.

Section 4
Empirical Study: Evaluation and Assessment

With increasing convenience and prevalence, the distant communication application has become a promising way for individuals who are eager to cooperate and interact virtually. This study explored the question of whether the collaborative interaction of the virtual teams has any effect on the conflict and network structure of virtual groups. A total of 150 participants were invited and randomly assigned to thirty groups with each group of five subjects. To function like real virtual groups, they were asked to communicate with their members through e-mail. Through genre analysis and social network analysis, nine communicative genres most frequently used in the collaborative groups were identified. Results of correlation analysis suggested that it was the communicative genres, not the network structure, that were associated with intra-group conflict of virtual group. Accordingly, whether the network structure of the virtual group is centralized or decentralized may not be instructors' or developers' major concern. Instead, they may wish to focus on a well-designed interface providing needed supports of communicative procedure for coordinating with distant members.

Chapter 16

McCarthy (1985) constructed the 4MAT teaching model, an eight step instrument developed in 1980, by synthesizing Dewey's experiential learning, Kolb's four learning styles, Jung's personality types, as well as Bogen's left mode and right mode of brain processing preferences. An important implication of this model is that learning retention is improved in the whole brain treatment group and thus this model is effective in retaining learning information as long term memory. Specifically, when examine the effectiveness of student scoring levels (high, median, and low), the results indicated that retention improved across all levels in the treatment group while results were inconsistent in the control group. When examine academic achievement and attitudes, interaction factor of both school and method showed a statistically significant difference.

Chapter 17

E-learning provides a convenient and efficient way for learning. Formative assessment not only guides student in instruction and learning, diagnose skill or knowledge gaps, but also measures progress and evaluation. An efficient and convenient e-learning formative assessment system is the key character for e-learning. However, most e-learning systems didn't provide methods for assessing learners' abilities but true-score mode. In this article, Sato's Student-Problem Chart (SP Chart) is applied to integrate with our proposed on-line assessment system. Teachers are able to analyze each learner easily and efficiently. In addition, the Bloom Taxonomy of Educational Objective supports each item in our assessment management system during the authoring time. In our proposed system, it provides groups of function for student, teacher, and system administrator. According to the SP Chart analysis and Bloom taxonomy of items, we can divide all items into four types, and students into six types. With these types of diagnosis analysis chart, teacher can modify or delete the items which are not proper. With diagnosis analysis chart of students, teachers can realize learners' learning situation easily and efficiently.

Chapter 18

The pervasive popularity of the Internet in the past decade has changed the way many students live and learn, in part, because modern technology has made it possible for learners to access Real-Time

Multimedia information on the Internet, or research any topic of interest to them from virtually any computer anywhere in the world. Students can also receive immediate feedback from their peers and/or their teachers when involved in collaborative projects. As a result, teachers of all disciplines need to incorporate the Internet and the concept of mobile learning into today's classrooms to take advantage of this technology. This research investigated the response of English majors to a mobile learning platform (NCCU-MLP) developed at National Chengchi University (NCCU) in which they were involved as participants. The goal of the NCCU-MLP is to improve the students' English ability as well as to update the teachers' understanding of how to use the technology. The purpose of this research was to investigate the responses of students to a mobile learning environment. The research involved 18 participants in a pilot study and 37 participants in a follow-up study who participated in a group activity involving mobile learning activities. The students were asked to complete the activity following which they completed a brief survey of their response to the mobile learning activity. The findings indicate a positive response from the participants regarding the content and procedures involved in the activity. Technical support for the project was found to need enhancement for future projects of this nature.

Chapter 19

Shoji Nishimura, Waseda University, China
Douglass J. Scott, Waseda University, China
Shogo Kato, Tokyo Woman's Christian University, Japan

In 2003, the School of Human Sciences, Waseda University (Japan), established the e-School, Japan's first complete undergraduate program enabling students to earn their bachelor degrees solely through e-learning. Supported by the widespread availability of high-speed Internet connections, it has become possible to economically transmit videotaped lectures with an image quality close to that of television across Japan and throughout the world. In addition, lecture contents are transmitted with an image quality that allows students to easily read what is written on the blackboard. Waseda's e-School has many features that contribute to its success, among these are the coupling of online and on-campus courses enhancing students educational experiences. In addition, online classes are relatively small—most are capped at 30 students—and new classes are created to respond to students' needs and interests. This article outlines the e-School's history, curriculum, administration, and management learning system. Various data are presented for the first four years of the e-School's operation (2003-2006), when the newly-created program was under the Ministry of Education's mandatory supervision period.

Preface

First electronic computer was developed in 1940s, and internetworking research was started in 1960s. Personal computers came to market in 1980s, and the Internet became popular in 1990s. In the past decade, with the evolution of Web 2.0 and wide use of smartphones, it becomes very easy for everyone to publish his/her personal contents via a variety of social media tools, such as SNS, blog, and micro-blog. User-generated contents produced and increased continuously. Now more digital bits (binary 1s and 0s) have been created in the digital space than stars in the physical universe. The Internet and Web have become the source of information, quarry of knowledge, and fount of wisdom.

First try to use computers to aid instruction, which is called CAI (Computer Aided Instruction), was taken place in mid-1950s to early 1960s by Stanford University and IBM. Since then, many innovative paradigms, technologies and support systems and standards, such as Computer Supported Collaborative Learning (CSCL), Web Based Learning (WBL), Blended Learning, Game Based Learning or Edutainment (Educational Entertainment), Learning Management System (LMS), Shareable Content Object Reference Model (SCORM) and IEEE LOM (Learning Object Metadata), have been proposed, developed, and applied in academic institutions and industrial organizations. Technology-enhanced distance learning has evolved from e-learning (provision of learning and education across time and distance), to m-learning (Mobile Learning, provision of learning and education at anytime and anywhere to anyone, with the means of mobile devices and communication networks), to u-learning (Ubiquitous Learning, provision of learning and education at the right time and the right place to the right person, with the means of ubiquitous/pervasive networking and context/situation aware computing technologies). The dramatic progress and wide utilization of information and communication technologies has greatly changed the way people work, live, play, and learn. With the emerging of distance education technologies and technology-enhanced learning paradigms, learning and education have been undergoing a big revolution.

This volume, grouped categorically into four sections, offers some of the latest advances in distance education technologies and new research achievements: newly developed methodologies, emerging support environments, and promising software systems.

Section 1, including the first five chapters, is called *New Frameworks and Architectures*. This section establishes the fundamentals of the most recent research into design and methodology behind distance education and learning, containing contributions from authors across the world.

Chapter 1 (*Collaborative Learning in Dynamic Group Environments* by Kamen Kanev, and Shigeo Kimura) is dedicated to Computer Supported Collaborative Learning (CSCL) employing dynamic groups, where at different stages students work independently, interact with each other in pairs, and conduct joint work in larger groups with varying numbers of participants. Their study features blended learning taking place in a face-to-face collaborative environment, where all students in the same room can move freely around and interact with each other while using digitally enhanced printed materials with direct point-and-click functionality. Flexible and efficient support for dynamic group management is ensured through the adopted Cluster Pattern Interface (CLUSPI) technology.

Chapter 2 (*A Systematic Framework of Virtual Laboratories Using Mobile Agent and Design Pattern Technologies* by Yi-Hsung Li, Chyi-Ren Dow, Cheng-Min Lin, Sheng-Chang Chen, and Fu-Wei Hsu) details a framework that aims at designing and implementing an agent-based virtual laboratory in a systematic way enhanced with design patterns, and by wrapping the existing CAI tools without reverser engineering the source codes. The authors' work has demonstrated that the feasibility of their proposed framework in several applications, including virtual digital circuit and signal processing laboratories.

In Chapter 3 (*A Computer-Assisted Approach for Conducting Information Technology Applied Instructions* by Hui-Chun Chu, Gwo-Jen Hwang, Pei-Jin Tsai, and Tzu-Chi Yang), a new model for conducting information technology applied instructions is proposed, which can assist teachers in designing information technology applied course content based on the features of subject materials and the learning status of the students. The proposed approach has been evaluated in a Chemistry course that is designed based on the model at a junior high school to show its effectiveness.

Chapter 4 (*A Highly Scalable, Modular Architecture for Computer Aided Assessment E-Learning Systems* by Krzysztof Gierłowski and Krzysztof Nowicki) proposes a novel e-learning system dedicated strictly to knowledge assessment tasks. It utilizes Web-based technologies, but its design differs radically from currently popular e-learning solutions which rely mostly on thin-client architecture. They employ a loosely-tied distributed system architecture of high scalability and modularity. The versatility of their work has been proved in classroom, distance, and blended learning environments.

Chapter 5 (*Recent Contributions to a Generic Architecture Design that Supports Learning Objects Interoperability* by Sotirios Botsios and Dimitrios A. Georgiou) concentrates and classifies recent research work and notices important points that can lead to an open, modular and generic architecture of a Learning Management System based on widely accepted standards. It offers an overview on adaptive navigation, presentation and content retrieval in a variety of e-learning systems, concerning the adaptivity parameters and standards. It further proposes a generic architecture based on the adaptivity parameters such as cognitive style, learning style, learning behavior (motivation), and knowledge level.

Section 2, which contains chapters 6-10, is titled *Promising Support Mechanisms and Technologies*. As the name suggests, the chapters in Section 2 describe support mechanisms for the frameworks and architectures proposed and detailed in Section 1, and move into technologies that advance distance education and learning.

Chapter 6 (*Statistical Inference-Based Cache Management for Mobile Learning* by Qing Li, Jianmin Zhao, and Xinzhong Zhu) proposes a statistical caching mechanism which makes use of prior knowledge (i.e., statistical data) to predict the pattern of user movement and then replicates and migrates the cache objects among different proxies. They further develop a statistical inference-based heuristic search algorithm to accommodate dynamic mobile data access in the mobile learning environment. Experimental studies show that this algorithm can obtain good performance on caching mobile data with an acceptable complexity.

Chapter 7 (*A 3D Geometry Model Search Engine to Support Learning* by Gary K. L. Tam, Rynson W. H. Lau, and Jianmin Zhao) investigates two important issues, namely, feature analysis that affects the general usage of a distance learning system for the construction of 3D geometry models, and the speed that affects the number of concurrent users. The focus in this work is on deformable models, i.e., similar models that may have different poses, and the method offers a mechanism to extract, index, match and efficiently retrieve stable features from these models.

Chapter 8 (*Supporting Interoperability and Context-Awareness in E-Learning through Situation-Driven Learning Processes* by Stefan Dietze, Alessio Gugliotta, and John Domingue) proposes Situation-Driven Learning Processes (SDLP), which describe learning processes semantically from two perspectives: the user perspective that considers a learning process as a course of learning goals which lead from an initial situation to a desired situation, and the system perspective that utilizes Semantic Web Services (SWS) technology to semantically describe necessary resources for each learning goal within a specific learning situation. Consequently, dynamic adaption to specific learning contexts as well as interoperability across different metadata standards and application environments can be achieved.

Chapter 9 (*A New Process Phase Diagnostic Technique: Visualized Interface for Diagnosing Learning Progress* by Pi-Shan Hsu and Te-Jeng Chang) details a new diagnostic technique combining measures of a learner's learning effort with associated performance in order to compare the efficiency of learning condition in a dynamic, real-time, and non-interfering instructional process. In the approach, the learning effort curve represents the quantitative value of the learning effort of each instruction unit, assessed by the proposed measurement technique.

Chapter 10 (*A FCA-Based Cognitive Diagnosis Model for CAT* by Yang Shuqun and Ding Shuliang) introduces a theoretical model of CD-CAT (Computerized Adaptive Testing with Cognitive Diagnosis) based on FCA (Formal Concept Analysis). It further describes the technology of item bank construction, item selection strategies in CD-CAT, and estimation methods, to design and implement a systemic CD-CAT, which diagnoses examinees on-line and offers remedial measure for examinees in time.

Section 3, called *Development of Practical Systems* and containing chapters 11-14, departs from the first two parts by adding a layer of pragmatism to the technologies and methodologies being developed. While the first two parts detail research and hypothesize about future goals and research directions, Section 3 describes what may be more practical in terms of developing new systems by utilizing promising distance learning techniques.

Chapter 11 (*Adaptivity in ProPer: An Adaptive SCORM Compliant LMS* by Ioannis Kazanidis and Maya Satratzemi) presents a Learning Management System (LMS) called ProPer, which conforms to SCORM specifications and provides adaptive hypermedia courses. ProPer manages and delivers SCORM compliant courses and personalizes them according to a learner's knowledge, goals and personal characteristics. In addition, the system monitors learners' progress and behavior, and gathers useful feedback, which is analyzed and used to improve course effectiveness.

Chapter 12 (*The Construction of an Ontology-Based Ubiquitous Learning Grid* by Ching-Jung Liao, Chien-Chih Chou, and Jin-Tan David Yang) attempts to incorporate adaptive ontology into ubiquitous learning grid to achieve a seamless learning environment, which uses ubiquitous computing environments to infer and determine the most adaptive learning contents and procedures in anytime, anyplace, and any device. A prototype of Ontology-Based Ubiquitous Learning Grid (OULG) has been constructed. Experimental results show that the proposed OULG is feasible and effective in supporting and facilitating ubiquitous learning.

Chapter 13 (*A Rule-Based System for Test Quality Improvement* by Gennaro Costagliola and Vittorio Fuccella) presents a rule-based e-testing system that assists tutors in obtaining question items of good quality through subsequent test sessions. After each test session, the system automatically detects items' quality, and provides the tutors with advice about what to do with each of them: good items can be reused for future tests; among items with lower performances, some should be discarded, while some can be modified and then re-used. The proposed system has been experimentally verified.

Chapter 14 (*An Understanding Information Management System for a Real-Time Interactive Distance Education Environment* by Aiguo He) proposes a so-called RIDEE-UIM system, an Understanding Information Management system for Real-time Interactive Distance Education Environment), for the lecturer to collect understanding information from each participant in real time distance education activities. Basic concept, design and implementation issues are discussed. Experimental use and analysis result show the usefulness of the proposed RIDEE-UIM system.

Finally, Section 4, called *Empirical Study: Evaluation and Assessment*, contains the final five chapters of the book, and details some of the latest research findings in terms of distance learnig evaluation and assessment, offering hints and suggestions for present implementation and practical utilization and future research opportunities.

Chapter 15 (*The Effects of Communicative Genres on Intra-Group Conflict in Virtual Student Teams* by Jung-Lung Hsu and Huey-Wen Chou) explores the question of whether the collaborative interaction of the virtual teams has any effect on the conflict and network structure of virtual groups in the learning situation. A total of 150 participants were invited and randomly assigned to 30 groups with each group of five subjects. Through genre analysis and social network analysis, nine communicative genres most frequently used in the collaborative groups were identified. Results of correlation analysis suggested that it was the communicative genres (not the network structure) that were associated with intra-group conflict of virtual group.

Chapter 16 (*Effect of Teaching Using Whole Brain Instruction on Accounting Learning* by Li-Tze Lee and Jason C. Hung) details the experimental design involving the applications of the whole brain instruction, based on the 4MAT teaching model, an eight step instrument developed in 1980 by synthesizing Dewey's experiential learning, Kolb's four learning styles, Jung's personality types, as well as Bogen's left mode and right mode of brain processing preferences. It reports the experimental results in an accounting course at three vocational high schools by examining students' academic achievement, attitude, and retention.

Chapter 17 (*Using S-P Chart and Bloom Taxonomy to Develop Intelligent Formative Assessment Tools* by Wen-Chih Chang, Hsuan-Che Yang, Timothy K. Shih, and Louis R. Chao) describes a new approach that integrates Sato's Student-Problem Chart (SP Chart) with their proposed online assessment system, where teachers are able to analyze each learner easily and efficiently. It further details the system architecture and implementation method, and shows test item diagnostic and analysis with concrete examples and interface snapshots of the proposed system.

Chapter 18 (*A Study of English Mobile Learning Applications at National Chengchi University* by Pei-Chun Che, Han-Yi Lin, Hung-Chin Jang, Yao-Nan Lien, and Tzu-Chieh Tsai) reports a case study of English mobile learning in a Taiwan university, which investigated the response of the participants to a mobile learning platform called NCCU-MLP in order to improve the students' English ability as well as to update the teachers' understanding of how to use the technology. Their finding indicates a positive response from the participants regarding the content and procedures involved in the activity.

Chapter 19 (*E-Learning Practice and Experience at Waseda E-School: Japan's First Undergraduate Degree-Awarding Online Program* by Shoji Nishimura, Douglass J. Scott, and Shogo Kato) offers a review on the history, curriculum, administration, and management structure, and system of the Waseda e-School, the first undergraduate degree-awarding full online e-learning program in Japan. Waseda e-School has many features that contribute to its success. This chapter also reports on the current status of the courses by analyzing the results of a questionnaire survey conducted after one year from their establishment and the state of credits registered and earned by students.

As Chapter 19 concludes the book, the volume is wrapped up with a fruitful discussion and conclusion about the future of distance learning and education, setting a model for similar institutions around the world to emulate. In all, this text offers a broad range of research, design, critical theory, design, implementation, assessment, and analysis of distance education technologies and emerging support systems. It should prove to be a vital resource to teachers and students, as well as instructional designers and administrators of distance learning and education.

Qun Jin
Waseda University, Japan

Section 1
New Frameworks and Architectures

Chapter 1
Collaborative Learning in Dynamic Group Environments

Kamen Kanev
Shizuoka University, Japan

Shigeo Kimura
Kanazawa University, Japan

ABSTRACT

This chapter is dedicated to Computer-Supported Collaborative Learning (CSCL) employing dynamic groups, where at different stages students work independently, interact with each other in pairs, and conduct joint work in larger groups with varying numbers of participants. A novel Dynamic Group Environment for Collaborative Learning (DGE/CL) that supports students in making informed and intelligent choices about how, when, and with whom to collaborate is introduced. A face-to-face collaborative scenario, where all students are in the same room and can move freely around and interact with each other while using digitally enhanced printed materials with direct point-and-click functionality is considered. Flexible and efficient support for dynamic group management is ensured through the adopted Cluster Pattern Interface (CLUSPI) technology, which, while preserving the original touch-and-feel of printed educational materials, supports additional affordances and allows employment of new, non-traditional paper-based interactions. Possibilities for DGE/CL enhancements with specialized surface code readers and laser-based digital surface encoding being developed by the authors are outlined and references to recent projects are given.

INTRODUCTION

Collaborative learning is a term denoting a multiplicity of educational approaches that stimulate learners to work closely together in joint intellectual efforts. Over the last half-century, collaborative learning has quickly turned into a strong promoter of groupwork in educational institutions at all levels (Gamson, 1994).

DOI: 10.4018/978-1-60960-539-1.ch001

Small groups with positive interdependence, where students work together to maximize personal and partner learning, have been traditionally used in *cooperative learning*. However, as discussed by Curtis (2001), cooperative learning has mostly dealt with tasks that are divisible into more or less independent subtasks, where cooperating parties work in parallel to process individual subtasks in an autonomous, independent way. In cooperative learning, the original task is thus solved by simply solving multiple subtasks in parallel.

Collaborative learning, on the other hand, is pertinent to situations where a joint solution to a problem is built synchronously and interactively, which implies discussions between the collaborating parties in the process of task engagement. As indicated by Pressley & McCormic (1995), this yields significant cognitive benefits since interactions and discussions among students have notable positive effects on their learning aptitude. In collaborative learning, participants brainstorm, share information, and learn from each other so their combined collaborative achievement considerably surpasses the simple sum of individual contributions.

Learner groups and groupwork play a central role, both in cooperative and in collaborative learning and attract significant research interest, especially when combined with instructional use of new and emerging educational technologies. In this context, Johnson & Johnson (1996) identify *formal cooperative learning*, *informal cooperative learning*, *base groups* and *academic controversies* as four major types of cooperative learning. Collaborative learning models, on the other hand, are classified into seven types by Hadwin et al. (2006), based on their *group size*, *temporal limitations*, *applied representations* and *collaborative roles*.

Our research reported in this paper falls in the domain of Computer-Supported Collaborative Learning (CSCL), although support of cooperative learning, based on the methods that we develop is also possible. The central idea of our approach is to build an educational environment based on

truly dynamic groups of learners. This is a challenging task, since traditional group management techniques when applied to dynamic groups incur too high a burden on the instructor and make implementations impractical. The viability of our idea and its practical implementation naturally depends, thus, on technical innovations and recent technological advancements. Our research addresses this issue by proposing a roadmap for the design and implementation of a CSCL system based on the innovative Cluster Pattern Interface (CLUSPI®) technology (Kanev & Kimura, 2005; Kanev & Kimura, 2006) that provides flexible and efficient support for dynamic group management.

DYNAMIC GROUPS IN COOPERATIVE AND COLLABORATIVE LEARNING

In the social sciences, the notion of *dynamic groups* stems from physiology and is mostly related to social psychology group dynamics and dynamic group therapy (Montgomery, 2002). Group related behaviors such as social loafing, free riding, group immaturity, etc. are also cited by some authors as (group) dynamics (Johnson & Johnson, 1996). In the exact sciences by contrast, dynamic groups are most often employed in distributed computing and communications, where the theoretical aspects of dynamic group management have been relatively well developed (Schiper, 2006). Our objective in this work is to propose a dynamic group framework that would support both the social aspects and the technological aspects of cooperative and collaborative learning activities.

We consider the collaborative learning process as an intelligent social activity, where at different stages students work independently, interact with each other in pairs, and conduct joint work in larger groups (Brine et al., 2006; Turk et al., 2006). Existing collaborative learning methods like JIGSAW (Gallardo et al., 2003), however, rely mostly on pairwork and groups with predetermined structures and sizes (Brine et al., 2006; Ellis, 2001). We, therefore, would like to provide a more flexible, dynamic group configuration in which students could make informed and intelligent choices about how, when, and with whom to pair or form multiperson groups.

In our approach we adopt some of the aspects of the intelligent collaborative e-learning systems (Miettinen, 2005); although, since students are mostly engaged in question-driven and open-ended queries, automated intelligent guidance appears to be rather difficult to implement. That is why, instead of attempting to guide students in an explicit way, we provide them with supportive information that builds *awareness* of the available resources and their dynamics (Ogata & Yano, 1998). A more formal discussion of *context awareness* and its use for group interaction support is available in (Ferscha et al., 2004) where focus is put on *location*, *identity*, *time*, and *activity* context information. In addition, Dimakis et al. (2006) describe a prototype system and corresponding software architecture for context-aware collaborative services that supports body tracking, face and audio source localization and participant identification.

In our approach, we concentrate on face-to-face collaborative learning, where all students are in the same room, can freely move around, and interact with each other. As explained by Ellis (2001), however, both face-to-face and asynchronous online communications bear different advantages and disadvantages as perceived by the students participating in the reported study. We have decided, therefore, to incorporate in our method some support for asynchronous online communications that could further enhance context awareness and facilitate interpersonal contacts. Suggested support is not about providing distant online communications but rather about establishing computer-assisted facilities supporting asynchronous collaboration. In this context, non-verbal communication and artifact-mediated collaboration (Dwyer & Suthers, 2006)

with support for paper-based interactions are of particular interest. The proposed approach is to use CLUSPI® enhanced printed materials with direct point-and-click functionality (Kanev & Kimura, 2006) instead of traditional paper documents. Such printed materials preserve the touch and feel of original educational documents while providing additional affordances, thus enabling students to interact with documents in new non-traditional ways (Kanev & Orr, 2006). One additional benefit of using CLUSPI® is the possibility for gathering CSCL process related feedback and quality assessment information in a transparent, unobtrusive way. Although at the moment, no particular quality-rating scheme has been selected, we believe that the one reported by Meier et al. (2007) might be a good initial choice.

INTERACTIVE PRINTED DOCUMENTS FOR COLLABORATIVE LEARNING

Traditional testing methodology maintains that once a written assignment is given to a student, it has to stay with that particular student for the entire length of the test. In a classic, paper-based test environment students would be asked to write their names on the assignment sheets and the instructor may have to prepare a list of student names and assignment numbers. In our case, however, we could eliminate the need of initial student-assignment association by allowing students to freely share and possibly exchange assignment sheets during exercises. Of course if students were to write their names and answers on the assignment sheets, such sharing would not be justifiable from a pedagogical point of view. Our solution, however, is based on printed materials with direct point-and-click functionality that supports answering questions without any need for physical writing.

To illustrate our method let us consider some simple *fact finding activity*. In computer science classes, when we teach fundamental data structures, we usually explain to our students the following important tree properties:

There is exactly one path connecting any two nodes in a tree and a tree with N nodes has exactly N-1 edges. A binary tree with N internal nodes has N+1 external nodes and the external path length of any binary tree with N internal nodes is 2N greater than the internal path length.

A mere disclosure of these properties is certainly not sufficient for proper retention, so we usually reinforce comprehension by asking questions such as:

1. How many edges does a tree with N nodes have?
2. What is the number of possible paths connecting two randomly chosen nodes in a tree?
3. How many external nodes are there in a binary tree with N internal nodes?

At earlier stages of learning, when students are still getting acquainted with the tree data structure concept, they can not easily recall the above important properties, so they need to get back to the descriptive text and look for answers. This becomes then a fact-finding activity, where students go through a given text and search for a specific statement that gives the right answer to a posed question. For the sample question No.1 above, the right answer would be "exactly N-1 edges".

Now let us consider how a student should answer such a question in a practical situation. If the question has been orally posed to the audience, students who find the answer could raise their hands or possibly, the first student to find the answer could just read it aloud. In a case of one-to-one interaction, the student could either read out the answer or just finger point to it. Please note that physical pointing to the correct answer in a difficult-to-read-and-comprehend original

text might be quite instructive, since it makes the student actually read and try to understand rather than just guess. Finally, if self-study is considered, neither oral answers nor finger pointing would work and therefore some other answer verification method should be used.

The approach we adopt is built around the natural finger-pointing gesture, but instead of bare fingers, students use the specialized CLUSPI® readers for pointing and clicking on digitally enhanced printed materials. This approach is applicable when questions are directed to an entire class, to a single student in one-to-one interactions and even in self-study situations. If, for example, a question is posed to a class of students during a lecture, they will have to read through their handouts, find the paragraph giving the correct answer, and then point and click on it with the CLUSPI® device. This can relay information to a database for later analysis or to the instructor to provide feedback on class comprehension. After allowing ample time for answering the question, the instructor may then show the answer on a video screen and give additional verbal explanations. This fact-finding activity has similarities with traditional quizzes that are routinely used to keep students focused, but our approach engages students even further; it keeps them involved at all stages of the educational process by allowing them to collaborate rather than remain passive observers. In contrast to paper-based quizzes that are essentially non-interactive, CLUSPI® based interactions can provide instant feedback both to the instructor and to the individual students. Please note that this is different from Computer Assisted Learning (CAL) where fully-fledged computerized workplaces are assigned to students. In our environment students can use compact, handheld CLUSPI® devices, and there is no need for individual keyboards, mice or screens, since students interact with printed educational materials in a direct straightforward way.

Figure 1. Direct interactions with CLUSPI® enhanced printed content

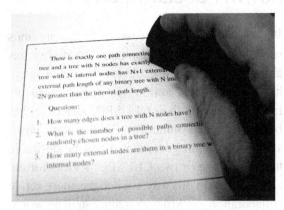

Figure 2. Sample CLUSPI® enhanced printed content with marked sensitive areas

> There is exactly one path connecting any two nodes in a tree and a tree with N nodes has exactly N-1 edges. A binary tree with N internal nodes has N+1 external nodes and the external path length of any binary tree with N internal nodes is 2N greater than the internal path length.
>
> Questions:
>
> 1. How many edges does a tree with N nodes have?
> 2. What is the number of possible paths connecting two randomly chosen nodes in a tree?
> 3. How many external nodes are there in a binary tree with N internal nodes?

For illustration, we have printed on CLUSPI® enhanced paper the earlier shown educational text along with the sample questions related to tree data structures. Direct interactions with the resulting digitally enhanced educational content are shown in Figure 1. Answering a question consists of two steps:

- the student selects a question by pointing and clicking with the CLUSPI® device anywhere on the printed text of the question, and
- the student points and clicks with the CLUSPI® device on the expression in the text that gives the correct answer.

CLUSPI® technology (Kanev & Kimura, 2005) is not based on OCR or other content feature extraction and recognition methods such as digital watermarking, so direct point and click functionality can freely be attached to surfaces of printed documents independently of their printed content. As an example, we show in Figure 2 how click-sensitive areas have been defined for the three questions and their answers in the sample tree-related educational text.

ASSIGNMENT MANAGEMENT AND PROGRESS MONITORING

When we envisage a Dynamic Group Environment for Collaborative Learning (DGE/CL), the very concept of dynamic groups implies a higher level of non-determinism and group volatility that makes it impossible to define group content and structure in an explicit way. Therefore, we believe that indirect, content based methods for governing the formation, development, and disbanding of groups should be considered. We continue then with a discussion of assignment management, including assignment distribution, tracking, progress monitoring and reporting.

In the DGE/CL, we initially present students with assignments printed on CLUSPI® enhanced sheets, similar to those shown in Figure 1 and Figure 2. Different students get assignment sheets with different content, and initial distribution of assignment sheets to students can be done at random. In fact, a stack of assignment sheets for the entire class could be provided and students could be instructed to freely take and use as many sheets as they wish. Please note that we suggest here a very general approach where the number of assignment sheets does not have to correlate with the number of students in the class. We do not, therefore, introduce any individual assignments that students have to solve independently, although we expect students to do some individual work, as we will explain later. In DGE/CL, it should be completely acceptable for a student to answer a few questions on an assignment sheet and then give the sheet to some other student. Since no writing on the sheet is done, the other student should be able to use it as if it were a new assignment sheet. On the other hand, if an assignment sheet gets returned to a student then the student should be allowed to proceed with answering only previously unanswered questions.

Implementation of the above described functionality is quite straightforward if CLUSPI® technology is used. As explained earlier, to answer a question, one first has to point and click on it with the CLUSPI® device. Based on acquired assignment sheet and question IDs, a database check is initiated and the status of the currently selected question is derived. System response will then be determined, based on the derived status and the current user information.

At this stage we assume that each student has an individual CLUSPI® device that is registered to the student ID and cannot be used by other students. This way, consecutive use of a single CLUSPI® device for answering multiple questions on one or more assignment sheets would indicate continuous work of a single student. Accordingly, altered use of more than one CLUSPI® device on a single assignment sheet would indicate interactions and possible collaboration among students.

It is important to realize that DGE/CL does not provide means for direct sensing of student-to-student interactions and collaboration. Indirect methods, based on tracking of assignments and student interactions with assignment sheets are used instead. For this purpose, student-to-assignment associations are first established and then updated with every CLUSPI® based interaction instance. In DGE/CL, however, such associations need not to be permanent and may actually change in the course of the exercise.

STUDENT IDENTIFICATION AND ACTIVITY OBSERVATION

We have based our discussion in the previous section on the presumption that each student has an individual CLUSPI® device. In such a setup, however, there is nothing to prevent students from exchanging their CLUSPI® devices, either by mistake or voluntarily. Furthermore, when students work in groups, it might be desirable to use just one or two CLUSPI® devices for the entire group. In this way, we believe, more active collaboration would develop, since students would have to share a few CLUSPI® devices while using together a multiplicity of assignment sheets. Within the scope of the DGE/CL, however, the number of groups and their participants are not known in advance and in fact would dynamically change in the course of the class work. Therefore, it would be difficult to estimate the number of CLUSPI® devices needed, and it would be practically impossible to establish and maintain any device-to-group relationships.

A more careful consideration reveals that if we know *who is doing what* at any time during the class activities, it might be possible to reconstruct student interactions, to identify collaboration between students and thus to gather sufficient information regarding group formation, development, and disbanding. The core component of our interaction interface is the CLUSPI® device that identifies assignment sheets and provides respective position and orientation feedback for direct point-and-click purposes. Based on this functionality, we have adopted a transparent binding model that allows flexible sharing and exchange of assignment sheets among students. Now we would like to apply this model to CLUSPI® devices and thus allow students to freely share and even switch them. We still must ensure, however, that we know who is doing what at all times, namely every point-and-click on an assignment sheet should be associated with the student that actually used the CLUSPI® device to effectuate the click.

Figure 3. The prototype CLUSPI®/RFID reader

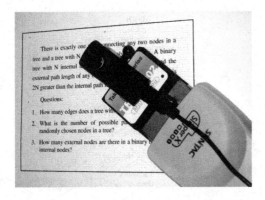

Figure 4. RFID tags

To achieve this, we have developed a new enhanced CLUSPI® device with added RFID sensing functionality. A prototype device consisting of an ordinary CLUSPI® reader combined with a compact 13.56 MHz RFID reader is shown in Figure 3. The integral device has the size of a standard mouse and can be operated in a pretty much similar way. Of course, since the CLUSPI® reader supports direct point-and-click functionality, in contrast to the mouse, the combined device does not need to be in constant contact with the material surface.

Combined device uses the standard CLUSPI® functionality to identify assignment sheets and respective positions and orientations, while the added RFID functionality identifies students and monitors their activities. Student identification is based on permanent RFID tags that once distributed and assigned to students can be used in many classes and for different purposes. A variety of forms and sizes of RFID tags are currently available, such as student identity card sized badges, necklace type, wrist wearable, different kinds of rings, etc. as shown in Figure 4. We have conducted experiments with RFID badges, and with wrist wearable and ring type RFID tags, where the latter demonstrated the best sensing and most reliable performance.

Sharing an RFID enhanced CLUSPI® reader occurs in a natural, self-explanatory way. Student identification by the RFID reader is completely transparent and unnoticeable for the student. No special preparation or registration is needed, since any student can just take the reader in his/her hand and immediately use it to point and click on a CLUSPI® enhanced assignment sheet. We have adopted ring shaped RFID tags mainly because they guarantee the closest possible proximity to the RFID reader when properly held. RFID badges, necklaces and wrist stripes leave more ambiguity, making it difficult to identify the student actually in control of the enhanced CLUSPI® device, especially when several students are working closely together.

Successful identification is only possible when the student wears a properly registered RFID tagged ring on the hand that holds the enhanced CLUSPI® reader. Identification of the student in control is a prerequisite for the correct CLUSPI® device operation, because it is used for deriving the user dependent context. In DGE/CL, CLUSPI® device functionality is inhibited when no user context is available, and in this way users without properly registered RFID rings will get no response from the CLUSPI® reader.

GROUP DYNAMICS MONITORING, REGISTRATION AND FEEDBACK

To encourage interaction and collaboration between students, we apply a data driven approach in which solutions of some problems require gathering information from multiple assignment sheets.

This way if a student uses a single assignment sheet, he/she can only solve part of the assignment problems. To solve the remaining problems, the student will need to obtain information from one or more additional assignment sheets, possibly already in possession of some other students. Based on this idea, here we attempt to elucidate the different stages and corresponding activities encountered in the unfolding CLUSPI® assisted learning and collaboration process. The DGE/CL method is put in the perspective of an experimental framework for investigating dynamic group support in the context of different collaborative learning approaches.

In the beginning of the class, students are given a class assignment printed on multiple sheets, where the number of sheets may be smaller, equal or greater than the number of the students in the class. By controlling the student-to-assignment sheet ratio different interaction patterns could be imposed. For example, if the number of assignment sheets is smaller than the number of students, some students will have to work together since the very beginning, and so they will not be involved in any individual work.

By manually distributing assignment sheets, the instructor could enforce initiation of either individual work, work in pairs or work in larger, predetermined groups. Alternatively, the instructor could allow students to freely take assignment sheets and thus to self-determine the initial individual, pair and grouping arrangements.

Individual Work

After students receive CLUSPI® enabled assignment sheets they read them and try to complete different activities by clicking on the printed text with their CLUSPI® scanning devices. The system knows which students are associated with which texts and activities by tracking the student RFID rings and the assignment sheet IDs. At this stage, the students read and try to complete activities individually.

Figure 5. Individual work

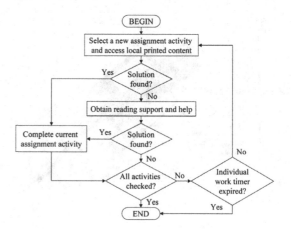

An example of these activities might be to read the text and answer general comprehension questions. If the student is able to complete the activity (for example, the student uses the CLUSPI® device to click on the parts of the text that contain the correct answers to the comprehension questions), the student is allowed to progress to the next reading activity. This process is controlled by the CLUSPI® system and all sequences of student clicks are recorded. If students cannot complete the activity on their own, then CLUSPI® gives them access to additional content and reading support. Students can click on the parts they find difficult to understand and CLUSPI® gives them the corresponding help until they can finish the activity as shown on the flowchart in Figure 5. During this process, the students have to read the same text repeatedly and thus, little by little they become "experts" that know the informative content of the assignment quite well.

In the following steps, some parts of the text might be missing or might not offer the necessary content to understand the text and/or complete all of the activities. At this point, the students realize that they need to exchange information with other class members. For example, they may have been presented with a text that contains gaps (Brine et al., 2007) and even with the CLUSPI® support they may not be able to fill all of the gaps.

Figure 6. Formation of groups

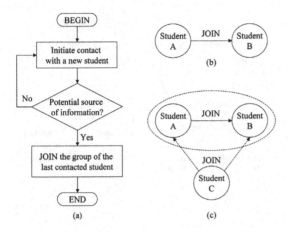

Since all students work in parallel, after some initial time period during which most students could process their locally answerable assignments, more and more students would begin seeking exchange of information with other students. Additionally, after the time limit for individual work expires, all remaining students may be automatically directed by CLUSPI® to begin searching for the missing information by talking to other class members and looking at their texts.

Formation of Groups

When a student realizes that the activity requires information from another class member, the student is motivated to initiate contacts with other students in the class.

As shown in Figure 6a, once a student identifies a new partner, namely another student that has potentially useful information for him/her, then the first student will join the group of the second student. This action is illustrated in Figure 6b, where student A joins student B who in this particular example does not belong to any group. The JOIN action is denoted by an arrow directed from the circle, representing student A (the information seeker) to the circle, representing student B. In this way, students contact each other to see if they can find potential sources of

information; information they need to complete their own activities. CLUSPI® registers the match once the students have established information links between the two texts. For example, Student A asks Student B for information. If Student B has the information, then Student A can attempt to complete components of the activity by clicking with the CLUSPI® device on the correct information in Student B's text. By clicking on a different but related text, CLUSPI® can invoke additional content, which is not available unless Student A clicks on parts of Student B's CLUSPI® encoded text.

A pair can be transformed into a group of three, four or even more persons, if other students approach the pair for information; however, in a stable group only one pair can be actively exchanging verbal information at any time. The other persons can listen to the information being exchanged while they wait for their turn, or they may be interacting with information that has been invoked by CLUSPI® when they access a matching activity sheet. In the illustration given in Figure 6c, the student C joins a two-student group, consisting of students A and B, where strictly speaking student C joins either student A or student B, depending on whom was first identified as a valuable information carrier. However, once a group of three students is formed and information flow within the group begins, new discoveries are likely to occur. While student C is observing the communication between students A and B for example, he/she might discover that both students (A and B) have different valuable information for him/her. We will use dashed arrows to denote such cases as shown in Figure 6c.

Groupwork Stage

Once students have registered a matching text or texts, CLUSPI® enables access to content that must be completed using a multiplicity of related texts. Student activities at the groupwork stage are outlined in Figure 7a. If the group can

Figure 7. Groupwork stage

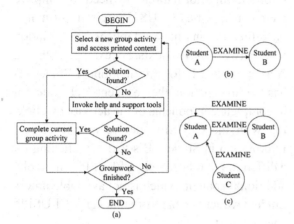

Figure 8. Group interactions and reforming

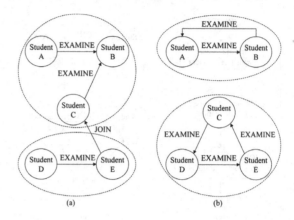

easily complete the given activity, then students can progress to the next stage of the task assignment. If they cannot complete the activity, which is made evident by a sequence of incorrect clicks or a direct request for more information, then CLUSPI® invokes support tools and content to help them to complete it.

Within the group, students discuss the content of their assignment sheets and consequently examine them by clicking and pointing with CLUSPI® (Figure 7b). Since a CLUSPI® response is context dependent, different students clicking on the same assignment sheet might get different feedback. Please note that more than one person can be examining a group member's text and accessing the CLUSPI® digital information at the same time. For example, in a group of three students, Student A is examining Student B's text. Student B and Student C are examining Student A's text. No one needs the information in Student C's text (Figure 7c).

Group Interactions and Reforming

Groups are joined on the basis of the information needed to complete an activity. For two groups to be joined, at least one person in one of the groups is required to be requesting information from a member of the other group (Figure 8a).

However, if only a single member of the first group needs information from the second group, the groups can separate into smaller groups. The members of these reformed groups can be either the same or different. For example, Students A and B are examining each other's activity sheet. However, they cannot provide any additional information to their group member, Student C. Student C then seeks out Student D as a potential source of information. Student E realizes that Student C has information that he/she needs as well. Student C has now left the group of Students A and B, and has joined the group consisting of Students D and E (Figure 8b). This way, students may stay with their groups and then membership changes will occur according to how the group merges and splits. Alternatively, individual students may resign from existing groups and join or form new groups. Please note that once a student has his/her part of the assignment completed, he/she may resign from his/her group and afterwards will participate in other groups only if invited.

Disbanding of Groups

As all individuals complete their activity sheets, the groups naturally dissolve. By this time, all examine and join actions should have been completed and students should have no incentives to seek further information exchange. Since all activity sequences and student answers have been recorded through CLUSPI®, the students can now be provided with feedback about their success and failures. Once the completion of the entire task assignment for the class has been registered with CLUSPI®, the students can also be individually administered with a final activity or quiz to demonstrate their overall understanding of the content presented during the task assignment.

DISCUSSION

Computer Supported Collaborative Learning (CSCL) aims at specialized tools and environments for collaborative learning support that enrich human understanding of the learning process and help enhancing current educational systems with new features and advanced functionalities (Dimitracopoulou, 2005). In line with this, we have designed our DGE/CL as a specialized environment for collaborative learning support and have incorporated in it dynamic group management features based on recent technological advancements. This makes it a powerful tool for conducting CSCL experiments with flexible multi-group learning environments where not only members of groups may change but also groups may merge, split and dissolve at any time.

Martin & Paredes (2004) have addressed formation and management of dynamic groups in adaptive collaborative hypermedia systems and Okada, Tarumi & Kambayasi (2000) have proposed a new dynamic group guidance method for distance learning systems. Reported approaches, however seem to be limited to web and network based interactions and might, therefore, be difficult to employ in face-to-face communications and class-based collaboration activities. Being specifically designed for classroom use, our approach in contrast, has the native support for

face-to-face collaborations already embedded in its core. In distinction to widely used screen-only collaboration environments the DGE/CL implements natural, paper-based collaboration through the adopted CLUSPI® technology.

It enables collaborating users to continue employing paper as a main collaboration medium and avoids major adjustments to their interaction habits and styles. We minimize this way the burden on the users while effectively establishing the technological background needed for supervision of the collaborative learning process. The framework also incorporates RFID-based tracking functionality that allows reliable, transparent identification of users and tracing of their collaborative learning activities. Combined with the CLUSPI® based identification of printed materials and tracking of employed content, this provides a unique opportunity for creating and storing for further analysis collaboration logs at any level of detail.

CONCLUSION

In this work, we have introduced a new experimental framework for collaborative learning in dynamic group environments. Since truly dynamic groups are difficult to maintain and support with the traditional group management techniques applicable to collaborative learning, we have considered new approaches including recent technological advancements and innovations. We have thus proposed a roadmap for design and implementation of a CSCL system based on the innovative Cluster Pattern Interface (CLUSPI®) technology that could provide flexible and efficient support for dynamic group management. In this context, management, tracking and progress monitoring of assignments is conducted through digitally enhanced printed documents with direct point-and-click functionality while student tagging, identification and activity observation is conducted through RFID. We have also elucidated the different stages of the dynamic group based collaborative learning process along with appropriate means for monitoring, registration and feedback control.

Since the inception of the DGE/CL, we have continued developing the underlying technologies and exploring various application possibilities in collaboration with other colleagues. A new class of optical input devices reported in Kanev et al. (2008) has been investigated in the context of augmented surface based interactions not only with printed materials but also with surfaces of physical objects and surrounding artifacts. In this relation new methods for laser-based digital encoding of physical surfaces and volumetric regions of 3D objects have been studied (Kanev et al., 2011). This could enable various physical objects to be directly integrated into the collaborative educational process and employed as tangible interface components (Kanev, 2008). Consequently a combination of technologies for information encoding and for multimedia annotation to enrich interactions with paper documents and physical objects both in desktop and mobile settings has been proposed in Bottoni et al. (2010). Conjunction with more traditional methods for testing and scoring has been discussed in Matsuda et al. (2009). Other aspects of learning process related to multilingualism (Barneva et al., 2009) and engagement of people with hearing difficulties (Kanev et al., 2009-2010) are also being addressed.

ACKNOWLEDGMENT

We would like to express our sincere appreciation to Thomas Orr, John Brine and Deborah Turk who have made valuable contributions to earlier stages of this project and coauthored previous papers.

REFERENCES

Barneva, R., Brimkov, V., & Kanev, K. (2009). Combining Ubiquitous Direction-Sensitive Digitizing with a Multimedia Electronic Dictionary for Enhanced Understanding. *International Journal of Imaging Systems and Technology, 2*(19), 39–49. doi:10.1002/ima.20189

Bottoni, P., Kanev, K., & Mirenkov, N. (2010). *Distributed and Context-focused Discussion on Augmented Documents and Objects.* In Proceedings of the 9th Int. Conf. on the Design of Cooperative Systems, pp.50-59.

Brine, J., Kanev, K., Turk, D., & Orr, T. (2007). Cloze Information Gap Tasks with Print-Based Digital Content Interfaces. In Proc. of the 7th IEEE International Conference on Advanced Learning Technologies (ICALT'07), pp. 318-319.

Brine, J., Turk, D., & Kanev, K. (2006). *Supporting Reading Jigsaws with Print-based Digital Content Interfaces.* Paper presented at JALTCALL'06 International Conference.

Curtis, D. D. (2001). Exploring Collaborative Online Learning. [JALN]. *Journal of Asynchronous Learning Networks, 5*(1), 21–34.

Dimakis, N., Polymenakos, L., & Soldatos, J. (2006). *Enhancing Learning Experiences Through Context-aware Collaborative Services: Software Architecture and Prototype System.* In Proc. of the 4th IEEE Int. Workshop on Wireless, Mobile and Ubiquitous Technology in Education (ICHIT'06).

Dimitracopoulou, A. (2005). Designing collaborative learning systems: Current trends & future research agenda. In Koschmann, T., Suthers, D., & Chan, T. W. (Eds.), *Proceedings of Computer Supported Collaborative Learning 2005: The next 10 years!* (pp. 115–124). Mahwah, NJ: Lawrence Erlbaum. doi:10.3115/1149293.1149309

Dwyer, N., & Suthers, D. D. (2006). Consistent Practices in Artifact-mediated Collaboration. *International Journal of Computer-Supported Collaborative Learning, 1*(4), 481–511. doi:10.1007/s11412-006-9001-1

Ellis, A. (2001). *Student-centred Collaborative Learning via Face-to-face and Asynchronous Online Communication: What's the Difference?* In Proc. of the 18th Annual Conference of the Australian Society for Computers in Learning in Tertiary Education (ASCILITE'01), pp. 169-177.

Ferscha, A., Holzmann, C., & Oppl, S. (2004). *Context Awareness for Group Interaction Support.* In Proc. of the Second Int. Workshop on Mobility Management & Wireless Access Protocols (MobiWac'04), pp. 88-97.

Gallardo, T., Guerrero, L. A., Collazos, C., Pino, J. A., & Ochoa, S. (2003). *Supporting JIGSAW-type Collaborative Learning.* In Proc. of the 36th Hawaii International Conference on System Sciences (HICSS'03).

Gamson, Z. F. (1994). Collaborative Learning Comes of Age. *Change, 26*(5), 44–49.

Hadwin, A. F., Gress, C. L. Z., & Page, J. (2006). *Towards Standards for Reporting Research: A Review of the Literature on Computer-Supported Collaborative Learning.* In Proc. of the Sixth Int. Conf. on Advanced Learning Technologies (ICALT'06).

Johnson, D. W., & Johnson, R. T. (1996). Cooperation and the Use of Technology. In Jonassen, D. H. (Ed.), *Handbook of Research for Educational Communications and Technology.* New York: Simon and Schuster.

Kanev, K. (2008). Tangible Interfaces for Interactive Multimedia Presentations. *Int. Journal of Mobile Information Systems: Special Issue on Information Assurance and Advanced Human-Computer Interfaces, 3*(4), 183–193.

Kanev, K., Barneva, R., Brimkov, V., & Kaneva, D. (2009-2010). Interactive Printouts Integrating Multilingual Multimedia and Sign Language Electronic Resources. *Journal of Educational Technology Systems, 2*(38), 123–143. doi:10.2190/ET.38.2.e

Kanev, K., Gnatyuk, P., & Gnatyuk, V. (2011). Laser marking in digital encoding of surfaces. *Advanced Materials Research, 222,* 78-81.

Kanev, K., & Kimura, S. (2005). *Digital Information Carrier. Patent Registration No 3635374.* Japan Patent Office.

Kanev, K., & Kimura, S. (2006). Direct Point-and-Click Functionality for Printed Materials. *The Journal of Three Dimensional Images, 20*(2), 51–59.

Kanev, K., Morishima, Y., & Watanabe, K. (2008). Surface Code Readers for Image Based Human-Computer Interfaces. In *Proceedings of the Eleventh Int. Conf. on Humans and Computers HC'08,* pp. 57-62.

Kanev, K., & Orr, T. (2006). Enhancing Paper Documents with Direct Access to Multimedia for an Intelligent Support of Reading. In *Proc. of the IEEE Conference on the Convergence of Technology and Professional Communication (IPCC'06),* pp.84-91.

Martin, E., & Paredes, P. (2004). Using Learning Styles for Dynamic Group Formation in Adaptive Collaborative Hypermedia Systems. Paper presented at *AHCW'04 held in conjunction with the International Conference on Web Engineering (ICWE'04).*

Matsuda, N., Kanev, K., Hirashima, T., & Taki, H. (2009). Ontology-based Annotations for Test Interpretation and Scoring. In *Proceedings of the 12th Int. Conf. on Humans and Computers HC'09,* pp.118-122.

Meier, A., Spada, H., & Rummel, N. (2007). A Rating Scheme for Assessing the Quality of Computer-supported Collaboration Processes. *International Journal of Computer-Supported Collaborative Learning, 2*(1), 63–86. doi:10.1007/s11412-006-9005-x

Miettinen, M., Kurhila, J., & Tirri, H. (2005). On the Prospects of Intelligent Collaborative E-learning Systems. In *Proc. of the 12th International Conference on Artificial Intelligence in Education (AIED'05)*, pp. 483-490.

Montgomery, C. (2002). Role of Dynamic Group Therapy in Psychiatry. *Advances in Psychiatric Treatment, 8*, 34–41. doi:10.1192/apt.8.1.34

Ogata, H., & Yano, Y. (1998). Knowledge Awareness: Bridging Learners in a Collaborative Learning Environment. *Int. Journal of Educational Telecommunications, 2/3*(4), 219–236.

Okada, A., Tarumi, H., & Kambayashi, Y. (2000). Real-Time Quiz Functions for Dynamic Group Guidance in Distance Learning Systems. In *Proc. of the First International Conference on Web Information Systems Engineering (WISE'00)*, pp.188-195.

Pressley, M., & McCormick, C. B. (1995). *Advanced Educational Psychology for Educators, Researchers, and Policymakers*. New York: Harper Collins.

Schiper, A. (2006). Dynamic Group Communication. *Distributed Computing, 18*(6), 359–374. doi:10.1007/s00446-005-0129-4

Turk, D., Brine, J., & Kanev, K. (2006). *Social Reading Activities Using Print-Based Digital Content Interfaces*. In Proc. of the 2nd IASTED International Conference on Education and Technology (ICET'06), pp. 51-55.

Chapter 2
A Systematic Framework of Virtual Laboratories Using Mobile Agent and Design Pattern Technologies

Yi-Hsung Li
Feng Chia University, Taiwan

Chyi-Ren Dow
Feng Chia University, Taiwan

Cheng-Min Lin
Nan Kai University of Technology, Taiwan

Sheng-Chang Chen
Feng Chia University, Taiwan

Fu-Wei Hsu
Sunplus mMobile Inc., Taiwan

ABSTRACT

Innovations in network and information technology have transformed traditional classroom lectures into new approaches that have given universities the opportunity to create a virtual laboratory. However, there is no systematic framework in existing approaches for the development of virtual laboratories. Further, developing a virtual laboratory from scratch is time consuming and costly. This article proposes a systematic framework to classify the activities between learners and instructors in the laboratory and to design the mobile agent-based virtual laboratory by wrapping the existing CAI tools without knowing the source code. Using the existing CAI tools can reduce the time and cost in constructing a virtual laboratory. The framework consists of three parts: mobile agent execution environment, mobile agent and learning platform. Moreover, various mobile agent design patterns are provided for users to design and implement virtual laboratories. This framework of patterns could make mobile agent based virtual

DOI: 10.4018/978-1-60960-539-1.ch002

laboratories easier to design and understand. The authors' framework has the following merits: adaptability, cost-effectiveness and collaboration. Their framework has demonstrated its feasibility in several applications, including digital circuit, language learning and digital signal processing laboratories.

INTRODUCTION

Virtual laboratories, virtual course-rooms, virtual collaboration rooms, virtual libraries and virtual private offices are categorized as part of the distance learning framework (Benmohamed *et al.*, 2005; Jiang *et al.*, 2001). In general, a traditional laboratory is composed of a number of physical instruments and a set of software applications. It is usually very expensive to construct a laboratory with physical instruments. Thus, virtual instruments and simulation tools can be used to construct a virtual laboratory. Currently, various virtual tools such as CAI/CAD systems are available in the market, but most of them are standalone tools. In order to include these standalone applications in a virtual laboratory and use them via networks, the source code for these systems must be modified to enable networking capability. Usually, to get the source code of these standalone applications is difficult. Therefore, reusing standalone applications in constructing a virtual laboratory without knowing the source codes is a great challenge.

The mobile agent (Perdikeas *et al.*, 1999) is an emerging technology that has potential for use as a convenient structuring technique in distributed and Internet-enabled applications. In order to assist students in the virtual laboratory, the mobile agents should have sufficient knowledge to solve problems and guide students to absorb the knowledge during the learning process. The mobile agent technique has been used to design and implement in several virtual laboratories (Dow *et al.*, 2002; Pantic *et al.*, 2005). However, these virtual laboratories and most of their system functions were implemented using an on-demand approach. Under these system environments, agents need to be redesigned and redeveloped for constructing a new virtual laboratory. Thus, it is necessary to provide design patterns

to help designers in developing mobile agent-based virtual laboratory applications.

This work proposes a framework to solve the above problems. The proposed framework provides various design patterns and features for virtual laboratory developers and end-users. In our framework, wrappers (Dow *et al.*, 2002; Dow *et al.*; 2006) are used as the middleware in virtual laboratories. Various agents are designed to provide collaboration between instructor and learner or between learner and learner in a virtual laboratory. Furthermore, ten activities for virtual laboratory were classified in the proposed system. Various existing CAI tools or on-line web sites can be incorporated into a virtual laboratory with the proposed framework. Thus, a framework that uses existing CAI tools and design patterns to develop virtual laboratories for saving time and resources is presented in this work.

The rest of this article is structured as follows. Section 2 briefly describes the background materials and related work. Section 3 describes the wrapping concepts and models for the proposed system architecture. The agents and design patterns for virtual laboratories are presented in Sections 4 and 5, respectively. The implementation of the virtual laboratories with the proposed method and experimental results are presented in Sections 6 and 7. Conclusions are described in Section 8.

RELATED WORK

There are many research areas related to our work, such as virtual laboratory, e-learning, mobile agents, wrappers and software patterns. With the growth of network technology and the increasing popularity of new learning methods, more and more researches focus on the virtual laboratory and e-learning (Benmohamed *et al.*, 2005; Bermejo, 2005; Chang *et al.*, 2000; Dow *et al*, 2002; Dow *et al.*, 2006; Gomez *et al.*, 2000; Jiang *et al.*, 2001; Jou, 2005; Muzak *et al.*, 2000; Tzeng *et al.*, 2000). The virtual laboratory proposed by Muzak *et al.* (2000) focuses on digital computers and is based on the client/server computing paradigm. A virtual laboratory changes the traditional lecture hall into a network enabled lecturing environment. Moreover, it focuses on the lecturing only and lacks some important activities such as an assessment system. Another virtual laboratory proposed by Tzeng & Tien (2000) for teaching electric machinery has realistic, interactive and flexible characteristics based on the client/server computing paradigm. Aside from the client/server based virtual laboratories, several researches have established virtual laboratories based on the World Wide Web, such as the virtual laboratory proposed by Gomez *et al.* (2000). Usually, these kinds of virtual laboratories are established for a specific device. Designers must design a new virtual laboratory for each different device. When a virtual laboratory becomes larger, traffic jams will occur in the network and virtual environments. Thus, the problems of adaptability for virtual laboratories are needed to be solved.

The mobile agent techniques (Concepcion *et al.*, 2002; Johansen *et al.*, 2002; Komiya *et al.*, 2002; Perdikeas *et al.*, 1999; Silva *et al.*, 2000; Sudmann *et al.*, 2001; Suwu *et al.*, 2001; Wang, 2000; Aglets, n.d.) have been widely used in many Internet applications. The merits (Silva, Soares, Martins, Batista, & Santos, 2000) of these technologies include a reduction in network traffic and latency in the client/server network computing paradigm, autonomy, dynamic adaptation, protocol encapsulation, heterogeneity, robust performance and fault tolerance. A mobile agent has the unique ability to move from one system in a network to another. Mobile agents, such as Aglets, characterized by the unique ability to transport their state and code with them, as they migrate among the components of a network infrastructure. When large volumes of multimedia data

are stored on remote hosts, these data should be processed close to the user. This reduces network traffic because processing commands do not need to be transferred over the network.

One important problem we faced when building a virtual laboratory is where to place an extra function for a standalone learning tool without knowing its source code. The wrapper (Sudmann *et al.*, 2001) is a technique that provides a convenient way to expand upon the existing application program functions without modifying its source code. Wrappers provide a way to compose applications from different parts. The fact that a mobile agent is wrapped should be transparent to other mobile agents in the system and potentially to the agent itself. Therefore, the union of a mobile agent and a wrapper looks just like another stationary agent. In our previous work (Dow *et al.*, 2002; Dow *et al.*, 2006), the agent-based virtual laboratories wrapped the existing CAI tools without knowing the source code. The concept is to use mobile agents as middleware for wrapping existing CAI tools.

Software patterns (Kienzle & Romanovsky, 2002) have their roots in Christopher Alexander's work in the field of building architecture. Patterns facilitate reuse of well-established solutions when known problems are encountered. The patterns that are adapted in the stage of object-oriented design (OOD) are called design patterns. Design patterns (Schelfthout *et al.*, 2002) are reoccurring patterns of programming code or components of software architecture that have succeeded as past solutions to design problems. The purpose of using design patterns is to increase the reusability and quality of code and at the same time to reduce software development effort. Design patterns are useful in achieving flexible and extensible designs, and they make future changes and modifications easier. There are different pattern formats (Deugo & Weiss, 1999). The minimal format contains the following headings or ones dealing with similar subject matters, including Name, Problem, Context, Forces and Solution.

SYSTEM ARCHITECTURE

I/O interception is in charge of exposing the functions of a CAI tool as a set of methods of an object by intercepting its I/O and commands. Each CAI tool has a fixed operation instruction set, such as hot keys, run-time parameters, etc. This component gives exact operation instructions to the CAI tool and triggers this tool to execute the corresponding functions. API is the interface for controlling the virtual laboratory. The software model, as shown in Figure 1, consists of four layers. The top layer is the application software, such as CAI tools. The second layer consists of services and user-defined mobile agents which interact with the Java native interface, the Windows API and the agent API. The third layer is the agent runtime layer, which consists of two parts: a core framework and a set of extensible system management components. The primary functions of the core framework are agent initialization and serialization/deserialization, class loading and transfer, agent references and garbage collection. Moreover, it provides core services for an executing agent, including creation, clone, dispatch, retraction, deactivation and activation. The management components are the cache manager, the security manager and the persistence manager. At the bottom are the communication API and its implementation. The wrapper concept provides both adaptability and cost-effectiveness in our virtual laboratory framework. From the system perspective, the framework supports object-oriented programming (OOP) in the development of a virtual laboratory; various standalone CAI tools can be easily reused in virtual laboratory by wrapping. Thus, the cost of time and system and educational resources can be reduced effectively. This reduces production costs; in particular, it reduces the amounts of time, computer system resources and educational resources that are required.

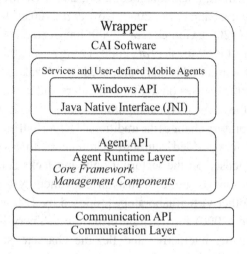

Figure 1. Software model

VIRTUAL LABORATORY AGENTS AND ACTIVITIES

In order to present a virtual laboratory just like a real laboratory, various objects are required in the virtual laboratory, including roles, hardware/software, network services and activities. The roles include instructors and learners. In the hardware/software aspect, the hardware consists of various physical experimental equipments, and the software includes teaching functions, learning functions and other functions. Because the virtual laboratory evolves from distance learning, it should provide the network capabilities and services for different networking paradigms. Thus, the instructors and learners can communicate with each other through the Internet.

The activity in our virtual laboratory has been classified into ten groups, includes guiding, monitoring, demonstrating, telling, cognizing, questioning, assessing, practicing, explaining and criticizing. These activities are described as follows.

1. **Guiding**: Through the guiding activity, instructors can give learners some hints to complete the experiment or help them to get the better solutions for their problems.

Besides, instructor can also lead learners to get into the unit levels that suit them by the guiding activity. With the guiding activity, learners can gain cognition easily.

2. **Monitoring**: In the traditional laboratory, the instructor can directly take care of learners. However, in the virtual laboratory world the instructor and learners are located in different places. Thus, we need a monitoring activity to know the learner's study schedule.

3. **Demonstrating**: Learners perform an experiment in the laboratory and usually need a demonstration by the instructor at the first time. Hence, the demonstration is an important activity for learners to be able to accomplish an experiment.

4. **Telling**: The instructor can teach learners new knowledge through the telling activity. Thus, the telling activity is a way to teach learners.

5. **Cognizing**: After the instructor teaches learners using the telling activity, learners will absorb knowledge through the cognizing activity. Thus, cognizing is indispensable in education.

6. **Questioning**: During the learning process, the instructor can give a topic or question for learners to find the answer. Learners can put forward questions to the instructor when they have problems during the learning process. Therefore, the questioning activity can help instructors and learners to complete the learning process.

7. **Assessing**: After learners complete their learning process, the instructor can use an assessment system to obtain the study effect of the learners' study. Learners can also use the assessment to understand how much they learned. Thus, the assessing activity is an important activity for instructors and learners.

8. **Practicing**: In the laboratory, practicing experiments plays an important part in a virtual laboratory. After the teacher uses the telling

and demonstrating activities, learners need practice to strengthen the memorization what they learned. With more practices, learners can get better learning effect.

9. **Explaining**: When learners have a question, the instructor needs to answer the question for learners. The explaining activity is an activity in which the instructor explains procedures and processes for learners. Learners can solve problems through the explaining activity.

10. **Criticizing**: During the learning process, it is not always through learning activities that a learner is taught by an instructor. Sometimes, an instructor and several learners will discuss some topics or subjects in a virtual meeting room. Through discussions with each other, learners can also learn very well.

In our virtual laboratory framework, various software agents and activities for instructors and learners as shown in Figure 2 are illustrated as follows:

1. **Guide Agent**: This agent proposes the guiding activity for an instructor. When learners get some problems during their experiment, the guide agent can lead them to complete the experiment automatically. Besides, the instructor can record the learning situation for learners and guide learners in different levels using a guide agent. With the guide agent, the instructor can understand and control the situation for learners.

2. **Monitor Agent**: This agent proposes a monitoring activity for the instructor. The monitor agent can act as the instructor to monitor the learner's actions and learning status.

3. **Demo Agent**: A demo agent uses the demonstrating activity to help an instructor or a learner. The agent is used to assist the instructor in demonstrating the steps of the learning for learners. Learners can also use

Figure 2. Relationships in a virtual laboratory

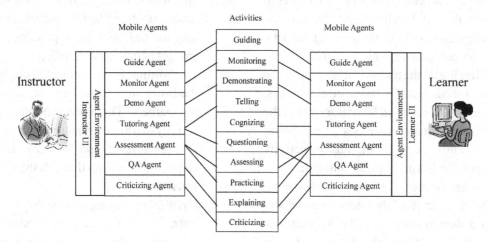

the agent to demonstrate the learning process to the instructor.

4. **Tutoring Agent**: A tutoring agent works with telling and questioning activities for instructor and the cognizing activity for learners. The agents dispatched by the instructor are telling and questioning for learners to cognize the learning materials.

5. **Assessment Agent**: Assessing and practicing activities are the main activities for an assessment agent. The instructor can use the assessment agent to give assessments to check the learner's learning results and provide different levels of assessment materials. The agent can also provide various practices for learners, such as homework.

6. **QA Agent**: A QA (Question and Answer) agent will accomplish the explaining activity for an instructor and the questioning and explaining activities for a learner. The QA agent can help the instructor to explain the regular questions when a learner posts a question in a virtual black board system.

7. **Criticizing Agent**: The criticizing activity will accomplish by a criticizing agent for instructors and learners. Instructors and learners can use the criticizing agent to discuss subjects with each other. This agent can also record the content of discussion to

help instructors to understand the learning status of learners.

In our virtual laboratory, the wrapper technique can be used in the demo agent and the tutoring agent for instruction. The wrapper technique utilizes two kinds of agents for wrapping existing CAI tools to quickly produce an example for learners. By using the previous seven agents and ten activities, as shown in Figure 2, the collaboration provided in our virtual laboratory enhances student learning.

In our proposed virtual laboratories, mobile agent techniques are used to construct the virtual laboratories. There are three major components in our virtual laboratory framework, including the mobile agent execution environments, agents and learning platforms. A mobile agent execution environment must be installed on both learner and instructor sides to provide a necessary runtime environment for agents to execute. The mobile agent has a principal role in the virtual laboratory. There are two kinds of mobile agents for our framework, agent wrappers and agent roles. The learning platform contains two parts: software environment and hardware environment. In the software part, it is an existing application program that could be a learning program as the CAI tool (e.g., a language learning tool), design software like the CAD tool, simulation tool (e.g.,

Code Composer, Matlab (Matlab, n.d.), Altera (Altera, n.d.), etc.) or on-line learning web site, which provides learners learning environments.

AGENT DESIGN PATTERNS

In order to design an agent-based virtual laboratory, we classify the components of mobile agent into seven design patterns, including system environment, nomadic management, delegation, behavior management, datacasting, coordination and auxiliary. These classification schemes make it easier to design and understand the virtual laboratory framework. It is very important that these seven design patterns make our virtual laboratory framework adaptability.

1. **System Environment Patterns**: The system environment patterns quickly construct an environment to provide mobile agent execution. The class diagram of system environment patterns is shown in Figure 3. The execution environment has two types: instructor and learner environments, which inherit from an abstract class called the system environment pattern that provides two abstract operations, initializeJob and routine-Job. It should be noted that each rectangle in Figure 3 denotes a UML class diagram (Oestereich, 2002). The three fields from top

to bottom in the UML class diagram, class name, attributes and operations, are divided from each other by a horizontal line. In the class diagrams of our design patterns, we focus on the illustration of the operations of the classes. Thus, the attribute fields are in blank.

2. **Nomadic Management Patterns**: The nomadic management patterns can be divided into two schemes, including one-way and round-trip migrations. The one-way migration means that a mobile agent will roam from the source to destination and not come back, such as a demo agent. The demo agent just needs to carry its demonstration data to a destination and does not need to carry any demonstration data back to the source. The round-trip type means that a mobile agent will roam from the source to destination and it will come back to the source to accomplish its task, such as the QA agent. The QA agent carries the questions from the questioner to the destination, and the QA agent brings the answers back to the source for the questioner. The class diagram for nomadic management patterns is shown in Figure 4.

3. **Delegation Patterns**: The delegation patterns contain sequential and parallel delegation schemes, which define schemes for mobile agents to complete their tasks. The delegation pattern class diagram is shown in

Figure 3. System environment patterns

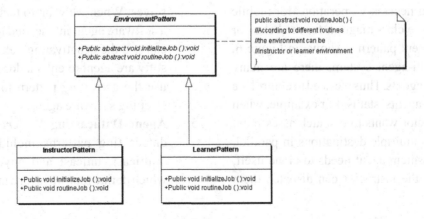

Figure 4. Nomadic management patterns

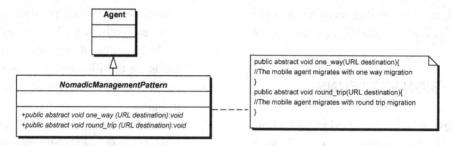

Figure 5. Delegation patterns

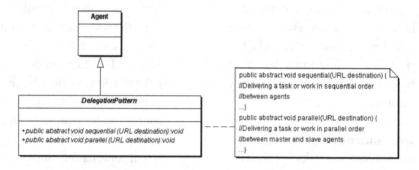

Figure 5. The instructor can design work or experiments that have several procedures for delivering information to the learners using the assessment agent. This facilitates learners to complete this work or experiment in a sequential order according to the content. These patterns provide collaboration models between instructors and learners or learners and learners.

4. **Behavior Management Patterns**: The behavior patterns include cloning, disposing, deactivating and activating patterns providing necessary operations for mobile agents. The class diagram for the behavior management pattern is shown in Figure 6. In a multi-agent system, there are many software agents. Thus we need to control the software agents' status. For example, when an instructor wants to dispatch assessment agents to multiple destinations in parallel, the assessment agent needs to clone itself, and then the instructor can dispatch them

to learners in parallel. Thus, four operating patterns are provided, including cloning, disposing, deactivating and activating patterns. We will use these behavior management patterns when the software agents accomplish their tasks. When we use one-way model for mobile agent's migration, we wish that the software agent would be disposed after it arrives at destinations. Thus, we use the disposing pattern. When we delegate several tasks in parallel, we can use the cloning pattern for software agents to clone themselves. When we want to temporarily store a software agent in a secondary storage, we can use the deactivating pattern to make a software agent to enter a dormant state and use the activating pattern to wake up the sleeping software agent.

5. **Agent Datacasting Patterns**: The agent datacasting patterns include broadcast, multicast, unicast and anycast patterns, which define four ways for a mobile agent to

Figure 6. Behavior management patterns

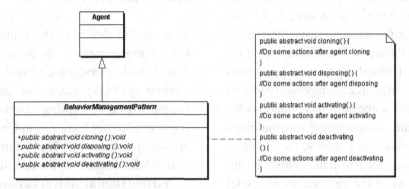

Figure 7. Agent datacasting patterns

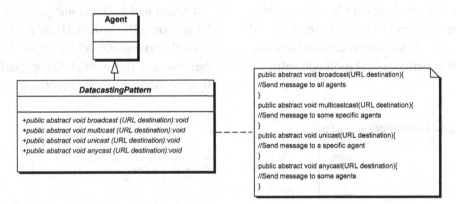

carry a message to other mobile agents. The class diagram of agent datacasting patterns is shown in Figure 7. Software agents can establish remote datacasts by using agent datacasting patterns, which make messages in the form of agents that carry and deliver messages between software agents. The unicast pattern can provide a software agent to send a message to a single software agent. The multicast pattern will let the software agent to send messages to a group of software agents. Broadcast pattern supports software agent to send messages to all the software agents which are alive in the virtual laboratory. The anycast pattern can provide a software agent to get messages from the nearest destination. In a multi-agent system, we can use these datacasting schemes to

pass messages between software agents. The network bandwidth can be managed through different message passing approaches.

6. **Agent Coordination Patterns**: The agent coordination patterns contain direct, blackboard, meeting-oriented and Linda-like (Cabri *et al.*, 2000) patterns, which define coordination schemes whereby a master agent can coordinate or exchange information with slave agents. The class diagram for the agent coordination patterns is shown in Figure 8. The coordination patterns are applicable in the following situations: (a) when software agents need to interact with other software agents with reliable and high-bandwidth network connections; (b) when software agents need to interact with other software agents with unreliable and

low-bandwidth network connections; and (c) when software agents need to interact with other software agents asynchronously.

7. **Auxiliary Patterns**: The auxiliary patterns include GUI, visual appearance, agent management and resource management patterns, which define some auxiliary functions for mobile agents. The class diagram of auxiliary patterns is shown in Figure 9. The auxiliary patterns are applicable in the following situations: (a) when software agents need GUI between users and software agents; (b) when software agents need some visual objects to represent themselves; (c) when users need to manage software agents' information; and (d) when software agents need to have collaboration between CAI tools and software agents.

IMPLEMENTATION

This section describes the implementations of virtual laboratories with the proposed framework. Two virtual laboratories, Virtual Digital System Laboratory (VDSL) (Dow *et al.*, 2002) and Virtual Digital Signal Processing Laboratory (VDSPL) (Dow *et al.*, 2006), are re-implemented with the proposed framework. The details of these two virtual laboratories are illustrated as follows.

Virtual Digital System Laboratory (VDSL): Previous work implemented a standalone virtual digital system laboratory, including a digital circuit board and a digital analyzer, without using the proposed framework (Dow *et al.*, 2002). We re-implemented the VDSL with the proposed framework in this work. In the standalone virtual digital system, the software contains wires, instru-

Figure 8. Agent coordination patterns

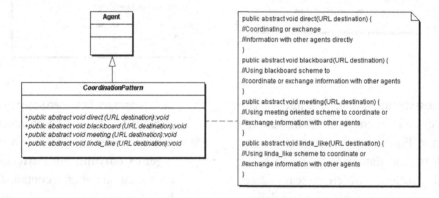

Figure 9. Auxiliary patterns

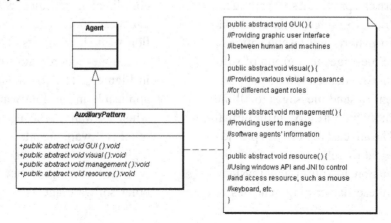

ments, layout tools and 44 kinds of ICs. Learners can practice design, simulation, debugging and layout. By using the proposed framework, we use wrapping technology to enable the network capability of the standalone virtual digital system. Hence, we design some mobile agents to wrap the original virtual digital system. In order to enable the network capability for the original virtual digital system, we constructed the tutoring agent and demo agent. Instructors use these agents to teach via the Internet. Learners can interact with instructors by the tutoring agent, and instructors can do some demonstrations of the virtual digital system for learners with the demo agent, as shown in Figure 10. In addition, the monitor agent and criticizing agent were implemented in the VDSL.

Virtual Digital Signal Processing Laboratory (VDSPL): The previous work creates virtual digital signal processing laboratory without the proposed framework. We re-implemented the VDSPL with the proposed mobile agents and design patterns. This was created using DMATEKs' TMS30C542 Evaluation Module (EVM) based on the Texas Instruments' (TI) Code Composer

Studio (CCStudio) development software. By using the proposed design patterns for VDSPL, we implemented five mobile agents, including a guide agent, a monitor agent, a demo agent, a tutoring agent and an assessment agent. Learners can use this virtual laboratory to learn DSP by a real-time multimedia demonstration and various agent functions. Furthermore, an instructor can also monitor and evaluate the results for learners by means of the guide, monitor and assessment agents. As shown in Figure 12, the mobile agents in the VDSPL were implemented by the proposed design patterns. With the proposed framework, the characteristics of mobile agents are clearly defined, and we can determine which mobile agent roles are needed to make the VDSPL learning experience fast and easy. Besides, with the different characteristics of mobile agents, we used the proposed design patterns to design the mobile agents. Furthermore, we created the network capability for the virtual laboratory by integrating mobile agent techniques without modifying existing system's source code. (see Figure 11)

EXPERIMENTAL RESULTS

Experiments were conducted in two parts. One is to evaluate the importance and satisfaction of

Figure 10. A snapshot of the demo agent in the VDSL

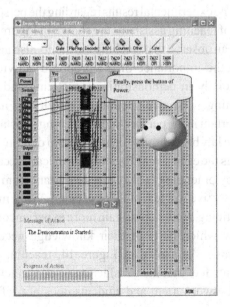

Figure 11. A snapshot of the guide agent in the VDSPL

Figure 12. The proposed design patterns used by the mobile agents in the VDSPL

Patterns	Agent	Guide Agent	Monitor Agent	Demo Agent	Tutoring Agent	Assessment Agent
System Environment Patterns	initializeJob	●	●	●	●	●
	routineJob	●	●	○	○	○
Nomadic Management Patterns	one_way	○	○	●	●	○
	round_trip	●	●	○	○	●
Delegation Patterns	sequential	○	○	●	○	○
	parallel	●	●	○	●	●
Behavior Management Patterns	cloning	●	●	●	●	●
	disposing	○	○	●	●	●
	activating	●	●	●	●	○
	deactivating	●	●	●	●	○
Agent Datacasting Patterns	broadcast	○	○	○	○	●
	multicast	●	●	○	●	○
	unicast	●	●	●	○	○
	anycast	○	○	○	○	○
Agent Coordination Patterns	direct	●	●	●	○	●
	blackboard	○	●	○	●	○
	meeting	○	○	○	●	○
	linda_like	○	○	○	○	○

● : Pattern was used by the mobile agent in VDSPL
○ : Pattern was not used by the mobile agent in VDSPL

the proposed activities for teaching assistants and students. Ten teaching assistants and twenty-five students in our department were recruited to conduct these experiments. We investigated the importance and satisfaction of the proposed activities, including guiding, monitoring, demonstrating, telling, cognizing, questioning, assessing, practicing, explaining and criticizing from the points of view of both teaching assistants and students. The other part is to evaluate the requirements from prospective users of the proposed design patterns. We investigated twelve users who have the experience of designing and implementing software agents in the software agent related projects or classes. The design patterns include system environment, nomadic management, delegation, behavior management, agent datacasting and agent coordination patterns. (see Figure 12)

In the first part, the experimental results regarding the perspective of students are shown in Figure 13. We can observe that students agree with the importance of the proposed activities, especially in guiding, demonstrating and explaining. In a lab-based course, instructors or teaching assistants, usually, teach students how to use or operate the instrument by demonstrating some examples. Guiding and explaining are two important activities for students when students encounter problems during their experiment. Activities with high levels of perceived importance would normally be expected to produce similarly high levels of satisfaction. Aside from the three most important activities from the perspective of students, we also found that the proposed activities are important for students, but the proposed activities in the traditional lab-based course was unable to satisfy them, except for the practicing activity, as shown in Figure 13. In the traditional lab-based course, it is hard for instructors or teaching assistants to teach students one-on-one. Instructors and teaching assistants can provide several practices so that students can know what they need to improve. Thus, students feel that most of the activities in the traditional lab-based course are not enough for learning, except for the practicing activity.

The experimental results regarding the perspective of teaching assistants are shown in Figure 14. We can observe that teaching assistants also agree with the importance of the proposed activities, especially in demonstrating, practicing and explaining. The demonstrating activity is most important in the perspective of teaching assistants. In the lab-based course, learning from demonstration is the easiest way for students to learn. Learning by practicing is also very important from the perspective of teaching assistants. With more practicing, students can gain more experience and know which parts of their knowledge need to improve. As shown in Figure 14, teaching assistants feel that the satisfaction of all the activities between them and students does not reflect

Figure 13. The importance and satisfaction of the proposed activities from students' perspective

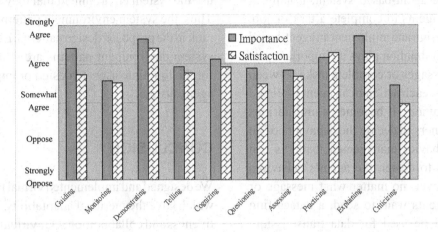

the importance of the activities. Due to insufficient manpower, teaching assistants cannot personally assist every student in the class. Teaching assistants want to guide each student attentively, but time constraints and class sizes prevent this.

If one considers these experimental results from the perspective of teaching assistants and students, certain focal points stand out. In general, a teaching assistant will find it hard to cope with a large number of students. Guiding all the students in the class at the same time is an impossible mission for a teaching assistant. A teaching assistant cannot do different demonstrations for different students at the same time. But a well-designed agent system will make this task pos-

sible. The proposed agent system can overcome the insufficiencies of the teaching assistant, and the proposed agent design patterns can design the agents for greater convenience.

In order to evaluate the requirements from prospective users of the proposed design patterns in the second part of the experiments, the proposed design patterns are provided for the users to give rank of the design patterns. The values 6 to 1 denote the rank values of the proposed design patterns from high to low. The experimental results regarding the perspective of users are shown in Figure 15. The top three of the proposed design patterns from the user are agent coordination, behavior management and agent datacasting

Figure 14. The importance and satisfaction of the proposed activities from teaching assistants' perspective

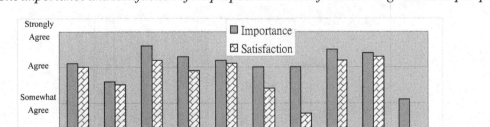

patterns. In the agent-based system, usually, it needs several agents to complete a task or job. Therefore, to design and implement an agent-based system, the coordination plays an important part to transmit messages or complete tasks between agents. Besides, each action of an agent is related to agent's behaviors. It becomes a multifarious work for designers to decide the behaviors of an agent. The behavior management patterns can help designers to design the agent's behaviors quickly. Moreover, no matter what message or information agents want to send, a datacasting method should be used for data transmission. Designers can use the agent datacasting patterns to reduce their workload. Therefore, these design patterns can be used by users to accomplish the complex and strenuous task when designing and implementing mobile agents.

Besides, the delegation, system environment and nomadic management patterns are the other three proposed design patterns. The mobility in the mobile agent-based system is important, but only mobile agents migrating to other places require the nomadic management and delegation patterns. Therefore, the requirement for these two patterns depends on the mobility of mobile agents. In general, users who have the experience of designing or implementing software agents will use the system environment that they are used to. Thus, the system environment patterns got lower rank in the proposed design patterns. Even though, system environment patterns are still important for the first time users to design or implement an agent system.

CONCLUSION

We designed and implemented virtual laboratories which have the merits of adaptability, cost-effectiveness and collaboration. Our virtual laboratory integrates mobile agent techniques and wrapper concepts to perform software re-engineering. Further, various design patterns are formulated for the virtual laboratory development. The proposed framework can be used to assist designers developing virtual laboratories in a formal approach and the existing CAI tools can be reused without modifying the source code from the original programs. In the meantime, various software agents have been designed and our virtual laboratory has been used for various applications, including digital circuit, language learning and digital signal processing. The experimental results show that the proposed activities between instructors and learners are important, and the need for an agent system is

Figure 15. The requirement rank from prospective users of the proposed design patterns

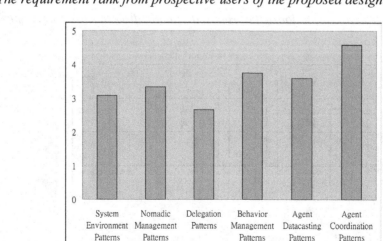

urgent. This work focuses on the development of virtual laboratories in e-learning. Our future plans are to integrate our framework with other components of e-learning and to implement more related design patterns. Future work includes the design and implementation of various knowledge management functions to these software agents in our framework.

ACKNOWLEDGMENT

The authors would like to thank the National Science Council of the Republic of China for financially supporting this research under Contract No. NSC96-2221-E-035-036.

REFERENCES

Aglets. (n.d.). Retrieved from http://aglets.source-forge.net/

Altera (n.d.). Retrieved from http://www.altera.com/

Benmohamed, H., Lelevé, A., & Prévot, P. (2005). Generic Framework for Remote Laboratory Integration. In *Proceedings of the 6th International Conference on Information Technology Based Higher Education and Training* (pp. T2B-11-T2B-16), Santo Domingo, Dominican Republic.

Bermejo, S. (2005). Cooperative Electronic Learning in Virtual Laboratories Through Forums. *IEEE Transactions on Education*, *48*(1), 140–149. doi:10.1109/TE.2004.837045

Cabri, G., Leonardi, L., & Zambonelli, F. (2000). MARS: A Programmable Coordination Architecture for Mobile Agents. *IEEE Internet Computing*, *4*(4), 26–35. doi:10.1109/4236.865084

Chang, S. K., Arndt, T., Levialdi, S., Liu, A. C., Ma, J., Shih, T., & Tortora, G. (2000). Macro University A Framework for a Federation of Virtual Universities. *International Journal of Computer Processing of Oriental Languages*, *13*(3), 205–221. doi:10.1142/S0219427900000168

Concepcion, A. I., Ruan, J., & Samson, R. R. (2002). SPIDER: A Multi-agent Architecture for Internet Distributed Computing System. In *Proceedings of the ISCA 15th International Conference on Parallel and Distributed Computing Systems* (pp. 147-152), Louisville, KY, USA.

Deugo, D., & Weiss, M. (1999). A Case for Mobile Agent Patterns. In *Proceedings of the Mobile Agents in the Context of Competition and Cooperation (MAC3) Workshop Notes* (pp. 19-22), Seattle, WA, USA.

Dow, C. R., Li, Y. H., & Bai, J. Y. (2006). A Virtual Laboratory for Digital Signal Processing. *International Journal of Distance Education Technologies*, *4*(2), 31–43. doi:10.4018/jdet.2006040103

Dow, C. R., Lin, C. M., & Chen, S. S. (2002). The Development of a Virtual Digital Circuit Laboratory Using VDSL. *The Journal of Chinese Institute of Electrical Engineering*, *9*(3), 251–257.

Dow, C. R., Lin, C. Y., Shen, C. C., Lin, J. H., & Chen, S. C. (2002). A Virtual Laboratory for Macro Universities Using Mobile Agent Techniques. *The International Journal of Computer Processing of Oriental Languages*, *15*(1), 1–18. doi:10.1142/S0219427902000509

Gomez, F. J., Cervera, M., & Martinez, J. (2000). A World Wide Web Based Architecture for the Implementation of a Virtual Laboratory. In *Proceedings of the 26th Euromicro Conference*, *2* 56-61. Maastricht, The Netherlands.

Jiang, G., Lan, J., & Zhuang, X. (2001). Distance Learning Technologies and an Interactive Multimedia Educational System. In *Proceedings of the IEEE International Conference on Advanced Learning Technologies* (pp. 405-408), Madison, WI, USA.

Johansen, D., & Lauvset, K. (2002). An Extensible Software Architecture for Mobile Components. In *Proceedings of the 9th Annual IEEE International Conference and Workshop on the Engineering of Computer-based Systems* (pp. 231-237), Lund, Sweden.

Jou, M. (2005). Development of an e-Learning System for Teaching Machining Technology. In *Proceedings of the 2005 International Conference on Active Media Technology* (pp. 347-352), Takamatsu, Japan.

Kienzle, J., & Romanovsky, A. (2002). A Framework Based on Design Patterns for Providing Persistence in Object-oriented Programming Languages. *IEE Software Engineering Journal*, *149*, 77–85. doi:10.1049/ip-sen:20020465

Komiya, T., Ohsida, H., & Takizawa, M. (2002). Mobile Agent Model for Distributed Objects Systems. In *Proceedings of the 5th IEEE International Symposium on Object-Oriented Real-Time Distributed Computing* (pp. 62-69), Washington, DC, USA.

MATLAB. (n.d.). Retrieved from http://www.mathworks.com/

Muzak, G., Cavrak, I., & Zagar, M. (2000). The Virtual Laboratory Project. In *Proceedings of the 22nd Internal Conference on Information Technology Interfaces* (pp. 241-246), Zagreb, Croatia.

Oestereich, B. (2002). *Developing Software with UML: Object-Oriented Analysis and Design in Practice*. Addison-Wesley.

Pantic, M., Zwitserloot, R., & Grootjans, R. J. (2005). Teaching Introductory Artificial Intelligence Using a Simple Agent Framework. *IEEE Transactions on Education*, *48*(3), 382–390. doi:10.1109/TE.2004.842906

Perdikeas, M. K., Chatzipapadopoulos, F. G., Venieris, I. S., & Marino, G. (1999). Mobile Agent Standards and Available Platforms. *Computer Networks Journal*, *31*(19), 1999–2016. doi:10.1016/S1389-1286(99)00076-6

Schelfthout, K., Coninx, T., Helleboogh, A., Holvoet, T., Steegmans, E., & Weyns, D. (2002). Agent Implementation Patterns. In *Proceedings of the OOPSLA 2002 Workshop on Agent-Oriented Methodologies* (pp. 119-130), Seattle, WA, USA.

Silva, L. M., Soares, G., Martins, P., Batista, V., & Santos, L. (2000). Comparing the Performance of Mobile Agent System: A Study of Benchmarking. *Computer Communications*, *23*(8), 769–778. doi:10.1016/S0140-3664(99)00237-6

Sudmann, N. P., & Johansen, D. (2001). Supporting Mobile Agent Applications Using Wrappers. In *Proceedings of the 12nd International Workshop on Database and Expert Systems Applications* (pp. 689-695), Munich, Germany.

Suwu, W., & Das, A. (2001). An Agent System Architecture for E-commerce. In *Proceedings of the 12nd International Workshop on Database and Expert Systems Applications* (pp. 715-726), Munich, Germany.

Tzeng, H. W., & Tien, C. M. (2000). Design of a Virtual Laboratory for Teaching Electric Machinery. In *Proceedings of the IEEE International Conference on Systems, Man, and Cybernetics*, *2*, 971–976.

Wang, Y. (2002). Dispatching Multiple Mobile Agents in Parallel for Visiting E-shops. In *Proceedings of the 3rd International Conference on Mobile Data Management* (pp. 61-68), Amsterdam, The Netherlands.

This work was previously published in International Journal of Distance Education Technologies (IJDET), Volume 7, Issue 3, edited by Qun Jin & Oscar Fuhua Lin, pp. 26-43, copyright 2009 by IGI Publishing (an imprint of IGI Global).

Chapter 3
A Computer–Assisted Approach for Conducting Information Technology Applied Instructions

Hui-Chun Chu
National University of Tainan, Taiwan

Gwo-Jen Hwang
National University of Tainan, Taiwan

Pei-Jin Tsai
National Chiao Tung University, Taiwan

Tzu-Chi Yang
National Chi-Nan University, Taiwan

ABSTRACT

The growing popularity of computer and network technologies has attracted researchers to investigate the strategies and the effects of information technology applied instructions. Previous research has not only demonstrated the benefits of applying information technologies to the learning process, but has also revealed the difficulty of applying them effectively. One of the major difficulties is due to the lack of an easy-to-follow procedure for inexperienced teachers to design course content with proper use of suitable information technologies. In this paper, a model for conducting information technology applied instructions is proposed. The novel approach can assist teachers in designing information technology applied course content based on the features of subject materials and the learning status of the students. An experiment on a Chemistry course in a junior high school was conducted to evaluate the performance of our novel approach.

DOI: 10.4018/978-1-60960-539-1.ch003

INTRODUCTION

With the popularity of computers and information technologies, systems and learning theories have been developed for web-based learning in higher education, while the effectiveness of these implementations has been empirically evaluated as well (Barrett & Lally, 1999). New technologies are presented each day in more activities and, of course, in education. This great innovation is changing the concept of information technology applied instruction, not only in terms of the teaching process itself, but also with respect to the methodologies applied. The new information age has changed the educational system, with the result being the birth of information technology applied instruction and computer-assisted learning.

Researchers have suggested that teachers examine the instructional strategies supported by various environments so as to determine the relative effectiveness of these environments. One of the major difficulties of information technology applied instructions is the lack of an easy-to-follow procedure for inexperienced teachers to design subject content such that suitable information technologies can be properly applied to the tutoring process. Chou (2003) indicated that teachers are the key to the successful use of the Internet for both teaching and learning. However, without any assistance, teacher's anxiety can often reduce the success of such technological and pedagogical innovations.

To cope with this problem, a systematic instructional design model is proposed to assist teachers in employing proper information technologies in the development of tutoring strategies and learning activities. The model provides a systematic procedure that guides inexperienced teachers to select proper information technologies or tools for the courses they teach by taking the features of the course content and the learning status of the students into consideration. With the help of this innovative approach, teachers can easily learn how to design a quality learning activity that employs proper information technologies to improve the learning performance of the students. An experiment on a Chemistry course in a junior high school was conducted to evaluate the performance of this novel approach. The results of this experiment show that the developed instructional design can significantly improve the learning performance of students, and hence we conclude that the present approach is desirable.

RELEVANT RESEARCH

The rapid progress in information technology can help instructors to teach more efficiently and effectively by employing new tutoring strategies with appropriate software tools and environments. Several studies have demonstrated the benefits of applying information technologies to instructions, such as Computer Scaffolding (Guzdial et al., 1996), CSCL (Computer-Supported Collaborative Learning) (Harasim, 1999), CSILE (Computer-Supported Intentional Learning Environments) (Scardamalia et al., 1989) and CiC (Computer-Integrated Classroom) (Eshet, Klemes, & Henderson, 2000).

The benefits of using Adaptive CAI (Computer-Assisted Instruction) systems make them desirable educational tools. A CAI system can be thought of as a tutorial system, which is a guided system to provide well-constructed information. Students can use this system to learn how to use a technical system or how to operate an instrument. For example, Oakley (1996) presented computer-based tutorials and a virtual classroom to teach circuit analysis. Meanwhile, Zhou, Wang, and Ng (1996) proposed a tutorial system using artificial intelligence technology. Later, Davidovic, Warren, and Trichina (2003) argued that greater efficiency can be achieved by basing the system development on the theoretical background of cognitive knowledge acquisition. In addition, some researchers have utilized auxiliary software to enhance their tutorial systems (Harger, 1996, Williams & Kline,

1994; Marcy & Hagler, 1996), while others have provided interactive tutorials for manuals with a graphical user interface (Wood, 1996) or with rich multimedia formats (Sears & Watkins, 1996; Lee & Sullivan, 1996).

Furthermore, owing to the rapid growth of network technologies, considerable work has been done on the use of the Internet as a distance-learning tool (Huang & Lu, 2003), especially the discussions and surveys concerning web-based educational systems and their applications (Shor, 2000) and the use of web-based simulation tools for education (Sreenivasan et al., 2000). Moreover, some practical usages of web-based educational systems in the control area have been reported (Poindexter & Heck, 1999). In addition to their obvious uses in a distance-learning scenario, computer and network technologies can also be used to enrich classroom experience through the use of a data projector (Ringwood & Galvin, 2002). For example, Exel et al. (2000) demonstrated a web-based remote laboratory for System Control courses. Meanwhile, Junge and Schmid (2000) showed how remote experiments could be conducted via the Internet. Several well-known software environments have been developed to support remote experiments, such as LabVIEW (Ramakrishnan et al., 2000) and MATLAB/Simulink (Apkarian & Dawes, 2000).

Although information technologies have provided a more interactive and flexible learning environment, educational researchers have indicated that teacher's anxiety can often reduce the success of such technological and pedagogical innovations (Gressard & Loyd, 1985; Heinssen, Glass, & Knight, 1987; Chou, 2003; Todman & Day, 2006). This anxiety is owing to the lack of sufficient knowledge to apply the computer systems to their classes, which has become a barrier to conducting information technology-applied instructions (Marcoulides, 1988). Consequently, instructional design with information technologies has become an important and challenging issue.

To cope with this problem, in the following sections, a systematic model is proposed.

MODEL FOR CONDUCTING INFORMATION TECHNOLOGY APPLIED INSTRUCTIONS

Esquembre (2002) classified information technologies that can be applied to the tutoring process into five categories:

1. **Tools for the acquisition and manipulation of data:** including examples ranging from the use of simple spreadsheets to the more advanced microcomputer-based laboratories (MBL) and video analysis.

2. **Multimedia software:** which is based on the concept of hypermedia, and presents information in a structured, usually graphical way.

3. **Microworlds and simulations:** which consist of very complex computer programs, constructed by experts, to implement a simulation of a wide range of physical processes and laws.

4. **Modeling tools:** which are software environments that allow students to build their own computer simulations.

5. **Telematics and Internet tools:** which exploit the capability of computer intercommunication, making use of all of the previous types of software.

Most of such software and tools are popular in schools. Table 1 shows seven candidate information technologies that have been frequently applied in the instruction of Chemistry courses (Tsai, Hwang, & Tseng, 2004). In conducting the arrangement of information technology applied instruction, the possible number of difficulty levels for a subject unit, as well as that of the learning levels for a student, is 3, 5 or 7 levels, as widely used in psychoanalysis (Hwang et al.,

Table 1. Illustrative examples of information technologies

Information Technology	Definition	Application
Search Engine (IT_1)	Web-based programs for searching data on the Internet	Searching for supplementary subject materials
BBS (IT_2)	Software systems to provide information exchange in public	Performing group-discussion on line Enabling use of an announcement board for each class
E-mail (IT_3)	Software systems to provide person-to-person information exchange with or without attached files.	Performing group-discussion on line Allowing the teacher to be a personal-consultant for each student Allowing students to discuss homework and to share information
Word Processor (IT_4)	Document editing software, such as Microsoft Word.	Enabling students to write reports
Presentations (IT_5)	Presentation software, such as Microsoft PowerPoint	Assisting the teacher to make presentations to the students Enabling students to present homework to the teacher and classmates
CAI (IT_6)	Computer-assisted instruction software.	Stimulating real-world phenomena Offering drill and practice functions for some specific courses Offering testing and evaluation functions for some specific courses
Spreadsheets (IT_7)	Computer software that offers analysis and statistical functions on the data represented in tabular form, such as Microsoft Excel.	Assisting teachers and students to present analysis and statistical results, such as Pie charts or bar charts.

2006). For example, in Table 2, three difficulty levels (namely "Easy", "Middle" and "Difficult") and three learning levels (namely "Naïve", "Average" and "Good") are used to describe the status of subject units and students. Assuming that the difficulty level is "Easy" and the learning level is "Naive", the weight of IT_1 (Search Engine) is greater than that of IT_3 (E-mail), which implies that IT_1 (Search Engine) is more appropriate for the subject unit than IT_3 (E-mail). For another situation, difficulty level "Easy" and learning level "Naive", the order of proper information technolo-

Table 2. Illustrative example of the systematic model for conducting information technology applied instructions

Difficulty Level	Learning Level	Degrees of Fitness
Easy	Naive	$IT_1(a_1)>IT_3(a_3)>IT_4(a_4)>IT_2(a_2)>IT_6(a_6)=IT_7(a_7)>IT_5(a_5)$
	Average	$IT_2(a_2)>IT_1(a_1)=IT_6(a_6)>IT_3(a_3)=IT_4(a_4)>IT_5(a_5)>IT_7(a_7)$
	Good	$IT_6(a_6)>IT_4(a_4)>IT_1(a_1)>IT_3(a_3)>IT_7(a_7)>IT_2(a_2)>IT_5(a_5)$
Middle	Naive	$IT_2(a_2)>IT_3(a_3)>IT_4(a_4)>IT_7(a_7)>IT_6(a_6)>IT_1(a_1)=IT_5(a_5)$
	Average	$IT_1(a_1)>IT_6(a_6)>IT_7(a_7)=IT_2(a_2)>IT_3(a_3)=IT_5(a_5)>IT_4(a_4)$
	Good	$IT_3(a_3)>IT_7(a_7)>IT_4(a_4)>IT_2(a_2)>IT_1(a_1)>IT_5(a_5)>IT_6(a_6)$
Difficult	Naive	$IT_4(a_4)>IT_2(a_2)>IT_1(a_1)>IT_7(a_7)=IT_6(a_6)>IT_5(a_5)>IT_3(a_3)$
	Average	$IT_4(a_4)>IT_5(a_5)>IT_6(a_6)>IT_3(a_3)>IT_1(a_1)>IT_2(a_2)=IT_7(a_7)$
	Good	$IT_5(a_5)>IT_7(a_7)>IT_3(a_3)>IT_2(a_2)>IT_6(a_6)>IT_1(a_1)>IT_4(a_4)$

Figure 1. Illustrative example of an AHP hierarchical model for a Chemistry course

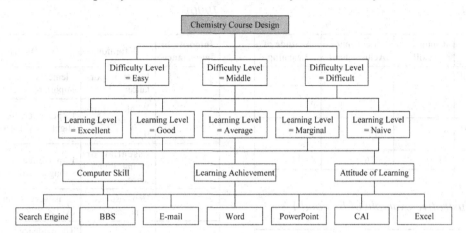

gies for the course is IT_1(Search Engine)>IT_3(E-mail)>IT_4(Word Processor)>IT_2(BBS)>IT_6(CAI) =IT_7(Spreadsheets)>IT_5(Presentations). Similarly, if the difficulty level is "Difficult" and the learning level is "Average", the arrangement of information technology applied instruction is IT_4(Word Processor)>IT_5(Presentations) >IT_6(CAI)> IT_3(E-mail)> IT_1(Search Engine)>IT_2(BBS) = IT_7(Spreadsheets).

In addition to the difficulty levels of subject units and the learning levels of the students, there are several other factors which need to be taken into consideration when applying information technologies to the tutoring process. It is difficult for experienced teachers to arrange learning activities and tutoring strategies for information technology applied instruction without any aid.

To cope with this problem, in this article, a systematic model for conducting information technology applied instructions is proposed based on the Analytic Hierarchy Process (AHP) method (Saaty, 1977, 1980), which is a systems analysis technique for solving decision-making problems. AHP provides a hierarchical framework within which multi-attribute decision problems can be structured. Its use of ratio scale along with paired relative comparison enables AHP to compare intangible attributes. AHP has the flexibility to combine quantitative and qualitative factors, to

handle different groups of actors, and to combine the opinions expressed by many experts. It can also help in stakeholder analysis (Ramanathan, 2001).

The methodology of AHP is basically to decompose a complex decision problem into elemental issues to create a hierarchical model. Without loss of generality, we shall use the design of a Chemistry course as an illustrative example to demonstrate our novel approach, consisting of four steps:

1. Structuring of the Decision Problem into a Hierarchical Model

In this step, the decision-making problem is decomposed into several elements according to their common characteristics, based on which a hierarchical model with different levels is constructed. For example, Figure 1 shows a hierarchical model of a Chemistry course with five levels. The top three levels are "Course Design", "Difficulty level" and "Learning level". The fourth levels are factors affecting "Learning level", such as "Computer Skill", "Learning Achievement" and "Attitude of Learning". The lowest level contains some candidate alternatives of applied information technology, such as "Search Engine", "BBS", "E-mail", "Word", "PowerPoint", "GSP" and "Excel".

Table 3. The pair-wise comparison matrix of the fourth level

A_{ij}	Computer Skill	Learning Achievement	Attitude of Learning
Computer Skill	1	1/7	1/3
Learning Achievement	7	1	3
Attitude of Learning	3	1/3	1
$X_j = \Sigma A_{ij}$	11	1.476	4.333

Table 5. Illustrative example of B_{ij}'s and Y_i's

B_{ij}	Computer Skill	Learning Achievement	Attitude of Learning	$Y_i = \Sigma B_{ij}/n$
Computer Skill	0.091	0.097	0.077	0.088
Learning Achievement	0.636	0.678	0.692	0.669
Attitude of Learning	0.273	0.226	0.231	0.243

Table 4. The AHP comparison scales (Vargas, 1990)

Intensity of importance	Definition	Description
1	Equal importance	Elements A_i and A_j are equally important
3	Weak importance of A_i over A_j	Experience and judgment slightly favor A_i over A_j
5	Essential or strong importance	Experience and judgment strongly favor A_i over A_j
7	Demonstrated importance	A_i is very strongly favored over A_j
9	Absolute importance	The evidence favoring A_i over A_j is of the highest possible order of affirmation
2, 4, 6, 8	Intermediate	When compromise is needed, values between two adjacent judgments are used
Reciprocals of the above judgments	If A_i has one of the above judgments assigned to it when compared with A_j, then A_j has the reciprocal value when compared with A_i	

2. Making Pair-Wise Comparisons and Obtaining the Judgmental Matrix

In this step, the elements of a particular level are compared pair-wise, with respect to a specific element in the immediate upper level. For example, the pair-wise comparison matrix of the fourth level of the hierarchical model in Figure 1 is given in Table 3. The meaning of each value used in the matrix is described in Table 4 (Vargas, 1990), where each A_{ij} value follows the rules: $A_{ij}>0$, $A_{ij}=1/A_{ji}$, $A_{ii}=1$ and $X_j = \Sigma A_{ij}$. For example, in Table 3, $A_{11}=1, A_{22}=1, A_{33}=1, A_{12}=1/7, A_{21}=7, A_{13}=1/3, A_{31}=3$, $X_1 = (1+7+3)=11$ and $X_2 = (1/7+1+1/3)=1.476$.

3. Determining Local Priorities and Consistency of Comparisons

Before calculating the local priorities, $B_{ij} = A_{ij}/X_j$ and $Y_i = \Sigma B_{ij}/n$ need to be computed first. For example, in Table 5, $B_{11} = 1/11 = 0.091$ and $B_{12} = (1/7)/1.476 = 0.097$, $Y_1 = (0.091+0.097+0.077)/3 = 0.088$ and $Y_2 = (0.636+0.678+0.692)/3 = 0.669$.

The matrix W_i is then calculated by summarizing the product of each column of matrix A, say Ai, and the corresponding Y_i as $W = \Sigma Y_i \times A_i$. For example,

```
W_i = 0.088× + 0.669 × +
0.243 × =
```

The Consistency Ratio (CR) can then be calculated by

```
CR = Consistency Index (CI)/ Random
Index (RI),
```

Therefore, $\lambda_{max} = [(0.265/0.088)+(2.014/0.669)+(0.73/0.243)]/3 = 3.008$, and CI $= (3.008-3)/(3-1) = 0.004$. In the above example, matrix size is 3, and hence RI=0.58, and CR = 0.004 / 0.58

Table 6. Average consistencies of random matrices

Size	1	2	3	4	5	6	7	8
RI	0	0	0.58	0.9	1.12	1.24	1.32	1.41

= 0.007. Since CR = 0.007<0.1, consistency of comparisons is acceptable.

4. Aggregation of Local Priorities

After calculating W_i for each level of pair-wise comparison matrices, the final priority can be derived. Let $W(P|Q)$ denote the priority weight of P under the circumstance that Q is true. In the example given above, by assuming that difficulty level = "Easy" and learning level = "Excellent", the priority weight of IT_i is:

```
W[Easy, Excellent, IT_i] =
W(difficulty level is "Easy") ×
W(learning level is "Excellent"|
difficulty level is "Easy") ×
W("Computer skill"| learning level
is "Excellent") × W("IT_i"| "Com-
puter skill")+W(difficulty level is
"Easy") × W(learning level is "Excel-
lent"| difficulty level is "Easy")
× W("Learning achievement"| learn-
ing level is "Excellent") × W("IT_i"|
"Learning achievement")+W(difficulty
level is "Easy") × W(learning level
is "Excellent"| difficulty level is
"Easy") × W("Attitude of learning"|
learning level is "Excellent") ×
W("IT_i"| "Attitude of learning"
```

After deriving the weight of each IT_i, the priorities of applying different information technologies under some specified considerations can be obtained.

Based on the constructed AHP hierarchical model, a standard interacting and computation procedure is then invoked to decide the priority of each candidate alternative to the top-level goal (Saaty, 1980). After deriving the weight of each IT_i, the priorities of applying different information technologies under some specified considerations can be obtained.

IMPLEMENTATION AND OPERATIONS OF I-DESIGNER

Based on the proposed model, the I-Designer, a web-based computer-assisted system for conducting information technology applied instructions has been implemented. The I-Designer aims to assist inexperienced teachers to plan learning activities and course content for applying information technologies to improve student learning performance. For most of the teachers who seldom or never use information technologies in their classes, this step-by-step guidance could be very helpful to them in preparing their classes.

The flowchart of the AHP-based model for conducting information technology applied instructions is given in Figure 2, which includes the following steps:

- **Step 1:** Input the name of the subject unit. Furthermore, specify the number of difficulty levels to classify the concepts in the subject unit (3, 5 or 7 levels) and the number of learning levels to identify the learning status of the students (3, 5 or 7 levels). For the example given in Figure 3, the teacher has entered "Chemical reaction" as the name of the subject unit, and chosen "3" as the number of difficulty levels, and "5" as the number of learning levels. That is, the candidate difficulty levels are "Easy", "Average" and "Difficult" and the candidate learning levels are "Excellent", "Good", "Average", "Marginal" and "Naive".

Figure 2. Flowchart of the systematic model

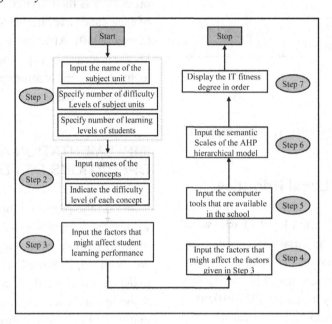

- **Step 2:** Input the names of the concepts in the "Chemical reaction" unit, and indicate the difficulty level of each concept. As shown in Figure 4, the teacher has identified "Atoms" as an "Easy" concept, "Chemical compounds" as an "average" concept, and "Chemical formulas" as a "Difficult" concept.
- **Step 3:** Input the factors that might affect student learning performance. I-Designer

has provided a manual containing several possible factors that might affect student learning performance. The teacher can either select feasible candidates from or enter new factors to I-Designer. The example given in Figure 5 shows that "attitude of learning", "computer skills" and "learning achievement" have been selected as the most critical factors affecting student learning performance in applying information technologies to the Chemistry course.

Figure 3. Illustrative example of operations in Step 1

Figure 4. Illustrative example of operations in Step 2

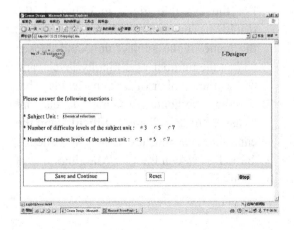

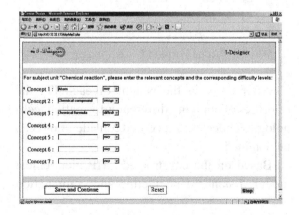

Figure 5. Illustrative example of operations in Step 3

Figure 6. Illustrative example of operations in Step 4

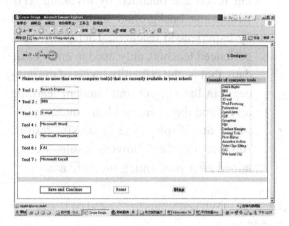

- **Step 4:** Input the computer tools that are available in the school. Those computer tools are the candidate information technologies that might be applied to the tutoring process of the course. A list of the most frequently used information technologies is displayed on the right side of the screen as a reference for inexperienced teachers to select possible candidate information technologies. In the example given in Figure 6, the teacher has entered "Search engine", "BBS", "E-mail", "Microsoft Word", "Microsoft PowerPoint", "CAI" and "Microsoft Excel" as the candidate information technologies.

- **Step 5:** Input the semantic scales of the AHP hierarchical model. I-Design will make pair-wise comparisons and present the analysis results according to the input semantic scale. Figure 7 demonstrates the user interface for inputting the semantic scale of the AHP hierarchical model. While comparing the importance of factors Ai and Aj, the input value "1" indicates that the two factors are of equal importance; "3" represents that experience and judgment slightly favor Ai over Aj; "5" implies that experience and judgment strongly fa-

vor Ai over Aj; "7" indicates that Ai is very strongly favored over Aj; "9" represents that the evidence favoring Ai over Aj is of the highest possible order of affirmation. In addition, when compromise is needed, values between two adjacent judgments (i.e. "2", "4", "6" and "8") are used. Note that the computations for determining the applicability of each information technology to each concept with different difficulty levels, the suitability of each information technology to the student with different learning levels, and the relationships among the factors that might affect student

Figure 7. Illustrative example of operations in Step 5

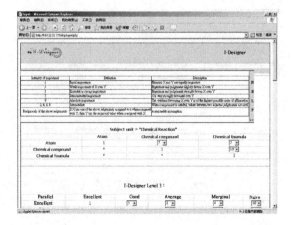

learning performance and student learning levels are obtained by invoking AHP with some background knowledge given by experienced teachers. Therefore, inexperienced teachers only need to enter basic data, that is, the difficulty levels of the concepts in the subject unit, student learning levels and the interested learning factors.

- **Step 6:** Display the analysis results. Assume that the following results are obtained after performing the AHP analysis:

```
IF      Subject unit "Chemical reac-
tion" and
Concept "Chemical formula" and
Difficulty level is "Difficult" and
Learning level is "Excellent"
THEN    Search Engine(21) > BBS(19)
> E-mail(17) > Microsoft Excel(15) >
Microsoft Word(14) > Microsoft Power-
Point(13) = CAI(13)
```

This rule shows that the priority weights of Search Engine, BBS, E-mail, Microsoft Excel, Microsoft Word, Microsoft PowerPoint and CAI are 21, 19, 17, 15, 14, 13 and 13, respectively. Consequently, the Search Engine is a more suitable tool for learning "Chemical formula" than BBS, and BBS is more suitable than E-mail... etc. As

Figure 8. Analysis results with ordered priority weights

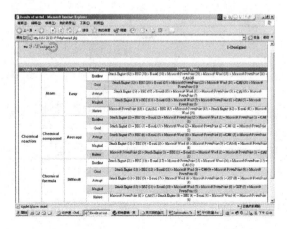

shown in Figure 8, I-Designer depicts the analysis results by showing a list of candidate information technologies ordered by the corresponding priority weights for each combination of subject unit, relevant concepts, difficulty levels, and learning levels.

EXPERIMENTS AND EVALUATION

To evaluate the efficacy for conducting information technology applied instructions, an experiment was conducted from March 2003 to June 2003 on a Chemistry course in a junior high school. One hundred and twenty-eight students participated in the experiment, and were separated into two groups, each consisting of sixty-four students.

The pre-test aimed to ensure that the students in the control group and experimental group had an equivalent basis for taking the course. The test sheet of the pre-test contained twenty multiple-choice questions. The t-test for the pre-test results of the control group and experimental group is shown in Table 7. The t-value is -0.891 and p-value is 0.374. Consequently, the pre-test results of the control group and experimental group are not significant at a confidence interval of 95%. That is, the students in the control group and the experimental group had equivalent ability when beginning the course.

After three months, a post-test was performed to compare the learning performance of the students in both groups. In this test, the students received twenty multiple-choice questions as in the pre-test. The t-test for the post-test results of

Table 7. Statistical results of pre-test

	Control Group	**Experimental Group**
N	64	64
Mean	6.31	5.94
Std. Dev.	2.363	2.396
$t = -0.891$ sig. $= 0.374$		

Table 8. Statistical results of post-test

	Control Group	Experimental Group
N	64	64
Mean	9.56	12.73
Std. Dev.	4.059	4.434
t = 4.222 sig. = 0.000		

the control group and experimental group is shown in Table 8. The t-value is 4.222 and p-value is 0.000. Consequently, the post-test results of the control group and experimental group are significant at a confidence interval of 95%. From the experimental results, it can be seen that the students in the experimental group achieved significantly higher performance than those in the control group, and hence we conclude that the new approach is helpful in enhancing student learning efficacy.

In addition, 33 teachers and 70 students who participated in several tutoring activities constructed by the I-Designer were asked to fill out questionnaires. Table 9 shows the analysis results of the questionnaires for the teachers. It can be seen that over 90% of the teachers indicated that the designed tutoring contents were able to promote learning motivation and help the students to understand the subject content. In addition, 77.8% of the teachers indicated that the novel

approach was helpful to them in designing the learning activities.

Table 10 shows the analysis results of the student questionnaires. It can be seen that over 80% of the students agreed that the designed tutoring content could promote their learning motivation and help them understand the subject content. Moreover, 84% of the students would like to attend courses using a similar tutoring style in the future. Consequently, we conclude that I-Designer is helpful in enhancing student learning efficacy.

To further analyze the attitudes of the teachers toward using the I-Designer, we reviewed the teachers' basic data and compared this data with the answers to the questionnaire items. Of the 33 teachers who participated in the experiment, there were nine who had rich experience of applying information technologies in the courses they teach. We found that three of them (33.3%) chose "disagree" for this item while four of them (44.4%) chose "neither agree nor disagree". That is, 77.7% of the experienced teachers did not agree (by choosing "disagree" or "neither agree nor disagree") that the I-Designer was helpful to them in designing the learning activities. Nevertheless, 100% of the inexperienced teachers agreed that the I-Designer was useful to them. Therefore, it can be seen that this innovative approach is more suitable for assisting inexperienced teachers in

Table 9. The results of the teacher questionnaire

Question	Strongly Disagree	Disagree	Neither Agree nor Disagree	Agree	Strongly Agree
The computer-assisted system (I-Designer) for conducting information technology applied instructions is easy to use.	0%	0%	3%	6.1%	90.9%
The planned tutoring contents are able to promote learning motivation.	0%	0%	6.1%	9.1%	84.8%
The planned tutoring strategy is helpful to the students to understand the subject content	0%	0%	9.1%	12.1%	78.8%
The computer-assisted system (I-Designer) is useful to me in designing the learning activities.	0%	9.1%	12.1%	12.1%	66.7%

Table 10. The results of the student questionnaire

Question	Strongly Disagree	Disagree	Neither Agree nor Disagree	Agree	Strongly Agree
The planned tutoring contents are able to promote learning motivation.	0%	8.6%	11.4%	32.9%	47.1%
The planned tutoring contents are helpful to the students to understand the subject content	0%	4.1%	14.3%	24.8%	56.8%
Would you like to receive courses with a similar tutoring style in the future?	0%	7.4%	8.6%	31.1%	52.9%

designing information technology-applied learning activities.

CONCLUSION

In this article, a systematic model for conducting information technology applied instructions is proposed. The novel approach can assist teachers to effectively employ information technologies in designing learning activities based on the features of the course content and the learning status of the students. Moreover, a web-based system has been developed based on the proposed model. To evaluate the performance of the novel approach, an experiment was conducted on a Chemistry course in a junior high school. The results of this experiment show that the novel approach is able to associate subject materials with proper information technologies and hence the students significantly appreciated the learning process.

For those elementary school teachers who seldom or never use information technologies in the courses they teach, the hints given by the I-Designer could be important and helpful; nevertheless, this does not imply that the approach is capable of solving all of the problems faced when applying information technologies in education. It should be clearly noted that the proposed approach can only be applied to assist teachers in designing the basic structure of the learning activities. The teachers still need to know the features of the courses they teach and make judgments based on

their past teaching experience when designing the learning activities.

Currently, we are applying the I-Designer to the planning of other courses, including English and Physics courses in a junior high school, and Natural Science and Social Studies courses in an elementary school, to evaluate the applicability of our approach.

ACKNOWLEDGMENT

This study is supported in part by the National Science Council of the Republic of China, under contract numbers NSC 96-2628-S-024-001-MY3 and NSC 97-2631-S-011-001.

REFERENCES

Apkarian, J., & Dawes, A. (2000). Interactive control education with virtual presence on the web. *Proceedings of the 2000 American Control Conference (ACC)* (Vol. 6, pp. 3985-3990). Chicago, IL: American Automatic Control Council.

Barrett, E., & Lally, V. (1999). Gender differences in an on-line learning environment. *Journal of Computer Assisted Learning, 15*(1), 48–60. doi:10.1046/j.1365-2729.1999.151075.x

Chou, C. (2003). Incidences and correlates of Internet anxiety among high school teachers in Taiwan. *Computers in Human Behavior, 19*(6), 731–749. doi:10.1016/S0747-5632(03)00010-4

Davidovic, A., Warren, J., & Trichina, E. (2003). Learning benefits of structural example-based adaptive tutoring systems. *IEEE Transactions on Education, 46*(2), 241–251. doi:10.1109/TE.2002.808240

Eshet, Y., Klemes, J., & Henderson, L. (2000). Under the microscope: Factors influencing student outcomes in a computer integrated classroom. *Journal of Computers in Mathematics and Science Teaching, 19*(3), 211–236.

Esquembre, F. (2002). Computers in physics education. *Computer Physics Communications, 147,* 13–18. doi:10.1016/S0010-4655(02)00197-2

Exel, M., Gentil, S., Michau, F., & Rey, D. (2000). Simulation workshop and remote laboratory: Two web-based training approaches for control. *Proceedings of the 2000 American Control Conference (ACC)* (vol. 5, pp. 3468-3472). Chicage, IL: American Automatic Control Council.

Gressard, C. P., & Loyd, B. H. (1985). Age and staff development experience with computers as factors affecting teacher attributes toward computers. *School Science and Mathematics, 85*(3), 203–209. doi:10.1111/j.1949-8594.1985.tb09613.x

Guzdial, M., Kolodner, J., Hmelo, C., Narayanan, H., Carlson, D., & Rappin, N. (1996). Computer support for learning through complex problem solving. *Communications of the ACM, 39*(4), 43–45. doi:10.1145/227210.227600

Harasim, L. (1999). A framework for online learning: The virtual-U. *Computer, 32*(9), 44–49. doi:10.1109/2.789750

Harger, R. O. (1996). Teaching in a computer classroom with a hyperlinked, interactive book. *IEEE Transactions on Education, 39,* 327–335. doi:10.1109/13.538755

Heinssen, R. K. J., Glass, C. R., & Knight, L. A. (1987). Assessing computer anxiety: development and validation of the Computer Anxiety Rating Scale. *Computers in Human Behavior, 3*(1), 49–59. doi:10.1016/0747-5632(87)90010-0

Huang, H. P., & Lu, C. H. (2003). Java-based distance learning environment for electronic instruments. *IEEE Transactions on Education, 46*(1), 88–94. doi:10.1109/TE.2002.808271

Hwang, G. H., Chen, J. M., Hwang, G. J., & Chu, H. C. (2006). A time scale-oriented approach for building medical expert systems. *Expert Systems with Applications, 31*(2), 299–308. doi:10.1016/j.eswa.2005.09.050

Junge, T. F., & Schmid, C. (2000). Web-based remote experimentation using a laboratory-scale optical tracker. *Proceedings of the 2000 American Control Conference (ACC)* (vol.4, pp. 2951-2954). Chicago, Illinois: American Automatic Control Council.

Lee, P. M., & Sullivan, W. G. (1996). Developing and implementing interactive multimedia in education. *IEEE Transactions on Education, 39*(3), 430–435. doi:10.1109/13.538769

Marcoulides, G. A. (1988). The relationship between computer anxiety and computer achievement. *Journal of Educational Computing Research, 4*(2), 151–158. doi:10.2190/J5N4-24HK-567V-AT6E

Marcy, W. M., & Hagler, M. O. (1996). Implementation issues in SIMPLE learning environments. *IEEE Transactions on Education, 39*(3), 423–429. doi:10.1109/13.538768

Oakley, B. (1996). A virtual classroom approach to teaching circuit analysis. *IEEE Transactions on Education, 39,* 287–296. doi:10.1109/13.538749

Poindexter, S. E., & Heck, B. S. (1999). Using the web in your courses: What can you do? What should you do? *IEEE Control Systems Magazine, 19*(1), 83–92. doi:10.1109/37.745773

Ramakrishnan, V., Zhuang, Y., Hu, S. Y., Chen, J. P., Ko, C. C., Chen, B. M., et al. (2000). Development of a web-based control experiment for a coupled tank apparatus. *Proceedings of the 2000 American Control Conference (ACC)* (vol. 6, pp. 4409-4413). Chicago, Illinois: American Automatic Control Council.

Ramanathan, R. (2001). A note on the use of the analytic hierarchy process for environmental impact assessment. *Journal of Environmental Management, 63*, 27–35. doi:10.1006/jema.2001.0455

Ringwood, J. V., & Galvin, G. (2002). Computer-aided learning in artificial neural networks. *IEEE Transactions on Education, 45*(4), 380–387. doi:10.1109/TE.2002.804401

Saaty, T. L. (1977). A scaling method for priorities in hierarchical structures. *Journal of Mathematical Psychology, 15*(3), 234–281. doi:10.1016/0022-2496(77)90033-5

Saaty, T. L. (1980). *The Analytic Hierarchy Process: Planning Setting Priorities, Resource Allocation* (p. 20). New York, NY: McGraw-Hill Press.

Scardamalia, M., Bereiter, C., McLean, R. S., Swallow, J., & Woodruff, E. (1989). Computer Supported Intentional Learning Environments. *Journal of Educational Computing Research, 5*(1), 51–68.

Sears, A. L., & Watkins, S. E. (1996). A multimedia manual on the world wide web for telecommunications equipment. *IEEE Transactions on Education, 39*, 342–348. doi:10.1109/13.538757

Shor, M. H. (2000). Remote-access engineering educational laboratories: Who, what, when, where, why and how? *Proceedings of the 2000 American Control Conference (ACC)* (vol. 4, pp. 2949-2950). Chicago, Illinois: American Automatic Control Council.

Sreenivasan, R., Levine, W. S., & Rubloff, G. W. (2000). Some dynamic-simulator-based control education modules. *Proceedings of the 2000 American Control Conference (ACC)* (vol. 5, pp. 3458-3462). Chicago, Illinois: American Automatic Control Council.

Todman, J., & Day, K. (2006). Computer anxiety: the role of psychological gender. *Computers in Human Behavior, 22*(5), 856–869. doi:10.1016/j.chb.2004.03.009

Tsai, P. J., Hwang, G. J., & Tseng, J. C. R. (July, 2004). *I-Designer: a Computer-Assisted System for Conducting Information Technology Applied Instructions*. Paper presented at The Eighth Pacific-Asia Conference on Information Systems (PACIS 2004), Shanghai, China.

Vargas, L. G. (1990). An overview of the analytic hierarchy process and its application. *European Journal of Operational Research, 48*(1), 2–8. doi:10.1016/0377-2217(90)90056-H

Williams, S. M., & Kline, D. B. (1994). An object-oriented graphical approach for teaching electric machinery analysis. *IEEE Transactions on Power Systems, 9*(2), 585–588. doi:10.1109/59.317686

Wood, S. L. (1996). A new approach to interactive tutorial software for engineering education. *IEEE Transactions on Education, 39*(3), 399–408. doi:10.1109/13.538765

Zhou, G., Wang, J. T. L., & Ng, P. A. (1996). Curriculum knowledge representation and manipulation in knowledge-based tutoring systems. *IEEE Transactions on Knowledge and Data Engineering, 8*(5), 679–689. doi:10.1109/69.542023

This work was previously published in International Journal of Distance Education Technologies (IJDET), Volume 7, Issue 1, edited by Qun Jin & Oscar Fuhua Lin, pp. 23-43, copyright 2009 by IGI Publishing (an imprint of IGI Global).

Chapter 4
A Highly Scalable, Modular Architecture for Computer Aided Assessment E–Learning Systems

Krzysztof Gierłowski
Gdansk University of Technology, Poland

Krzysztof Nowicki
Gdansk University of Technology, Poland

ABSTRACT

In this chapter, the authors propose a novel e-learning system, dedicated strictly to knowledge assessment tasks. In its functioning it utilizes web-based technologies, but its design differs radically from currently popular e-learning solutions which rely mostly on thin-client architecture. The authors' research proved that such architecture, while well suited for didactic content distribution systems is ill-suited for knowledge assessment products. In their design, they employed loosely-tied distributed system architecture, strict modularity, test and simulation-based knowledge and skill assessment and an our original communications package called Communication Abstraction Layer (ComAL), specifically designed to support communication functions of e-learning systems in diverse network conditions (including offline environment and content aware networks). The system was tested in production environment on Faculty of Electronics, Telecommunications and Informatics, Technical University of Gdansk with great success, reducing staff workload and increasing efficiency of didactic process. The tests also showed system's versatility in classroom, remote and blended learning environments.

INTRODUCTION

The task of knowledge assessment is one of the fundamental elements of didactic process. It was also one of the first didactic tasks to be conducted by various electronic learning devices employed to support didactic process.

Currently there are many e-learning solutions supporting knowledge assessment both as their

DOI: 10.4018/978-1-60960-539-1.ch004

main functionality and as an additional module (Sakai, 2010; Moodle, 2010).

Almost any advanced e-learning tool offers this functionality. In light of those facts we could conclude that this area of e-learning is a well explored one and suitably supported in practical e-learning products.

Our experience with e-learning systems both as their users and designers, leads us to conclusion that the above statement is far from correct. Vast majority of currently available electronic knowledge assessment tools are extremely similar and offer strictly limited functionality. Such products offer almost exclusively knowledge assessment based on various choice tests and their automatic grading mechanisms most often are not very comprehensive and fit to support different grading scenarios.

In complex e-learning systems knowledge assessment functionality is treated as mandatory element, but also receives no special consideration, which often results in a simple implementation of choice test. Specialized knowledge testing solutions (employed for example by Microsoft during their computer proficiency exams) include more advanced mechanisms, like adaptive question selection, but they are few and still do not go beyond the basic scenario of choice test (Bersin & Associates, 2004; Jesukiewicz, P. et al., 2006).

Apart from these weaknesses, one of the most serious problems with currently available products and especially the most popular ones based on web-based thin-client architecture is their strict dependence on network connectivity. Majority of such products require constantly active network connection during e-learning session and few are fit to function under other circumstances, such as periodic or no network connectivity, and still remain a part of managed e-learning system. The quality of network service is also a factor in case of many of such products (Gierłowski K. & Gierszewski T., 2004).

Having analyzed above limitations of currently available knowledge assessment products, we de-

signed and created our own dedicated knowledge assessment system. It was designed to provide highly modifiable platform for various knowledge testing tools, able to provide its functions in any network connectivity conditions (including no connectivity scenario). The system can scale from very simple setup (adequate for servicing a single exercise) to a large, distributed solution fit to support an enterprise. Strictly modular architecture allows users to employ only a selected set of its mechanisms and extremely easily integrate it with third-party solutions. The selection of employed modules depends completely on user needs – there is no mandatory control module or management platform which must be present.

We created a number of client modules with full support for low/no-connectivity scenarios, for example:

1. the classic, but highly configurable and versatile, multiple choice knowledge testing solution,
2. an unique simulation-based knowledge and skill assessment module, dedicated to exercises concerning Asynchronous Transfer Mode (ATM) and Frame Relay networks,
3. a module allowing a real-time grading of students performance during exercises.

Our system also addresses security aspects of remote, computer based knowledge testing, in both test distribution and results gathering preserving user anonymity to unauthorized parties.

As an key element of the system, we have created an innovative Communication Abstraction Layer (ComAL) - a set of mechanisms designed to provide e-learning system designers with API containing a comprehensive set of communication functions which can make an e-learning system independent of underlying network connectivity conditions. ComAL completely isolates e-learning solution programmer from the details of network communication and can be employed to easily create networked e-learning solutions, allowing creation of an integrated, managed e-learning system even in environment without network connectivity.

OVERALL SYSTEM DESIGN

During design and creation of our system we aimed to provide a solution fit to accommodate needs to assess students' knowledge in the widest possible set of scenarios. To fulfill this task we considered its following aspects:

1. compatibility with the widest possible set of hardware and operating systems,
2. ability to function in variety of network connectivity environments (including lack of such connectivity) while still retaining capability to function as globally managed solution,
3. security and reliability of the system, including safety of the system itself, test content, students' solutions and personal data,
4. information storage and manipulation capabilities, to allow creation of central database of results and grades, complete with easy access methods,
5. knowledge assessment functionality including: multiple choice tests with highly customizable automatic grading and real time grading by a teacher,
6. comprehensive management interfaces for administrators and teachers,
7. ease of deployment, customization, modification and integration with third-party solutions.

To fulfill these requirements, we have chosen a client-server architecture for our system, which is a pretty standard solution today, but in contrast to the most common practice we decided to abandon thin-client technology in favor of full-client approach.

From our experience, web-based thin-client architecture despite its undisputed compatibility and ease of deployment, is not especially well suited for knowledge assessment systems, as it requires a constant network connectivity for operation and lacks a sufficient degree of control over user environment, which impairs system reliability and allows unauthorized actions on part of the users. Operating system and web browser security mechanisms are also an important issue here, as their incorrect configuration can lead to abnormal or partial client software behavior (Nowicki K. & Gierłowski K., 2004).

Full-client approach allows client to conduct much wider range of operations compared to thin-client. This allows inclusion of more advanced internal mechanisms providing improved functionality, much better reliability and security of client operation. With proper design full-client utilizing web-based technologies can also operate independently of server which gives our system versatility, necessary to handle limited network connectivity scenario. It also helps to create strictly modular system architecture and provide high level of scalability (as many tasks can be conducted client-side and data transfers minimized).

The most serious limitations of full-client approach, deployment and system compatibility, are also possible to overcome by employing easily deployable, platform independent clients (for example Java-based). Such solution allows for all advantages of full-client and web-based technologies, while still retaining high level of hardware and system compatibility and easy (even web-based) deployment.

The second of our fundamental design decisions was maintaining a strict modularity of our product. All basic elements are constructed as modules capable of operating independently, and are employing only standardized, self-describing data format for inter-module data transfer - Extensible Markup Language (XML). The format is compatible with QTI (Question & Test Interoper-

Figure 1. Partial system deployment and integration with 3rd party solutions

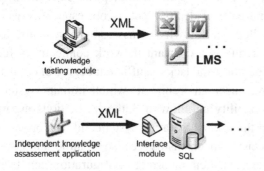

ability) version 2 specification (QTI, 2008), but defines additional extensions.

Modular system structure complicates design and implementation, as it requires the use of additional inter-module communication mechanisms, but these difficulties are easily compensated by our ComAL API, described in later chapter.

On the other hand modular structure brings enormous advantages, as it is possible to substitute customized solutions in place of some standard modules or include additional elements into standard system data paths to provide additional data analysis/translation functionality (Figure 1). Advantages of these possibilities are clear, as they allow easy modification and customization of the system, including creation of dedicated interfaces for third-party systems and applications. Moreover, there are already many such solutions accepting XML input and providing XML output (for example MS Office, OpenOffice etc.).

There is also a possibility which had proven even more useful then these mentioned above during test deployments of our system – it is possible to deploy only selected elements and/or integrate it directly with third-party solutions supporting XML language.

An ability to deploy only a chosen set of modules allows for deployment precisely tailored to individual needs. If system user is interested only in simple multiple choice solution for a small number of students there is no need for a system

server – it is enough to deploy only a testing/grading module and read resulting offline data files directly with MS or Open Office. In an opposite situation, where the user is interested only in system's data storage and access functions, he can easily deploy the system's server part, substituting its clients with his own, as long as they support XML output or can provide appropriate translating interface.

This partial-deployment ability also makes transition to new system much easier, as it can be conducted in phases, by gradually exchanging existing infrastructure with modules of the system.

The most common usage scenarios include:

1. No server-side / third-party scenario – client modules are operating independently or export results to a third-party application/system.
2. Single server scenario – client modules are managed by client communication module and access central database, all data storage and control functions are available.
3. Multi-server distributed architecture – able to support large number of clients (performance) and allows different organizational units to operate independent (but integrated) servers.

COMMUNICATION ABSTRACTION LAYER

Inter-module communication mechanisms are among the key elements of modular system. The task of providing local communication (between modules on the same machine) is relatively simple, because we can precisely predict environment characteristics.

Remote connectivity (communication between modules on different machines) is another matter. It is dependent on various characteristics of available network infrastructure. Providing

Figure 2. Overall ComAL architecture

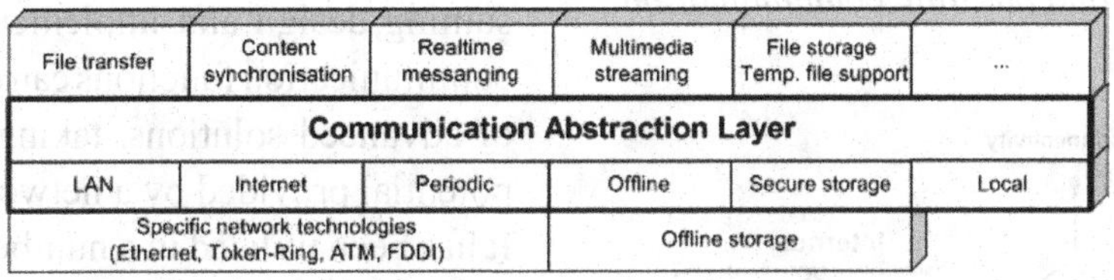

File transfer	Content synchronisation	Realtime messanging	Multimedia streaming	File storage Temp. file support	...
Communication Abstraction Layer					
LAN	Internet	Periodic	Offline	Secure storage	Local
Specific network technologies (Ethernet, Token-Ring, ATM, FDDI)			Offline storage		

reliable communication and satisfying quality of service requirements of an e-learning system in wide range of network scenarios and conditions is a difficult and work intensive task (Gierłowski K. & Gierszewski T., 2004). Its complication and cost most often lead to abandoning such attempts and creation of products which require constant and stable network connectivity lacking mechanisms for handling other scenarios (for example: the popular thin-client architecture) or employ no advanced communication functions at all.

While such approach may be sufficient for didactic content distribution systems, knowledge assessment requires a higher degree of communication between client (which interacts with user) and server part of the system (usually responsible for control, management, task assignment and results gathering).

To help developers in building a robust, networked e-learning systems we have created a set of mechanisms called Communication Abstraction Layer (ComAL) specifically designed to provide network communication functions required by e-learning environment (Figure 2). This set of mechanisms can employ a variety of communication methods, automatically choosing the one most appropriate for current working conditions, and is responsible for all communication tasks – both local and remote. It isolates e-learning system developer from particulars of implementing network communication mechanisms by providing him with high level API.

From our experience in developing networked e-learning systems, we divided most often encountered network conditions into four scenarios:

1. Local Area Network – efficient and reliable, permanent network connectivity.
2. Internet – an environment where we have a permanent network connectivity at our disposal, but there are no Quality of Service (QoS) or reliability guarantees.
3. Periodic connectivity – most commonly encountered in case of dialup connections.
4. Offline – there is no network connectivity, but there is still a possibility of communication by offline methods (floppy, CD/DVD, USB-storage…).

ComAL provides dedicated means for maintaining a stable communication in all of these environments, and is able to detect the correct scenario automatically and keeps monitoring the situation to detect if the scenario changes.

Communication functions provided by ComAL to e-learning system creator can accommodate a wide variety of application types, ranging from sending simple messages, through high volume file transfers and content synchronization, to reliable, real-time interactive message exchanges and multimedia transmissions. Of course, not all of these functions can be made available in all of the above scenarios. To deal with such limitations, ComAL provides feedback mechanisms informing higher application layers about functionality available under current network conditions, state of currently conducted communication activities, overall status of network connectivity and its changes.

For transport of data ComAL currently employs (Figure 3): direct TCP and UDP connectivity, SOAP over HTTPS, encrypted SOAP over SMTP

Figure 3. Knowledge assessment system client-server architecture and possible communication scenarios

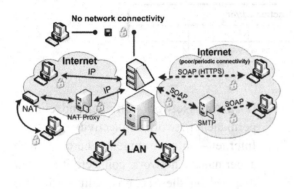

and advanced, automatic, secure file export/import functions. Some of these methods (SMTP and file-based) allow communication between system modules behind NAT. Moreover, we are currently developing a media proxy module functionality, allowing destinations behind NAT to communicate with TCP/UDP and indirect (but still secure) SOAP over HTTPS.

Recently, ongoing development of new modules for our knowledge assessment system pointed to a popular need for local storage functions on the part of system modules. As such function can be regarded as an external to a given module's functionality, we decided to extend ComAL to cover this requirement, and a number of functions providing both permanent and temporary storage have been implemented.

All communications and file storage operations can be protected with use of strong security mechanisms, ensuring their confidentiality, integrity and mutual authentication of communicating parties. The communication can also be digitally signed to ensure non-repudiation of submitted data (for example test solutions). The ComAL utilizes both symmetric and public-key cryptography and supports automatic key/certificate generation for clients.

We believe that creation of such abstraction layer, able to free e-learning system developers

from difficult, specialized, costly and work consuming design and implementation of network communication functions can encourage creation of advanced solutions, taking full advantage of potential provided by a networked environment. It has been utilized in a number of our e-learning products (Nowicki K. & Gierłowski K., 2004; Gierłowski K. & Nowicki K., 2002; Gierłowski K. et al., 2003), greatly reducing design complexity and implementation work required. It was also successfully employed to extend functionality of strictly local e-learning solution, to allow network based management.

ComAL is a basis of all inter-module communication in our knowledge assessment system, enabling our system to function as manageable entity in most diverse communication scenarios.

Content Aware Networks

The most recent research and development direction for our communications layer concerns possible integration with and usage of Content Aware Networks (CANs). Due to a number of existing approaches to creating such networks, which results in many architectures and solutions, largely different in both employed mechanisms and provided functionality, we have decided to concentrate on Content Delivery oriented CANs (Borcoci E. et al., 2010).

Such networks employ sophisticated content identification, description (metadata), distributed storage and caching, searching, and delivery mechanisms. This functionality, as will be shown in the following chapter, corresponds very well to our system's distributed architecture's needs, which allows us to perform many of data management tasks (such as, for example, content distribution and synchronization) network-side – without the need to handle them at ComAL layer. The layer, however, requires extension, to handle CAN-specific signaling and access functions.

Our research and design work indicates so far, that the integration of complex e-learning system and CAN network can be not only beneficial, but also relatively easy task, due to, for example, similarities in content description – for example between SCORM compliant (SCORM, 2007) didactic materials and some content delivery CAN solutions.

To test the efficiency of e-learning-CAN integration, we are currently deploying our system as a part of Future Internet Engineering (Future Internet Engineering Project, 2010) project, which includes a designs, implementation and deployment of a country-wide CAN infrastructure, complete with an example set of applications.

Our research into the field of CAN networks seems to suggest that emergence of such networks can be directly beneficial for e-learning systems, as in a high number of frequently required, high level communication-related tasks is supported directly by the network. This results in both easier implementation and more efficient data handling due to possibility of network-based data transfer optimizations.

SYSTEM ARCHITECTURE

As our knowledge assessment system follows a client-server design, its modules can be divided into two basic groups: client and server modules. Communication between system elements is conducted with use of ComAL to support various network environments.

Client modules interact directly with student or teacher during didactic process and are responsible for providing majority of system's functionality in accordance with configuration information obtained from servers and under their control. Results of knowledge assessment conducted by client modules are returned to servers for processing and storage.

There can be many client modules providing different types of knowledge assessment or supporting functions. Currently we have implemented the following client modules:

1. Test-based knowledge assessment module.
2. Unique simulation-based e-learning model, allowing knowledge and skill assessment.
3. Teacher's interface for grading student's progress during training session.

All of these modules are able to function as independent applications and support full ComAL capabilities, including strictly offline scenario – in such case configuration and test packages are provided to them as cryptographically protected files (automatically generated by server), and results are returned to server in the same way. Also they are able to monitor presence of network connectivity and initiate automatic upload of results gathered in offline mode.

Server part of the system is a distributed database containing both didactic content and system's complete configuration information. A single server consists of a database (most often an SQL server) and at least one of two modules: system maintenance module and/or client communication module.

A system maintenance module is responsible for creating and maintaining distributed information base. It also provides a web-based administrative interface allowing administrator to create and control the system.

An administrator is responsible for creating distributed system architecture by defining communication links between system servers, and deciding which of ComAL transport mechanisms are permitted for each link. If a server cannot maintain current transport mechanism it will switch do less demanding one if such is permitted, otherwise it will mark link as down. A simple link-state path selection protocol is then used to ensure communication between all nodes, utilizing as link metrics information from ComAL network monitoring mechanisms.

Over such communication structure works a data indexing mechanism, allowing full access to distributed information base from any system node. This distributed database includes complete

Figure 4. Server part of the system – distributed database: A, B – replicated configuration data, 1-8 – indexed didactic content

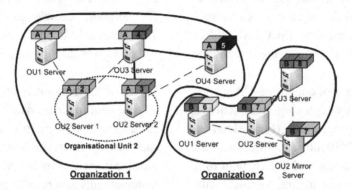

information about system-wide configuration (system structure, global users and access rights, link states, distributed database state) which is replicated to all servers and didactic content (test content, grading rules, student lists, test results and grades etc.) which is kept locally on specific server and is not replicated, but can be searched and accessed from any server if there is connectivity present, and access rights are sufficient (Figure 4).

Such architecture allows largely independent operation of a particular server (supporting for example a single course or organization department), while still allowing administration of the system as a whole and easy access to information stored on different servers. It will give various teachers or departments the freedom of independent operation and still provide means of global data access. As a result servers can be connected and disconnected from the distributed system at will with no negative effect for them or the system (other than loss of access to disconnected resources).

If a given server will communicate with client modules, it must include a client communication module. It is responsible for communication with other modules using ComAL, supplying client modules with configuration and didactic content, gathering and processing incoming results and providing teacher's interface to the system.

The teacher's interface allows its user to create test packages and assign it to specific combination of students, network workstations or time frames – it is possible to provide student witch a choice of available tests. Such test package contains all information to conduct a test, namely: test content adequate for specific client module, grading rules and additional information concerning test execution (time limit, randomization of content, means of results upload etc.).

Teacher's interface allows a full read access to gathered results and ability to modify or add data concerning teacher's own tests, as well as generation of basic reports and statistics. There is also an option of importing external data in XML format into the system and exporting system data in the same format.

The new, planned addition of CAN-related functionalities to the ComAL allows it to offload a number of the tasks necessary to support the described distributed infrastructure to the CAN network itself. In our opinion the following aspects of system's functioning can largely benefit from being deployed in a content aware network environment:

- Automatic handling of efficient didactic material publication – the CAN is able to automatically distribute the required didactic content to the servers and cache it in network nodes. The network takes into account the spread of user requests and a current transmission network state, to provide necessary QoS parameters for user's access combined with minimized network resource consumption.

• Information searching mechanisms – as CAN network incorporates advanced search mechanisms based on metadata descriptions of data units, such mechanism can be easily incorporated into our system, which utilizes similar description method compliant with a SCORM standard (SCORM, 2007),

• Synchronization, replication and indexing tasks – CAN network's content distribution mechanisms can also be employed as means of handling synchronization, replication and information searching between system's servers. Offloading such tasks to network-based mechanisms can vastly reduce the necessary complexity of e-learning systems.

As we can see, the list includes the crucial distributed system's mechanisms. We should also note, that properly implemented and functioning CAN network can provide the above services based on the current network resource state, traffic conditions and content's QoS requirements (for example: QoS and resource aware path selection).

Such possibility leads to high quality service and optimization of network resource usage.

CLIENT MODULES

Client modules are critical for the system as they are its point of contact with the student, responsible for many essential tasks, such as presentation of test content, enforcing configured test conditions (time, test randomization, etc.), performing it and sending all necessary information back to the system for processing and storage, etc. The grading of tests can be conducted client-side, by client modules, or server-side, by client communication module. Server side grading is more secure but less scalable and versatile solution.

Test-Based Knowledge Assessment Module

This first and most often employed client module of our system allows knowledge assessment by means of diverse choice tests. While the method itself is very popular in case of e-learning products, we designed this module to provide functionality unique among similar products.

Module's user interface (Figure 5) allows presentation of wide range of multimedia content including formatted text, bitmap and vector graphics, sound and movies which provides teacher with

Figure 5. Test-based knowledge assessment module – user interface

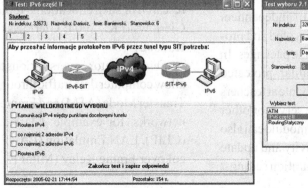

great versatility when preparing test content. Test questions can be randomly selected from a larger set, and order of both questions and answers can be randomized.

Automatic grading mechanisms support both single and multiple choice questions in single test, and use simple scripting language which allows to utilize any of popular methods of assigning points for test answers. The total test result can be normalized to a provided value and/or mapped to a grade. The module returns to server or external application a complete information about student's solution (which can be later used by, for example, server side grading mechanisms), such as: personal data, test id, timeframe of test, client-side grading results of all questions and total grade, all answers, operating system computer name and user name, IP address etc.

Module configuration allows teacher to enforce various additional test characteristics, such as necessity of solving questions in order, lack of ability correct already answered questions, time limit for a whole test or every single question etc.

Apart from already described functionality, one of our primary priorities was to take full advantage of ComAL communication capabilities allowing the software to function as part of managed system even without network connectivity. Such scenario is most often ignored by designers of modern e-learning solutions as it prohibits the use of web-based thin-client architecture. At the same time it is a very popular scenario in case of network-related courses, as obtaining network connectivity is often the final goal of laboratory exercises on the subject.

The module is fully capable of independent offline operation according to encrypted and protected configuration files and course packages. In such case results are stored in similar, protected files and can be decrypted by the module at teachers request for manual transfer to the server or other application such as MS Excel. The module can also detect available network connectivity and update its status by obtaining new configuration settings/

Figure 6. Didactic model of connecting LAN systems by WAN networks – user interface

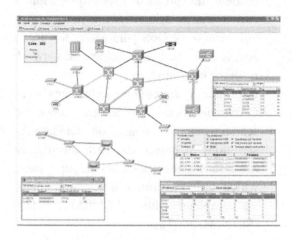

course packages from the server and uploading cached test results automatically.

As a result we have at our disposal one of the most advanced (apart from adaptive choice tests) knowledge testing products utilizing choice test method, which can function as a standalone application or as a part of managed system regardless of network connectivity available, due to integrated ComAL functionality.

Didactic Model of Connecting LAN Systems by WAN Networks

"Didactic model of connecting LAN systems by WAN networks" (Figure 6) has been developed as a part of our research concerning simulation-based didactic and e-learning tools. It is a didactic simulator (Kindley R., 2002), designed and implemented according to results of our original research of such educational tools (Nowicki K. & Gierłowski K., 2004; Gierłowski K. & Nowicki K.,2002).

Our simulator covers various technologies that allow computer data traffic through Asynchronous Transfer Mode (ATM) and Frame Relay wide area networks, for example: Classical IP over ATM (CLIP), LAN Emulation (LANE) or Multiprotocol over Frame Relay (MPoFR).

Due to its original design (Gierłowski K. & Nowicki K., 2002) it can be employed in a variety of didactic roles:

1. knowledge distribution – a comprehensive, context sensitive help system is included, containing theoretical information concerning various elements of simulated environment. Coupled with simulator's ability to illustrate the knowledge with interactive, modifiable examples it creates a highly efficient knowledge distribution solution.
2. skill development – didactic simulation product is one of the best tools for building practical skills on the base of theoretical knowledge, bridging theory and practice.
3. self-study and experimentation – didactic simulation product (with its ability to save and restore simulated system state) can be used by students for self-study, as they are able to experiment in real-like environment without fear of damaging or critically misconfiguring the equipment.
4. design, troubleshooting and optimization exercises – ability to interact with much more complicated systems than possible under laboratory conditions allows for these highest level exercises, able to build not only basic skills but also give user experience in efficiently dealing with these complex tasks.

Among these roles a knowledge and skill assessment can also be found – our simulation product includes mechanisms for automatically measuring various aspects of simulated system performance (available bandwidth, data loss, transmission delay etc.), which allows automatic grading mechanisms to assess competence of simulated system's designer and administrator.

The module is able to receive task files by ComAL from the server. A tasks file consists of a starting simulation setup, a set of goals which user must reach (for example: create connectivity between selected devices, optimize system ef-

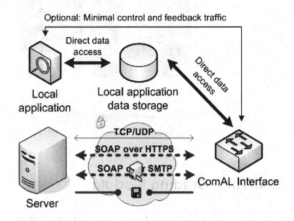

Figure 7. Integration of local e-learning solution with networked system with ComAL-database interface

ficiency by a certain threshold etc.) and grading rules. User's solutions along with their grades are uploaded to the server.

The module was originally created as a standalone application supporting SCORM-compliant data files (SCORM, 2007), but by employing a dedicated interface interacting with product's information store and ComAL communication functionality it has been upgraded to a networked product, able to fully integrate with our knowledge assessment system (Figure 7). Modifications of product code were not necessary to archive that result, and that fact can be considered as another evidence of ComAL vast usefulness and versatility. A number of minor user interface modifications were also made to improve functionality of the product.

A didactic simulator can be a powerful e-learning tool as its capabilities cover wide range of scenarios. Its inclusion of as a module in our system offers us a unique ability to test not only theoretical knowledge, but also student's ability to employ it in a given situation (user's skill), and even his efficiency in dealing with various real-life situations (experience). These tests can be conducted in both simple and very complex systems, which would otherwise never be available for didactic tasks.

Figure 8. Real-time grading module - user interface

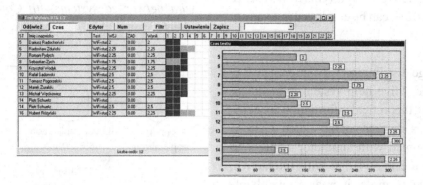

Real-Time Grading Module

Real-time grading module has been designed to support classical theoretical and laboratory exercises. It is an interface for a teacher, allowing him to grade students during such activities, by marking their progress through assigned tasks.

The main element of the module's user interface (Figure 8) is a table containing all students participating in the current class in the rows and task numbers in columns. A teacher can assign percent grades (including above 100% for exceptional performance) for specific tasks, and the system will calculate resulting total grade automatically and in real-time.

The list of students can be obtained from the system server or any other application with use of any ComAL-supported mechanisms including offline files. For example, if students are required to take an entry test before the class, their list, complete with additional information such as their place number and entry test grade will be displayed. Of course other means of creating such list can also be used (such as dedicated system module for checking in or a teacher prepared list) and provided to module by the server automatically or by simple file import.

Apart from user list, module can also take into account different point weights for different tasks, and such information is obtained by the module in the same way as the list of students.

This module can be an enormous help for a teacher, as he has complete information about his students at his disposal including name, place, and if entry test was taken, its result. That way he knows the entry level of theoretical knowledge of his students and can assign his attention accordingly. Also student's progress during current class is easy to track and graded automatically. Results can be uploaded to system server via any of ComAL transport methods.

As this module would be particularly useful on mobile platform, allowing teacher to use it not only during lectures (when teacher is able to use a stationary computer), but also during classes when a teacher's mobility is a requirement, we have also developed such version, designed to run on Symbian 6.0 v3 compliant mobile devices. Apart from already described, basic functionality, the mobile version introduces elements of location awareness as an element of e-learning system.

The location awareness services used by the module are provided by ComAL mechanisms, which in turn has been extended to support popular wireless technologies: WiFi (IEEE Standards Library, 2007) and Bluetooth (IEEE Standards Library, 2002).

The first mechanism of location awareness, designed for computer laboratories, utilizes mobile device's Bluetooth interface. The system locates nearby Bluetooth interfaces (installed in student's computers) by measuring their received signal

Figure 9. ComAL extended for wireless-based location services

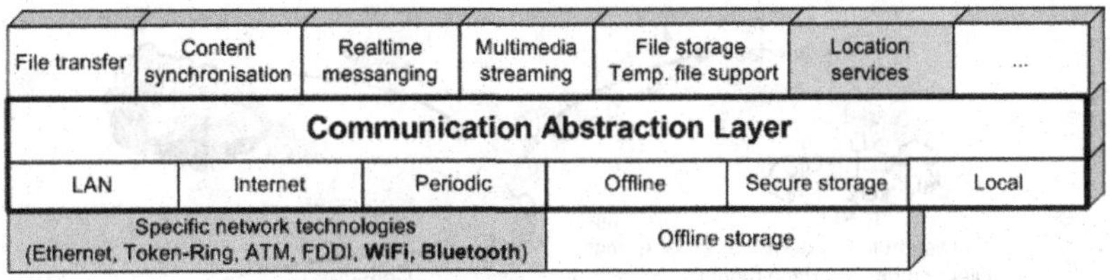

File transfer
Content synchronisation
Realtime messanging
Multimedia streaming
File storage Temp. file support
Location services
...
Communication Abstraction Layer
LAN
Internet
Periodic
Offline
Secure storage
Local
Specific network technologies (Ethernet, Token-Ring, ATM, FDDI, WiFi, Bluetooth)
Offline storage

strength. Hardware address of a Bluetooth interface with the strongest signal is then checked with a preconfigured list of such addresses to obtain a computer number (place number). In practice it means that all a teacher has to do is to approach a student (instead of entering place ID manually), and the module will display student's information and allow teacher to enter the grade.

The second solution, designed for larger environments (for example lecture halls). In contrast with the Bluetooth-based solution described above, it depends on measuring a signal received form teacher's device by multiple WiFi access points (APs). Our test proved, that with 3-4 APs (we used Cisco Aironet 1100 APs) deployed in a simple (as far as radio propagation is concerned) environment of a lecture hall, it is possible to pinpoint location of wireless client with about 5 meter accuracy. While it is insufficient to identify a particular place in the hall, we use this information to narrow down the list of possible place ID, which are then presented to teacher to choose from.

Both of above solutions are in testing phase, but they are already functioning fairly stable. The main problem concerns a proper configuration of the required infrastructure: Bluetooth interfaces should be of the same type or at least transmit with similar power, they need to be configured as "shown" (as opposed to "hidden" where they will not transmit their identity information), the table of Bluetooth hardware addresses and their corresponding place IDs need to be constructed as well as the table allowing translation of WiFi signal strengths to locations, etc. To offset this problem, we are currently working on tools designed to automate many of the above tasks.

Web Publication Module

This module is responsible for communication with system's living users (not software clients) and allows teacher to easily publish test related information to his students. The module provides its own teacher's interface (which can be integrated into client communication module's interface) and can operate on the entire distributed data store.

To fulfill this task the web publication module requires a web server with PHP language support as its working environment. The module can be divided (Figure 10) into management part (which provides teacher's interface and manages publications) and publishing part (which provides services to users) – they interact with use of a shared database space.

The most important function of this module is a knowledge assessment results publication. The teacher can easily create and publish on the web automatically generated lists of results from

Figure 10. Web publishing module (WPM) divided into management (M) and publishing (P) parts

WPM(P)
Users
Publishing web server
Distributed system with client comm. interface module
WPM(M)
Teacher's interface
Other datasource
Publishing web server

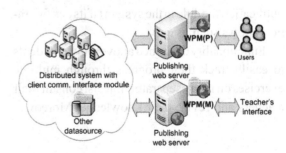

Figure 11. Analysis module - external data exchange

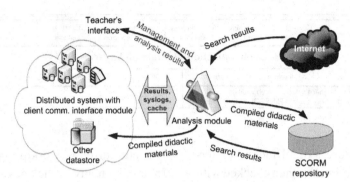

system's database. Two methods of list creation are supported: manual selection of results to include or using a rule which automatically publishes matching results.

The lists can contain results of a single or a number of exercises in which case each of them is represented as additional table column. Moreover, a final grade can be calculated from a set of exercises.

Another possible form of results publication is a student oriented one. After providing correct login information student can access all his grades stored in the system.

Results published in any form can also be automatically supplemented with additional information present in the system, for example: teacher's contact information, correct solutions of test questions, cross references to study materials etc.

Each publication can be configured by the teacher either as local or universal. Local publications are available only from the web publication module from where there were configured. Universal publications are available from any web publication module in the system (if its configuration allows such usage).

Functionality described above allows students to easily track their progress through multiple exercises on many separate subjects, consult their teachers and revise their knowledge. Moreover,

the fact that any and all web publication modules can be used to access all the information stored in the system, provide students with easy and reliable access to a complete and current (all changes in the database are instantly visible) grading information in uniform layout.

Teachers in turn gain very easy, work conserving and error resistant method of result, solution and contact information publishing.

The second function of the module is to provide strictly web-based choice test functionality. The module allows teachers to use test packages prepared for knowledge assessment module described in chapter 6.1 (full-client) in thin-client environment. The test can be are carried out with any modern web browser with JavaScript enabled. Of course all described limitations of thin-client approach apply and only a subset of the full-client module's functionality is available. Still, it is a good tool to conduct simple tests without preparations or in emergency situations.

The last function of web publication module is the web-based deployment of full-client software to client computers. It is currently under development and will provide web-based guide and wizard (Java) to check client computer configuration, advise user in necessary system configuration changes and automatically install desired (and allowed by administrator for a particular user) full-client modules.

Analysis Module

This module is devoted to a detailed analysis of test packages and gathered knowledge assessment results stored in the system database (Figure 10). Additionally it allows monitoring of system operation and usage.

Its functionality consists of:

1. statistical analysis of test results and student grades,
2. assessment of test quality based on test results (under development),
3. semi-automatic generation of didactic content, helpful in acquiring knowledge appropriate to a given test,
4. creating reports concerning system operation and usage.

The first option allows teacher to calculate various statistical properties of knowledge assessment results, such as maximum/minimum/ mean grade, percentage of students passing the test, grade distribution etc.

Choice test results can also be used to assess quality of the questions (defined as correct level of their difficulty and high discrimination (Costagliola G. et al., 2007). We are currently testing our own analysis engine for the task, based on experiences described in (Costagliola G. et al., 2007) and other works referenced there.

The third of module options can be used to semi-automatically prepare electronic learning material appropriate for a given choice test. It can then be used for pre-assessment study or during test results revision. To fulfill this useful and usually time-consuming task we use three basic methods.

In case of the most direct approach, learning content can be included directly in XML test definition. It can be linked to a test as a whole, or to separate questions and even answers. As such method is obviously not the most efficient one (in terms of data management), learning content objects can also be referenced by URI links, in-

stead of including them directly. In such case the system compile an appropriate learning package fully automatically. Unfortunately it is also a work intensive solution for a teacher.

The second and third methods are based on automatic search of appropriate material on the Internet using highly configurable Google search engine (Google, 2007) or in a repository of SCORM compliant material (SCORM, 2007).

The second method requires test author to provide keywords in XML test definition. They can be supplied as separate XML elements or just as marked parts of questions and answers. Such information is then used in the search.

The third method does not require any additional input except test definition. The search phrases submitted to search engines are automatically constructed from test definitions by removing popular words, and obtaining keywords by means of:

1. word frequency analysis,
2. checking word positions in sentences,
3. comparing results of searches for candidate keywords with remainder of test definition.

As these automatic methods can produce unpredictable results (which is especially true in case of Internet search) a teacher's revision of results is necessary. The module provides teacher with a preview of search results which should be manually verified and can be subsequently used to construct a SCORM compliant package. The teacher constructs such package by connecting desired materials with SCORM sequencing and navigation relations (SCORM, 2007) using module's web interface. Resulting SCORM package can be utilized in a wide variety of SCORM compliant e-learning systems.

Apart from these education-related tasks, the module is also able to gather event logs and usage statistics from the system nodes, to create overall reports concerning its operation, efficiency, usage and to inform administrator about important events occurring in the system.

DEPLOYMENT RESULTS

To test its efficiency in production environment we deployed the system in selected classes (mainly computer science and computer networks) of Faculty of Electronics, Telecommunications and Informatics, Technical University of Gdansk during the last three years. A total of over 4500 students participated in the tests generating about 45000 separate test results.

The system allowed to drastically reduce workload of the teachers by automatically creating attendance list, conducting and grading tests and generating lists of results. It lowered time consumed by knowledge assessment related tasks from over 10 min. to 1 min. on average, for a single laboratory group. It also allowed to minimize number of errors occurring in this process (for example: name mistypes, lost results,) by about 70%, which makes the resulting error rate almost null (1-2 mistakes for about 4000 test results). It was also well received by our students, which is visible in the opinion poll results presented below.

A combination of test-based knowledge assessment and real-time grading modules has been particularly effective during laboratory exercises, as it allowed to instantly grade exercises composed of theoretical test and practical laboratory work. Its ability to function in offline environment and upload results when connectivity becomes available made it suited even for computer networks laboratories.

To guide us in further development of our system, we conducted an opinion pool amongst the students and teachers using it.

Of a 200 students participating in the poll, 83% think that deployment of the system was a desirable change (from classical pen and paper tests and assorted computerized knowledge assessment

Table 1. Results of a survey concerning deployment of the proposed system – Gdansk University of Technology.

	Better	Indifferent	Worse	Total
Students	166 (83%)	30 (15%)	4 (2%)	200
Teachers (early post-deployment)	6 (50%)	3 (25%)	3 (25%)	12
Teachers (6 month post-deployment)	10 (84%, +34%)	2 (16%, -9%)	0 (0%, -25%)	12

solutions), 15% is indifferent, and 2% preferred previous methods employed for the purpose.

The most common positive remarks concerning the system include (in order of frequency):

1. very fast publication of results,
2. a single, well known location and universal format of results,
3. an uniform knowledge testing interface for many subjects and teachers.

As a downside of the system students pointed to its strictness in enforcing test limits (such as time limit or need to answer the question in order) and tendency to overdo such limitations by the teachers.

Of 12 teachers using the system for about a year, 10 rate it as a better solution that the ones they employed before and 2 are indifferent. It is a significant improvement over the first teacher's opinion poll, conducted one month after the system was deployed – the opinions then included: 6 for better, 3 indifferent, and 3 for less useful than previous solutions. We attribute that results and their subsequent change to an additional work required to learn operation of the system and prepare didactic materials (tests definitions etc.).

That conclusion is supported by remarks provided by the teachers. They include, in order of importance to pool respondents and frequency:

Table 2. Most popular positive student's remarks concerning deployment of proposed knowledge assessment system.

Strict time limit enforcement	10%
Too many enforced limitation during test	8%
Choice test as a method of knowledge assessment	8%
Change from previously known solution/UI	6%
Other remarks	2%

1. almost fully automatic and very easy result gathering and publication,
2. ability to perform test in non-networked environments,
3. easy and automatic test deployment and execution.

As a drawback teachers mentioned the need to learn how to use a completely new tool of advanced functionality.

Also, no irreversible data loss (in storage and in transmission) occurred in 3 years of system operation. There are also no indications of successful security breach in any element of the system.

CONCLUSION

In this article we described a dedicated knowledge assessment system, designed to supplement existing e-learning solutions, as they implement such functionality in inadequate manner. The design of our system includes a number of original solutions and often exceeds similar products in terms of functionality. It also differs from currently popular e-learning solutions in such base aspects as system architecture, because our research shows that knowledge assessment functionality requires significantly different approach then content distribution tasks which constitute most of popular e-learning systems' functionality. Our system relies heavily on web-based technologies (Java, XML, HTML, standardized media files,

Table 3. Most popular positive student's remarks concerning deployment of proposed knowledge assessment system.

Fast publication of results	41%
Single, well known location of results	23%
Choice test as a method of knowledge assessment	22%
Lack of technical problems during knowledge testing	16%
Low level of grading/publishing mistakes	10%
Uniform knowledge testing interface	10%
Multimedia tests support	6%
Instantaneous publication of any modifications	5%
Other remarks	7%

streaming media, SOAP, SMTP, MIME, etc.), but their usage differs from currently popular trends.

The uniqueness of our e-learning solution lies in its architecture of independent modules, full-client approach, distributed server-side structure and inclusion of ComAL functionality.

As a result we have a system which can be deployed fully or partially and easily integrated with third party solutions. Possible deployment scenarios range from a single workstation with knowledge testing module exporting results to MS Excel, to a collection of interconnected servers (each controlling a large number of knowledge-testing client modules) allowing global information searches. The system has proven to be extremely scalable. Complication of system configuration also scales, which means that simple setups are as easy to prepare and maintain as installing and running a standalone application, while only more advanced require additional system configuration and administration.

Distributed server part configuration is also easy due to automatic information routing mechanisms. System servers function independently and can be connected and disconnected from the system almost at will with no impairment of their basic functionality, apart from global search ability. That independence allows various departments of an organization to autonomously organize their own elements of the system and retain access to full system information base.

Client modules are implemented in full-client version, as our research proves it to be superior to thin-client approach in case of knowledge assessment systems, in contrast with systems mainly devoted to didactic content distribution.

Our, currently implemented, client modules allow both classical knowledge assessment by use of choice tests and unique functionality of skill assessment by employment of didactic simulation-based tool. There is also a module allowing teacher to easily grade students during classroom exercises and interface to import/export XML data between the system and external sources.

Additionally, we are currently developing additional server modules which will handle supporting tasks, such as advanced results publication, statistical analysis, question quality assessment and semi-automatic didactic material compilation.

All system modules employ our original ComAL communication package designed especially for e-learning systems. Allows e-learning product designers to use communication functions independent of available network connectivity, and allows dynamic environment detection and automatic selection of data transmission mechanisms including strictly offline methods (automatically controlled file import/export). Such functionality allows creation of centrally managed systems even in environment where there is no network connectivity available. Moreover, the ComAL is currently being extended to interface with newly developed content aware networks (CANs) to offload many of communication tasks to network itself, as well as provide additional functionality.

All of these traits make our system one of the most versatile, expandable and easy to deploy knowledge assessment solutions available and positive feedback from its users seems to confirm our confusions.

Usefulness of the system has been verified by its successful deployment in production environment, where over 40000 tests were processed, and by means of student and teacher opinion pool. The results confirmed its value in various learning environments and provided us with further development directions.

ACKNOWLEDGMENT

This work has been partially supported by the Polish Ministry of Science and Higher Education under the European Regional Development Fund, Grant No. POIG.01.01.02-00-045/09-00 (Future Internet Engineering Project).

REFERENCES

Bersin., & Associates. (2004). *Study: Learning Management Systems 2004*. Bersin & Associates, http://www.bersin.com/

Borcoci, E., et al. (2010). *A Novel Architecture for Multimedia Distribution Based on Content-Aware Networking*. 2010 Third International Conference on Communication Theory, Reliability, and Quality of Service (CTRQ), 162-168.

Costagliola, G., et al. (2007). *A Web-Based E-Testing System Supporting Test Quality Improvement*. Proceedings of the 6th International Conference on Web-based Learning, pp.190-197

Future Internet Engineering Project. (2010). *Future Internet Engineering Project Working Raports*. Retrieved from http://www.iip.net.pl

Gierłowski, K., et al. (2003). *Didaktische simulationsmodelle für E-learning in der IK-ausbildung*. Proceedings of 7th Workshop Multimedia für Bildung und Wirtschaft, pp. 77-82, Ilmenau, Septamber 2003, Tech. Univ. Ilmenau, Ilmenau.

Gierłowski, K., & Gierszewski, T. (2004). *Analysis of Network Infrastructure and QoS Requirements for Modern Remote Learning Systems.* Proceedings of the 15th International Conference on Systems Science Wroclaw, September 2004, Oficyna Wydawnicza Politechniki Wrocławskiej, Wroclaw.

Gierłowski, K., & Nowicki, K. (2002). *Simulation of Network Systems in Education.* Proceedings of the XXIVth Autumn International Colloquium Advanced Simulation of Systems(pp. 213-218), Krnov, September 2002, MARQ, Ostrava.

Google Documentation. (2007). Retrieved from http://www.google.com/

IEEE Standards Library. (2007). IEEE 802.11-2007, Wireless LAN Medium Access Control (MAC) and Physical Layer (PHY) Specifications for Wireless Local Area Networks (WLANs), June 2007.

IEEE Standards Library. (2007). IEEE 802.15.1-2002, Wireless Medium Access Control (MAC) and Physical Layer (PHY) Specifications for Wireless Personal Area Networks (WPANs), June 2002.

Jesukiewicz, P., et al. (2006). *ADL Initiative Status and ADL Co-Lab Network.* Academic ADL CoLab archives, http://www.academiccolab.org/

Kindley, R. (2002). The Power of Simulation-based e-Learning. *The e-Learning Developers' Journal*, https://www.elearningguild.com/show-file.cfm?id=95.

Moodle Course Management System Documentation. (2010). Retrieved from http://moodle.org/

Nowicki, K., & Gierłowski, K. (2004). *Implementation of Didactic Simulation Models in Open Source and SCORM Compliant LMS Systems.* Proceedings of XXVIth International Autumn Colloquium, Advanced Simulation of Systems, pp. 161-166, Sv Hostyn, September 2004, MARQ, Ostrava

QTI Public Draft Specification Version 2. (2008). Retrieved from http://www.imsproject.org/question/

Sakai: Collaboration and Learning Environment for Education Documentation. (2010). Retrieved from http://sakaiproject.org/

SCORM. 2004 3rd Edition Documentation. (2007). Advanced Distributed Learning Initiative. Retrieved from http://www.adlnet.gov/

Chapter 5
Recent Contributions to a Generic Architecture Design that Supports Learning Objects Interoperability

Sotirios Botsios
Democritus University of Thrace, Greece

Dimitrios A. Georgiou
Democritus University of Thrace, Greece

ABSTRACT

Adaptation and personalization services in e-learning environments are considered the turning point of recent research efforts, as the "one-size-fits-all" approach has some important drawbacks, from the educational point of view. Adaptive Educational Hypermedia Systems in World Wide Web became a very active research field and the need of standardization arose, as the continually augmenting research efforts lacked interoperability capabilities. This article concentrates and classifies recent research work and notices important points that can lead to an open, modular and generic architecture of a Learning Management System based on widely accepted standards.

INTRODUCTION

As the Internet and World Wide Web are rapidly developed, the technologies that support the educational processes come closer to the traditional educational systems. More and more teachers provide

their teaching material to their students through simple or more sophisticated electronic means and experts in various fields continually provide knowledge to the public, usually in the form of web pages. A recent research by Liaw, Huang, & Chen (2007) demonstrated that instructors have very positive perceptions toward using e-learning as a teaching assisted tool. Regarding to learners'

DOI: 10.4018/978-1-60960-539-1.ch005

attitudes, self-paced, teacher-led, and multimedia instruction are major factors one expects to affect learners' attitudes toward e-learning. According to Brusilovsky and Miller (2001), Adaptive and Intelligent Web-Based Educational Systems provide an alternative to the traditional 'just-put-it-on-the-Web' approach in the development of Web-based educational courseware. In their work Brusilovsky and Pyelo, (2003) mention that Adaptive and Intelligent Web-Based Educational Systems attempt to be more adaptive by building a model of the goals, preferences and knowledge of each individual student and using this model throughout the interaction with the system in order to be more intelligent by incorporating and performing some activities traditionally executed by a human teacher – such as coaching students or diagnosing misconceptions.

According to Brusilovsky and Pyelo, (2003) existing Adaptive and Intelligent Web-Based Educational Systems are very diverse. They offer various kinds of support for both students and teachers involved in the process of Web-enhanced education. In their introductory article they address several technologies appeared (until 2003) in Adaptive and Intelligent Web-Based Educational Systems and provide a catalog of sample systems that provide these technologies.

Also Brown et al (2005) mention that the ultimate objective of Adaptive Educational Hypermedia is to create the 'perfect' online lesson for every learner – utilizing a common set of learning resources. The 'rules' that are used to describe the creation of such a system are not yet standardized, and the criteria that need to be used pedagogically effective rule-sets (i.e. adaptation parameters) are, as yet, poorly mentioned. Many experimental Adaptive Educational Hypermedia Systems have been created – each to their own unique specifications. As yet, however, no combined effort has been made to extract the common design paradigms from these systems.

The scope of this article is to provide a starting point for the development of a generic, open and

modular architecture for the retrieval of learning objects from disperse learning objects' repositories (LORs) to an e-learning environment. Rehak and Mason (2003) consider learning object as a digitized entity which can be used, reused or referenced during technology supported learning. Practically, LOs acquisition is achieved by querying LORs distributed over the internet. This LO "journey" must comply with widely accepted standards. A brief description of research work is also presented. This description classified according to the adaptivity strategy published by several authors aiming to underline the need of unification. Properly modified techniques and methods from the referenced work are suggested for application to the architecture's foundation to provide an open, modular and distributed solution, closely coupled to given standardizations.

The rest of the article is structured as follows. In chapter 2 there is a brief description of the different areas of e-learning systems' adaptive behavior, namely adaptive navigation, presentation and content retrieval. In chapter 3 the most commonly cited adaptivity parameters are classified and several research efforts are mentioned in order to justify the connection of each parameter with the e-learning procedure. An overview of the most commonly accepted standards for e-learning is given in chapter 4. In chapter 5 we provide a review table of the research efforts that connect adaptivity behaviors with some adaptivity parameters and standards. Following, a first attempt for the design of a generic, open and modular architecture for LOs retrieval from LORs is described and the relations of the proposed architecture with other ones found in literature are given. Chapter 7 consists of the properly modified methods and techniques found in literature which could be applied in the modules and become the foundations of the proposed architecture. This article closes with some conclusions and an overview of our planned future work.

ADAPTIVE NAVIGATION, PRESENTATION AND CONTENT RETRIEVAL

Brusilovsky (2001), revising his previous classification Brusilovsky (1996), defined a generally accepted and very commonly cited taxonomy of adaptation types. He defined two main categories as content level adaptation (adaptive presentation) and link level adaptation (adaptive navigation) in order to distinguish accordingly various areas of e-learning systems' adaptive behavior.

The first class includes paradigms of systems that can adapt the presentation of the provided learning material to a stored student model. Examples could be the presentation of visual material instead of text, or the presentation of audio instead of visual. Another example could be the change of the text paragraphs content to display more or less info at the same time (conditional text). The general idea is that the system has the ability to present alternative views to a user, according to some adaptivity parameters which are discussed later on. This ability requires that the content is already constructed in alternative views or the content is constructed at run-time from finer grained elementary material.

Systems that provide adaptive navigation support can suggest and implement, direct navigation, free navigation (through a menu) or different variants of link hiding, disabling, removal, creation, annotation, dimming etc. Again, these links variations can be built at authoring time or at run-time.

The problem that arises –and still is an open one- is the bridging of the gap between these adaptation techniques and free, distributed, standardized learning material from different authors in the hyperspace. Restated, how can an e-learning system put in the most appropriate order and present in the best way "bits and pieces" of LOs placed in disperse LORs of the vast hyperspace.

Authors provide adaptive content retrieval alternatives to approach the previously stated problem. Course Sequencing (Brusilovsky & Vassileva, 2003), or Adaptive Content Scheduling (Watson, Ahmed, & Hardaker, 2007) techniques is the kernel of such scientific efforts. These techniques create a research field close to the field of adaptive navigation support.

ADAPTIVITY PARAMETERS

In this section, we provide brief analysis and literature review of some commonly cited adaptivity parameters. Other parameters could also be found in literature, not very commonly though, such as user context of use (location, technology, time), visual or other impairments, etc. (Brusilovsky & Millan, 2007) The review and analysis of such parameters are out of the scope of this article.

Cognitive Style - Cognitive Abilities

The roots of the word cognition lie on the Latin word cognosco, which in turn comes from the ancient Greek word γιγνώσκω ~ gignosko. The closest translation of the Greek word is I am aware of or I have the property of understanding. There exists a great variety of models and theories in the literature regarding learning behavior and cognitive characteristics i.e. Learning Styles (LSs) or Cognitive Styles (CSs) (Sternberg & Zhang, 2001). Although some authors do not distinguish between LSs and CSs (Rezaei & Katz, 2004), there are others who clearly do (Papanikolaou, Mabbott, Bull, & Grigoriadou, 2006; Sadler-Smith, 2001). According to Riding and Rayner (1998), CS refers to an individual's method of processing information. The building up of a learning strategies repertoire that combine with CS, contribute to an individual's LS (see next subsection). In particular, as Jonassen and Grabowski (1993) reported, LSs are applied CSs, removed one more level from pure processing ability usually referring to learners' preferences on how they process information and not to actual ability, skill or processing tendency. According to Lemaire (1999), Cognitive Abilities are mechanisms that allow humans to acquire and recognize pieces of information, to convert them into representations, then into knowledge, and finally to use them for the generation of simple to complex behaviors.

According to Antonietti and Giorgetti (1997) three main kinds of data can be used to measure cognitive styles: behavioral, self-report, and physiological. Behavioral data can be obtained by recording the final results of a given task or the procedure applied when performing the task. Most of the time, the task consist of filling out a paper-and-pencil test, a multiple choice test or a sorting test. Self-reports require that people evaluate themselves by describing introspectively the way they performed tasks by checking personal habits or preferences, or by endorsing statement about what they think of themselves (for example keeping diary). Finally, some physiological measures can be interpreted as hints of particular cognitive preferences in processing stimuli. Observations of physiological measures have indicated that, when someone is asked a question that requires some thinking, eyes make an initial movement to the left or right.

There are many different classifications of cognitive styles as different researchers emphasize on different aspects (Riding & Cheema, 1991). Field dependence/independence is probably the most well-known division of CSs and, as Witkin et al (1997) notice, it refers to a tendency to approach the environment in an analytical, as opposed to global, way. Their research indicated that field dependent learners are less likely to impose a meaningful organization on a field that lacks structure and are less able to learn conceptual material when cues are not available.

Many experimental studies have demonstrated the impact of field dependence/independence on the learning process. Research by Jonassen and Wang (1993) indicates that students with different CSs choose different strategies for learning. Furthermore, they argue that field independent

learners generally prefer to impose their own structure on information rather than accommodate the structure that is implicit in the learning material.

In their work, Triantafillou et al (2004), investigate the hypothesis that adaptive hypermedia accommodating CSs can be beneficial for the observed learning outcomes. A prototype system, designed to be adapted to individual CSs, was developed and an empirical study was conducted. A list of teaching strategies, applied as adaptation techniques, is adopted in their prototype system for field dependent and field independent learners. For example, a menu from which learners can choose to proceed in the course in any order is provided for field independent learners. This menu is hidden from field dependent users' interface. Their results, both quantitative and qualitative, support the evidence that students of their experimental group (teaching strategies applied) performed significantly better than students in the control group (teaching strategies not applied).

Bernard and Mammar (2005) present an environment called "Cognitive User Modeling for Adaptive Presentation of Hyper-Document". The aim of their proposed environment is to adapt a hyper-document presentation by selecting the elements that best fit the user cognitive profile/abilities. The environment is based on four components: a cognitive user model, a hyper-document generator, an adaptive engine and a generic style sheet to present the adapted hyper-documents. They view the presentation adaptation as a process of selection of the most suitable combination of multimedia items (text, images, audio and video) that describe a concept or provide an explanation. The best combination is the one that most fits the user cognitive abilities. In order to model these abilities, they have defined a cognitive profile, which is a set of valued indicators representing elementary cognitive functions. To validate their approach they defined an innovative protocol, which consists of proposing adaptation based on randomized profile and analyzing performances according to the distance between the real and

Figure 1. Kolb's learning cycle

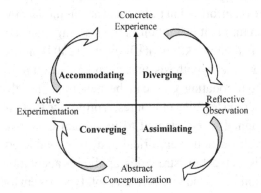

Table 1. Description of D. Kolb's LSs

As-similator	Their characteristic question is "What?". This type of learners prefers information that is presented in an organized way and likes to have time for reflection.
Con-verger	The characteristic question for this learning type is "How?". They like to work actively on well-defined tasks and learn by trial-and-error.
Ac-como-datror	The characteristic question for this learning type is "What if?". They like applying course material in new situations to solve real problems.
Di-verger	The characteristic question is "Why?". They respond well to explanations of how course materials relate to their experience, interest and future careers.
Milosevic, Brkovic et al (2007)	

the randomized profile. The results showed that adaptive presentation of hyper-documents can significantly contribute to the improvement of the performance of users in memorizing and understanding hyper-documents.

In Karampiperis et al (2006) work, authors selected two cognitive characteristics, namely working memory capacity and inductive reasoning ability (available from the Cognitive Trait Model (Kinshuk & Lin, 2004), to create adaptivity algorithms. According to Miller (1956), working memory is the cognitive system that allows us to keep active a limited amount of information for a brief period of time to temporarily store the outcome of intermediate computations during problem solving to perform further computations on these temporary outcomes. Inductive reasoning skill is described by Heit (2000) as the ability to figure out the rules/theories/principle from observed instances of an event, described as working opposite to deduction, moving from specific observations to broader generalizations and theories. In their experiment they simulated different learner behaviors in navigating a hypermedia LOs space, and measured the selection success of the proposed selection decision model as it is dynamically updated using the simulated learner's navigation steps. The simulation results provide evidence that the proposed selection methodology can dynamically update the internal adaptation logic leading to refine selection decisions.

Learning Style

The issue of estimating a learner's LS in the scope of providing tailored education has been addressed in the literature several times. Learning theories converge to the fact that students learn and acquire knowledge in many different ways, which has been classified as LSs. Felder and Silverman (1988) claim that students learn by observing and hearing; reflecting and acting or by reasoning logically and intuitively. Students also learn by memorizing and visualizing; drawing analogies and building mathematical models. LS classifications have been proposed by Kolb (1999) and others (Honey & Mumford, 2000; Dunn & Dunn, 1992; Felder & Silverman, 1988). Most of the authors categorize them into groups and propose certain inventories and methodologies capable of classifying learners accordingly.

The Kolb's LS model (Kolb, 1984; Kolb, 1984) is one of the most well know and widely used in research. According to the model students have a preference in the way they learn: a. Concrete Experience or Abstract Conceptualization and b. Active Experimentation or Reflective Observation. The model is represented in a two dimensions graph, as shown on Figure 1. The preference is diagnosed by analysing subject's responses in given questions of a questionnaire. (Table 1)

In his work, Brusilovsky (2001) noticed that several systems that attempt to adapt to LS had been developed, however it was still not clear which aspects of LS are worth modelling, and what can be done differently for users with different styles. Since then great efforts have been made and a quite large number of surveys have been published that remark the benefits of adaptation to LS.

ACE (Adaptive Courseware Environment) is a WWW-based tutoring framework, developed by Specht et al (1998), which combines methods of knowledge representation, instructional planning and adaptive media generation to deliver individualized courseware over the WWW. Experimental studies within ACE showed that the successful application of incremental linking of hypertext is dependent on students' LS and their prior knowledge. In their research, Graf et al (2007) show how cognitive traits and LSs can be incorporated in web-based learning systems by providing adaptive courses. The adaptation process includes two steps. Firstly, the individual needs of learners have to be detected and secondly, the courses have to be adapted according to the identified needs. The LS estimation in their work is made by a 44-item questionnaire based on Felder-Silverman LS model.

In another work, Papanikolaou, Mabbott et al, (2006) conducted empirical studies on two educational systems (Flexi-OLM and INSPIRE) to investigate learners' learning and cognitive style, and preferences during interaction. The Index of Learning Styles questionnaire was used to assess the style of each participant according to the four dimensions of the Felder-Silverman LS model. It was found that learners do have a preference regarding their interaction, but no obvious link between style and approaches offered, was detected. Other examples which implement different aspects of the Felder-Silverman Index of Learning Styles are WHURLE (E. J. Brown & Brailsford, 2004; Moore, Brailsford, & Stewart, 2001) and ILASH (Bajraktarevic, Hall, & Fullick, 2003).

Part of the Carver, Howard et al (1999) work was to develop an adaptive hypermedia interface that provided dynamic tailoring of the presentation of course material based on the individual student's LS. By tailoring the presentation of material to the student's LS, the authors believe students learned more efficiently and more effectively. Students determine their LS by answering a series of 28 questions. These forms were based on an assessment tool developed at North Carolina State University (B.S. Solomon's Inventory of Learning Styles). In iWeaver from Wolf (2002) the Dunn and Dunn model is used.

The Milosevic, Brkovic et al (2007) approach tend to pursue adaptation according to generated user profile and its features which are relevant to the adaptation, e.g. the user's prefernces, knowledge, goals, navigation history and prossibly other relevant aspects that are used to provide personilized adaptations. They discuss lesson content's design tailored to individual users by taking into consideration LS and subject matter learning motivation. They also mention how LOs metadata can be used for LO retrieval according to the specific needs of the individual learner. They relied on the Kolb's learning style model. They suggest that every LS class should get a different course material sequencing.

Learning Behavior - Motivation

In this article with the term Learning Behavior we address the easily changeable psychological-emotional state of the learner while interacting with an e-learning system. Boredom, frustration, motivation, concentration, tiredness are emotional conditions that, among others, are considered important for the effectiveness of the learning process.

Tracing learner's behavior in real time is a quite challenging task. In her work, Conati (2002) address the problem of how an interactive system can monitor the user's emotional state using multiple direct indicators of emotional arousal. A Dynamic Decision Network was used to represent the probabilistic dependencies in a unifying framework between possible causes and emotional states (anger, reproach, motivation, arousal) on one hand, and between emotional states and the user bodily expressions they can affect on the other hand (following the Ortony, Clore and Collins cognitive theory of emotions). Detection of user's body expressions, such as eyebrow position, skin conductance and heart rate, requires special sensors. The system was applied on computer-based educational games instead of more traditional computer-based tutors, as the former tend to generate a much higher level of students' emotional engagement.

Another approach that exploits novel methods of resolution for fine-grained user profiling based on real-time eye-tracking and content tracking information is presented in Gutl et al (2004) work. The authors introduced the Adaptive e-Learning with Eye-Tracking System, a system that utilizes a monitor mounted camera that records the eye of the participant and trace the gaze in a scene through imaging algorithms. Real- time information of the precise position of gaze and of pupil diameter can be used for assessing user's interest, attention, tiredness etc.

Both of the above mentioned examples utilized a kind of sensors to capture users' behavioral indicators. In Chen et al (2005) work, authors propose a Dynamic Fuzzy Petri Net inference engine that monitors "browsing time" and "browsing count" of users' interaction with their system. According to them, whenever the learner spends too much time on a specific section, he/she is very interested in it or confused by it. Regardless, the auxiliary learning content should be provided. With fuzzy rules like this one, the engine provides an appropriate dynamic learning content structure and normalizes the exercise grade using a course intensity function.

Milosevic et al (2006) examined the users' motivation as a factor of learning efficiency. According to the authors motivation is a pivotal concept in most theories of learning. It is closely related to arousal, attention and anxiety. Increasing learner's motivation during online course is one of the key factors to achieve a certain goal. For example, highly motivated students tend to learn faster and to accept learning material in larger quantities, while low motivators must be presented with smaller knowledge chunks with appropriate feedback, trying to increase their motivation. They propose a pre-course test to assess the user's motivation level, which they import it in user model to adapt the provided learning material.

Knowledge Level

Some researchers emphasize that personalization in e-learning systems should consider additional adaptivity parameters such as different levels of learner knowledge, and learning goals. Brusilovsky (1996) pointed out that AH systems can be useful in any application area where a hypermedia system is expected to be used by people with different goals and knowledge and where the hyperspace is reasonably big. Brusilovsky (2003) notices that users with different goals and knowledge may be interested in different pieces of information presented on hypermedia page and may use different links for navigation. AH tries to overcome this problem by using knowledge represented in the user model to adapt the information being presented, limit browsing space and consequently minimize the cognitive load. In most cases researchers who taken into account knowledge level, goals and/or course material difficulty proposed solutions that provided adaptive navigation (or course sequencing) services.

Two works published by Specht & Kobsa (1999) and Brusilovsky & Rizzo (2002), experimented on adaptive navigation methods with subjects of different previous knowledge level. Both of them concluded that learners with higher previous knowledge seem to prefer non-restricting adaptive methods, while learners with low previous knowledge can profit from the guidance of more restrictive adaptive methods.

The idea of Baldoni et al (2004) is to introduce the pre-requisites and effects of each instruction material unit (LO). Given a set of LOs, annotated by pre-requisites and effects, it is possible to compose reading sequences by using the standard planners based on graph algorithms. In their work, they also introduced some learning strategies, i.e. sets of rules for selecting those LOs which are the most suitable to the student, expressed only in terms of competences.

Chen et al (2006) proposed a system based on modified Item Response Theory which provides learning paths that can be adapted to various levels of difficulty of course materials and various abilities of learners. Meanwhile, the concept continuity of learning pathways is also integrated by analyzing concept relation degrees for all database courseware while applying personalized curriculum sequencing. To prevent the learner from becoming lost in course materials, the system provides personalized learning guidance, filters out unsuitable course materials to reduce cognitive loading, and provides a fine learning guidance based on individual user profile. Experimental results indicated that their system can recommend appropriate course materials to learners based on individual ability, and help them to learn more effectively in a web-based environment.

STANDARDS FOR E-LEARNING

Nowadays e-Learning applications are getting widely spread in the Internet. As a result, an increasing demand for reusable and sharable LOs arises. Groups such as SCORM (Shareable Content Object Reference Model), IEEE LTSC (IEEE Learning Technology Standards Committee), IMS (Instructional Management Systems) and AICC (Aviation Industry CBT Committee) have undertaken significant work on LOs schemas. The SCORM standard was developed by the Depart-

ment of Defense's ADL (Advanced Distributed Learning) initiative.

Today SCORM is a widely accepted collection of standards in e-Learning applications. SCORM seeks to establish a collection of specifications and standards adapted from multiple sources to provide a comprehensive suite of e-Learning capabilities that support the interoperability, accessibility and reusability of web-based learning content (SCORM, 2004) ((ADL), 2006). It can be considered as a collection of "technical books" which are presently grouped under three main topics: a. Content Aggregation Model (CAM), b. Run-time Environment (RTE) and c. Sequencing and Navigation (SN).

SCORM CAM defines how learning resources are defined with the XML metadata. Learning resources in SCORM are assets, Sharable Content Objects (SCOs) and Activities. Assets are electronic representations of media that can be collected together to build other assets. If this collection represents a single launchable learning resource that utilizes SCORM RTE to communicate with an LMS, it is referred to as an SCO. An Activity is a meaningful unit of instruction that may provide learning resources (assets or SCOs) or be composed of several subactivities. SCORM CAM consists of three different parts: a. Content Model which describes the low level components of instruction (assets, SCOs and content aggregations), b. Metadata, i.e. information describing the instruction material, and c. Content Packaging. ((ADL), 2006)

SCORM RTE defines the communication procedures between a Learning Management System and the instruction material. It consists of three parts: a. Launch, which defines a common way for LMS to start Web-based learning resources, b. Application programmable interface, which is the communication mechanism for informing the LMS of the state of the learning resource and c. a standard set of elements used to define the information being communicated, the Data Model. ((ADL), 2006)

SCORM Sequencing and Navigation (SN) defines a method for representing the branching and flow of learning activities in any SCORM conformant LMS. The learning resources flow could be both predefined by the content author and run-time created by user interactions with content objects. ((ADL), 2006)

IMS Learner Information Package specification LIP is a collection of information about a learner or a producer of learning content. The specification addresses the interoperability of internet based Learner Information systems with other systems that support the Internet learning environment. Storing information regarding recording and managing learning-related history, goals, preferences and accomplishments is described in LIP specification. ((IMS), 2001)

ADAPTIVITY PARAMETERS AND STANDARDS

As mentioned in the introduction, one of this article's contributions is to provide a classification of research efforts that connect adaptivity parameters and standards (see table 2). Each article examines adaptivity parameters which appear in the second column and adaptivity types (adaptive presentation, navigation, content retrieval) which are placed in the third column. The forth column provides the reference to given standardizations and specifications and the fifth column provides some information about the assessment method used to capture the adaptivity parameter. Specific, properly adopted, methods and techniques from research efforts of table 2 are selected to underlie the generic architecture, which is described in the next section.

One can notice that some of the referenced scientific work is annotated as standards extension proposals. Authors of these articles propose certain standards additions in order to create adaptive courses. In specific, Ray-Lopez et al (2006) argue that current standards do not fully support content

personalization. They study the adaptation possibilities of the SCORM standard and present an extension to permit the instructors to create adaptive courses with flexible structures, as well as to define the rules that permit the system to decide which activities are the most appropriate for a particular student. The adaptivity is provided at two levels: SCO level and activity level. Adaptivity at SCO level is achieved by defining a new type of SCO: the self-adaptive SCO, which self-configures based on a set of user's characteristics. Adaptivity at activity level consists in offering different combinations of subactivities to achieve the objective of the parent activity.

Other examples of standard extension proposals are the Rumetshofer et al (2003) work, where the parent element <Psychological> is suggested to be added in IEEE LOM, and Sampson's et al (2002) effort, where extensions over the IMS content packaging specification are suggested.

GENERIC ARCHITECTURE: A FIRST APPROACH

General Description

In this section a brief description of the proposed generic architecture is given (Figure 2). The model describes a solution to the scenario of distributed LOs adaptive retrieval and presentation from a web-based Learning Management System (LMS), as it seems to be the dominant practice. Practically, LOs acquisition is achieved by querying LORs distributed over the internet, using LOs metadata standards. The database queries must have solid structure with strictly defined parameters.

The criteria of the retrieval, presentation and navigation (sequencing of the LOs) are in accordance with the adaptivity parameters examined in section 3.

- Cognitive Style, cognitive abilities
- Learning Style

Table 2. Classification of recent research which reference to standardization and adaptivity parameters

	Adaptivity Parameter	Assessment Method	Reference to Standardization	Adaptivity Type
Milosevic, et al (2007)	learning style	Kolb Learning Style Inventory	<learningResourceType>	adaptive navigation
	motivation	pre-, post- tests	<SemanticDensity>	adaptive presentation
Yordanova (2007)	general	-	<title> <language> <description> <keyword> <format> <learningResourceType> <interactivityLevel> <difficulty> <taxonPath>	-
Watson et al (2007)	knowledge level	SCO performance assessment	SCORM interaction elements	adaptive content retrieval
Karampiperis et al (2006)	cognitive style > working capacity	monitoring navigation steps	<aggregationLevel> <interactivityType> <interactivityLevel> <semanticDensity> <difficulty> <typicalLearningTime> <learningResourceType>	adaptive content retrieval
Chen et al (2006)	knowledge level	modified Item Response Theory	<description> <keyword> <difficulty>	adaptive content retrieval
Chen et al (2005)	learning behavior	Dynamic Fuzzy Petri Net	Activity Tree of <organization> SCORM Rollup Rules	adaptive content retrieval
Baldomi et al (2004)	knowledge level	-	<purpose> <taxon>	adaptive navigation
Rey-Lopez et al (2008)*	dependent to each LMS	dependent to each LMS	<adaptation> <organization> <item>	adaptive content retrieval adaptive presentation
Rumetshofer et al (2003)*	cognitive style learning strategy skill	assessment center (questionnaires)	<psychological> <cognitive style> <learning strategy> <learning modality> <skills>	adaptive content retrieval, presentation, navigation
Sampson et al (2002)*	learner profile (general)	questionnaire to create an IMS LIP based profile	<rules> <domain ontology> <LO meta-data> <questions & tests> <competencies> <user profiles>	adaptive content retrieval
*standards extension				

- Learning Behavior, motivation
- Knowledge level

The above parameters are considered independent to each other, by the means of absence

of influence. The values of these parameters are resulted from separate modules, accordingly.

The numbered list which follows, describes the most important aspects of the architecture's modules. The "x" symbol in the corner of some

Figure 2. A first approach of the generic architecture

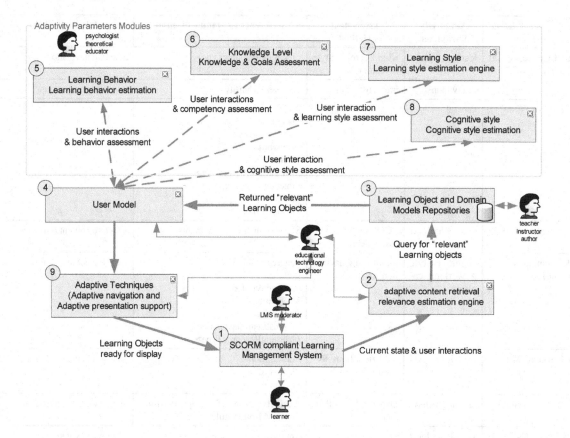

boxes implies that the module could be disabled or not present, without disturbing the LO's retrieval, but, of course, disabling some, or all, of these modules the system becomes less parametric or less "intelligent".

1. Learning Management System (LMS). The beginning and the end of the e-learning experience. The LMS captures user interactions and forwards them to next modules. Also, the LMS is responsible to receive and display the returned LOs. Of course, both captured user interactions and received LOs must be standardized.

2. According to visited LO (in figure 2: current state) and user interactions –information that is send from the LMS- the relevance estimation engine is responsible to create the appropriate query to "ask" LORs for

"relevant" LOs. Algorithms proposed by Chen et al (2006) (C. M. Chen, Liu, & Chang, 2006) and Watson et al (2007) (Watson, et al., 2007) could be applied to provide a taxonomy of "relevant" LOs. Taking under consideration user interactions and LOM, these algorithms are inference engines that provide selection rules to filter LOs from disperse and vast LORs.

3. Learning Objects and Domain Models Repositories receive a query and return a number of "relevant" LOs. A catalogue of some large LORs with sharable LOs can be found in Nash (2005) (Nash, 2005).

4. The User Model is responsible to store (keep personal user data, preferences data and history related data) and forward user interactions to adaptivity parameters modules (see 5, 6, 7 and 8), receive their assessments

and export a final filtered taxonomy of the Learning Objects that have received from 3.

5. Learning Behavior. This module is dedicated to learning behavior diagnosis. A suggestion for estimating learning behavior from user's interaction is proposed by Chen et al (2005) (J. N. Chen, et al., 2005) and Milosevic et al (2007) (Milosevic, et al., 2007) (see table 2).

6. Competence Level. This module supports the assessment of user's knowledge and goals. The modified item response theory from Chen et al (2006) (C. M. Chen, et al., 2006) or SCO performance assessment from Watson et al (2007) (Watson, et al., 2007) are two alternatives for this purpose (see table 2).

7. Learning Style. Similarly to 5 and 6, this module produces results for user's LS. Milosevic et al (2007) (Milosevic, et al., 2007) developed a solution that "connects" user's LS to specific LOM (see table 2).

8. Cognitive Style. This module is dedicated to estimate the user's CS. The module receives user interaction related data and exports an assessment. An example application is the Karampiperis et al (2006) (Karampiperis, et al., 2006) work. Data about user navigation is used to export LOM (see table 2).

9. All the algorithms to provide adaptive navigation and adaptive presentation services are the last stage of this architecture. This module receives user model information and produces a filtered taxonomy of learning objects, applies the appropriate algorithms and forwards the data to be displayed in the interface of the LMS.

We must also mention that our model, as an AEHS, is created in favor of the learner, but it should be supported by others, such as:

1. Instruction material providers (educators, teachers, authors etc)

2. System moderators
3. Cognitive Psychologists (assessment engines)
4. Administrators
5. Educational Technology Engineers

Relations to Other Architectures

The proposed architecture has some similarities to components of other architectures one can find in literature. As already mentioned, one of this article's objectives is to gather, formalize and generalize other research efforts on this field. In referenced work, researchers seek to create an architecture which meets specific needs, but the basic aspects of their efforts can be considered as the following:

1. A pool, database, repository of the instruction material and the domain models (possible relation to instruction material) → (3)

2. An assessment method: An engine that tries to capture some user characteristics → (5, 6, 7, 8)

3. A user model generation process: Techniques that gather results from the assessment engines and create a dynamic user "instance" which is used throughout the e-learning experience → (4)

4. An adaptation process: Techniques based on rules that map user model to the instruction material → (4 to 9)

5. A user interface generator: An engine which produces the final screenshot of the e-learning experience which is displayed to the user's screen → (9 to 1)

6. Agents that capture user interactions with the interface → (1 to 2)

Note that agents or society of agents function between each component.

In his work, Oliveira (2002) presents a generic architecture for AEHSs, which is resulted from known AEHS architectures' analysis and other adaptive systems, as well. In our article we refer to the very significant parameter of standards, which has not been included in his work.

Some of the above modules can be found in Bernard and Mammar (2005) work. Authors present an environment called "Cognitive User Modeling for Adaptive Presentation of Hyper-Document". The proposed environment is based on four components, namely a cognitive user model, a hyper-document generator, an adaptive engine, and a generic style sheet to present the adapted hyper-documents. Adaptive presentation is viewed as a process of selection of the most suitable combination of multimedia items (text, images, audio and video) that describe a concept. The best combination is the one that better fits the user cognitive abilities.

A generic architecture is also described in Karampiperis et al (2005) work. It follows a two layer architecture: a Runtime Layer and a Storage Layer. The Runtime Layer consists of an Educational Content Presenter, a Behavior Tracker and an Adaptation Rule Parser. The Storage Layer consists of a User Model, an Adaptation Model, the Educational Resources (LOs) themselves and a Domain Model, where the connections of Educational Resources with concepts are held. These connections are represented in the <classification> element of the IEEE LOM standardization. An interesting part of that work is the use of the IMS LIP specification for representing User Model elements. For example user's LS is represented with Accessibility/Preference/typename and Accessibility/Preference/prefcode IMS LIP elements.

Another example that utilizes some of the above mentioned modules is found in Chen et al work (2006). The modular system architecture consists of a courseware analysis module, a courseware recommendation agent, which is responsible to match user interaction with course material, and finally a learning interface agent.

METHODS AND TECHNIQUES

In what follows a short description of a new approach to certain model's components functionality is presented

Relevance Estimation Engine

The establishment of a LOs taxonomy concerning the "distance" each LO of a certain LOR has from the LO currently in use, is still an open problem. Watson et al (2007) ask: How would the student select the correct learning objects to achieve the learning objectives, when assuming that he/she has access to the repository filled with various learning objects? If the student is allowed to pick learning objects, the pathway could become illogical and confusing. On the other hand, if the student followed a static linear pathway through the learning objects, the outcome would not necessarily match his/her individual needs. Facing questions of this kind, we seek to estimate the concept relation degree of two LOs. Several methods have been proposed, such as "estimation of concept relation degree" proposed by Chen et al (2006) or "Pathway generator" proposed by Watson et al (2007). For the scope of this article we will briefly describe a slight modification of Chen's vector space model. Each LO is represented as a vector in a multidimensional Euclidean space. Each axis in this space corresponds to a linguistic term obtained from word segmentation process of specific LOM fields (<title>, <description>, <keyword>, <coverage> from the <general> element and the children elements of the <contribute> element). These fields are selected following the Najjar et al (2005) research results and recommendation of an iterative usability study conducted to examine the usability of a search tool used to find learning objects in ARIADNE Knowledge Pool System. The coordinate of the ith LO in the direction corresponding to the kth linguistic term can be determined as follows:

$$w_{ik} = tf_{ik} \cdot \log \frac{N}{N_{lo_k}}$$

where w_{ik} represents the weight that express the participation of the kth term in the ith LO, tf_{ik} is the term frequency of the kth term, which appears in the ith LO; N denotes the total number of LOs and N_{bk} is the number of LOs containing the kth term.

Assume that there are m terms in total under union of all linguistic terms of the ith LO and j^{th} LO. The concept relation degree, r_{ij}, between the ith and j^{th} LO can be found using the cosine-measure, listed as follows:

$$r_{ij} = \frac{\sum_{h=1}^{m} w_{ih} w_{jh}}{\sqrt{\sum_{h=1}^{m} w_{ih}^2 \sum_{h=1}^{m} w_{jh}^2}}$$

where $c_i = [w_{i1}, w_{i2}, \ldots, w_{ik}, \ldots, w_{im}]$ and $c_j = [w_{j1}, w_{j2}, \ldots, w_{jk} \ldots, w_{jm}]$, respectively, represent the vectors in a multidimensional Euclidean space for the ith and j^{th} LO.

Assume that there are totally n LOs in a LOR, the concept relation matrix for all courseware can be expressed by the matrix R, and listed as follows:

$$R = \begin{bmatrix} r_{11} & r_{12} & \cdots & r_{1n} \\ r_{21} & r_{22} & \cdots & r_{2n} \\ \cdots & \cdots & \cdots & \cdots \\ r_{n1} & r_{n2} & \cdots & r_{nn} \end{bmatrix}_{n \times n}$$

Obviously the value of the items of the main diagonal is 1.

In the following example we provide results from our preliminary experimentation on the algorithm. The obtained results provide a measure of relation between LOs that reflect on our intuitional hypothesis of relevance. Table 3 present the value of the <description> node of metada file from selected LOs. The first 4 lines display real LOs, retrieved from the open LOR "Australian Flexible Learning Toolboxes". The last two

Table 3. The description metadata value from 6 LOs

LO Identifier	Description Metadata Value
1	The multimedia designer Jacob introduces a number of key concepts about digital imaging, photography and digital video including file types for specific applications (bitmaps, jpegs, gifs, tifs etc), bit depth, resolution, compresssion, video dvd, connectivity, video legal colours, image scanning, health and safety and asset managment while working with digital images, video and or multimedia.
2	In this project the learner will have to measure performance and usability of a site they've created and create a report based on those findings. The learner is situated in a fictitious company (Arachnoid Web Services) having commenced work as a Junior Web Designer.
3	This activity describes a pratical multimedia project that involves image manipulation, sound editing and multimedia design and export. A local travel agency, Top Travel has asked us to produce a second multimedia presentation for their web site promoting the various attractions on offer in this region. We need approximately 30 digital photos of the local area incorporated with a sound track into a multimedia sequence. This presentation will incorporate text that encourages tourism to our local area. We will use Movie Maker to assemble the whole presentation There are 7 other activities in this series that contribute understanding required to undertake the whole project. These are: All about Images Digital Cameras Prepare for a Photo Shoot Image Manipulation Removing Red Eye Digital Sound Movie Maker As you work through this series you will develop your tourism project.
4	This activity describes how to remove red eyes in digital images caused by flash bounce. As you remove red eye from an image, you will learn to use a number of Photoshop tools and processes including eyedropper, filters, paintbrush, hues and blends.
5	Measuring the importance and performance of a web site, from a Web Designer's point of view.
6	Alice in the Wonder Land. Some pictures from the book.

lines display imaginary LOs. The first of these is considered as "relevant" to one of the real LOs, while the second is irrelevant to every single one of the real LOs. We should mention that, for the scope of this preliminary experimentation, we applied the algorithm only in the <description> node's values, because we just wanted to get some indication of the algorithm's efficiency.

Following the LOs selection, we applied word segmentation techniques. We removed articles, pronouns, prepositions, words that do not significantly contribute to a text's meaning and also considered every word without its ending (for example we removed the –ing, -er, -ist, -s and other endings of the words). The result of the application of these techniques is a set of 140 linguistic terms. The application of the relevancy estimation engine resulted in the following 6x6 relation matrix:

$$R = \begin{bmatrix} 1.000 & 0.086 & 0.207 & 0.210 & 0.081 & 0.025 \\ 0.086 & 1.000 & 0.168 & 0.133 & 0.344 & 0.104 \\ 0.207 & 0.168 & 1.000 & 0.216 & 0.099 & 0.077 \\ 0.210 & 0.133 & 0.216 & 1.000 & 0.037 & 0.019 \\ 0.081 & 0.344 & 0.099 & 0.037 & 1.000 & 0.067 \\ 0.025 & 0.104 & 0.77 & 0.019 & 0.067 & 1.000 \end{bmatrix}$$

The given results justify intuitional considerations. (Figure 3)

Learning Style

As mentioned earlier in this article, user's LS is considered as an important parameter which should be taken under consideration in the e-learning experience. Each user's LS is extracted by applying methods proposed by cognitive scientists. As an example of LS estimation in an on-line system we can address the Botsios et al work (2008). Their work is based on Kolb's Learning Style Inventory (Kolb, 1999; Kolb, 1999). Instead of using just a static questionnaire to estimate

the learner's LS, authors implemented the Fault Implication Avoidance Algorithm (FIAA) and a Probabilistic Expert System. Taking into account the structure of Kolb's Learning Style Inventory, FIAA dynamically creates a descending shorting of learner's answerers per question, decreases the amount of necessary input for the diagnosis, which in turn can result to limitation of possible controversial answers. The applied Probabilistic Expert System analyzes information from responses supplied by the system's antecedent users (users that complete the questionnaire before the present user) to conclude to a LS diagnosis of the present user. Evidence is provided that the effect of some factors, such as cultural environment and lucky guesses or slippery answers, that hinder an accurate estimation, is diminished. Their system gives a "clear" LS estimation (no "grey" estimation areas), making the results of practical use in an AEHS.

After diagnosing user's LS, the user model match diagnosed LS to a LO in optimum way. Milosevic et al (2007) discuss about designing lesson content tailored to individual users, taking into consideration, among others, LS and how LOM could be used for LO retrieval according to the specific needs of the individual learner. They

Figure 3. LOs relevancy distribution

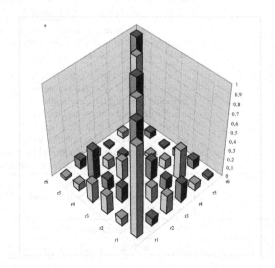

Table 4. Teaching activities (LOs) and learning resources types according to user's LS

Teaching activities	AC/RO (assimilator)	AC/AE (converger)	CE/AE (accommodator)	CE/RO (diverger)
theory	1 lecture	0	0	1 lecture
examples	2 slides, examples	1 experiment, simulation	2 simulation, experiment	2 simulation
practicing	0	2 self assessment, exercise	1 problem statement	0
tests	3 exam	3 exam	3 exam	3 exam
optional links				
index	+3	+3	+3	+1
problem sets	+1	+2	+2	+3
case study	+2	+1	+1	+2
(Milosevic, et al., 2007)				

relied on the Kolb's LS model. They suggest that every LS class should get a different course material sequencing. Specifically, they take advantage of the LOM element <learningRersourceType>, which, according to IEEE LOM recommended vocabulary, it takes one of the following values: exercise, simulation, questionnaire, diagram, figure, graph, index, slide, table, narrative text, exam, experiment, problem statement, self assessment, lecture. They also propose that learning material should contain knowledge modules: theory, examples, practice and test, represented with appropriate LOs. Besides, each page should provide optional links to Index, Problem sets, Case study and Group discussion ordered according to the LS diagnosis conducted earlier. The table summarizes teaching activities enclosed in adaptation algorithm. A value (1,2,3) is assigned to each knowledge module stating its importance. Contents that have value 0 assigned to them denote that such content type should not be presented to the learner. (Table 4)

In their paper Milosevic et al (2007) provide the following example. Assimilator LS should be presented with (1) theoretical content, followed by (2) example and then (3) test. Practicing should not be presented as obligatory knowledge module, since people of this LS don't like studying through application on knowledge. In the optional part,

links should be ordered by 1) problem sets, 2) case study and 3) index, without group discussions.

Cognitive Style

As mentioned earlier, learners of different cognitive characteristics require content presentation tailored to their learning needs. In Karampiperis et al (2006) (Karampiperis, et al., 2006) work, authors selected two cognitive characteristics, namely the working memory capacity and the inductive reasoning skill to create adaptivity algorithms. Working memory capacity diagnosis and the adaptation rules are briefly described in the next paragraph.

Working memory capacity diagnosis is made by tracing user's navigation patterns. Lin (2003) (Lin, 2003) suggests that non-linear navigation in the learning space, constant reverse navigation and frequent revisit of learned material are indications, among others, of low working memory capacity. When the working memory capacity of the learner is low then a. the number of the paths and the amount of information presented to the learner should decrease to protect the learners from getting lost in the vast amount of information, b. the relevance of the information should increase to raise the possibility that the learners will get the

Table 5. Working memory capacity and LOM elements

	Low	**High**
InteractivityType	Expositive	Active
InteractivityLevel	Very low, low	Very high, high
SemanticDensity	Very low, low	Very high, high
Difficulty	Very easy, easy	Very difficult, difficult
(Karampiperis, et al., 2006)		

most important information and c. the concreteness of the information should increase so the learner can grasp the fundamental rules first and use them to generate higher-order rules. The opposite should happen if the working memory capacity of the learner is high (linear navigation pattern, rare or none reverse navigation, infrequent or none revisit of learned material). The LOM elements that are relevant to the pedagogical adaptation to working memory capacity are <Interactivity-Type>, <InteractivityLevel>, <SemanticDensity> and <Difficulty> of the <Educational> parent element. (Table 5)

Motivation – Learning Behavior

By the term "level of user's motivation" is denoted the measure of student's focus of attention on the teaching process, especially on the learning material presented to the student. User's motivation can be assessed recording users' interaction. Chen et al (2005) propose two characteristics that need to be monitored, namely: browsing time and browsing count. Browsing time is the total time a learner persists in a certain learning section. <typicalLearningTime> element of the <Educational> parent node can keep such an information. Whenever the learner spends too much time on such a LO, he/she is either very interested in it or confused by it. Regardless, the motivation level can be considered as high. Browsing count is the frequency with which a

particular LO is addressed. Browsing count can also be an indication of motivation and confusion. In their work Milosevic et al (2007), they chose to incorporate the element <SemanticDensity> of the <Educational> parent element, denoting the complexity and the semantic quantity of LO. Each LO can have semantic density between 1 and 5, i.e. providing low motivators with LOs that have <SemanticDensity> smaller than or equal to 2, moderate motivated students with LOs of smaller or equal to 4 <SemanticDensity> and finally high motivators with LOs annotated 5 to their <SemanticDensity> tag.

Knowledge Level

In this paragraph we describe the mapping of the user's ability or knowledge to LOs' difficulty level, which can be annotated in the <Difficulty> node of the <Educational> element. The algorithm is proposed by Chen et al (2006) in their "courseware recommendation agent". The courseware recommendation agent first estimates learner ability using a Bayesian estimation procedure, then evaluates the modified information function value of LOs in the LOR and creates a LO descending sorting. A LO, which is high in this taxonomy, is considered as the most suitable for the user's current knowledge level.

To estimate the learner's ability, the item characteristic function with a single difficulty parameter is used. The formula is defined as follows:

$$P_j(\theta) = \frac{e^{D(\theta - b_j)}}{1 + e^{D(\theta - b_j)}}$$

where $P_j(\theta)$ denotes the probability that learners can understand the jth LO of the LOR at a level below their ability level θ, b_j is the value of <difficulty> node of the jth LO and D is a constant 1.702. For the estimation of user's ability level, θ, a Bayesian procedure is described in the same paper (Chen et al, 2006). The quadrature form to approximately estimate learner's ability is given by the following formula:

$$\hat{\theta} = \frac{\sum\limits_{k}^{q} \theta_k A(\theta_k) \prod\limits_{j=1}^{n} P_j(\theta_k)^{u_j} \left[1 - P_j(\theta_k)\right]^{1-u_j}}{\sum\limits_{k}^{q} A(\theta_k) \prod\limits_{j=1}^{n} P_j(\theta_k)^{u_j} \left[1 - P_j(\theta_k)\right]^{1-u_j}}$$

where $\hat{\theta}$ denotes the learner's ability of estimation, θ_k is the kth split value of ability in the standard normal distribution, $A(\theta_k)$ represents the quadrature weight at a level below the θ_k ability level and $u_j=1$ or $u_j=0$ if the answer is understood or not understood from the learner, respectively (this value is obtained from leaner feedback to the jth LO). In this algorithm, learner abilities are limited between $\theta=-1$ and $\theta=1$. That is, learners with ability -1 are viewed as the poorest, those with ability 0 are viewed as having moderate abilities and those with ability 1 are viewed as having the best abilities. Finally, the maximum information functions is used to create a descending sorting of LOs. The maximum information is defined as follows:

$$I_j(\theta) = \frac{(1.7)^2}{\left[e^{1.7(\theta-b_j)}\right]\left[1 + e^{-1.7(\theta-b_j)}\right]^2}$$

where $I_j(\theta)$ is the information value of the jth LO at a level below user's ability level θ, b_j is the difficulty parameter of the jth LO. A LO with the maximum information function value indicates that the system gives the highest recommendation priority.

CONCLUSION AND FUTURE WORK

There exist a wide variety of diverse Adaptive and Intelligent Web-Based Educational Systems. The 'rules' that are used to describe the creation of such systems are not yet fully standardized,

and the criteria that need to be used pedagogically effective rule-sets (i.e. adaptation parameters) are, as yet, poorly mentioned (Brown et al., 2005) (E. Brown, et al., 2005). In this article we provide a starting point for the development of a unified architecture capable to retrieve LOs from disperse LORs and to direct them to every user tailored to his/her needs. This LO "journey" must comply with widely accepted standards. The model is based on a distributed architecture. Interoperability, information sharing, scalability and dynamic integration of heterogeneous expert fields are considered as the major advantages of the proposed model. a. Interoperability: support for available standards, technology and platform independent. b. Information Sharing: user information, learning objects, services and assessment tools. c. Scalability: continuous update of each module's functionality (Learning Objects, monitoring tools, cognition and learning style theories, sequencing and navigation algorithms). d. Integration of heterogeneous expert field: independent module development and dynamic adaptation to the latest criteria.

This article aims to gather step by step recent research work concerning adaptivity parameters, to investigate their connection with widely accepted LO standards and to provide suitable methods and techniques from the literature which can be applied in a generic architecture for the retrieval of learning objects from disperse learning objects' repositories to an e-learning environment. Further detailed development of the above described generic architecture may be in focus of software engineers' attention. Also, a further literature review will might bring in light more elegant methods and might discover most recent approaches in adaptivity parameters diagnosis.

ACKNOWLEDGMENT

This work is supported in the frame of Operational Programme "COMPETITIVENESS", 3rd

Community Support Program, co financed by the public sector of the European Union – European Social Fund And by the Greek Ministry of Development – General Secretariat of Research and Technology.

REFERENCES

A. D. L. (2006). *SCORM 2004 3rd Edition, Sharable Content Object Reference Model*. Advanced Distributed Learning.

Antonietti, A., & Giorgetti, M. (1997). The Verbalizer-Visualizer Questionnaire: A review 1. *Perceptual and Motor Skills, 86*(1), 227–239.

Bajraktarevic, N., Hall, W., & Fullick, P. (2003). *ILASH: Incorporating Learning Strategies in Hypermedia*. Paper presented at the Fourteenth Conference on Hypertext and Hypermedia.

Baldoni, M., Baroglio, C., Patti, V., & Torasso, L. (2004). *Reasoning about learning object metadata for adapting SCORM courseware*. Paper presented at the EAW'04.

Botsios, S., Georgiou, D., & Safouris, N. (2008). Contributions to AEHS via on-line Learning Style Estimation. *Journal of Educational Technology & Society, 11*(2).

Brown, E., Cristea, A., Stewart, C., & Brailsford, T. (2005). Patterns in authoring of adaptive educational hypermedia: A taxonomy of learning styles. *Educational Technology and Society, 8*(3), 77–90.

Brown, E. J., & Brailsford, T. (2004). *Integration of learning style theory in an adaptive educational hypermedia (AEH) system*. Paper presented at the ALT-C Conference.

Brusilovsky, P. (1996). Methods and techniques of adaptive hypermedia. *User Modeling and User-Adapted Interaction, 6*(2-3), 87–129. doi:10.1007/BF00143964

Brusilovsky, P. (2001). Adaptive hypermedia. *User Modelling and User-Adapted Interaction, 11*(1-2).

Brusilovsky, P. (2003). Adaptive navigation support in educational hypermedia: The role of student knowledge level and the case for meta-adaptation. *British Journal of Educational Technology, 34*(4), 487–497. doi:10.1111/1467-8535.00345

Brusilovsky, P., & Millan, E. (2007). User Models for Adaptive Hypermedia and Adaptive Educational Systems. In P. Brusilovsky, A. Kobsa, & W. Nejdl (Eds.), *The Adaptive Web* (Vol. 4321, pp. 3-53). Berlin Heidelberg: Springer-Verlag.

Brusilovsky, P., & Miller, P. (2001). Course Delivery Systems for the Virtual University. In T. Della Senta & T. Tschang (Eds.), *Access to Knowledge: New Information Technologies and the Emergence of the Virtual University* (pp. 167-206). Amsterdam: Elsevier Science.

Brusilovsky, P., & Pyelo, C. (2003). Adaptive and Intelligent Web-based Educational Systems. *International Journal of Artificial Intelligence in Education, 13*(2-4), 159–172.

Brusilovsky, P., & Rizzo, R. (2002). Map-based horizontal navigation in educational hypertext. *Journal of Digital Information, 3*(1).

Brusilovsky, P., & Vassileva, J. (2003). Course sequencing techniques for large-scale web-based education. *International Journal of Continuing Engineering Education and Lifelong Learning, 13*(1-2), 75–94.

Carver, C. A. Jr, Howard, R. A., & Lane, W. D. (1999). Enhancing student learning through hypermedia courseware and incorporation of student learning styles. *IEEE Transactions on Education, 42*(1), 33–38. doi:10.1109/13.746332

Chen, C. M., Liu, C. Y., & Chang, M. H. (2006). Personalized curriculum sequencing utilizing modified item response theory for web-based instruction. *Expert Systems with Applications, 30*(2), 378–396. doi:10.1016/j.eswa.2005.07.029

Chen, J. N., Huang, Y. M., & Chu, W. C. C. (2005). Applying dynamic fuzzy petri net to web learning system. *Interactive Learning Environments, 13*(3). doi:10.1080/10494820500382810

Conati, C. (2002). Probabilistic assessment of user's emotions in educational games. *Applied Artificial Intelligence, 16*(7-8), 555–575. doi:10.1080/08839510290030390

Dunn, R., & Dunn, K. (1992). *Teaching elementary students through their individual learning styles.* Boston: Allyn and Bacon.

Felder, R. M., & Silverman, L. K. (1988). Learning and teaching styles in engineering education. *English Education, 78*(7), 674–681.

Graf, S., & Kinshuk (2007). *Considering Cognitive Traits and Learning Styles to Open Web-Based Learning to a Larger Student Community.* Paper presented at the International Conference on Information and Communication Technology and Accessibility.

Gutl, C., Pivec, M., Trummer, C., Garcia-Barrios, V. M., Modritscher, F., Pripfl, J., et al. (2005). AdeLE (Adaptive e-Learning with Eye Tracking): Theoretical Background, System Architecture and Application Scenarios. *European Journal of Open, Distance and E-Learning (EURODL).*

Heit, E. (2000). Properties of inductive reasoning. *Psychonomic Bulletin & Review, 7*(4), 569–592.

Honey, P., & Mumford, A. (2000). *The Learning Styles Helper's Guide.* Maidenhead: Peter Honey Publications.

I. M. S. (2001). *IMS Learner Information Packaging Information Model Specification.* Instructional Management Systems.

Jonassen, D. H., & Grabowski, B. L. (1993). *Handbook of individual differences: Learning and instruction.* Hillsdale, New Jersey: Lawrence Erlbaum Associates.

Jonassen, D. H., & Wang, S. (1993). Acquiring structural knowledge from semantically structured hypertext. *Journal of Computer-Based Instruction, 20*(1), 1–8.

Karampiperis, P., Lin, T., & Sampson, D. G., & Kinshuk. (2006). Adaptive cognitive-based selection of learning objects. *Innovations in Education and Teaching International, 43*(2), 121–135. doi:10.1080/14703290600650392

Karampiperis, P., & Sampson, D. (2005). Adaptive learning resources sequencing in educational hypermedia systems. *Educational Technology and Society, 8*(4), 128–147.

Kinshuk, & Lin, T. (2004). Cognitive profiling towards formal adaptive technologies in web-based learning communities. *International Journal of Web Based Communities, 1*(1), 103-108.

Kolb, D. A. (1984). *Experimental learning: Experience as the source of learning and development.* Jersey: Prentice Hall.

Kolb, D. A. (1999). *Learning Style Inventory - version 3: Technical Specifications*: TRG Hay/McBer, Training Resources Group.

Lemaire, P. (1999). *Psychologie Cognitive.* Bruxelles: De Boeck Universite.

Liaw, S. S., Huang, H. M., & Chen, G. D. (2007). Surveying instructor and learner attitudes toward e-learning. *Computers & Education, 49*(4), 1066–1080. doi:10.1016/j.compedu.2006.01.001

Lin, T. (2003). *Cognitive Trait Model for Persistent and Fine-Tuned Student Modelling in Adaptive Virtual Learning Environments.* Massey University, Palmerston North, New Zealand.

Miller, G. A. (1956). The magic number seven, plus or minus two: Some limits on our capacity for processing information. *Psychological Review, 63*(2), 81–96. doi:10.1037/h0043158

Milosevic, D. (2006). Designing Lesson Content in Adaptive Learning Environments. *International Journal of Emerging Technologies in Learning, 1*(2).

Milosevic, D., Brkovic, M., Debevc, M., & Krneta, R. (2007). Adaptive Learning by Using SCOs Metadata. *Interdisciplinary Journal of Knowledge and Learning Objects, 3,* 163–174.

Moore, A., Brailsford, T. J., & Stewart, C. D. (2001). *Personally tailored teaching in WHURLE using conditional transclusion.* Paper presented at the Proceedings of the ACM Conference on Hypertext.

Najjar, J., Klerkx, J., Vuorikari, R., & Duval, E. (2005). Finding appropriate learning objects: An empirical evaluation, *Lecture Notes in Computer Science (including subseries Lecture Notes in Artificial Intelligence and Lecture Notes in Bio-informatics)* (Vol. 3652 LNCS, pp. 323-335).

Nash, S. S. (2005). Learning Objects, Learning Object Repositories, and Learning Theory: Preliminary Best Practices for Online Courses. *Interdisciplinary Journal of Knowledge and Learning Objects, 1,* 217–228.

Oliveira, J. M. P. d. (2002). *Adaptation Architecture for Adaptive Educational Hypermedia Systems.* Paper presented at the World Conference on E-Learning in Corporate, Government, Healthcare, and Higher Education 2002.

Papanikolaou, K. A., Mabbott, A., Bull, S., & Grigoriadou, M. (2006). Designing learner-controlled educational interactions based on learning/cognitive style and learner behaviour. *Interacting with Computers, 18*(3), 356–384. doi:10.1016/j.intcom.2005.11.003

Rehak, D., & Mason, R. (2003). Keeping the learning in learning objects. In A. Littlejohn (Ed.), *Reusing Educational Resources for Networked Learning.* London: Kogan.

Rey-Lopez, M., Fernadez-Vilas, A., Diaz-Redondo, R. P., Pazos-Arias, J. J., & Bermejo-Munoz, J. (2006). Extending SCORM to create adaptive courses. *Lecture Notes in Computer Science (including subseries Lecture Notes in Artificial Intelligence and Lecture Notes in Bioinformatics), 4227 LNCS,* 679-684.

Rezaei, A. R., & Katz, L. (2004). Evaluation of the reliability and validity of the cognitive styles analysis. *Personality and Individual Differences, 36*(6), 1317–1327. doi:10.1016/S0191-8869(03)00219-8

Riding, R., & Cheema, I. (1991). Cognitive styles - An overview and integration. *Educational Psychology, 11*(3-4), 193–215. doi:10.1080/0144341910110301

Riding, R., & Rayner, S. (1998). *Cognitive Styles and Learning Strategies.* London: David Fulton Publishers.

Rumetshofer, H., & Wo, W. (2003). XML-based adaptation framework for psychological-driven E-learning systems. *Educational Technology and Society, 6*(4), 18–29.

Sadler-Smith, E. (2001). The relationship between learning style and cognitive style. *Personality and Individual Differences, 30*(4), 609–616. doi:10.1016/S0191-8869(00)00059-3

Sampson, D., Karagiannidis, C., & Cardinali, F. (2002). An architecture for web-based e-learning promoting re-usable adaptive educational e-content. *Educational Technology and Society, 5*(4), 27–37.

Specht, M., & Kobsa, A. (1999). *Interaction of domain expertise and interface design in adaptive educational hypermedia.* Paper presented at the Proceedings of Second Workshop on Adaptive Systems and User Modeling on the World Wide Web.

Specht, M., & Oppermann, R. (1998). ACE - adaptive courseware environment. *New Review of Hypermedia and Multimedia, 4,* 141–161. doi:10.1080/13614569808914699

Sternberg, R. J., & Zhang, L. F. (2001). Perspectives on Thinking, Learning, and Cognitive Styles. *The Educational Psychology Series*, 276.

Tarpin-Bernard, F., & Habieb-Mammar, H. (2005). Modeling elementary cognitive abilities for adaptive hypermedia presentation. *User Modeling and User-Adapted Interaction*, 15(5), 459–495. doi:10.1007/s11257-005-2529-3

Triantafillou, E., Pomportsis, A., Demetriadis, S., & Georgiadou, E. (2004). The value of adaptivity based on cognitive style: An empirical study. *British Journal of Educational Technology*, 35(1), 95–106. doi:10.1111/j.1467-8535.2004.00371.x

Watson, J., Ahmed, P. K., & Hardaker, G. (2007). Creating domain independent adaptive e-learning systems using the sharable content object reference model. *Campus-Wide Information Systems*, 24(1), 45–71. doi:10.1108/10650740710726482

Witkin, H. A., Moore, C. A., Goodenough, D. R., & Cox, P. W. (1977). Field-dependent and field-independent cognitive styles and their educational implications. *Review of Educational Research*, 47(1), 1–64.

Wolf, C. (2003). *iWeaver: Towards 'Learning Style'-based e-Learning in Computer Science Education*. Paper presented at the Proceedings of the Fifth Australasian Computing Education Conference on Computing Education 2003.

This work was previously published in International Journal of Distance Education Technologies, Volume 7, Issue 4, edited by Qun Jin, pp. 17-47, copyright 2009 by IGI Publishing (an imprint of IGI Global).

Section 2
Promising Support Mechanisms and Technologies

Chapter 6
Statistical Inference-Based Cache Management for Mobile Learning

Qing Li[1]
Zhejiang Normal University, China

Jianmin Zhao
Zhejiang Normal University, China

Xinzhong Zhu
Zhejiang Normal University, China

ABSTRACT

Supporting efficient data access in the mobile learning environment is becoming a hot research problem in recent years, and the problem becomes tougher when the clients are using light-weight mobile devices such as cell phones whose limited storage space prevents the clients from holding a large cache. A practical solution is to store the cache data at some proxies nearby, so that mobile devices can access the data from these proxies instead of data servers in order to reduce the latency time. However, when mobile devices move freely, the cache data may not enhance the overall performance because it may become too far away for the clients to access. In this article, we propose a statistical caching mechanism which makes use of prior knowledge (statistical data) to predict the pattern of user movement and then replicates/migrates the cache objects among different proxies. We propose a statistical inference based heuristic search algorithm to accommodate dynamic mobile data access in the mobile learning environment. Experimental studies show that, with an acceptable complexity, our algorithm can obtain good performance on caching mobile data.

INTRODUCTION

Mobile data management has been an increasingly hot research problem over the past few years, as

DOI: 10.4018/978-1-60960-539-1.ch006

it is crucial to the successful deployment into a number of applications including mobile learning. An important topic (sub-problem) there is efficient data access in a mobile learning system, especially from the perspective of data caching and quality of services (QoS). Generally speaking, a local memory space is necessary for a mobile device to cache, in advance, some data objects since the data server on the Internet may need to handle tens of thousands of requests simultaneously. But it becomes unpractical to cache a lot of data on the so-called light-weight mobile devices (particularly, cell phones) due to their very limited capability. Instead, data caching over the proxies becomes a viable approach in order to enable the mobile clients to access the learning objects (data) efficiently. The proxies may serve as a secondary level cache if a mobile device can maintain a small local cache, or serve as a direct cache if the mobile device cannot hold a local cache at all. However, how to dynamically maintain the cache data across the multiple proxies in order to enhance the overall performance of a mobile learning system is a challenging problem.

There are two main difficult problems for maintaining the cache data on the proxies. First of all, a proxy is limited by its hardware capability, which may prevent it from caching all the required data for the mobile clients. When a mobile device needs to access some data from a location whose proxy does not have the data cached, the proxy must decide if it should replicate/migrate the data from other proxies, depending on the actual situations and constraints. Because an earlier decision may impact the subsequent performance, it is very complex and costly to find a global optimal replication/migration algorithm. Secondly, global knowledge on mobile clients' movement and data access patterns is hard to obtain accurately, if not impossible. Yet even a rough approximation of such global knowledge will surely be useful for making sensible decisions.

In this article, we propose to develop an efficient mobile learning system through devising a statistical caching mechanism, in which each proxy makes use of prior knowledge (statistical data) to decide whether any cache objects should be replicated, migrated or deleted. Our method is different from the traditional approaches, e.g., Markov Chain-based models. Such kinds of mod-

els typically have an assumption which may not simulate real-life user movement accurately, and some of them even incur a very high computational cost. In contrast, our mechanism converts the distributed caching problem into a heuristic search problem and uses statistical inference to supervise the decision.

The rest of the article is organized as follows. We give a brief review of related work in the next section, after which our system architecture including the performance metrics is introduced. Next, we discuss the statistical caching mechanism in detail, followed by presenting our experiment results. In the last section, we summarize our work and offer a few research directions.

RELATED WORK

In this section, we review some earlier research works related to our research. Such relevant works can be divided into three categories: mobility model (movement prediction), data migration and data caching.

Mobility Model

Several user mobility models can be found in previous research papers for modelling the user movement. The fluid flow model (Thomas, R., Gilbert, H., & Mazziotto, G., 1998) is one of the early models widely used, in which mobile users are assumed to be uniformly populated and the users carrying terminals are moving at an average velocity with uniformly distributed moving-direction over $[0, 2\pi]$. During the last fifteen years, other mobility models have been suggested, such as random way point model, city model, highway model etc. Most of these models assumed that user behaviour is absolutely random. Kobayashi et.al. introduced a new mobility model based on HSMM process and used it to facilitate resource allocation in wireless networks (Kobayashi, H., Yu, S. Z., & Mark, B. L., 2000). To study and predict the movement of mobile users, (George, L., & Gerald, M. J., 1993) takes another approach in which modelling the behaviour of individual mobile user is composed of two parts: a random movement component and regular movement component. In turn, the regular movement consists of identical movement patterns of each mobile user, which represents the special behaviour of the movement of the user within a defined period of time; the MT/MC model is proposed to model the regular movement of mobile users. Ben and Haas (2003) presented a novel scheme which takes full advantage of the correlation between a mobile's current velocity and location and its future velocity and location based on Gauss-Markov random process. In Xuemin, Mark, & Jun (2003) an adaptive fuzzy inference system is developed to predict the probabilities that a mobile user will be active in the nearby cells at future moments using the real-time measurement data of the pilot signal powers received by the mobile user.

Data Migration

Data migration in distributed database systems has been a classical problem of research, and there are a good number of papers published in this area. In S. Khuller et al. (2003) studied a particular kind of data migration problem, namely: given several data items, find a migration schedule using the minimum number of rounds to migrate these items from their source disks to the destination disks. Each disk can transfer, either as a sender or receiver, only one data item. The underlying network is assumed to be fully connected and data items are all of the same size. This problem is NP-hard and the authors suggested a polynomial-time approximation algorithm.

Research has also been conducted on how to find the optimal solution to satisfying a sequence of requests in a distributed environment (Manasse, M. S., McGeoch, L. A., & Sleator, D. D., 1990; Chrobak, M., Larmore, L. L., Regingold, N., & Westbrook, J., 1997). Page replication and migra-

tion problems arise in a multi-processor system where each processor has its own local memory. For a writable page, only one page copy can be kept; for a read-only page, many copies can be kept in the network. There are two kinds of algorithms proposed: online and offline ones. The former works under an uncertain future and the latter assumes to have knowledge of the future request sequence. An online algorithm for a given problem is said to be c-competitive when the cost incurred by the algorithm is at most c times the cost incurred by the optimal offline algorithm. However, these algorithms did not consider the space constraint of a server, which may not work when the data volume involved becomes large.

H. M. Gladney (1989) suggested a method to replicate copies in different locations but these replicas are not synchronized with the source data "eagerly" when an update occurs. An algorithm is proposed by the author to record the used portion of the source database, as a way to identify obsolete replicas. This approach performs well in a large scale, weakly connected network.

Data Caching

The third category of related work is on traditional database caching systems. We review such (non-mobile) data caching systems briefly through some representative works.

R. P. Klemm described the WebCompanion in 1999 as a friendly client-side Web prefetching agent. It pursues a prefetching strategy based on estimated round-trip times for Web resources that are referenced. The longer the estimated round-trip time for a resource is, the more likely it will be prefetched. Of special interest to us is that, the solution was guided by the design goal of avoiding a penalty to the user for accessing the Web through WebCompanion, and to prefetch as many resources as possible while limiting network and server overhead as well as local resource consumption.

D. Kossmann et al. (2000) studied the problems of query optimization and distributed data placement together. By integrating query optimization and data placement, the performance looks beyond the one of a single query. M. Altınel et al. introduced a new database object called "cache table" that enables persistent caching of the full or partial content of a remote database table (Altınel, M., Bornhövd, C., Krishnamurthy, S., Mohan, C., Pirahesh, H., & Reinwald, B., 2003). The content of a cache table is either defined declaratively and populated in advance at setup time, or determined dynamically and populated on demand at query execution time. Both D. Kossmann et al. (2000) and M. Altınel et al. (2003) have a common characteristic that they consider query and data placement together in order to get higher performance.

A. Ailamaki et al. (2001) in their work "weaving relations for cache performance" demonstrate that in-page data placement is the key to high cache performance. A natural extension of that work into a distributed caching environment can thus re-confirm the importance of a well organized distributed cache structure for such applications as stream media data access.

SYSTEM MODEL AND EVALUATION METRICS

Our mobile learning system architecture assumes a three-tier hierarchy model for cellular systems, as depicted in Figure 1.

A data server S_j in Figure 1 provides multimedia courseware access services over the Internet, which may handle tens of thousands of requests simultaneously. There are N proxies, numbered as B_1, B_2,…, B_N, respectively, that can serve as data cache for mobile users. Several cells compose a Location Area (LA). A single proxy is assigned to a LA to ensure that the proxy can detect user location update conveniently, and all users' requests from a LA will be processed by the corresponding proxy. Each B_i is responsible for forwarding a user's request (including server IP, port, user name, password, and starting time) to a designated data server S_j, the latter handles the request and returns the requested content via B_i.

In our model, the cache mechanism of a mobile device is implemented on the proxies. In this way, if a data item is cached already, future users who want to access the same data item need not go through the process of downloading the data from a data server. As we stated before, there can be many requests at the same time but the hardware capability may prevent a data server from handling all of them instantly, thus user requests may end up with being queued up on the data server for a long time. While there have been a good number of research results obtained on reducing the wireless channel/bandwidth, the communication delay between a proxy and a data server has been largely overlooked, which nevertheless contributes to the total effect of quality of services (QoS) substantially. In this paper, we aim

Figure 1. Architecture of data access model for mobile learning

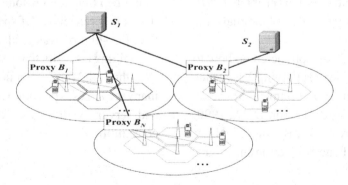

Figure 2. Data structure of each proxy's caching mechanism

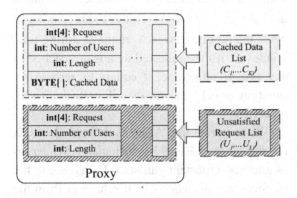

Table 1. Data types appeared on the proxy

Name	Type	Explanation
Req	int (Ben, L., et al., 2003)	The ID of the data
N	int	The number of users within B_i whose request has the same value as $B_i.Req$
Len	int	The length of the data
Data	BYTE[]	The data object

at reducing the communication delay by devising an efficient caching mechanism on the proxies.

Figure 2 shows the detailed data structure of the caching mechanism on each proxy. From Figure 2, we can see that each proxy maintains two types of data, namely, "cached data list" and "unsatisfied request list". The cached data list on a proxy B_i is formed by a number of cache objects $C_1, C_2, \ldots, C_{Ki}$, where each C_p ($1 \leq p \leq Ki$, and Ki is the number of cache objects of proxy B_i) has the data structure as shown in the upper left gray box of Figure 2. Other mobile clients within the cells of B_i whose requested data is not cached are listed in B_i's unsatisfied request list, denoted as $U_1, U_2, \ldots, U_{Li}$, where each U_q ($1 \leq q \leq Li$, and Li is the number of unsatisfied objects of B_i) has the data structure as shown in the lower left box.

The two lists are implemented by using two hash tables for fast access. Notice that with a large number of requests from a LA, there is a concern of how many records can be held in these two lists. In our model, we assume a proxy has enough space to store the two lists because the size of each record is very small. In the case that a cached data list gets overflowed, some cached data will have to be removed from the proxy – a subproblem to be addressed in the next section. Table 1 gives a detailed explanation of the elements appeared in C_p and U_q.

In addition, a data object is allowed to be cached in multiple proxies simultaneously. If a proxy B_i is determined to be necessary to cache a data object, it calculates the corresponding Req using MD5 sum and broadcasts it to its nearby proxies, each of which compares the Req with its local records upon receiving the broadcast. If a proxy B_j has a $B_j.C_p.Req$ equal to Req, it replies a confirmation to allow B_i to copy the data object from B_j, thereby saving the waiting time for B_i to fetch the data from a server. In the case that B_i does not get any reply, it has to contact the corresponding data server for the data object to cache.

To enable pertinent / objective evaluation of our overall system performance, particularly the caching mechanism to be described in next section, two popular metrics called BHR and ASD are incorporated and utilized, as described below.

Byte Hit Ratio

Byte Hit Ratio (BHR) is widely used as a metric which takes into account the differences among different cache objects (Paknikar, S., Kankanhalli, M., Ramakrishnan, K. R., Srinivasan, S. H., & Ngoh, L. H., 2000). In particular, BHR is defined as the ratio of total bytes satisfied by the cache to the total bytes transferred to the client. Because we have maintained cached data list and unsatisfied request list, the total bytes from cached objects and the total bytes requested by mobile users can be easily calculated. Therefore, one of the design aims of our caching mechanism is, according to the data structure in Figure 2, to maximize BHR under the following constraint:

$$\sum_{p=1}^{K_i} (B_i.C_p.Len + 6) + 6L_i < Q_i, \forall i = 1, ..., N \tag{1}$$

This objective can be achieved by replicating / migrating cache data blocks among the proxies, a problem we term as "cache data scheduling". Note that in the expression Q_i stands for the storage quota of data cache blocks for proxy B_i.

There are other performance metrics introduced in the related fields, e.g. Backbone Traffic Reduction Ratio (BTRR) (Jin, S. D., Bestavros, A., & Iyengar, A., 2002). However, metrics such as BTRR can be calculated using the same formula as BHR, since BTRR is defined as the fraction of the total bytes that are served by a cache. So for simplicity, we only use BHR in our work to measure the benefit brought up by using the data caching mechanism.

Average Service Delay

In addition to BHR, we adopt another metric named Average Service Delay (ASD) since to reduce the waiting time spent on the data transferring is another major objective of our caching mechanism.

A request from a mobile device A_x to a proxy B_i has to be forwarded to a data server if none of the nearby proxies has the requested data in its cache, in which case B_i puts the request into an unsatisfied request list. Therefore A_x would wait for a longer time for the desired data. Adapted from (Jin, S., et al., 2002) the ASD of A_x is mathematically calculated by formula (2).

$$ASD(A_x) = \frac{1}{R} \sum_{x=1}^{R} \left[\frac{\overline{B}(A_x, T)}{b(A_x, T)} - T \right]^+ \tag{2}$$

In formula (2), $b(A_x, T)$ stands for the bandwidth that a requested server reserves to a mobile device A_x, and $\overline{B}(A_x, T)$ equals to the number of bytes the mobile device A_x requests during time window T if the requested data is not cached in any proxy; otherwise, it equals to zero. Also, function $u = [v]+$ means that if $v < 0$, then $u = 0$; otherwise, $u = v$.

We re-iterate that ASD, as defined above, is not the same as BHR. In particular, ASD serves as another important yardstick for assessing the performance of data cache mechanism from the user's perspective.

STATISTICAL CACHING

In this section, we detail our statistical caching mechanism for efficient data access in mobile learning systems. Since the problem of finding an optimal solution is NP-complete (Shladover, S. E., 1992), a statistical inference based approach is targeted at which can provide a good performance with an acceptable complexity.

Cache Block Scheduling

As mentioned previously, our approach to maximize the BHR metric is to replicate / migrate the cached data among the proxies dynamically. Box 1 outlines our approach to addressing this cache scheduling problem for two cases: (1) a mobile device A_x accesses a cache block from proxy B_n and, (2) a mobile accesses a cache block from proxy B_n and, (2) a mobile device A_x stops its access to or leaves from proxy B_m.

Specifically, Algorithm_access(A_x, B_n) in Figure 3 can be executed on proxy B_n and Algorithm_stop_access (A_x, B_m) on proxy B_m, respectively.

Note that Algorithm_stop_access (A_x, B_m) in our system is relatively simple. As shown in lines 1' to 2', if B_m has a cached object serving for A_x,

Box 1. Pseudo-code for cache scheduling

```
Algorithm_access(A_x, B_n)
1.          if ∃p ∈ [1, K_n], A_x.req = B_n.C_p.req
2.              increase B_n.C_p.N by 1;
3.          else if enough space to cache A_x
4.              create cache data for A_x;
5.          else
6.              make a decision based on statistical data
Algorithm_stop_access(A_x, B_m)
1'.         if ∃p ∈ [1, K_m], A_x.req = B_m.C_p.req
2'.             decrease B_m.C_p.N by 1;
3'.             if B_m.C_p.N=0
4'.             destroy B_m.C_p and free its memory;
5'.         else
6'.             find ∃p ∈ [1, L_m] so that A_x.req = B_m.U_p.req;
7'.             decrease B_m.U_p.N by 1;
8'.             if B_m.U_p.N=0
9'.             destroy B_m.U_p and free its memory.
```

its recorded number of users (N) is decreased by 1 after A_x stops its access; the cached object will be destroyed and the space released if no more mobile device uses it, as lines 3' to 4' indicate. On the other hand, lines 5' through 9' cope with the situation when A_x does not find the data cached on B_m, in which case proper bookkeeping is done accordingly based on the data structure of Figure 2.

For Algorithm_access(A_x, B_n), the situation is more complicated due to the fact that there are three possible cases to be dealt with. Specifically, lines 1 to 2 correspond to the simplest case that there is already a cached object in B_n which is identical to A_x's request, so A_x can access it directly. Lines 3 to 4 depict the second case where B_n does not have the required object cached but still has sufficient space for caching new data. In this case, a cached object $B_m.C_p$ from a nearby proxy B_m is copied to B_n using the broadcasting method as mentioned before. The third case, captured by lines 5 and 6, is the most complex one. In this circumstance, the data object requested by A_x is not cached on proxy B_n, and there is no enough space in B_n to

cache it. There are two possible choices for B_n: the first one is to put A_x's request into the unsatisfied request list; the second choice is to remove one or more existing cached objects and use the freed space to accommodate the data requested by A_x. Because B_n does not have the whole picture to predict the consequence of the choices on the overall performance, in line 6, B_n puts together all such messages (from the same time window) for strategic consideration in order to maximize the global BHR; the detailed algorithm is discussed in the next subsection.

Note that the messages are considered together by the proxy B_n based on the same time window $T=[t_1, t_2]$, which can in principle lead to a better result than by handling each message one by one (Wu, K. L., Yu, P. S., & Wolf, J. L., 2001). But a problem may occur when there are a large number of messages sent within the same time window to the proxy for handling. In particular, a large number of messages would lead to an expensive decision-making process by the proxy with an exponential complexity. In section 4.3, we will address this problem by using a statistical inference based algorithm. But first, we detail in the following the two choices faced by an individual proxy (with a view on their consequences over BHR value change).

Effect of the Two Choices

We now describe, for the two choices depicted in lines 5 and 6 of Figure 3 in section 4.1, the calculation of the new BHR after A_x's access.

Note that in the second choice, it would cost a lot to find a proper set of cached blocks to remove and cache the new data block brought in by A_x. The best solution is to find such a set $C_g = \{C_{p'} \mid p'=1,...,Y\}$ from $\{B_n.C_p \mid p=1,...,K_n\}$ under the constraint:

$$\sum_{p'=1}^{Y} B_n.C_{p'}.Len > A_x.Len$$

(where Ax.Len means the size of the data requested by Ax), so as to minimize

$$\sum_{p'=1}^{Y} (B_n.C_{p'}.N \bullet B_n.C_{p'}.Len).$$

To find this best solution is, however, a fractional knapsack problem without taking partial items, which is known as NP-complete (Papadimitriou, C. H., 1994). In order to avoid the expensive calculation, we devise a heuristic approach as depicted in Box 2. Intuitively, the algorithm in Box 2 is to find an optimized C_g to remove if proxy B_n decides to go for data replacement (this decision is however supervised by the SIBheus algorithm to be presented in next section), so that a relatively large value of BHR can be obtained. The computational complexity of Algorithm_findreplace() depends on the 3rd step, which yields a computational cost of $O(K_n \log_2 K_n)$.

SIBheus Algorithm

As stated earlier in this section, when a data object requested by A_x is not cached on proxy B_n, and there is no enough space in B_n to cache it, we have two possible choices for B_n: put A_x's request into the unsatisfied request list or remove one or more existing cache objects and use the freed space to accommodate the new data. However, B_n does not know which decision would be better to maximize the global BHR. To this end, we transform the decision-making process into a search problem over a complete binary tree G, in which the cost function between a node and its direct subnode (denoted as an edge e of G) can be defined as the change of BHR value by each decision. In this context, the immediate problem of our caching mechanism is to find the shortest path from the root (s) to one of the leaves in G. As mentioned, a large number of messages within a time window

Box 2. Pseudo-code for finding C_g in B_n

```
Algorithm_findreplace()
7.          for p = 1 to Kn
8.              Mp = Bn.Cp.Len ● Bn.Cp.N ;
9.          let M1' < M2' < ... < MKn' be the ascending order of {M1,...,MKn} ;
10.         let sum = 0, p = 1;
11.         while sum < Len.Ax
12.             sum = sum + Mp';
13.         return M1,...,Mp.
```

T would lead to an expensive decision-making process by a proxy with an exponential complexity, hence it must be addressed realistically for practical applications.

As studied in (George, L., & Gerald, M. J., 1996), user movement in cellular systems is regular to a great extent, and each user has his/her mobility pattern. However, it is difficult to mathematically model this pattern in an accurate way. Previous prediction algorithms as mentioned in section 2 are incapable of finding a mathematically accurate pattern. In addition, even if we can sometimes find the pattern and predict a user's location, it would be difficult and costly to update /inform the information for every proxy promptly. Generally speaking, a distributed decision making mechanism without assuming the availability of a mathematically accurate moving pattern is needed instead. Our proposed method is enlightened from SA search (Zhang, B., & Zhang, L., 1992). based on statistical inference, which assumes every branch of the search tree follows a specific statistical distribution. In particular, SA search consists of a statistical inference method and Best-First (BF) heuristic search, which can be treated as a two-phased loop operation. In the first phase, it identifies quickly the most promising subtree using a(n) (global statistics or subtree statistics). In the case of a binary tree, in particular, the two search directions, i.e., the subtrees $T(n_{11})$ and $T(n_{12})$ rooted at nodes n_{11} and n_{12}, are examined for possible rejection if it does not satisfy the null hypothesis (Kiefer, J. C., 1987). SA takes the nodes of each subtree in the next level as its input (called "observed samples"). The subtrees which contain the "goal" g (a leaf node with maximum BHR) with a low probability are rejected / pruned. The one which is not pruned by the above steps is the most promising subtree to be accepted for phase two's further processing. During phase two, SA expands nodes within the accepted subtree using a node evaluation function b(n) (local statistics or node statistics). This constitutes a complete

round of SA search, and the next round is started recursively until the goal is found.

Knowing that SA can employ different statistical inference methods which may result in different search results, we use asymptotic efficient sequential fixed-width confidence intervals for the mean, or ASM (Zhang, B., et al., 1992) for short, as a testing hypothesis. The advantage of our algorithm is that it is not necessary to know the distribution of the subtree evaluation function a(n), which is hard to obtain in a distributed caching system anyway. Our caching algorithm uses ASM as the statistical inference method. Assume that $\{x_i\}$ (i=1,...,n) are identically and independently distributed variables, which have a common distribution function F with a finite fourth moment (Rosenblatt, M., 1974). Given $\delta>0$ and $0<\gamma<1$, the stopping variable $R(\delta)$, adopted from ASM, is defined as the minimal integer which satisfies formula (3):

$$R \geq \frac{a^2}{\delta^2}\left\{\frac{1}{R}\left[1 + \sum_{i=1}^{R}\left(x_i - \overline{x}_R\right)^2\right]\right\} \qquad (3)$$

where $\overline{x}_R = \frac{1}{R}\sum_{i=1}^{R}x_i$, $\varphi(x) = \frac{1}{\sqrt{2\pi}}\int_{-\infty}^{\infty}e^{-t^2/2}dt$, and $a = \varphi^{-1}(\frac{1+\gamma}{2})$.

Let μ be the mean of $\{x_i\}$, formula (3) has the property that $\forall F$, the probability of $\mu \in (\overline{x}_R - \delta, \overline{x}_R + \delta)$ is greater than γ, where $(\overline{x}_R - \delta, \overline{x}_R + \delta)$ is a fixed-width confidence interval denoted by $I(\overline{x}_{R(\delta)}, \delta)$. Consequently, the smaller δ is, the more precise our prediction of μ will be.

The whole search procedure begins with the root. First, given R=1, formula (3) is tested. If formula (3) holds, interval $I(\Gamma, \delta)$ is computed (where Γ is a wild card); otherwise, newly observed samples are tested against formula (3).

However, if a statistical inference method is directly used here, it may impose a rejection

Box 4. SIBheus algorithm (Proc2)

```
Algorithm_search()
1.          given α₀;
2.          for i = 0 to D
3.              let γ=1- α₀ and δ=c/4;
4.              let x₁=e₁(i) and x₂=eᵣ(i);
5.              for j = 1 to 2
6.                  calculate x̄ʀ₍δ₎ using formula 4;
7.                  let I(pⱼ, δ) = I( x̄ʀ₍δ₎, δ);
8.              if I(p₁, δ) does not intersect I(p₂, δ)
9.                  increase i by 1;
10.                 if p₁<p₂
11.                     prune the right branch;
12.                 else
13.                     prune the left branch;
14.                 break;
15.             else
16.                 δ = δ/2;
17.                 decrease i by 1.
```

(hence "service failure") problem. In particular, it is possible that all subtrees at a certain level are rejected by the algorithm. This is not a desirable property, since such a failure would stop our cache mechanism from providing continuous services. So, we make some modifications to the search procedure. The basic idea is as follows: Given an arbitrary constant δ_1, confidence intervals $I(p_i, \delta_1)$ (i=1, 2) are obtained according to the definition, where p_i is the ith subnode at current level. If $I(p_1, \delta_1)$ intersects with $I(p_2, \delta_1)$, a new constant $\delta_2 (<\delta_1)$ is tried in place of δ_1, and the whole process gets repeated until we find a δ_n, so that $I(p_1, \delta_n)$ does not intersect with $I(p_2, \delta_n)$. So, finally, the algorithm consists of two parts. The first part is the statistical learning procedure (Proc1), and the second part is the SIBheus search procedure (Proc2).

Box 4, $e_1(i)$ stands for the cost function from node i to its left subnode, while $e_r(i)$ stands for the cost function from node i to its right subnode. Also, D is the depth of the search tree G. The variable α_0, which is given at the top, is called

the significance level in statistical inference.[2] Practically, the smaller the value of α_0 has, the more accurate result we can obtain. However, if α_0 is too small, the possibility that $I(p_1, \delta)$ does not intersect with $I(p_2, \delta)$ will be high, which can make the "if" condition false in line 8 and increase the number of loops. This suggests that a trade off between accuracy and efficiency is inevitable for the real world applications.

With Proc1 and Proc2, the entire search algorithm runs as follows: The proxy B_n does the initialization work by calling Proc1 to get the value of c, which will be used in Proc2. Proc2 is executed once per time window T to get the near-best solutions. Note that the computational cost of Proc1 in Box 3 is $O(2^D)$ which is a little bit high, as it takes several time windows to run line 3 to find the optimal goal g. So, in comparison with Proc 2, Proc1 is called much less frequently to refresh c as the (latest) estimation of the distribution pattern of the search tree G.

Box 3. Statistical learning in SIBheus (Proc1)

```
Algorithm_stat()
1.          let i = 0, left = right = 0;
2.          find goal g by Branch-and-Bound search;
3.          while g ≠ s
4.            m = the parent node of g
5.            if g is the left subnode of mleft=left+Subroutine_sum(g);
6.            else
      right=right+Subroutine_sum(g);
7.              g=m;
8.              increase i by 1;
9.          return c=(left-right)/i.
Subroutine_sum(N)
10'.          sum = 0;
11'.          for i = 1 to N
12'.            sum = sum+e_l(i)+e_r(i);
13'.          return sum.
```

Theoretically, our proposed statistical searching algorithm has a complexity of an upper bound $O(D\ln^2 D)$ and the error probability $2\alpha_0$, as shown by the following two claims.

Claim 1: *Assume that $\{\alpha_k(\Gamma)\}$ (where Γ is a wild card) satisfies the null hypothesis H_0 and has a finite fourth moment. Given (α_0, β_0), let $\alpha=min(\alpha_0, \beta_0)$, $A=\sum_{i=1}^{\infty}(\frac{m}{i^2}).$*

The computational complexity of the statistical inference based binary tree search algorithm is of $O(D\ln^2 D)$.

Proof: *Given the significant level (α_0, β_0), we use a significant level*

$$\left(\alpha_i = \frac{\alpha}{(i+1)^2}, \beta_i = \frac{\alpha}{(m-1)(i+1)^2}\right)$$

in ASM, where m is the number of subtrees within level i. If the number of observation surpasses a given threshold d_j

$$d_j = 2b_2 \ln(j+1) \cdot \ln\frac{j+1}{\alpha}, b_2 = \frac{4m\sigma^2}{(\mu_1 - \mu_0)^2}$$

then, the hypothesis H_0 is rejected for i=0, 1. search pointer is under level $(\alpha, \frac{\alpha}{m-1})$.

In i-th depth, the threshold is:

$$d_j = 2b_2 \ln(j+1) \cdot \ln\frac{j+1}{\alpha} \sim C\ln^2(j+1)$$

So, the upper bound of the complexity is

$$\sum_{j=1}^{N} C\ln^2(j+1) \sim O(D \cdot \ln^2 D)$$

Claim 2: *Assume that $\{\alpha_k(\Gamma)\}$ (where Γ is a wild card) satisfies the null hypothesis H_0 and has a finite fourth moment. Given (α_0, β_0), let $\alpha_0=min(\alpha_0, \beta0)$, $A=\sum_{i=1}^{\infty}(\frac{m}{i^2}).$*

The goal g can be found by the search under α with probability≥ 1-b, b$\leq \alpha_0 + \beta_0$.

Proof: *The probability of the occurrence of type I error in deciding on i-subtrees is $\leq \alpha/(i+1)^2$ and the probability of the occurrence of type II is $\leq (m-1)\alpha/(i+1)^2$, where m is number of subtrees within level i. Because the error probability in deciding on i-subtrees is $\alpha*m/(i+1)^2$, the total error probability P_e is therefore:*

$$P_e \leq \sum_{i=1}^{N-1} \left(\frac{\alpha m}{(i+1)^2} \right) < \alpha \sum_{i=1}^{\infty} \left(\frac{m}{i^2} \right) = \alpha A = \min(\alpha_0, \beta_0)$$
$$\leq \alpha_0 + \beta_0$$

Discussion

Traditional caching algorithms based on LRU (Least Recently Used), LFU (Least Frequently Used), and FIFO (Fist In First Out) are all essentially of depth-first search nature if we treat the decision procedure as a binary tree search problem. However, depth-first search cannot find the best result in most cases. In contrast, our SIBheus algorithm is a more accurate approach to find a near-optimal solution. It consists of a periodical learning procedure (viz., Proc1) and a searching procedure (Proc2) with an acceptable complexity $O(D\ln^2 D)$.

Our algorithm is characterized by applying statistical inference into the heuristic search, so that the searching procedure is guided by the statistic knowledge. During the searching procedure, only one branch is kept and the other is pruned at each level, which resembles the same behaviour as depth-first search. But our method deviates from depth-first search in that the decision it makes is not simply dependent on the cost function between a node and its subnodes. Instead, it uses statistical inference to choose a branch to prune, which is more accurate than that of the depth-first search. More specifically, the probability that the searching algorithm can find the optimal solution is $1-2\alpha_0$.

EXPERIMENT

As part of this research, a simulation system has been developed to evaluate the effect and performance of our proposed caching mechanism. First, we give a brief description of the experiment set up as a necessary context for our subsequent discussions.

User Distribution

The mobile user distribution simulation comes from a tilt data file (Shladover, S. E., 1992), which includes more than 60,000 points. 8,000 of them are randomly selected, representing the initial user positions on the map, with each position being of (x, y) format where x and y range within [0, 10000].

User Movement

Movement of each user is depicted by a state chain, where each state stands for the user location represented by the cell number. We use the user mobility models in (George, L., et al., 1996). which assumes that user movement is of two parts: random part and regular part. In the regular part, a period T_p is defined and user movement will represent periodicity based on T_p. Intuitively, this situation is close to our daily life. In each T_p, a user chooses a random point as the destination and the speed of movement follows Zipf distribution in [10/T, 20/T] (skewed towards 0). After reaching the destination, the user will randomly choose another point to move on. In the random part, some tiny Gaussian white noises are added over the regular part.

Access Pattern

Each data object is randomly assigned with a value representing its popularity. The mobile users choose data objects based on such values. The larger a value is, the more possible that users

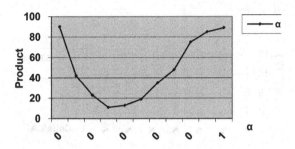

Figure 3. Efficiency-accuracy trade off against α

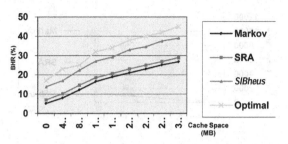

Figure 4. Performance comparison with BHR against cache space

may access that object. We assume the time of accessing each data object to be following Zipf in [60T, 600T] based on the result of (Chesire, M., Wolman, A., Voelker, G. M., & Levy, H. M., 2001), in which the distribution of client requests of data objects is observed to be Zipf-like (α around 0.5).

Proxy Allocation

We group several cells into one LA and assign a proxy to it. The number of cells per LA can be regarded as a parameter and we can adjust it dynamically. At first no data is cached on any proxy, and once users begin to move, each proxy starts to adopt our statistical caching algorithm to dynamically replicate / migrate data objects.

As mentioned in the previous section, there is a trade off between efficiency and accuracy in the binary tree searching. We use "product = error rate * number of loops" as a measure on the effect of this trade off. The error rate is calculated as the mean square error of the costs from root s to g and g', where g is the leaf node with maximum BHR value (viz., the "goal" in section 4), and g' is the actual leaf node found by our algorithm.

Figure 3 plots the product curve against α based on the simulation data, from which we can see that when α is about 0.34, product has the smallest value.

To test the performance of our caching mechanism, we compare our SIBheus algorithm with two other caching policies, namely, SRA (Loukoupoulos, T., & Ahmad, I., 2000)., and a Markov

model-based prediction algorithm (Ben, L, 2003). The comparisons are in terms of their BHR values against each proxy's cache space. As shown in Figure 4, our algorithm outperforms the other two strategies under various cache spaces. We also see that the performance of our algorithm is not far from optimal replication/migration under the exhaustive search of the decision tree. Although for this test case, we set the time interval T=1s, cache block size = 40KB and the cell radius equal to 500, similar relationships among the three curves are obtained with different values on the parameters.

Figure 5 shows the performance of our caching mechanism against time with the proxy's cache space equal to 600MB, and the parameter c being refreshed once every 80 time windows. Here we compare the three caching policies from another point of view. As depicted in Figure 5, when time increases, BHR curves of SRA and Markov based algorithm are nearly a straight line with little change. However, BHR becomes a zigzag curve for our algorithm, which can be explained as fol-

Figure 5. Performance comparison with BHR against time

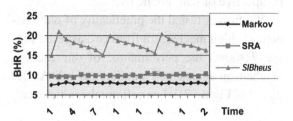

Figure 6. Computing time comparison against message numbers per time window

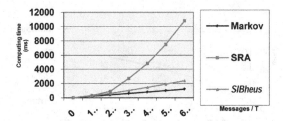

Figure 7. Performance of SIBheus against cell numbers

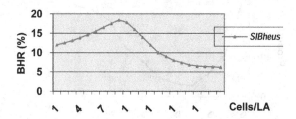

lows: Each time when a proxy learns from the historic data and calculates a new value of c, BHR will have an abrupt jump because our algorithm also predicts the future requests. However, with the change of the user movement pattern over time, this prediction becomes less accurate, and the original c could no longer lead to a near-optimal solution. This explains the gradual decrease of BHR after each jump.

Similarly, we can compare with SRA and Markov based algorithm from the perspective of Average Service Delay (ASD). Not surprisingly, the ASD of our algorithm is also a zigzag curve against time, but is almost of an inverse shape to that of BHR.

The comparison of the computation time of these three algorithms is given in Figure 6. We can see that due to statistical estimation, SIBheus (with complexity $O(Dln^2D)$ outperforms SRA (with complexity $O(D^2)$) in all cases. In fact, when there are a large number of accesses within a short time window, SRA becomes unpractical for realistic mobile applications. For the Markov-based model, the computing time is the best due to its linear algorithm, but the relatively poor performance on BHR (and ASD) against time and space still leaves it unfavorable and unacceptable from the perspective of real mobile users.

We further tested the practicality of our SIBheus caching mechanism from two aspects. Figure 7 shows the performance of our caching mechanism against cell numbers per LA. As depicted in Figure 7, when cell numbers increases,

BHR will increase at first, and then decrease after reaching a peak value. This can be explained as follows: When a LA has a small number of cells, each proxy cannot benefit much from statistical caching because user movement information is insufficient, which leads to a poor prediction. However, when a single LA has many cells, although a proxy can statistically learn much from historical data and decide more precisely, the storage quota of each proxy would prevent it from caching all the data objects that are already determined to cache. So for different situations, we may have different optimal cell numbers. As depicted in Figure 7, the optimal cell number under our simulation conditions is about 11.

Figure 8 shows the extra communication cost induced by our caching mechanism against cell numbers per LA. As depicted in Figure 8, communication cost will decrease along with the increase of cell numbers per LA. This is natural because when a LA has more cells, inter-cell broadcasting messages and replication/migration cost will decrease. We can see that when a LA has about 10 cells, the extra communication cost

Figure 8. Extra communication cost of SIBheus against cell numbers

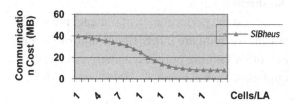

is around 20M bytes, which is practically acceptable for ordinary mobile data services.

CONCLUSION

Mobile data management including mobile data access has become an increasingly hot research problem due to its applicability to practical mobile/wireless applications, particularly mobile learning. In this article, we have presented a practical caching mechanism for data access in mobile learning systems. This caching mechanism makes use of prior knowledge (statistical data) to predict the user mobility pattern. Based on the statistical heuristic search, a statistical caching algorithm is developed. Experimental studies show that our caching mechanism can obtain good performance on caching courseware data for mobile learning systems, with a computational complexity of $O(Dln^2D)$, which is acceptable for most (if not all) mobile learning applications.

Admittedly, there are issues remaining to be addressed. We are currently studying some other testing hypothesis methods different from ASM (Zhang, B., et al., 1992), as well as the effect of the selection of a testing hypothesis method on the performance. While our cache mechanism described in this paper works for mobile learning systems, we also plan to adapt the statistical caching mechanism into supporting streaming media (eg, lecture videos) data access in the mobile learning environment.

ACKNOWLEDGMENT

The authors thank Mr. Li Xiang and Mr. Zhai Jian for their contribution to the experimental research of this project. The work has been supported by the Natural Science Foundation of China with the project 60773197 and Zhejiang Natural Science Foundation under grant numbered Y107750.

REFERENCES

Ailamaki, A., DeWitt, D. J., Hill, M. D., & Skounakis, M. (2001). Weaving Relations for Cache Performance. In Proceedings of VLDB conference.

Altınel, M., Bornhövd, C., Krishnamurthy, S., Mohan, C., Pirahesh, H., & Reinwald, B. (2003). Cache Tables: Paving the Way for an Adaptive Database Cache. In Proceedings of VLDB conference.

Ben, L., & Haas, Z. J. (2003, October). Predictive Distance-Based Mobility Management for Multidimensional PCS Networks. *IEEE/ACM Transactions on Networking, 11*(5).

Chesire, M., Wolman, A., Voelker, G. M., & Levy, H. M. (2001). Measurement and Analysis of a Streaming-Media Workload. In Proceedings of the USENIX Symposium on ITS. (Best paper award).

Chrobak, M., Larmore, L. L., Regingold, N., & Westbrook, J. (1997). Page Migration Algorithms Using Work Functions. *Journal of Algorithms, 24*(1), 124–157. doi:10.1006/jagm.1996.0853

Gal, A., & Eckstein, J. (2001). Managing Periodically Updated Data in Relational Databases: A Stochastic Modeling Approach. *Journal of the ACM, 48*(6), 1141–1183. doi:10.1145/504794.504797

George, L., & Gerald, M. J. (1996). A class of mobile motion prediction algorithms for wireless mobile computing and communications. *Mobile Networks and Applications, 1*, 113–121. doi:10.1007/BF01193332

Gladney, H. M. (1989). Data Replicas in Distributed Information Services. *ACM TODS, 14*(1), 75–97. doi:10.1145/62032.62035

IETF. http://www.ietf.org/rfc/rfc1321.txt

Jin, S. D., Bestavros, A., & Iyengar, A. (2002). Accelerating Internet Streaming Media Delivery using Network-Aware Partial Caching. In Proceedings of ICDCS conference.

Kangasharju, J., Roberts, J., & Ross, K. W. (2002, March). Object replication strategies in content distribution networks. *Computer Communications*, 25(5), 376–378. doi:10.1016/S0140-3664(01)00409-1

Khuller, S., Kim, Y. A., & Wan, Y. C. (2003). Algorithms for Data Migration with Cloning. In Proceedings of PODS conference.

Kiefer, J. C. (1987). *Introduction to statistical inference*. Springer-Verlag.

Klemm, R. P. (1999). WebCompanion: A Friendly Client-Side Web Prefetching Agent. *IEEE TKDE*, 11(4), 577–594.

Kobayashi, H., Yu, S. Z., & Mark, B. L. (2000). An integrated mobility and traffic model for resource allocation in wireless networks. In Proceedings of the Third ACM International Workshop on Wireless Mobile Multimedia (pp. 39-47).

Kossmann, D., Franklin, M. J., & Drasch, G. (2000). Cache Investment: Integrating Query Optimization and Distributed Data Placement. *ACM TODS*, 25(4), 517–558. doi:10.1145/377674.377677

Lim, E. J., Park, S. H., Hong, H. O., & Chung, K. D. (2001). A Proxy Caching Scheme for Continuous Media Streams on the Internet. In Proceedings of ICIN conference.

Loukoupoulos, T., & Ahmad, I. (2000). Static and Adaptive Data Replication Algorithms for Fast Information Access in Large Distributed Systems. In Proceedings of ICDCS conference.

Manasse, M. S., McGeoch, L. A., & Sleator, D. D. (1990). Competitive Algorithms for Server Problems. *Journal of Algorithms*, 11(2), 208–230. doi:10.1016/0196-6774(90)90003-W

Paknikar, S., Kankanhalli, M., Ramakrishnan, K. R., Srinivasan, S. H., & Ngoh, L. H. (2000). A Caching and Streaming Framework for Multimedia. In Proceedings of ACM MM conference.

Papadimitriou, C. H. (1994). *Computational complexity*. Addison-Wesley.

Rosenblatt, M. (1974). Random processes. Springer-Verlag. RTSTP. http://www.rtsp.org/

Shen, B., Lee, S. J., & Basu, S. (2003). Performance Evaluation of Transcoding-Enabled Streaming Media Caching System. In Proceedings of MDM conference.

Shladover, S. E. (1992). The California PATH Program of IVHS Research and Its Approach to Vehicle-Highway Automation. In Proceedings of the ACM Symposium on IV.

Thomas, R., Gilbert, H., & Mazziotto, G. (1988, September). Influence of the movement of mobile station on the performance of the radio cellular network. In Proc. of 3rdNordic Seminar, Copenhagen.

Wang, B., Sen, S., Adler, M., & Towsley, D. (2002). Optimal Proxy Cache Allocation for Efficient Streaming Media Distribution. In Proceedings of INFOCOM conference.

Wang, Z. J., Kumar, M., Das, S. K., & Shen, H. P. (2003). Investigation of Cache Maintenance Strategies for Multi-cell Environments. In Proceedings of MDM conference.

Wu, K. L., Yu, P. S., & Wolf, J. L. (2001). Segment-Based Proxy Caching of Multimedia Streams. In Proceedings of WWW conference.

Xuemin, S., Mark, J. W., & Jun, Y. (2000). User mobility profile prediction: An adaptive fuzzy inference approach. *Wireless Networks*, 6, 363–374. doi:10.1023/A:1019166304306

Zhang, B., & Zhang, L. (1992). *Theory and Applications of Problem Solving*. North-Holland.

ENDNOTES

[1] Main part of the work by this author was done when he was on leave from City University of Hong Kong, HKSAR, China.

[2] In the theory of statistical inference, there are two types of judging errors, namely, type I error (if the alternate hypothesis H_1 is chosen when in fact the null hypothesis H_0 is true) and type II error (the opposite to type I error). The significance level α_0 controls the possibility of occurrence of type I error. In our model, we let H_0 be the negation of H_1 and let the possibility of occurrence of the type II error β_0 be the same as α_0 for simplicity.

This work was previously published in International Journal of Distance Education Technologies, Volume 7, Issue 2, edited by Qun Jin, pp. 83-99, copyright 2009 by IGI Publishing (an imprint of IGI Global).

Chapter 7
A 3D Geometry Model Search Engine to Support Learning

Gary K. L. Tam
Durham University, UK & Zhejiang Normal University, China

Rynson W. H. Lau
Zhejiang Normal University, China & City University of Hong Kong, Hong Kong

Jianmin Zhao
Zhejiang Normal University, China

ABSTRACT

Due to the popularity of 3D graphics in animation and games, usage of 3D geometry deformable models increases dramatically. Despite their growing importance, these models are difficult and time consuming to build. A distance learning system for the construction of these models could greatly facilitate students to learn and practice at different time and geographical locations. In such a system, an important component is the search engine, which serves as both the source of teaching materials and a platform for sharing resources. Although there have been a lot of works on text and multimedia retrieval, search engines for 3D models are still in its infant stage. In this article, we investigate two important issues: feature analysis, which affects the general usage of a system, and speed, which affects the number of concurrent users. Our method offers a mechanism to extract, index, match and efficiently retrieve features from these models.

INTRODUCTION

The Internet has become an important place for educational resources in recent years. Ranging from instructor-led learning to self-study, students are encouraged to actively learn from this free library. To find relevant information and learning materials from this huge knowledge collection, an effective search engine is typically needed, which means that the search engine may be considered as the entry point to the Internet. One notable search engine for text documents is Google. Taking a simple example of searching for a mathematic equation, a student may type in some descriptive keywords of the equation and the search engine will return its definition and usage. Hence, the search

DOI: 10.4018/978-1-60960-539-1.ch007

engine may also be considered as an important educational tool to help locate useful information from this huge information/knowledge/resource database of the Internet.

In the past, education was generally conducted through text books. With the advance in multimedia technology, we are beginning to see a lot of multimedia educational materials that include images, animation and videos. The use of multimedia in presentations not only promotes students' interests and interactivity but also helps prolong their memory on the subject materials (Smith, 2000). Similar to text and documents, there is a growing demand for more effective search engines that support multimedia information too. 3D geometry models, being a type of multimedia information, are getting popularity in recent years due to their widespread use in animation and games. However, geometry models can also be used in many 3D applications for education too. For example, Li (2004) discusses how to progressively transmit geometry models in a 3D training system or a 3D engine for educational games. Despite the advance in 3D modeling tools, geometry models are still difficult and time consuming to build. Students often need to spend a long time to learn and to construct geometry models because of the deep learning curve and the effort in producing fine geometry details. Here, a learning system that guides the students in constructing the desired models from existing models of similar type may help reduce the learning time, model construction time and encourage model sharing. To support this type of applications, an efficient geometry search engine that facilitates sharing and reuse of geometry models is essential. A typical scenario is that one may want to construct a model by combining parts coming from multiple existing models created by others. This may require the retrieval of some desired models based on some user defined specifications (Funkhouser, 2004). With the retrieved models, the user may then cut and paste parts to form the new model.

As geometry models are becoming more popular, we are beginning to see geometry search engines that are developed for retrieving various 3D geometry data from the Internet or a 3D database, e.g., medical data (Keim, 1999), protein molecules (Kastenmüller, 1998), cultural artifacts (Rowe, 2001), and mechanical parts (Berchtold, 1997). For example, a search engine may help trainee medical doctors search for similar organs, archaeology students search for antiques, and mechanical students search for mechanical parts from a geometry database. Hence, a geometry search engine is useful in many applications including education.

Currently, there is a substantial amount of work devoted to matching and retrieving rigid geometry models efficiently and accurately. For example, Princeton University has developed a search engine (Funkhouser, 2003) where benchmarking is also available (Shilane, 2004). The method presented here, however, targets a more general type of models: the deformable models, i.e., models with similar skeletons but different postures. These models are very useful in designing and creating 3D applications for education and computer games. There are not many search engines designed for 3D deformable models, and they are generally slow because they need to apply graph matching techniques. In our recent work (Tam, 2007), we have presented an effective method for extracting and matching deformation-stable features. However, in order to build a search engine for web-based or distance learning systems, there are two challenges to overcome. First, it should be accurate in retrieval. Second, it should be fast enough to support many concurrent users (Herremans, 1995). In this article, we focus our discussion on the necessary information for building a search engine that supports distance learning.

The rest of this article is organized as follows. Section 2 briefly surveys related work. Section 3 presents an overview of the whole matching framework. Section 4 discusses the representation and storage of features. Sections 5 and 6 discuss the algorithms for matching and indexing. These are the essential building blocks of a search engine. Section 7 provides some experimental results. Finally, Section 8 briefly concludes the work presented in this article and discusses some possible future works.

RELATED WORK

The earliest retrieval systems for multimedia content may date back several decades ago. Since we focus this article on search engines that support geometry models, in particular deformable models, we would like to refer readers to (Lew, 2006) for a full survey of existing retrieval work on images, videos and audios. In this section, we briefly survey existing work on 3D geometry model retrieval. Classical 3D retrieval methods can be categorized into four approaches: geometry-based, transform-based, image-based, and topology-based. The first three methods can only handle non-deformable models, whereas the fourth can handle deformable models.

Non-Deformable Geometry Models

Geometry-based, transform-based, and image-based approaches focus on retrieving non-deformable 3D models only. The geometry-based approach concerns properties that are related to the shape and size of a model. In general, methods of this approach can be classified into three types: methods based on extracting physical properties (Elad, 2001; Kazhdan, 2004), methods based on computing histograms or some distribution functions (Osada, 2001) and methods based on computing energy for morphing a model (Tangelder, 2003; Yu, 2003). The transform-based approach analyzes 3D models in a different feature domain. Transformation functions used include Fourier Transform (Vranic, 2001) and Zernike Transform (Novotni, 2003). Funkhouser (2003), Kazhdan (2004) and Novotni (2003) propose Spherical Har-

monic for extracting rotation-invariant features. The image-based approach captures features from 2D image views of a 3D model for comparison (Chen, 2003; Ohbuchi, 2003).

Deformable Geometry Models

The topology-based approach is the only approach that supports matching of deformable models through analyzing the model with skeletal or topological information. As this approach is the focus of our work, we discuss these methods in more detail here.

In (Hilaga, 2001), the Multiresolution Reeb Graph (MRG) is proposed. It first partitions a model into nodes using integral geodesic at different resolutions. Unlike Euclidean distance, geodesic measures distances on the surface and is not affected by model deformation. Thus, integral geodesic indicates how far a point is from the surface center. MRG then constructs an MRG tree by analyzing the adjacency of each node in the current and lower/higher resolutions. In each node, it uses area and length as geometric features. To match two MRG trees, a heuristic graph-matching algorithm is applied in a coarse-to-fine manner. It starts from the root nodes of the two trees and traverses down the trees following the child nodes with maximum similarity. When all high-resolution nodes are exhausted, the matching process traces back to the lowest resolution nodes again. All similarity values computed are added up as the final similarity value.

In (Sundar, 2003), a voxel thinning method is proposed to extract the skeleton from a voxelized model. In each skeletal node, the radial distribution of edges is preserved for local shape matching. To speed up the query process, a topological feature vector is generated for each skeletal graph as an index to the database. Nearest neighbor search is then applied for model retrieval. To further verify the correctness of the retrieved models, an enhanced maximum cardinality minimum weight bipartite matching algorithm is used. Instead of using the skeletal graph, Tal (2004) analyzes models based on the component graph. A model is first split by mesh decomposition with each component node described by one primitive. An optimal error-correcting subgraph isomorphism algorithm is then applied to match two component graphs.

In summary, topology-based methods handle deformable models using skeletal information. However, several research issues have still not been explored yet. First, although most of these methods work well in discriminating dissimilar-skeleton models, none of them consider the issue of discriminating similar-skeleton models as they use only local geometric features. Second, due to the large feature size or the use of slow graph matching techniques (Tal, 2004), these methods are generally slow in practice and do not scale well to large databases. Third, although (Sundar, 2003) proposes an indexing scheme for large databases, it may still suffer from the accuracy problem when answering nearest neighbor queries as it separates topological matching and geometric matching into two processes. To improve the recall rate, it needs to return a large number of models in the first pass, causing a performance penalty to the indexing scheme.

OVERVIEW

The framework of a content-based 3D model retrieval system is shown in Figure 1. It is composed of several components: user interface, query processor and 3D geometry database. To build a 3D geometry database, 3D models are first converted into compact and representative features through the feature extraction process (refer to Section 4). An indexing structure is then built to store the features in an efficient manner. A typical approach for query processing is called query by example. First, the user inputs a sample model. The system then extracts the representative features from this model and match them with each set of the features extracted from the models stored in

Figure 1. A search engine for 3D geometry models

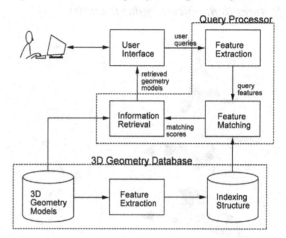

the 3D geometry database using a feature matching technique (refer to Section 5). Models in the database with similar features will be returned to the user. To speed up the searching process, the system may employ the k-nearest neighbor search on the database index to find models that are most relevant to the given query and return retrieval results through the search engine interface (refer to Section 6).

FEATURE REPRESENTATION

The identification of compact and representative features is essential in content-based retrieval system for two main reasons. First, it is usually far more efficient to compare compact features than the raw data. For example, in the case of videos, there can be over several gigabytes of video data. If a search engine compares all the video data frame by frame, it would take a long time before it can return any results. This is certainly not a good searching experience for general users. Second, using representative features to represent the original data may allow certain kind of invariance analysis. For example, in the case of 3D models comparison, it is necessary that the system can handle rotation invariance and scale invariance. While scale invariance can be achieved

Figure 2. Compact and representative topological features (left: objects, right: features)

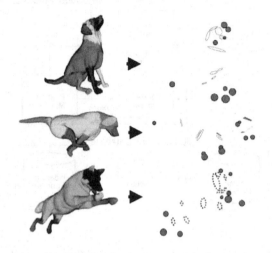

by simple normalization, rotation invariance may not be trivial. To achieve rotation-invariant representation, Fourier analysis (Vranic, 2001) and Spherical Harmonic analysis (Funkhouser, 2003; Kazhdan, 2003) are proposed to convert rotation dependent features into rotation independent form. This is done by transforming the features into a different feature domain. Similarly, to handle 3D deformable models, we must obtain compact and representative features that are stable towards scaling, rotation and deformation. Considering the examples shown in Figure 2, it is impossible to compare the wolf with the dog directly without taking care of their different postures.

To handle the change in postures, existing algorithms extract skeletal or topological information from 3D deformable models as features. These features are inter-connected to form a graph with each graph representing a deformable model. However, graph matching techniques are computationally expensive and it is difficult to describe these features geometrically and globally. Hence, we propose a different approach to represent the geometrical information of 3D models. We extract two types of features:

- Topological points and rings to represent the skeletal information, and
- Local and global geometric features to characterize each of these points and rings.

A topological point is defined as the salient point located at a protrusion tip, and a topological ring is defined as the border that separates two significant components in a model. Since these topological points and rings are located at protrusion tips and joints, they follow the model skeleton and thus are stable towards posture deformation. As an example, we represent different components of the three models (wolf and dog) in different colors as shown in Figure 2. The border of two color regions represents a topological ring. To further show the locations of topological points and rings, we have also presented them explicitly on the right of Figure 2. We can see that even though the two dogs have different poses, they have similar topological points and rings at similar locations.

Apart from topological features, it is also necessary to define geometric features to characterize each of the topological features so that the system can discriminate deformable models that may have similar topological points and rings (say, wolf and dog, or boy and baby). In our system, we consider two types of features, local (importance and spatial locations) and global features (three types of geodesic distribution data). The importance describes the weight of a topological feature. We note that the importance of a topological feature located in a finger should be smaller than that located in the leg. This is intuitive as removing a leg from a 3D model gives a larger perceptual impact than removing a finger. In our system, importance is represented by a scalar value which is equal to the surrounding area of a topological feature. To specify where a topological feature is, we calculate a scalar value using normalized integral geodesic. The function of integral geodesic was proposed in (Hilaga, 2001) for partitioning a mesh into different sections. We apply this function because integral geodesic measures the centricity of a

Figure 3. Geodesic distribution with respect to a topological ring in a leg

Figure 4. Topological features and their corresponding geometric features

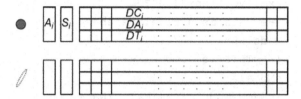

model surface (Tam, 2007). Importance and spatial location are local features because they describe the topological features locally.

Apart from local features, we also consider three global geometric features: curvature, area and average distance. We construct three vectors from these features by first dividing the model into many bands according to their geodesic distances from a given topological feature. Since geodesic is calculated on the surface, the resulting feature vectors are stable towards mesh deformation. As an example, we divide two dog models shown in Figure 3 into geodesic bands relative to a topological ring located at one of the legs. Bands of the same color indicate that they are within the same geodesic interval from the ring. We can see that although the two dogs have different poses, the locations of the color bands are similar. In each of these bands, we capture the three types of geometric information: curvature, area and average distance. Curvature measures the local deformation of each band, area measures the size of each band, and average distance measures the thickness of each band. We can see that these bands and features are similar across similar models with similar skeleton. These features are global because they capture the overall global shape of a model.

We summarize topological features and their geometric features in Figure 4. A_i and S_i represent the importance and spatial location, respectively. DC_i, DA_i and DT_i represent curvature, area and average distance (thickness) distribution, respectively. We store all these features in XML format, as it is convenient for debugging. A sample XML database is shown in Box 1.

FEATURE MATCHING

Given the representative features of two geometry models, we need a distance function to measure how similar they are with each other. If the distance between the two sets of features is small, the two models are considered as similar. In general, an efficient distance function cannot be trivially defined for a search engine as it must conform to the metric properties in order for an indexing technique to be applied. On the other hand, since we have different numbers of topological features for different models, direct application of the Euclidean distance is difficult.

In order to be able to compute a distance value efficiently while supporting indexing, we apply the Earth Mover Distance (EMD) approach here. Given a predefined ground distance function, EMD calculates the similarity between two mass distributions in some features space. Supposing that one mass distribution is a collection of "earth" and the other mass distribution is a collection of holes, EMD measures the minimum amount of energy required to fill all holes with earths. The EMD approach computes its solution based on a transportation problem between the supplier and the consumer. Given some amount of goods and the cost of transporting one single unit of goods between a supplier and a consumer, the transportation problem is to find the best flow of goods that is least-expensive. Similarly, computing the distance between two set of features can be modeled as a transportation problem by defining one set of features as the suppliers (earth) and the other as the consumers (holes), and let the cost

Box 1. An example XML 3D model database

```
<?xml version="1.0"?>
<!-- This is a model database -->
<ModelDB>
<!-- This is a model -->
 <Model>
  <Name>Model File Name</Name>
  <Group>Model Grouping</Group>
  <Features>
   <!-- a feature -->
   <Feature>
    <ID>…</ID>
    <type>POINT</type> <!-- or RING -->
    <importance>…</ importance>
    <spatial>…</ spatial >
    <KgHist KgHistSize="…" kg01="…" … kg20="…"/>
    <areaHist areaHistSize ="…" a01="…" … a20="…"/>
    <ptDistHist ptDistHistSize="…" d01="…" … d20="…"/>
   </Feature>
  <!-- another feature -->
   <Feature>………
   </Feature>
  </Features>
 </Model>
 <!-- another model -->
 <Model>………
 </Model>
</ModelDB>
```

function of transportation between suppliers and consumers be the predefined ground distance. Then, EMD computes the best flow (minimum energy) required. In our approach, we consider a topological feature as an EMD point and define importance (weight) as the amount of goods to transport. To describe the cost of transporting one unit of goods between two EMD points, we define a ground distance function Dist() based on geometric features as follows:

$$Dist(U_1, U_2) = W_1 \times |G'_{norm}(U_1) - G'_{norm}(U_2)|$$

$$+ W_2 \times L_{2,norm}(K(U_1), K(U_2))$$
$$+ W_3 \times L_{2,norm}(A(U_1), A(U_2))$$
$$+ W_4 \times L_{2,norm}(H(U_1), H(U_2))$$

There are several advantages of using EMD. First, though EMD has a high computation complexity, it is very efficient practically as it is based on the simplex algorithm. Second, EMD can also be used to measure the distance between two multi-dimensional features. For example, it is intrinsically difficult in our case to define the distance between two models because our features are very complex: each model is described as a

Figure 5. Construction of a VP-tree and kNN search

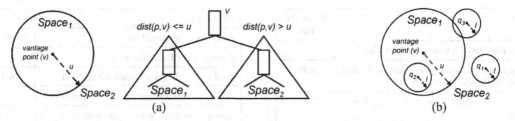

(a)   (b)

set of topological features with each of them characterized by local and global geometric features. Third, since our ground distance is a metric and we normalize all models to have equal weights, EMD becomes a true metric naturally by definition (Rubner, 2000).

INDEXING AND K-NN SEARCH

A search engine should return results accurately and within an acceptable period of time. As most users are only interested in the first few ten items of the returned results, most search engines would employ an indexing structure so that relevant information can be retrieved without the need to traverse the whole database. For content-based retrieval systems, this is particularly important as the database is generally very large. One of the general approaches is to define features as k-dimensional points and apply existing spatial access indexing methods, like R-tree and KD-tree for fast retrieval. However, as explained in our previous section, our features are complex and it is difficult to transform them into k-dimensional points while preserving their distances. To support fast retrieval, we apply the vantage point (VP) tree (Chiueh, 1994) to construct an indexing structure here.

The VP-tree is similar to the KD-tree in that both partition the metric space into separate spaces and build the search tree hierarchically on these spaces. However, while the KD-tree chooses the median as the separating point by projecting data to a dimension axis with maximum spread, the

VP-tree partitions the space based on relative distances between data points and a particular vantage point. As shown in Figure 5(a), the VP-tree algorithm chooses a vantage point (v) and partitions the feature space by a radius u. The space inside the circle represents features that are at most u distance away from v, whereas the space outside represents features that are at least u distance away from v. A VP-tree can then be constructed with the left branch storing features inside the circle ($Space_1$) and the right branch storing features outside the circle ($Space_2$). This partitioning process is applied recursively on all the features.

To apply the VP-tree in our 3D search engine, a distance function that satisfies the metric properties is required. Our method is based on the EMD approach, which can be proven to be a true metric. Therefore, our distance function is designed to fit into the VP-tree indexing structure. To search for the most relevant models with respect to an input query, it is equivalent to performing a k-Nearest Neighbor (kNN) search on the VP-tree. According to (Fu, 2000), kNN search on the VP-tree is like tree traversal while pruning away unnecessary walks on the tree. Given a query q, as shown in Fig 5(b), a kNN search is to find all neighbors within distance l, where l is dynamically adjusted to the distance of the kth nearest neighbor. Considering query q_1, since the query space does not overlap with $Space_1$ of vantage point v, the traversal of left side of the tree can be avoided. Similarly for q_2, since there is no overlap between the query space and $Space_2$, the traversal of right side of the tree can be avoided.

Table 1. Matching and retrieval times of a query

Operation	Required Time
Average total time for matching one model	1ms
Average total time for one query (sequential search of whole database)	0.88s
VP-tree construction time from XML feature database	778.7s
Average time for 1-nearest neighbor search	0.39s
Average time for 2-nearest neighbor search	0.42s
Average time for 3-nearest neighbor search	0.47s
Average time for 4-nearest neighbor search	0.54s
Average time for 10-nearest neighbor search	0.77s

Table 2. Storage size after feature extraction

Data Type	Storage Size
Total size of all model files	487 MB
Average size of each model file	831 KB
Total size of the feature database (in XML)	26.7 MB
Average no. of topological features per model	30
Average size of the features per model (in XML)	45.6KB
Average memory space used for each model	16.2 KB
Size of the index file (VP-tree)	11 KB

This kind of pruning can significantly reduce the computational and disk-IO costs. For query q_3, where the query space overlaps with both $Space_1$ and $Space_2$, the search traverses both branches of the tree.

EXPERIMENTAL RESULTS

We have constructed a database of 600 deformable models, stored in XML format, which is easier for display and for debugging. In this section, we show some of the experimental results.

Feature Compactness

As seen in Table 1, sequential search is generally slow. It takes 0.88s for a full search of our database. This figure will scale up as the size of the database increases. After we apply indexing, however, the total speed is improved. This is particularly useful when the user just wants the first few relevant results. In the extreme case, if only the most relevant result is shown, it takes only 0.39s (43% of original full search time).

Matching Time

As seen in Table 2, after feature extraction, the total data size is reduced from 487MB to 26.7MB, which is about 5% of the original data size. We expect that the storage size can be further reduced if we store the models in a binary format instead of XML.

Matching Accuracy

From our experiment, our feature representation is very efficient and effective. Figure 6 shows some of the experimental results and our web interface.

CONCLUSION

In this article, we have proposed a search engine for 3D geometry (in particular deformable) models to support multimedia learning. Our method offers a mechanism for extracting, matching, indexing and efficient retrieval of deformation stable features. We have demonstrated the effectiveness of the proposed method with some experimental results. We have also shown that a geometry search engine can be useful in many learning-based systems. However, there is still much work to do in order to build a fully functional system.

Here, we briefly summarize several possible future works. From a user-centric point of view, a better interface is indeed needed. Currently,

Figure 6. The search engine interface and sample results

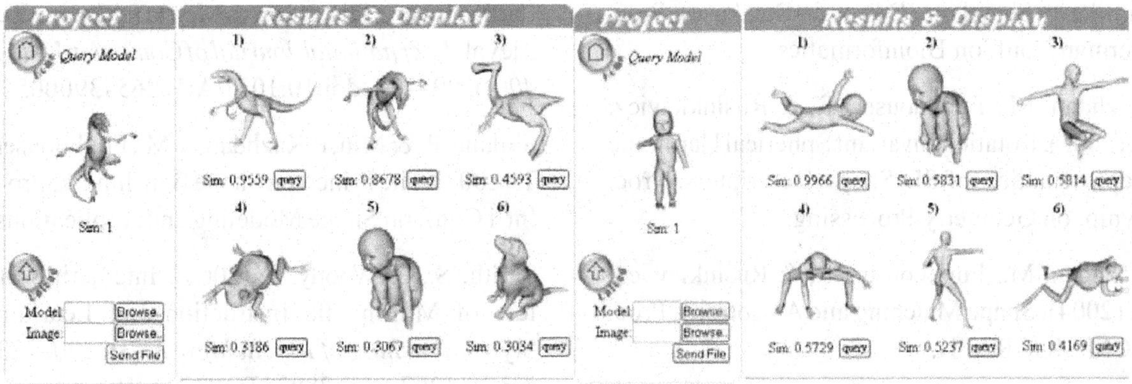

we allow users to upload a simple model or re-use an existing model as query input. Though it matches general use, it is not very user-friendly. One possible extension is to allow the user to sketch and build their query models on the fly. Tools for cutting, copying, pasting or deforming may also be provided for the users to build their query models. From the technique-centric point of view, searching-by-parts (also called partial-matching) may be provided. This may allow, for example, a mechanical student who has an unknown part to query for all machineries in the database that contain the given part. Finally, from the application-centric point of view, an education platform should be customizable to different communities like teachers, students, doctors, animators. Profiling may be used to help improve the learning experiences.

REFERENCES

Berchtold, S., & Kriegel, H. (1997). S3: Similarity search in CAD database systems. *Proc. SIGMOD*, 564–567.

Chen, D., Tian, X., Shen, Y., & Ouhyoung, M. (2003). *On Visual Similarity Based 3D Model Retrieval*. Proc. Eurographics.

Chiueh, T. (1994). Content-Based Image Indexing. Proc. VLDB, 582–593.

Elad, M., Tal, A., & Ar, S. (2001). Content Based Retrieval of VRML Objects - An Iterative and Interactive Approach. Proc. EG Multimedia, 97–108.

Fu, A., Chan, P., Cheung, Y., & Moon, Y. (2000). Dynamic VP-Tree Indexing for N-Nearest Neighbor Search Given Pair-Wise Distances. VLDB Journal.

Funkhouser, T., Kazhdan, M., Shilane, P., Min, P., Kiefer, W., Tal, A., et al. (2004). Modeling by Example. Proc. ACM SIGGRAPH.

Funkhouser, T., Min, P., Kazhdan, M., Chen, J., Halderman, A., Dobkin, D., & Jacobs, D. (2003). A Search Engine for 3D Models. *ACM Transactions on Graphics*, *22*(1), 83–105. doi:10.1145/588272.588279

Herremans, A. (1995). Studies #02 New Training Technologies. UNESCO Paris and ILO International Training Centre.

Hilaga, M., & Shinagawa, Y. Kohmura, & T., Kunii, T (2001): Topology Matching for Fully Automatic Similarity Estimation of 3D Shapes. Proc. ACM SIGGRAPH.

Kastenmüller, G., Kriegel, H., & Seidl, T. (1998). Similarity Search in 3D Protein Databases. Proc. German Conf. on Bioinformatics.

Kazhdan, M., Funkhouser, T., & Rusinkiewicz, S. (2003). Rotation Invariant Spherical Harmonic Representation of 3D Shape Descriptors. Proc. Symp. on Geometry Processing.

Kazhdan, M., Funkhouser, T., & Rusinkiewicz, S. (2004). Shape Matching and Anisotropy. Proc. ACM SIGGRAPH.

Keim, D. (1999). Efficient Geometry-based Similarity Search of 3D Spatial Databases. Proc. SIGMOD, 419–430.

Lew, M., Sebe, N., Djeraba, C., & Jain, R. (2006). Content-based Multimedia Information Retrieval: State-of-the-art and Challenges. *ACM Trans. on Multimedia Computing, Communication, and Applications*, 2(1), 1–19. doi:10.1145/1126004.1126005

Li, F., & Lau, R. (2004). A Progressive Content Distribution Framework in Supporting Web-Based Learning. Proc. ICWL, 75–82.

Novotni, M., & Klein, R. (2003). 3D Zernike Descriptors for Content Based Shape Retrieval. Proc. ACM Symp. on Solid Modeling and Applications.

Ohbuchi, R., Nakazawa, M., & Takei, T. (2003). Retrieving 3D Shapes Based On Their Appearance. Proc. ACM SIGMM Workshop on Multimedia Information Retrieval.

Osada, R., Funkhouser, T., Chazelle, B., & Dobkin, D. (2001). Matching 3D Models with Shape Distributions. Proc. Int'l Conf. on Shape Modeling and Applications, 154–166.

Rowe, J., Razdan, A., Collins, D., & Panchanathan, S. (2001). A 3D Digital Library System: Capture, Analysis, Query, and Display. Proc. Int'l Conf. on Digital Libraries.

Rubner, Y., Tomasi, C., & Guibas, L. (2000). The Earth Mover's Distance as a Metric for Image Retrieval. *International Journal of Computer Vision*, 40(2), 99–121. doi:10.1023/A:1026543900054

Shilane, P., & Min, P. Kazhdan, & M., Funkhouser, T. (2004). The Princeton Shape Benchmark. Proc. Int'l Conf. on Shape Modeling and Applications.

Smith, S., & Woody, P. (2000). Interactive Effect of Multimedia Instruction and Learning Styles. *Teaching of Psychology*, 27(3), 220–223. doi:10.1207/S15328023TOP2703_10

Sundar, H., Silver, D., Gagvani, N., & Dickinson, S. (2003). Skeleton Based Shape Matching and Retrieval. Proc. Int'l Conf. on Shape Modeling and Applications.

Tal, A., & Zuckerberger, E. (2004). Mesh Retrieval by Components. Technical Report, Faculty of Electrical Engineering, Technion, CCIT–475.

Tam, G., & Lau, R. (2007)... *Deformable Model Retrieval Based on Topological and Geometric Signatures, IEEE Trans. on Visualization and Computer Graphics*, 13(3), 470–482.

Tangelder, J., & Veltkamp, R. (2003). Polyhedral Model Retrieval Using Weighted Point Sets. Proc. Int'l Conf. on Shape Modeling and Applications, 119–129.

Vranic, D., & Saupe, D. (2001). 3D Shape Descriptor Based on 3D Fourier Transform. Proc. ECMCS, 271–274.

Yu, M., Atmosukarto, I., Leow, W., Huang, Z., & Xu, R. (2003). 3D Model Retrieval with Morphing-based Geometric and Topological Feature Maps. Proc. IEEE CVPR.

This work was previously published in International Journal of Distance Education Technologies, Volume 7, Issue 2, edited by Qun Jin, pp. 100-112, copyright 2009 by IGI Publishing (an imprint of IGI Global).

Chapter 8
Supporting Interoperability and Context–Awareness in E–Learning through Situation–Driven Learning Processes

Stefan Dietze
Open University, UK

Alessio Gugliotta
Open University, UK

John Domingue
Open University, UK

ABSTRACT

Current E-Learning technologies primarily follow a data and metadata-centric paradigm by providing the learner with composite content containing the learning resources and the learning process description, usually based on specific metadata standards such as ADL SCORM or IMS Learning Design. Due to the design-time binding of learning resources, the actual learning context cannot be considered appropriately at runtime, what limits the reusability and interoperability of learning resources. This paper proposes Situation-driven Learning Processes (SDLP) which describe learning processes semantically from two perspectives: the user perspective considers a learning process as a course of learning goals which lead from an initial situation to a desired situation, whereas the system perspective utilizes Semantic Web Services (SWS) technology to semantically describe necessary resources for each learning goal within a specific learning situation. Consequently, a learning process is composed dynamically and accomplished in terms of SWS goal achievements by automatically allocating learning resources at runtime. Moreover, metadata standard-independent SDLP are mapped to established standards such as ADL SCORM and IMS LD. As a result, dynamic adaptation to specific learning contexts as well as interoperability across different metadata standards and application environments is achieved. To prove the feasibility, a prototypical application is described finally.

DOI: 10.4018/978-1-60960-539-1.ch008

INTRODUCTION

The increasing availability of learning resources raises the need to discover and deliver the most appropriate learning resources to the learner to satisfy his/her learning needs within the actual learning situation. A learning *situation* constitutes the actual *context* which has to be addressed and is defined by e.g. the used technical environment or specific learner characteristics such as his/her native language.

The current state of the art in E-Learning is mainly represented by approaches based on software systems, such as *learning content management systems (LCMS)* which provide a learner with composite learning contents – the so called *learning objects (LO)*. Usually, a LO contains a description of a learning process - the learning path which has to be followed by the learner to fulfil his current learning objective – which is referred to a set of learning resources, whether these are data or services. Interoperability between LCMS is currently supported through metadata standards such as IEEE LOM (Duval, 2003), ADL SCORM (ADL SCORM, 2004) – based on IMS Simple Sequencing - or IMS Learning Design (IMS LD) (IMS Global, 2003) supporting the description of learning processes as well as learning objects. To satisfy a given learning need, a learning designer manually describes the learning process and allocates learning resources. Even though current E-Learning metadata standards try to address dynamic context-adaptability by introducing facilities such as the IMS LD Level B properties, their capabilities are limited and still rely on the manual pre-allocation of resources and a pre-defined selection strategy. Due to the design-time binding of learning process and learning resources, the actual runtime context of the learning process cannot be considered appropriately and therefore, a learning object cannot adapt dynamically to the specific context or learner needs. Consequently, reusability of a LO across distinct learning contexts or E-Learning applications is limited.

The use of *Web services* instead of data addresses these issues partially. However, since Web services are deployed using purely syntactic technologies such as SOAP (W3C, 2003a), WSDL (W3C, 2001), and UDDI (W3C, 2003b), which do not provide information about the semantic meaning of the service functionalities, utilized data or usage constraints, services cannot be discovered, composed and invoked automatically. *Semantic Web Services (SWS)* technology (Fensel et al., 2006) aims at the automatic discovery of distributed Web services as well as underlying data on the basis of comprehensive semantic descriptions utilizing ontologies (Gruber, 1995) as formal specification of a service conceptualization. First results of SWS research are available, in terms of reference ontologies – e.g. OWL-S (Joint US/EU ad hoc Agent Markup Language Committee, 2004) and WSMO (WSMO Working Group, 2004) – as well as comprehensive frameworks - e.g. DIP project results (http://dip.semanticweb.org) - and applications. Whereas existing SWS frameworks enable the semantic description of Web services and data exposed by a Web service, they do not entirely encourage the representation of learning situations and processes, in which resources are used. In other words, SWS descriptions represent a process from a system perspective as an orchestration process which involves the invocation of services and the manipulation of data. In contrast, process metadata descriptions such as IMS LD or ADL SCORM provide non-semantic descriptions about a learning process from a user perspective.

The approach described in this paper bridges the gap between learning situations and resources based on semantic *Situation-driven Learning Processes (SDLP)* that consider the user as well as the system perspective of a process. Learning processes are described as sequences of learning goals which lead from an initial to a final situation, where each goal is supported through dynamic SWS goal invocations. SDLP are composed dynamically and accomplished by automatically allocating learning resources (data, services) at runtime to adapt to different learning contexts. To achieve this vision, our approach is based on the following principles: abstraction from learning resources and semantic contextualization of learning process models.

The abstraction from the actual resources – data as well as services – supports the semantic representation of the system-perspective of a process through established SWS technology and is aimed at the automatic discovery of resources which provide the required capabilities for a given context. Based on semantic descriptions of functional capabilities of available Web services, a SWS broker automatically selects and invokes Web services appropriate to achieve a given user goal. The contextualization of learning process models aims at the semantic representation of learning processes as sequences situation-specific learning goals to support the user-perspective of a process. It makes use of *Semantic Web (SW)* technology to provide the necessary contextualized descriptions and is mapped to different metadata standards to enable their interoperability.

The rest of the paper is organized as follows. The following Section 2 introduces our motivation which led to our vision of context-adaptive learning processes described in Section 3 together with our proposed approach. Section 4 then introduces the utilization of SWS to abstract from learning resources whereas Section 5 explains a metamodel for Situation-driven Processes (SDP). SDP are derived for the E-Learning domain in Section 6 and their deployment within a context-adaptive E-Learning application is described in Section 7. We compare our approach with the current state of the art in E-Learning in Section 8, and report some related work in Section 9. Our contributions are summarized and discussed in the last Section 10.

MOTIVATION

Current technologies aimed at supporting learning processes are mainly based on the following practices:

- *Widespread use of proprietary, non-semantic metadata standards,* such as IMS LD and ADL SCORM, to describe a learning process. A process is described based on a common syntax – the metadata specification – but not enriched with descriptions of a semantic meaning in a machine-processable way.

- *Manual allocation of learning resources at design-time of a process.* Data and services are manually associated with specific learning objectives based on the limited knowledge and subjective decisions of a specific individual. Since process descriptions rely on syntactic descriptions only, the allocation of appropriate resources requires the manual interpretation of the semantics of a process model. Moreover, the allocation of learning resources at design-time of a process - i.e. when the specific learning process metadata is described - contradicts the consideration of the actual learning context, what is possible at runtime only.

- *Workflow-centred notion of a learning process.* Learning processes usually focus on the description of the learning workflow to be followed rather than on the learning context – e. g. the specific requirements of the addressed learning situation.

For instance, to support a learner who intends to learn a particular language, e.g. French, usually a learning designer manually provides a learning object which contains the learning process based on a particular metadata standard and allocates learning assets to each of the learning activities. Imagine a learning process consisting of two learning activities, where the first introduces basic knowledge about the French language and the second one adds advanced vocabulary and grammar information. Each activity will be associated manually with a set of audio-visual learning assets or is referred at design-time to a Web service which retrieves appropriate learning resources. The composed LO is provided to the learner, for instance through open E-Learning platforms such as OpenLearn (http://openlearn.open.ac.uk/), and finally presented within a metadata compliant runtime environment or LCMS.

Due to these facts, the following limitations have been identified (Amorim et al., 2006)(Collis and Strijker, 2004)(Knight, Gasevic & Richards, 2006):

L1. *Limited reusability across different learning contexts and metadata standards.* A learning process model – including references to associated resources - suiting the context and the preferences of a specific learner cannot be used across distinct learning contexts. Moreover, the conformance of a learning process model with a specific metadata standard ensures interoperability across systems following the same standard, but does contradict the usage of the same model in information systems adopting different standards. As a result, distinct learning process models have to be developed to meet multiple contexts and learner needs.

L2. *Limited appropriateness and dynamic adaptability to actual learning contexts.* A learning object usually is composed of both, the workflow of learning activities and the set of required learning resources. Due to the designtime-binding of learning resources and learning process metadata, the actual learning context – known at runtime only – cannot be considered appropriately. Moreover, the use of data excludes the dynamic adaptability to a specific context a priori. The use of services instead of data addresses some of these issues but does not enable context-adaption based on the automatic allocation of services at runtime.

L3. *Limited use of distributed heterogeneous learning resources.* Since learning resources usually are allocated manually at designtime, distributed heterogeneous data and services are neither widely reused nor

integrated into learning application environments sufficiently. Nevertheless, standardized methodologies to solve heterogeneities between terminologies used by distinct data or service providers are not available. Therefore, interoperability and scalability of current E-Learning applications is limited.

L4. *High development costs.* Due to L1, L2, and L3 distinct learning objects – including distinct learning process models and learning resources - have to be developed to support different learning contexts appropriately. Therefore, high development costs have to be taken into account to provide appropriate process support.

CONTEXT-ADAPTIVE LEARNING PROCESSES: VISION AND APPROACH

This section describes our vision and approach to context-adaptive learning process composition and accomplishment aimed at overcoming the limitations L1 – L4 described in Section 2.

Vision: Situation-Driven Learning Processes

We consider the automatic, situation-aware allocation of resources at runtime of a learning process based on dynamic service invocations. Learning processes are described semantically as a composition of user goals within a specific learning situation, the actual context. Learning goals are achieved dynamically through automatic discovery of appropriate services for a given goal within a specific situation. Figure 1 depicts this vision of a situation-driven learning process.

Semantic learning process models abstract from specific resources – whether data or services - and metadata standards. Given an initial situation and knowledge about the desired final situation, learning processes are composed dy-

Figure 1. Situation-driven learning processes

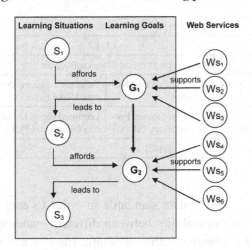

Figure 2. Conceptual framework to gradually abstract from learning process resources and contextualize learning process models

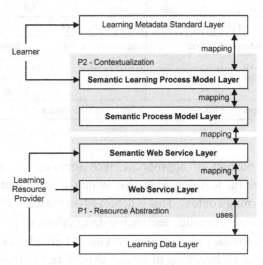

namically and accomplished automatically. Based on semantic descriptions of available resources, the most appropriate resource is selected automatically to achieve a certain learning goal within the actual learning (runtime) context. This vision enables a highly dynamic adaptation to different learning contexts and learner needs. Moreover, using adequate mappings, standard-independent semantic learning process models can be transformed into existing (non-semantic) metadata standards in order to enable their reuse within existing standard-compliant runtime environments.

By addressing limitations L1 – L3, the described vision consequently reduces the efforts of creating learning process models (L4): one unique learning process model can adapt dynamically to different process contexts and can be translated into different process metadata standards.

Approach

Our approach is fundamentally based on realizing the following principles:

- Learning resource abstraction.
- Contextualization of learning processes.

To support these principles, we introduce a layered approach to achieve a gradual abstraction and finally, a gradual mapping between resources – data and services – and process metadata (Figure 2).

P1. Learning Resource Abstraction

To integrate heterogeneous resources, we foresee the abstraction from existing learning data and content. A *Web Service Layer* is considered which exposes functionalities appropriate to fulfill specific learning objectives. These functionalities range from querying learning data repositories to filtering of data or the computation of competency gaps. This abstraction from learning process data enables a dynamic discovery of appropriate data to suit a specific context and objective. Services exposed at this layer may make use of semantic descriptions of available learning data to accomplish their functionalities.

In order to abstract from these functionalities (Web services), we introduce an additional layer – the *Semantic Web Service Layer*. This layer enables the dynamic selection, composition and

Table 1. Overview on approach followed to address L1-L4

Adressed lacks:	L4			
	L3		L1, L2	
Design principles:	P1: Learning Resource Abstraction		P2: Learning Process Contextualization	
Conceptual layers:	Web Service Layer	Semanti Web Service Layer	Semantic Process Model Layer	Semantic Learning Process Model Layer
Ontologies:		Web Service Modelling Ontology (WSMO)	Situation-Driven Process Ontology (SDPO)	Learning Process Modelling Ontology (LPMO)
Supportive software:	Supporting Web services	IRS-III		

invocation of appropriate Web services for a specific learning objective within a particular learning context. This is achieved on the basis of formal semantic, declarative descriptions of the capabilities of available services to enable the dynamic matching of service capabilities to specific user goals. Due to the semantic abstraction from learning resources, additional distributed resources can be integrated into the application framework by simply adding semantic resource descriptions following a common SWS standard, such as WSMO (WSMO Working Group, 2004) or OWL-S (Joint US/EU ad hoc Agent Markup Language Committee, 2004). Please note, that the aforementioned layers make use of established standard Web service and SWS technologies.

P2. Contextualization of Learning Processes

Whereas the aforementioned layers utilize existing technologies, the contextualization of learning processes introduces two novel semantic layers. A first layer concerned with the semantic contextualization of current learning process metadata standards is the *Semantic Learning Process Model Layer*. It allows the comprehensive description of situation-driven processes within the domain of E-Learning as a composition of learning goals which occur in specific learning situations described by parameters such as the current learning environment or the actual user preferences. This layer is mapped to semantic representations of current learning metadata standards in order to enable the interoperability between different standards and furthermore, the automatic transformation between them.

To achieve a further abstraction from domain-specific process models – whether it is e. g. a learning process, a business process or a communication process – we consider an upper level process model layer – *Semantic Process Model Layer*. This layer enables the description of contextualized domain-independent processes and introduces the high-level concepts – e. g. process goals, roles or process parameters – which are subject across different process domains. Thus, this layer enables a mapping between different domain-specific process model layers - for instance the mapping between learning objectives and business objectives.

Based on semantic mappings, upper level layers can utilize information at lower level layers. It is important to note, that we explicitly consider mappings not only between multiple semantic layers but also within a specific semantic layer. For instance, within the Semantic Learning Process Model Layer different semantic conceptualizations could be utilized and aligned with each other in order to support reusability across different application scenarios each using a distinct terminology and conceptual E-Learning model.

The following Table 1 provides an overview of our approach, mapping the lacks introduced in Section 2 with the elements of our approach that address them at different levels of abstraction: design principles, conceptual layers, implementation aspects. The implementation aspects (ontologies and supporting software) are elaborated further in the following sections.

Design principle P1 addresses the identified lack L3 (Section 2), whereas P2 is aimed at overcoming L1 and L2. Both, P1 and P2 target L4 by aiming at a decrease of development efforts. To follow P1 the Web Service as well as the Semantic Web Service Layers have been introduced, whereas the Semantic Process Model Layer and the Semantic Learning Process Model Layer support the contextualization of learning processes (P2). To implement the Semantic Web Service Layer, established SWS technology has been utilized: the *Web Service Modelling Ontology (WSMO)* and the Semantic Execution Environment *IRS-III* (Cabral et al., 2006) (Section 4). The *Situation-Driven Process Ontology (SDPO)* populates the Semantic Process Model Layer (Section 5), while the *Learning Process Modelling Ontology (LPMO)* derives SDPO for E-Learning and facilitates the Semantic Learning Process Model Layer (Section 6). Nevertheless, several Web services - aimed at learning-related functionalities such as LO retrieval, competency gap calculation or learning process composition - have been implemented and incorporated as SWS into the SWS-oriented application framework (Section 7).

ABSTRACTING FROM LEARNING RESOURCES THROUGH SEMANTIC WEB SERVICES (WSMO) AND IRS-III

In this Section we introduce the abstraction from learning process resources through a Web Service Layer and a Semantic Web Service Layer, which are based on established Web service and SWS technologies. The introduction of a Web Service Layer enables the integration of distributed heterogeneous learning data sources (Data Layer) into an open E-Learning application environment. Furthermore, services can provide any kind of learning-related functionality, such as data transformations or the computing of a competency gap between a desired learning objective and specific competencies of a learner. Whereas Web services technology facilitates the reuse of distributed software functionalities through the Web, it does not support the automatic integration and discovery of appropriate services and thus, always requires the manual allocation of appropriate Web services. By providing formal descriptions with well defined semantics, SWS technology facilitates the machine interpretation of Web service descriptions.

Introducing the Semantic Web Service Layer enables the automatic discovery, orchestration and invocation of appropriate services based on comprehensive semantic formalizations of distributed services. SWS are based on a Semantic Web Service broker which hosts semantic descriptions of available services to enable the automatic discovery and composition of appropriate services. Since utilized data is a crucial important aspect of a Web service, semantic descriptions of data are an implicit part of a SWS description. Thus, the Semantic Web Service Layer enables abstraction not only from services but also from data, and consequently their integration based on formal semantics.

We adopt the Web Service Modelling Ontology as reference ontology model for SWS descriptions. WSMO is a formal ontology for describing the various aspects of heterogeneous services. The conceptual model of WSMO defines four top level elements:

- Ontologies provide the foundation for describing domains semantically. They are used by the three other WSMO elements.
- Goals define the tasks that a service requester expects a Web service to fulfill. In this sense they express the requester's intent.

- Web service descriptions represent the functional behavior of an existing deployed Web service. The description also outlines how Web services communicate (choreography) and how they are composed (orchestration).
- Mediators handle data and process interoperability issues that arise when handling heterogeneous systems.

WSMO includes ontologies as one of its main entities; thus it is not limited to SWS descriptions exclusively. Therefore, all semantic layers – Semantic (Learning) Process Model Layer as well as Semantic Web Service Layer – can be supported by a unique Semantic Execution Environment based on WSMO.

IRS-III (Cabral et al., 2006) the Internet Reasoning Service, is a Semantic Execution Environment (SEE) that also provides a development and broker environment for SWS based on WSMO. A client sends a request which captures a desired outcome or goal – specified as WSMO Goal - and, using the set of Semantic Web Service capability descriptions, IRS-III proceeds through the following steps:

1. Discover potentially relevant Web services.
2. Select set of Web services which best fit the incoming request.
3. Invoke the selected Web services whilst adhering to any data, control flow and Web service invocation constraints.
4. Mediate any mismatches at the data or process level.

IRS-III adopts ontological descriptions to achieve the automatic discovery of appropriate services. In particular, IRS-III incorporates and extends WSMO as core epistemological framework of the IRS-III service ontology which provides semantic links between the knowledge level components describing the capabilities of a service and the restrictions applied to its use.

SITUATION-DRIVEN PROCESSES FOR SEMANTIC WEB SERVICES

To achieve the vision described in Section β, the Semantic Process Model Layer aims at providing the semantic representation to incorporate SWS descriptions into reasonable process settings. Therefore the Semantic Process Model Layer introduces the domain-independent notion of semantic *Situation-driven Processes (SDP)* which describe two perspectives on a process:

1. *The user perspective*: describes the process as composition of user Goals
2. *The system perspective*: which describes the process in terms of services which support each user Goal.

A semantic SDP Model consists of *SDP Situations* (*S*) and *SDP Goals* (*G*) as main entities. Utilizing the notion of concepts as described in (Gangemi, Mika, 2003), a situation is described by a set of concepts *C*. Consequently, an initial situation *Si* is defined by a set of *x* concepts:

$$Si = \left\{c_1, c_2, .., c_x\right\}, c_i \in C$$

A desired final situation is defined by the union of *Si* and a set of *y* additional desired concepts *cd*.

$$Sf = Si \cup \left\{cd_1, cd_2, .., cd_y\right\}, cd_i \in C$$

A SDP Goal represents a particular objective from a user perspective. Each Goal assumes a specific situation, described in its Goal assumption description *Ga* by a set of *a* concepts and describes the state after its invocation as its effect *Ge* by utilizing a set of *e* concepts:

$$Ga = \left\{c_1, c_2, .., c_a\right\}, \ Ge = \left\{c_1, c_2, .., c_e\right\}$$

A Situation-driven Process *SDP* is a particular ordered set of *n* user Goals:

$$SDP = \{G_1, G_2, .., G_n\},$$

where each goal G is described in terms of its assumption G_a and its effects G_e. The initial situation is a subset of the assumption of the first goal of *SDP*

$$Si \subseteq Ga_1,$$

and the final situation *Sf* represents a subset of the union between *Si* and the set of all concepts which are described in the set of effects *Ge* of each of the *n* Goals of the *SDP*:

$$Sf \subseteq Ga_1 \cup Ge_1 \cup Ge_2 \cup ... \cup Ge_n$$

Moreover, each particular Goal G_i is supported by a set of p_i *SDP Brokered Goals BG* which are linked to SWS and describe the outcome of a Web service from the system perspective (Section 4). BG provide the union of all concepts described as the effects of Goal G_i:

$$Ge_i \subseteq BGe_1 \cup BGe_2 \cup .. \cup BGe_{p_i}$$

For instance, to enable the accomplishment of a specific SDP Goal within a learning process, i.e. to acquire a specific competency, one BG could be aimed at providing required E-Learning assets out of specific databases whereas another aims at computing a specific calculation, such as the current competency gap of the learner. In this way, the achievement of Brokered Goals at runtime subsequently progresses the actual situation, for instance by adding additional resources, until a desired user situation is reached. For instance in Figure 3, BG_1 and BG_2 are achieved at runtime while gradually progressing situation S_1 to $S_{1.1}$

Figure 3. Utilizing SWS to support situation-driven process goals

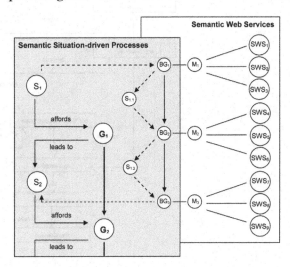

and $S_{1.2}$. Finally, achievement of BG_3 ensures that S_2 is satisfied.

Brokered Goals are instantiated as domain-specific derivations of WSMO-based SWS Goals and thus, are mapped through *Mediators (M)* to SWS in order to enable the dynamic achievement at runtime through a SWS broker engine in terms of SWS service discovery, orchestration and invocation. Therefore, a SDP model extends the expressiveness of SWS facilities by enabling the incorporation of SWS Goals into meaningful process contexts. We would like to emphasize that process situations are highly dependent on the domain and nature of a process – for instance, whether it is a business or a learning process – since each domain emphasizes different situation parameters. For instance, a learning process situation is strongly dependent on parameters such as the competencies of the learner, whereas a business situation may focus on parameters such as the costs for a specific business task. Therefore, the SDP metamodel is not meant to be instantiated directly, but has to be derived in terms of domain-specific SDP models. Such conceptual models of domain contexts based on the SDP metamodel provide the facilities to represent

Figure 4. Core concepts of the SDP ontology (SDPO)

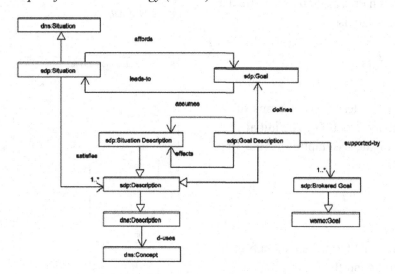

existing process metadata schemas to enable the transformation of semantic SDP into non-semantic metadata standard manifestations. Our vision foresees a SDP lifecycle consisting of 3 stages which have to be supported by a SDP compliant application to suit a given user situation:

1. Automatic composition of domain-specific SDP.
2. Transformation of SDP into metadata manifestation.
3. Accomplishment of SDP-based process in terms of BG achievements.

The abstract metamodel of SDP is defined in terms of a *SDP Ontology* (*SDPO*) expressed by using the OCML representation language (Motta, 1998). SDPO describes a metamodel of processes as composition of situations (contexts) and Goals independent from their specific domain setting. In order to enable a high level of interoperability of the SDPO, it is aligned to an established foundational ontology: the Descriptive Ontology for Linguistic and Cognitive Engineering (DOLCE) (Gangemi, Guarino, Masolo, Oltramari, Schneider, 2002) and, in particular, its module Descriptions and Situa-

tions (D&S) (Gangemi, Mika, 2003). Figure 4 depicts the central concepts and relations of SDPO.

SITUATION-DRIVEN LEARNING PROCESSES

The Semantic Learning Process Model Layer (Section 3) is supported through the *Learning Process Modelling Ontology (LPMO)* which supports the semantic description of learning processes and process contexts following the SDP metamodel (Section 5). Besides its alignment to SDPO, LPMO is aligned to E-Learning metadata standards to enable interoperability. Figure 5 depicts an overview of the major semantic representations which have been provided.

LPMO extends the SDPO by specifying (a) the concepts that can be used in domain-specific descriptions of E-Learning situation, (b) a set of Brokered Goals supporting learning Goals.

Figure 6 depicts the main elements used to define learning situation descriptions.

A situation description of the semantic SDP model is specialised into a E-Learning situation description *(lpmo:Situation Description)* in terms of specific *functional roles* and *situation param-*

Figure 5. Stack of ontologies to support situation-driven learning processes

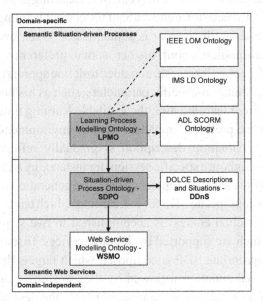

eters (d-uses). Roles and parameters are inherited from the D&S ontology through the SDP Ontology. The former are the roles of *actors* and *resources* in learning situations. The latter are the characteristics that describe the learning situation.

It is important to note that the LPMO allows the description of learning situations in domain-specific terms by using domain-specific parameters *(lpmo:Parameter)* such as competencies *(lpmo:Competency).* The situation description *(lpmo:Situation Description)* is of central character, since it describes the entire context of a specific learning situation, such as the learning domain *(lpmo:Domain)*, the actual learner *(lpmo:Actor)* or his/her actual objective *(lpmo:Objective).* Specific parameters, for instance the learner *(lpmo:Actor)*, are described by a dedicated description (e.g.

Figure 6. Learning process model ontology as domain-specific SDP derivation

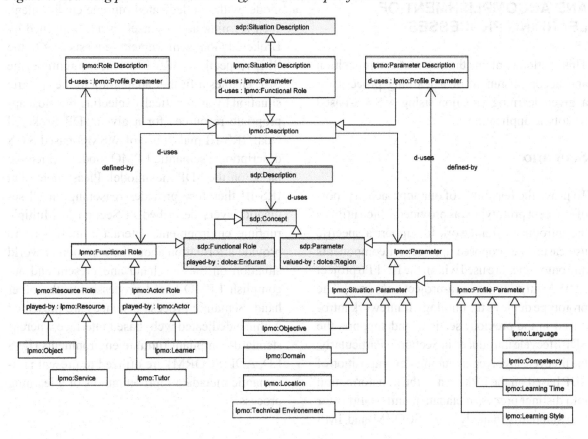

lpmo:Actor Profile) using specific parameters (e.g. *lpmo:Profile Parameters*).

Moreover, we would like to highlight that a specific domain – such as E-Learning - can be populated through the use of the LPMO, but also through several distinct ontologies which are aligned to the SDP metamodel. The alignment between different conceptual models of one specific domain can be achieved by concrete mappings as well as the use of mediation facilities as described in Section 4. Based on semantic representations of E-Learning-specific metadata standards – IMS LD and ADL SCORM - and the manual description of mappings to LPMO, standard compliancy with non-semantic metadata standards as well as interoperability between them is supported. Further elaboration of these mappings can be found in (Dietze et al., 2007a).

SITUATION-DRIVEN COMPOSITION AND ACCOMPLISHMENT OF LEARNING PROCESSES

This section explains the automatic composition and accomplishment of a learning process for a given learning situation using a SWS-based prototype application.

Scenario

To prove the feasibility of our approach, a proof-of-concept prototype was provided which utilizes the introduced framework to support a specific use case. The proposed application components and ontologies are used within the EU FP6 project LUISA (http://www.luisa-project.eu/www/). The prototype deploys the ontology framework introduced in the previous sections and supports the SDP lifecycle introduced in Section 5. Particularly, the lifecycle involves the automatic composition of SDP based on the LPMO, and the transformation into distinct process metadata manifestations for two standards, namely ADL SCORM and IMS

LD, and the automatic process accomplishment, in terms of dynamic achievements of learning goals.

To reach awareness about the current learning situation, the learner is authenticated to retrieve information about his/her actual preferences. Moreover, learners are enabled to define appropriate situation-specific parameters, such as his/her current learning aim, the available learning time or the preferred metadata runtime environment. The situation description is gradually refined throughout a specific session, for instance by adding the actual competency gap. The generation of an appropriate SDP for E-Learning, which targets the actual context is accomplished in two steps which are supported by distinct services: first an appropriate SDP is composed which targets the actual situation followed by the transformation of a metadata-independent SDP into the desired metadata standard. Figure 7 depicts the utilized architecture

During runtime presentation of the process model within a dedicated runtime environment, each learning activity itself is accomplished by Brokered Goal achievement requests sent to the SEE, respectively IRS-III. Hence, at runtime, the SEE enables a further adaptation to the specific situation by automatically selecting the most appropriate resources for a given SDP Brokered Goal. IRS-III makes use of WSMO-based SWS descriptions, semantic LPMO models which are based on the SDP metamodel. Please note, that IRS-III therefore provides reasoning on all semantic layers described in Section 3. Multiple runtime environments interact with IRS-III to provide information about the current real-world situation on the one hand and present and accomplish LPMO-based processes on the other hand. Semantic process instances are presented within a dedicated web- based interface whereas standard-compliant runtime environments (IMS LD, ADL SCORM) are utilized to present non-semantic metadata representations of a learning process.

Situation-Driven Composition of Learning Goals

Utilizing the gradual mapping between E-Learning-specific Brokered Goals and WSMO Goals, not only processes but also entire application scenarios are accomplished by automatically achieving Brokered Goals at runtime through the Semantic Execution Environment. Therefore, to follow our scenario, a sequence of high level Brokered Goals is achieved at runtime to support S1 – S3. Figure 8 depicts the utilized Goals.

After a gradual refinement of the available information about the actual situation context – learner authentication (*BG.1*), situation refinement (*BG.2*), computation of competency gap (*BG.3.1*) – a Goal is achieved to provide a learning process (*BG.3.2*). The learning process, respectively the SDP for E-Learning, has to suit the given situation and in particular the desired metadata standard. Hence, *BG.3.2* is decomposed into two sub Goals which are aimed at composing a semantic context-aware learning process model (*BG.3.2.1*) based on the LPMO and transforming the process

Figure 7. Architecture to support runtime reasoning on SDLP and SWS

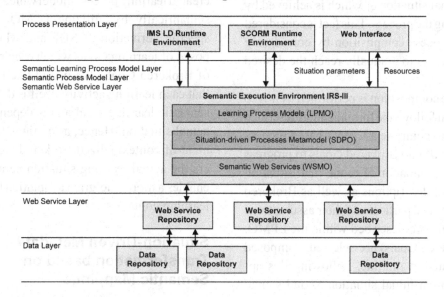

Figure 8. Goal orchestration to create context-adaptive and metadata-compliant learning processes

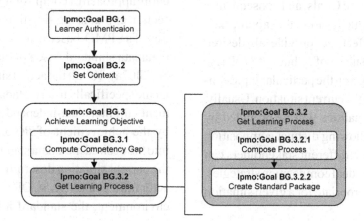

model into a metadata format appropriate for the given context (*BG.3.2.2*).

The first one (*BG.3.2.1*) is accomplished by a Web service which takes into account specific situation parameters of *Si*, for instance the preferred educational method of the learner or his/her available learning time. In order to reason about the desired final situation *Sf* of the learner, a particular situation parameter is taken into account, the *Aim* of the learner. Each particular Aim, for instance "Learning French", is linked to a set of desired competencies, for instance "French Language Advanced Level" and "French Language Expert Level". Therefore, these competencies are part of the final situation *Sf* which is achieved by accomplishing the process. This fact is considered during the process composition by considering specific activities to gradually reach the desired final situation.

The entire composition is performed by a Web service, which follows the formalization described in Section 5 to compose a LPMO-based process as a set of Goals and Brokered Goals to progress from the initial situation *Si* to the final situation *Sf*. Since Goal descriptions as well as Brokered Goal descriptions, particularly their assumptions and effects, are pre-described within the LPMO, Goals (Brokered Goals) are selected, composed and instantiated at runtime. Following this approach, given an initial situation *Si* and a final situation description *Sf*, a *SDP* (based on the LPMO) to progress from *Si* to *Sf* can automatically be composed of specific Goals, and consequently Brokered Goals, which show the appropriate assumptions and effects to provide all desired concepts which are subset of *Sf* but not *Si*. These are then instantiated given the particular input concepts which describe the current situation. Usually, composition functionalities will be provided by different services following distinct composition strategies. In this way, different stakeholders can implement their individual composition strategies, whereas the most appropriate for a given situation

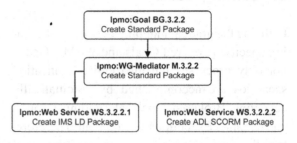

Figure 9. Semantic Web Services to provide metadata standard compliant learning packages

context is discovered and invoked at runtime by the Semantic Execution Environment.

The outcome of *BG.3.2.1* is a dynamically created learning process model which is described semantically by utilizing LPMO as domain-specific derivation of SDP and which is composed of learning Goals which each refer to a set of Brokered Goals. We would like to highlight, that each learning activity itself is described as a semantic learning Goal and is dependent on the actual situation. Hence, at runtime, the achievement of contextualized Brokered Goals considers the actual learning situation parameters and enables a more fine-grain adaptation to the actual learning context.

Situation-Driven Metadata Transformation based on Semantic Mappings

Whereas the previous section was focused on the entire approach of composing SDP at runtime, this section explains the situation-driven transformation of a LPMO-based process into a non-semantic metadata standard based on mappings (Dietze et al., 2007a). To suit the actual situation – in particular the specifically used metadata runtime environment – the metadata-independent process provided by the achievement of *BG.3.2.1* is transformed into the desired metadata standard. For instance, if the current situation description indicates that the actor utilizes an ADL SCORM compliant runtime environment, the standard independent LPMO-

Figure 10. SWS capability description of WS.3.2.2.1

lpmo:WebService

```
(DEF-CLASS CREATE-IMSLD-PACKAGE-WEB-SERVICE
          (LPMO-GOAL)
          ?GOAL
          ((HAS-INPUT-ROLE
            :VALUE
            HAS-PROCESS
            :VALUE
            HAS-CONTEXT)
           (HAS-INPUT-SOAP-BINDING
            :VALUE
            (HAS-PROCESS "string")
            :VALUE
            (HAS-METADATA-STANDARD "string"))
           (HAS-OUTPUT-ROLE :VALUE HAS-PACKAGE-URL)
           (HAS-OUTPUT-SOAP-BINDING
            :VALUE
            (HAS-PACKAGE-URL "string"))
           (HAS-PROCESS :TYPE LPMO-PROCESS)
           (HAS-METADATA-STANDARD :TYPE LPMO-METADATA-STANDARD)
           (HAS-URL :TYPE STRING)))

(DEF-CLASS CREATE-IMSLD-WEB-SERVICE-CAPABILITY
    (CAPABILITY)
    ?CAPABILITY
    ((USED-MEDIATOR :VALUE GET-LEARNING-DATA-MED)
       (HAS-ASSUMPTION
         :VALUE
         (KAPPA
           (?WEB-SERVICE) (= (WSMO-ROLE-VALUE ?WEB-SERVICE 'HAS-
           CONTEXT)"IMS LD")))))
```

based process model is transformed into an ADL SCORM compliant metadata manifestation which represents the generated LPMO-based process and is contained in an IMS content package.

The transformation into appropriate metadata standards is accomplished by SWS invocations, such as *WS.3.2.2.1* and *WS.3.2.2.2* as depicted in Figure 9.

As depicted above, these Web services are published as SWS and associated with Goal *BG.3.2.2* via a dedicated Web Service-Goal-Mediator (WG-Mediator). The actual situation parameters are utilized by the Semantic Execution Environment to identify and invoke the most appropriate service – in this case whether *WS.3.2.2.1* or *WS.3.2.2.2* - for the given context on the basis of semantic capability descriptions.

We would like to highlight, that for each metadata standard transformation, different Web services can be provided which each follow a distinct transformation strategy. This may be necessary, since the semantics of a metadata schema are usually not completely unambiguous and thus, their interpretation and finally, their

semantic alignment can vary and completeness may not be feasible.

The following listing shows a portion of the OCML code of the SWS description of *WS.3.2.2.1* aimed at providing an IMS LD compliant manifestation based on a given process (see Figure 10).

Please note, that the capability description indicates that the grounded Web service provides packages compliant with the metadata standard IMS LD and thus, this service is only invoked in case this metadata standard is desired. The authors would like to emphasize, that each transformed metadata manifestation still follows the SDP approach of describing user and system perspective on a process. This is achieved by referring user goals within a metadata manifest to SDP Brokered Goal achievements through HTTP references to a web applet which requests the achievement of a BG from a SEE. Particularly, the Web service reported here (WS.3.2.2.1.) not only dynamically generates the IMS LD content package but also a set of JavaScript files which are included into the package. These scripts – one for each Brokered Goal of the learning process – are capable of sending achievement requests for the

Figure 11. Screenshots of distinct interfaces presenting LPMO-based processes

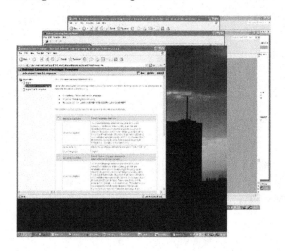

respective BG to the Semantic Execution Environment IRS-III at runtime of the process - further details can be found in (Dietze et al., 2007b) - and hence, they implement our vision of SDP as described in Section 5.

Runtime Accomplishment of SDP through Dynamic Goal Achievements

At runtime, a process is presented either in a metadata standard-specific runtime environment or a runtime environment dedicated to interpret semantic LPMO-based process models. As introduced in Section 5, each activity within a SDP-based process is described in terms of a situation-specific Goal from the user perspective and a set of Brokered Goals which define the Goal from the system perspective. This principle applies to dynamically created LPMO-based process models as they are domain-specific derivations of the SDP metamodel, and particularly to metadata standard-compliant manifestations of LPMO-based processes. Figure 11 depicts screenshots of three different process runtime environments, each presenting a distinct representation of a LPMO-based process. Whereas a specifically

Figure 12. Learning goals supported by a sequence of brokered goals

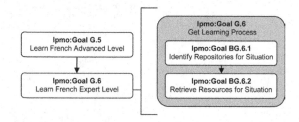

developed user interface is utilized to interpret and present semantic process instances of the LPMO, two player applications of the RELOAD-project (http://www.reload.ac.uk/) are utilized to present dynamically created XML-manifestations following the IMS LD and ADL SCORM standard.

Each of the interfaces depicted above presents a representation of a dynamically composed process aimed at teaching the French language at different levels. In this individual learning situation, a specific situation description described by a learning aim to acquire French language skills for a specific learner competency profile and setting requirements led to the composition of a learning process which is described in terms of two distinct learning activities, respectively learning Goals *G.5* ("Learn French Advanced Level") and *G.6* ("Learn French Expert Level") which are depicted in Figure 12.

Each learning Goal – such as *G.5* and *G.6* – is supported through the runtime achievement of two Brokered Goals which enable to progress from the initial situation to the desired situation. In case of *G.6*, the initial situation is defined by the learner's profile parameters, such as the native language or technical environment and in particular the learner's competency profile parameters. The actual situation description includes in particular that the previous learning Goal *G.5* is achieved and its prospective competency ("French Language, Advanced Level") is achieved and is part of the current situation description.

The two Brokered Goals *BG.6.1* and *BG.6.2* gradually modify the actual situation by adding specific parameters. *BG.6.1* provides a list of matching learning resource repositories, whereas *BG.6.2* provides a selection of learning resources which support the entire situation. In that way, the initial situation of *G.6* is gradually modified by achieving Brokered Goals through SWS Goal achievements via a Semantic Execution Environment until the final situation of *G.6*, defined in the semantic effect description of *G.6*, is reached. Similar Goal achievements are orchestrated to achieve each activity of a specific process at runtime.

We would like to highlight, that following the SDP approach enables not only the dynamic composition of a specific process for a specific situation but also the achievement of each activity at runtime, and consequently considers situation-specific parameters at runtime to enable selection of appropriate resources within a specific context setting.

EVALUATION

In this section, we introduce an evaluation model that provides an attempt to formalize and compare the efforts required to develop learning processes by following the common current practice in contrast to the approach proposed in this paper.

Current State of the Art

Let us consider a number of real world learning processes p, which have to be supported based on a number of process descriptions *m*. Each description has to be developed by spending an effort e_m. The latter represents the amount of work to annotate a learning process by using one of the existing metadata specifications (e.g. IMS LD, SCORM), and it has been considered constant. In particular, we consider s different process metadata standards.

The actual learning context for every process can be defined by *n* context parameters $\{c_1..c_n\}$, such as the technical platform or the native language of the learner. Each context parameter has got a number of possible parameter values:

$$\forall c_i \in \{c_1..c_n\}, v(c_i) = |c_i| + 1$$

where $|c_i|$ represents the number of all possible values of each parameter, and the unit defines the "no-specification" case. We assume that different process data is available to fit all different context parameter values and that process models for all different kind of process contexts have to be provided.

According to the limitations introduced in Section 2, the necessary cumulative development effort e_{cum} to support all learning processes, learning contexts and metadata specifications by following the traditional approach can be formalized as follows:

$$e_{cum} = f(m) = e_m * m$$

i.e. creating all the necessary process descriptions m, where:

$$m = f(p) = p * (\prod_{i=1}^{n} v(c_i) - 1) * s.$$

i.e. we have to create a different process description for each possible process, context and metadata specification. Therefore, the necessary effort can be summarized with:

$$e_{cum} = f(p) = e_m * p * (\prod_{i=1}^{n} v(c_i) - 1) * s$$

Based on this formula, we can expect an enormous linear increase in the development costs with an increase in the number of processes that have to be supported.

Figure 13. *Comparison between SCP-based and current state of the art-based approaches, according to the proposed model*

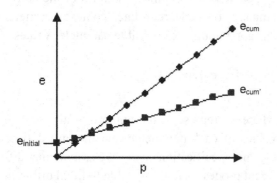

Figure 14. *Comparison of development efforts between SDP-based and traditional-based approaches in the introduced scenario*

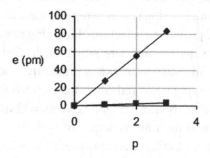

APPLYING LEARNING SDP

Let us refer to the formalization introduced in the previous subsection. According to our approach and differently to the current state of the art, the number of process models *m* necessary to support different processes *p* is equal to *p*: the same SDP description can be used within different contexts and automatically mapped into different metadata specifications. However, we have to consider a first effort $e_{initial}$ to fully provide the facilities to support our semantic framework; i.e. the semantic representations of the process contexts, the mappings to metadata standards, as well as the SWS descriptions. Thus, the cumulative effort in our approach can be summarized as follows:

$$e_{cum'} = f(p) = e_{initial} + p * e_{SDP}$$

where e_{SDP} is the effort to represent a process according to the semantic descriptions of our approach. Given our experience, we can assume that $e_m \cong e_{SDP}$. Therefore:

$$e_{cum'} = e_{initial} + p * e_m$$

Figure 13 depicts a generic comparison of this effort with the efforts of traditional approaches.

We foresee that the advantages of our vision can be observed with an increasing number of learning processes, since it benefits from lower process description development efforts, but requires an initial amount of work to provide necessary facilities. In the following subsection, we provide a concrete comparison, based on the scenario introduced in Section 7.1.

Validation Based on Example Scenario

To support the use case scenario which is currently being supported through our prototype application, we have to describe two different learning processes: "Modelling with Fourier Series" and "Speaking French Language". Therefore, *p=2*. In addition, we have to support two learning context parameters *c*: the native language of the learner and the learning domain. The former can be valued by 5 different values *v* (English, German, French, Spanish and an unknown native language); the latter can be valued by 3 different values (Languages, Math and an unknown domain). Furthermore, two different metadata standards *s* have to be supported (IMS LD and ADL SCORM). Therefore, the cumulative effort to describe the necessary process descriptions can be expressed as follows:

$$e_{cum} = f(p) = e_m * 2 * (5 * 3 - 1) * 2 = e_m * 56$$

while the effort to develop the prototype application introduced in Sections 7 can be estimated as follows:

$$m = f(p) = p = 2$$

with

$$e_{cum}' = f(p) = e_{initial} + 2 * e_m$$

If we assume an effort e_m of 1 person-month (pm), as well as the availability of all facilities enabling our development approach – i.e. we do not have to consider the initial development effort $e_{initial}$, we obtain the comparison in Figure 14.

Figure 14 illustrates the point, that supporting the example scenario by following the traditional approach does require an amount of 56 pm. Every new learning process has to be taken into account with a necessary amount of 28 pm to satisfy just the simple requirements of the example use case. In contrast, by following our SCP-based approach, every new learning process can be supported with just 1 additional mm.

We want to highlight that generalizing the effort of creating different learning process models is a simplistic approach. Therefore, it was just adopted to enable a quantification and comparison of expected efforts. Moreover, the choice of assuming the initial effort $e_{initial}$ null follows the idea of comparing the running framework (i.e. ready for use for learning designers) with the existing practices in E-Learning. In fact, the initial effort $e_{initial}$ could even be higher. For example, to implement the application described in Section 7.1, we spent 10 pm. However, considering 2 processes to represent, our approach already provides an advantage.

RELATED WORK

Given the framework and ontologies described above, L1-L4 (Section 2) are addressed by supporting the dynamic composition of context-adaptive learning processes, their transformation into distinct metadata standards and their automatic accomplishment in terms of SWS Goal achievements.

Several other existing approaches follow the idea of using Semantic Web or Web service technologies to provide dynamic as well as personalized, and context-sensitive support for learning objectives, each addressing a subset of the mentioned lacks L1-L4 (Section 2). To quote a few examples, Knight et al. (2006) as well as Baldoni, Baroglio, Patto and Torasso (2002) are concerned with bridging learning contexts and resources by introducing semantic learning context descriptions. This allows the adaptation to different contexts based on reasoning over provided context ontologies, but does not provide solutions for building complex adaptive learning applications by reusing distributed learning functionalities. Moreover, Knight et al. (2006) base their work entirely on IMS LD and thus, it does not envisage to bridge between different metadata standards.

Baldoni, Baroglio, Brunkhorst, Henze, Marengo and Patti (2006) follow the idea of using a dedicated personalization Web service which makes use of semantic learning object descriptions to identify and provide appropriate learning content. Neither is the integration of several distributed learning services within the scope of this research, nor is the allocation of services at runtime. Further related research on a Personal Reader Framework (PRF) introduced in Henze (2006) and Henze, Dolog, Nejdl (2004) allows a mediation between different services based on a so-called "connector service". However, the composition of complex learning applications based on distributed services is not within the scope of the PRF.

The work described in Schmidt and Winterhalter (2004) and Schmidt (2005) utilizes Semantic Web as well as Web service technologies to enable adaptation to different learning contexts by introducing a matching mechanism to map between a specific context and available learning data. However, neither it considers approaches for automatic service discovery nor it is based on common standards. Hence, the reuse and automatic allocation of a variety of services or the mediation between different metadata standards is not supported. These issues apply to the idea of "Smart Spaces" for learning as well (Simon, Dolog, Miklos, Olmedilla, Sintek, 2004).

Apart from these research efforts, even the specifications of existing E-Learning metadata standards such as IMS LD or ADL SCORM provide facilities for context-adaptive behavior. For instance, IMS LD Level B properties (IMS Global, 2003) and the sequencing elements of IMS Simple Sequencing, utilized by ADL SCORM enable the description of strategies for conditional selection of learning resources. However, since these facilities still rely on a manual pre-selection of learning resources at design-time, the issues described in Section 2 are not finally solved.

Whereas the majority of the described approaches enables context-adaptation based on runtime allocation of learning data, none of them enables the automatic allocation of learning functionalities or the integration of new functionalities based on open standards. Nevertheless, all approaches do not envisage mappings between different learning metadata standards to enable interoperability not only between learning contexts but also across platforms and metadata standards.

CONCLUSION

In this paper, we proposed an approach aimed at bridging the gap between learning contexts and learning resources based on Situation-driven Learning Processes (SDLP), which abstract from learning data and services – the actual resources - as well as learning process metadata. By introducing semantic descriptions of contextualized learning processes, which are aligned through SWS to learning resources on the one side and learning process metadata descriptions on the other side, our approach finally enables the context-aware composition of learning processes and their accomplishment by automatically allocating learning resources for a given learning need within a specific learning situation.

To support this vision, we provided the semantic representations to support SDLP, respectively an ontology which represents the SDP metamodel (SDPO) and another which derives SDP for the E-Learning domain (LPMO). Given a specific learning situation, a semantic learning process based on LPMO is composed dynamically and is accomplished in terms of SWS Goal achievements, utilizing the gradual derivation of learning goals within a learning process from WSMO Goals. Furthermore, an implementation architecture to support reasoning on these semantic layers was introduced based on the Semantic Execution Environment IRS-III. IRS-III serves as central reasoning environment and SWS broker, hosting ontological descriptions of available learning resources as well as semantic conceptualizations of situation-driven learning processes. Thus, IRS-III is able to compose and deliver appropriate resources to satisfy a given learning objective within a specific learning situation. Consequently, by addressing L1-L4 described in Section 2, neither manual design and composition of learning processes nor manual allocation of resources is required in contrast to traditional E-Learning applications.

Apart from that, the authors would like to highlight the openness of the described approach: additional resource providers can be integrated into the application framework by simply providing semantic descriptions of available resources and publishing these to the Semantic Execution Environment. By utilizing dedicated mediation facilities, heterogeneities related to data formats or terminologies used by distinct providers, can be solved to ensure the autonomy of all integrated resource providers.

It is apparent that the approach described in this paper requires a preliminary effort, to provide the semantic facilities described in the previous sections as well as comprehensive semantic descriptions of learning resources and that their maintenance may be a challenging task. However, given these facilities - as exemplarily provided for the described prototype - our approach represents a generalisable framework which can be applied and reused across distinct E-Learning application scenarios to enable context-adaptive learning process composition and accomplishment.

Moreover, the authors are aware, that the E-Learning community may be suspicious about trusting a reasoning engine based on semantic knowledge representations instead of manual process design and resource allocation. This is of particular concern as there may not be the one and only point of view on the semantics of a resource or a situation and distinct philosophies and perspectives are common on the question, which resource may be most appropriate for a given learning situation. To take this aspect into account, we particularly foresee the provision of distinct semantic descriptions of one learning entity, such as a learning resource, and of a variety of Web services which compose and transform learning processes. The most appropriate Web service is selected at runtime as this is a key feature of the Semantic Execution Environment IRS-III.

To enable the high applicability of our approach, future work will consider the development of semantic mappings to a wider variety of metadata standards. Furthermore, it may be beneficial, to consider further SWS standards, such as OWL-S and their alignment to the SWS layer (Section 3). Nevertheless, as we attempt to provide a domain-independent metamodel for SDP, the consideration of further process domains

is within the scope of our work, to enable a mapping of learning processes to additional process domains – for instance business processes – and their conjoint support through a unique SWS based application framework. We are strongly convinced that applying the idea of SDP in further process domains is feasible, since processes across several domains share similar notions and concepts and have to deal with related issues, such as process design, process resource allocation, and context-sensitivity.

REFERENCES

ADL SCORM. (2004). Advanced Distributed Learning (ADL) SCORM 2004 Specification, from http://www.adlnet.org.

Amorim, R. R., Lama, M., Sánchez, E., Riera, A., & Vila, X. A. (2006). A Learning Design Ontology based on the IMS Specification. *Journal of Educational Technology & Society*, *9*(1), 38–57.

Baldoni, M., Baroglio, C., Brunkhorst, I., Henze, N., Marengo, E., & Patti, V. (2006). A Personalization Service for Curriculum Planning. In proceedings of *14th Workshop on Adaptivity and User Modeling in Interactive Systems*, Hildesheim.

Baldoni, M., Baroglio, C., Patti, V., & Torasso, L. (2002). Using a rational agent in an adaptive web-based tutoring system. In proceedings of the *Workshop on Adaptive Systems for Web-Based Education, 2nd Int. Conf. on Adaptive Hypermedia and Adaptive Web-based Systems, pages 43-55*, Malaga, Spain.

Cabral, L., & Domingue, J. (2005). Mediation of Semantic Web Services in IRS-III. In Proceeding of the *Workshop on Mediation in Semantic Web Services in conjunction with the 3rd International Conference on Service Oriented Computing*, Amsterdam, The Netherlands.

Cabral, L., Domingue, J., Galizia, S., Gugliotta, A., Norton, B., Tanasescu, V., & Pedrinaci, C. (2006). IRS-III: A Broker for Semantic Web Services based Applications. In roceedings of the *5th International Semantic Web Conference (ISWC 2006)*, Athens, USA.

Coalition, O. W. L.-S. (2004). *OWL-S 1.1 release.* from http://www.daml.org/services/owl-s/1.1/

Collis, B., & Strijker, A. (2004). Technology and Human Issues in Reusing Learning Objects. *Journal of Interactive Media in Education*, 2004(4). Special Issue on the Educational Semantic Web, from www- jime.open.ac.uk/2004/4.

De Bruijn, J., Lausen, H., Krummenacher, R., Polleres, A., Predoiu, L., Kifer, M., & Fensel, D. (2005). *Web service Modeling Language (WSML).* Final Draft, from http://www.wsmo.org/TR/d16/d16.1/v0.21/20051005/

Dietze, S., Gugliotta, A., & Domingue, J. (2007a). *Using Semantic Web Services to enable Context-Adaptive Learning Designs. Special Issue on IMS Learning Design and Adaptation of Journal of Interactive Media in Education.* JIME.

Dietze, S., Gugliotta, A., & Domingue, J. (2007b). Context-aware Process Support through automatic Discovery and Invocation of Semantic Web Services. In proceedings of *IEEE International Conference on Service-Oriented Computing and Applications (SOCA'07)*, Newport Beach, California.

Domingue, J., Galizia, S., & Cabral, L. (2005). Choreography in IRS-III- Coping with Heterogeneous Interaction Patterns in Web services. In Proceedings of *4th International Semantic Web Conference*, Galway, Ireland.

Duval, E. (2003). 1484.12.1 *IEEE Standard for learning Object Metadata*, IEEE Learning Technology Standards Committee, from http://ltsc.ieee.org/wg12/

Fensel, D., Lausen, H., Polleres, A., de Bruijn, J., Stollberg, M., Roman, D., & Domingue, J. (2006). *Enabling Semantic Web Services – The Web service Modelling Ontology.* Springer.

Gangemi, A., Guarino, N., Masolo, C., Oltramari, A., & Schneider, L. (2002). Sweetening Ontologies with DOLCE. In A. Gómez-Pérez, V. Richard Benjamins (Eds.) *Knowledge Engineering and Knowledge Management. Ontologies and the Semantic Web: 13th International Conference, EKAW 2002*, Siguenza, Spain.

Gangemi, A., & Mika, P. (2003). Understanding the Semantic Web through Descriptions and Situations. In Meersman, R., Tari, Z., and et al. (Eds), *On The Move Federated Conferences (OTM'03)*, LNCS. Springer Verlag.

Global, I. M. S. (2003). *IMS Learning Design Specification,* from http://www.imsglobal.org

Gruber, T. R. (1995). Toward principles for the design of ontologies used for knowledge sharing. *International Journal of Human-Computer Studies, 43*(4-5), 907–928. doi:10.1006/ijhc.1995.1081

Henze, N. (2006). Personalized E-Learning in the Semantic Web. Extended version of 4. [iJET]. *International Journal of Emerging Technologies in Learning, 1*(1).

Henze, N., Dolog, P., & Nejdl, W. (2004). Reasoning and Ontologies for Personalized E-Learning. *Journal of Educational Technology & Society, 7*(4).

Joint US/EU ad hoc Agent Markup Language Committee (2004), *OWL-S 1.1 Release*, from http://www.daml.org/services/owl-s/1.1/

Knight, C., Gašević, D., & Richards, G. (2006). An Ontology-Based Framework for Bridging Learning Design and Learning Content. *Journal of Educational Technology & Society, 9*(1), 23–37.

Mika, P., Oberle, D., Gangemi, A., & Sabou, M. (2004). Foundations for Service Ontologies: Aligning OWL-S to DOLCE, In proceedings of the *13th International Conference on World Wide Web*.

Motta, E. (1998). An Overview of the OCML Modelling Language, In proceedings of the *8th Workshop on Methods and Languages*.

Schmidt, A. (2005). *Bridging the Gap Between E-Learning and Knowledge Management with Context-Aware Corporate Learning (Extended Version), In proceedings of Professional Knowledge Management (WM 2005)*. Springer.

Schmidt, A., & Winterhalter, C. (2004). User Context Aware Delivery of E-Learning Material: Approach and Architecture [JUCS]. *Journal of Universal Computer Science, 10*(1).

Simon, B. Dolog., P., Miklós, Z., Olmedilla, D. and Sintek, M. (2004). Conceptualising Smart Spaces for Learning. *Journal of Interactive Media in Education*. 2004(9), from http://www-jime.open.ac.uk/2004/9

World Wide Web Consortium. W3C (2001). *WSDL: Web services Description Language (WSDL) 1.1*, from http://www.w3.org/TR/2001/NOTE-wsdl-20010315

World Wide Web Consortium. W3C (2003a). *Simple Object Access Protocol (SOAP)*, Version 1.2 Part 0: Primer, from http://www.w3.org/TR/soap12-part0/

World Wide Web Consortium. W3C (2003b). *Universal Description, Discovery and Integration: UDDI Spec Technical Committee Specification v. 3.0*, from http://uddi.org/pubs/uddi-v3.0.1-20031014.htm

WSMO Working Group. (2004). D2v1.0: Web service Modeling Ontology (WSMO). WSMO Working Draft, from http://www.wsmo.org/2004/d2/v1.0/

This work was previously published in International Journal of Distance Education Technologies, Volume 7, Issue 2, edited by Qun Jin, pp. 20-43, copyright 2009 by IGI Publishing (an imprint of IGI Global).

Chapter 9

A New Process Phase Diagnostic Technique:
Visualized Interface for Diagnosing Learning Progress

Pi-Shan Hsu
Ching Kuo Institute of Management and Health, Taiwan

Te-Jeng Chang
National Taiwan Normal University, Taiwan

ABSTRACT

By improving the imperfections of previous diagnostic techniques, the new process phase real-time diagnostic technique is developed to be suitable for an adaptive e-learning instructional process. This new diagnostic technique combines measures of a learner's learning effort with associated performance in order to compare the efficiency of learning condition in a process phase, real-time, and non-interfering instructional process. The learning effort is represented as a visualized learning effort curve which is a user-friendly interface to enhance the decision making of learning path through the effective interaction between instructors and learners in an adaptive e-learning instructional process. The situated experiment was designed based on the new diagnostic technique and applied on 165 university students. In-depth group interview was conducted right after accomplishing the experiment. Results indicate that the learning effort curve is a capable real-time and non-interfering tool to diagnose learning progress in adaptive e-learning process.

INTRODUCTION

The learning effectiveness a learner can achieve in an instructional process is highly relevant to the learner's expertise in associate domain. The level of a learner's expertise influences mental effort directly according to Cognitive Load Theory (CLT). Therefore, many diagnostic techniques of assessing expertise related factors had been developed over past decades. Under adaptive

DOI: 10.4018/978-1-60960-539-1.ch009

e-learning context a learner's learning condition is required to be assessed in a process phase, real-time, and non-interfering approach which is not fulfilled by those diagnostic techniques presented in past studies. Hence, the purpose of this research is to design a new diagnostic technique suitable for adaptive e-learning context by improving the imperfections of previous diagnostic techniques. Furthermore, this new diagnostic technique is demonstrated with a visualized learning effort curve which is an effective user-friendly interface to enhance a learner's decision making in an adaptive e-learning instructional process.

The literature review of past studies on diagnostic techniques of assessing expertise under static and dynamic conditions was conducted in order to identify the requirements and dimensions of a new dynamic diagnostic technique of assessing expertise under a process phase, real-time, and non-interfering base in the instructional process of adaptive e-learning. The requisite assessment mechanisms for individual dimensions of this new dynamic diagnostic technique were developed accordingly (Hsu et al., 2009). Based on this new dynamic diagnostic technique a situated experiment was applied on 165 university students. The experimental results were transformed into characteristic learning effort curves by the assessment mechanisms of this new developed process phase, real-time, and non-interfering diagnostic technique.

OVERVIEW OF DIAGNOSTIC TECHNIQUES

Static Diagnostic Techniques of Assessing Expertise

CLT inquires interactions between information structures and knowledge of human cognition to determine instructional design (van Merriëboer et al., 2005). The expertise reversal effect is an interaction between several basic cognitive load effects (split-attention, modality, and worked example effects) and level of expertise (Kalyuga et al., 2003; Kalyuga et al., 2010). The effect is demonstrated when instructional methods that work well for novice learners have no effects or even adverse effects when learners acquire more expertise. In short, the level of expertise of the learner directly influences cognitive load; furthermore, an effective instructional design for different instructional contexts should be developed with the consideration of expertise. Therefore, the diagnostic techniques are needed to assess the levels of expertise of learners in such a way that cognitive load is taken into account. A review of past studies on diagnostic techniques of assessing expertise under static conditions is presented in this research. The assessments are taken at a specific stage of instruction instead of being conducted dynamically in the instructional process. The following different diagnostic techniques of assessing expertise related factors are presented.

1. **Static Assessments of Performance**: The traditional assessment in education primarily deals with learning performance which presents a learner's achievement measured by the test score or the time spent on task. Performance is one assessment dimension of cognitive load. Higher cognitive load often results in lower test score and less performance (Pass & van Merriëboer, 1994). The test score or the time spent is assessed at the stage of accomplishing a specific learning task, that is, the performance is assessed statically.

2. **Static Assessments of Mental Effort**: However, the other assessment dimensions of cognitive load are at least equally important for the assessment of expertise. They include mental load originated from the interaction between task characteristics and learner characteristics, which yields a priori estimate of cognitive load and mental effort (Pass & van Merriëboer, 1993). The

mental effort being expended by learners is considered essential to obtaining a reliable estimate of cognitive load. Van Gerven et al. (2004) conclude that the use of subjective rating scales to measure mental effort at the stage of accomplishing a specific learning task remains popular.

3. **Instructional Efficiency – Static Diagnostic Technique**: For many practical cases, it is feasible for two people to achieve the same performance levels with devoting different effort levels. Hence, both people have identical performance but expertise might be higher for the person who performs the task with less effort than for the person who devotes substantial effort. Therefore, an appropriate diagnostic technique of expertise should include assessments of mental effort and performance.

Paas and van Merriëboer (Pass & van Merriëboer, 1993; van Gerven et al., 2004) developed a computational approach to combine assessments of mental effort with assessments of associated performance in order to compare the efficiency of instructional condition. Using this approach, high task performance associated with low mental effort is called high-instructional efficiency, whereas low task performance with high mental effort is called low-instructional efficiency. But this approach can only be used after gathering all data from learners working under different instructional conditions. Definitely it is not able to be utilized in the context of adaptive e-learning. Alternative methods are demanded for the continuous diagnosis of expertise of individual learners in instructional process.

Dynamic Diagnostic Techniques of Assessing Expertise

From previous studies (Pass & van Merriëboer, 1993; van Gerven et al., 2004), instructional efficiency is a proper indicator of assessing learn-ers' expertise in a static condition. It is not able to be applied in a dynamic condition whereas in the context of adaptive e-learning. Salden, Paas and van Merriëboer (2006) argued adaptive e-learning as a straightforward two-step cycle: (1) the dynamic selection of the next learning task, and (2) assessment of a learner's expertise.

1. **Dynamic Task Selection – Mental Efficiency**: Camp et al. (2001) and Salden et al. (2004) compared the effectiveness of four approaches: (1) a fixed sequence of learning tasks ordered from simple to complex, (2) dynamic task selection based on mental efficiency, (3) dynamic selection based on performance, and (4) dynamic selection based on mental effort. Mental effort and performance were both assessed and measured by subjective rating scale. In the dynamic conditions, the next task was selected depended on the assessment results. In both studies, dynamic task selection proved superior to the use of a fixed sequence of tasks. In the study of Salden et al. (2004), the mental efficiency condition appeared more effective than the mental effort and performance conditions.

2. **Dynamic Assessments of Performance – Non-interfering**: In the study of Salden et al. (2004), both mental effort and performance are assessed and measured by subjective rating scale which resulted in interfering learning while a learner conducts subjective rating to discontinue learning in the instructional process. In order to obtain an optimal diagnostic technique of a learner's expertise, Kalyuga and Sweller developed an approach that could be implemented in a computer-based learning environment for dynamically adapting instruction to changing levels of leaner expertise in a domain, which is a different approach than Camp et al. (2001) and Salden et al. (2004). The approach is to produce a dynamic diagnostic

technique of expertise for the context of adaptive e-learning through utilizing the concept of instructional efficiency, first step - task selection and rapid assessment test.

The concept of a central executive explains working memory operations in lower level cognitive tasks (Baddeley, 1986), which determine what information learners attend to and what cognitive activities they engage in at any specific stage of cognition (Kalyuga & Sweller, 2005). When dealing with high-level cognitive processes, a central executive is not considered as a permanent processor in working memory, but as an entity constructed for every specific task at hand by retrieving appropriate schemas from long-term memory (Sweller, 2003). The relative weight of schemas and instructional explanations in a learner's central executive for a task depends on the level of learner expertise (Kalyuga & Sweller, 2005).

Instructional designs have to be tailored to changing levels of expertise for specific domains in order to optimize cognitive load. Instructional procedures should be user-tailored and require diagnostic techniques of assessing a learner's expertise that could be used in real time during instructional process. The availability of schema-based knowledge structure is the major factor determining expert-novice differences, which can be obtained by asking learners to rapidly indicate their first step toward solution of a task (Kalyuga & Sweller, 2005).

Kalyuga and Sweller proposed a "Rapid Assessment Test" (RAT) to assess the quality of learners' schemas that guide their problem-solving process (Kalyuga & Sweller, 2004). In RAT learners are asked to indicate their first step towards solution of a task. As the example presented below, students may respond the algebraic problem $(4X - 6)/2=7$ in one of the following ways when asked to report their first step:

- The first step reported is incorrect or the learner indicates that he does not know the answer. Then this learner is categorized as a pre-novice with no relevant schemas.
- $4X-6=14$ is indicated as the first step, this learner is categorized as a novice.
- $4X=20$ is indicated as the first step, this learner is categorized as having intermediate ability.
- $X=20/4$ is indicated as the first step, this learner is categorized as an advanced student.
- $X=5$ is indicated as the first step, this learner is categorized as an expert.

The assumption that higher quality schemas allow for the skipping of steps in solving an algebra equation is central to this type of rapid assessment. The skipping of steps is an important characteristic of higher levels of expertise because well learned or automated solution procedures incorporate cognitive rules together that consistently follow each other in performing particular tasks (Blessing & Anderson, 1996; Sweller et al., 1983). Kalyuga and Sweller (2005) found high correlations (up to .92) between performance on RAT and traditional performance tests that required complete solutions of corresponding tasks. This indicates that the first step – task selection is indeed a good indicator of the quality of available problem-solving schemas (Kalyuga & Sweller, 2005).

3. **Cognitive Efficiency - Dynamic Diagnostic Technique**: Kalyuga and Sweller (2005) developed a dynamic diagnostic technique that the rapid measures of schematic knowledge were combined with measures of cognitive load based on the subjective ratings of mental effort. In the domain of algebra, RAT is used to measure performance and a subjective rating scale is used to measure mental effort. Cognitive efficiency (E) is defined as $E=P/R$, where R is the metal effort rating and P is the performance measure on the

same task. Cognitive efficiency is similar to the instructional efficiency developed by Paas and van Merriënboer (Pass & van Merriëboer, 1993; van Gerven et al., 2004) but it is for the continuous diagnosis of expertise of individual learners in their instructional process.

As the example presented below for assessing performance by RAT, learners may respond the algebraic problem $4X - 6 = 10$ in one of the following ways when asked to report their first step. Scores ranging from 0 to 4 are allocated as following:

- The first step reported is incorrect or the learner indicates that he does not know the answer, score 0 is allocated.
- $4X=10+6$ is indicated as the first step, score 1 is allocated.
- $4X=16$ is indicated as the first step, score 2 is allocated.
- $X=16/4$ is indicated as the first step, score 3 is allocated.
- $X=4$ is indicated as the first step, score 4 is allocated.

After learners type their first solution step, they are asked to rate how difficult this task is by clicking the mental effort rating on the same task. The mental effort rating (R) of each task is combined with the performance measure (P) on the same task to provide an indicator of cognitive efficiency (E), where E is defined by $E = P \div R$.

PROCESS PHASE, REAL-TIME, AND NON-INTERFERING DIAGNOSTIC TECHNIQUE

The cognitive efficiency indicator is used to monitor learners' progress during instruction process in the study of Kalyuga and Sweller (2005) which fits the requirements of dynamic diagnostic technique

of expertise in the context of adaptive e-learning in terms of (1) subjective evaluation, (2) first step –task selection, (3) dynamic process and dynamic task selection, (4) real-time assessment, and (5) user-tailored instructional process.

The performance of the cognitive indicator is assessed and measured by RAT according to first step – task selection. It fulfills with those requirements of dynamic diagnostic technique of expertise in the context of adaptive e-learning. But the mental effort of the cognitive efficiency indicator is assessed and measured by subjectively clicking the mental effort rating, which is still handled by the traditional measurement technique applied at the moment of accomplishing task (called node phase) rather than assessing the mental effort in a real-time and non-interfering process (called process phase). The defect of interfering instructional process to discontinue continuous learning activities is the essential disadvantage of the node phase diagnostic technique compared with process phase diagnostic technique. Technically the cognitive efficient indicator is not able to be the continuous optimal assessment of expertise of individual learners in their instructional process because of node phase assessment of mental effort.

Requisite Elements of the Assessment Technique of Learning Effort

Thus this research is aimed to developing a new assessment technique of learners' effort to be feasible in monitoring learners' learning progress during instructional process in a process phase, real-time and non-interfering based approach. The learner's effort is defined as the "learning effort" in a dynamic process which is able to be assessed and measured by subjective real-time evaluation and learner-controlled task selection without interfering continuous learning. This new assessment technique of learning effort is designed to fulfill following requisite elements which makes it be feasible to be applied in real-life instructional context and also aligned with those requirements of dynamic diagnostic techniques of assessing expertise.

1. **Intelligent Tutoring System (ITS)**: The concept of ITS is used as the baseline of the adaptive e-learning platform in developing the new diagnostic technique of expertise in this research. The architecture of the system is approached by curriculum sequencing according to mastery learning theory.

Mastery learning is a theoretical perspective of education that has attracted much attention in the past. The article by Bloom (1968) on mastery learning is widely regarded, which compares two models of education: the traditional model and the mastery model. The traditional model uses the same instruction for an entire class, regardless of aptitude. The test is applied after instruction to measure the information learners have retained. Consequently, learners with an aptitude to learn the requisite material quickly move forward while slower learners fall behind and receive lower performance. In contrast, the mastery model varies instruction according to aptitude, resulting in higher levels of learning for all learners.

Curriculum sequencing is a well-established technology in the field of ITS based on mastery learning theory. The idea of curriculum sequencing is to generate an individualized course for each student by dynamically selecting the most optimal instructional operation (presentation, example, or assessment) at any given moment (Huang et al., 2007).

The steps of the ITS platform utilized in this research are outlined as following:.

- Step 1. Formative assessment A: It is a diagnostic instrument or process.
- Step 2. Corrective activity (hint): Activities to correct may involve alternative materials or any type of learning activity that al-

low for a difference in sensory or motivational preference.

- Step 3. Formative assessment B: A second assessment parallel in form to the first formative assessment for the instructional unit, which is not identical but covers the same concepts and material as the first assessment. It is asked in a slightly different way or format.
- Step 4. Culminating demonstration: It is a full presentation to demonstrate what learners should learn to solve assessment B correctly. The presentation is delivered by tutoring in different forms such as step-by-step text explanation or virtual operation through motion picture.

The instructional process of the steps mentioned above is presented in Figure 1. The learning paths and learner selection points indicated in Figure 1 are learner-controlled process through interactive models of formative assessment which is aligned with subjective evaluation and dynamic task selection.

2. **Integration of Assessment in Teaching – Emergence of Dynamic Assessment**: In the study of Allal and Ducrey (2000), dynamic assessment encompasses a variety of measurement techniques and instruments which all share a common feature: element of teaching, in the form of examiner intervention, tutoring, coaching, or mediation, are integrated in the assessment sequence as a means of obtaining more complete measures of learners' cognitive abilities and more accurate predictions of future learning. In the perspective of integrating assessment in teaching, the most common dynamic assessment procedure employs a test-train-test paradigm which results in providing quantitative data through the measurement mechanism designed in the dynamic assessment process of this research. The interactive

Figure 1. Instructional process of ITS (Intelligent Tutoring System) e-learning platform

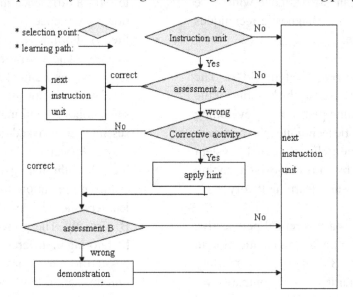

models of formative assessment based on learner-instructor interactions through computerized interactive tools in e-learning environments is designed in ITS platform in this research, which are particularly relevant to the integration of assessment in teaching.

Mechanisms of the Assessment Technique of Learning Effort

The basic concept of assessing learning effort in process phase, real-time, and non-interfering base tends to monitor learners' progress during instructional process includes two approaches: (1) quantitative measurement mechanism of structured learning paths and (2) assessment mechanism of task selection points. Both approaches are operated in a learner-controlled base. A learner conducts an assessment at each task selection point then selects the learning path he (or she) will proceed next according to his (or her) learning effort level in such instructional condition (refer to Figure 1), which is aligned with first step – task selection. Consequently, the learning effort of a leaner is

able to be assessed and quantitatively measured by selecting different learning path in process phase, real-time, and non-interfering base. The quantitative measurement mechanism of learning effort is described as following:

1. **Learning Effort in Basic Instructional Conditions**: In Table 1, five basic instructional conditions are categorized with quantitative value from the instructional process of ITS e-learning platform presented in Figure 1.
    ◦   Null Condition (c): Whereas the learning activity is not operated, thus there is no learning effort developed by instruction. Score 0 is allocated.
    ◦   Hint: The corrective activity (here named hint) in any format such as work examples applied on different learners will alter learners' effort level (Sweller et al., 1998). Therefore, the hint is categorized into effective and un-effective hint depended on whether the hint results in reducing or increasing learners' effort.

○ Effective hint (d): Learners' learning effort is reduced after applying hint to answering assessment correctly. Score -1 is allocated. The negative number presents that the effort is reduced.

○ Correct answer (e): Learners are able to answer assessment correctly without applying hint. The effort of "correct answer" is lower than the condition of "effective hint". Score -2 is allocated.

○ Wrong answer (b): Learners are not able to answer assessment correctly without applying hint. The effort in such condition is at the equally opposite side of the "correct answer". Score 2 is allocated.

○ Un-effective hint: Extra effort is taken place caused by applying hint but not able to answer assessment correctly. The effort in such condition is even higher than "wrong answer". Score 3 is allocated.

2. **Learning Effort in Composite Instructional Conditions**: In Table 2, seven composite instructional conditions by different learning path combinations from the instructional process presented in Figure 1 are categorized with quantitative calculation based on composing basic instructional conditions presented in Table 1.

Table 1. Learning effort in basic instructional conditions

Code	Learning effort	Basic instructional condition
a	3	un-effective hint
b	2	wrong answer
c	0	null condition
d	-1	effective hint
e	-2	correct answer

Learning Effort Curve

The learning effort curve is dynamically created under real-time and non-interfering base through the qualitative assessment and measurement mechanism in the instructional process. The process learning effort is acquired by the superposition of learning effort measured in each instruction unit. An example is presented in Table 3, the learning effort curve presented in Figure 2 is created by connecting the points of coordinates presented in Table 3 through the instructional process.

Mechanisms of the Assessment Technique of Learning Performance

Learning performance is assessed while a learner conducts formative assessments according to the scoring mechanism of RAT in the instructional process. As the instructional process of ITS e-learning platform presented in Figure 1 three conditions are scored by RAT mechanism. A learner may respond in one of the following conditions when asked to report answers. Scores of learning performance ranging from 0 to 2 are allocated as following:

• The learner indicates that he or she does not know the answer or has wrong answers through assessment A and B, score 0 is allocated.

Table 2. Learning effort in composite instructional conditions

condition code	composite learning effort	composite instructional conditions	remark
A	0	c	0
B	-2	c + e	0+(-2)
C	2	c + b	0+(2)
D	1	c + b +d	0+(2)+(-1)
E	5	c + b + a	0+(2)+(3)
F	0	c + b + e	0+(2)+(-2)
G	4	c + b + b	0+(2)+(2)

Figure 2. Learning effort curve

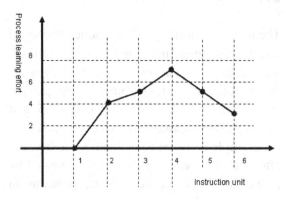

Table 3. Process learning effort chart

Instruction unit	1	2	3	4	5	6
Condition code	F	G	D	C	B	B
Learning effort	0	4	1	2	-2	-2
Superposition of learning effort	0	0+4	4+1	5+2	7-2	5-2
Process learning effort	0	4	5	7	5	3

- The learner answers correctly in assessment A, score 2 is allocated.
- The learner answers wrongly in assessment A but correctly in assessment B, score 1 is allocated.

Learning Process Efficiency - Process Phase, Real-Time, and Non-Interfering Diagnostic Technique

The learning effort (R_p) and learning performance (P_p) are able to be assessed and measured through the process phase, real-time, and non-interfering assessment technique in this research. Once the mental effort indicator (R) and performance indicator (P) in the cognitive efficiency model ($E = P \div R$) of Kalyuga and Sweller is replaced by the learning effort indicator (R_p) and learning performance indicator (P_p), the dynamic diagnostic technique of assessing expertise in the context of adaptive e-learning is constructed as learning process efficiency (E_p), where E_p is defined as $E_p = P_p \div R_p$ and the subscript "p" presents "process phase" to make a distinction between node phase indicators used in cognitive efficiency and process phase indicators used in learning process efficiency.

SITUATED EXPERIMENTS

165 students from two universities in northern and southern part of Taiwan, who were interesting in participating IC[3] (Internet and Computing Core Certifications) examinations, took adaptive e-learning courses by using IC[3] Mentor platform which is an adaptive e-learning system developed by Certiport (Certiport is the world's only globally recognized, standards-based credential for validating Microsoft® Office Specialist certification) for global IC[3] users. IC[3] Mentor fulfills those requisite elements of the assessment technique of learning effort argued in this research. The standard operation process (SOP)was developed and applied to 165 students when they conducted e-learning on IC[3] Mentor platform in order to control the associated variances such as learning content, duration, and learning environment. 31 instruction units were commonly applied for every learner in 45 minutes experiment. The learning process records of individual learners were recorded by the learning management system of IC[3] Mentor platform named IC[3] Management.

165 students were grouped into 5 groups, 3 groups were from the university in northern part of Taiwan and another 2 groups were from the university in southern part of Taiwan, the same experiment was applied to each group by following the SOP. A 30 minutes semi-structured in-depth group interview was conducted to each group once accomplishing the experiment. The questions

Figure 3. Characteristic learning effort curve – high learning process efficiency group

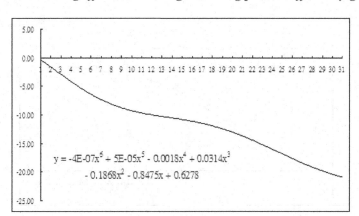

of the group interview were mainly focusing on inquiring: (1) which instruction units were easier, (2) which instruction units were more difficult, (3) what's the overall feeling when the learner dealt with easier instruction units, (4) what's the overall feeling when the learner dealt with more difficult instruction units, (5) whether the overall progress tended to lost control or steady-state condition. The group interview report was cross checked by the interviewer (authors) and subjects (students) to receive common agreement on the report content. Then authors cross referred the interview report and characteristic learning effort curves to verify whether the meaning interpreted by the learning effort curves was in line with the finding from group interview at the same range of instruction units.

RESULTS

We extracted data from the database of IC[3] Management and transformed it into the quantitative data of learning effort and learning performance for each individual learner by using the diagnostic technique developed in this research. Furthermore, the learning process efficiency of each individual learner was calculated. 165 students (learners) were segregated into two groups: (1) high learning process efficiency group with negative value of learning process efficiency, (2) low learning process efficiency group with positive value of learning process efficiency. The learning effort curves of individual learners were drew and classified in high learning process efficiency and low learning process efficiency groups accordingly. The characteristic learning effort curve of each group was created by conducting 6-order polynomial approximation on the learning effort curves in each group. The characteristic learning effort curve of high learning process efficiency group was presented in Figure 3. The characteristic learning effort curve of low learning process efficiency group was presented in Figure 4.

In Figure 3 the process learning effort tends to decrease for the individual learner with high learning process efficiency in the instructional process. In Figure 4 the process learning effort tends to increase for the individual learner with low learning process efficiency in the instructional process. Between the instruction units 5 to 19 the progress of learning effort tends to increase and results in less decrease of process learning effort for the learners with high learning efficiency. For the learners with low learning process efficiency the progress of learning effort between instruction units 5 to 19 tends to increase significantly and results in sharply increase of process learning effort.

Figure 4. Characteristic learning effort curve – low learning process efficiency group

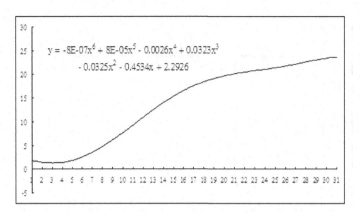

Through the group in-depth interview with learners we found that most of instruction units are neutral identified by the learners from five groups except units 5 to 19. Learners identified instruction units 5 to 19 were more difficult to learn compared with rest of instruction units. All five groups had the same comment on contributing more learning effort on instruction units 5 to 19. Thus, based on the findings of group interview and characteristic learning effort curves we infer that a learner's learning effort is positively correlated with the difficulty of the instruction content and represented by increasing learning effort. If the learners in both groups having similar learning performance while confront the learning difficulty then the learning effort of the high learning process efficiency group will be less increase compared with the learning effort of the low learning process efficiency group. This inference is consistent with the results indicated in Figure 3 and 4 that the progress of the learning effort for high learning process efficiency group tends to be less decrease than the one for low learning process efficiency group.

In addition, 4 of 5 groups commented that the progress of the experiment tended to a steady-state condition. In other word, 80% learners claimed that they experienced saturated learning through the learning process. The saturated learning condition is consistent with the results indicated in Figure 3 and 4 that the progress of the characteristic learning effort curve for both high and low learning process efficiency groups tends to approach a steady-state condition.

CONCLUSION

Based on the research results we conclude that the progress of the process learning effort tends to decrease for the learners with high learning process efficiency in the instructional process. In contrast, the progress of the process learning effort tends to increase for the learners with low learning process efficiency in the instructional process. The conclusions are in accordance with the arguments of CLT that lower effort results in higher performance (Kalyuga et al., 2000; Kalyuga, 2007; Mousavi et al., 1995; Sweller et al., 1998).

In addition, the learning effort curve is a user-friendly tool to be used as a visualized interface by both instructors and learners. Instructor and learners are able to visually recognize the process phase progress of the process learning effort in the instructional process. By the high speed calculation ability of computers the learning effort curve of a learner can be created under real-time base that makes feasible real-time interaction between instructor and learner. By using the learning effort curve and qualitative indicator of learning process efficiency a learner's learning progress is able to be diagnosed in process phase, real-time and non-interfering base in an adaptive e-learning instructional process.

Further research is recommended to develop the normal patterns of characteristic learning effort curves for the targeted categories of subjects. The characteristic learning effort curve is able to be used for forecasting specific learners' learning progress in their instructional process once the normal pattern is established as a norm for specific category of subjects. It will be a valuable research to construct a diagnostic technique for the next generation of e-learning called personalized e-learning.

ACKNOWLEDGMENT

I, the first author of this article, would like to represent highly appreciation to Dr. Ming-Hsiung Wu. Dr. Wu devoted time and effort to construct this research together with the team and coordinate in adopting experiments in order to accomplish required data collection successfully.

REFERENCES

Allal, L., & Ducrey, G. P. (2000). Assessment of – or in – the zone of proximal development. *Learning and Instruction*, *10*, 137–152. doi:10.1016/S0959-4752(99)00025-0

Baddeley, A. D. (1986). *Working Memory*. New York, NY: Oxford University Press.

Blessing, S. B., & Anderson, J. R. (1996). How people learn to skip steps. *Journal of Experimental Psychology. Learning, Memory, and Cognition*, *22*, 576–598. doi:10.1037/0278-7393.22.3.576

Bloom, B. S. (1968). Mastery learning. *Evaluation Comment*, *1*, 1–16.

Camp, G., Paas, F., Rikers, R., & van Merriënboer, J. J. G. (2001). Dynamic problem selection in air traffic control training: a comparison between performance, mental effort and mental efficiency. *Computers in Human Behavior*, *17*, 575–595. doi:10.1016/S0747-5632(01)00028-0

Hsu, P. S., Chang, T. J., & Wu, M. H. (2009). A new diagnostic mechanism of instruction: A dynamic, real-time and non-interference quantitative measurement technique for adaptive e-learning. *International Journal of Distance Education Technologies*, *7*(3), 85–96. doi:10.4018/jdet.2009070105

Huang, M. J., Huang, H. S., & Chen, M. Y. (2007). Constructing a personalized e-learning system based on genetic algorithm and case-based reasoning approach. *Expert Systems with Applications*, *33*, 551–564. doi:10.1016/j.eswa.2006.05.019

Kalyuga, S. (2007). Expertise reversal effect and its implications for learner-tailored instruction. *Educational Psychology Review*, *19*, 509–539. doi:10.1007/s10648-007-9054-3

Kalyuga, S., Ayres, P., Chandler, P., & Sweller, J. (2003). The expertise reversal effect. *Educational Psychology*, *38*, 23–31. doi:10.1207/S15326985EP3801_4

Kalyuga, S., Chandler, P., & Sweller, J. (2000). Incorporating learning experience into the design of multimedia instruction. *Journal of Educational Psychology*, *92*(1), 126–136. doi:10.1037/0022-0663.92.1.126

Kalyuga, S., Renkl, A., & Paas, F. (2010). Facilitating flexible problem solving: A cognitive load perspective. *Educational Psychology Review*, *22*, 175–186. doi:10.1007/s10648-010-9132-9

Kalyuga, S., & Sweller, J. (2004). Measuring knowledge to optimize cognitive load factors during instruction. *Journal of Educational Psychology*, *96*, 558–568. doi:10.1037/0022-0663.96.3.558

Kalyuga, S., & Sweller, J. (2005). Rapid dynamic assessment of expertise to improve the efficiency of adaptive e-learning. *Educational Technology Research and Development, 53*(3), 83–93. doi:10.1007/BF02504800

Mousavi, S. Y., Low, R., & Sweller, J. (1995). Reducing cognitive load by mixing auditory and visual presentation modes. *Journal of Educational Psychology, 87*(2), 319–334. doi:10.1037/0022-0663.87.2.319

Paas, F., & van Merriënboer, J. J. G. (1993). The efficiency of instructional conditions: an approach to combine mental effort and performance measure. *Human Factors, 35*, 737–743.

Paas, F., & van Merriënboer, J. J. G. (1994). Instructional control of cognitive load in the training of complex cognitive tasks. *Educational Psychology Review, 6*, 51–71. doi:10.1007/BF02213420

Salden, R. J. C. M., Paas, F., Broers, N. J., & van Merriënboer, J. J. G. (2004). Mental effort and performance as determinants for the dynamic selection of learning tasks in air traffic control training. *Instructional Science, 32*(1-2), 153–172. doi:10.1023/B:TRUC.0000021814.03996.ff

Salden, R. J. C. M., Paas, F., & van Merriënboer, J. J. G. (2006). A comparison of approaches to learning task selection in the training of complex cognitive skills. *Computers in Human Behavior, 22*(3), 321–333. doi:10.1016/j.chb.2004.06.003

Sweller, J. (2003). Evolution of human cognitive architecture. *Psychology of Learning and Motivation, 43*, 215–266. doi:10.1016/S0079-7421(03)01015-6

Sweller, J., Mawer, R., & Ward, M. (1983). Development of expertise in mathematical problem solving. *Journal of Experimental Psychology. General, 112*, 639–661. doi:10.1037/0096-3445.112.4.639

Sweller, J., van Merriënboer, J. J. G., & Paas, F. (1998). Cognitive architecture and instructional design. *Educational Psychology Review, 10*(3), 251–285. doi:10.1023/A:1022193728205

Van Gerven, P. W. M., Paas, F., van Merriënboer, J. J. G., & Schmidt, H. G. (2004). Memory load and the cognitive papillary response in aging. *Psychophysiology, 41*, 167–174. doi:10.1111/j.1469-8986.2003.00148.x

Van Merriënboer, J. J. G., & Sweller, J. (2005). Cognitive load theory and complex learning: recent developments and future directions. *Educational Psychology Review, 17*(2), 147–177. doi:10.1007/s10648-005-3951-0

Chapter 10
A FCA–Based Cognitive Diagnosis Model for CAT

Yang Shuqun
Fujian Normal University, China

Ding Shuliang
Jiangxi Normal University, China

ABSTRACT

There is little room for doubt about that cognitive diagnosis has received much attention recently. Computerized adaptive testing (CAT) is adaptive, fair, and efficient, which is suitable to large-scale examination. Traditional cognitive diagnostic test needs quite large number of items, the efficient and tailored CAT could be a remedy for it, so the CAT with cognitive diagnosis (CD-CAT) is prospective. It is more beneficial to the students who live in the developing area without rich source of teaching, and distance education is adopted there. CD is still in its infancy (Leighton at el.2007), and some flaws exist, one of which is that the rows/columns could form a Boolean lattice in Tatsuoka's Q-matrix theory. Formal Concept Analysis (FCA) is proved to be a useful tool for cognitive science. Based on Rule Space Model (RSM) and the Attribute Hierarchy Method (AHM), FCA is applied into CD-CAT and concept lattices are served as the models of CD. The algorithms of constructing Qr matrice and concept lattices for CAT, and the theory and methods of diagnosing examinees and offering the best remedial measure to examinees are discussed in detail. The technology of item bank construction, item selection strategies in CD-CAT and estimation method are considered to design a systemic CD-CAT, which diagnoses examinees on-line and offers remedial measure for examinees in time. The result of Monte Carlo study shows that examinees' knowledge states are well diagnosed and the precision in examinees' abilities estimation is satisfied.

INTRODUCTION

Teachers, parents, and students look forward to know students' knowledge deficiencies because it benefits teaching quality and reduces the burden on students, but it is not easy to achieve. Amplified by the current No Child Left Behind, Act of 2001 (No Child Left Behind Act, 2001), contemporary assessments are expected to provide more infor-

DOI: 10.4018/978-1-60960-539-1.ch010

mative diagnostic reports to students, parents, teachers and principals that enable successful instructional intervention. In 2009, The Obama administration announced "Race to the Top" Assessment Program would provide $350 million in competitive grants to support the development of a new generation of multi-state assessment systems including cognitive diagnosis assessment. A paper in "SCIENCE" discussed the potential of technology to launch a new era of integrated, learning-centered assessment systems, especially for cognitive diagnosis (Edys S, 2009). That is, teachers should know students' knowledge states, and offer corresponding remedial measures.

CD is treated as the core of new generation of psychology and education measurement theory, and it is the production of the combination of cognitive psychology and statistical measurement. It involves some concepts, such as cognitive attribute and state of knowledge. An attribute refers to a cognitive component or sub-process. To be precise, an attribute is a task, subtask, cognitive process, or skill involved in answering an item (Cheng & Chang, 2007). If the number of attributes involved in an exam is n, then a n-dimension vector, whose element is 0 or 1, could describe the knowledge state of an examinee. Provided that the j-th element is 1, it shows the examinee grasps the j-th attribute, and 0, otherwise. Some researchers had thought different examinees grasped the same knowledge points but to different degree, and the difference derived from their different abilities. So DiBello et al. (DiBello, Stout, & Rousso, 1995) pointed out that the foundation of CD is that the performance of examinees is described by abilities and knowledge states. And CD is considered important not only in teaching but also in intelligent tutoring system.

For large-scale testing/examination, it is impossible that feedback for CD is given immediately. Even in class, teachers hardly can make a diagnosis for students on line and present timely response. But diagnosing on line and responding in time is

one of the effective ways to improve teaching and learning. At present, many researchers focus on CAT which can estimate examinee' ability in time but can not make cognitive diagnosis. This kind of CAT is called a traditional CAT. Item response theory (IRT) (Hambleton & Swaminathan, 1985) supports CAT and CAT is a successful application of IRT. For every examinee, an optimal exam would be constructed by CAT which is efficient, rapid, fair and personalized and it is popularized in Occident and Australia. In China, CAT has been launched now. For example, a CAT developed by The Fourth Military Medical University has been applied in the recruitment, and the nice effect is reported. In order to diagnose examinee's knowledge state, the length of traditional cognitive diagnostic test must be long. The reason is that if an examinee has not grasped a knowledge point, no matter how easy items are, the examinee could not answer them correctly. But if traditional CAT enlarges its function and can make cognitive diagnosis, then CD-CAT can overcome this drawback since CD-CAT would not select the items including the attribute which has been judged by CD-CAT and examinees have not grasped.

A great progress has been made about the theory of CD at present. There are more than 60 kinds of cognitive diagnostic models (CDM). But these models have some flaws: generally some of them are complicated, and some are too complicated to recognize parameters (DiBello, Stout, & Roussos, 1995; DiBello, Stout, & Hartz, 2000); the accurate rate of diagnosis is low (Henson & Douglas, 2005), and it is lower when there are many attributes involved in a test; traditional paper-and-pencil test often include many items, which easily causes the examinees' fatigue and influence the result.

If CD is combined with CAT, the efficiency and adaptability of CAT can avoid many flaws of traditional CAT. But most of researches pay attention to paper-and-pencil testing of 0-1 scoring, but for the combination of CD and CAT there are few researches. At present, for CD-CAT, the reports are a few, such as the papers (Tatsuoka & Tatsuoka, 1997; McGlohen, 2004; Cheng, 2008). Although also it has been studied by Lin and Ding (Lin & Ding, 2007), but few theories have been touched.

Incidence matrix, which relates attributes with items, plays an important role in cognitive diagnosis (Tatsuoka, 1983; Tatsuoka, 1995; Leighton, Gierl, & Hunka, 2004; DiBello, Stout, & Hartz, 2000). Some properties were given about Q-matrix in (Tatsuoka, 1995), which was called the theory of Q-matrix. Tatsuoka pointed out that the columns or rows in Q-matrix under some operations formed Boolean algebra (Tatsuoka, 1995; Tatsuoka, 1991). In fact, the rows of Q matrix could not be guaranteed to form a Boolean lattice. It is well known that the number of the elements in a finite Boolean lattice must be 2^t, where t is a positive integer (Kolman, et. al.,1996). For the k by k Guttman scale matrix, say $k=3$, 5, 6, its rows do not form a Boolean lattice (Boolean algebra). So there are problems in Tatsuoka's Q-matrix theory. Tatsuoka employed a Boolean descriptive function and thought the Boolean descriptive function was a mapping between the attribute space spanned by latent attribute variables and the item response space spanned by item score variables (Tatsuoka, 1991; Tatsuoka, 1995), and the theory foundation of Boolean descriptive function is Q-matrix theory. Hence, the modification of Q-matrix theory is significant.

In the view of formal concept analysis (FCA) (Ganter & Wille, 1999), considering attribute hierarchy, the concept lattices are gained from Q-matrices, which modifies Tatsuoka's Q-matrix theory and forms the Q-matrix theory based on FCA. The concept lattices derived from Q-matrices are applied to CD, and regarded as the models of CD. Considering the searching method with heuristics and other technologies, CD-CAT is to be constructed.

In the present paper, concept lattice becomes the foundation of Q-matrix theory, the flaws of Q-matrix theory are modified, and the structure

of concept lattice is constructed for Q-matrix theory. Considering RSM and AHM, an initiatory and systemic CD-CAT is designed, Monte Carlo study is carried out and the result shows that it effective and efficient empirically.

Basic Concepts and Relative Knowledge

Computerized Adaptive Testing

The development of psychometric and educational measurement can be divided into two phases: the first is classical testing theory before 1950s; the second is generalizability theory (GT) and item response theory (IRT) (Hoi, 1990) except classical testing theory, which is labeled as multi-theory phase. IRT, generally considered a new theory in psychometric and educational measurement, opens out the relationship between examinees' items response activities and examinees' latent traits, which is described through item characteristic curve.

CAT is one of the successful applications of IRT. The objective of CAT is to construct an optimal test for each examinee, and its development can also be categorized into two stages: One is probing. The ability of an examinee, which has not been known at the beginning of the testing, can be estimated roughly through a batch of probing items. The specific method is described as follows: a mid-difficult item may be taken out randomly from the item pool. If the examinee responded it correctly, a more difficult item would be taken out. Or else, the easier item would be employed. The probing phase will stop when the examinee's response information shows that the examinee has answered some items correctly and some wrongly. The reason is that maximum likelihood estimation can estimate the examinee's ability only if the examinee has answered some items correctly and answered some items wrongly simultaneously; the other is precise estimating stage. The rough data estimated in the first stage couldn't provide enough information to estimate examinee's ability because inadequate items had been provided to the examinee. Hence, the examinee should be tested continuously to get more information to renew the estimated value of his/her ability. The principle of CAT is "testing examinees tailored". As for different examinees, the first item that should be selected, the number of items to be taken out, and the last item is different. Generally, examinees with high ability answer more difficult items and those with low ability answer easier ones. The trait level estimated finally may match the ability of the examinees.

Rule Space Model and Attribute Hierarchy Method

Rule Space Model (RSM) is proposed by Tatsuoka and her colleagues (Tatsuoka, 1983; Tatsuoka, 1995), and it is employed for validating the cognitive processing model and for classifying the subjects into the students' latent states of knowledge on the GRE-Q, SAT, and PSAT. Then it has been developed into an approach to CD-CAT in 1997 (Tatsuoka & Tatsuoka, 1997). Gierl, Leighton, and Hunka logicized Tatsuoka's approach in 2000 (Gierl, Leighton, & Hunka, 2000). Leighton, Gierl, and Hunka furthered the studies and presented attribute hierarchy method (AHM) in 2004 (Leighton, Gierl, & Hunka, 2004). The postulate of RSM depends on a set of specific skills or competence called attributes the examinees need possess in order to answer the items without slips or errors. AHM adopts some formal concept and methods in RSM. One of differences between AHM and RSM is the different time of getting attributes and their hierarchy. AHM emphasizes logically getting attribute hierarchy before test construction, but RSM admits of getting attributes and attribute hierarchy after a testing. Tatsuoka defined the sufficient Q-matrix: If the pairwise comparison of attribute vectors in the Q-matrix with respect to the inclusion relation yields the reachability matrix R, then the Q-matrix is said to

be sufficient for representing the cognitive model of a domain of interest (Tatsuoka, 1995). Tatsuoka took notice of attribute hierarchy, but did not fully emphasize it. Hence, combining with AHM, the researchers of the present research modify the theory of Q-matrix.

One purpose of AHM is to obtain expected response patterns which correspond to knowledge states. Every expected response pattern is a class. Pattern classification method is used to make cognitive diagnosis for examinees. In AHM, firstly, attributes should be identified and then be made up hierarchy. Hierarchy describes the dependent relations among the attributes. For example, the attributes used by an examinee to solve the fraction problem include: addition of integers (attribute 1 or A1), multiplication of integers (A2), conversion of mixed numbers into improper fractions (A3), and division of integers (A4) (Gierl, Leighton, & Hunka, 2000). These four attributes can be ordered into a hierarchy based on their logical and/or psychological properties. A1, A2 and A3 are prerequisites to A2, A3 and A4 respectively, so the hierarchy is linear. Four basic types of attribute hierarchy are given in AHM (Leighton, Gierl, & Hunka, 2004). Secondly, a binary adjacency matrix (A matrix) is specified by the relationship among attributes. The adjacency matrix expresses the direct relationship among attributes. Thirdly, a reachability matrix (R matrix) is performed through the adjacency matrix. The reachability matrix expresses the direct and indirect relationships among attributes. Fourthly, an incidence matrix (Q matrix) is formed, and a reduced incidence matrix and an ideal attribute matrix (Ea matrix) are obtained. Here, the incidence matrix is constructed by all combinations of attributes. If the number of attributes is n, the incidence matrix is $2^n - 1$, *because items represent combinations of attributes that must fit the constraints of specified attribute hierarchy, and* the incidence matrix (Q matrix) should be reduced to form the reduced Q matrix (Qr matrix) by imposing the

Figure 1. An Attribute hierarchy

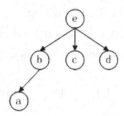

constraints of the attribute hierarchy as defined in the *R* matrix. *Ea* matrix is the transposition of *Qr* matrix. In the *Ea* matrix, the rows have two facets of meaning: one is typical examinees (examinee's knowledge state), and the other is typical item model (Leighton, Gierl, & Hunka, 2004). Here, the word "typical" means that not only examinee's knowledge state but also the attributes of items should satisfy attribute hierarchy. In the situation without slip or guess (briefly, ideal situation), for a typical examinee (a row of *Ea* matrix), if the set of attributes of a typical item (a row of *Ea* matrix) is the subset of the set of attributes (knowledge state) that the examinee has grasped, the typical examinee can correctly answer the typical item under the ideal situation. Finally, an expected response pattern (T) is obtained from

Ea -matrix. A general example is provided as follows. Figure 1 is an attribute hierarchy, Table 1 shows *A* matrix, *R* matrix, *Q* matrix, *Qr* matrix, *Ea* matrix and *T* matrix derived from Figure 1.

Formal Concept Analysis

Standard denotations of FCA (Ganter & Wille, 1999) are adopted in the present research.

Definition 1. A formal context is a triple of sets (G, M, I), where G is called a set of objects, M is called a set of attributes, and $I \subseteq G \times M$.

From Table 2, the set of objects is {1, 2, 3, 4, 5, 6, 7, 8, 9, 10, 11, 12}, and the set of attributes is {a, b, c, d, e}.

Two monotone operators: Given a formal context (G, M, I), P(A) stands for the power set of A,

$$\forall A \in P(G), A* = \{ m \in M \mid g \, \mathrm{I}m, \forall g \in A \} \in P(M)\} \tag{1}$$

$$\forall B \in P(M), B* = \{ g \in G \mid g \, \mathrm{I}m, \forall m \in B \in P(G)\} \tag{2}$$

Table 1. Some matrices related to diagnosis derived from Figure 1

A	R	Q	Qr	Ea	T
00000	10000	01000110101011111000110101011111	000010001101	00001	100000000000
10000	11000	00100101000110110100101000011011	010011011111	01001	110000000000
00000	00100	00010011010101110010011010010111	001000111011	00101	101000000000
00000	00010	00001000111110100010001111111101	000101100111	00011	100100000000
11110	11111	10000000000000001111111111111111	111111111111	11001	110010000000
				01011	110101000000
				00111	101100100000
				01101	111000010000
				11101	111010011000
				11011	110111000100
				01111	111101110010
				11111	

Note that *A* is the adjacency matrix, *R* is the reachability matrix, *Q* is the incidence matrix, *Qr* is the reduced *Q* matrix, *Ea* is the *Ea* matrix, and *T* is the expected response patterns.

Table 2. A formal context

Attributes/objects	a	b	c	d	e
1	0	0	0	0	
					1
2	0	1	0	0	1
3	0	0	1	0	1
4	0	0	0	1	1
5	1	1	0	0	1
6	0	1	0	1	1
7	0	0	1	1	1
8	0	1	1	0	1
9	1	1	1	0	1
10	1	1	0	1	1
11	0	1	1	1	1
12	1	1	1	1	1

It can be proved that ** is a closure operator.

For example, A is a set of objects from Table 2, and $A = \{4, 6\}$. Because $< 4, d > \in I$, $< 4, e > \in I$, $< 6, d > \in I$, and $< 6, e > \in I$, $A^* = \{d, e\} \in P(M)$. Because $< 7, d > \in I$, $< 7, e > \in I$ $< 10, d > \in I$, $< 10, e > \in I$, $< 11, d > \in I$, $< 11, e > \in I$, and $< 12, d > \in I$, $A^{**} = \{4, 6, 7, 10, 11, 12\}$.

Definition 2. (G, M, I) is a formal context, (A, B) is an ordered pair, $A \in P(G), B \in P(M)$.

if $(A, B) \in P(G) \times P(M)$, $A^* = B$ and $B^* = A$, then (A, B) is called a concept.

Suppose that (A_1, B_1) and (A_2, B_2) are concepts, the order operator "$\leq$" is defined by (3).

$$(A_1, B_1) \leq (A_2, B_2) \Leftrightarrow (A_1 \subseteq A_2)(or B_1 \supseteq B_2) \tag{3}$$

The set of all concepts in a formal context forms a concept lattice $L(G, M, I)$. The greatest lower bound and the least upper bound are defined as (4) and (5), respectively.

$$(A_1, B_1) \wedge (A_2, B_2) = (A_1 \cap A_2, (B_1 \cup B_2)^{**}) \tag{4}$$

$$(A_1, B_1) \vee (A_2, B_2) = ((A_1 \cup A_2)^{**}, B_1 \cap B_2) \tag{5}$$

For example, Figure 2 shows the concept lattice from Table 2, and 1.5 is a weigh value.

Definition 3. Suppose that (A_1, B_1) and (A_2, B_2) are concepts, if $(A_1, B_1) \leq (A_2, B_2)$, and there is no concept (A_3, B_3) such that

$$(A_1, B_1) \neq (A_3, B_3), (A_2, B_2) \neq (A_3, B_3),$$
$$(A_1, B_1) \leq (A_3, B_3) \leq (A_2, B_2).$$

Figure 2. The concept lattice from Table 2

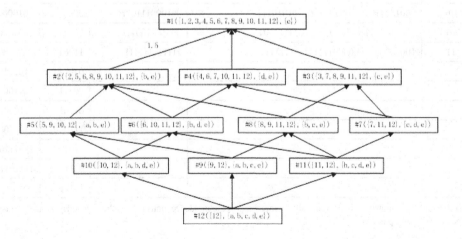

Figure 3. Tatsuoka's algorithm

Algorithm: Tatsuoka's algorithm	
Input:	R, R is a reachability matrix of S;
Ouput:	Q, which is a Qr matrix
01:	{create a matrix with $2^n - 1$ columns and named it Q;
02:	for (every column r of the matrix)
03:	
04:	*temp*=zero vector;
05 :	If r does not meet attribute hierarchy
06:	r is deleted from the matrix;
07:	endif
08:	endfor
09:	}

Then (A_1, B_1) is called a lower neighbor of (A_2, B_2), and (A_2, B_2) is called a upper neighbor of (A_1, B_1) in this paper. It is denoted by $(A_1, B_1) \prec (A_2, B_2)$.

The Theory of CD-CAT Based on FCA

The Construction of Ea Matrice

Tatsuoka's Method

An *Ea* matrix is the transposition of a *Qr* matrix, which is formed by imposing the constraints of the attribute hierarchy. S is an attribute hierarchy with n attributes, which means that there may be $2^n - 1$ valid items. The rest after deleting all invalid items is the *Qr* matrix. The method Tasuoka proposed is called Tatsuoka's algorithm which is shown in Figure 3.

For example, Figure 1 is an attribute hierarchy with 5 attributes. The number of potential items is 31, 19 of which do not meet Figure 1, so they should be deleted. The left 12 items comprise the *Qr* matrix which is shown in Figure 4.

Incremental Augment Algorithm

We proposed the incremental augment algorithm (Yang, et. al, 2010) to generate *Qr* matrice. The incremental augment algorithm is given in Figure 5.

For example, Figure 1 is an attribute hierarchy, and initial value of Q is an empty matrix. Let R is partitioned according to its columns, i.e.,

$R = \left(r_1, r_2, r_3, r_4, r_5 \right)$. In the first cycle, r_1 is added to Q and denoted by q_1; in the second cycle, r_2 is added to Q and denoted by q_2. $q_1 \oplus r_2$ is computed. If the Boolean sum is different from q_1, it is a new item and put it into Q. But in this cycle, no new item is generated; in the third cycle, r_3 is added to Q and denoted by q_3. $q_1 \oplus r_3 \neq q_i$ ($i = 1, 2$) and $q_2 \oplus r_3 \neq q_i$ ($i = 1, 2$), which means that $q_2 \oplus r_3$ and $q_1 \oplus r_3$ are two new items. They are added to Q and denoted by q_4 and q_5; in the fourth cycle, r_4 is added to Q and denoted by q_6. After computing $q_i \oplus r_4$ ($i = 1, 2, 3, 4, 5$), 5 new items are generated and denoted by $q_7, q_8, q_9, q_{10}, and, q_{11}$; in the fifth cycle, r_5 is added to Q and denoted by q_{12}. After computing $q_i \oplus r_5$ ($i = 1, ..., 11$), a new items are generated and denoted by q_{12}. At this point, all items are generated, which consisted of the Qr matrix. Figure 6 shows the proceeding of the generating of the Qr matrix.

Figure 4. The Qr matrix of Figure 1

$$\begin{pmatrix} 0 & 0 & 0 & 0 & 1 & 0 & 0 & 0 & 1 & 1 & 0 & 1 \\ 0 & 1 & 0 & 0 & 1 & 1 & 0 & 1 & 1 & 1 & 1 & 1 \\ 0 & 0 & 1 & 0 & 0 & 1 & 1 & 1 & 0 & 1 & 1 \\ 0 & 0 & 0 & 1 & 0 & 1 & 1 & 0 & 0 & 1 & 1 & 1 \\ 1 & 1 & 1 & 1 & 1 & 1 & 1 & 1 & 1 & 1 & 1 & 1 \end{pmatrix}$$

Figure 5. The incremental augment algorithm

Algorithm: Incremental augment algorithm	
Input:	R, R is a reachability matrix of S; Q is a empty matrix ;
Ouput:	Q, which is a Qr matrix for S
01:	$r_1, r_2, ..., r_n$ are the columns of R ;
02:	$m = 0$;
03:	for $i = 1$ to n
04:	$\{ m = m + 1$;
05 :	$q_m = r_i$; % q_m is a new column in Q
06:	for $t = 1$ to $m - 1$
07:	if ($r_i \oplus q_t$ is not in Q) % $\oplus$ means the Boolean addition
08:	then $\{ m = m + 1$; $q_m = r_i \oplus q_t$;$\}$
09:	endif
10:	endfor t
11:	endfor i

Concept Lattices Based on CD-CAT

Leighton et al. (2004) contributed four types of hierarchical structures in AHM, i.e., linear, convergent, divergent, and unstructured (Leighton, Gierl, & Hunka, 2004). Obviously, the linear, the divergent and the unstructured are tree-shaped. But other structures are assumed to exist. From a Texas state reading test for Grade 3 students in spring 2002 (McGlohen, 2004), there were six independent attributes about the reading test including: determining guessing the meaning of words in a variety of written texts, identifying supporting ideas in a variety of written tests, summarizing a variety of written texts, perceiving relationships and recognizing outcomes in a variety of written texts, analyzing information in a variety of written texts in order to make inferences and generalizations, recognizing points of view, and /or statements of fact and opinion in a variety of texts. Hence, attribute hierarchy is classified reasonably into three basic types: diamond-shaped, tree-shaped and isolated vertices.

Definition 4. If attribute x (i.e., node x) is prerequisite to attribute y then x is called a restricted attribute of y or a restricted node of y. An attribute is called a start attribute or a start node if and only if any node which is prerequisites to the attribute does not exist. The node is not prerequisite to any attribute is called leaf node.

Attribute "e" is a start node in Figure 1, and attributes "a", "c", and "d" are leaf nodes. Attribute "e" and "f" are start nodes in Figure 7, and attributes "c" and "h" are leaf nodes.

The basic structures can construct compound structures. Due to the number of the start node(s), compound attribute hierarchy is divided into the attribute hierarchy with one start node and attribute hierarchy with multi-start-nodes.

Every type of the attribute(s) hierarchies can be converted into *Ea-matrices*. Afterwards, a matrix E stands for the *Ea* matrix in this paper.

Based on the Graph Theory, some properties could be solicited as follows:

Property 1. Suppose that S is an attribute hierarchy, E is derived from S, then every row of E can express a sub-graph (S_1) of S.

Proof: Because every row must satisfy the constraint of the attribute hierarchy, then the result is easily proved.

This completes the proof.

For example: Figure 7 is a graph, $<\{a, b, c, d, e, f, g\}, \{(e, b), (e, c), (e, d), (b, a), (f, g)\} >$, where $\{a, b, d, e, f, g\}$ is the set of vertices and

Figure 6. The illustration of incremental augment algorithm

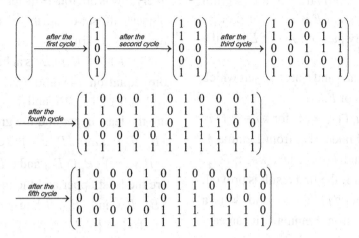

{*(e, b), (e, c), (e, d), (b, a), (f, g)*} is the set of edges. An item is {1100111} in Figure 7,which is a sub-graph (i.e., <{*a, b, e, f, g*}, {*(e, b), (b, a), (f, g)* }>) of Figure 3, where {*a, b, e, f, h*} is the set of vertices and {*(e, b), (b, a), (f, g)* } is the set of edges.

Property 2. Suppose that S is an attribute hierarchy with n attributes ($n \geq 2$), E is from S, for every $k \in \{1, 2, ..., n\}$, at least there is a row of E, such that the sum of elements of the row is k. If E is expressed by $(a_{ij})_{m \times n}$, then E can be arranged to satisfy $\sum_{i=1}^{n} a_{i+1,j} - \sum_{i=1}^{n} a_{i,j} = 0$ or $\sum_{i=1}^{n} a_{i+1,j} - \sum_{i=1}^{n} a_{i,j} = 1$ for $i \in \{1, ..., n-1\}$, where the rules of Boolean add is as follows: 0+0=0, otherwise 1; Boolean multiply is that: $1 \times 1 = 1$, otherwise 0.

Proof: S can express a row of E obviously from property 1. A leaf node of S is deleted. Suppose that the rest of S is called S_1, S_1 must satisfy the constraints of S. So S_1 also expresses a row of E. The rest may be deduced by analogy. Therefore, for every $k \in \{1, 2, ..., n\}$, at least there is a row of E, such that the sum of elements of the row is k. Obviously, if the order of row(s) is decided by the order of the sum of element(s) of row(s), the row(s) of E can be arranged to satisfy the result.

This completes the proof.

E is arranged according to its row sum next.

Lemma 1. Suppose that E is from S, S_1 is a sub-graph of S, S_1 can express a row of E if and only if S_1 includes all restricted nodes of every node of S_1.

Proof: The Necessary Condition is easily obtained by property 1.

If S_1 includes all restricted nodes of every node of S_1, then from the definition of E, S_1 can express a row of E.

This completes the proof.

Suppose that φ denotes the vector, the elements of which are 0, φ could not express any item because an item at least has an attribute. If a row of E denotes a set of attributes (e.g., the row 11001 in Table 1 can denote {*a,b,e*}), the φ is the empty set.

Figure 7. A compound attribute hierarchies with multi-start-nodes

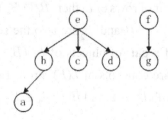

Lemma 2. Suppose E is from S, intersection $\cap$ of every pair of rows of E is a row of E or φ, and the join $\cup$ of every pair of rows of E is still a row of E.

Proof: Suppose that r_1 and r_2 are two sets which denote a pair of rows of E.

Case 1, $r_1 \cap r_2$. If $r_1 \cap r_2 \neq \varphi$, for $\forall i \in r_1 \cap r_2$ and k is a restricted node of i, from Lemma 1, we get that $k \in r_1$ and $k \in r_2$, i.e., $k \in r_1 \cap r_2$. According to Lemma 1, the first result is proved.

Case 2, $r_1 \cup r_2$. For $\forall j \in r_1 \cup r_2$ and k is a constraint node of j, from Lemma 1, it can easily get $k \in r_1$ or $k \in r_2$, i.e., $k \in r_1 \cup r_2$. According to Lemma 1, the second result is also proved.

This completes the proof.

If every row of E is served as an object, then E is obviously a formal context and E can form a concept lattice. In fact, Table 2 is the formal context from the Ea matrix in Table 1, and can get concept lattice (Figure 2). Specially, a concept lattice from an Ea matrix is called $L(E)$.

Theorem 1. Suppose that S is an attribute hierarchy, E is derived from S, $L(E)$ is the concept lattice from E. If S is a diamond-shaped attribute hierarchy, a tree-shaped attribute hierarchy, or a compound attribute hierarchy with one start node, then the set of concepts is $\{(\{i\}^{**}, \{i\}^*) \mid i$ is an object of $E\}$. If S belongs to a isolate vertices attribute hierarchy or a compound with multi-start-nodes attribute hierarchy, then the set of concepts is $\{(\{i\}^{**}, \{i\}^*) \mid i$ is an object of $E\} \cup \{(\varphi^*, \varphi)\}$.

Proof: Case 1, S is a diamond-shaped attribute hierarchy, a tree-shaped attribute hierarchy, or a compound attribute hierarchy with one start node. Obviously S has only one start node, so if B_1 and B_2 are a pair of rows of E, then $B_1 \cap B_2 \neq \phi$ and $B_1 \cup B_2 \neq \phi$. B_1 and B_2 are also the sets of attributes of a pair of objects of E. (B_1^*, B_1) and (B_2^*, B_2) are concepts of $L(E)$. From Lemma 2, we get $B_1 \cap B_2 \in E$ and $B_1 \cup B_2 \in E$. Because

every row is obviously different, there is only one object with set of attributes of $B_1 \cup B_2$. Hence, by the definition of the operator *, $(B_1 \cup B_2)^{**} = B_1 \cup B_2$ is achieved. According to the equation (4) and (5), it is known that $((B_1 \cap B_2)^*, B_1 \cap B_2)$ and $((B_1 \cup B_2)^*, (B_1 \cup B_2)^{**})$ are the least upper and the great lower bound of (B_1^*, B_1) and (B_2^*, B_2) respectively, i.e., $((B_1 \cap B_2)^*, B_1 \cap B_2)$ and $((B_1 \cup B_2)^*, B_1 \cup B_2)$ are the least upper and the great lower bound of (B_1^*, B_1) and (B_2^*, B_2) respectively.

If $C = \{(\{i\}^{**}, \{i\}^*) \mid i$ is an object of $E\}$, $J = \{a \mid a$ is a object in $E\}$, for an object i of J, only one concept $(\{i\}^{**}, \{i\}^*)$ corresponds to it in $L(E)$. a mapping f can be defined from J to C. $f: J \to C$, for every object i of J, such that $f(i) = (\{i\}^{**}, \{i\}^*)$. For every pair of objects i, j in J, if $i \neq j$, then i and j are different items. Hence $\{i\}^* \neq \{j\}^*$ and $(\{i\}^{**}, \{i\}^*) \neq (\{j\}^{**}, \{j\}^*)$, i,.e., f is injection. So we get that f is one-to-one mapping, $f(E) = C$.

For every pair of objects i, j in J, $(\{i\}^{**}, \{i\}^*)$ and $(\{j\}^{**}, \{j\}^*)$ are a pair of concepts of C (see Box 1).

It is easily obtained that $\{i\}^* \cap \{j\}^*$ and $\{i\}^* \cup \{j\}^*$ are rows of E, so

$$(\{i\}^{**} \cap \{j\}^{**}, \{i\}^* \cup \{j\}^*) \text{ and}$$

$$((\{i\}^{**} \cup \{j\}^{**})^{**}, \{i\}^* \cap \{j\}^*)$$

are in C, which means that the least upper and the great lower bound of every pair of concepts of C are in C. So we have that the partial ordered set $(C, \leq)$ is the concept lattice from E. Because $L(E)$ is the concept lattice from E, so we get $(C, \leq)$ is $L(E)$. Hence, the first result is proved.

Case 2, S belongs to the isolate vertices, the connected compound with multi-start-nodes, or

Box 1.

$$({\{i\}}^{**}, {\{i\}}^{*}) \wedge ({\{j\}}^{**}, {\{j\}}^{*}) = ({\{i\}}^{**} \cap {\{j\}}^{**}, ({\{i\}}^{*} \cup {\{j\}}^{*})^{**}) = ({\{i\}}^{**} \cap {\{j\}}^{**}, {\{i\}}^{*} \cup {\{j\}}^{*})$$

$$({\{i\}}^{**}, {\{i\}}^{*}) \vee ({\{j\}}^{**}, {\{j\}}^{*}) = (({\{i\}}^{**} \cup {\{j\}}^{**})^{**}, {\{i\}}^{*} \cap {\{j\}}^{*})$$

the non-connected compound attribute hierarchy. From Lemma 2 and case 1, if $B_1 \cap B_2 \neq \varphi$, then $B_1 \cap B_2$ and $(B_1 \cup B_2)^{**}$ are still in E. If $B_1 \cap B_2 = \varphi$, because $\varphi \notin E$ and (φ^*, φ) is the least upper of (B_1^*, B_1) and (B_2^*, B_2), so (φ^*, φ) is a concept of $L(E)$. Hence, the second result has been proved.

This completes the proof.

Definition 5. Suppose that B_1 and B_2 are finite sets, $D(B_1, B_2)$ is defined by

$$D(B_1, B_2) = \frac{|B_1 \cap B_2|}{|B_1|} \qquad (6)$$

Obviously, if $(A_2, B_2) \leq (A_1, B_1)$, then $D(B_1, B_2) = 1$.

Theorem 2. Suppose that S is an attribute hierarchy, E is derived from S, $L(E)$ is the concept lattice from E. (A_1, B_1) and (A_2, B_2) are concepts of $L(E)$, and (A_1, B_1) is the upper neighbor of (A_2, B_2), then $D(B_1, B_2) = 1$ and $|B_2| - |B_1| = 1$, where $|B|$ donate the number of elements of B.

Proof: Because $(A_2, B_2) \prec (A_1, B_1)$, according to definition 3, $(A_2, B_2) \leq (A_1, B_1)$ can be obtained, and then $B_1 \subseteq B_2$ by equation (3).

Suppose that the number of attributes of S is n, $|B_1| = k$ ($k \leq n-1$), because $B_1 \subseteq B_2$, then $|B_2| \geq k+1$. If $|B_2| > k+1$, then B_2 can express a sub-graph S_1 of S. Suppose that $B_C = B_2 - B_1$, it can get $|B_C| > 1$ and B_C at least includes a leaf node i of S_1. i is deleted from S_1 and the rest of S_1 forms an item B_3, such that $B_1 \subseteq B_3 \subseteq B_2$, $|B_3| \geq k+1$. If $A_3 = B_3^*$, then (A_3, B_3) is obviously a concept of $L(E)$. From the equation (3), it can get $(A_1, B_1) \leq (A_3, B_3) \leq (A_2, B_2)$, which is contrary to definition 3, so $|B_2| > k+1$ is not true, i.e., $|B_2| = k+1$.

This completes the proof.

According to the Theorem 1 and Theorem 2, it can easily obtain that the algorithm of constructing of concept lattices (Yang, et. al., 2008).

It is known that E is not only an accident matrix but also a formal context. It is known that E has two meanings: one is typical examinee (examinee's knowledge state), another is typical item. The set of attributes of every concept of $L(E)$ (except (φ^*, φ)) correspond to a row of E (i.e., a knowledge state), so concepts of $L(E)$ can represent knowledge states. Concept lattice indicates a special partial relation among concepts, and the relation is hierarchy, so concept lattice describes knowledge states in a domain and the relation among them. Cognitive diagnosis is detecting examinees' knowledge states. The partial relation of knowledge states makes concept lattice being a nice model of cognitive diagnosis. The model combines with CAT to form CD-CAT, and then cognitive diagnosis and estimation of ability are realized in the model.

For an examinee, there must be the set of attributes of a concept is the examinee's knowledge state. Cognitive diagnosis is the procedure of searching examinees' knowledge states.

Definition 6. E is an Ea matrix from S, and $L(E)$ is derived from E. (A, B) is a concept in $L(E)$. If an examinee can answer correctly the items including B, then it can be thought that the examinee can reach (A, B).

Definition 7. E is an Ea matrix from S, and $L(E)$ is derived from E. (A_1, B_1) is a cocept in $L(E)$. (A_1, B_1) is called an examinee's concept if and only if the examinee can reach (A_1, B_1), but can not reach (A_2, B_2), where (A_2, B_2) satisfies $(A_1, B_1) \neq (A_2, B_2), (A_2, B_2) \leq (A_1, B_1)$.

Obviously, the set of attributes of the examinee's concept is the examinee's knowledge state.

Theorem 3. E is an Ea matrix from S, and $L(E)$ is derived from E. M is a set of concepts which an examinee can reach in $L(E)$. The partial order relation "$\leq$" is defined as concept lattices, then $(M, \leq)$ is a partial set, $(M, \leq)$ is the sublattice of $L(E)$, and its great element is same with $L(E)$.

Proof: Because "$\leq$" is an partial order operator, $(M, \leq)$ is a partial set.

For every pair concept of M, (A_1, B_1) and (A_2, B_2), according to the knowledge in FCA, the greatest lower bound and the least upper bound of the two concept are $(A_1 \cap A_2, (B_1 \cup B_2)**)$ and $((A_1 \cup A_2)**, B_1 \cap B_2)$. From Theorem 1, the greatest lower bound of the two concepts is $(A_1 \cap A_2, B_1 \cup B_2)$. The examinee can reach (A_1, B_1) and (A_2, B_2), so the examinee can reach $(A_1 \cap A_2, B_1 \cup B_2)$. It is obvious that the examinee can reach $((A_1 \cup A_2)**, B_1 \cap B_2)$. So $(A_1 \cap A_2, (B_1 \cup B_2)**)$ and $((A_1 \cup A_2)**, B_1 \cap B_2)$ will fall into M. Hence, $(M, \leq)$ is a lattice and a sub-lattice of $L(E)$.

This completes the proof.

$(M, \leq)$ is called the examinee's concept lattice of cognitive diagnosis in this paper.

Inference 1. If $(M, \leq)$ is an examinee's concept lattice of cognitive diagnosis, then the set of attributes of the greatest lower bound of $(M, \leq)$ is the examinee's knowledge state.

Property 3. Suppose that $L(E)$ is from E, if (A_1, B_1) is a concept an examinee can not reach, and there is a concept (A_3, B_3), such that $(A_3, B_3) \leq (A_1, B_1)$, then the examinee can not reach (A_3, B_3); If (A_1, B_1) is a concept the examinee can reach, and there is a concept (A_2, B_2), such that $(A_1, B_1) \leq (A_2, B_2)$, then the examinee can reach (A_2, B_2).

If $(M, \leq)$ is an examinee's concept lattice of cognitive diagnosis, a path will be gotten from the least upper to the great lower of $(M, \leq)$ which is a proceeding of cognitive diagnosis. So cognitive diagnosis is the proceeding of searching the great lower of $(M, \leq)$. The depth-first searching with heuristic information (Nilsson, 1998) is the right strategy for probing examinees' knowledge states and property 3 is the heuristic information. If i is an examinee's concept, then the attributes the examinee has not grasped must not be included in the set of attributes of i. So the attributes the examinee lacks can be acquired through cognitive diagnosis. A diagnosis without remedy is not intact and inhumane, which seems likely that a doctor does not prescribe for patients after diagnosing. Remedy should be provided after examinees' lacks have been found diagnostically. Generally, an attribute is diagnosed one time. If many attributes need to be provided with remedy, then an order of remedy should be decided. The order is called remedial instruction.

Theorem 4. $L(E)$ is a concept lattice from E, if i is an examinee' concept lattice, and j is a concept the examinee wants to reach, $N = \{k \mid j \leq k \leq i, k \text{ is a concept in } L(E)\}$, then $(N, \leq)$ is a sub-lattice of $L(E)$. i and j are the least upper bound and the greatest lower bound of $(N, \leq)$, respectively.

Proof: Because "$\leq$" is an order operator, $(N, \leq)$ is a partial set.

For every pair concept of N, (A_1, B_1) and (A_2, B_2), it is known that the greatest lower bound and the least upper bound of the two concept are $(A_1 \cap A_2, B_1 \cup B_2)$ and $((A_1 \cup A_2)**, B_1 \cap B_2)$. Because $j \leq (A_1, B_1) \leq i$ and $j \leq (A_2, B_2) \leq i$,

$$j \leq (A_1 \cap A_2, B_1 \cup B_2) \leq i \text{ and}$$

$$j \leq ((A_1 \cup A_2)**, B_1 \cap B_2) \leq i,$$

i.e., $(A_1 \cap A_2, (B_1 \cup B_2)**)$

and $((A_1 \cup A_2)**, B_1 \cap B_2)$

must be in N. Hence, $(N, \leq)$ is a lattice and a sub-lattice of $L(E)$.

This completes the proof.

$(N, \leq)$ is called the examinee's concept lattice of remedial instruction.

Inference 3. If $(N, \leq)$ is an examinee's concept lattice of remedial instruction, then a path from the examinee's knowledge state to the least lower of $(N, \leq)$ is a remedial instruction.

Proof: Because the attributes examinee has not grasped and the path from the examinee's knowledge state to the least lower of $(N, \leq)$ can be obtained, the result is proved.

This completes the proof.

The Application of FCA in CD-CAT

Making Cognitive Diagnosis for Examinees

Since every row of E is served as an object, and the row expresses a typical examinee, which have been mentioned to above, every concept of $L(E)$ expresses the relationship between examinees (objects of the concept) and knowledge states (the set of attributes of the concept), which indicates that what examinees can reach. For example, Table 2 is an Ea matrix from an attribute hierarchy

(Figure 1). It has 12 rows, which means it has 12 objects. Figure 2 is a concept lattice from Table 2 For concept #9({9, 12}, {a, b c, e}), {a, b, c, e} (i.e., (11101)) is a knowledge state, and object 9 and 12 can reach #9.

The order operator "$\leq$" means the relationship among the knowledge states, which expresses the order of logic/psychology in attribute learning. According to Theorem 2, it is thought that concept lattices from E are the suitable models of cognitive diagnosis. Examinees' abilities can be computed when the attributes they have grasped are probed. So concept lattices are also the suitable models of cognitive diagnosis in CAT.

For the convenience in writing and reading, some new concepts will be given. To probe whether an examinee can reach a concept (A, B) or not is called that the examinee learns the concept (A, B). If the examinee can reach (A, B), the examinee can pass (A, B), or else the examinee will fail. For a concept lattice which is the model of cognitive diagnosis, probing starts from the upper bound of the concept lattice. If the set of attributes of the upper bound is not empty, then the examinee learns the upper bound, or else the examinee learns the lower neighbor of the upper bound. From Theorem 2, in new learning, a new attribute is added to be learned. If the examinee passes a concept, the examinee learns the concept's lower neighbor which has not be learned, but if there is no lower neighbor or the examinee can not reach the concept, he or she returns to the upper neighbor of the concept. The probing is not finished until the probing could not continue (i.e., could not add any new attribute) or until the examinee passes the lower bound of the concept lattice. In probing, three problems should be considered: the technology of item bank construction, item selection strategies, and estimation method of the knowledge state or ability. In this way, the examinee's knowledge state can be probed and the attributes the examinee lacks can be obtained, and then the most efficient remedial instruction from Theorem 3 could be achieved.

A concept corresponds to a knowledge state. So when a concept is learned, the item bank should be constructed by the items, the attributes of which are the attributes of the set of attributes of the concept. Although how to construct good item bank has not discussed at present, item bank construction based on FCA at least gives the attributes included in item bank.

Two stages are applied to CD-CAT. The first stage focuses on cognitive diagnosis, i.e., the procedure of searching the lower bound of examinees' concept lattice of cognitive diagnosis, and the second stage concentrates on ability estimation. In CAT, tests depend on examinees, the processes of testing are different, and testing for each student couldn't be designed firstly. During learning, item selection strategies of traditional CAT should be improved. Since item selection strategy means how to select suitable items for every examinee, for an examinee α, the item bank is divided into four parts: the set of attributes grasped by α (grasped attributes), the set of attributes which haven't been grasped by α (non-grasped attributes), the attribute α is learning (learning attribute), and the set of attributes α hasn't been learned (non-learning attributes). Provided that S_α is the candidate set of items, the set of attributes of S_α must include the learning attribute, and may include grasped attributes, and couldn't include non-grasped attributes and non-learning attributes. In S_α, the item is selected approaching to the ability of α.

For example, in Figure2, an examinee α starts to learn concept #1 of which the set of attribute is {e}, if α passes #1, i.e., α can reach concept #1, which means α has grasped the attribute e. Then the expected a posteriori (EAP) (Baker, 1992) is used to estimate the ability of α. A begins to learn concept #2 of which the set of attribute is {b, e}. The items, which are suitable for the present ability of α and include attribute b and e, are selected for α. If α can not pass, then it means that α has not grasped attribute b and should return to con-

cept #1, and then to learn concept #3. After ability estimation, items, which are suitable for the present ability of α and include attribute c and e, are selected for α. If α passes it then turns to concept #8. The reason is that concept #8 is less than or equal to concept 2 and α can't reach concept #2. So α can not reach concept #8 and α must turn to learn concept #7. If α can reach concept #7, then the learning stops since concept #11 is less than or equal to concept #2. Then, knowledge state of α is 00111, which means α grasps attribute c, d, and e. Sometimes examinees can not answer correctly items for mistakes, so examinees are given 3 opportunities, which means that if examinees can't pass a learning at the first time and second time, the easier items would be selected from S_α for examinees. The process of cognitive diagnosis is shown in Process 1.

In second stage (i.e., ability estimation stage), item selection strategy is the same as the cognitive diagnosis stage. The items examinees have grasped are selected, and traditional item selection strategy are adopted until enough information for ability estimation is obtained. The CAT with variable length is applied in this paper.

Providing Remedial Instruction

Remedy needs cost. Tatsuoka defined cost by Maharanobis distance (Tatsuoka & Tatsuoka, 1997). Suppose that the costs are given among knowledge states in concept lattices (e.g., 1.5 in Figure 2). The cost is called learning cost (the computing of learning cost is not considered in this paper). If the cost of a remedial instruction is the lowest from a concept to another concept then the remedial instruction is considered the best. From Property 3, Dijkstra's shortest path (Dijkstra, 1959) is adopted to get the lowest cost and to get the best remedial instruction.

Usually, if the number of attributes is lower, then the attributes examinees lack are easier to be detected. Because the smaller a concept is, the bigger the number of attributes of the concept is.

Process 1.

```
Process 1. (L(E),an examinee)
   { create an empty stack;
     i=the upper bound of L(E);
     push i into the stack;
     for (the stack is not empty)
       {i=the top element of the stack;
        if (the set of attributes of i is not φ and i has an attribute
j which has not marked) /
j is marked means the examinee has grasped it./
           {n=1;
          while (n<=3)
{ create an item which includes all attributes of i;
           the item is being tested by the examinee;
           if (the examinee passes the testing)
               {mark j;
                 if (i has lower neighbor k which has not been tested)
                     {push k to the stack; break;}}
               else { if (n=3)  pop an element from the stack; else n=n+1;}
}
           }
        else
          if (i has lower neighbor(s) which has (have) not been tested)
             push a lower neighbor into the stack;
          else output i;
      } }
```

The number of attributes of the great element is the least in a *L(E)*, so width-first searching method is considered to search remedial instruction. In Figure 2, if an examinee's concept is #3({3,7,8,9,11,12},{c,e}) and the examinee wants to #9, a shortest path that can be gained is #3->#8->#9. Then the list of attributes that the examinee lacks could be achieved from the shortest path. The list is (a,b). Attribute b should be firstly remedied. According to the width-first searching method, #2({2,5,6,8,9,10,11,12},{b,e}) is the biggest concept including b, so the examinee is suggested study the items #2 first in the remedy. If attribute b is successfully remedied, the attribute a should be remedied next. For the same reason, concept #5({5,9,10,12},{a,b,e}) is suitable to remedy attribute a. If attribute a is also successfully remedied then the remedy is well done.

The process of getting remedial instruction is as follows in Process 2.

The Design and Realization of CD-CAT

Remedial instruction can only be carried out in teaching, so the present paper just simulates cognitive diagnosis.

Monte Carlo Simulation is applied to simulating item bank, examinees and examinees' responses to the items. The experiment is based on the design above. The procedure of the experiment is as follows:

Firstly, an attribute hierarchy is given; the *Ea* matrix is formed, and a concept lattice is constructed from the *Ea* matrix;

Process 2.

```
Process 2. (L(E), an examinee's concept in a L(E), the concept that the exam-
inee wants to reach)  { The shortest path is gotten from the examinee's con-
cept to the concept the examinee wants to reach by Dijkstra's algorithm;
A list of attributes that the the examinee lacks is gotten from the shortest
path;
     for every attribute j in the list
     {create an empty queue;
      enqueue the upper bound of L(E) to the queue;
      while (the queue is not empty)
       {
        the head of the queue dequeue and is assigned to i;
        if (i includes j)
            output i and start to remedy j according to i;
        else
            enqueue all upper neighbor of i to the queue;
       }
     }
  }
```

The attribute hierarchies are different in different cognitive domains. A tree-shaped structure, isolated vertices structure with 6 nodes, Figure 1, and Figure 7 are considered in the experiment.

Secondly, for every concept, items and examinees are drawn from the given distributions. In detail, the ability parameters, the difficulty parameters, and the logarithm of the discriminant parameters are drawn from the standard normal distribution, i.e., $N(0,1)$. And the responses of the examinees are simulated as follows. For the given item response function P_{ij} (such as one-parameter Logistic model (1PLM), two-parameter Logistic model (2PLM) or 3PLM), and for every i, j, compute P_{ij}, and draw a random number r from the uniform distribution $U[0,1]$. If $r \leq P_{ij}$, let $X_{ij} = 1$, else $X_{ij} = 0$. Then the score matrix X is obtained. And the parameters of items and the parameters of the abilities of examinees are estimated;

First, the examinees and items of isolated vertices are from a primary school (McGlohen, 2004). It offers the score matrix of 2000 true examinees and 36 true items, Q matrix, the parameters of items and the parameters, and the estimation of knowledge states. For other attribute hierarchy, according to all possible items and knowledge states, a batch of items is simulated, and examinees are tested to get the score matrix. From the score matrix, parameter estimation is done, and the parameters of items and the parameters of the abilities of examinees are acquired.

Then, item bank and examinees are simulated. Because the items parameters are similar for the items with same attribute hierarchy (Yu, 2001), the parameters of items with same attribute hierarchy are changed a little from the items parameters by (i). Examinees simulation is in the same way.

Thirdly, items bank and examinees are simulated, then the examinees are diagnosed and their abilities are estimated;

Fourthly, the comparison between the diagnostic results and the knowledge state from simulation is done, which results in the ratio of pattern match (*RPM*), and the indexes of estimation, such as The test length (*TL*), precision of ability estimation, i.e. *ABS*, the efficiency of testing (*ET*), the uniformity of exposure (*UE*), the number of item(s) of over exposure (*NIOE*), the overlapping coefficient of testing (*OCT*).

The meanings of all indexes are as follows:

$$RPM = \frac{\text{The number of examinees of pattern match}}{M}$$

here M stands for the number of examinees.

Because of its conceptual importance, the *RPM* index needs to be examined a bit more closely.

Suppose that there are K attributes included in the cognitive diagnostic test. The set of 'true' knowledge states and the set of estimate knowledge states are denoted as *Truestate* and *Estimatestate* as follows, respectively:

Truestate=$\{ \alpha_i \mid \alpha_i$ is the true knowledge state of examinee $i \}$,

Estimatestate=$\{ \hat{\alpha}_i \mid \hat{\alpha}_i$ is estimate knowledge state of examinee $i \}$

If $\alpha_i = \hat{\alpha}_i$, let $h_i = 1$, else $h_i = 0$, and let $RPM = \sum_{i=1}^{M} h_i / M$, where M is the number of examinees.

Obviously, the knowledge states are latent vectors, the 'true' knowledge state is not realistic. But in Monte Carlo simulation, the 'true' knowledge state could be obtained.

$$ABS = \frac{1}{M} \sum_{j=1}^{M} abs(\hat{\theta}_j - \theta_j)$$, here $abs(\hat{\theta}_j - \theta_j)$

stands for the absolute value of the difference of the true ability of the j-th examinee and its estimation. The smaller its value is, the better the precision of ability estimation is.

$$TL = \frac{\sum_{j=1}^{M} L_j}{M}$$

Here L_j stands for the test length of examinee j.

$$ET = \frac{\sum_{j=1}^{M} \inf_j}{\sum_{j=1}^{M} L_j}$$

Here $\inf_j$ stands for the information of examinee j. ET stands for the average information of all items.

$$UE(\chi^2) = \sum_{i=1}^{N} \frac{[A_i - (\sum_{i=1}^{N} A_i / N)]^2}{\sum_{i=1}^{N} A_i / N}$$

Here N stands for the number of items of item bank, A_i stands for the ratio of exposure of i-th item ($A_i = \dfrac{\text{the usage times of the i-th item}}{M}$), the smaller is χ^2, the safer is the CAT and more uniform the exposure is.

$$OCT = \frac{TO_{all} / C_M^2}{(\sum_{j=1}^{M} L_j) / M} = \frac{2TO_{all}}{(M-1)\sum_{j=1}^{M} L_j}$$

Here TO_{all} stands for the number of items, $TO_{all} = \sum_{i=1}^{N} C_{m_i}^2$, m_i stands for the usage times of the *i*-th item. *OCT* is less, implying that the possibility of same items among items examinees answer, the security of test is higher.

NIOE is an index which is dependent on the predetermined exposure rate. In this paper, the rate is equal to 0.2, which is the lowest boundary, i.e., the number of items whose exposure rate is greater than 0.2 is included and cumulated.

The results of experimental tests are shown in Table 3. The result from isolated vertices with 6 nodes is described. 3000 examinees and 3000 items are simulated, the length of testing limited to 30 items. From Table 3, examinees' knowledge states are well diagnosed and the precision in examinees' abilities estimation is satisfying.

From Table 3, the *RPM* is higher than that provided by Henson and Douglas (Henson & Douglas, 2005) since the correct classification rates of attribute patterns (which identifies with the *RPM* here) for 8 attributes case is less than 0.4 for DINA and RUM models. For 4 attributes case, the *RPM* is no more than 0.948 for DINA model, it is no more than 0.86 for RUM.

For the accuracy of estimate ability is high and the other indexes for evaluating the CAT are available.

CONCLUSION

The present paper gives the theory about CD-CAT based on FCA and constructs CD-CAT. Attribute hierarchy is rationally classified into diamond-shaped, tree-shaped and isolated vertices. The basic structures construct attribute hierarchy with one start node and attribute hierarchy with multi-start-nodes. An *Ea* matrix from an attribute

hierarchy is served as a formal context and forms a concept lattice. The number of concepts of the concept lattice equals to that of rows of the *Ea* matrix for the attribute hierarchy with one start node, and the result is the same except for the concept, the set of attribute of which is empty set for the attribute hierarchy with multi-start-nodes. The concept lattice is also hierarchy structure. If a concept has a lower neighbor, then the set of attributes of the concept is subset of that of its lower neighbor, and the number of attributes is 1 less than that its lower neighbor. The concept lattice is suitable to be a model of cognitive diagnosis. For an examinee, there are two sub-lattices of the concept lattice. One is the examinee's concept lattice of cognitive diagnosis, and the other is the examinee's concept lattice of remedial instruction if he/she needs according to the concept the examinee wants to reach. The lower bound of the examinee's concept lattice of cognitive diagnosis is the upper bound of the examinee's concept lattice of remedial instruction. Cognitive diagnosis is the procedure of searching the lower bound of an examinee's concept lattice of cognitive diagnosis. A remedial instruction with minimal cost can be gotten from the examinee's concept lattice of remedial instruction. An initiatory and systemic CD-CAT has been designed. As for cognitive diagnosis in CAT, Monte Carlo study shows the result is satisfying.

Concept lattice is one good tool of knowledge representation. The concept lattices from *Ea* matrices describe the relation among items; teaching result is required to be known and cognitive

Table 3. The results of experimental tests

Attribute hierarchy	SIB	RPM	ABS	TL	ET	UE	NIOE	OCT
A tree-shaped	3000	89.57%	0.19	25.70	0.92	23.12	20.12	0.11
Isolated vertices with 6 nodes	2500	99.16%	0.26	27.32	0.54	48.49	29	0.13
Figure 1	500	98.84%	0.25	25.30	0.76	33.11	24.20	0.12
Figure 7	500	94.26%	0.20	22.14	0.89	46.40	27	0.14

NOTE: SIB stands for the size of item bank.

diagnosis can provide the detail information. So CD-CAT based on FCA benefits intelligent tutoring systems.

The theory in the present paper is the modification of Q-matrix theory. It is known that a concept in $L(E)$ can express a typical examinee or a typical item. For a concept (a typical examinee/item), searching out the concepts which the concept is less than or equal to ($\leq$) can get the typical examinee's expected response pattern. In fact, the set of ideal response pattern could be obtained by the typical examinee's concept lattice of cognitive diagnosis. Hence, the theory of this paper is also the modification of RSM.

A first perspective concerning this work consists of the validation of the efficiency of remedial instruction. It seems that the CAT model is flawless. In fact, it is always difficult to construct attribute hierarchy, so another perspective would be transferring concepts to items, which benefits the generation of items (Isaac et. al., 2003). Attributes marking is also a problem we should be studied.

ACKNOWLEDGMENT

The work is supported by the Natural Science Foundation of China (Grant No. 30860084), the Natural Science Foundation of China (Grant No. 60263005), the Fund of the Ministry of Education for Doctoral Programs in Universities (Grant No. 8020070414001), the Backbone young teachers Foundation of Fujian Normal University (Grant No. 2008100244), and supported by the Youth Foundation of Humanities and Social Science Research Projects of the Ministry of Education (Grant No. 10YJCXLX049).

REFERENCES

Baker, F. B. (1992). *Item Response Theory: Parameter estimation techniques*. NY: Marcel Dekker Inc.

Bejar, I. I., Lawless, R. R., Morley, M. E., & Wagner, M. E. (2003). A Feasibility Study of On-the-Fly Item Generation in Adaptive Testing. In R.E. Bennett & J. Revuelta (Eds.), *The Journal of Technology, Learning, and Assessment, 2*(3), 3-29.

Cheng, Y. (2008). *Computerized Adaptive Testing-New Developments and Applications*. Unpublished doctoral thesis, University of Illinois at Urbana-Champaign.

DiBello, L., Stout, W., & Hartz, S. (2000). *On identificability of parameters in the unified model for cognitive diagnosis*. Proceeding of the Annual Meeting of Psychometric Society, Vancouver, Canada.

DiBello, L., Stout, W., & Roussos, L. (1995). Unified cognitive/psychometric diagnostic assessment likelihood-based classification techniques. In Nichols, P. D., Chipman, S. F., & Brennan, R. L. (Eds.), *Cognitively Diagnostic Assessment* (pp. 361–389). Hillsdale, NJ: Lawrence Erlbaum Associates.

Dijkstra, E. W. (1959). A note on two problems in connection with graphs. *Numer Math, 1*, 269–271. doi:10.1007/BF01386390

Edys, S. (2009). Quellmalz James W. Pellegrino. Technology and Testing. *Science, 323*(2), 75–79.

Ganter, B., & Wille, R. (1999). *Formal Concept Analysis. Mathematical Foundations*. Springer.

Gierl, M. J., Leighton, J. P., & Hunka, S. M. (2000). Exploring the logic of Tatsuoka's Rule-Space Model for test development and analysis. *Educational Measurement: Issues and Practice*, 34–44.

Hambleton, R. K., & Swaminathan, H. (1985). *Item Response Theory: Principles and Applications*. Boston: Klumer-Nijhoff publishing.

Henson, R., & Douglas, J. (2005). Test construction for cognitive diagnosis. *Applied Psychological Measurement, 29*(4), 262–277. doi:10.1177/0146621604272623

Hoi, K. S. (1990). *Principles of Test Theories.* Hillsdale, NJ: Lawrence Erlbaum Associates.

Kolman, B., Busby, R. C., & Ross, S. (1996). *Discrete Mathematical Structures* (p. 261). Upper Saddle River, NJ: Prentice Hall.

Leighton, J. P., & Gierl, M. J. (2007a). Why cognitive diagnostic assessment? In Leighton, J. P., & Gierl, M. J. (Eds.), *Cognitive Diagnostic Assessment for Education: Theory and Applications* (pp. 3–18). Boston, MA: Cambridge University Press. doi:10.1017/CBO9780511611186.001

Leighton, J. P., Gierl, M. J., & Hunka, S. M. (2004). The attribute hierarchy method for cognitive assessment: A variation on Tatsuoka's Rule Space approach. *Journal of Educational Measurement, 41*(3), 205–237. doi:10.1111/j.1745-3984.2004.tb01163.x

Lin, H., & Ding, S. (2007). An Exploration and Realization of Computerized Adaptive Testing with Cognitive Diagnosis. *Acta Psychologica Sinica, 39*(4), 747–753.

McGlohen, M. K. (2004). *The application of cognitive diagnosis and computerized adaptive testing to a large-scale assessment.* Unpublished doctoral thesis, University of Texas at Austin.

Nilsson, N. J. (1998). *Artificial Intelligence: A New Synthesis.* San Francisco, CA: Morgan Kaufmann.

Shuqun, Y., Shuliang, D., & Qiulin, D. (2010). The Incremental Augment Algorithm of *Qr* matrix. *Transactions of Nanjing University of Aeronautics and Astronautics, 27*(2), 183–189.

Tatsuoka, K. K. (1983). Rule Space: An approach for dealing with misconceptions based on item response theory. *Journal of Educational Measurement, 20*(4), 345–354. doi:10.1111/j.1745-3984.1983.tb00212.x

Tatsuoka, K. K. (1991). *Boolean algebra applied to determination of universal set of knowledge states. RR-91-44-ONR* [R]. Princeton, NJ: ETS.

Tatsuoka, K. K. (1995). Architecture of knowledge structure and cognitive diagnosis: A statistical pattern recognition and classification approach. In Nichols, P. D., Chipman, S. F., & Brennan, R. L. (Eds.), *Cognitively Diagnostic Assessment* (pp. 327–361). Hillsdale, NJ: Lawrence Erlbaum Associates.

Tatsuoka, K. K., & Tatsuoka, M. M. (1997). Computerized cognitive diagnostic adaptive testing: effect on remedial instruction as empirical validation. *Journal of Educational Measurement, 34*(1), 3–20. doi:10.1111/j.1745-3984.1997.tb00504.x

U.S. House of Representatives. (2001). *Text of No Child Left Behind Act.* Cheng, Y., & Cheng, H. (2007). *The modified maximum global discrimination index method for cognitive diagnostic CAT.* In D. Weiss (Ed.), Proceedings of the 2007 GMAC Computerized Adaptive Testing Conference.

Yang, S., Ding, S., Cai, S., & Ding, Q. (2008). An Algorithm of Constructing Concept Lattices for CAT with Cognitive Diagnosis. *Knowledge-Based Systems, 21*(8), 852–855. doi:10.1016/j.knosys.2008.03.056

Yu, J. (2001). The analysis on different cognitive trait items with Item Response Theory. *Journal of Nanjing Normal University Social Sciences, 1*, 99–103.

Section 3
Development of Practical Systems

Chapter 11
Adaptivity in ProPer:
An Adaptive SCORM Compliant LMS

Ioannis Kazanidis
University of Macedonia, Greece

Maya Satratzemi
University of Macedonia, Greece

ABSRACT

Adaptive Educational Hypermedia Systems provide personalized educational content to learners. However most of them do not support the functionality of Learning Management Systems (LMS) and the reusability of their courses is hard work. On the other hand some LMS support SCORM specifications but do not provide adaptive features. This article presents ProPer, a LMS that conforms to SCORM specifications and provides adaptive hypermedia courses. ProPer manages and delivers SCORM compliant courses and personalizes them according to learner's knowledge, goals and personal characteristics. In addition learner's progress and behavior is monitored and useful feedback is returned to tutors. ProPer will be used for an adaptive Java Programming course distribution to CS1 students. Statistical feedback will be gathered by tutors in order to improve course effectiveness. The technology background is briefly given and the system's architecture and functionality are analyzed.

INTRODUCTION

The nature of the Internet is an ideal platform for beliefs and data sharing all over the world. As a consequence the Internet is used for knowledge distribution. Over the last years connection speeds have become faster and the coverage of the Inter-

net's global population has grown impressively. Thus, more quantitative and qualitative data can be delivered to a larger number of people. Nowadays, knowledge from almost all domains and sciences is distributed via the Internet. The main advantage of web-based learning is the ability to deliver educational content to a wide number of learners regardless of their place of lodging, age or traditional constraints such as study time. Further-

DOI: 10.4018/978-1-60960-539-1.ch011

more, web-based courses support asynchronous learning processes and require less development and maintenance efforts than traditional ways of knowledge distribution. They can be used either as supplementary to directly-communicated education, complementing the conventional educational process or as an independent integrated solution for distance learning.

Learners with different personal characteristics, culture, needs, and previous knowledge can study a proposed learning content. Moreover, learners can navigate freely inside a course or visit a variety of pages, even when not related to the course, in various ways according to their goals and personal characteristics. This, however, can simultaneously be a weakness of web-based courses since they cannot satisfy the wide range of learners' needs. A course or a system that is designed with a particular class of learners in mind may not suit learners of another class (Weber, 1999). A learner may be confused or overwhelmed by the variety of options and functions a system provides. More so, a learner can feel that a course is either too easy or too difficult for their knowledge level. Furthermore, it is possible for a learner to become "lost in hyperspace" (Conklin, 1987) not knowing where they are nor how to get to where they want to (Murray et all, 2000). Research has documented major problems of web-based courses related to the above situations. These problems summarized in (Murray et all, 2000) are Disorientation, Cognitive Overload, Narrative and conceptual flow, and Content readiness. Consequently, a possible solution to these problems could be the development of web-based applications that offer interactivity and adaptability (Weber, 1999).

Adaptive Educational Hypermedia Systems (AEHS) were introduced as a promising solution. These systems integrate several technologies from both hypermedia systems and Intelligent Tutoring Systems (ITS), by combining both the tutor-driven learning process of ITS and the flexibility of a student centered Hypermedia System (Eklund & Zeilenger, 1996). With AEHS the navigation process, the educational content and its presentation can be dynamically personalized to a particular learner, according to their individual needs, characteristics, goals and current progress. Therefore, with these systems each learner can have both an individual view and navigation through the educational content that hypermedia systems deliver.

The evolution of the Internet and e-learning led to the appearance of Learning Management Systems (LMS). Nowadays the use of an LMS is a very popular way to distribute learning content to the end-user. However, the use of LMS raises some issues. A course distributed by a LMS most times cannot be used by another system due to incompatibility. In addition, sometimes after an update of the LMS, hosted courses must also be updated in order to be distributed properly. Constituting specifications for all the learning units of educational content is required in order for the above problems to be avoided. Some of the most common e-learning and metadata specifications and standards that were applied are SCORM, LOM, IMS, AICC etc. SCORM, is at present the most popular specification. SCORM (ADL, 2004) known as Shareable Content Object Reference Model was proposed by the Advanced Distributed Learning (ADL) initiative and it counts on previous standards from other organizations (AICC, ARIADNE, IMS, IEEE LTSC). Its goal is to provide courses that can be interoperable (operate with a variety of operating systems, hardware etc.) and durable (no modifications required after system software updates). Respectively, SCORM provides reusable educational content by different courses and supports its indexing so as to achieve better accessibility. Consequently, a SCORM compliant course can be distributed by any SCORM compliant LMS. Thus, better quality courses can be delivered by more LMS to the end-user.

This article presents a system called ProPer, whose name comes from the initial characters of the Greek words "PROsarmostiko PERivallon" that mean Adaptive Environment. ProPer is an integrated environment that provides administration facilities and conforms to SCORM specifications but at the same time provides adaptive and adaptable web-based courses to learners. It comprises a combination of an adaptive hypermedia system (AHS) and a LMS, while providing a variety of additional educational features for the learner (Java Editor, dynamic F.A.Q. Draft notes etc) and the teacher (course-user statistics, courses management option etc.). It therefore takes advantage of the strengths of both systems.

Related Work

According to Brusilovsky (2004) the first adaptive hypermedia systems were developed in the early 1990s. Since then, several adaptive systems have been developed and can be distinguished into three generations. First generation systems (1990-1996) were experimental and developed to explore innovative ideas (Brusilovsky, 2004). However, the rapid increase of Internet use in the mid-1990s led researchers to develop a second generation of AEHS intended to help with real world problems (Brusilovsky, 2004).

Till 2002 the majority of the web-based courses relied on LMSs and not AEHS. Nevertheless, AEHS are not inferior to LMSs but it seems that they cannot be adapted to the needs of practical Web-based education (Brusilovsky, 2004). Researchers have been working on this following several streams. One of these streams focuses on new features such as system interoperability and content reusability, applying a number of standards stated above. Since 2002 these new projects have comprised the third generation of AEHS.

Many of the systems from all the generations are similar to our prototype. Some of them are the following (Brusilovsky, 2004):

ELM-ART is an intelligent Web-based tutor for LISP. It was one of the first adaptive systems and many of the posterior adaptive systems have their roots in it. KBS-HyperBook is an adaptive hypermedia system for an introductory course on computer science (CS1), which uses the constructivist educational process. The Knowledge Sea system generates links relevant to the content studied by the learner.

Some adaptive systems provide functionality to authors to develop adaptive courses such as:

InterBook is a tool for authoring and delivering adaptive content following ELM-ART's adaptive methodology. NetCoach is similarly a tool which supports the development of adaptive hypermedia and derives from ELM-ART. AHA! is an open source software and compared to the above systems is distinguished for its simplicity. MetaLinks is also an authoring tool that can adapt content of the page depending on where the learner came from.

Other systems rely on Cognitive Styles like:

INSPIRE generates courses separating learner's performance into three levels: Remember, Use and Find. For the presentation of the educational content, learners have to be characterized as one of the following types: Activists, Pragmatists, Reflectors and Theorists. The system uses the same learning material each time focusing on different perspectives of the presented topic according to the above learner types. AES-CS is another system which adopts the Field Dependence/Independence (FD/ FI) styles theory in order to state which instructional strategy can be applied to any particular learner. CSC383 belongs in the same category, which performs adaptive presentations adopting the Felder-Silverman learning style model.

Finally, there are some systems which attempt to follow the new educational content standards such as SCORM. One such is OPAL, whose learning content consists of SCOs (Sharing Content Objects) and uses AEHS techniques. It can be adaptive at the content delivery stage, removing or hiding at any particular time individual types of content. Another system that adopts SCORM standard is VIBORA (Morales, 2003) but it is adapted only to user knowledge evaluating it through tests, and providing the user with extra activities if necessary. On similar axes research was done (Conlan et all, 2002) on systems that can integrate separate adaptive hypermedia services with learning environments. While the above researches try to combine AHS with LMS there are some others like (Monova, 2005) which attempt to use SCORM specifications to develop adaptive courses. However, they cannot provide adaptive techniques such as adaptive link annotation, which is discussed in detail later.

ProPer's strength through the above systems is that it provides a variety of LMS functionality and conforms to SCORM specifications that AHS do not support. Furthermore, it provides adaptive features in one integrated environment that most of the SCORM compliant systems cannot do.

TECHNOLOGY BACKGROUND

In this section the technology background that ProPer adopts is presented. ProPer uses technologies both from AHS as well as from SCORM conformant LMS. Adaptive hypermedia technology is first introduced and SCORM standard and LMS technology follows.

Adaptive Hypermedia Technology

A general structure comprising mainly of three components is adopted by almost all the AHS. These components are the domain model (DM), the user model (UM) and the adaptation module (AM).

In brief, the domain model represents the domain knowledge of the system. The user model represents the learner's knowledge of the domain as well as his/her individual characteristics. The adaptation module defines the adaptation rules that point the way that an adaptation will be applied and which items will be adapted.

Domain Model

The role of the DM is to represent the knowledge about the teaching domain. Although many types of domain models have been applied, a typical DM could be divided into three layers.

The first layer consists of concepts. Concepts are elementary pieces of knowledge. The amount of domain knowledge that every concept represents can differ between systems depending on the domain size, the application area and the designer's choice (Brusilovsky, 2003). Each concept can correspond to one or more web pages that comprise the second layer. A web page consists of smaller fragments such as text, images, animation etc (Prentzas & Hatziligeroudis, 2001). These smaller fragments constitute the third layer of the domain model.

The simplest form of the domain model is when concepts are independent. On the other hand, the domain model is sometimes more complex, where concepts can have relationships with each other and constitute a conceptual network which represents the domain's structure (Brusilovsky, 2003). The most popular relationship between concepts is the hypertext link when a concept is linked to another. Another usual relationship is that of the prerequisite. A concept is a prerequisite of another when the learner should first have read the first concept before visiting the second. Other relations are the "part of" when some concepts are part of another concept and the "is a" relation which links a concept to others that are its typical instances (Prentzas & Hatziligeroudis, 2001).

User Model

An AHS has to be aware of user's initial and current knowledge of the domain, as well as of his/her individual characteristics. All this information about the user is stored into the User Model (UM) and can be separated into two main categories (Kavcic, 2000).

The first category contains the information about user knowledge of the domain. It stores data about the user for each concept of the DM. This data can be the user's estimated knowledge, study time etc. The second category contains all the domain independent information about the user such as user profile and individual characteristics, preferences, learning style etc. The UM data can be either static when gathered during the initialization of the UM using tests and forms and does not change during the educational process (user individual characteristics, preferences, capabilities etc), or dynamic when it is collected during the learning process (learner's study progress, current knowledge, actions taken, navigation preferences etc.) (Cormona & Cionejo, 2004; Kavcic, 2000). Most times, learner's personal characteristics are static data while their knowledge is dynamic. Sometimes the user, in the middle of a course has the right to modify data that generally is considered static, like their learning goals, previous knowledge, preferences etc. Even if the user model can store a lot of information, special care should taken in order for the UM not contain more than the necessary information so that the system is not overburdened with useless interactions (Cormona & Cionejo, 2004).

Several techniques have been developed for UM construction. The most widely used technique is the overlay model, where user's knowledge of the domain is considered as a part of the expert's knowledge in the particular domain (Kavcic, 2000). The UM stores a value (binary, qualitative or integer quantitative) for every domain model concept that represents user's knowledge on this concept (Brusilovsky, 2003). The requisite data can be obtained either by a test (data about knowledge or cognitive style etc.), by learner's declaration (user goals, cognitive style, user preferences etc.) or from learners interaction with the system. One simpler technique is the stereotype model (Kavcic, 2000). Stereotypes define specific classes of users with common characteristics. When a user adopts a stereotype, s/he is categorized into the corresponding class inheriting its properties. The stereotype and overlay models can be combined by initially categorizing users applying stereotypes and then gradually redefining this model as an overlay model acquiring data from the user's progress into the course (Brusilovsky, 1998). Other techniques of user knowledge representation are the perturbation or buggy model, where a part of the DM and some user misconceptions are placed in a group which represents user knowledge. Finally there are some models based to uncertainty (Prentzas & Hatziligeroudis, 2001).

Adaptation Module

The AM, through a set of rules, applies various adaptation technologies in order to adapt courses to the user.

AEHS have inherited adaptation technologies both from ITS and AHS. According to Brusilovsky there are two main groups of adaptation hypermedia technologies in AEHS: the adaptive presentation which provides content-level adaptation and the adaptive navigation which reside in the link-level adaptation of the system (Brusilovsky, 1998).

Adaptive presentation can be applied via text and multimedia adaptation technologies. According to this technology, a hypermedia page is dynamically generated by a number of educational content elements (texts, images, audio, video, animation), properly selected so that it is appropriate to the knowledge, goals and other characteristics of the particular user. Many systems provide a full or a kind of adaptive presentation such as AHA! and INSPIRE.

Adaptive navigation support is divided into (Brusilovsky, 1998):

- **Link hiding:** when system hides a link to an inappropriate concept for study, displaying only a simple text;
- **Link disabling:** when the user can see the link but cannot click on it (Prentzas, 2001);

- **Link removal:** when the system removes an inappropriate link (Prentzas, 2001);
- **Link sorting:** when the sequence of links can be changed;
- **Link annotation:** when links are annotated corresponding to the user model;
- **Direct guidance:** where the system proposes the next best concept for study; and finally
- **Hypertext map adaptation:** when the system provides and changes appropriately a graphical representation of the link structure like AHA! does.

Almost every AEHS uses one or more of the adaptive navigation support technologies.

SCORM Technology

SCORM is a set of technical specifications for the development of web-based instruction content. It describes how to create web-based educational content, how this content can be delivered by SCORM compliant LMS and what a LMS must do in order to deliver and track that educational content. There are three main parts of the SCORM technical specification: the Content Aggregation Model (CAM), the Run-Time Environment (RTE) and the Simple Sequencing and Navigation specification (SSN).

CAM describes the format of the content structure (using Extensible Markup Language (XML)), how to package the content components for exchange between SCORM compliant systems, how to describe them and how to define sequencing information for those components (ADL, 2007). CAM is made up of five components: i) Assets which are the most basic form of data that can be delivered to a web-client like image, sound, text etc. ii) Sharable Content Objects (SCOs) that are collections of one or more assets. Unlike assets SCOs can communicate with the LMS. iii) Activities: a learning activity may provide a SCO or Asset to the learner or it can just be composed

of sub-activities. iv) Content Organization which is a map that shows how the structured units (activities) relate to one another and v) Content Aggregation which is a virtual map that describes the composition of related content objects so that the whole set can be delivered to the learner.

The second part of SCORM specification is the RTE, which deals with requirements about: the delivery of a content object, the way a content object communicates with a compliant LMS, the information a content object has to track, and the way a LMS manages that information. SCOs can communicate via an API Instance with the LMS and retrieving or storing data like score, time limits etc.

The SSN is based on the IMS Simple Sequencing Specification. It introduces a set of sequencing and navigation rules which describe the navigation inside a course. All the SCORM compliant LMS should interpret these rules in a consistent manner.

To sum up SCORM concerns the tagging, packaging, delivering and communicating of the learning content and assumes the presence of a LMS for the learning content distribution. In SCORM, learning content consists of Sharable Content Objects (SCOs). Each SCO includes one or more Assets. The SCOs can communicate with the LMS in order to retrieve or store data. ADL has developed a LMS, which using a Run-Time Environment (RTE) implements SCORM and its specifications. As described later ProPer comprises an extension of SCORM 2004 RTE.

SYSTEM ARCHITECTURE

The System's architecture is a combined architecture of SCORM LMS and AEHS. As shown in simplified form, in figure 1, we adopt the typical SCORM Run Time Environment (RTE) structure adding an adaptation module and extending the preexistent Domain and User Models. Thus, the prototype involves four main modules:

Figure 1. Architecture of the system

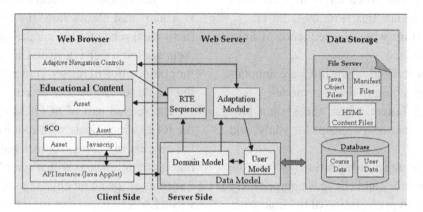

- the Domain Model that represents the domain knowledge of the system,
- the User Model that represents the particular user's knowledge of the domain as well as his/her individual characteristics; both these models comprise the Data Model of the system,
- the Adaptation Module (AM) which interacts with DM and UM in order to provide adaptive navigation to the course, and
- the RTE Sequencer triggered by course navigating controls, it interacts with DM and delivers the appropriate educational content to the learner.

Educational content can be delivered either as Sharable Content Objects (SCOs) or Assets. While SCOs can interact with DM and UM via a specific SCORM specified API Instance and provide some kind of adaptation, Assets, are static hypermedia content (text, images etc.). Finally, for data storage we use both a Database and File server.

Domain Model

The domain model represents system's domain knowledge, providing the essential educational content, in forms of concepts with specific properties and relationships between them. ProPer's DM contains the entire mandatory data from

SCORM Content Aggregation Model and SCORM RTE Data Model (ADL, 2007), for every single concept of the course. All the information of the DM is stored into a Java Object File and in the system's Database in a Table entitled "ItemInfo". Moreover, additional data, required for the adaptation process, was added to ProPer's DM. A boolean variable that states the learner's option to manually define whether or not s/he has learned the corresponding concept of a unit has been appended to the ItemInfo table. Furthermore, new tables were created that store information about groups of goals for different classes of learners, and Frequent Asked Questions (FAQ) for every course unit with their related answers.

The DM of every course originates from a course manifest file, comprised of course structure and concept properties (like the relationship data of the concepts, concept weight etc.), course educational content and tutor preferences for each course unit that are acquired by the system's forms.

As presented in Figure 2, each concept (SCO) is structured from one or more topics (web pages) and each topic contains some elementary pieces of knowledge named Assets (text, images etc.). Every SCO has some attributes that define its position inside a course, its relationship with other SCOs, its weight in the course's total score, the minimum local score in order to consider the study of that SCO successful, its behavior under

Figure 2. Domain and user models

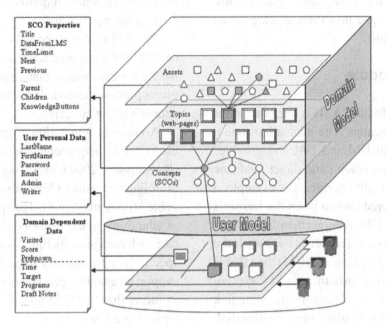

specific learner's actions, the options that a learner will have when studying content connected to a particular SCO and FAQ relative to SCOs content.

User Model

ProPer provides adaptation according to user model information. A multilayered overlay model is used for user knowledge representation, like the majority of AEHS. The User model is comprised of three main categories of data: i) user knowledge of the domain, ii) user actions and goals (time spent studying a concept, number of visits, goals) and iii) domain independent data (such as, user name, password, mail, language and privileges). A graphical representation of the UM and its connection with DM is shown in Figure 2.

User personal data is retrieved through the registration of the user and is static. For user knowledge representation, like the majority of AEHS, we use a multilayered overlay model which consequently follows the domain structure. Its DM unit consists of several corresponding data, which are in a number of different layers. The first layer

stores navigation history, data that presents if the learner has studied a particular concept and if s/he has actually visited the corresponding web page. The second layer contains learner's estimated knowledge on a particular concept. The learner's estimated knowledge is derived from the study of a concept and is represented as a percentage score. The third layer describes the learner's previous knowledge of the domain and can be declared initially or during the course in an appropriate form. Consequently, by this data being stored in different layers enables an independent update to take place. Therefore, user knowledge data from one layer does not overwrite identical data from another layer.

The third category of data stores the time a learner spends on a specific concept, the number of times that s/he has visited the web page and whether or not a concept is considered one of his/her goals. The user goals model is a combination of the overlay and stereotype models since user can manually define his/her goals (overlay model) or select one of the tutor's created groups of goals according to a category i.e. novice – expert (stereotype model). Finally, learner's draft notes, feedback for tutors and Java Programs are stored for every course unit.

Adaptation Module

The Adaptation Module (AM) is responsible for the system's adaptation. The adaptation model interacts both with UM and DM and provides link annotation (see below) and direct guidance through a set of adaptation rules. For example, a concept is considered known when the learner's score (retrieved by UM) is bigger than the required minimum concept score (retrieved by DM). If the user already knew that concept (UM) then that is also considered known. In both cases a "√" symbol appears on the title icon of the corresponding link in the Table of contents (adaptive navigation-link annotation). Some adaptation rules are presented in a simplified way below:

if (studyScore > requiredMinimumScore) OR (preknowledge) then known=true

if (known) then print "√" over the corresponding title icon

if (numberOfVisits>0) then visited = true

If (visited) then print an open book.

if (isGoal and !known and !current and !suggestedFound and requiredMinimumScore >0 and...) then {suggested = true; suggestedFound =true}

If (suggested) print a green book

All the rules above concern the system's adaptive annotation and have been placed into a javascript file named "mtmcode.js". The data required by the rules is comprised of the DM and UM data, which has been retrieved from the Java Object File and Database. The corresponding code has been placed into the file code.jsp of the RTE.

Furthermore, a new function was created for the direct guidance feature.

The AM is also responsible for the store procedures of the required adaptation data. Thus new jsp files were created that acquire and store the user's previous knowledge of the domain and the course's target concepts.

Additional adaptation rules are applied by the SCORM Sequencing and Navigation Model (Brusilovsky, 2004), providing link hiding, link disabling and random link order to the links in the Table of contents. SCORM can provide some kind of adaptivity in the event that the course author takes advantage of its functionality. Thus, under specific conditions and rules SCOs are able to support an adaptive presentation of their contents in forms that SCORM specification and course authoring allow.

RTE Sequencer

The RTE Sequencer is the actual sequencing engine that any SCORM compliant LMS has. It is triggered by course navigating controls, interacts with DM and delivers the appropriate educational content to the learner. Its main operation is to set up the user navigation process applying SCORM specifications and rules. When a learner chooses one of the navigation options, RTE Sequencer has to execute the navigation process. If adaptive navigation control (direct guidance) is chosen, RTE Sequencer cooperates with the AM in order to complete the operation.

SYSTEM ADAPTIVITY AND ADAPTABLE FUNCTIONALITY

Our prototype is a LMS that provides adaptive hypermedia courses adopting SCORM standards and specifications. Adaptive functionality can be provided in two ways: using the system's Adaptation Module or taking advantage of SCORM func-

Figure 3. Table of contents and symbols' explanation

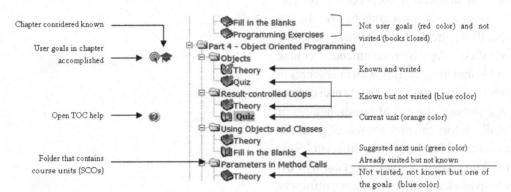

tionality at the course authoring phase; designing a course in tis way provides a kind of adaptation.

Adaptive navigation: ProPer provides adaptive navigation in two ways. First, via the AM through which direct guidance and link annotation are provided. Direct guidance is provided with a "Next" button on the screen and delivers the most appropriate material for study according to current UM. The second way is with link annotation where all links in the Table of contents are annotated properly according to UM. Links are annotated for five instances: already visited links, links whose corresponding concepts are considered known, links that constitute learner's goals, links of the current opened web page, and finally the proposed next link for study. Moreover, the system respectively at the course and main units levels, annotates whether they are considered known and whether the user goals on them have been accomplished. Figure 3 presents a Table of Contents (TOC) screenshot with symbol explanations.

Another two adaptive navigation techniques, link hiding and link disabling are supported (such as AHA! and Anes) with appropriate course design. These techniques plus random link order can be applied with specific SCORM conditions to the course's DM.

Adaptive presentation: Like the majority of AEHS our system provides adaptive presentation. Adaptive presentation can be provided utilizing SCORM functionality. In SCORM a course can involve a number of objectives. The author can write conditions that let the system present content in a specific way, counting the completion of the objectives. This means that course structure and HTML files corresponding to educational content have to be designed in an appropriate way. In this way the author can apply much, more or less, intelligent course built-in functionality, such as: adaptive presentation displaying appropriatly selected content of SCO; either provide or not "Back" and "Next" buttons; specify cases to hide the TOC; the appearance of personal messages; define prerequisite concepts; change the design of the presentation, etc.

Adaptable functionality: Learners can modify their UM at any point of the educational operation. They can select their goals like Interbook or they can manually state their previous or current knowledge of the domain. An extra feature was added to help novice learners. Take into account that learners with little or no prior knowledge of the subject may not be capable of defining their goals; the system provides a mechanism to tutors to define some possible sets of goals. Therefore, novice learners can choose one of the alternative sets according to their needs. Furthermore, ProPer provides adaptable functionality to all tutors, who have the option to adapt any SCORM compliant course to their preferences modifying specific attributes of the DM course. Firstly, they can provide

FAQ with their answers for every course concept. Secondly, they can allow a learner to have the option of specifying themselves whether or not they have learned a concept. We recommend all course units provide that functionality with the exception of those units whose role is to estimate user current knowledge through the use of questionnaires or tests. Thirdly, tutors can provide sets of goals for specific classes of learners or for different levels of desired knowledge acquisition. This will especially help novice learners who have difficulty estimating their educational targets on their own.

Additional functionality: Many auxiliary features for both learners and teachers are appended to ProPer. The system provides an interactive FAQ mechanism, inspired by a system called See Yourself IMproved (Tsinakos & Margaritis, 2001). The learner can ask their tutor a question via an html form. The tutor can later answer that question and make it visible to all registered on the course if s/he considers that the answer to this question would be beneficial to other learners. Thus, a database of FAQ can be built, where learners are able to read all the visible questions with their corresponding answers. In the case where tutors have uploaded a course to more than one server, the FAQ data can be exported to a Java Object file and later imported to the other server's course.

Another provided functionality is the draft notes that learners can keep on every course activity. All their notes are stored in the database. The learners have the option to either read only their notes on the current activity or to view all their notes as a whole.

ProPer is intended to support a Java Programming course, thus it will be used for Java Programming instruction. We integrated a Java Editor – Compiler (Figure 4) that enables learners to write, compile and execute Java Programs. In order to compile and execute user programs the Runtime.getRuntime().exec(…) is used. This command calls windows programs. In this case we call javac and java programs followed by appropriate arguments. It is worth noting that the Java

Figure 4. Java editor-compiler

Editor is able to run Java programs that consist of one or more files and classes. Furthermore, a user can predefine keyboard input that is later read by the executed program. The Java editor also supports the program's store and retrieval functions. As presented in the flowchart in Figure 5 after any compilation of a java program, the editor stores the program's current version code, the time that the user spent writing the program, as well as the number of program compilations. Furthermore, a simple grade mechanism counts an estimated program's score according to compilation and program execution output. Appropriate messages help the user in the case of a failed program compilation or execution. Authors can insert optional input text - that will be read during program execution – as well as the desirable execution output for program marking. Authors also have the option of providing the program score's weight in the corresponding unit's final score. Feedback about user programs can be sent to the course tutor. As there is a security issue with the Java Editor functionality, where a person could write and execute a program that harms the server PC, we have taken care of this problem by performing a security check before program

Figure 5. The flow of performing program compilation and execution

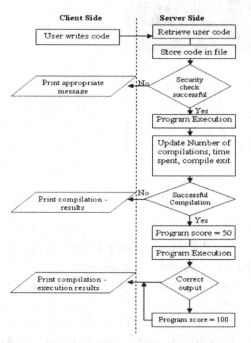

compilation (Figure 5). The Java editor does not allow the user to compile programs with specific commands inside the program's code, such as Runtime.getRuntime().exec(…) which executes windows programs.

Student's motivation playes an important role in education and therefore in distance learning and web courses as well (Jenkins, 2001; Karsenti, 1999). Research on the right ways to motivate students has been carried out (Bonk, 2003), which shows that motivation can be applied in several ways. We believe that providing direct feedback about learner's progress works as a kind of motivation which stimulates learners to carry on studying. ProPer measures progress by providing the learner's with two scores on their progress. One score is for the overall course progress and the other is in regards to the learner's goals. So, at any time the learner knows their percentage of both the course and the goals covered.

The system provides a detailed state of the learner's progress (Figure 6) for any course with

Figure 6. User course status

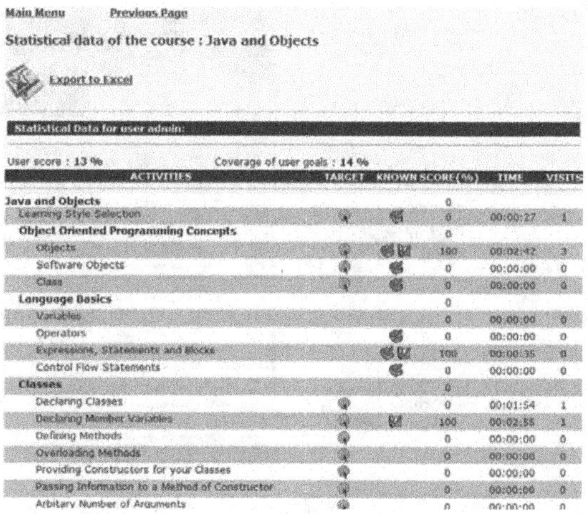

statistics about the overall course score, study time, number of visits for every unit etc. The learner can either view or download in Excel format the state of their course status.

Finally, ProPer provides login/logout services, allows learners to register/unregister for the available courses and permits them to modify their profile.

ProPer as a LMS provides course administration options to tutors. Since our prototype is a SCORM compliant LMS, it lets tutors import, manage and deliver any course developed by a SCORM compliant authoring tool, such as Reload and Trident. Once a course is imported the tutor can adapt the course's appropriare model and define sets of goals for different learners' classes. Furthermore, they can define the units where manual knowledge definition will be permitted to the learners. In addition, a number of course parameters can be specified, such as password protection and time limitation to course availability or write brief information about the course. Tutors can also manage a FAQ, course database and check for feedback. Keeping in mind that a course can be uploaded to more than one server, ProPer can save all the above information into a file. Therefore, a tutor who uploads a course to another server can directly import the course's

Figure 7. System's interface

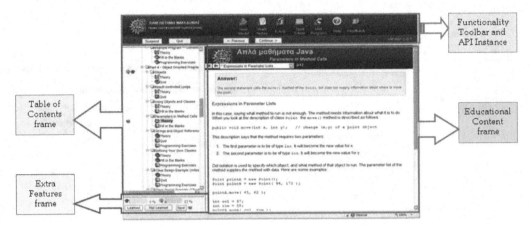

model from the saved file. Additionally, the system provides general statistics about a course related to all learners' behavior Data can automatically be exported to an Excel formatted file for better statistical analysis. Tutors can also see statistics for particular course users, which can assist them to estimate learners' understanding and possible problems in any particular course unit. This will help tutors improve course effectiveness.

SYSTEM IMPLEMENTATION

Our system derives from SCORM 2004 Sample RTE Version 1.3.3 based on the latest SCORM 2004 third edition specification. Therefore, its architecture is typical of a SCORM compliant LMS (Figure 1). We use Apache Tomcat 5.5 as a web and application server and MySQL 5 as a database server. Our prototype resides on a Windows XP operating system. The system retrieves course files initially from a zip file, which contains a manifest xml file and all the html and media required files. The initial DM data that is exported by the manifest file and the tutor's additional data about the course units are stored together in a java object file. Additional data about the course, however, is stored in the database. UM data is stored into separate Java

Object Files while domain independent data of UM is also stored in the database.

For the system interface a multi-frame web page is used. Educational content is delivered from the server, in the form of HTML files, into the "Educational Content frame" (Figure 7) of the web browser. HTML files can include appropriate Javascript that allow them to communicate with the system's DM. In this operation an API instance is involved, that is, an applet on the top frame of the browser (the "Functionality Toolbar and API Instance frame") which mediates between Javascript and DM. The TOC is delivered into the "Table of Contents frame" of the web browser, while adaptive navigation techniques have been applied to it via Java servlets and Java Server Pages (JSP). Current user score, direct guidance button and manual knowledge definition buttons appeared on the "Extra Features frame". All the runtime data about user actions and performance is stored in Java Object Files via JSP and Java servlets. The system creates one Java object file per user and course. Users' Java programs are also stored in.java,.txt and.class files in the user directory. All other supportive functions of the LMS are applied via JSP and the required data is stored in the system's database.

EVALUATION OF PROPER

Evaluation Method

ProPer includes a number of features (either adaptive or not), which need to be tested. Each feature as well as the whole system needs to be evaluated with specific measurements according to the goals of the evaluation. Hence, the evaluation goals have to be determined in advance.

The Technology Acceptance Model (TAM) (Davis, 1989) attempts to anticipate technology acceptance by individual users. According to TAM the adoption of a technology is mainly depended on the perceived ease of use and the perceived usefulness of that technology by the user. Therefore these two determinants potentially affect the actual use of a system by individual users. Actual use can be determined either by the time a user spends using the system or by the frequency of system use.

Thus, one of our goals during the development of the system was to achieve the greatest possible actual use of the system. Consequently usefulness and easy use of the system should be carefully evaluated.

Thereupon the goals of the formative evaluation are to find out:

- any possible effect on the learning process and proposed knowledge of subjects
- any possible effect on the requisite time for completing the course
- the usefulness of either the overall or separate system features (adaptive or not)
- the usability of the system

The formative evaluation of our system is divided into two parts. In the first part experts inspected the system for usability issues and in the second part an end-user evaluation was applied in order to inspect usability issues as well as educational effectiveness.

The Tessmer Model (Tessmer, 1993) is adopted in this study, which identifies the four following phases:

- Expert Review
- One–to-one evaluation
- Small group
- Field trial

These phases are conducted in the above stated order and revision of the system is carried out at the end of each phase completion. However, Expert Review and One to One evaluation are most times carried out simultaneously. At this time the first two phases have been completed and small group evaluation and field trial are going to be applied.

Expert Review

Even though presentations of the informal system to colleagues and simple users, offer initial feedback, formal inspection by experts has proved to be especially effective and useful. The experts should be specialized in either the application domain or computer-human interaction. Expert review does not require a lot of preparation, can be accomplished relatively fast, and at a low cost.

In the expert review a semi-structured interview was used so as to record experts' opinions about ProPer design and its functionality. The system and its functionalities were first introduced to the experts followed by a semi-structured interview based on a questionnaire. The questionnaire, in accordance with the evaluation goals, was based on four aspects: the easy use of the system, the system's usefulness, the inspection of the system's adaptive features, and additional recommendations from experts.

Similar to other studies (Nam&Smith-Jackson 2007; Turner, 1998) two experts acted as evaluators. Their educational background is computer science and they teach computer science courses in both secondary schools and universities.

There was overall positive feedback from the experts along with some remarks and recommendations. In general, they found the system easy to use, although the first expert requested for better help support. Also, the second expert recommended there was clearer annotation of the title of the current activity in the TOC. Actions were taken to comply with these suggestions. A detailed manual for every feature of the system was written and correspondent links added at certain points of the system. In addition, the line's background of the current activity title was colored orange in order to distinguish it from the other titles in the TOC.

The two experts found the system very useful for both students and teachers. Furthermore, they were satisfied with almost all the system's features. One feature that experts questioned was the way the system marks user programs (by program compilation and output). This problem had already been dealt with allowing learners to manually define whether or not they had learned the activities that require program writing.

Moreover, both experts identify the navigation process of the system and the adaptive annotation as the system's strong points. However, the second expert expressed that the annotation symbols were quite difficult. We appended a separate section in the manual giving an in-depth explanation of the annotation symbols and we added a link to the corresponding entity in the manual at the start of the current activity link in the TOC.

Finally, to the question "What do you suggest should be appended to the system?" the first expert proposed providing learners with the option to send feedback to the authors/teachers about the course activities. The proposed feedback option was appended to the system's toolbar.

Teacher Review

In a classroom situation, it is the teacher who decides whether or not to use an AEHS. Studies (Mahmood & Swanberg, 2001; Venkatesh & Davis, 2000) have shown that the perceived usefulness of computer technology provides strong motivation for teachers to use that technology. Similarly, when a system is perceived as being easy to use, this likewise affects the teachers' intention to use that particular computer technology (Will, 2005). Thus, evaluation should additionally check teachers' responses and opinions on the system.

The teacher can either create the entire course or simply find a SCORM ready course and load it onto ProPer. The first case is beyond the scope of this study as it is related to authoring of SCORM courses. In this research, we assume that a teacher has a SCORM course and wants to upload it onto ProPer.

The teachers' evaluation of the system was similar to that of the experts'. We first introduced the system and its adaptive features to the teachers and then we focused on the system's author functionality. A semi-structured interview followed according to a predefined questionnaire. The questionnaire given to the teachers focused on 3 aspects: course insertion and the modulation of course capabilities, the usability, and the usefulness of the system.

Two teachers (Gagne 1992) evaluated ProPer. The first teacher (BE (Civil), MSc, PhD Candidate in Civil Engineering) teaches at the Technological Educational Institute of Kavala, while the second (Bc Mathematics, MSc Medical Informatics) has teaching experience in Greek secondary schools. They both found the system and its features very useful. More specifically, both agreed that all the system's author features were very useful, and in particular the course statistics option as well as the mechanism that the system provides on F.A.Q. The first teacher disputed the need for the option where learners have to manually define whether or not they had learned the content of an activity, in opposition to the second teacher who found it very practical. In the usability aspect, the first teacher expressed doubt as to whether the system was suitable for users with a low level of experience in computers and suggested providing better help. As mentioned earlier, an integrated manual was developed for this purpose. On the whole, both teachers had a positive view about the usability of the system. As far as usefulness is concerned, they found ProPer very effective for course presentation and they would like to use it in the future. The components of the system that they liked the most included the navigation structure, FAQ and the course statistics state. On the other hand, the second teacher noted that if one wants to create a new course they have to know SCORM rules and some programming. Our reply to that was if we want to take advantage of SCORM functionality, the system must conform to this standard and its limitations.

Finally, the first teacher made some comments about the way the statistics results and usernames were printed on the screen. We made all the necessary changes in order to comply with the suggestions.

Student Review

Prior to the field test taking place, we had two students simulate the subjects of the study in order to preclude any unexpected problems that the system may produce. A bug was found at the user registering process. The bug was instantly repaired. The students were asked about the usability and the usefulness of the system and their overall opinion was very positive.

The first part of the system evaluation was accomplished with the students' review. In order to detect possible bugs in the system there will be a follow up of small group evaluations. Following, a field trial will be carried out to ascertain the system's usefulness as well as any weaknesses that may be present.

The field trial will comprise of an adequate number of students participating in the pilot lessons. The students are required to complete a pre-test to determine their previous knowledge on the domain as well as create their personal profiles. According to the pre-test results, the students will be divided into two equal groups. For the first group, the lessons will be conducted using ProPer,

while the second group will apply SCORM RTE 1.3.3. At the end of the sessions, the subjects will fill in a post-test questionnaire in order to check their acquired knowledge. The first group subjects will also complete an assessment questionnaire about ProPer. Moreover, quantitative results will be gathered from the system's records, which will be analyzed and any possible improvements in either the prototype or Java course will be made.

CONCLUSION

In this article, a presentation was made of the system ProPer and its functionality. Further, a brief reference was made to the background technology and similar systems, and finally, the early phases of the assessment process were presented. ProPer is an AEHS system that was developed at the Department of Applied Informatics at the University of Macedonia, Northern Greece. It is a LMS that provides adaptive hypermedia courses adopting SCORM standards and specifications. The main aim of the system is to manage and deliver SCORM compliant courses, adapt those courses accordingly to the UM, provide some auxiliary study tools to learners, and monitor their progress and course effectiveness by providing feedback to tutors. The system supports adaptive navigation and under specific conditions, adaptive presentation of its educational content.

We believe that ProPer will help users avoid the major problems of web courses (Murray et al, 2000) such as:

- Dissoriantation problems can be addressed by the adaptive link annotation that ProPer provides. The results of the first evaluation phase seem to confirm this assumption.
- As stated in (Kazanidis & Satratzemi 2007) we believe that Cognitive Overload can be addressed with the use of adaptive presentation. Moreover, ProPer has been carefully designed with clear options in

order to prevent users becoming confused with its features.

- Content Readiness and Narrative Flow can be addressed both with adaptive annotation techniques and adaptive presentation (Kazanidis & Satratzemi 2007).

Moreover, system auxilary feautures, like FAQ, Java Editor and draft notes help users in their studies. Both experts and tutors agree that these features are very helpful.

In addition, ProPer helps tutors improve their courses providing them with detailed feedback, allowing them to adapt courses to particular classes of learners and reuse the educational SCORM compliant content in other courses.

The essential feature of ProPer is the combination of technologies from both AEHS and SCORM compliant LMS, which is its main advantage over identical systems. Most AEHS do not support SCORM specifications while SCORM compliant systems do not provide the range of adaptivity that our system does.

Concerning adaptivity and adaptive technologies, ProPer follows the typical structure of AEHS using DM, UM and AM. A multilayered overlay model is used and adaptation to user knowledge and goals is applied. Authors can adjust specific elements of the DM and users can change their UM any time during the learning process. ProPer provides adaptive navigation while adaptive presentation can be applied using SCORM functionality. Finally, it must be mentioned that the system provides administration functionality like the majority of LMS.

The system was revised taking into consideration the comments made by experts and tutors. The system's formative evaluation will be completed with the small goup evaluation and the field trial phase. Both the usability and usefulness of the system and its features will be assesed. Finally, learners' comments will be taken into account in order to revise the system and proceed to summative evaluation.

REFERENCES

ADL. (2007). Advanced Distributed Learning, Sharable Content Object Reference Model (SCORM®) 2004 3rd Edition. Retrieved December 20, 2007, from http://www.adl.org

Bonk, J. (2008). Motivational Strategies. Retrieved January 14, 2008, from http://www.indiana.edu/~bobweb/mt_web.html

Brusilovsky, P. (1998). Methods and Techniques of Adaptive Hypermedia. P. Brusilovsky, A. Kobsa, J. Vassileva (Ed.), *Journal of User Modeling and User-Adapted Interaction 6 (2-3), Special Issue on Adaptive Hypertext and Hypermedia*, 87-129.

Brusilovsky, P. (2003). Adaptive navigation support in educational hypermedia: The role of student knowledge level and the case for meta-adaptation. *British Journal of Educational Technology, 34*(4), 487–497. doi:10.1111/1467-8535.00345

Brusilovsky, P. (2003). Developing Adaptive Educational Hypermedia Systems: From Design Models to Authoring Tools. Murray, T., Blessing S., & Ainsworth, S. (Ed.), *Authoring Tools for Advanced Technology Learning Environments: Toward cost-effective adaptive, interactive, and intelligent educational software*, (pp. 377-409). Norwood, Ablex.

Brusilovsky, P. (2004). Adaptive Educational Hypermedia: From generation to generation. *Proc. Fourth Hellenic Con. Information and Communication Technologies in Education (*pp 19-33).

Carmona, C., & Cionejo, R. (2004). A Learner Model in a Distributed Environment. P. De Bra, W. Nejdl (Ed.)., *Third Int'l Conf. Adaptive Hypermedia and Adaptive Web-Based Systems (AH'04), Lecture Notes in Computer Science*, vol. 3137, (pp. 353-359). Berlin, Springer Verlag.

Conklin, J. (1987). Hypertext: An Introduction and Survey. IEEE. *Computer, 20*(9), 17–41. doi:10.1109/MC.1987.1663693

Conlan, O., Wade, V., Gargan, M., Hockemeyer, C., & Albert, D. (2002). An architecture for integrating adaptive hypermedia services with open learning environments. P. Barker and S. Rebelsky, eds., *Proc. ED-MEDIA'2002 - World Conf. Educational Multimedia, Hypermedia and Telecommunications*, (pp. 344-350). Denver, CO, AACE.

Davis, F. D. (1989). Perceived Usefulness, Perceived Ease of Use, and User Acceptance of Information Technology. *Management Information Systems Quarterly*, *13*(3), 319–340. doi:10.2307/249008

Eklund, J., & Zeilenger, R. (1996). Navigating the Web: Possibilities and Practicalities for Adaptive Navigation Support. *Proc. Ausweb96: The Second Australian World-Wide Web Conference* (pp. 73-80), Southern Cross University Press.

Gagne, R. M., Briggs, L. J., & Wager, W. W. (1992). *Principles of instructional design* (4th ed.). Orlando: Harcourt Brace Jovanovich College Publishers.

Jenkins, T. (2001). The Motivation of Students of Programming. *Proc. Integrating Technology into Computer Science Education Conf. (ITiCSE'01)* (pp. 53-56).

Karsenti, T. (1999). Student Motivation and Distance Education on the Web: Love at First Sight? *Proc. Fifth Int'l Conf. Web-Based Learning* (pp. 119-134).

Kavcic, A. (2000). The Role of User Models in Adaptive Hypermedia Systems. *Proc. Tenth Mediterranean Electrotechnical Conference*, Lemesos, Cyprus

Kazanidis, I., & Satratzemi, M. (2007). Adaptivity in a SCORM compliant Adaptive Educational Hypermedia System. *Proc. Sixth International Conference Web-based Learning (ICWL'2007)*, *LNCS 4823*, Springer.

Mahmood, M. A., & Swanberg, D. L. (2001). Factors affecting information technology usage: a meta-analysis of the empirical literature. *Journal of Organizational Computing*, *11*, 107–130. doi:10.1207/S15327744JOCE1102_02

Monova–Zheleva, M. (2005). Adaptive Learning in Web-based Educational Environments. *Journal Cybernetics and Information Technologies*, *5*(1).

Morales, R. (2003). The VIBORA project. G. Richards, eds, *Proc. World Conf. E-Learning in Corporate, Government, Healthcare, and Higher Education* (pp. 2341-2344).

Murray, T., Shen, T., Piemonte, J., Condit, C., & Tibedau, J. (2000). Adaptivity for conceptual and narrative flow in hyperbooks: The Metalink system. *Adaptive Hypermedia and Adaptive Web-based system. Lecture Notes in Computer Science*, *1892*, 155–166. doi:10.1007/3-540-44595-1_15

Nam, C. S., & Smith-Jackson, T. L. (2007). Web-Based Learning Environment: A Theory-Based Design Process for Development and Evaluation. *Journal of Information Technology Education*, *6*, 23–43.

Prentzas, D., & Hatziligeroudis, I. (2001). Adaptive Educational Hypermedia: Principles and Services. *Proc. First Panhellenic Conf. Open and Distance Learning*, Greece. (in Greek).

Prentzas, D., Hatziligeroudis, I., Koutsogiannis, K., & Rigou, M. (2001). The architecture of a Web-based Intelligent Tutoring System for the Instruction of New Informatic's Technologies. *Proc. First Panhellenic Conf. Open and Distance Learning*. Patra, Greece (in Greek).

Tessmer, M. (1993). *Planning and Conducting Formative Evaluations: Improving the Quality of Education and Training*. London: Kogan Page.

Tsinakos, A., & Margaritis, K. G. (2001). See Yourself IMprove (SYIM) Implementing an educational environment for the provision of personalized distance education services and the formulation of student models. *Proc. World Conf. of the Web Society (WebNet 2001)*.

Turner, S. G. (1998). *A Case Study Using Scenario-Based Design Tools and Techniques in the Formative Evaluation Stage of Instructional Design: Prototype Evaluation and Redesign of a Web-Enhanced Course Interface*. Doctoral dissertation, Virginia Polytechnic Institute and State University, Virginia

Venkatesh, V., & Davis, F. D. (2000). A theoretical extension of the technology acceptance model: four longitudinal studies. *Management Science*, *46*(2), 186–204. doi:10.1287/mnsc.46.2.186.11926

Weber, G. (1987). Adaptive learning systems in the World Wide Web, *Proc. Seventh Int'l Conf. User Modeling* (pp. 371-377).

Weber, G. (1999). Adaptive learning systems in the World Wide Web. *Proc. Seventh Int'l Con. User Modeling* (pp. 371-377).

Will, W. M., Andersson, R., & Streith, K. O. (2005). Examining user acceptance of computer technology: an empirical study of student teachers. *Journal of Computer Assisted Learning*, *21*(6), 387–395. doi:10.1111/j.1365-2729.2005.00145.x

This work was previously published in International Journal of Distance Education Technologies, Volume 7, Issue 2, edited by Qun Jin, pp. 44-62, copyright 2009 by IGI Publishing (an imprint of IGI Global).

Chapter 12
The Construction of an Ontology–Based Ubiquitous Learning Grid

Ching-Jung Liao
Chung Yuan Christian University, Taiwan

Chien-Chih Chou
Chung Yuan Christian University, Taiwan

Jin-Tan David Yang
Ming Chuan University, Taiwan

ABSTRACT

The purpose of this study is to incorporate adaptive ontology into ubiquitous learning grid to achieve seamless learning environment. Ubiquitous learning grid uses ubiquitous computing environment to infer and determine the most adaptive learning contents and procedures in anytime, any place and with any device. To achieve the goal, an ontology-based ubiquitous learning grid (OULG) was proposed to resolve the difficulties concerning how to adapt learning environment for different learners, devices, places. OULG through ontology identifying and adapting in the aspects of domain, task, devices, and background information awareness, so that the adaptive learning content could be delivered. A total of 42 freshmen participate in this study for four months to learn Java programming. Both of pretesting and posttesting are performed to ensure that the OULG is useful. Experimental results demonstrate that OULG is feasibile and effective in facilitating learning.

INTRODUCTION

An ontology-based ubiquitous learning grid (OULG) proposed in this study is aim to achieve ubiquitous learning. On the other hand, although

DOI: 10.4018/978-1-60960-539-1.ch012

the components of most current learning management systems conforms to SCORM standards (ADL, 2004), SCORM standards do not govern service and learning procedures between learning management systems, which makes learning services on different learning systems cannot share and communicate. In this sense, although learning management system (LMS) and network infrastructure are widespread, there exists two main problems: incapability between learning management systems, which makes sharing difficult, and the fact that learning material can not be delivered to different types of client devices and to different learner preferences, which fails the fundamental objectives of ubiquitous learning. As network infrastructure is maturing, some scholars, advocating transforming traditional electronic learning to ubiquitous learning, propose realizing the concept of u-Learning through the use of various mobile devices for ubiquitous computing. Most learning management systems, for example, Blackboard (2007), WebCT (2007) and open-source Sakai (2007), Moodle (2007), Claroline (2007), focus more on the authoring and delivery of learning material and assessment and learning progress management, and address less about the statement of environment awareness capability, therefore, learning services can not be easily shared between different learning management systems, despite most Learning Objects, or LOs, conform to SCORM specification.

OULG was constructed with adaptive ontology and ubiquitous computing environment to infer and determine the most adaptive learning contents. Current learning management systems have less description about context awareness capability. Grid services is a method in a grid computing that comprises learning service. The key issue about achieving adaptive learning with grid services is how to adapt learning. Adapting learning refers to making adjustment based on the input and output of a learning process, therefore, adding ontology to ubiquitous learning grid is a way to strengthen adaptiveness. Ontology uses a controlled hierarchy of terminology to describe knowledge structure, abstracting the ontology of concepts, and to distinguish different classes and individuals and can also define the relation between concepts. Therefore in this study, a set of ontology were used to enhance capability of the ubiquitous learning grid in the aspect of seamless

learning. Since the production of learning material could be costly and the components incorporated into learning management are rarely shared and reused, Learning Ontology, or OntoL is used, to rectify this drawback. In addition, Context Awareness Ontology, or OntoCA is used to detect new client devices and, with the reference to learner preference settings, the system can and automatically convert learning material to be more user-friendly.

The study uses current ubiquitous learning grid as foundation and, on the grid middleware, globus toolkit, build prototyping of the OULG. JSP (Java Server Pages) technology is employed to implement Grid portal, while Java-related development technology is employed to develop other components needed for this research, on the Fedora Core, a Unix-like operating system. On the other hand, ontology design is conducted with Protégé (2007), which is developed by Stanford Medical Informatics. In the aspects of learning and context awareness, this research utilizes six ontologies definitions to cover the scope of research: domain ontology, task ontology, service composition ontology, device ontology (FIPA, 2002), preference ontology and adaptation ontology. Although there are numerous parameters and complex rules governing them, this research only look into those parameters relevant to the designing and defining of the Ontology used in the research.

The remainder of this paper is organized as follows: related work are discussed in Section 2. Section 3 details the proposed framework of OULG. Section 4 presents and discusses the system implementation and experimental results. Finally, Section 5 gives conclusions and directions for future research.

RELATED WORK

The works related to our proposed framework are presented here in a way how we leverage existing solutions from grid technologies and ontology to provide the learing adaption.

Grid Technologies

Grid computing owns better abilities of workflow collaboration and sharing resources for integrating e-Learning platforms. The sharing resource of grid computing primarily focuses on direct access to computers, software, data, and other resources, as required by various collaborative problem-solving and resource-brokering strategies emerging in industry, science, and engineering (Foster, 2002). Currently, grid architecture has demonstrated a shift toward service-oriented concepts. For example, web service is a key technology in service-oriented technology. A grid service with web service technologies is a new development trend and gradually obtains enterprise's support. A service can be considered a platform-independent software component, which is described by using a descriptive language and published as part of a directory or registry by a service provider. A service request can then locate a set of services by querying the registry, a process called resource discovery. Moreover, a adaptive service can finally be selected and invoked, which called binding. Service-oriented concepts solve the problems associated with "Naming", and employ open standards and protocols to enable the concepts and solutions for enterprise systems to be viewed.

The Evolution of Ubiquitous Learning

Recently, e-Learning has been widely employed by many enterprises and schools in training or lectures, replacing the conventional ways of learning and effectively saving costs with better efficiency (Abbas, 2005). In case of absence from class and workplace, for example, students and employees can still engage in learning or training anytime through e-Learning system. At present, as more and more people use mobile phones to communicate, a logical extension of e-Learning emerges, which is named Mobile Learning (m-Learning). It has the potential to make learning even more widely available and accessible than the existing e-Learning systems. People could use mobile phones or wireless devices to access the learning systems. Mobile learning could contribute to the quality of education in communication and interaction. It also enable people on the move to learn, and offers opportunities the optimization of interaction between lectures and learners, among learners, and among members of Communities of Practice (COPs) (Brown, 2005).

u-Learning has characteristics of highly mobility and highly embeddedness, which enables people learning at anytime, any place, and any device. Learner conducts learning through learning device and Internet without the limitation of place and space. However, systems like that do not provide personalized learning information and make so consideration of context awareness information. On the other hand, ubiquitous learning, through ubiquitous computational environment, gathers context awareness information anytime, anywhere and with any device, and infer and judge to provide learners with adaptive learning content and sequence. The critical point is providing learners adaptive learning information at perfect timing, in other words, the convenience about learning is not so much about mobility but adding the context awareness capability (Ogata, 2003). It bears more importance to deliver adaptive information regardless of circumstances and embed the information in the learning sequence than merely to allow people to learn on the move. Rogers (2005) also proposed that for u-Learning, indoor learning can be integrated with outdoor learning, enhancing learning performance. If learning performance is to be enhanced, it is essential to make learning easier for learners. In contrast, u-Learning mainly focuses on automatically providing adaptive learning content, options and procedures, minimizing learners' burden for decision-making and inputs and achieving a more convenient learning environment.

RDF, OWL, SCORM, and CC/PP

Resource Description Framework (RDF) is a framework that describes resources on the Internet, which, in concept, is similar to but essentially more than metadata, rather; RDF describes and exchange metadata. There are three important elements to RDF: Resource, Property and Statement. The Resource can be anything that has Uniform Resource Identifier (URI), that is, all Web pages on the Internet, while Property is the name of a known resource, used to indicate the characteristic of resource, and Statement combines Resource, Property and value of their attributes. Other than its fundamental elements, there is also distinctive nature to RDF design, for example, independence; interchange; scalability; Properties are Resources; value can be Resources, Statements can be Resources etc. RDF is a framework built on XML. Because the original XML structure is rather loose, an XML may represent a tree structure, graphs or text strings. On the other hand, RDF is carefully defined to process above-mentioned fundamental element and characteristic; simply speaking; its focus is directed to describing internet resources.

Web Ontology Language (OWL) is a language designed to meet the requirements of the Internet for Ontology, presenting abstract concepts in a structured fashion. The bases of OWL are XML and RDF, therefore; OWL has XML's advantage in format and RDF's in resource description (McGuinness, 2004). However, since OWL is intended to process information content and not to be used by humans, is more thorough and complete than RDF in the aspect of providing Web content and vocabulary. Using standardized content, it would be easier for more machines to decode the content that OWL describes.

SCORM is a standard for e-Learning which combines XML based technologies to define and describe each e-Learning material as a learning object. Different LOs can be inter-recognized so it can exchange among different learning systems that support these standards. Ontology is a concept representation. Cui (2004) propose a kind of flexible educational platform architecture integrated educational ontology for e-learning, which is named OntoEdu.

CC/PP is a standard, which can be used to transmit their capabilities and user preferences for various devices (Klyne, 2003). For example: mobile phone, PDA, and so on. It was originally design to be used when a device requests web content via a browser so that servers and proxies can customize content to the target device. In u-Learning grid, it can be used to detect what kind of device connects to the portal so that broker can send the adaptive learning content service to the client device. Ubiquitous learning should make users be able to learn any information, anytime, anyplace, with any devices.

Ubiquitous Learning Grid with Ontology

Ontology-based ubiquitous learning grid is essentially a ubiquitous learning grid incorporated with ontology, which serves to define domain knowledge in the system and device profile. In this study, instead of using CC/PP, ubiquitous learning grid uses device ontology identify client devices, and it utilizes OWL DL as metadata for reasoning and, to define ontology's class and instance. Therefore, domain knowledge and context awareness information will be presented with ontology. Since the production of learning material for learning management system could be costly, and those components embedded in the system are rarely shared and reused, these problems could be resolved with learning ontology (OntoL). The advantages of using learning ontology are:

1. Consistent terminology: For different domains, sometimes different terminologies are used to represent the same concept (for

example, for grid computing, there are more than two interpretations in Chinese, but the same meaning). Consistent terminology will facilitate the system to search and process learning objects.

2. Easy to manage and divide learning objects: Ontology uses hierarchical architecture to describe domain knowledge, and ontology of a domain is often consisted of different subjects. The author of learning material design the relation between learning objects in the hierarchical architecture based on his/her understanding of the curriculum structure, his/her teaching experience and the characteristic of the lecture. Learning ontology, on the other hand, defines the hierarchical architecture of description of domain. Through learning ontology, the author of learning material can find learning objects that suit the curriculum and uses existing learning resources to edit.

3. Increase the ability to share and the usability of learning objects: Ontology enables authors of learning material to access learning repositories that distributed at different levels on the Internet.

For example, after identifying the year of the learner and the lectures the learner has taken before, the system can infer and decide the best learning content for further learning. Take the subject of grid applications for example, some learners may have taken fundamental lecture on that subject with basic understanding of grid computation and then, through Service Composition Ontology and the inference and conclusion made by domain ontology and task ontology, the system provides the learner the lecture of grid service under the grid applications as the learning material (one of options). In the aspect of adaptability to client devices, device ontology is utilized to identify new devices. At the same time, preference ontology is used to infer with related context awareness parameters while adaptation

ontology is used to provide reference of client device's display capability and to adjust learning content. As long as OULG has device ontology provided by device manufacturers, when a new kind of client device is connect to OULG, OULG can find out attribute information of the device. This information will be used as a criterion to when learning content is converted for output, so that learning content is made adaptive for display in the client device's screen resolution and color capability. In addition, combining ontology and ubiquitous learning grid make it possible to take not only the advantage of ontology's ability in describing domain concept, but also ubiquitous learning grid's adaptiveness and grid's ability to share heterogeneous resources, streamlining learning process. Additionally, it simplifies the operation with portable device, making learning easier.

SYSTEM FRAMEWORK OF OULG

An OULG prototype was proposed in this study. It includes four parts, which will be explained in the ensuing chapters. Figure 1 shows the system architecture of the prototype.

The main purpose of Presentation Layer which deals with the interface with learners. For example, it may contain login/logout, learning material processing, data I/O etc. All of the system functions are mainly presented in this layer. The

Figure 1. System layer of OULG

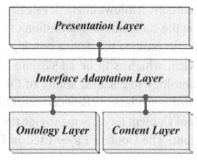

Figure 2. Scenario of conceptual design

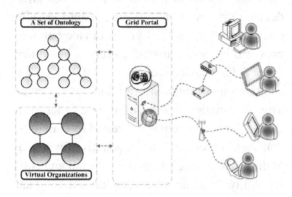

purpose of Interface Adaptation Layer is focused in coordination of the adaptation between upper layer Presentation Layer, and lower layers, Ontology layer and Content layer. The function of Ontology layer focuses on the establishment and definition of Ontology. For example, Learning Ontology and Context Awareness Ontology (OntoCA) use tree-like structure to define Ontology, mainly using format that based on OWL DL to define all Concepts, Statements and Instances. When these definitions pertaining to different domains are made, the capability is necessary for parsing these definition data to correctly determine appropriate content to be presented to learners. Ontology Layer is employed Ontology to enhance capability of OULG to support seamless learning. OntoL and OntoCA can engage in mutual support to derive proper learning content for learners. Furthermore, with its open format and standards, the content of OntoL can be expanded when experts in different domains contribute relevant OntoL. OntoCA, on the other hand, defines variables that concerns user devices and factors that affects learners. It allows client device providers, basing on the standards and definition of Device Ontology, to provide the device ontology of the new device, which is to be added into OULG' device ontology to enhance ability of OULG to identify different kinds of client devices. The main function of Content Layer is to provide the learning content. The Content Layer used in OULG

learning objects that conform to SCORM 2004 standard. These learning objects will be packaged as service and deployed to each virtual organization and registered in the OULG portal registry, so that Grid portal can make use of the learning resources in the portal. And because the learning objects conforming to SCORM 2004 format are used, it is possible for content provider to furnish different content catered for different field, making the learning system more encompassing.

System Prototyping Development

The conceptual design for the OULG was shown in Figure 2. Users are allowed to connect to Grid services portal through different devices, such as, PCs, Laptops, PDAs or Smartphones. Grid portal functions as a broker, which, using reference to preset Device Ontology, identify the client device and its attributes before determining what content to be put forward.

Second, according to the conceptual design, the detailed functionality of OntoL and OntoCA will be designed. In OULG, OntoL is used to manage the interface that concerns learning content, for example, service and learning material. For OULG, service and learning material is like the raw data in a database system, and it contains no standards and definitions about the functionality of the system. Here learning service and learning material and associate them together is defined in OntoL, making the use of learning service and learning material more flexible. On the other hand, OntoCA defines the interface that concerns context awareness, for example, device profiles and user preferences. Through device description, device type can be determined. For example, if a Smartphone is connected to OULG, then using the device description in OntoCA, the information about the make, model number, screen resolution and number of colors of display of the Smartphone can be gathered. With this information, present correct learning content best suited to the display device. User preferences, on the other hand, can add user-friendliness to the learning experience, for example, the information about the location of the learner, when the learner connects to the system, learning objectives etc. Therefore, the OULG can be more user-friendly, providing learning content that best match the user's needs. OULG includes two main parts: OntoCA and OntoL. OntoCA consists of Device Ontology, Preference Ontology and Adaptation Ontology, while OntoL consists of Domain Ontology, Task Ontology and Service Composition Ontology. OntoL mainly handles learning services and learning materials, while OntoCA processes device profiles and user preferences. OntoL will provide learning content for OntoCA to adapt and deliver the adapted content to client device.

Learning Adaptation by Ontology

For this study, Ontology is intended to enhance the adaptability of the system to the needs of learning. For example, Ontology can describe characteristics of a learning service such as target learner, previously-acquired competence (this may be determine by what subjects the learner has studied) and the competence is expected of the learner after learning. All these attributes is placed under Service Composition Ontology to describe, facilitating the system to adapt to different learning situation. Context awareness parameters at least can be current time, place of learning, expected time needed for learning, learning objectives, learning records and client device of learning. These information can be automatically determined by the system or through the interaction with the learners. With these information about the user available, the OntoCA can determine what learning content and procedure would best suit the learner and can achieve personalization by incorporating user preferences. For example, when a user connects to the system while on the commute abroad subway, the user's device will provide the system the information that the user is currently on the subway (parameter: Lplace for

learning place), and he has about 30 minutes learning time (parameter: Ltimeavailable for expected time needed for learning) and the domain skill of learning at this time (parameter: Lgoal for learning objectives). The system can then automatically obtain the time of learning (parameter: Ltime for current time), learning records of the learner has taken with the concept of Grid computing (parameter: Lportfolio for learning records) and the client device (parameter: Ldevice for client device, other parameters may also be obtained, including the make, name and display capability of the device in use). The results of query and inference can be obtained by entering above-mentioned parameters into a set of Ontology in the system, dynamically tailoring learning experience with personal choice, content and sequence. With above-mentioned parameters, OULG will make inference in the following steps:

1. Define classes and individuals for the six Ontology based on the needs of OULG.
2. Check consistency and classification process through the reasoner and then obtain inferred model.
3. Input parameters needed for the six Ontology to OULG.
4. With these input parameters and using specific logic of OULG, OULG search in inferred Ontology model and declared Ontology model to obtain results for output.

Figure 3 shows the how OULG works with Ontology. It can be learned that OULG obtains parameters from user's input or by automatic gathered. In this example, the parameters obtained from user's input and by automatic gathered. The parameters will then be input to the OntoL and OntoCA that have been already established. Through query and inference of Interface Adaptation Layer through the reasoner, learning content can then be adapted. When the adaptation is complete, the adapted content can be forwarded to the Presentation Layer, at which time the content will

Figure 3. Illustration of the OULG works with ontology

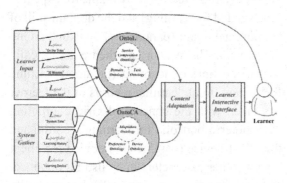

appear in the client device of the user. Let's see another example where adaptive learning content is obtained after the domain skill the learner has entered is inferred. In Preference Ontology, the concept of Skill was defined, which is about the concepts related to domain skills. Therefore, it is used to be the input parameter, L_{goal} to Preference Ontology for the system to begin infer to obtain recommended lecture. Under the concept of Skill, there is MIS related sub-concept, Skill.MIS, which has following statements as shown in Table 1.

From Table 1, it can be seen that Description. Skill.MIS is used to describe the domain skill of

Skill.MIS, while Keyword.Skill.MIS defines the keywords concerning Skill.MIS, to be used for searching. Under Keyword defined the sub-concept of Keyword.Skill.MIS, and in its individual defined related keywords of Skill.MIS, to be used to search for capability index, Capability. The statements of Keyword.Skill.MIS are as shown in Table 2. From Table 2, Skill.MIS contains the individuals of the concept Keyword. Under Capability, there are three Capability defined in this research: Capability.Grid.GridConcept (Capability of Grid concept), Capability.Grid.Grid-Computing (Capability of Grid computing) and Capability.Grid. GridService (Capability of Grid service). From Figure 4, these three Capability are similar concept and have similar Statement. Table 3 lists the Statements for Capability.Grid. GridConcept as an example. From Table 3, it can be seen that Capability.Grid.GridConcept has a corresponding Skill, which is Skill.MIS. From above-mentioned Statement, the model derived after Preference Ontology is inferred can be obtained. That is to say, when the learner enter the keywords about the domain skills he/she wishes to learn, for example, "MIS", "IT" etc, OULG will take these keywords as parameters for infer-

Table 1. Statements of Skill.MIS

Condition	Statement	Protégé Expression
Necessary & Sufficient	Some instances are Skill Skill.MIS	∃ isSkill Skill.MIS
Necessary	Has Description.Skill.MIS as its Description	∃ hasDescriptioin Descriptioin.Skill.MIS
	Has Keyword.Skill.MIS as its Keyword	∃ hasKeyword Keyword.Skill.MIS

Table 2. Statements of Keyword.Skill.MIS

Condition	Statement	Protégé Expression
Necessary & Sufficient	Some instances are Keyword Keyword.Skill.MIS	∃ isKeyword Keyword.Skill.MIS
Necessary	Some instances are Keyword of Skill.MIS	∃ isKeywordOf Skill.MIS

Figure 4. Asserted model of preference ontology

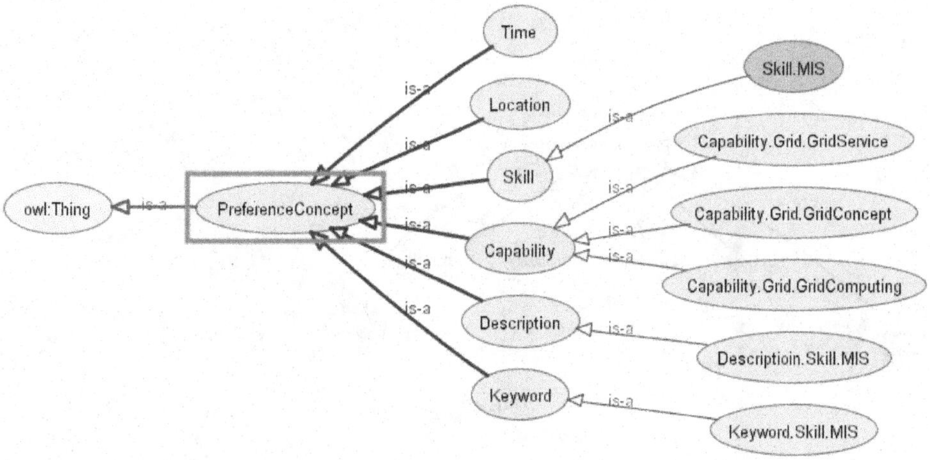

ence and search for individuals that contains these keyword in the class Skill in the Preference Ontology, thusly obtaining corresponding the concept of domain skill. In this example, Keyword.Skill. MIS will be obtained.

As in Figure 5, for the model after classification, OULG will infer that capability index, Capability, which concept is similar to Keyword. Skill.MIS, has Capability.Grid.GridConcept, Capability.Grid.GridComputing and Capability. Grid.GridService. Suppose that learning history, $L_{portfolio}$ covers Capability.Grid.GridConcept, OULG will mark the recommended learning portfolio as learned or it is ignored. Figure 6 illustrates Preference Ontology obtaining Capability from keywords.

Through these capabilities, which are obtained from inference, corresponding lectures can be obtain from domain ontology, learning sequence from service composition ontology and learning

content from adaptation ontology. According to the above-mentioned design of logical structure, the entire OULG system framework was devised, as illustrated in Figure 7. Users can connect to OULG portal using any type of client devices, such as PCs, laptops, PDAs and Smartphones. The connections can be Internet, Intranet, or telecommunication services like GPRS, CDMA and WCDMA. When the OULG portal receives the request of connection from a client device, the portal will acquire the description of the client device based on the device information sent by the client device, and obtained the statement of the device from the already-defined device ontology. This description would be used to coordinate ensuing learning content, forming learning service. After virtual organization in the grid generates service instance of learning object, the instance will be forwarded to the client device for binding. When the binding between service instances is

Table 3. Statements of Capability.Grid.GridConcept

Condition	Statement	Protégé Expression
Necessary	Has Skill.MIS as its Skill	∃ hasSkill Skill.MIS
	Some instances are Capability Capability.Grid. GridConcept	∃ isCapability Capability.Grid.GridConcept

Figure 5. Inferred model of preference ontology

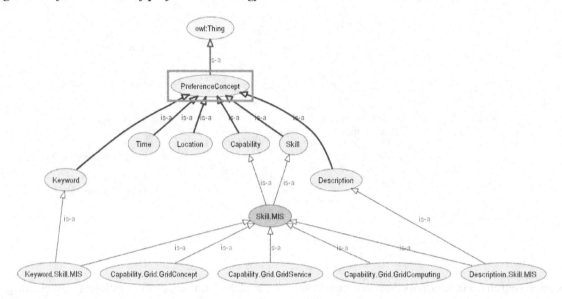

completed, the learner can begin learning and interacting with OULG. Learning records will be recorded through grid service portal, so that learning records from different learning management systems, achieving information sharing, which is a basic concept of using grid service in this study.

SYSTEM IMPLEMENTATION AND EXPERIMENTAL RESULTS

System Environment and Implementation

The methodology used in this study is system development method; its life cycle model uses

Figure 6. Illustration of preference ontology inference

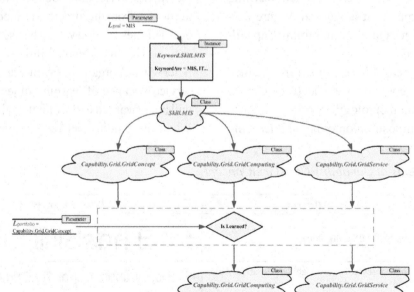

Figure 7. System framework of OULG

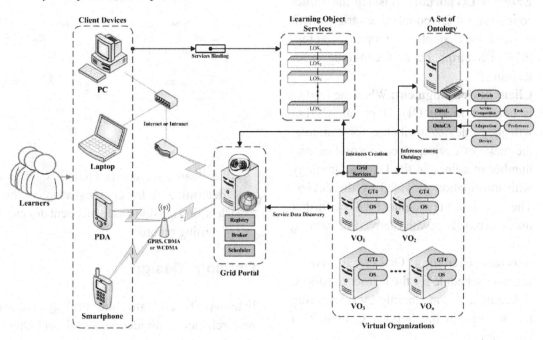

prototyping. Each step in the experiment will be explained in detail, including the operation, role, method, input and output of each step, and were given as following:

1. **Ontology creation:** First, Protégé used to create Ontology needed for OULG, this is mainly done by Ontology provider and experts in each domains. As explained earlier, OULG contains six Ontology: Domain Ontology, Task Ontology, Service Composition Ontology, Device Ontology, Preference Ontology and Adaptation Ontology. Six Ontology will be created in this stage for the use by OULG at a later time.

2. **Learning contents creation:** In this step, the learning content was created that will be used in OULG. Ready-made learning content can be adopted in the research. Since learning content can be scattered in different learning management systems, therefore, resources sharing can be achieved. In the experiment,

RTE is used to simulate a learning management system, and package learning content to SCORM format before it is registered to RTE. To be used when accessed by the learner in OULG.

3. **Learning services deployment:** In this step, learning service of OULG will be deployed in the nodes of the Grid. A learning service may handle one or more learning content to organize a learning process. Therefore, learning service should include learning content, procedure and other authentication procedure with other learning management systems to obtain learning content forward to learners.

4. **Register learning services:** In this step, learning service deployed in the Grid nodes will be registered with OULG portal. Registered information is stored with PostgreSQL. Through registration, OULG service broker and identify learning service when it is retrieved.

5. **Enter OULG portal:** In this step, the learner connects to OULG portal using various client devices, for example, desktop PC, Laptop, PDA or Smartphone, before logging in for learning.

6. **Client device judgment:** When the learner is connect to the OULG portal, OULG will judge device attributes, for example, the make of device, screen resolution and number of colors, in the Device Ontology with information provided by the device. The results of the judgment will be further used as a reference when delivering learning content.

7. **Services scheduling:** OULG will make a learning schedule for the learner to follow. Scheduling is done mainly by referencing the settings in the Service Composition Ontology.

8. **Learning contents adaptation:** In this step, learning content will be adapted. The purpose of the adaptation is to make the learning content adaptive for presentation on the client device, so the learner has no worries over what device should be used. OULG will provide the learning content best adaptive for the device in use based on the definition in the Adaptation Ontology.

9. **Services binding:** After OULG has decided the learning content adaptive with the client device, learning content and device should be bound. After binding, the learner can view learning content in the client device and conduct learning and quiz.

10. **Record learning history:** Learner portfolio will be generated after learning, for example, the time when learning begins, the time when learning ends, quiz results and the Capability gained. These records will be stored in the OULG portal for its reference when providing learning recommendation at later time.

11. **Re-enter OULG:** Learning will not be a one-off event, so the learner is expected to re-enter OULG for further learning. When

Figure 8. A set of ontology in this study

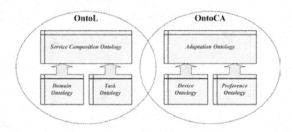

the learner re-enters OULG, OULG will determine the lectures best adaptive for this learning session based on client devices and learning records.

Ontology Design

In terms of functionality, the ontology used in this research can be divided as OntoL and OntoCA. OntoL mainly manages learning material and learning service, while OntoCA is responsible for coordinating user preference and terminal device. The ontology is illustrated in Figure 8. The OntoL includes Domain Ontology, Task Ontology and Service Composition Ontology, while OntoCA includes Device Ontology, Preference Ontology and Adaptation Ontology. In Figure 8, the overlap indicates that these Ontology can conduct inter-Ontology communication through interface classes and attributes. The interaction within Ontology is coordinated and operated through the Presentation Layer. As an example, Domain Ontology is discussed there in after.

Protégé v3.1.1 (2007) is adopted for Ontology development in this research, which is developed by Stanford Medical Informatics. Protégé is fully compatible with OWL and supported by a great variety of plug-ins that enhances the function of graphic display, which makes it easy for us to present the structure of the Ontology, therefore; it is an ideal choice to develop the Ontology for this study with Protégé. In addition, OWL is used to implement Ontology and construct the structure of the entire Ontology and each related individu-

Figure 9. Asserted model of domain ontology

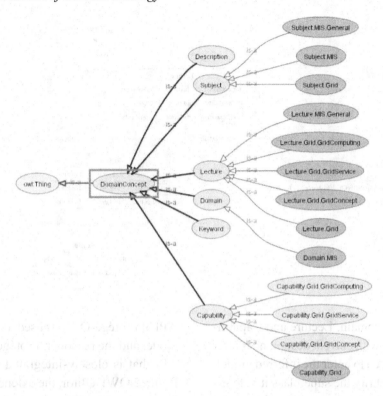

als in each Ontology. In other words, all Ontology in OULG has to adhere to its respective norm in the field of Ontology. Since there is more stringent norm about the input individuals, ensuing inference and query of individuals will be more streamlined.

Domain Ontology defines the concept within a domain. For this research, the concept of a domain is divided into domain, subject, lecture and capability, the asserted model of Domain Ontology is shown in Figure 9. Using domain of Management Information Systems (MIS) as an example, Domain.MIS was defined as a subclass under the concept of Domain; Subject.Grid and Subject.MIS under Subject; Lecture.Grid, Lecture.MIS.General, Lecture.Grid.GridConcept, Lecture.Grid.GridComputing and Lecture.Grid.GridService under Lecture; and lastly define Capability for these Lecture: Capability.Grid, Capability. Grid.GridConcept, Capability.Grid.GridComputing and Capability.Grid.GridService. Capability are

defined for the needs for the experiment without pedagogical consideration and are taken into the design consideration for the communication interface between Ontology.

Form this asserted model, it can be seen that the concept of domain contains two independent subclasses: Keyword and Description, both of which can be used to conduct a search. When Domain Ontology receives keywords entered by the learner, if OULG can't directly identify the learner's needs, it still can use the individual settings of these keywords to list possible domain, subject or lecture for the learner to choose from, or infer the learner's need by adding other parameters of context awareness into the system. Furthermore, from the asserted Domain Ontology model, it can be seen that there is only one layer of subclass under the concept of Domain. For example, Subject has only one level of subclass; it includes Subject.Grid, Subject.MIS and Subject. MIS.General, which are at the same level. So are

Figure 10. Statements of domain ontology

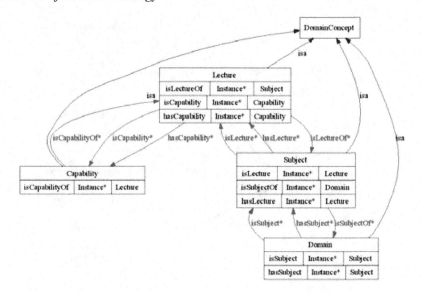

other classes like Domain, Lecture and Capability. For the system with current design, no matter which node is chosen to enter the inferred model, it is possible to identify the superclass it belongs to by querying the superclass one level up in its Ontology asserted model. Therefore, searching for its major superclass is more simplified and system performance is enhanced.

With the defined classes, it needs statement to tell the relations between classes to conduct the inference on related domains that follows. Statement can be achieved with the definition of the attributes of class. With the example of Domain Ontology, the conceptual relation is domain→subject→lecture→capability. For example, hasSubject was defined to describe what subjects there will be under a domain. For the domain of MIS as an example, Subject.MIS and Subject. Grid have been defined to correspond to Domain. MIS. Attributes and Statements for this class are shown in Figure 10.

After the Statements of the classes have been defined, the asserted model of Ontology can be started to reason. The reasoner uses RacerPro v1.9.0 (2007) to conduct inference through DIG (Description Logic Implementation Group). The

API of Protégé-OWL is used to operate Ontology model and the reasoner. Protégé-OWL is a set of API that is closely-integrated with Jena. Since Protégé-OWL editor, the extended module of the Protégé, is developed from this API, its main purpose is to support OWL and RDF. Therefore, operating OWL using this API will have the results using Protégé. So there is an API that has been implemented a system and on the other hand, it can be used in the integrated development environment of the Protégé. For this research, this helps us to verify the research results more effectively. After defining Statements of classes and processed with the reasoner, an inferred model will be arrived, as shown in Figure 11. Form this model, derived from the inference of the reasoner, the hierarchy of the entire Ontology and the association between different concepts can be seen clearly.

In this research, Ontology is divided into several parts with different functionality to achieve effective division of maintaining Ontology. However, communication between Ontology is needed to integrate different Ontology. Within each Ontology, a class was designed for interface communication, which allows Ontology to inter-

Figure 11. Inferred model of domain ontology

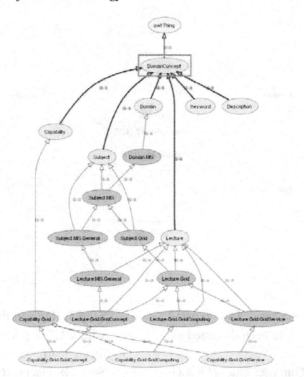

act and use Protégé-OWL and RacerPro DIG to handle these Ontology. The way of interface communication is shown as Figure 12.

From Figure 12, it can be seen that these Ontology communicate with each other through Capability and some attributes related to the characteristic of Device. In other words, Device Properties in Figure 12 are conducting communication across Ontology. When preference parameters are obtained from Preference Ontology and the corresponding Capability class is also obtained, needed content can then be obtained from the remaining Ontology through this class. For example, with Capability.Grid.GridConcept, Lecture.Grid.GridConcept can be obtained from Domain Ontology, and then Content. Grid. GridConcept, learning content from Adaptation Ontology that corresponds to the display parameter derived from the query of the Device Ontology, can also be obtained. As a result, learning content that suits the needs of the learner can be put forward to the learner through Presentation Layer.

Scenario Simulation

In this study, research experiment design is conducted with scenario simulation. The scenario is designed in accordance with OULG system framework. The scenario for the simulation is as follows:

- Suppose learner A, B and C are at home, aboard subway and in the school, respectively, and enter OULG using desktop computer, PDA and Smartphone. OULG first present logon page that suits the learners' client devices based on the device parameters provided by the devices. Learners A, B and C can begin learning with content best suited to their device after learning options have been confirmed. Base on

Figure 12. The way of interface communication between ontology

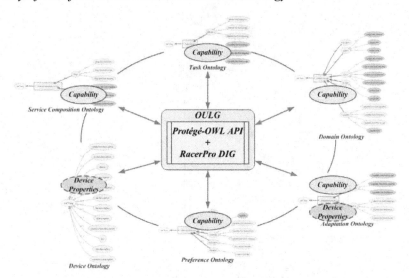

the fore-mentioned scenario, two experiments for simulation had been designed as following:

- **Experiment One:** One user enters OULG with different devices. The learning record is continuous regardless of different devices are used. The purpose of this simulation is to see if OULG meets fundamental requirements of a learning system and, furthermore, to assess its feasibility. Simulation procedure were given as following:

- **Step 1:** Ontology of learning related such as Domain Ontology, Task Ontology and Application Ontology has to be set up by Ontology builder. Device Ontology is also needed from device provider. OULG maintainer, on the other hand, provides Preference Ontology and the definition and maintain of Adaptation Ontology, ensuring user to obtain suit content when connecting to OULG anytime through any device.

- **Step 2:** In accordance with defined OntoL, learning content provider provides learning content of specific domain and deploying Grid nodes of virtual organization in OULG.

- **Step 3:** Register deployed learning content with OULG portal, allowing portal to allocate learning resource.

- **Step 4:** Users connect to OULG portal through PC and login to the system. At this point OULG will authenticate the learner's identity.

- **Step 5:** OULG portal, acting as a broker, acquire device description and relevant learning information from pre-defined Ontology.

- **Step 6-7:** OULG portal returns active learning services for learners to choose from and enter the lecture to take.

- **Step 8:** OULG portal, per learners input, coordinates learning processes.

- **Step 9:** Grid nodes of virtual organization, per requests from portal, generate learning service instance.

- **Step 10:** PC begins binding the generated learning service instance.

- **Step 11:** Learner's learning record will be written back, through the interaction between client device and the system, to OULG and saved for learner's next learning session with OULG.

- **Step 12-13:** Repeat steps 4-11 to complete the simulation for this experiment. The result is the continuous learning record for learner.

- **Experiment Two:** Different learners choose the same lecture, using different devices. In this experiment, OULG will be verified, when dealing with multiple learners at the same time, can provide different learning content adaptive for the client devices of different learners. Simulation procedure were given as following:

- **Step 1-3:** Same as steps 1-3 in Experiment One.

- **Step A1-A8:** Same as steps 4-11 in Experiment One.

- **Step B1, C1:** Essentially the same as steps A1-A8. At this point, it is expected that the same lecture content will be presented differently on different client devices.

Simulation Results and Discussion

The following operation of OULG is based on the scenario simulation and experiment design and software and hardware configuration had been planned in before. As described earlier in the experiment procedures, the learner must use client device and Web browser (for example, Internet Explorer, Netscape etc.) to connect to the OULG portal. It is assumed herein that the learner uses PC at home and Internet Explorer to connect to the Internet and reach OULG portal by entering the URL of the OULG. After the user name and password are entered, the learner will be arrived the page as shown in Figure 13.

From the screenshot of the system after login, it can be seen that, for this example, the system gather the information about "Your username", "You have capabilities before" and "Maybe use client device as", for which there are two options: PC and Laptop. After login OULG, that will begin to query Device Ontology to obtain most adaptive device properties, for example, the size of UI,

Figure 13. Screenshot of the OULG after login first time

number of display colors etc. Since for the moment, the learner uses PC, along with IE of Windows XP, to access OULG portal, so the system will not list PDA and Smartphone as options. It indicates that OULG will automatically detect the device in use and present minimal options for the learner to enter. It in another case where a PDA or a Smartphone is used, the system will present those options relevant to PC and Smartphone for the learner to choose from; it reduce the trouble of making settings when switching to different client devices to conduct learning.

Next simple description will be entered of subject to be learned into the system, as shown in Figure 14. If the learner, for example, wants to learn about MIS-related subjects, the learner can enter "MIS" in the text field, and then OULG will begin to infer and query on Preference Ontology. In this experiment, the system will use the keyword entered by the learner to infer Capability related to MIS. Through the definition of the concepts and statements in the Ontology and the results of the reasoner checking consistency and classification, needed parameters will be input to Ontology. The inference is done by acquiring output through the model that the system has inferred and queried upon. With the concept Capability interface for

Figure 14. An example of OULG getting recommended lectures and procedure

Figure 15. An example of adapted learning content provided by OULG

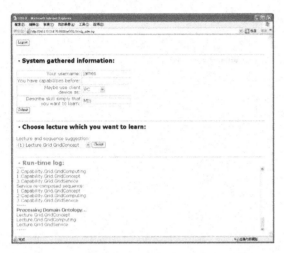

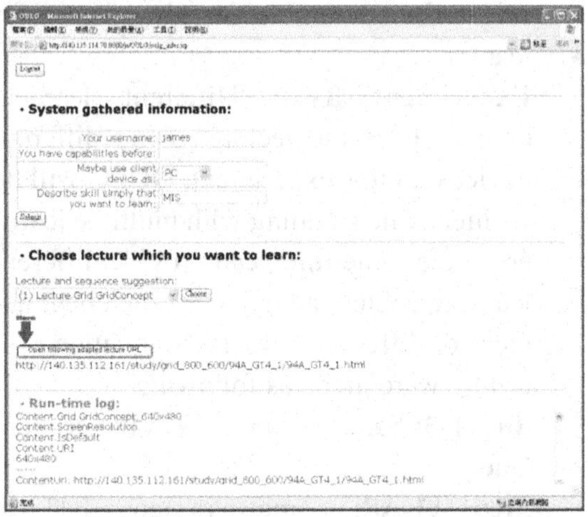

communication, the system enters Domain Ontology to get the inferred relevant learning content. Referring to the learning procedures established in the Service Composition Ontology, the system will also organize adaptive suggestion of learning procedure to the learner. For example in this experiment, the system establishes three lectures: Lecture.Grid.GridConcept, Lecture.Grid.GridComputing, Lecture.Grid.GridService, but the lectures established in Domain Ontology do not include suggestions about learning procedure. When the system enters Service Composition Ontology, OULG will make reference of the definition in the model declared by the Ontology to obtain the previous and next Capability. Through the correspondence between Capability and Lectures, recommended learning procedure can be obtained for the learner's reference, allowing the learner understand where to begin learning and reducing learning barrier.

And then, Lecture.Grid.GridConcept will be selected for learning. After options are entered, OULG will load Adaptation Ontology to infer and also make reference the attributes related to UI that has been obtained by Device Ontology. In this experiment, since the default display setting is 800x600, when OULG is unable to identify the UI size of the client device, the Adaptation Ontology will use default setting. Under normal situation when UI size can be identified, UI attributes obtained through Device Ontology will be used to determine the learning objects adaptive for delivery to the learner. As seen in Figure 15, after OULG has inferred, a learning object of size of 800x600 will be provided to the learner. When learning is finished, the learner can take a quiz to conclude the lecture. The system will record the Capability the learner has just acquired to the OULG database, so that next time when the same learner logs in to OULG, the learner will be reminded of the lecture that he/she has taken and old lecture will not be delivered to the learner as shown in Figure 16. Since the learner has previously finished Lecture.Grid.GridConcept, correspond with Capability.Grid. GridConcept will be obtained. When the learner logs in OULG at a later time, OULG will mark the previously-learned lecture as "Learned", reminding the learner not to re-take the same lecture. It should be noted that regardless of the client devices used to connect to OULG, learning record is based on Capability, not the actual learning content delivered.

Next, a situation is presumed that the learner is connecting to OULG and learning using GPRS service with his PDA aboard subway on the way to school. After the learner has launched Internet Explorer on his/her PDA and connected to OULG portal by entering its URL, the OULG portal appears in the PDA as shown in Figure 17. A situation was presumed that the learner connected to OULG and learning using GPRS service with his PDA aboard subway on the way to school. After the learner has launched Internet Explorer on his/her PDA and connected to OULG portal by entering its URL, the OULG portal appears in the PDA as shown in Figure 17(a). After the learner has successfully logged in OULG through same portal, OULG will once again obtain device from Device Ontology that has the same display capability using request headers of device, and easier

Figure 16. An example of learning records in OULG

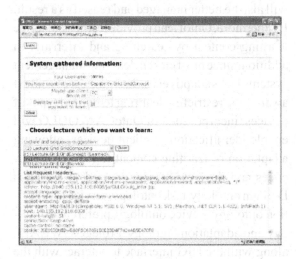

options is provided. Figure 17(b) shows the connection to OULG by PDA. After querying Device Ontology, the system found iPAQ hx2790 has the same display capability with the client device, so that the options presented to the learner are all small devices, for instance, PDA or Smartphone. As in the previous example with PC, after the keyword, "mis", and the system will return same learning items. Since Capability.Grid.GridConcept is the Capability the learner has previously learned with PC, Lecture.Grid.GridConcept will be marked as "Learned", as shown in Figure 17(c) and Figure 17(d). Here, Lecture.Grid.GridComputing was chosen, which is not previously learned. According to previously-obtained device attributes, OULG will obtain learning content adaptive for learner's device from Adaptation Ontology. In this case, since PDA's display size is 240x320, the learning content will be adapted to the display size of 240x320, as shown in Figure 17(e) and Figure 17(f). From previous operations, it can be seen a lecture will be distinguished by the Capability acquired by the learner, so that even if a different client device is used for learning, the same lecture will not be repeated again, which is feature of seamless learning environment. In other words, it satisfies the objectives of ubiquitous learning.

From the scenario experiments on OULG, the following results can be drawn:

- **Experiment One:** A learner uses different devices to connect to OULG at different time. In this scenario, a learner can

Figure 17. Some experimental results of OULG with PDA

  (a)   (b)   (c)   (d)   (e)   (f)

engage learning at different time using different devices, and the learning record will be continuous. In addition, OULG will adapt learning content to the attributes and the display capability of the client device, which enabling correct display of learning content.

- **Experiment Two:** Different learners learn the same lecture using different client devices. In this scenario, it is found that when different users uses different devices to learn, their learning records will be maintained individually by system and will not be confused.

- From the previous two experiments, it is confirmed that OULG is equipped with fundamental functionality seen in general learning system and, through the continuous development of Ontology, it can be more adaptive. Therefore, seamless learning can be achieved through OULG.

A Comparative Study

To realize the impact of OULG on students' achievement, this section presents the results of a comparative study. Forty-two freshmen participate in this experiment to learn the course of Java programming from March to June 2007. The students are divided into two groups, one is control group for using general LMS, and the other one is experimental test group for using OULG. All of the students are asked to take a pretest before performing OULG and a posttest at the ending of semester. The pretest and posttest contained 50 questions, respectively. The reliability of the pretest sheet was 0.7, and the posttest sheet was 0.8 based on Cronbach's value (Cronbach, 1970). The experimental results in Table 4 indicate an obvious grade improvement in two groups. Moreover, the students in Experimental group has higher achievement than those who in the Control group.

Table 4. Comparative study

Group	Pre-test		Post-test	
	M	**SD**	**M**	**SD**
Experimental (N=21)	33.29	12.673	48.62	17.46
Control (N=21)	33.76	12.004	43.33	18.101
M = Mean score SD = Standard Deviation				

CONCLUSION

In this study, an ontology-based ubiquitous learning grid was proposed to resolve the difficulties of ubiquitous learning environment in adapting to different learners, time and space. General learning management systems, though conforming to SCORM in learning objects, do not offering sharing across different systems, as a result, learning service can only be applied to certain type of learning system. By adding OntoL to OULG, that is aim to resolve the problem. Learning services will also be better managed and reused as a result. Furthermore, OntoL can provide learners adaptive learning content by searching and inferring. In addition, since most current learning management systems lacks adaptiveness in the aspect of context awareness, restricting learning to limited types of devices, incorporation of OntoCA to OULG will enable identification of client devices, allowing adaptation of learning content to learner preferences and devices. Protégé is used to establish Domain ontology, task ontology, service composition ontology, device ontology, preference ontology and adaptation ontology. Protégé-OWL API, along with the DIG interface to interact with the reasoner. Apache and Tomcat are laid on Fedora Core to provide the service as Web server. Since the API of the development tools used are Java-based, for example, GT4 and Protégé-OWLAPI, in this research, Java-based component technologies are employed to implement OULG.

With user-input parameters to OULG, along with some parameters obtained by the system,

OULG follows specific logic and rules to operate these six Ontology and obtain the results of inference. These results can be used in determining learning lectures and learning sequence. On the other hand, the Device Ontology in the OntoCA can be updated with the description of latest devices, making OULG more adaptive to wider range of client devices. The experimental results of comparative study present the feasibility and good performance of OULG.

In summary, with the addition of ontology to the adaptability of ubiquitous learning grid to client devices, OULG is able to identify and adapt in the aspects of learning domain, service procedure, devices and context awareness, providing better learning experience with adaptive content under various circumstances and achieving seamless learning environment. From this study, the following recommendations can be drawn for further:

- Incorporating different ontology into OntoL and, in the aspect of acquiring tacit knowledge, evaluate their value in the area of knowledge management.
- Implement more on the parameters of OntoCA to obtain diverse results of inference.
- Performance comparison for larger ontology and various reasoners and to evaluate the strategy to achieve performance optimization of ontology-based systems.

REFERENCES

Abbas, Z., Umer, M., Odeh, M., McClatchey, R., Ali, A., & Ahmad, F. (2005). A Semantic Grid-based E-Learning Framework (SELF). *Proceedings of the 5th IEEE/ACM International Symposium on Cluster Computing and the Grid*, (pp. 11-18). Cardiff, UK.

Advanced Distributed Learning (ADL). (2004). Sharable Content Object Reference Model (SCORM) 2004 2nd Edition Overview. Retrieved from http://www.adlnet.org/.

Blackboard. (2007). http://www.blackboard.com/us/index.aspx.

Brown, T. H. (2005). Towards a Model for m-Learning in Africa. *International Journal on E-Learning, 4*(3), 299–315.

Claroline. (2007). http://www.claroline.net/.

Cronbach, L. J. (1970). *Essentials of Psychological Testing*. New York: Harper & Rowe.

Cui, G., Chen, F., Chen, H., & Li, S. (2004). OntoEdu: A Case Study of Ontology-Based Education Grid System for e-Learning. *Global Chinese Journal of Computers in Education, 2*(2), 59–72.

Foster, I., Kesselman, C., Nick, J. M., & Tuecke, S. (2002). *The Physiology of the Grid*. Retrieved from http://www.globus.org/research/papers/ogsa.pdf.

Foundation for Intelligent Physical Agents (FIPA). (2002). *FIPA Device Ontology Specification*. Retrieved from http://www.fipa.org/specs/fipa00091/XC00091C.pdf.

Klyne, G., Reynolds, F., Woodrow, C., Ohto, H., Hjelm, J., Butler, M. H., & Tran, L. (2003). Composite *Capability/Preference Profiles (CC/PP): Structure and Vocabularies*. http://www.w3.org/TR/2003/WD-CCPP-struct-vocab-20030325/.

McGuinness, D. L., & Harmelen, F. v. (2004). *OWL Web Ontology Language Overview*. Retrieved from http://www.w3.org/TR/2004/REC-owl-features-20040210/.

Moodle. (2007). http://moodle.org/.

Ogata, H., & Yano, Y. (2003). How Ubiquitous Computing can Support Language Learning. *Proceedings of the First International Conference on Knowledge Economy and Development of Science and Technology (KEST 2003)*, (pp. 1-6). Honjo City, Japan.

Protégé. (2007). http://protege.stanford.edu/.

RacerPro. (2007). http://www.racer-systems.com/.

Rogers, Y., Price, S., Randell, C., Fraser, D. S., Weal, M., & Fitzpatrick, G. (2005). Interaction design and children: Ubi-learning Integrates Indoor and Outdoor Experiences. *Communications of the ACM, 48*(1), 55–59. doi:10.1145/1039539.1039570

Sakai Project. (2007). http://www.sakaiproject.org/.

WebCT. (2007). http://www.webct.com/.

Chapter 13
A Rule-Based System for Test Quality Improvement

Gennaro Costagliola
University of Salerno, Italy

Vittorio Fuccella
University of Salerno, Italy

ABSTRACT

To correctly evaluate learners' knowledge, it is important to administer tests composed of good quality question items. By the term "quality" we intend the potential of an item in effectively discriminating between skilled and untrained students and in obtaining tutor's desired difficulty level. This article presents a rule-based e-testing system which assists tutors in obtaining better question items through subsequent test sessions. After each test session, the system automatically detects items' quality and provides the tutors with advice about what to do with each of them: good items can be re-used for future tests; among items with lower performances, instead, some should be discarded, while some can be modified and then re-used. The proposed system has been experimented in a course at the University of Salerno.

INTRODUCTION

E-testing, also known as *Computer Assisted Assessment (CAA)*, is a sector of e-learning aimed at assessing learner's knowledge through computers. Through *e-testing*, tests composed of several question types can be presented to the students in order to assess their knowledge. *Multiple choice* question type is frequently employed, since,

among other advantages, a large number of tests based on it can be easily corrected automatically.

The experience gained by educators and the results obtained through several experiments (Woodford & Bancroft, 2005) provide some guidelines for writing good *multiple choice* questions (*items*, in the sequel), such as: "use the right language", "avoid a big number of unlikely *distractors* for an item", etc.

It is also possible to evaluate the effectiveness of the items, through the use of several statistical

DOI: 10.4018/978-1-60960-539-1.ch013

models, such as *Item Analysis* (IA, 2008) and *Item Response theory* (*IRT*). Both of them are based on the interpretation of statistical indicators calculated on test outcomes. The most important indicators are the *difficulty* indicator, which measures the difficulty of an item, and the *discrimination* indicator, which represents the information of how effectively an item discriminates between skilled and untrained students. More statistical indicators are related to the *distractors* (wrong options) of an item. A good quality item has a high discrimination potential and a difficulty level close to tutor's desired one.

Despite the availability of guidelines for writing good items and statistical models to analyze their quality, only a few tutors are aware of the guidelines and even fewer are used with statistics. The result is that the quality of the tests used for exams or admissions is sometimes poor and in some cases could be improved.

The most common Web-based e-learning platforms, such as *Moodle* (Moodle, 2008), *Blackboard* (Blackboard, 2008), and *Questionmark* (Questionmark, 2008) evaluate item quality by generating and showing item statistics. Nevertheless, their interpretation is left to the tutors: these systems do not advise or help the tutor in improving items.

In this article we propose an approach and a system for improving items: we provide tutors with feedback on their quality and suggest them the opportune action to undertake for improving it. To elaborate, the approach consists of administering tests to learners through a suitable *rule-based system*. The system obtains item quality improvement by analyzing the test outcomes. After the analysis, the system provides the tutor with one of the following suggestions:

- "Keep on using the item" in future test sessions, for good items;
- "Discard the item", for poor items;
- "Modify the item", for poor items whose defect is originated by a well-known cause.

In this case, the system also provides the tutor with suggestions on how to modify the item.

Though item quality can be improved after the first test session in which it is used, the system can be used for subsequent test sessions, obtaining further improvements.

Rule-based systems are generally composed of an *inferential engine*, a *knowledge-base* and a *user interface*. Our system follows this model. The *inferential engine* works by exploiting *fuzzy classification*: the items are classified on the basis of the values of some parameters calculated on test outcomes. *Fuzzy classification* has been successfully employed in technological applications in several sectors, from weather forecast (Bradley et al.; 1982) to medical diagnosis (Exarchos et al.; 2007). In our system, it has been preferred over other frequently used classification methods based on machine learning due to the following reasons:

- *Knowledge availability*. Most of the knowledge is already available, as witnessed by the presence of numerous theories and manuals on *psychometrics*.
- *Lack of data*. Other types of classification based on data would require the availability of large data sets. Once they have been gathered, in such a way to have statistically significant classes to perform data analysis, such methods might be exploited.

The *knowledge-base* of the system has been inferred from *IA* and other statistical models for the evaluation of the items.

The system has been given a Web-based *interface*. Rather than developing it from scratch, we have preferred to integrate the system in an existing Web-based e-testing platform: *eWorkbook* (Costagliola et al.; 2007), developed at the *University of Salerno*.

An experiment on system's performances has been carried out in a course at the *University of*

Salerno. As shown in the experiment, we can obtain items which better discriminate between skilled and untrained students and better match the difficulty estimated by the tutor.

The article is organized as follows: the next two sections are introductive to fuzzy classification and to the statistical models for evaluating the effectiveness of the items, respectively; the approach for item quality improvement is presented in the fourth section. In the fifth section, we describe the system: its architecture and its instantiation in the existing *e-testing* platform; the sixth section presents an experiment and a discussion on its results; the following section contains a comparison with work related to ours; lastly, several final remarks and a discussion on future work conclude the article.

FUZZY CLASSIFICATION

The approach presented in this article employs a *fuzzy classification* method. *Classification* is one of the most widespread *Data Mining* techniques (Roiger & Geatz; 2004). It lies in grouping *n* entities of a given knowledge domain into *m* knowledge containers, often called *classes*, *sections*, *categories*, etc. To perform a *classification*, several attributes of the entities must be analyzed. These are called *input attributes*. The class in which the entity will be inserted is an *output attribute*. A good *classification* consists of classes with high *internal cohesion* and *external separation*. *Classification* differs from *clustering*. The difference lies in the final classes, which are *predefined* only for the former problem. In *clustering*, instead, the classes (*clusters*) are discovered during the process. For this reason, we say that classification is a *supervised* process.

Classification has been employed in several fields for solving real problems, such as:

- In medicine, for medical diagnosis;

- In pattern discovery, for fraud detection. E.g., the FALCON system (Brachman et al.; 1996), created by the HNC Inc. is used for detecting possible transactions;
- In economy and financing, for risk management, for classifying the credit risk of a person who has requested funds.

Several methods can be used for *classification*. Some of them, such as *decision trees*, use *machine learning* for extracting knowledge from data. The most frequently used *machine learning* approaches divide data in two sets: the *training set* and the *test set*. The former is used to produce the knowledge, the latter to test the effectiveness of the approach. The *decision tree* lends itself to be used in classification, but it gives just one output categorical attribute. Furthermore, the *decision tree* produces particularly easy to explain results and can be suitable in the case of unknown data distribution. Nevertheless, it can be advisable to employ other methods, such as the *Bayesian classifier*, when all or most of the input attributes are numerical: the tree could have too many conditional tests to satisfy to be informative.

When data are missing, and the knowledge is already available, a *rule-based* system is a suitable solution for classification. A *rule-based* system is a system whose knowledge-base is expressed under the form of *production rules*. Rule-based systems have been employed in many applications for decision making. Such systems can also be used for classification. The *production rules* can be inferred directly from the expertise or obtained through *machine learning* methods. In general, the rules are in the following form:

```
IF <antecedent conditions>
THEN <consequent conditions>
```

The *antecedent conditions* define the values or the value intervals for one or more input attributes. The *consequent conditions* define the values or the value intervals for one or more output attributes. In the case of *classification*, the *consequent conditions* determine if a given entity belongs to a class. In *rule-based* systems, it is often necessary to deal with *uncertainty*. To this aim, *fuzzy logic* is often employed, e.g. it has been used for economic performance analysis (Zhou et al.; 2005).

Fuzzy logic is derived from *fuzzy sets* theory. *Fuzzy sets* were first introduced by Zadeh (1997), and have been applied in various fields, such as decision making and control (Bardossy & Dukstein; 1995). *Fuzzy set* theory deals with reasoning that is approximate rather than precisely deduced from classical predicate logic. A *fuzzy set* is characterized by a *membership function* which maps a value that might be a member of the set to a number between zero and one indicating its actual *degree of membership*. The *triangular membership function* is the most frequently used function and the most practical, but other shapes, continuous or discrete, are also used.

A variable used in a *fuzzy production rule* is also called a *linguistic variable* and is associated to a *linguistic value* (*term*). Each *linguistic value* is associated to a *fuzzy set*.

A *fuzzy system* is a set of *fuzzy rules* connecting fuzzy input and fuzzy output in the form of IF-THEN sentences. Once we have the rules and the fuzzy sets for defining the values of the *linguistic variables*, the *fuzzy inference* can be applied. The most commonly applied method is the 4-phases procedure introduced by Mamdani & Assilian (1999). The four steps are the following:

- *Fuzzyfication*: conversion of the input values in the corresponding membership levels in each fuzzy set;
- *Inference*: the membership levels are combined in order to obtain a degree of fulfillment for each rule;
- *Combination*: combination of all the values obtained for the rules to obtain a unique fuzzy set;

- *Defuzzyfication*: conversion of the fuzzy set obtained at the previous phase into a value.

A *fuzzy classifier* is a function that at each entity associates a set of Boolean functions defining the possibility (*Degree of Fulfillment, DoF* briefly) that an instance belongs to the output classes. The *fuzzy classifier* produces a categorical value as final output. Often, the classification is performed by selecting the class for which the *DoF* is the highest. This method corresponds to the case of *maximum* method for *combination* and *maximum* method for *defuzzyfication*.

ITEM QUALITY: ITEM AND DISTRACTOR ANALYSIS

This section describes the main statistical models on which the knowledge-base of our system is based. In particular, it focuses on *Item Analysis IA*, whose statistical indicators are used in our system's rules. The tests administered through our system make use of *multiple choice* items for the assessment of learners' knowledge. Those items are composed of a *stem* and a list of *options*. The *stem* is the text that states the question. The only correct answer is called the *key*, whilst the incorrect answers are called *distractors* (Woodford & Bancroft, 2005).

As mentioned in the introduction, two main statistical models are available for evaluating item quality: *IA* and *IRT*. Although today *IRT* is the pre-dominant measurement model, *IA* is still frequently employed by psychometricians, test developers, and tutors for a number of reasons. First, concepts of *IA* are simpler than those of their *IRT* counterpart: even the tutors without a strong statistical background can easily interpret the results without going through a steep learning curve. Second, *IA* can be computed by many popular statistical software programs, including *SAS*, while *IRT* necessitates use of specialized software packages such as *Bilog, Winsteps, Multilog, RUMM* (Yu and Wong, 2003; Yu, 2005). One great advantage of *IRT* is the invariance of ability and item parameters: it is the cornerstone of IRT and the major distinction between *IRT* and *IA* (Hambleton & Swaminathan, 1985). One drawback, however, of *IRT* is that a big sample size is necessary for the estimation of parameters. Nevertheless, empirical studies, examining and/or comparing the invariance characteristics of item statistics from the two measurement frameworks, have observed that it is difficult to find a great invariance or any other obvious advantage in the *IRT* based item indicators (Stage, 1999).

For our study, *IA* has been preferred over *IRT* due to the following main reasons: it needs a smaller sample size for obtaining statistically significant indicators; it is easier to use *IA* indicators to compose rule conditions. The following statistical indicators are available from *IA* and other models, such as *distractor analysis*:

- *difficulty*: a real number between 0 and 1 which expresses a measure of the difficulty of the item, intended as the proportion of learners who get the item correct.
- *discrimination*: a real number between -1 and 1 which expresses a measure of how well the item discriminates between skilled and untrained learners. *Discrimination* is calculated as the *point biserial* correlation coefficient between the score obtained on the item and the total score obtained on the test. The *point biserial* is a measure of association between a continuous variable (e.g. the score on the test) and a binary variable (e.g. the score on a *multiple choice* item).
- *frequency(i)*: a real number between 0 and 1 which expresses the frequency of the i-th option of the item. Its value is calculated as the percentage of learners who choose the i-th option.
- *discrimination(i)*: a real number between -1 and 1 which expresses the discrimina-

tion of the i-th option. Its value is calculated as the *point biserial* correlation coefficient between the result obtained by the learner on the whole test and a dichotomous variable that says whether the i-th option was chosen (yes=1, no=0) by the learner or not.

- *abstained_freq*: a real number between 0 and 1 which expresses the frequency of the abstention (no answers given) on the item. Its value is calculated as the percentage of learners who did not give any answer to the item, where allowed.
- *abstained_discr*: a real number between -1 and 1 which expresses the discrimination of the abstention from giving a response to the item. Its value is calculated as the *point biserial* correlation coefficient between the result obtained by the learner on the whole test and a dichotomous variable that says whether the learner refrained or not (yes=1, no=0) on the item.

Discrimination and *difficulty* are the most important indicators. They can be used for both determining item quality and choosing advice for tutors. As experts suggest (Massey, 2007), a good value for *discrimination* is about 0.5. A positive value lower than 0.2 indicates that the item does not discriminate well. This can be due to several reasons, including: the question does not assess learners on the desired knowledge; the stem or the options are badly/ambiguously expressed; etc. It is usually difficult to understand what is wrong with these items and more difficult to provide a suggestion to improve them, so, if the tutor cannot understand the problem her(him)self, the suggestion is to discard the item. A negative value for *discrimination*, especially if joined with a positive value for the discrimination of a *distractor*, is a sign of a possible mistake in choosing the key (a data entry error occurred). In this case it is easy to recover the item by changing the key.

If *difficulty* is too high (>0.85) or too low (<0.15), there is the possibility that the item does not correctly evaluate the learners on the desired knowledge or subject. This is particularly true when such values for *difficulty* are sought together with medium-low values for *discrimination*. Furthermore, our system allows the tutor to define the foreseen difficulty for an item.

In a test, in order to better assess a heterogeneous class with different levels of knowledge, it is important to balance the difficulty of the items: for example, in the preparation of the *Michigan Educational Assessment Program* (*MEAP*, 2007), "easy" and "difficult" items are used in every form to balance the difficulty level of the items. Having a precise estimation of item's difficulty allows the tutor to correctly assign it to a test section on the basis of its difficulty, when composing tests. Thus, the closer a tutor's estimation of item *difficulty* is to the actual calculated difficulty for that item, the more reliable that item is considered to be.

When *difficulty* is too high or underestimated, this can be due to the presence of a *distractor* (noticed for its high frequency) which is too plausible (it tends to mislead a lot of students, even skilled ones). Removing or substituting that *distractor* can help in obtaining a better item. Sometimes, the item has its intrinsic difficulty and it can be difficult to adjust it, so the suggestion can be to modify the tutor's estimation.

As for *distractors*, they can contribute to form a good item when they are selected by a significant number of students. When the frequency of the *distractor* is too high, there could be an ambiguity in the formulation of the stem or of the *distractor*. A good indicator of *distractors'* quality is their discrimination, which should be negative, denoting that the *distractor* was selected by untrained students. In conclusion, a good *distractor* is the one which is selected by a small but significant number of untrained students.

High abstention is always a symptom of high difficulty for the item. When it is accompanied by a high (not negative or next to 0) value for its discrimination and a low value for item *discrimina-*

tion, it can tell that the question has a bad quality and it is difficult to improve it.

THE APPROACH

Our approach for obtaining better items consists of administering tests to the learners through a suitable e-testing *system*. On the basis of test outcomes, the system evaluates the items and suggests the tutor the most suitable action to undertake on each of them. This is possible after a test has been administered to a statistically significant number of learners. In general, the quality improvement is obtained in two ways:

- through the increment of item *discrimination*. This objective is pursued by both eliminating and opportunely modifying items with low *discrimination*.
- by having the tutor's estimation of the *difficulty* closer to the calculated difficulty for the item. In the most desirable cases (when possible), the system suggests how to modify the item. Otherwise, the estimation must be modified.

Though item quality can be improved after the first test session in which it is used, the items can be evaluated by the system through subsequent test sessions, following the lifecycle shown in Figure 1. The figure shows a *UML activity diagram*, in which the role of the tutor and the role of the system are specified in two different swimlines.

The item starts its lifecycle when it is created by the tutor. Then, the tutor selects the item for a test session. The test is administered to the learners through the system in a test. At the end of the session, the system stores learners' outcomes. Such outcomes are used to calculate statistical indicators, which are used in the *production rules* for item evaluation. The output of the evaluation is the *state* of the item, whose value is expressed through a traffic light. Later on, according to the

Figure 1. Item lifecycle

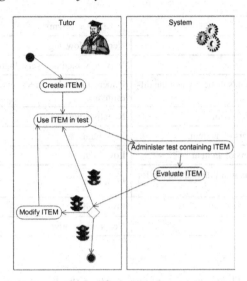

system output, the tutor decides the destiny of the item as follows:

- **State = Green**: the item has good performances and can be re-used for future test sessions.
- **State = Red**: the item has bad performances and should be discarded.
- **State = Yellow**: the item has bad performances, but its quality can be improved. The system suggests how. The item is modified by the tutor and can be re-used for future test sessions.

It is worth noting that the system just suggests the tutor the most suitable action. Figure 1 shows the case in which the tutor follows the suggestion of the system. Nevertheless, the tutor can choose not to follow the system's suggestion if s/he thinks it is opportune.

THE SYSTEM

Typically, rule-based systems are composed of an *inferential engine*, a *knowledge-base* and a

user interface (Momoh et al.; 2000). Our system follows this model.

The *knowledge-base* has been mostly inferred by translating into rules the verbal knowledge presented in the third section. Since such knowledge does not completely cover all of the aspects considered in our system, it has been integrated with knowledge extracted from data.

The *inferential engine* works by performing a *classification* of the items. Several classes of items have been identified, and each class is associated to a *production rule*. Fuzzy sets have been used in order to cope with *linguistic uncertainty* contained in the rules: sources of uncertainty in our system are associated to both the conditions in the antecedents of the rules and to the combination of the rules themselves. The *DoF* of a rule tells the membership of the item to the corresponding class. The classification is performed by selecting the class for which the *DoF* is the highest. This model fits well our question item classification problem, since, in most cases (except for Class 1, see Table 3), the belonging to a class indicates the presence of a defect affecting the item. By choosing to classify the item to the class to which the item belongs with the maximum degree, a decision is taken according to the heaviest problem affecting the item.

The system has been equipped with a Web-based *user interface*. Rather than developing it from scratch, we have preferred to integrate the system in an existing Web-based e-testing platform. To elaborate, the system has been implemented as a Java *Object Oriented* framework, called *Item Quality Framework*, which can be instantiated in any Java-based e-testing platform. Our choice is fallen on *eWorkbook*, already in use at our faculty.

The Knowledge-Base

This section describes the process for obtaining the *fuzzy production rules* from the knowledge. As already pointed out, the rules have been mostly

Table 1. Variables and terms

Variable	Explanation	Terms
discrimination	Item's discrimination (see sec. 3)	Negative, low, high
difficulty	Item's difficulty (see sec. 3)	Very_low, medium, very_high
difficulty_gap	The difference between the tutor's estimation of item's difficulty and the difficulty calculated by the system	Underestimated, correct, overestimated
max_distr_discr	The maximum discrimination for the distractors of an item	Negative, positive
max_distr_freq	The maximum (relative) frequency for the distractors of an item.	Low, high
min_distr_freq	The minimum (relative) frequency for the distractors of an item	Low, high
distr_freq	The (relative) frequency of the distractor with maximum discrimination for an item	Low, high
abst_frequency	The frequency of the abstentions for an item	Low, high
abst_discrimination	The discrimination of the abstentions for an item	Negative, positive

inferred from the verbal knowledge presented in the third section and integrated with knowledge extracted from data. The integration has only been necessary for modeling a few *membership functions*.

Variables and Fuzzyfication

The set of variables used are reported, together with an explanation of their meaning and the set of possible values they can assume (*terms*), in Table 1. These variables are directly chosen from the statistical indicators presented in the third section or derived from them.

The *discrimination* and *difficulty* variables are the same indicators for item *discrimination* and *difficulty* defined in the third section. The same discourse is valid for the variables related to the abstention, *abst_frequency* and *abst_discrimination*. *difficulty_gap* is a variable representing the error in tutor's estimation of item *difficulty*: through the system interface, the tutor can assign one out of three difficulty levels to an item (easy =0.3; medium=0.5; difficult=0.7). *difficulty_gap* is calculated as the difference between the tutor estimation and the actual difficulty calculated by the system.

Three variables representing the frequency of the *distractors* for an item have been considered: *max_distr_freq, min_distr_freq, distr_freq*. Their value is not an absolute frequency, but relative to the frequency of the other *distractors*: it is obtained by dividing the absolute frequency by the mean frequency of the *distractors* of the item. In the case of items with five options, as our system has been tested, their value is a real number varying from 0 to 4.

Membership Functions

As for the *membership functions* of fuzzy sets associated to each *term*, *triangular* and *trapezoidal* shapes have been used. Most of the values for the *bases* and the *peaks* have been established using the expertise. Only for some variables, the *membership functions* have been defined on an experimental basis. While we already had clear ideas on how to define most of them, we did not have enough information from the knowledge on how to model *membership functions* for the variables related to abstention (*abst_frequency* and *abst_discrimination*). A calibration phase was required in order to refine the values for the bases and peaks of their *membership functions*. As a calibration set, test results from the *Science*

Table 2. Anomalous values for variables related to abstention

Question Id	abst_discrimination	abst_frequency
23	0.03	0.26
29	0.10	0.53
33	0.14	0.42
34	0.18	0.32
61	0.17	0.42
Mean	**0.12**	**0.39**

Faculty Admission Test of the 2006 year were used. The *calibration set* was composed of 64 items with 5 options each. For each item, about one thousand records (students answers) were available, even if only a smaller random sample was considered. Test items and their results were inspected by a human expert who identified items which should have been discarded due to low *discrimination* and anomalous values for the vari-

ables related to abstention. We have found 5 items satisfying the conditions above: the mean values for *abst_discrimination* and *abst_frequency* were, respectively, 0.12 and 0.39, as shown in Table 2.

Due to the limited size of the calibration set, the simple method of choosing the peaks of the functions at the mean value, as shown in (Bardossy & Duckstein; 1995), has been used. When more data will be available, a more sophisticated method will be used for the definition of membership functions, such as the one proposed in (Civanlar & Trussel; 1986). Charts for the membership functions are shown in Figure 2.

Rules

From the verbal description of the knowledge presented in the third section, the rules summarized in Table 3 have been inferred. The first three columns in the table contain, respectively, the class of the item, the rule used for classification and the item

Figure 2. Membership functions

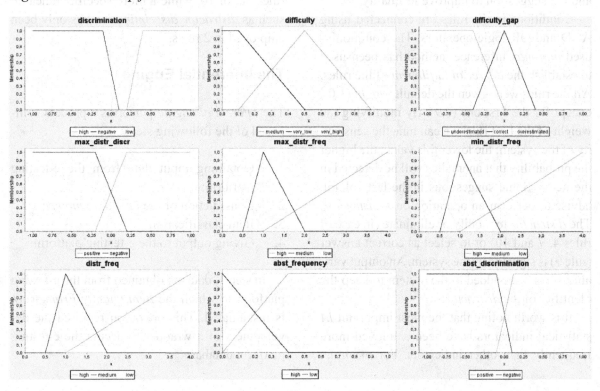

Table 3. Rules

Class	Rule	State	Problem and Suggestion
1	discrimination IS high AND abst_discrimination IS negative WITH 0.9	Green	/
2	discrimination IS low AND abst_frequency IS high AND abst_discrimination IS positive	Red	/
3	difficulty IS very_low AND discrimination IS low	Red	/
4	difficulty IS very_high AND discrimination IS low AND max_distr_freq IS high	Yellow	Item too difficult due to a too plausible distractor, delete or substitute distractor x.
5	difficulty_gap IS overestimated AND discrimination IS low	Yellow	Item difficulty overestimated, avoid too plausible distractors and too obvious answers.
6	difficulty_gap IS overestimated AND discrimination IS NOT low	Yellow	Item difficulty overestimated, modify the estimated difficulty.
7	difficulty_gap IS underestimated AND max_distr_freq IS high	Yellow	Item difficulty underestimated due to a too plausible distractor, delete or substitute distractor x.
8	difficulty_gap IS underestimated AND max_distr_freq IS NOT high	Yellow	Item difficulty underestimated, modify the estimated difficulty.
9	max_distr_discr IS positive AND discrimination IS negative	Yellow	Wrong key (data entry error), select option x as the correct answer.
10	discrimination IS high AND max_distr_discr IS positive AND distr_freq IS NOT low	Yellow	Too plausible distractor, delete or substitute distractor x.

state. For items whose state is yellow, the fourth column contains the problem affecting the item and the suggestion to improve its quality.

Conditions in the rules are connected using AND and OR logic operators. The commonly-used *min-max* inference method has been used to establish the *degree of fulfillment* of the rules. All the rules were given the default *weight* (1.0), except for the first one (0.9). By modifying the weight of the first rule, we can tune the sensitivity of the system: the lower this value, the higher the probability that anomalies will be detected in the items. Some suggestions in the last column advise to perform an operation on a *distractor*. The *distractor* to modify or eliminate (in case of rules 4, 7 and 10) or to select as correct answer (rule 9) is signaled by the system. An output variable *x* has been added to the system to keep the identifier of the *distractor*.

It is worth noting that the most important *IA* statistical indicators have been employed more frequently than other indicators. For example,

the *discrimination*, which is a good indicator for the overall quality of an item, is present in 8 rules out of 10, while a more specific indicator, such as *distractor discrimination* has only been employed in 2 rules.

The Inferential Engine

The *inferential engine* performs a process composed of the following steps:

1. Obtaining input data from the e-testing platform;
2. Construction of the *item data matrix*;
3. Item classification;
4. Giving output to the e-testing platform.

In step 1, data are obtained from the e-testing platform in which the *Item Quality Framework* is instantiated. This operation required the development of a wrapper to access the e-testing platform database.

The input data obtained at the previous step, are used in step 2 for the construction of the *item data matrix* which reports, for each item, the value of the following attributes:

- *N*: number of options;
- *key*: the index of the right option;
- *discrimination*: item discrimination;
- *difficulty*: item difficulty;
- *tutor_difficulty*: tutor's estimation for item difficulty;
- *discrimination (1); ... ; discrimination(N)*: N columns containing the discrimination of each option.
- *difficulty (1); ... ; difficulty(N)*: N columns containing the difficulty of each option;
- *abstained_discr*: discrimination of the abstention on the item;
- *abstained_freq*: frequency of the abstention on the item.

Item classification is performed, at step 3, by firing the rules. Before the rules can be fired, their variables must be assigned to values directly taken from the *item data matrix* (e.g. *discrimination*, *difficulty*, etc.) or derived from them (e.g. *difficulty_gap*, *max_distr_freq*, etc.). Then, the rules are fired and a new matrix containing the *DoF* for each item and for each class is obtained. As stated before, the item is classified in the class with the maximum *DoF*.

Lastly, at step 4, the output with item state, problem and suggestion, is passed to the *e-testing* platform.

System Implementation and Interface

The system was implemented in two phases:

1. Development of the *Item Quality Framework*;
2. Its instantiation in an existing Web-based e-testing platform, called *eWorkbook*.

The Item Quality Framework

The system has been implemented as a Java Object Oriented framework. In this way, it would have been easily integrated in any e-testing java-based platform. The *Item Quality Framework* offers the following functionalities:

- Implements the inferential engine;
- Provides an *Application Programming Interface* (*API*) for both the construction of the *item data matrix* and the access to output data.

For the development of the *inferential engine*, a free java library implementing a complete Fuzzy inference system, called *jFuzzyLogic* (jFuzzy-Logic, 2008), has been used. The system variables, fuzzyfication, inference methods and the rules have been defined using the *Fuzzy Control Language* (FCL, 1997), supported by the *jFuzzyLogic* library. The advantage of this approach, compared to a hard-coded solution, is that *membership functions* and rules can be simply changed by editing a configuration file, thus avoiding to build the system again. Data can be imported from various sources and exported to several formats, such as spreadsheets or relational databases. The data matrix and the results can be saved in persistent tables, in order to avoid to perform calculations every time they must be visualized.

The *API* is composed of two different Java classes, which allow to perform input and output to the *Inferential Engine*, respectively. The former contains methods for adding rows to the *item data matrix*. The latter contains methods for obtaining the *state* of an item (*green*, *yellow*, *red*) and, in case of *yellow state*, the *suggestion* for improving the item quality. It is worth noting that suggestions can be internationalized, that is, they can easily be translated into any language by editing a text file.

Instantiation in eWorkbook

eWorkbook is a Web-based e-testing platform that can be used for evaluating learner's knowledge by creating (the tutor) and taking (the learner) on-line tests based on *multiple choice* question type. The questions are kept in a *hierarchical* repository. The tests are composed of one or more sections. There are two kinds of sections: *static* and *dynamic*. The difference between them is in the way they allow question selection: for a static section, the questions are chosen by the tutor. For a dynamic section, some selection parameters must be specified, such as the difficulty, leaving the platform to choose the questions randomly whenever a learner takes a test. In this way, it is possible with *eWorkbook* to make a test with banks of items of different difficulties, thus balancing test difficulty, in order to better assess a heterogeneous set of students.

As shown in Figure 3, *eWorkbook* has a layered architecture. The *Jakarta Struts framework* (Struts, 2008) has been used to support the *Model 2* design paradigm, a variation of the classic *Model View Controller* (*MVC*) approach. In our design choice, *Struts* works with *JSP*, for the *View*, while it interacts with *Hibernate* (Hibernate, 2008), a powerful framework for *object/relational persistence* and query service for Java, for the *Model*. The application is fully accessible with a Web browser. No browser plug-in installations are needed, since its pages are composed of standard HTML and *ECMAScript* (EcmaScript, 2008) code. The Web browser interacts with the *Struts Servlet*, at the *Controller Layer*, that processes the request and dispatches it to the *Action Class*, responsible for serving it, according to the predefined configuration. It is worth noting that the *Struts Servlet* uses the JSP pages to implement the user interfaces. The *Action Classes* interact with the modules of the *Business Layer*, responsible for the logic of the application. At this layer, the functionalities of the system are implemented in four main sub-systems:

Figure 3. eWorkbook Architecture (after the instantiation of the item quality framework)

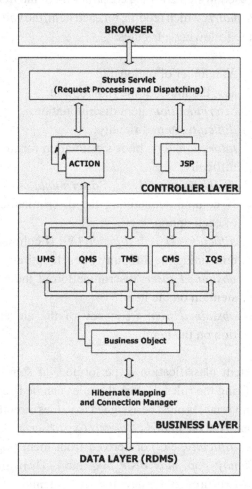

- *User Management Subsystem* (UMS), responsible for user management. In particular, it provides insert, update and delete facilities.
- *Question Management Subsystem* (QMS), which manages the *eWorkbook*'s question repository and controls access to it.
- *Test Management Subsystem* (TMS), which manages the *eWorkbook*'s test repository.
- *Course Management Subsystem* (CMS), responsible for course management. In particular, it allows the insertion, update and deletion of a course.

Figure 4. eWorkbook interface

Text	Vers	#DIF	#DIS	State
A cosa serve il tag <HR>	1	0,248	0,650	
Il "tag" DIV serve a:	1	0,192	0,369	
Per creare una nuova cella all'interno di una r...	1	0,212	0,544	
I seguenti elementi sono obbligatori in un coo...	1	0,300	0,471	
Quali affermazioni sono corrette ?	1	0,225	0,740	
Quali delle seguenti affermazioni sull'indiriz...	1	0,288	0,784	
La seguente istruzione HTML: <META HTTP-EQUIV="...	2	0,619	0,441	
Cosa fa l'attributo HSPACE?	2	0,450	0,299	
Cos'è onChange?	1	0,420	0,592	
Quali delle seguenti affermazioni sono corrette:	1	0,245	0,629	
Cos'è onBlur?	1	0,500	0,774	
I valori degli attributi degli elementi XML dev...	1	0,140	0,648	
Quali delle seguenti frasi sono vere:	1	0,157	0,688	
Cosa fa il seguente codice:Element root= new El...	1	0,720	0,414	
La specifica <!ELEMENT Articolo(Rubrica*,...)>s...	1	0,299	0,714	

(a)

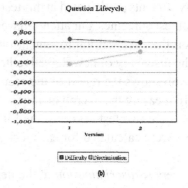

(b)

The *Business Layer* accesses to the *Data Layer*, implemented through a Relational Data Base Management System (RDBMS), to persist the data across the functionalities provided by the *Hibernate* framework.

The integration of the new functionalities in *eWorkbook* has required the development and integration in the platform of new modules at all the layers. In particular, a new sub-system, called *Item Quality Sub-System* (IQS), responsible for instantiating the framework and providing input, output and visualization functionalities, has been added at the *Business Layer*.

Further minor modules have been added at the other layers: input of data is performed by a wrapper module that reads data from *eWorkbook*'s database and calls the *API* to fill the data matrix of the framework; the interface for browsing the item repository in *eWorkbook* has been modified in order to show item's performances (*difficulty* and *discrimination*) and state (*green, yellow* or

red). In this way, defective items are immediately visible to the tutor, who can undertake the opportune actions (delete or modify). A screenshot of the item report is shown in figure 4a.

Furthermore, the platform has been given a *versioning functionality*: once an item is modified, a newer version of it is generated, keeping the old data in the question repository. Through this functionality, the tutor can analyze the entire lifecycle of an item, thus having a feedback on the trend of statistical indicators over time. In this way he/she can verify that the changes he/she made to the items positively affected their quality. Figure 4b shows the chart of an item improved across two sessions of tests. The improvement is visible both from the increase in the item *discrimination* (the green line), and in the convergence of the calculated difficulty with the tutor's estimation of the difficulty (the continuous and dashed red lines, respectively).

EXPERIMENTAL RESULTS

We experimented the system by using it across two test sessions in a university course, and measuring the overall improvement of the items in terms of discrimination capacity and matching to the tutor's desired difficulty. A database of 50 items was arranged for the experiment. In the first session, an on-line test, containing a set of 25 randomly chosen items, was administered to 60 students. After, items were inspected through the system interface in order to check those to substitute or modify. Once the substitutions and modifications were performed, the modified test was administered to 60 other students.

Figure 7a shows a table, exported in a spreadsheet, containing a report of the items presented in the first test session and their performances. The items to eliminate are highlighted in red, while those to modify are highlighted in yellow. According to the system analysis, 5 out of 25 items must be discarded, while 4 of them must be modified.

Actually, among the items to modify, for two of them (those with id 1-F-4 and 1-E-1) the *difficulty* was underestimated due to a *distractor* that was too plausible (class 7), whose text was opportunely modified. In another case (1-B-16), the difficulty was different from that estimated by the tutor, due to the intrinsic difficulty of the item (class 8). The action undertaken was to adjust the tutor's estimation of the difficulty. Lastly, the item with id 1-F-1, with a negative *discrimination*, presented a suspect error in the choice of the key (class 9).

To give the reader a more precise idea, two modified items (opportunely translated from Italian) have been reported in Figure 5 and Figure 6. In item 1-F-4 (Figure 5a), a *distractor* (option D) was sought to be "too plausible". Since the *distractor* was chosen by too many learners (26 out of 60 = 0.43%), the item was much more difficult (*difficulty* = 0.79) than expected (medium = 0.5). The tutor modified the distractor by changing the text from "Refreshes the content of the page http://www.expedia.it/info.htm in 20 seconds" to "Refreshes 20 times the content of the page http://www.expedia.it/info.htm" (Figure 5b). Such a modification significantly decreased the distractor plausibility, thus obtaining a difficulty level (0.43) for the item closer to the desired one, in the second session.

By inspecting item 1-F-1 (Figure 6a), the tutor verified that the chosen *key* was not correct, even though the *distractor* labeled as *correct* by the system was not the right answer: simply, the item did not have any correct answer. The text of the key was modified to provide the right answer to the stem (Figure 6b).

A new test was prepared, containing the same items, except for the 5 discarded ones, substituted by 5 unused items, and for the 4 modified ones, which were substituted by newer versions. A new set of sixty students participated in this test. In the analysis of test outcomes, our attention was more focused on the eventual improvement obtained than on the discovery of new defective items.

Figure 6b shows the report of the second test session. To measure the overall quality improvement across the two test sessions, the following parameters were calculated for each tests:

- the average *discrimination* of the items;
- the average of the differences |*tutor_difficulty – difficulty*| for the items of the tests;

As for parameter 1, we have observed an improvement from a value of 0.375, obtained in the first session, to a value of 0.466, obtained in the second session. As for parameter 2, we had a decrement in the mean difference between

Figure 5. The versions of item 1-F-4 used for the first (a) and the second (b) test session

1-F-4. The following HTML statement:
<META HTTP-EQUIV="refresh" CONTENT="20;URL=http://www.expedia.it/info.htm">
A. Includes the first 20 rows of the page http://www.expedia.it/info.htm into the one containing the statement
B. Includes the page http://www.expedia.it/info.htm into the one containing the statement in 20 seconds
C. *Loads the specified page http://www.expedia.it/info.htm in 20 seconds*
D. Refreshes the content of the page http://www.expedia.it/info.htm in 20 seconds
E. Refreshes the content of the current page in 20 seconds

(a)

1-F-4. The following HTML statement:
<META HTTP-EQUIV="refresh" CONTENT="20;URL=http://www.expedia.it/info.htm">
C. Includes the first 20 rows of the page http://www.expedia.it/info.htm into the one containing the statement
B. Includes the page http://www.expedia.it/info.htm into the one containing the statement in 20 seconds
C. *Loads the specified page http://www.expedia.it/info.htm in 20 seconds*
D. Refreshes 20 times the content of the page http://www.expedia.it/info.htm
E. Refreshes the content of the current page in 20 seconds

(b)

the difficulty estimated by the tutor and the one calculated by the system, passing from a value of 0.19 to 0.157 across the two sessions.

It is worth noting that, in our experiment, the tests have been administered to learners enrolled to the same university course, even if across different exam sessions. The results can be considered valid with respect to the above requirement. Due to the dependency of *IA* results on the learners' ability, there is no warranty that the system behaves in the expected way also when radically changing the context between different sessions.

RELATED WORK

Several different applications supporting e-testing, such as the most common Web-based e-learning platforms, (*Moodle, Blackboard*, and *Questionmark*), evaluate item quality by generating and showing item statistics. Nevertheless, in most cases, the interpretation of their results is left to the tutors: these systems do not advise or help the tutor in improving items.

Several commercial stand-alone applications are available for improving test quality through

Figure 6. The versions of item 1-F-1 used for the first (a) and the second (b) test session

1-F-1. What is the role of the HSPACE attribute?
A. *It sets the horizontal space among images*
B. It inserts a Java Applet in the page
C. It sets the horizontal space between text attributes
D. It sets the vertical space among images
E. It sets the horizontal space between images and page borders

(a)

1-F-1. What is the role of the HSPACE attribute?
A. *It sets the horizontal space between the image and surrounding text*
B. It inserts a Java Applet in the page
C. It sets the horizontal space between text attributes
D. It sets the vertical space among images
E. It sets the horizontal space between images and page borders

(b)

Figure 7. Results after test sessions

Question Id	Options	Correct	Discrimination	Tutor Diff	Difficulty
1-F-1	5	1	-0,04	0,7	0,76
1-B-10	5	3	0,51	0,5	0,24
1-B-6	5	4	0,6	0,5	0,58
1-A-19	5	4	0,22	0,5	0,29
1-D-2	5	2	0,7	0,5	0,82
1-B-4	5	5	0,42	0,5	0,34
1-A-13	5	1	0,33	0,3	0,08
1-F-4	5	3	0,32	0,5	0,79
1-B-18	5	4	0,55	0,3	0,53
1-A-15	5	5	0,37	0,5	0,66
1-B-2	5	5	0,59	0,5	0,45
1-E-4	5	4	0,4	0,5	0,79
1-C-1	5	1	0,67	0,5	0,39
1-B-12	5	4	0,48	0,3	0,74
1-A-24	5	2	0,36	0,3	0,37
1-D-3	5	5	0,15	0,5	0,53
1-C-4	5	1	0,16	0,5	0,74
1-B-16	5	3	0,41	0,5	0,76
1-A-9	5	3	0,57	0,3	0,53
1-B-20	5	5	0,38	0,3	0,47
1-A-2	5	2	0,21	0,3	0,34
1-B-8	5	5	0,49	0,5	0,29
1-C-5	5	1	0,17	0,7	0,87
1-B-15	5	4	0,52	0,5	0,42
1-E-1	5	4	0,44	0,5	0,87
Average Discrimination			0,3752		
Average Difficulty Gap			0,19		

(a)

Question Id	Options	Correct	Discrimination	Tutor Diff	Difficulty
1-F-1	5	1	0,48	0,7	0,67
1-B-10	5	3	0,54	0,5	0,20
1-B-6	5	4	0,58	0,5	0,57
1-D-4	5	3	0,08	0,5	0,76
1-D-2	5	2	0,62	0,5	0,78
1-B-4	5	5	0,42	0,5	0,30
1-A-13	5	1	0,39	0,3	0,07
1-F-4	5	3	0,47	0,5	0,43
1-B-18	5	4	0,63	0,3	0,45
1-A-15	5	5	0,40	0,5	0,71
1-B-2	5	5	0,56	0,5	0,39
1-E-4	5	4	0,40	0,5	0,88
1-A-17	5	5	0,44	0,3	0,45
1-B-12	5	4	0,46	0,3	0,65
1-A-24	5	2	0,38	0,3	0,29
1-D-3	5	5	0,13	0,5	0,44
1-A-23	5	3	0,38	0,3	0,32
1-B-16	5	3	0,40	0,7	0,84
1-A-9	5	3	0,50	0,3	0,52
1-B-20	5	5	0,45	0,3	0,46
1-F-3	5	5	0,76	0,7	0,72
1-B-8	5	5	0,55	0,5	0,25
1-B-5	5	5	0,66	0,3	0,50
1-B-15	5	4	0,59	0,5	0,49
1-E-1	5	4	0,37	0,5	0,58
Average Discrimination			0,4660		
Average Difficulty Gap			0,1573		

(b)

IA (Integrity, 2008; Berk & Griesemer, 1976; Lertap, 2008) or *IRT* (RASCAL, 2008; Gierl & Ackerman, 1996). These can import test data from e-testing systems through a text file. Some of them are Web-based applications, such as *Integrity* (Integrity, 2008). It can perform a detailed test analysis which also identifies problem areas and includes relevant recommendations for addressing them. Differently from our system, parameters are not combined in rules: a recommendation is given when for a given parameter an anomalous value is sought.

Some other systems run under specific platforms (OS or spreadsheets). A program running under MS Windows is *ITEMAN* (Berk & Griesemer, 1976). *ITEMAN* analyzes data files (ASCII format) of test item responses produced by optical mark readers (scanners) or by manual data entry to compute conventional item analysis statistics. *ITEMAN* offers a multiple-keying option that allows items to have more than one correct answer (e.g., for a poorly-written item), and will flag those answers which appear to function better than the keyed answer. Our system does something similar by firing rule 9.

An application running in a spreadsheet is *Lertap* (Lertap, 2008), an Excel-based classical item and test analysis program. A nice feature of this program is the so called *Visual Item Analysis*, suggesting an ocular approach to item analysis, and exemplifying some of the graphics made by *Lertap*.

A model for presenting test statistics, analysis, and to collect students' learning behaviors for generating analysis result and feedback to tutors is described in (Hsieh et al., 2003).

In other approaches, the qualitative characteristics of the items are considered for different aims: *IRT* has been applied in some systems (Ho & Yen, 2005) and experiments (Chen et al., 2004; Sun, 2000) to select the most appropriate items for examinees based on individual ability. In (Chen et al., 2004), the *fuzzy set* theory is combined with the original *IRT* to model uncertainly learning response. The result of this combination is called *Fuzzy Item Response Theory*. Winters et al. (2005), mining the data of their educational institutions, found some scores that could be analyzed with the purpose of identifying those items that were particularly good or particularly bad, giving instructors feedback that will hopefully train them to ask better questions more consistently.

A work closely related to ours is presented in (Hung et al., 2004). It proposes an e-testing system, where rules can detect defective items, which are signaled using traffic lights. It proposes an analysis model based on *IA*. Statistics are calculated by the system both on the items and on the whole test. Unfortunately, the four rules on which the system is based seem to be insufficient to cover all of the possible defects which can affect an item. Moreover, these rules are not inferred from consolidated statistical models and use crisp values (i.e., one of them, states that an option must be discarded if its frequency is 0, independently from the size of the sample). Furthermore, it does not contain any experiment which demonstrates the effectiveness of the system in improving assessment. Nevertheless, this work has given us many ideas, and our work can be considered a continuation of it. To elaborate, our system improves the above cited one in the following aspects:

- it broadens and improves the rules used to check the items;
- it gives advice to tutors to improve item quality;
- it manages rules uncertainty (using fuzzy logic);
- it has been evaluated in an experiment.

Lastly, most of the scientific literature about *e-testing* and structured tests focuses on item generation with automatic (Mitkov & Ha, 2003; Brown et al., 2005) or semi-automatic (Wang et al., 2007; Hoshino & Nakagawa, 2007; Chen et al., 2006) processes based on *Natural Language Processing* (*NLP*) techniques, performed on instructional documents in an electronic format. The automatic systems generate the items, while the semi-automatic ones assist the user in their generation. In general, the human intervention is anyhow necessary for verifying the good sense of the items before using them in a test. Only in a few cases, the quality of the generated items is verified through statistical model such as *IA* or *IRT*. In most cases they are inspected and eventually modified by the tutor. The evaluation of the whole system is performed by checking the percentage of the reliable items out of the number of generated ones.

In conclusion, we believe that tools that automatically generate items or assist the tutor in their creation, as those described before, can be very useful, since they permit to reduce the times of the onerous item construction phase. Nevertheless, they are still far from offering optimal performances and many of the analyzed systems are tailored for a specific educational subject, mostly foreign language teaching. Our approach is more general and can be applied to any subject. Furthermore, many tutors will keep on using their own items and our system is still applicable to generated items, for further improving their quality. Our system, compared to automatic or semi-automatic ones, requires a longer time for item construction, but allows us to obtain better quality items on the following aspects:

- a better discrimination capacity;
- evaluation of the learners on tutor's desired knowledge;
- a difficulty level closer to tutor's desired one.

CONCLUSION

In this article we have presented a *rule-based e-testing system*, capable of improving item quality. Our system's knowledge-base is mostly taken from several statistical models for item evaluation and partly extracted from data.

The system detects anomalies on *multiple choice* items and gives tutors advise for their improvement. Obviously, the system can only detect defects which are visible by analyzing results of *item* and *distractor analysis*.

The strength of our system is in the possibility for all the tutors, and not only experts of assessment or statistics, to improve test quality, by discarding or, when possible, by modifying defective items. An initial experiment carried out at the University of Salerno has produced encouraging results, showing that the system can effectively help the tutors to obtain items which better discriminate between skilled and untrained students and better match the difficulty estimated by the tutor. More accurate experiments, involving a larger set of items and students, are necessary to better measure the system capabilities.

Our system performs a classification of items, carried out by evaluating fuzzy rules. At present, we are collecting data on test outcomes. Even though fuzzy classification has proven itself to perform well, we intend to investigate also other classification methods, such as *decision trees* and *Bayesian classifiers*, once a large database of items and learner's answers will be available.

REFERENCES

Bardossy, A., & Duckstein, L. (1995). *Fuzzy Rule-Based Modeling with Applications to Geophysical, Biological, and Engineering Systems*. Boca Raton, USA: CRC Press.

Berk, R. A., & Griesemer, H. A. (1976). Software Review: ITEMAN: An Item Analysis Program for Tests, Questionnaires, and Scales. *Educational and Psychological Measurement, 36*(1), 189–191. doi:10.1177/001316447603600122

Blackboard (2008). Available at http://www.blackboard.com.

Brachman, R. J., Khabaza, T., Kloesgen, W., Piea-tetsky-Shapiro, G., & Simoudis, E. (1996). Mining Business Databases. *Communications of the ACM, 39*(11), 42–48. doi:10.1145/240455.240468

Bradley, R. S., Barry, R. G., & Kiladis, G. (1982). *Climatic fluctuations of the western United States during the period of instrumental records. Final report to the National Science Foundation.* Amherst: University of Massachussets.

Brown, J. C., Frishkoff, G. A., & Eskenazi, M. (2005). Automatic Question Generation for Vocabulary Assessment. *Proceedings of the conference on Human Language Technology and Empirical Methods in Natural Language Processing* (pp 819-826).

Chen, C. M., Duh, L. J., & Liu, C. Y. (2004). A Personalized Courseware Recommendation System Based on Fuzzy Item Response Theory. *Proceedings of the IEEE International Conference on e-Technology, e-Commerce and e-Service*, Taipei, Taiwan (pp. 305—308).

Chen, C.-Y., Liou, H.-C., & Chang, J. S. (2006). FAST: an automatic generation system for grammar tests. *Proceedings of the COLING/ACL on Interactive Presentation Sessions* (pp 1-4).

Civanlar, M. R., & Trussel, H. J. (1986). Constructing membership functions using statistical data. *Fuzzy Sets and Systems, 18*, 1–14. doi:10.1016/0165-0114(86)90024-2

Costagliola, G., Ferrucci, F., Fuccella, V., & Oliveto, R. (2007). eWorkbook: a Computer Aided Assessment System. *International Journal of Distance Education Technologies, 5*(3), 24–41. doi:10.4018/jdet.2007070103

ECMAScript. (2008). Standard ECMA-262, EC-MAScript Language Specification, available at http://www.ecma-international.org/publications/files/ECMA-ST/Ecma-262.pdf.

Exarchos, T. P., Tsipouras, M. G., Exarchos, C. P., Papaloukas, C., Fotiadis, D. I., & Michalis, L. K. (2007). A methodology for the automated creation of fuzzy expert systems for ischaemic and arrhythmic beat classification based on a set of rules obtained by a decision tree. *Artificial Intelligence in Medicine, 40*(3), 187–200. doi:10.1016/j.artmed.2007.04.001

FCL. (1997): Fuzzy Control Prog. Committee Draft CD 1.0 (Rel. 19 Jan 97), http://www.fuzzytech.com/binaries/ieccd1.pdf.

Gierl, M. J., & Ackerman, T. (1996). Software Review: XCALIBRE — Marginal Maximum-Likelihood Estimation Program, Windows Version 1.10. *Applied Psychological Measurement, 20*(3), 303–307. doi:10.1177/014662169602000312

Hambleton, R. K., & Swaminathan, H. (1985). *Item Response Theory - Principles and Applications.* Netherlands: Kluwer Academic Publishers Group.

Hibernate (2008), available at http://www.hibernate.org.

Ho, R. G., & Yen, Y. C. (2005). Design and Evaluation of an XML-Based Platform-Independent Computerized Adaptive Testing System. *IEEE Transactions on Education, 48*(2), 230–237. doi:10.1109/TE.2004.837035

Hoshino, A., & Nakagawa, H. (2007). A Cloze Test Authoring System and Its Automation. *Proceedings of 6th International Conference on Web-Based Learning* (pp. 174- 181).

Hsieh, C. T., Shih, T. K., Chang, W. C., & Ko, W. C. (2003). Feedback and Analysis from Assessment Metadata in E-learning. *Proceedings of the 17th International Conference on Advanced Information Networking and Applications*, Xi'an, China, (pp. 155—158).

Hung, J. C., Lin, L. J., Chang, W. C., Shih, T. K., Hsu, H. H., Chang, H. B., et al. (2004). A Cognition Assessment Authoring System for E-Learning. *Proceedings of the 24th Int. Conf. on Distributed Computing Systems Workshops* (pp. 262—267).

IA. (2008). *Item Analysis*. Available at http://www. washington.edu/oea/pdfs/resources/item_analysis.pdf.

Integrity (2008). Integrity - Item analysis and collusion detection tools. http://integrity.castlerockresearch.com/

jFuzzyLogic (2008): Open Source Fuzzy Logic (Java). Available at http://jfuzzylogic.sourceforge. net/html/index.html.

Lertap (2008). Lertap 5! http://www.lertap.curtin. edu.au/

Mamdani, E. H., & Assilian, S. (1999). An experiment in Linguistic Synthesis with a Fuzzy Logic Controller. *International Journal of Human-Computer Studies*, *51*(2), 135–147. doi:10.1006/ ijhc.1973.0303

Massey (2007). The Relationship Between the Popularity of Questions and Their Difficulty Level in Examinations Which Allow a Choice of Question. *Occasional Publication of The Test Dev. and Res. Unit*, Cambridge.

MEAP. (2007). State of Michigan – Department of Education. *Design and Validity of the MEAP Test*. Available at http://www.michigan.gov/ mde/0,1607,7-140-22709_31168-94522--,00. html.

Mitkov, R., & Ha, L. A. (2003). Computer-Aided Generation of Multiple-Choice Tests. *Proceedings of the HLT-NAACL 03 workshop on Building educational applications using natural language processing - Volume 2* (pp. 17-22).

Momoh, J., Srinivasan, D., Tomsovic, K., & Baer, D. (2000). Expert Systems Applications. In Tomsovic, K., & Chov, M. Y. (Eds.), *Tutorial on Fuzzy Logic Applications in Power Systems*.

Moodle (2008). Available at http://moodle.org.

Questionmark (2008). Available at http://www. questionmark.com.

RASCAL. (2008). RASCAL - Rasch Analysis Program. http://www.assess.com/xcart/product. php?productid=253&cat=29&page=1

Roiger, R. J., & Geatz, M. W. (2007). *Introduzione al Data Mining*. McGraw-Hill. (in Italian)

Stage, C. (1999). A Comparison Between Item Analysis Based on Item Response Theory and Classical Test Theory. A *Study of the SweSAT Subtest READ*. Available at http://www. umu. se/ edmeas/ publikationer/ pdf/ enr3098sec.pdf.

Struts (2008), The Apache Struts Web Application Framework, http://struts.apache.org

Sun, K. T. (2000). An Effective Item Selection Method for Educational Measurement. *Proceedings of the International Workshop on Advanced Learning Technologies* (pp. 105—106).

Wang, W., Hao, T., & Liu, W. (2007). Automatic Question Generation for Learning Generation in Medicine. *Proceedings of 6th International Conference on Web-Based Learning* (pp. 198-203).

Winters, T., & Payne, T. (2005). What Do Students Know? An Outcomes Based Assessment System. *Proceedings of the 2005 international workshop on Computing education research* (pp. 165-172).

Woodford, K., & Bancroft, P. (2005). Multiple Choice Items Not Considered Harmful. *Proceedings of 7th Australian Conference on Computing Education* (pp. 109—116).

Yu, C. H. (2005). A Simple Guide to the Item Response Theory (IRT) http://seamonkey.ed.asu. edu/~alex/computer/sas/IRT.pdf

Yu, C. H., & Wong, J. W. (2003). Using SAS for classical item analysis and option analysis. *Proceedings of 2003 Western Users of SAS Software Conference*. http://www.lexjansen.com/wuss/2003/DataAnalysis/c-using_sas_for_classical_item_analysis.pdf

Zadeh, L. A. (1977). *Fuzzy Sets and Their Applications to Pattern Classification and Clustering*. River Edge, NJ, USA: World Scientific Publishing Co. Inc.

Zhou, J., Li, Q., Xu, D., Chen, Y., & Xiao, T. (2005). Fuzzy Rule-based Integrated System Multi-indicators Economic Performance Evaluation and Decision Making Support Framework. *Proceedings of International Conference on Computational Intelligence for Modelling, Control and Automation/ International Conference on Intelligent Agents, Web Technologies and Internet Commerce* (pp. 714-720).

This work was previously published in International Journal of Distance Education Technologies, Volume 7, Issue 2, edited by Qun Jin, pp. 63-82, copyright 2009 by IGI Publishing (an imprint of IGI Global).

Chapter 14
An Understanding Information Management System for a Real-Time Interactive Distance Education Environment

Aiguo He
The University of Aizu, Japan

ABSTRACT

A real-time interactive distance lecture is a joint work that should be accomplished by the effort of the lecturer and his students in remote sites. It is important for the lecturer to get understanding information from the students which cannot be efficiently collected by only using video/audio channels between the lecturer and the students. This article proposes RIDEE-UIM (Understanding Information Management system for Real-time Interactive Distance Education Environment) for collecting understanding information from each participant to the lecturer during real time distance education activities. The usefulness of RIDEE-UIM has been confirmed by experiments. This article describes the basic idea, implementation and experiments of RIDEE-UIM.

INTRODUCTION

A distance education activity, such as a distance lecture, a distance exercise or distance seminar, is a joint work accomplished by the participants (the lecturer and his students), who interact by using audio/video communication equipment or computer support systems.

There are two kinds of computer system for supporting distance educational activities: asynchronous support system and synchronous support system. Asynchronous support system can be realized based on the normal Internet for providing learning resources to people who want to study by themselves and/or make asynchronous communication with their instructors by email, etc.. Moodle(Moodle home page, 2008) is a good example of asynchronous system. There are also systems based on SCORM(Advanced Distributed Learning. Sharable Content Object Reference Model, 2008) or other standard/methodology (Jardim, Neto, & Ribas, 2005) (Nordmann &

Neumann, 2008)(Zhang, Cheng, Huang, He, & Koyama, 2003).

By the spread of high-speed computer communication network and audio/video technology, synchronous support system can be easily constructed(Erol & Li, 2005). Synchronous support systems allow real-time education activities to be performed between remote sites with high quality audio/video equipment and shared multimedia materials over broadband communication environment such as satellite communication systems(Araki, Yagi, Sugitani, & Minoh, 1999)(Suzuki et al., 2000)(Tanaka & Kondo, 1999)(Space Collaboration System Project, 2008) and high-speed network(Kohsaka, Nomura, & Shibata, 1997)(Segawa, Sugino, & Miyazaki, 2000)(Watanabe et al., 2000)(Yoshino & Munemori, 2002). Synchronous support system is important for people who want to study under real-time instructions from other person. By the audio/video channel between the lecturer and the students, interactive virtual classroom can be constructed(Deshpande & Hwang, 2001). Researches were done about video data(Liu & Kender, 2004) and lecture materials (Wang, Ngo, & Pong, 2003)

But almost real time distance learning support systems only support the information flow from lecturer side to student side. The lecturer has to catch information from students only by the video picture from remote sites. A skilled lecturer can properly give questions to the students to collect information about their understanding situation, but this is not efficient for such students who do not want talk positively. Therefore, it is necessary to collect understanding information from the students efficiently.

In author's university, a research project named "Real-time Interactive Distance Educational Environment (RIDEE for short)" has been promoted since 2000 (Cheng et al.,2000)(He et al., 2001). To solve the above-mentioned problem, we proposed an RIDEE-UIM (RIDEE Understanding Information Management system)(He & Cheng, 2004), the usefulness of which has been confirmed by experiments.

In the remainder of this paper, the outline of RIDEE and the basic idea of RIDEE-UIM are described in Section "RIDEE-UIM"; its detail design and its implementation are described in Section "Design and Implementation by Java"; its experimental evaluation is described in Section "Experiment and Evaluation".

RIDEE-UIM

RIDEE and RIDEE-SPS

RIDEE is a distributed computing platform for support of real-time distance education activities(He, Zhang, & Cheng, 2004). It realizes a virtual classroom consisting of more than one physical site, each of which can be a classroom or a studio, over high-speed network(Figure 1).

High-quality video/audio channels exist among the sites to support real-time interactive activities. All the sites are equipped with video cameras, projection screens, microphones and speakers for constructing the video/audio channels.

Every participant(lecturer or student) joins the computer supported activities using their own information processing equipment(at present, assuming they are personal computers); and the audio/video equipment can be remotely controlled from other sites.

By now, RIDEE has three subsystems developed by Java technology: RIDEE-CCP(RIDEE-Communication Control Platform) for Java object-based communication(He, Cheng, Huang, & Koyama, 2002), RIDEE-FCS (RIDEE-Floor Control System) for floor control in education activities(He, Cheng, Koyama, et al., 2002) and RIDEE-SPS (RIDEE Slide Presentation System)

Figure 1. Image of RIDEE

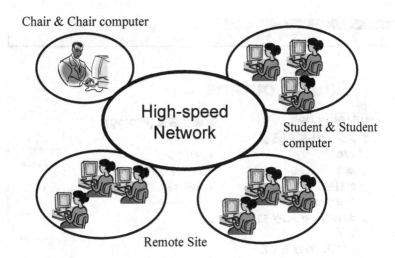

for material management and presentation(He et al., 2003).

RIDEE-SPS distributes lecture materials from lecturer computer to others, synchronizing the contents displayed on each computer with the lecturer's operation. The lecture materials are sets of JPEG format pictures (slides), which can be created by a tool such as Microsoft PowerPoint(Microsoft Powerpoint, 2008). Those pictures satisfactorily convey information for most educational purposes and can be easily shared and managed over network.

Figure 2 shows the user interface of RIDEE-SPS, by which the participants can perform the following operations:

- Load a slide set from a local computer. The slides will be automatically transmitted to all other computers in this virtual classroom.
- Add text or free hand lines on the displayed slide, by the keyboard or mouse.
- Select a set or a slide to be shared.
- Use a white board.
- Select the foreground color of the text or free hand lines on the slide.

Understanding Information Management

Understanding Information is the information sent from the student side to the lecturer side which expresses how much the materials offered by the lecturer have been understood by the students. The following are the requirements to understanding information management for real-time education support systems:

- The students can easily send their understanding information to the lecturer for each slide showed by the lecturer.
- The statistical results of the understating information should be immediately showed to the virtual classroom and easily used by the lecturer in the ongoing distance lecture.
- Understanding information saved according to students can be used later, for the analysis and instruction of individual student, and the improvement of the lecture materials.

Figure 3 shows the model of RIDEE-UIM which works based on RIDEE-SPS.

Figure 2. GUI of RIDEE-SPS

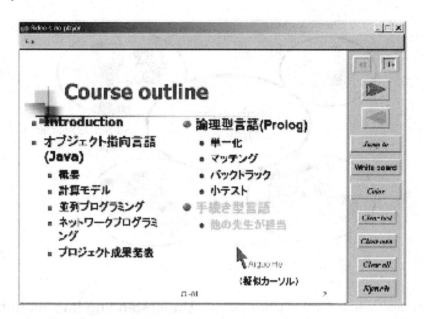

Figure 3. System model of RIDEE-UIM

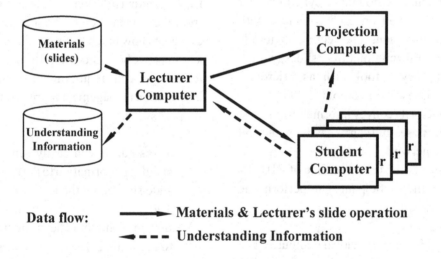

At the beginning of the distance lecture, the lecturer sends materials (slides) from lecturer computer to all the student computers. During the lecture, the students input their understanding information on each slide, which then be sent to the lecturer computer. Those information will be saved in the lecturer computer for immediately or later use. Also, the statistical results of the understanding information will be showed on each projection computer and student computer. Slide is the minimum unit of the materials used in RIDEE. So it is convenient to manage the understanding information about each slide.

For a lecture, the set V of understanding information data can be expressed as:

$$V = \{v_{ij} | 1 \leq i \leq S, \ 1 \leq j \leq P\}$$

Figure 4. Software architecture of RIDEE-UIM

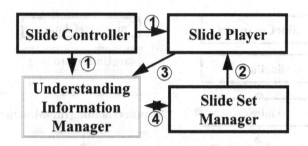

① **Slide change message**
② **Slide Data**
③ **Slide Information**
④ **Understanding Information**

S is the number of the slides offered by the lecturer; P is the number of students in the virtual classroom.

v_{ij} is a value of understanding degree.

$$v_{ij} \in \{d_k | 1 \leq k \leq D\}$$

D is the number of understanding degree.

For slide(i), its average value of understanding can be obtained by:

$$U_{sa}(i) = \frac{1}{P} \sum_{j=1}^{P} v_{ij}$$

And its statistical value of understanding can be expressed as:

$$U_{ss}(i) = \{a_k | 1 \leq k \leq D\}$$

a_k is the number of $v_{ij} = d_k$ in subset $V_i = \{v_{ij} | 1 \leq j \leq P\} \in V$.

For student(j), his average value of understanding can be obtained by:

$$U_{pa}(j) = \frac{1}{S} \sum_{i=1}^{S} v_{ij}$$

Besides the above-mentioned data, the understanding operation log data recording the transition of understanding value is also useful for various analysis after the lecture. This kind of data can be expressed as:

$$L = \{R_i | i = 1, 2, ...\}; R_i = \{p_i, s_i, v_i, t_i\}\}$$

R_i is one record of the operation log data, meaning that a student(p_i) had input his understanding value(v_i) on a slide(s_i) at time t_i.

DESIGN AND IMPLEMENTATION BY JAVA

Software Architecture

Figure 4 shows the software architecture of RIDEE-UIM, which consists of three components belonging to RIDEE-SPS: Slide Controller, Slide Player and Slide Set Manager, and one new component, Understanding Information Manager.

Slide Controller contains all the buttons on the RIDEE-SPS's GUI (see Figure 2), accepting the slide operation from the lecturer or student, transmitting slide change messages to the Slide Players in the virtual classroom.

Slide Player forms the slide area on the RIDEE-SPS's GUI, receiving messages of slide data and slide operation data (cursor position, slide change,

Figure 5. Class hierarchy of RIDEE-UIM

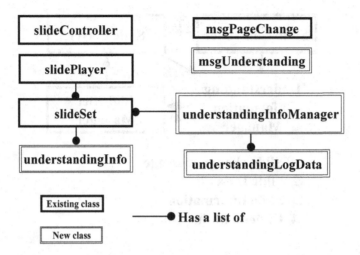

online note, etc.) from Slide Controller(s), rendering them on the computer display.

Slide Set Manager manages one set of slides to be displayed by the Slide Player. Because the understanding information are attached to each slide, Slide Set Manager is the best component for saving the understanding information data.

Understanding Information Manager forms a GUI area on the computer screen, accepting the understanding information input form students for each slide, taking the statistic of the information, showing the statistical results. It also communicate with the Understanding Information Managers on other computers, transmitting and receiving understanding information.

When a slide change message is received from a Slide Controller, the Slide Player whips out the designated slide data stored in the Slide Set Manager, displaying it on the slide area.

The Understanding Information Manager will receive the same slide change message after the Slide Player finished the slide display, then it (1) gets the information about displayed slide from the Slide Player; (2) gets the understanding information of that slide form the Slide Set Manager, initializing its GUI.

When an understanding information message is received, the Understanding Information Manager will pass the message to Slide Set Manager to save the received data.

Class Hierarchy

Figure 5 shows the class hierarchy of RIDEE-UIM. The following classes are newly designed:

- understandingInfoManager achieves the functions of Understanding Information Manager. It shares the list of the slideSet objects with the slidePlayer.
- The list of understandingInfo stores the understanding information data set V. It also has functions to access V.
- The list of understandingLogData stores the understanding operation log data set L. It also has functions to access L.
- msgUnderstanding achieves the understanding information input from the students. it will be created by the understandingInfoManager when a student input his understanding information. msgUnderstanding will be sent by the understandingInfoManager to all other computers.

Figure 6. GUI of RIDEE-SPS and RIDEE-UIM

slidePlayer and slideSet are existing classes in RIDEE-SPS, but are enhanced for RIDEE-UIM.

slideController and msgPageChange are existing classes in RIDEE-SPS, relating to RIDEE-UIM.

Communication between those classe objects is realized by RIDEE-CCP(He, Cheng, Huang, & Koyama, 2002).

About Understanding Degree

In current version, the number of understanding degrees D and $\{d_k | 1 \le k \le D\}$ are as follows:

$$D = 3$$
$$\{d_k | 1 \le k \le D\} = \left\{ \begin{array}{l} \text{Well understand} \\ \text{Aomost understand} \\ \text{Not understand} \end{array} \right\}$$

GUI

Figure 6 shows the new GUI of RIDEE-SPS enhanced by RIDEE-UIM, which is a small window under the slide area, offering following functions:

- Inputing understanding information: By clicking a radio button, Understand well, Understand almost or Not understand, the student can input his understanding information about the slide showed on the slide area.
- Statistical Graph: This graph shows the total understanding situation about the slide showed on the slide area. For example, in Figure 6, for the current slide, about 50% of the students say they well understand, about 13% of them say almost understand, about 12% of them say not understand, about 25% of them have not input their understanding information yet.

Figure 7 shows an application of the understanding information. This is a list of slides offered by the lecturer. On each slide, its statistical result graph is displayed. By these graphs, the lecturer can easily know which slide should be explained to the students again.

Experiment and Evaluation

Distance lecture experiments were performed in the University of Aizu to evaluate RIDEE-UIM. Those experiments were combined with an actual normal class, Communication and Networking,

Figure 7. Slide list with understanding information

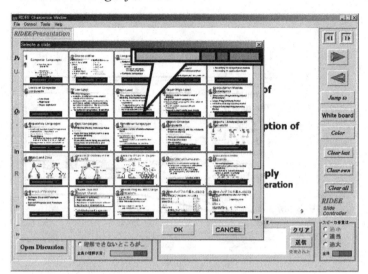

which was performed in the lecturer theater of the University of Aizu. The lecturer site was the lecturer theater and the remote classroom site was an office room. In the experiments, part of the normal class students were attended in the remote classroom. In the remote classroom, every student has a computer, sharing the teaching materials (slides) with the lecturer. A projection screen was used to display the video of the lecturer site. The students heard the voice of the lecturer, watching the mouse moving on the slides, inputing their understanding level value timely for each slide.

Figure 8 shows the sight of the remote classroom site. The video and audio data between the two sites was transmitted by using a TV conference system, Polycom made by the Polycom Ltd..

The experiments were done two times, totally attended by 21 students as experimental subjects. After each experiment, a questionnaires was answered by the students. The questions of the questionnaire were as follows:

Q1　Is this system easy to use?
Q2　Is this system a burden to you?
Q3　Can a distance class with RIDEE-UIM get the efficient like in a face-to-face style class ?
Q4　Did this system function smoothly?

Figure 8. The remote classroom site

Q5　Is the statistic graph of RIDEE-MIU useful to you?
Q6　Is the number of understanding levels enough to describe your understanding ?
Q7　Is this system useful for distance classes?
Q8　Could you learn efficiently using this system compared with a face-to-face style class?

The answer values for Q1-Q8 are among 1(poor) to 5(very good). The result of the questionnaire are shown in Figure 9.

80% of the experimental subjects answered "very good" or "good" in Q1 and Q2. These results

Figure 9. Evaluations of RIDEE-UIM

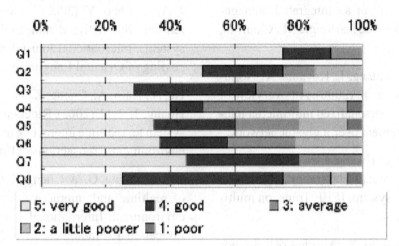

show that the operation of RIDEE-UIM is easy, and is not a burden to the students. 18% of the experimental subjects answered "a little poor" in Q3, and 20% of them answered "a little poor" or "poor" in Q4. The reason for this results is that in the first experiment, a computer crashed because its user unexpectedly pulled out its power supply at the beginning of this class, and this lost about 5 minutes of that class. 60% of the experimental subjects answered "very good" or "good" in Q5, 80% of them answered "very good" or "good" in Q7. These results mean that the statistical graph is useful and RIDEE-UIM is effective to the distance class. 70% of the experimental subjects answered "very good" or "good" in Q8. This result shows that students could efficiently understand the teaching materials offered by the teacher compared with traditional class.

CONCLUSION

The importance of understanding information collection support in real-time interactive distance education environment has turned out from our current education practices. To solve this problem, RIDEE-UIM, was developed. RIDEE-UIM provides easy functions to feedback the personal un-

derstanding situation of the students/participants to the lecturer/presenter in real-time, and show the statistical results to the classroom without to open private information such as student's name.

Several distance lectures were performed and RIDEE enhanced by RIDEE-UIM was applied. It was confirmed by the questionnaire's result that RIDEE-UIM is effective to distance classes, and distance classes near the face-to-face style class become possible by using RIDEE-UIM.

The future work about RIDEE-UIM are as follows:

- The improvement of RIDEE-UIM for supporting students who are late for the distance class, or leave early from the class.
- Evaluation from the view point of user interface and the improvement of evaluation methodology.

REFERENCES

Advanced distributed learning (adl). sharable content object reference model. (2008). Available from http://www.adlnet.org/scorm/

Araki, M., Yagi, K., Sugitani, K., & Minoh, M. (1999). Development of an integrated management system of distance learning. JDLA Journal, 1 , 28-32.

Cheng, Z., He, A., Huang, T., Koyama, A., Noguchi, S., Honda, N., et al. (2000). An overview of an interactive and personalized multimedia tele-education environment over a gigabit network.

Deshpande, S. G., & Hwang, J.-N. (2001). A real-time interactive virtual classroom multimedia distance learning system. IEEE Trans. on multimedia, 3 , 432 -444.

Erol, B., & Li, Y. (2005). An overview of technologies for e-meeting and e-lecture. In Proceedings of ieee international conference on multimedia and expo (icme). Los Alamitos, CA, USA: IEEE Computer Society.

He, A., & Cheng, Z. (2004). A design of understanding information management system for realtime interactive distance education environment. In Proceedings of 2nd international conference on knowledge economy and development of science and technology (p. 89-95). Beijing, China:Tsinghua University Press.

He, A., Cheng, Z., Huang, T., & Koyama, A. (2002). The development of a communication control platform for realtime interactive distance education support systems. In Proceedings of 2002 international workshop on multimedia distance education systems and technologies (p. 420-428). San Francisco, California, USA: Knowledge Systems Institute.

He, A., Cheng, Z., Huang, T., Nakatani, R., Amadatsu, Y., Koyama, A., et al. (2001). Design of a realtime interactive tele-exercise classroom for computer exercises over a gigabit network. In Proceedings of the 15th international conference on information networking (p. 757-762). Los Alamitos, CA, USA: IEEE Computer Society.

He, A., Cheng, Z., Koyama, A., Huang, T., Dehart, J. A., & Zhao, Y. (2002). A working model for realtime interactive distance education support systems. International Journal of Computer Processing of Oriental Languages, 15 , 19-31.

He, A., Kara, A., Cheng, Z., Go, K., Koyama, A., Huang, T., et al. (2003). Ridee-sps: a presentation system for realtime interactive distance education environment. Transactions of ISPJ , 44 ,700 -708.

He, A., Zhang, G., & Cheng, Z. (2004). A design of realtime and interactive distance education environment. International Journal of Distance Education Technologies, 2 , 1-12.

Jardim, C. H., Neto, R. B., & Ribas, H. B. (2005). Web services enabling context-aware applications:Lessons learned by integrating e-learning applications. nwesp, 400-405.

Kohsaka, Y., Nomura, T., & Shibata, Y. (1997). Design and evaluation of flexible multimedia remote lecturing support system. IPSJ SIGNotes, DPS-82-15 , 81-86.

Liu, T., & Kender, J. R. (2004). Lecture videos for e-learning: Current research and challenges. ismse, 574-578.

Microsoft powerpoint. (2008). Available from http://office.microsoft.com/en-us/powerpoint/

Moodle home page. (2008). Available from http://moodle.org/

Nordmann, M., & Neumann, J. (2008). Learning application suite creating and playing scorm compatible web and computer based training. In Icalt'08. eighth ieee international conference on advanced learning technologies (p. 572-573). Los Alamitos, CA, USA: IEEE Computer Society.

Segawa, N., Sugino, E., & Miyazaki, M. (2000). The consideration of the distance learning between iwate prefectural university and miyaki junior college division, iwate prefectural university. IEICE technical report. Education technology, ET2000-49 , 23-28.

Space collaboration system project. (2008). Available from http://www.nime.ac.jp/SCS

Suzuki, H., Wakabayashi, R., Eguchi, K., Muto, K., Shimada, K., & Takahata, F. (2000). Vsat network distance learning system by each station functioning control in turn. JDLA Journal, 2 , 16-20.

Tanaka, K., & Kondo, K. (1999). Configuration of inter-university satellite network (space collaboration system). IEICE Transactions on Information and Systems, 82-D-I , 581-588.

Wang, F., Ngo, C.-W., & Pong, T.-C. (2003). Synchronization of lecture videos and electronic slides by video text analysis. In Proceedings of the eleventh acm international conference on multimedia (p. 315 - 318). Berkeley, CA, USA: ACM.

Watanabe, K., Otani, M., Tanaka, H., Isagai, Y., Okawa, K., Kokuryo, J., et al. (2000). Distance classroom using high quality video stream on the japan gigabit network. IEICE technical report. Education technology, ET2000-86 , 71-77.

Yoshino, T., & Munemori, J. (2002). Application and evaluation of distributed remote seminar support system remote wadaman ii over tow years. Transactions of ISPJ , 43 , 555-565.

Zhang, G., Cheng, Z., Huang, T., He, A., & Koyama, A. (2003). A distance learning support system based on effective learning method sq3r. IPSJ Journal, 44 , 709 -721.

This work was previously published in International Journal of Distance Education Technologies, Volume 7, Issue 1, edited by Qun Jin, pp. 44-57, copyright 2009 by IGI Publishing (an imprint of IGI Global).

Section 4
Empirical Study:
Evaluation and Assessment

Chapter 15
The Effects of Communicative Genres on Intra-Group Conflict in Virtual Student Teams

Jung-Lung Hsu
National Central University, Taiwan

Huey-Wen Chou
National Central University, Taiwan

ABSTRACT

With increasing convenience and prevalence, the distant communication application has become a promising way for individuals who are eager to cooperate and interact virtually. This study explored the question of whether the collaborative interaction of the virtual teams has any effect on the conflict and network structure of virtual groups. A total of 150 participants were invited and randomly assigned to thirty groups with each group of five subjects. To function like real virtual groups, they were asked to communicate with their members through e-mail. Through genre analysis and social network analysis, nine communicative genres most frequently used in the collaborative groups were identified. Results of correlation analysis suggested that it was the communicative genres, not the network structure, that were associated with intra-group conflict of virtual group. Accordingly, whether the network structure of the virtual group is centralized or decentralized may not be instructors' or developers' major concern. Instead, they may wish to focus on a well-designed interface providing needed supports of communicative procedure for coordinating with distant members.

INTRODUCTION

The advance of computer mediated communication (CMC) not only releases the constraints of time and location for individuals while interacting, but also changes the way of interpersonal communication. As a result, it draws much attention of researchers from various domains. Some researchers of interest to virtual teams continue to

DOI: 10.4018/978-1-60960-539-1.ch015

explore the outcomes of using CMC to interact with virtual team members (Lee, 2004; Wilson, Straus, & McEvily, 2006; Van der Meijden & Veenman, 2005). Others provide alternative aspect to this issue, in that diversity such as different cultural and psychological backgrounds among team members adds complexity to the functioning of virtual teams (Lapinski & Rimal, 2005; Zoller, 2005; Kreijns, Kirschner & Jochems, 2003). In this study, we distinguish research of interest to virtual teams into two streams, namely psychotechnical perspective and sociotechnical perspective. The former mainly focus on the relationships between technology and psychological status, whereas the latter frequently deals with relationships between technology and social practice. While agreeing both streams have shed light on this issue, we think that both streams are potentially intertwined but are seldom put together in the past research. Consequently, this provides a motivation for this study to supplement our understandings of virtual teams by synthesizing both perspectives.

Media richness theory, for example, is one of the most common groundings for research with psychotechnical perspective. Based on the tenet of media richness theory, attributes of the media refers to the determinant that affects individuals' usage and message content of the CMC, and consequently leads to outcomes of distant interaction. In this regard, communicating via CMC may not always be beneficial for participants. Compared to face-to-face communication, CMC provides a reduced cues environment that is ill-suited to emotional, expressive or complex communications. In sum, the lens of psychotechnical research suggests that it is the features of CMC that affects individuals' uses and outcomes of interacting in virtual ways. Accordingly, it is foreseeable that any technological feature that is potential to eliminate individuals' psychological distance is welcome in this stream.

On the contrary, research with sociotechnical perspective, which mainly based on social cognitive theory, suggests that an individual's behavior is partially shaped and controlled by the influences of social network (i.e., social systems). More specifically, the use and impact of CMC are dependent on the type of tie connecting communicators, which in turn determines the ways, means, and expression of communications. Furthermore, the social influence model posits that perceptions of media characteristics are in part socially constructed and that the selection of a medium frequently reflects social forces in addition to attributes of the medium. Researchers have explored the impact of social relationships on media use, suggesting that the use of communication technology is socially constructed (Orlikowski, Yates, 1998). In contrast to research with psychotechnical perspective, the lens of this stream proposes an alternative contention suggesting that social relationships determine the adoption of medium and then constitute the meaning of a message.

Prior studies based on the psychotechnical perspective have ignored the importance of social influence. Consequently, this study synthesizes perspectives of both streams and primarily focus on the relationships among individuals' psychological status, social relations and practical content. More specifically, this paper addresses the question of whether the collaborative interaction of the virtual teams has any effect on the conflict and network structure of virtual groups.

LITERATURE REVIEW

Network Structure of Virtual Groups

"Communication" means which one informs of whom through which route, and that finally brings what result. In the other words, interpersonal communication may create a structure which in turn affects what else gets said and done and by whom (Keyton, 1999). In this regard, groups are inherently networked because their members have to interact with one another to settle down the shared goals (Rulke & Galaskiewicz, 2000).

Communicative structure influences not only individual's feelings of participation, independence, responsibility, but also efficiency, speed, and accuracy of the delivering messages. With different nature of the communicative structure, groups demonstrate various outcomes of mutual interactions. For instance, when task is simple and communicative structure is a circle type, the delivering speed of communication is slow because extra people are involved in communication (Leavitt, 1951). On the contrary, a wheel network needs only the minimal communication required to succeed in a simple task. In addition, some researchers separate communicative structure into two categories in terms of degree of centralization, namely centralized and decentralized structure. In his study, Shaw (1964) find that groups with decentralized communicative structure take less time than that with centralized communication while facing a complex or non-routine task. So far, it appears that past research focus most on the explicit representation of communication. However, there is few study investigate the contextual meanings while individuals communicate. Drawing on social network analysis, this study introduces communication betweenness and communication density to help us investigate the contextual meanings of learners' communication messages.

Communication Betweeness

Brokerage relations are connected among disorganized others. The broker carrying information from one individual to another retains a position as intermediary and possesses control of the information. In social network analysis, it can be measured by betweenness, the extent to which an actor sits between others in the network. Interactions between two nonadjacent actors might depend on the other actors in the set of actors, especially the actors who lie on the paths between the two. These "other actors" potentially might have some control over the interactions between the two nonadjacent actors.

As an intermediary, the individual with high degree of betweenness refers to play an important information role as a broker or gatekeeper filtering and importing information to the network. Thus, one may state that the "actor in the middle" have more "interpersonal influence" on the others (Freeman, 1979). Furthermore Bavelas (1950) has indicated actors located on many interaction paths are indeed central to the network. Leavitt (1951) has similar thought, he argued that an actor is central if it lies between other actors on their interaction, and could communicate with others without anyone. Group betweenness allow us to compare different networks with respect to the heterogeneity of the betweeness of the members of the networks (Freeman, 1979).

$$B = \frac{\sum_{i=1}^{g}[B(n^*) - B(n_i)]}{(g-1)}; j \neq i$$
$$B(n_i) = \sum_{j<k} g_{jk}(n_i) / g_{jk}$$

Freeman's group betweenness index has numerator

$$\sum_{i=1}^{g}[B(n^*) - B(n_i)],$$

where B(n*) is the largest realized actor betweenness index for the set of actors. Where g_{jk} is the number of connections linking the two actors. And $g_{jk}(n_i)$ is the number of connections linking the two actors that contain actor i. $B(n_i)$ is simply the sum of these estimated probabilities over all pairs of actors not including the ith actor.

Communication Density

Cohesiveness describes attributes of the whole network, indicating the presence of strong interaction relationships among network members, and also the likelihood of their having access to the same information or resources. Density, like other measures of cohesion, indicates the extent to which all members of a population interact with all other members. Information in the low-density graph can flow through only one route, whereas information in the high-density graph can flow from and to a number of different actors. Actors in a high-density network are more in touch with all others in the network than actors are in a low-density network. Information can be expected to flow more freely among members of a higher density network than a lower density network.

The density of a network is the proportion of possible lines that are actually present in the graph. However the frequency level of communication between any two members of a group is different, thus we follow other network researchers in using communication or interaction frequency as a measure of relational strength to indicate communication density (Uzzi, 1999):

$$D = \frac{\sum_{i=1}^{g}\sum_{j=1}^{g} Z_{ij} \, / \, \max(Z_i)}{g(g-1)}, j \neq i$$

Where Z_{ij} is the frequency at which team member I reports communication with team member j, $\max(Z_{ij})$ is the largest of i's reported ties to anyone on the team, and g is the number of members in the team. Density varies from zero (no communication between team members) to one (maximum strength communication between all team members).

Communicative Genres

A genre is a patterning of communication created by a combination of the individual, social, and technical forces implicit in a recurring communicative situation. The concept of genre has a long tradition in rhetorical and literary analysis. Recently a number of researchers began to use the notion of genre as typified social action in cultural and design studies. (Crowston & Williams, 2000; Dillon & Gushrowski, 2000; Schryer, 2005). Orlikowski and Yates (1994) applied the notion of genres to organizational communication. They studied, among others, the evolution from the formal business letter (through informal business letter and memorandum) to electronic mail, and analyzed the genre repertoire in the e-mail of a team of computer language designers, paying attention to the function of memos, language proposals, dialogs and ballots.

In accordance with modern genre theory, Orlikowski and Yates (1994) conceived genres as socially recognized types of communicative actions, and identified them by their purpose and by their common characteristics of form. The purpose of a genre is not based on an individual's private motive, but rooted in social agreement, also in an organization. Form refers to three observable aspects of communication: medium (such as paper or e-mail), structure (text formatting) and linguistic features. Within the organizational framework, genres are part of a dynamic process of production, reproduction and modification. As Yates & Orlikowski (1992) had proposed, since every communication action may differ from each other in terms of its specific purpose and form, genre can be accordingly classified into several types.

Genres tend to be linked or networked together in a way that constitutes a coordinated communicative process (e.g. a conference may start with a call for proposals, followed by abstracts and concluded with papers). Such a cluster forms a genre system and is useful for studying the interaction between people in a community (Orlikowski & Yates, 1998). As mentioned above, different communication interaction results in various genres. Thus, it is the nature of different communication purpose makes genres become variable and complex, which facilitate the progress of interaction and then lead to communicators' intention.

Conflict

Conflict is an awareness on the part of the parties involved of discrepancies, incompatible wishes, or irreconcilable desires. Jehn and Mannix (2001) proposed that conflict in work group be categorized into three types: relationship, task, and process conflict. Relationship conflict, an awareness of interpersonal incompatibilities, includes affective components such as feeling, tension, and friction. Besides it also includes personal issues such as dislike among group members and feelings. Task conflict is an awareness of differences in viewpoints and opinions pertaining to a group task. And it pertains to conflict about ideas and differences of opinion about the task. Process conflict is defined as an awareness of controversies about aspects of how task accomplishment will proceed. More specifically, process conflict pertains to issues of duty and resources delegation, such as who should do what and how much responsibility different people should get.

One of the casual explanations may be that activity leads to interaction and which leads to sentiment. Accordingly, frequent interaction leads to positive sentiment and which in turn reduces conflict (Amir, 1975). Moreover, Nelson (1989) investigated the relationship between social networks and conflict in 20 organizational units. He classified the relationships into strong ties or weak ties. Thus, strong ties are frequent contacts that almost invariably have affective, often friendly and may include reciprocal favors. Weak ties are infrequent contacts that, because they are episodic, do not necessarily have affective content. The results indicated that low-conflict organizations are characterized by higher numbers of intra-group strong ties.

As mentioned before, if interactions of groups are tracked over a period of time, they exhibit a pattern of communication and reveal what has been referred to as network structure (Burkhardt & Brass, 1990). Although there are several genres which appeared during the process of interaction has been identified. Research about whether varies genres affect group's network structure and conflict has not yet been studied. Moreover, Ahuja et al. (2003) suggest individuals' structural position within the virtual groups mediates the effects of functional role, status, and communication role on individual performance. However, they only study interaction frequency within the group, but not take communication content into consideration. This review suggests that researchers need to study virtual groups by examining its contextual interaction, structure, and conflict. In particular, we are interested in answering the following questions: Whether the collaborative communication of the virtual group has any relationship with intra-group conflict and team conflict and communicative genre?

RESEARCH DESIGN

Samples

A total of 150 participants were randomly assigned to thirty groups with each group of five subjects. In accordance with the features of virtual group, familiarity among members should be taken into consideration. Participants were first-year undergraduate students from a university in Taiwan and they were from five classes of two departments: Foreign Languages and Early Childhood Care and Education. In order to form a group, one subject was randomly selected from each class. A pretest on subjects' computer literacy and familiarity of CMC tools were employed and no significant differences were found. Furthermore, to match the features of virtual group, group members were all dispersed in locations. Participants were asked to fulfill a questionnaire of familiarity to indicate their acquaintance with the others in the same group, after they were informed of their members. The questionnaire contains 4 items, such as "Before the team was established, some members had been acquainted with me.", "Before the team was established, some members had known my name.", "Before the team was established, I had known some members' personhood." and "Before the team was established, some members are friends of mine.". Those items were rated on a 5-point Likert scale anchored by 1 = "None" and 5 = "A lot". Nine groups were dropped since the average level of familiarity were higher than 3 (94% response rate). In other words, data analyzed in the following section were collected from the remaining 21 groups, which meant that messages were from about 105 subjects.

Synchronous and asynchronous communications are two usable ways for learners to interact virtually. Synchronous communication, such as MSN, Skype and so on, is one way of CMC that enables senders and receivers interact simultaneously with each other whenever they are both online. It is more convenient than using e-mail because its nature of synchronicity shortens the time of correspondence. However, a coordinate schedule seems required for learners so that they can have virtual meetings by the instant applications. In this study, over a half of participants had a job during the day and were students at the night. Therefore, finding out a vacant time to have a date with one another was quite difficult for them all. Furthermore, participants of this study were not major in computer-related disciplines, instead, they were major in Foreign Languages or in Early Childhood Care and Education, indicating a terrible skill in using computer. As a result, installing these applications may involve costs of coordinating schedule and operating the software may also impose cognitive cost on learners as well.

Another communication way that has been widely adopted is asynchronous communication. Of the most prevalent asynchronous communication is e-mail. In fact, we believed the asynchronous ways for participants to interact with their members was a better solution in this study. First of all, unlike MSN and Skype, after enrolling in

school each student got his own account without any further registering procedure. Moreover, many of them had a job in the day, and consequently it was difficult for them to seek out a stable time to regularly discuss online. Actually, the qualitative analysis showed that some group members had ever asked others for MSN account in order to shorten the communication time. However, since students had inconsistent time to be online, they found interacting with members by e-mail was convenient than by using MSN, particularly, when many of them did not hear about MSN before this study.

Procedure

All groups were asked to communicate with their members through e-mail, no matter the purpose of interaction was to discuss, collaborate or allocate the assignment. The assignment was required to be finished within four weeks. And the question is: "*Please describe what the matter is worthy to pay more attention in order to avoid scam while conducting e-shopping. Moreover what's the relationship between IC cards and e-shopping, how does IC card take effect on online transaction, and how will it influence the implementation of e-government*". Because subjects are not major in information technology related department, thus such an assignment is difficult to them. Since the purpose of the teams was to complete team assignment, all teams adopted the assignment due dates as their timeline goals.

Data were collected from months of Sep 2004 through Jan 2005. Team members sent e-mail messages to one another in order to participate in discussion to the assignment. Not only the message content was recorded, but also the mailing list in the fields of "send to" (TO) and "carbon copy" (CC) were automatically archived. Both quantitative and qualitative methods of inquiry were used to capture the dynamic interaction within groups.

Data Collection

The survey data we used in our analysis were collected by questionnaire to examine subjects' perception of task, relationship, and process conflict. Meanwhile the genre analysis was used to find out the most general genres in every group over the process of collaboration, and social network analysis was exploited to evaluate network structure of each group. Task and relationship conflict in the group was measured by the Intragroup Conflict Scale (Jehn, 1995), whereas process conflict items were adopted from Jehn and Shah's (1997) scale and were surveyed at the end of this experiment. These survey items asked participants to indicate their perception level of relationship, task and process conflict, which they perceived in their team. Those items focusing on the presence of conflict were rated on a 5-point Likert scale anchored by 1 = "None" and 5 = "A lot".

RESULTS

To evaluate learners' perception of task conflict, process conflict and relationship conflict, all subjects were asked to complete a post-questionnaire (88% response rate). The coefficients of Cronbach α of task conflict, process conflict and relationship conflict were 0.86, 0.84, 0.9, respectively.

Communicative Genres

The primary data for our study consisted of a subset of the 2546 messages during four weeks of the assignment for which e-mail archives exist. These messages were analyzed both qualitatively and quantitatively by one doctorial student and one graduated student. These two assistants read hundreds of messages and translated all of these messages for an iteratively developed coding scheme (see Table 1), which was used to analyze a sample of the messages. The coding scheme was based on the two identifiable dimensions of

genre: purpose and form, which were originally proposed by Orlikowski and Yates (1994). Purpose categories referred to the socially recognizable purposes of a message. Because we observed that many messages had multiple purposes, one or more of eight purposes could be indicated. Form categories referred to a message's formatting features and linguistic features, such as subject line, greeting, smiley face ^_^ created by alphanumeric characters, and so on.

A research assistant used this scheme to code all the electronic message transcripts. To judge coding reliability, one of the researchers independently coded a stratified sample of 776 messages selected randomly to represent all coding categories. As shown in Table 1, intercoder reliabilities were high for all categories and could be used primarily to locate interesting phenomena for later qualitative analysis.

After reading all the e-mails of the mailing list, these categories were coded simply as present or absent. A particular genre of communication was then determined by the occurrence or not of combinations of these purpose and form categories. Certain of these categories were included in the definition of the used genres as shown in Table 2. Overall, the used genres in our mailing list were more or less similar to the ones employed by Orlikowski and Yates in their study of genres emerging from organizational communication in mailing lists (Orlikowski & Yates, 1994; Yates, Orlikowski & Okamura, 1999). Additionally, three most important directions of communication flow, downward, upward, and horizontal communication, were taken into consideration.

Table 3 shows the content of communicative genres about developing relationships and coordinating collaboration in virtual environment. Figure1 shows the percentage of communicative genres identified in this study. Since genres were dependent on the overall content of the message, the most common characteristics of the collaboration process were analyzed within a discussion thread. This provided us a general perspective of

Table 1. Definition, reliability, and distribution of coding categories (N=2546)

Coding Category	Definitions of Coding Categories	Cohen K	N	%
Purpose	Purpose of message[more than one coded]			
Response	Reply to previous message or messages	0.84	675	27%
Solicitation	Request for ideas or information	0.85	771	30%
Apology	Offer of an apology for some action, message, etc	0.98	133	5%
Report	Documentation of an event or change in affairs	0.99	623	24%
Announcement	Statement indicating an event or change in affairs	0.96	884	35%
Command	Statement of having someone to do something	0.93	114	4%
Coordination	Expression of work dispatching, scheduling, etc.	0.75	238	9%
Form: Formatting features				
Self-introductory greeting	Presence of personal introduction or identification	0.97	137	5%
Embedded message	Inclusion of all or part of a previous message(s)	0.92	631	25%
Edited embedded message	Previous message(s) was edited before inclusion	0.97	14	1%
Cited content	Inclusion of homepage content from Internet	0.93	154	6%
Word/phrase emphasis	Presence of emphasizing symbols or mark	0.91	393	15%
Graphic devices	Presence of graphical elements	0.97	5	0.2%
List	Presence of lists to indicate parallel items in text	0.94	107	4%
Signature	Presence of closing remark, signoff, or signature block	0.99	493	19%
Hyperlink	Presence of hyperlink	0.95	107	4%
Attachment	Presence of embedded file	0.98	436	17%
Form: Linguistic features				
Chinese subject line	Presence of any Chinese characters in subject line	0.93	2289	90%
English subject line	Presence of any English characters in subject line	0.88	340	13%
Social symbol	Presence of network symbol(e.g.,^_^, @_@, etc)	0.99	216	8%
Apologetic language	Presence of self-effacing language or modest tone	0.88	139	5%
Jocose language	Presence of jocose tone	0.92	129	5%
Accusative language	Presence of reprehensive language	0.95	29	1%
Authoritative language	Presence of commanding language	0.94	203	8%
Grateful language	Presence of grateful language or tone	0.99	351	14%
Encouraging language	Presence of self-effacing language or modest tone	0.98	399	16%

the discussion rather than isolated examples detached from context.

Announcement genre (27%) was used to notify members of the information extracted from outside of the group. The most salient feature of this genre was that it usually emerged by way of broadcasting. As a result, all members of the group received the messages. In this study the main purpose of announcement genre for the message

Figure 1. Percentage of communicative genres identified (clockwise)

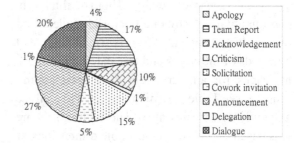

Table 2. Definition and distribution of genres

Genres	Genre definitions
Announcement	purpose=announce and not response, form=no embedded message
Delegation	purpose=coordination and command, form=word/phrase emphasis, list, and no embedded message
Solicitation	purpose=solicitation, not response, form=no embedded message
Cowork invitation	purpose=solicitation, coordination and not command, form=no embedded message
Criticisms	purpose=not report, not solicitation, form=accusative, not social symbol and not jocose
Team Report	purpose=report, form=attachment
Acknowledgement	purpose=not solicitation, not command and not coordination, form=grateful
Apology	purpose=apology, not command, not report, not coordination, form=apologeic
Dialogue	purpose= response, form=embedded message

Table 3. Communicative genres content

Announcement genre: Hey, Guys. Our teacher said the report should have at least 8 pages, no more than 15. please use letter 12 with 1.5 space spare (#32)
Delegation genre: This is our work assignment, everybody take a look. 1.What is network transaction?......(#101). 2. Network fraud classification, How to avoid these fraud?....(#102). 4. What is IC card?..... (#101). 5. How does IC card take effect on network transaction?......... (#103). 6.What is e-gorverment?....... (#104). 7.Organization (WORD and PowerPoint)....... (#105).
Cowork Invitation genre: Hello, everybody, I tried to divide our work into 2 sections as the following. Thanks! 1.Please describe what the matter is worthy to pay more attention in order to avoid scam while conducting e-shopping (2 persons). 2.What's the relationship between IC cards and e-shopping, how does IC card take effect on online transaction, and how will it influence the implementation of e-government (3 persons). Please think about which topic would you like to choose before this Friday. Best regards. (#84)
Solicitation genre: Hi, Jean, how are you? Sorry for asking the work so frequently. Because our members still have some troubles with this assignment, I think you should mail us the final report once you've done the work. Please reply me as soon as possibly. THX. (#65)
Team report genre: I've finished the report, you guys may take a look in the attached file. (#21)
Criticisms genre: How dare you can show up right now! Won't it be too late for doing the assignment now? This is a group assignment, so that you can not do the homework whenever you want to do. (#89)
Acknowledgement genre: At first I supposed this assignment would be very difficult to accomplish. However, I have completely changed my mind! I'm so glad to have wonderful members like you. Although we never met one another, I can feel everyone is really care about the assignment. I'm touched. ~ ><"" Thank you for your hard working!! (#72)
Apology genre: Hello, I'm sorry for coming so late. Because I am busy these days, there are so many things delayed. I'm not looking for any excuse, I just want to tell you I am not in purpose. This is group assignment, so I can imagine how troubled it could be once someone else disappeared. However, I just wish you can forgive me. If there were any thing not yet completed, just tell me. I'll do my best this time to finish the task. (#18)
Dialogue genre: hey, can you send to us ASAP. then, we could study it to catch some points. thanks a lot. Regards brian 11/30. ---The following is original content---. Hello. When do I should give you my data? (#61)

senders was to make sure their group members having a consistent aspect of the assignment specification. Thus, the role of the announcement genres played in virtual groups was like a message gate, which was responsible for importing external information. As members consecutively broadcasted and disseminated information, virtual groups were more likely to establish a shared memory, and thereby their members could continuously obtained and retrieved knowledge.

The role of leadership was an interesting aspect of the virtual groups. Although this study did not ask each group to choose someone as a group leader, we found some groups consistently revealed that an individual within the group volunteered to coordinate the group task. Therefore, the team leader in this study was identified as the individual who was responsible for delegating someone to do something. The delegaters took leadership of the virtual group and coordinated the schedule, such as making deadline of having accomplished individuals' subtasks and regulating checkpoints for monitoring individuals' efforts. Unlike the well known obligation of scheduling and monitoring the group task, the delegaters' capability to determine if those late for the assignment were forgivable was novel and seldom noticed in the past. Based on our observation, the procrastinators had no chance to provide their contribution as they were back, unless team leaders provided a new suggestion and asked others how about reallocating the entire assignment. Since reallocation meant that the effort they had taken might be gone, and those late would probably share the outcome in an easy way. It was reasonable that members might be reluctant to propose such a suggestion. As a leader in virtual group, the delegaters suffered more responsibilities than others, leading them to propose such an embarrassing suggestion.

While having no public and open information such as progress status to indicate whether the situation of each subtask proceeded well, participants were used to employing solicitation genres (15%) to inquiry how others' subtasks were going as well as to ask for renewing the subtask deadline when someone perceived their subtasks couldn't be finished on time. Because subtasks might have different deadlines and they were interdependent, the entire group assignment was then constrained not only by limited time but also by the sequential order of every members' subtasks. For example, the group assignment was achieved only when the subtasks had been finished individually and were entirely integrated into a new one. Therefore, renewing a predefined deadline might cause the whole group schedule changed.

Team report genre (17%) emerged when members had collected relevant documents or had finished their own subtask at hand. In this study,

team report usually contained attached files, which provided outcomes of individual's corresponding efforts. With this genre, participants could justify their members' performance and imagine what the final outcome of the group assignment would be like. Accordingly, participants could make clear each other's idea and have sufficient information to help improve the assignment.

In this study, having such visible information helped participants do not need to worry about whether their efforts would be in vain. Moreover, team report provided opportunities for those who had temporarily missed in the ongoing group assignment quickly understand what should be done next. In this study, we referred this phenomenon to a "trade off". As mentioned before, because participants in this study had different careers, computer usage behaviors, and vacant time, they were hardly to make a stable and consistent time to contact one another, even by the virtual way. With public and complete information concerning what others had been working, those who had finished their own subtasks might voluntarily help the busy or troubled members to settle down the tasks. Meanwhile, those temporarily missed members could involve in the assignment once again as soon as they had never left before.

Criticisms genre (1%) emerged only when those late asked others for pardon. However, the number of criticism genres in this study was surprisingly few. At first, we suspected that members might frequently blame those late and ask them to provide ideas about how to finish the assignment to compensate for their free riding. However, our results showed that members employed dialogue (20%) to clarify ambiguous thoughts more frequently rather than employed criticism (1%) to dispute with others. The reason might be that being unfamiliar with group members, and they really need one another to accomplish the assignment. So that members consciously avoided words that were acrimonious, and frequently used responses such as "dialogues" instead of criticizing.

Most groups were used to treat those late by ignorance instead of criticism. Members usually had consensus not to respond any information about whether those late were forgivable or not. In fact, members seldom mentioned about how to punish those procrastinators. No matter they were all waiting for one another's suggestion of how to deal with the issue or they had never think about it. However, through the way of doing nothing participants had substantially punished those free riders and the other members, including themselves.

Acknowledgement (10%) usually emerged when groups had accomplished the whole assignment. However, this genre may not always appear in each group. Based on our results, members who felt grateful and comfortable to the overall process of collaboration transmitted messages about acknowledgement. Moreover, its messages usually include some network smiley symbol such as:-) ^_^ or @@. This kind of smiley symbol, according to the result, mostly appeared in acknowledgement genre.

Messages about asking someone for pardon were identified as apology genres. In this study, this genre appeared when someone had been late for this group assignment. As mentioned before, whether those who had been late were forgivable were not dependent on the message content or any excuse they proposed. Rather, only the one who played the role of delegater in the group could provide a chance for those who were late by asking other members to relocate the task at hand.

Dialogue was emerged when the receivers had responded to the senders. Content of the dialogue usually contained information from previous messages. As the name implies, dialogue continued interacting with group members. Thus, dialogue genre played a significant role in idea clarifying and process status confirming, in turn, leading to threaded mail between the message senders and the receivers.

Correlation Analysis

E-mail messages were coded into a binary matrix, with rows representing messages senders, and columns representing messages receivers. A value of "1" in the intersection of row X and column Y indicates a communication link between X and Y, whereas "0" indicates lack of such a link. These matrices were utilized as inputs to the Social Network Analysis software package UCINET which was used to compute values of communication betweenness and density. However, in order to accurately represent delivering flow of messages in a group, only threaded messages were included for the computation of betweenness values.

Table 4 shows the correlations with communicative genres, network structure, and intra-group conflicts. Communicative genres such as acknowledgement, solicitation, criticism, dialogue, announcement and delegation were significantly associated with network structure of the virtual group or intra-group conflict. More specifically, density of network structure was positively associate with acknowledgement (r=0.72) and negatively related to criticism (r=-0.55), whereas betweenness of network structure was positively associated with dialogue (r=0.6) and negatively related to announcement (r=-0.51). In a nutshell, both acknowledgement and criticism were used by learners to express their feelings. Therefore, functions of these two genres focused mainly on learners' psychological status. For instance, if learners are grateful to group members for their help, they may send messages for thanks. Similarly, they may probably blame someone by mailing messages with displeasure content if they feel angry. Dialogue and announcement focused primarily on work related issues. With these two genres, learners made clear what was going on and what should be done next, and consequently led to a decentralized network structure.

Task conflict, in this study, correlated with criticism (r=0.52) and, particularly, delegation (r=0.74). Our findings indicated that relationship conflict had similar results to that of task conflict, however, it was much more related to criticism (r=0.83) than to delegation (r=0.45). In addition, process conflict were positively associated with solicitation (r=0.45), criticism (r=0.44), and delegation (r=0.57). Although network structure in this study was measured and represented by the communication density and the communication betweenness, this study revealed that only communication density was associated with one of the three conflicts: relationship conflict (r=-0.59). This result showed that compared to the network structure, the communicative genre was useful in explaining learners' perception of intra-group conflict. In sum, delegation was referred to a double-side sword. Although beneficial to the completeness of group assignments, delegation usually accompanied with potential conflicts to the groups. Accordingly, an approach that facilitates allocation of subtasks and meanwhile inhibits the probability of potential conflicts was helpful for learners to cooperate online. In combination, density was correlated with intra-group conflict because it was negatively associated with criticism, and which in turn led to engendering of disagreement in social, task and process conflict.

DISCUSSION

Although previous literature indicates that task conflict may have been misperceived as personal criticism and been interpreted as relationship conflict (Amason, 1996), this study finds that delegation, although critical for task coordination, has effects on increasing the potential possibilities of task conflict and relationship conflict. This finding is interesting because there were few explicit complaints demonstrated as the delegaters proposed a subtask allocation and asked members to follow. In fact, other members may have other opinions or comments in their mind. However, having no explicit cue to make sure others' thinking, they may choose to "sacrifice" their own ideas to conform the

"group decision". In this study, we suspect that it is the reason that leads delegation genre positively correlated with task and relationship conflicts. In this regard, instructors or educators may wish to urge learners to regulate a sound strategy of allocating the task. According to justice theory (Skarlicki & Folger, 1997), procedural justice and distribution justice are critical lines when groups regulate satisfactory rules of task allocation. For example, practitioners can make some suggestions about how to divide the assignment based on each student's relative advantages, and then give each of them a different score in terms of student's actual contribution to the group. This study, therefore, supposes that any approach that satisfies learners' requirement of procedural and distribution justice can then effectively alleviate their disagreements in social, task and process conflict. Future researchers of interest to this issue may consider take this proposition into account.

As shown by the qualitative analysis, members usually asked others to renew the deadline when they were unable to finish their own task on time. Not surprisingly, most members responded to the messages and agreed with their requests. However, some respondents frequently asked the requesters for indicating how their task is going to prevent rescheduling again. This phenomenon was especially severe when many of their tasks were highly interdependent and were in sequence. Sometimes, solicitation also stands for reviewing one's the efforts that had been made. Given that the group assignment was usually divided into several subtasks, each member was responsible for one part of the assignment, and then had somebody integrated every member's contribution into a final report. As a result, learners were forced to change their own working habits to satisfy one another, and consequently leading to high possibility of controversy. This study therefore suggests that an integrated discussion interface incorporating functions of online interaction and indicators of individual task completion is required for learners to grasp the overall status of group assignment.

For instance, system developers may refer to the guidelines of workflow or courses from project management to design packages that function in sequence. Therefore, the system may trace the remaining steps required to finish a given task to calculate the current proportion of group task completion.

Research regarding to group cooperation has acknowledged the importance of sense of belonging. Likewise, this study also found that it was lacking of willingness to participate, plan and allocate group assignment that accompanies with intra-group conflicts. In fact, most of these are social interaction issues. Lacking of sufficient cues makes learners are more sensitive to this issue in case they are free rode by other members. With a short period of time for team building and the limitations of the distant collaborating, learners do not have much time on conducting social practice. Therefore, this study suspect that learners in virtual group may have many doubts about their group members since there is no sufficient grounding to sustain their mutual trust. If this proposition is confirmed, practitioners thus may need to ask some social activities at the beginning stage of grouping. On the other hand, developers may wish to think deeply in how to facilitate individual's trust toward others whom he has never met before.

From the correlation analysis, some genres are associated with network structure; others correlate to conflicts in virtual groups. From a psychno-technical standpoint, features of communication tools have been acknowledged to have effects on individuals' usage and message content. More specifically, media richness theory suggests that different task requires different channel size to communicate. Fore example, people are seldom to frequently coordinate jobs to finish a routine task, whereas they may spend much effort to attain a shared cognition before doing a non-routine task. A task is routine when it is generally and constantly executed. Therefore, individuals usually have cultivated sufficient experiences to figure out the

course of actions. Furthermore, a routine task can be separated into a set sequence of steps to do, indicating a highly structured nature. As a result, doing a routine task seems require less effort to coordinate operations and make decisions, and consequently reducing the number of interactions and changing the content of genres.

CONCLUSION

This study sought to find out whether and how communicative genres affect conflicts and network structure of the virtual teams. While a great deal of recent research has focused on CMC features and its performance on groups, there has been less focus on structural properties, intra-group conflicts, and communicative interaction of virtual groups. In this exploratory study we offered empirical evidence regarding the relationships between communicative genres and network structure and intra-group conflicts of the virtual groups for a particular kind of work. Along with the results, future research of interest to phenomena from virtual groups may consider the association links of the variables that have been identified in this study.

Our results showed that the communicative genre has potential to influence the level of participation and interaction among members, and has the capacity to provide a meaningful supplement to regular group discussions. While virtual collaboration provides an interactive educational setting to increase opportunities for participants to learn from each others, however, making this happened seems require a more elaborated environment. Specifically, an integration of communication interface that incorporating needed genres for learners to fluently and transparently coordinate is suggested to develop as having individuals to collaborate virtually.

These findings hold implications for a contingency model of the relationship between communicative interaction, group network structure and conflict. Of course as we did not vary the type of task in this study, we can only speculate about this link. However, previous research suggests that integrative structures yield higher performance in non-routine, complex work by joining unique expertise within a group.

Clearly, communicative genre is not the only antecedent of network structure and conflict in virtual groups. However the limitation of this research raises a reasonable argument. Conflict may alter network structure and message content, perhaps reducing one's intention to communicate with members. More likely, causality is reciprocal, but the scope and methods of this study were inadequate to address the issue. Future research should focus on network structure as both a cause and a consequence of conflict in different virtual group settings. In addition, more research is needed to analyze how task properties affect communicative genres in virtual environment.

One limitation of this study is the experimental nature of the course itself. This study invited subjects from only one university and asked them use e-mail to supplement regular group discussions. All the results must be viewed in the context in which they were obtained because the study was not designed to produce results that could be generalized to other courses. Furthermore, these groups all came from university and might be affected by unique features of the organization such as its culture.

REFERENCES

Ahuja, M., Galletta, D. F., & Carley, K. (2003). Individual centrality and performance in virtual R&D groups: An empirical study. *Management Science*, *49*(1), 21–38. doi:10.1287/mnsc.49.1.21.12756

Amason, A. C. (1996). Distinguishing the effects of functional and dysfunctional conflict on strategic decision making: Resolving a paradox for top management teams. *Academy of Management Journal*, *39*(1), 123–148. doi:10.2307/256633

Amir, Y. (1975). The role of intergroup contact in change of prejudice and ethnic relations. In Katz, D. (Ed.), *Toward the elimination of racism* (pp. 245–308). New York: Pergamon Press.

Bavelas, A. (1950). Communication pattern in task-oriented groups. *The Journal of the Acoustical Society of America*, *22*, 725–730. doi:10.1121/1.1906679

Burkhardt, M., & Brass, D. (1990). Changing patterns or patterns of change: The effects of a change in technology on social network structure and power. *Administrative Science Quarterly*, *35*(1), 104–127. doi:10.2307/2393552

Crowston, K., & Williams, M. (2000). Reproduced and emergent genres of communication on the World-Wide Web. *The Information Society*, *16*(3), 201–215. doi:10.1080/019722240050133652

Dillon, A., & Gushrowski, B. A. (2000). Genre and the Web: Is the personal home page the first uniquely digital genre? *Journal of the American Society for Information Science American Society for Information Science*, *51*(2), 202–205. doi:10.1002/(SICI)1097-4571(2000)51:2<202::AID-ASI11>3.0.CO;2-R

Freeman, L. C. (1979). Centrality in social networks: Conceptual clarification. *Social Networks*, *1*, 215–239. doi:10.1016/0378-8733(78)90021-7

Jehn, K. A. (1995). A multimethod examination of the benefits and detriments of intragroup conflict. *Administrative Science Quarterly*, *40*, 256–282. doi:10.2307/2393638

Jehn, K. A., & Mannix, E. A. (2001). The dynamic nature of conflict: A longitudinal study of intragroup conflict and group performance. *Academy of Management Journal, 44*(2), 236–251. doi:10.2307/3069453

Jehn, K. A., & Shah, P. P. (1997). Interpersonal relationships and task performance: An examination of mediating processes in friendship and acquaintance groups. *Journal of Personality and Social Psychology, 72*(4), 775–790. doi:10.1037/0022-3514.72.4.775

Keyton, J. (1999). Relational communication in groups. In Frey, L. R. (Ed.), *The handbook of group communication theory and research* (pp. 192–222). Thousand Oaks, CA: Sage.

Kreijns, K., Kirschner, P. A., & Jochems, W. (2003). Identifying the pitfalls for social interaction in computer-supported collaborative learning environments: A review of research. *Computers in Human Behavior, 19*(3), 335–353. doi:10.1016/S0747-5632(02)00057-2

Lapinski, M. K., & Rimal, R. N. (2005). An explication of social norms. *Communication Theory, 15*(2), 127–147. doi:10.1111/j.1468-2885.2005.tb00329.x

Leavitt, H. J. (1951). Some effects of certain communication patterns on group performance. *Journal of Abnormal and Social Psychology, 46*(2), 38–50. doi:10.1037/h0057189

Lee, E. J. (2004). Effects of visual representation on social influence in computer-mediated communication: Experimental tests of the social identity model of deindividuation effects. *Human Communication Research, 30*(2), 234–259. doi:10.1093/hcr/30.2.234

Nelson, R. E. (1989). The strength of strong ties: Social networks and intergroup conflict in organizations. *Academy of Management Journal, 32*(2), 377–401. doi:10.2307/256367

Orlikowski, W. J., & Yates, J. (1994). Genre repertoire: Examining the structuring of communicative practices in organizations. *Administrative Science Quarterly, 39*, 541–574. doi:10.2307/2393771

Orlikowski, W. J., & Yates, J. (1998). Genre systems as communicative norms for structuring interaction in groupware. CCS WP205. Available at http://ccs.mit.edu/papers/CCSWP205/

Rulke, D. L., & Galaskiewicz, J. (2000). Distributions of knowledge, group network structure, and group performance. *Management Science, 46*, 612–625. doi:10.1287/mnsc.46.5.612.12052

Schryer, C. F. (2005). Genre theory, health-care discourse, and professional identity formation. *Journal of Business and Technical Communication, 19*(3), 249–278. doi:10.1177/1050651905275625

Shaw, M. (1964). Communication networks. In Berkowitz, L. (Ed.), *Advances in Experimental Social Psychology* (pp. 111–147). New York: Academic Press. doi:10.1016/S0065-2601(08)60050-7

Skarlicki, D. P., & Folger, R. (1997). Retaliation in the workplace: The role of distributive, procedural, and interactional justice. *The Journal of Applied Psychology, 82*(3), 434–443. doi:10.1037/0021-9010.82.3.434

Uzzi, B. (1999). Embeddedness in the marketing of financial capital: How social relations and networks benefit firms seeking financing. *American Sociological Review, 64*, 481–505. doi:10.2307/2657252

Van der Meijden, H., & Veenman, S. (2005). Face-to-face versus computer-mediated communication in a primary school setting. *Computers in Human Behavior, 21*(5), 831–859. doi:10.1016/j.chb.2003.10.005

Wilson, J. M., Straus, S. G., & McEvily, B. (2006). All in due time: The development of trust in computer-mediated and face-to-face teams. *Organizational Behavior and Human Decision Processes, 99*(1), 16–33. doi:10.1016/j.obhdp.2005.08.001

Yates, J., & Orlikowski, W. J. (1992). Genres of organizational communication: A structurational approach to studying communications and media. *Academy of Management Review, 17*(2), 299–326. doi:10.2307/258774

Yates, J., & Orlikowski, W. J. (2002). Genre systems: Structuring interaction through communicative norms. *Journal of Business Communication, 39*(1), 13–35. doi:10.1177/002194360203900102

Yates, J., Orlikowski, W. J., & Okamura, K. (1999). Explicit and implicit structuring of genres: Electronic communication in a Japanese R&D organization. *Organization Science, 10*(1), 83–103. doi:10.1287/orsc.10.1.83

Zoller, H. M. (2005). Health activism: Communication theory and action for social change. *Communication Theory, 15*(4), 341–364. doi:10.1111/j.1468-2885.2005.tb00339.x

This work was previously published in International Journal of Distance Education Technologies, Volume 7, Issue 1, edited by Qun Jin, pp. 1-22, copyright 2009 by IGI Publishing (an imprint of IGI Global).

Chapter 16
Effect of Teaching Using Whole Brain Instruction on Accounting Learning

Li-Tze Lee
The Overseas Chinese Institute of Technology, Taiwan

Jason C. Hung
The Overseas Chinese Institute of Technology, Taiwan

ABSTRACT

McCarthy (1985) constructed the 4MAT teaching model, an eight step instrument developed in 1980, by synthesizing Dewey's experiential learning, Kolb's four learning styles, Jung's personality types, as well as Bogen's left mode and right mode of brain processing preferences. An important implication of this model is that learning retention is improved in the whole brain treatment group and thus this model is effective in retaining learning information as long term memory. Specifically, when examine the effectiveness of student scoring levels (high, median, and low), the results indicated that retention improved across all levels in the treatment group while results were inconsistent in the control group. When examine academic achievement and attitudes, interaction factor of both school and method showed a statistically significant difference.

INTRODUCTION

Vocational education in the secondary education level has had a great influence on the economic growth in Taiwan for the past forty years because the major labor force it provides. As Yang (2001) noted, the goal of vocational high school education is to prepare students with appropriate skills for them to enter the labor force right after graduation. Also, Jones (1979) explained that the educational movement in secondary vocational schools in the United States has transformed the focus from subject matter to employment and providing practical

DOI: 10.4018/978-1-60960-539-1.ch016

and introductory job knowledge is essential in this educational setting.

However, due to rapid societal changes in Taiwan, a large percentage of students in vocational high schools are now inclined to pursue higher degrees (Chuang, 2001; Yang, 2001). According to information released by the Taiwan Ministry of Education (2008), nearly four times more vocational high school graduates pursue higher degrees than they did ten years ago (1994, 16.22%; 2005, 69.79%). Achievement and competency should be equally valued in vocational technical education (Jorgensen, 1979). In Taiwan, with the push to close the gap between vocational high school and academic high school, academic performance has consequently become another educational focus of current secondary vocational education in Taiwan (Taiwan Ministry of Education, 2008).

The American Accounting Association (1986) reported that the major goal for general accounting courses is to equip students not only with content knowledge, but also with the competency to relate learning to lives. The Accounting Education Change Commission (AECC) (1990) reported that the purpose of accounting education is to help students become independent learners and continue to learn in their professional lives. Developing students as information providers and communicators for business decisions are two major areas of focus in the first course in accounting, and the teaching method in such a course should focus on student involvement and learning interaction (AECC, 1992). The structure of accounting education is out-of-date and transformation is needed (Albrecht & Sack, 2000).

Accounting education in Taiwan follows the American system in many ways. According to Chuang (2001), accounting courses in business vocational high schools in Taiwan have been delivered passively without any connection to real life; the lecture method of content delivery dominates. The test oriented, abstract, and serious nature of accounting makes it a subject in which many students do not have interest. In addition,

researchers (Wang, Sheu, & Chen, 2008) noted that the major teaching method in accounting course in Taiwan focuses on depositing learning materials and memorization.

Diversity exists in every classroom. Nevertheless, schools do not provide students many alternatives in ways of learning or testing (O'Neil, 1990). Students bring their own experiences, interests, and preferences in learning to the classroom (Erlauer, 2003; Stronge, 2002). These learning differences should be equally valued and respected in every classroom (McCarthy, 2000). Teaching business classes in vocational high schools should encompass different alternative delivery options (materials, media, and methods), and teachers should realize these alternatives provide several classroom management strategies allowing teachers to become facilitators instead of broadcasters of new information (Jones, 1979). Applying a proper teaching methodology not only helps students to overcome learning obstacles, but increases their learning performance (O'Neil). Education professionals should understand the function of the human brain as a whole and adopt brain related research since it can fill the classroom with energy, motivating teachers and thereby validating good teaching techniques (Jensen, 2005; Nunnelley, Whaley, Mull, & Hott, 2003). Sharing the same idea, Loo (2002) suggested that educators should use flexible teaching techniques to approach different learning styles in a class. Furthermore, McCarthy (1985) constructed the 4MAT teaching model, an eight step instrument developed in 1980, by synthesizing Dewey's experiential learning, Kolb's four learning styles, Jung's personality types, as well as Bogen's left mode and right mode of brain processing preferences. This 4MAT teaching cycle contains eight steps: connect, attend, imagine, inform, practice, extend, refine, and perform (McCarthy, 2000, p. 227). In Borkowski and Welsh's (1996) early adoption of this model confirmed that 4MAT is an advantageous instruction tool in accounting courses.

Statement of the Problem

The goal of accounting education in the United States is to develop future business professionals. However, accounting programs no longer attract as many students. For example, according to Sanders (2001), the numbers of students obtaining bachelor's and master's degrees in accounting has decreased nation-wide from 1998-2000. In 1998-99, there were 47,895 degrees granted, but in 1999-2000, this number dropped to 45,095. Compared to 1995-1996, the numbers decreased 20% and 24% for each academic year respectively. One of the reasons for such a decline in enrollment is that the accounting curriculum and teaching methodology have remained the same for several decades (Albrecht & Sack, 2000). Accounting education has seldom been taught in ways other than lectures, quizzes, and examinations. In addition, by interviewing heads of accounting departments and other practicing accountants, Albrecht and Sack found that "accounting education, as currently structured, is outdated, broken, and needs to be modified significantly" (p. 1). If these practitioners were pursing their degrees again, some of them would choose other majors than accounting.

The AECC (1990), after investigating a group of practitioners, educators and researchers with different viewpoints, announced that accounting students should learn in effective ways and be able to utilize valuable learning strategies to become lifelong learners. Accounting education should develop students as future professional accountants to acquire diverse abilities when they enter the work force. The decrease in student enrollment and graduates as Albrecht and Sack (2000) claimed, as well as the announcement by the AECC, has indicated that accounting education needs to be reformed. Some accounting programs have made changes in curricula through the transformation in instruction; however, these changes are still not significant or persistent enough.

In Taiwan, accounting classes in business vocational high schools have been delivered passively without any link to the real world environment and are regarded as a serious, abstract, and unexciting subject by many students (Chuang, 2001). According to Freire (2000), "Education thus becomes an act of depositing, in which the students are the depositories and the teacher is the depositor. Instead of communicating, the teacher issues communiqués and makes deposits which the students patiently receive, memorize, and repeat" (p. 72). Traditional classroom teaching, without the chance to learn from peers, limits student ability to think and use creativity to find multiple correct solutions to problems (Jensen, 2005). The lecture method may seem to be effective in the short-term but the amount of material presented at one time may lead to confusion and overload (Stronge, 2002). According to Jensen, the brain is very effective when processing learning, especially when learning involves new experiences and simulations.

It is important to understand that the roles of teachers may need to be changed: teachers should become aware of how different students learn and find ways to facilitate different teaching strategies (Erlauer, 2003; Genesee, 2000; Jensen, 2005; Magnuson, 2002), and students should be encouraged to participate actively in their learning (AECC, 1990).

Purpose of the Study

The Principles of Accounting course provides accounting and non-accounting majors the essential and fundamental knowledge, skills, and abilities to be successful in their course work; therefore, the Principles of Accounting course should receive additional attention (AECC, 1990). Researchers (Chen, 2002; Chuang, 2001) have sought diverse teaching strategies in accounting courses in Taiwan, and others have used whole brain instruction in subject areas, such as math, music, science, language arts, or early childhood

(Appell, 1991; Bowers, 1987; Vaughn, 1991; Wilkerson & White, 1988). However, seldom address the issue of accounting.

The purpose of this study was to examine student academic achievement, attitudes, and retention in a Principles of Accounting course by employing an experimental design involving the application of whole brain instruction at three vocational high schools in Taiwan. The following research questions were therefore presented.

Research Questions

Three questions have emerged to guide this study:

1. Is there a significant difference in academic achievement, as measured by a standardized content test, among Principles of Accounting students who received whole brain instruction and those who received conventional instruction?
2. Is there a significant difference in learning attitudes, as measured by a Likert scale survey, among Principles of Accounting students who received whole brain instruction and those who received conventional instruction?
3. Is there a significant difference in learning retention, as measured by the results of comparing content posttest one and posttest two, among Principles of Accounting students who received whole brain instruction?

Limitations

There are several limitations beyond the control of this study. First, there was no control to assign students in each class since this was done by the registration office of each school. Thus, classes were intact and lacked randomization. In addition, accounting curriculum is directed by the department of education in Taiwan. This study had to follow the guidelines dictated by the curriculum in the Principles of Accounting course. Third, there could have been some degree of communication between the students in the treatment and the control groups. This may also have affected student learning performance in this study. Fourth, class schedules for the Principles of Accounting course differed from class to class; some were taught in the morning, others in the afternoon. Finally, teachers may not have been able to remove their personality characteristics from their teaching methods.

Delimitations

Several delimitations existed in this study.

1. This study was delimited to 10th grade vocational high school students. This will limit the ability to generalize the finding to a broader population.
2. This study involved three schools with two classes of each located in three different cities in the central area of Taiwan.
3. Treatment and control classes were not taught by the same teacher
4. The intervention duration was delimitated to four weeks as the treatment period.
5. The units of instruction were whole-brain designed for the first three chapters in the textbook used by three schools.
6. Retention was measured by the content test again four weeks after the first posttest.
7. The Principles of Accounting course was the only subject tested in this study. This is the fundamental course taken by all business students. Any finding of this study may only apply to this course and not to other subject areas.

Significance of the Study

In a traditional school system, students are taught in the same way and learn to be linear thinkers and to adopt new knowledge passively without linking concepts to their real lives. Researchers (Chen,

2002; Chuang, 2001; Wang, Sheu, & Chen, 2008) in Taiwan have been trying different innovations in teaching accounting in vocational high schools, but have seldom addressed the issue of learning styles and the whole brain instructional teaching method. Studies in the United States examined whole brain instruction in many fundamental content areas, such as science, math, and English but few tackled the topic of accounting (Getz, 2003; Kitchens, Barber, & Barber, 1991; Wilkerson & White, 1988). This study attempted to bridge the gap between these two aspects by employing whole brain instruction to a vocational high school accounting course in Taiwan. The significance of this study is three fold from the perspective of accounting education, vocational high schools students, and teacher education.

Accounting Education

With the decreasing number of student enrollment indicated by Sanders (2001), accounting professionals have called for accounting educational reform. As Francis, Mulder, and Stark (1995) suggested, accounting instructors should develop instruction techniques to meet student needs for learning as mature learners and undertake different learners' perceptions. Therefore, matching teaching strategies to diverse student brain hemisphere preferences will aid in motivating learners and help them achieve academic success.

Vocational High School Students

The compulsory education in Taiwan is nine years, from grade one to nine. Students have several options if they decide to pursue further education after junior high school: academic high school, comprehensive high school, or a vocational high school. However, students who choose vocational high schools are regarded as less academically inclined than those in academic high schools. It is assumed that they have less interest in learning. Therefore, this study investigated whether whole brain instruction can benefit the academic performance and attitudes toward learning of students in a vocational high school setting.

Teacher Educators

The results of this study may determine the effect whole brain instruction has on student academic achievement, learning attitudes, and learning retention. The findings of this study may provide some insight for vocational high school inservice or for preservice teacher educators. In addition, principles or administrators may also benefit from this study if they undertake some innovative changes in instruction methods at their schools.

LITERATURE REVIEW

The purpose of this study is to examine academic achievement, attitudes, and retention of accounting students by employing an experimental research design involving the application of whole brain instruction called the 4MAT teaching model in six Principles of Accounting classes at three vocational high schools in Taichung, Taiwan.

Conditions of Learning

Information Processing

[T]he brain is not a passive consumer of information … The stored memories and information-processing strategies for our cognitive system interact with the sensory information received from the environment, selectively attend to this information, relate it to memory, and actively construct meaning for it. *(Wittrock, 1990, p. 348)*

Thanks to the technological development in simulating human behavior and in mathematical psychology, a picture of the relation of short-term to long-term memory has immerged (Atkinson & Shiffrin, 1971). They noted that the memory system is triggered by information as a stimulus moving to short-term memory, and if the stimulus is retained, it will become embedded in long-term memory. In other words, short-term memory is a part of long-term memory that can be triggered when needed to control the process of new information.

The information processing model described by Atkinson and Shiffrin in 1968 was modified and improved; however, the constructive mind still remains as the essence of this theory (Mayer, 1996). As Mayer stated, the two distinctive perspectives of the information-processing model are the literal view and the constructive view. The literal view perceives information as inputs and outputs much like the functioning of computers while the constructive view looks at the information processing as humans being creators of their knowledge structures.

Discovery Learning or Expository Learning

Bruner (1961) believes that learning occurs when learners actively participate in constructing new information using prior knowledge. When constructing new information based on the theory of discovery learning, learners are not provided with the final form of learning concepts but rather are required to coordinate new learning with their own thinking.

In contrast, Ausubel (1968) argued that most school learning should provide students with an organized form of learning materials since the constructive way of learning is time consuming and the diverse discovery approaches and their results vary with the abilities of different learners. This kind of teaching method produces reception learning. There was a strong debate about whether the discovery method or reception learning method is better. However, a guided discovery combining both discovery and reception learning is suggested as a practical classroom teaching strategy (Lefrancois, 1999).

Instructional Design

Several elements involved in Gagné's (1985) learning stages are: (a) alertness, (b) expectation, (c) recall from prior experiences, (d) selective awareness, (e) encoding to long-term memory, (f) behavioral response, (g) feedback, and (h) recall (p. 304). Gagné's learning model combines behaviorism and cognitive theories and focuses on not only external stimuli but also internal cognitive structures of individuals; learning activities should not depend on teaching alone but should follow a sequence or order to make learning happen (Gagné & Brigg 1979; Gagné).

Learning and the Brain

"The latest revolution in education is brain based learning" (Becktold, 2001, p. 95). According to Bruer (1999), "cognitive neuroscientists are beginning to study how our neural hardware might run our mental software, how brain structures support mental functions, [and] how our neural circuits enable us to think and learn... but it is also a very young one" (p. 649). As Jensen (2000) noted, brain-based learning or brain-compatible learning is a new revolution of shaping the paradigm through the cooperation of knowledge from different fields like neuroscience, biology, and psychology. Therefore, as it combines with brain research and learning, education has moved to an exciting and new era—the brain era (Erlauer, 2003).

Left and Right Brain Hemispheres

Sperry (1975) discovered that the right and left hemispheres of the human brain provide distinct functions: the left hemisphere is responsible for speaking, writing, reading, and mathematical calculation, while the right hemisphere is responsible for aesthetics, spatial analysis, and problem solving. Springer and Deutsch (1998) also noted that the left hemisphere functions in a verbal, chronological, rational, and analytic way while the right hemisphere functions in a nonverbal, image-like, and innate way. Thus, the left hemisphere dominated person is more linear, logical, and perceives the parts before the whole while the right hemisphere dominated person is more global, creative, and perceives the whole picture before the parts.

Jacobs and Scheibel (1993) conducted research and found out that students with more challenging and demanding school tasks had more synaptic densities than those who did not. In this sense, human brains change physically and became more complicated. Bruer (1999) stated that even the process of visual imagery relies on the left hemisphere, the verbal communication and reading skills do not merely rely on the left hemisphere, and numerical comparisons depend on subsystems functioning in both the left and right hemispheres. As McCarthy (2000) described, distinct purposes and functions are served in the two halves of the human cerebral cortex: left hemisphere people tend to succeed in cause and effect analysis, detail observation, and abstract conceptualizing whereas right hemisphere people tend to succeed in perceiving the whole, symbols, and sensation and looking for correlations as well as connections.

"Research about brain anatomy, chemistry, and processes applied to how humans learn is still in its infancy" (Jorgenson, 2003, p. 368). Jorgenson's report also claimed that educators should be aware of interpreting neuroscientific brain research and applying it to education and using cause and effect study results to draw unjust conclusions; however, it is believed that this new paradigm will eventually transform the current educational system. Jensen (2005) added to previous thought about the hemispheres by claiming that advanced musicians and beginning math learners are left hemisphere oriented while beginning music learners and mathematicians are right hemisphere oriented. Therefore, as Sousa (2001) noted, "Teachers try to change the human

brain everyday. The more they know about how it learns, the more successful they can be" (p. 3).

Emotion

Learners must feel that something is true before they believe it. Bar-On (2000) proposed a developmental stage of human emotional intelligence and maintained that proficiencies can be designed at a particular stage to reach the goal of enhancing emotional intelligence. According to Dwyer (2002), it is difficult for human brains to be attentive to all concepts taught, owing to the selection function of the brain, dissimilarity and personal meaningfulness are retained in the brain. Therefore, with this prioritized or selective function in the brain, when perceiving a physical or psychological threat, the logical system in the human brain will be closed down and chemicals will be released preparing for physical reactions; however, this impedes the learners' ability to learn (Dwyer).

Emotion, as a meaningful learning intermediary, performs as a channel to encourage or discourage learning; thus positive emotions can better reorganize memory systems to interpret learning content which relates to individual learners (Greenleaf, 2003). Dwyer (2002) contended that the brain responds to juxtaposed ideas and personally meaningful stimulation but shuts down when exposed to threats. A moderate stress level allows learners to become emotionally engaged and gives motivation to learn. Teaching techniques such as using role playing or simulation practices, and teaching learning to learn skills can help to cultivate emotional intelligence.

Once a student can sense physical and emotional safety, they can start to concentrate on their school work (Sousa, 2001). Therefore, as Jensen (2005) once suggested "Good learning engages feelings … emotions are a form of learning" (p. 81).

Enriched Environment

The study of Bennett, Diamond, Krech, and Rosenzweig (1964) investigated the relations of the weight and thickness of the brain cortex to the enriched environment. Two major findings in this study were: first, cortical tissue weights and thickness were not related to motor skill activities, isolation stress, or the growth of the brain; and second, an enriched training environment increased the weight and depth of rats' cortical tissues. The work of Rosenzweig, Love, and Bennett (1968) measured the brain effects by giving rats different hours of stimulation. They concluded that a few hours of an enriched environment provides adequate stimulation to digest information as an all day long enriched environment. In addition, to study whether body movement such as running, gaming, or working out can cause changes in rats' brains, Black, Isaacs, Anderson, Alcantara, and Greenough (1990) conducted an experiment to inspect the formation of synapses. Their study reported that rats increased their synaptic densities as a result of the simulative surrounding, not the body movement or the exercise condition.

The work of Karni et al. (1995) showed that adults can improve their motor skills in a slow developing, enduring training as a result of practice during an experimental period. In fact, Bruer (1998) claimed that "the brain can reorganize itself for learning throughout our lifetimes" (p. 18).

Bransford, Brown, and Cocking (1999) noted that challenges that do not bore or discourage learners should be posed at the appropriate difficulty levels while still motivating learners. Jensen (2005) also pointed two elements to facilitate an enriched environment as being: challenging learners to go beyond their comfort zones and communicating about the progress of their work.

Some educational writing (Erlauer, 2003; Genesee, 2000; Magnuson, 2002) reported that brain based teaching does not necessarily abandon traditional methods of teaching but rather should invite new teaching strategies to evolve and transform to a new paradigm. Moreover, Sparapani (1998) noted that many schools face time limitations, fixed mind-sets of teachers and students, out-dated learning equipment, lack of mobility in the classroom setting, and lack of variety of evaluation methods. Brain-based education, which integrates the curriculum, uses thematic teaching, cooperative learning, and portfolio-based measurement, can be a solution to encourage a higher-level of thinking in middle or high school students.

Four levels of brain study interpretation are: (a) learning models, (b) scientific findings, (c) medical experiments on human subjects, and (d) field research. According to these categories, the most reliable way to explain brain studies is to apply field research or the real world setting (Jensen, 2005). Genesee (2000) shared the same thought by encouraging teaching professionals to step out and develop research according to their classroom experiences and understanding of how the brain works for learning. Effective and successful changes in education depend on time, effort, and valid brain compatible studies which can all support this new information in learning (Erlauer, 2003; Magnuson, 2002).

4MAT Teaching Model

McCarthy (1985) noted that existing teaching methods, such as lectures and question and answers, benefit the one type of learner and she noted that the educational setting is mostly left-brain oriented. To address this problem, McCarthy constructed the 4MAT teaching model by synthesizing Dewey's experiential learning, Kolb's four learning styles, Jung's personality types as well as Bogen's left mode and right mode of brain processing preferences. The instrument, developed in 1980, is an eight step model of integrating student diverse learning styles (imaginative, analytical, common sense, and dynamic) with right and left brain hemispheric processing preferences (McCarthy). Eight steps of 4MAT teaching cycle are labeled: connect; attend; imagine; inform; practice; extend; refine; and perform. (McCarthy, 2000, p. 227)

Kelly (1990) claimed that the traditional approach to teaching law only reaches Quadrant Two learners without promoting other types of learners. The 4MAT system provides activities to help law school students in applying their knowledge to real ethical problems. Weber and Weber (1990) reported that Quadrant Two learning style students enjoy classroom lectures while the other types of learners struggle with this kind of teaching. Teaching the 4MAT system to gifted groups of 5th and 7th grade students helped students to learn to make better oral presentations by applying the 4MAT system. The results of this study showed that the 4MAT system promotes on-task engagement and helps students to modify their ways of presenting information by addressing varied listeners in the class.

With a belief that better teaching should be more than just lecturing, Borkowski and Welsh (1996) designed a curriculum that employed 4MAT as their method to teach students with different strengths. They also noted that the 4MAT teaching method, a proper pedagogy to teach accounting concepts and theories, enhanced students' abilities to work and communicate in groups, to learn creatively, and to make content more meaningful and appealing.

By tapping different talents, as Kaplan (1998) noted, the 4MAT approach allows learners to comprehend, use, and integrate information as well as encouraging different learners to make contributions and achieve success. His report showed that most participants strongly agreed that the 4MAT workshop met the goal of school leadership development.

It is believed that an active teaching approach has a positive impact on student learning (Lindquist, 1995; McInerney, McInerney, & Marsh, 1997; O'Neil, 1990; Ravenscroft, Buckless, McCombs, & Zuckerman, 1995). According to McCarthy (2000), the 4MAT teaching model, as a complete instructional model, represents a natural cycle of learning. It begins with learners' previous experiences, and adds new perceptions, which lead to individual conceptualizations. Learners act and try out their understanding and therefore the learning becomes more part of their personal useful lives. In this learning cycle, there are no hierarchies because all steps are equally necessary and equally valued.

METHODOLOGY

In this study, the major issue focused on student learning and attitudes in a Principles of an Accounting course by applying whole brain instruction as an intervention in three vocational high schools in Taiwan.

Procedures

Teacher Training

Before research starts, it is essential to have inservice training for teachers participating in studies of the effect of instructional methods (Boone & Newcomb, 1990). Thirty hours of whole brain learning workshop was given by a whole brain expert, Dr. Robert Croker, at Ivy Bilingual High School at Taichung, Taiwan. Teachers from more than 10 high schools attended this workshop. After this workshop, three teachers who completed the training hours and taught the Principles of Accounting course volunteered to participate in this study.

Lesson Plan Development

Three instructors teaching the Principles of Accounting course volunteered to participate in this study were invited to developed whole brain learning lesson plans with the researcher and the whole brain learning expert.

Whole Brain Instruction

During the four week treatment period of twenty hours of class, students in the treatment group received whole brain instruction using the eight step whole brain learning cycle, while the control group received the conventional instruction using textbook lectures. Communication was frequent between the researcher and the three teachers via emails, telephones, and mails.

Assessment

A standardized content test and an attitudinal survey were administered to both groups of students as the posttest to assess whether there was a difference in student academic achievement and learning attitudes.

To test student retention of the learning content, Abu and Flowers (1997) administered their same test three weeks after the first posttest. In this study, the standardized content test was administered again four weeks after the treatment to assess whether there was a difference in student learning retention.

Three output measurable variables are: first content test, second content test, and result of student attitudinal survey. First content test was used to evaluate academic achievement. Second content test was used to evaluate student learning retention. Student attitudinal survey was used to evaluate learning attitudes.

Participants

One private and two public vocational high schools in the central area of Taiwan participated in this study. Students were either assigned as the control or the treatment group and they did not have any prior accounting knowledge since this is the first accounting course for them. No students have been exposed to any whole brain instruction in their past learning experiences.

These three teachers from three different schools were assigned as the whole brain instruction group, while three other teachers who did not attend the whole brain learning workshop were assigned to the conventional instruction group. These six classes initially consisted of 259 students (130 students from the treatment group and 129 from the control group). Due to inconsistent answers toward the positive and negative questions in the attitudinal survey, eleven students were removed from the subject pool of this study. Therefore, the final number of students in this study was 248 (126 students from the treatment group and 122 from the control group).

Sampling

Students were assigned to classes by the registration office when they applied to high schools, so this study's samples included pre-existing classes. Three instructors were invited to participate in the treatment group in this study after they attended in the whole brain learning workshop. As Gall, Gall, and Borg (2003) noted, convenience samples are pre-existing subjects in a population which are accessible for the researcher to approach. Convenience sampling was used in this study.

Instrumentation

Two instruments were employed in this study. The first instrument was to test students' academic achievement based on content knowledge learned in the three-chapter unit. There were 33 multiple choice questions in this instrument. This is a standardized content test given to all accounting students and is contained in the accounting textbook. The second instrument, a student learning attitudinal survey, was to measure student learning attitudes toward teaching method, group work, and accounting itself. This attitudinal survey was a 24 question instrument, employing a four-point Likert scale, ranging from strongly agree, agree, disagree, to strongly disagree. The Likert scale, measuring differences in opinions, is regarded as the most common and reliable way to assess attitudes (Gall, Gall, & Borg, 2003; Oppenheim, 1992).

Validity and reliability are essential characteristics to ensure the quality of this survey instrument (Gall, Gall, & Borg, 2003). As Oppenheim (1992) stated, reliability should be considered before validity since it is a prerequisite to the validity. Reliability refers to the consistency to ensure the instrument is stable itself and score variations under different circumstances are highly proportionate.

Reliability

When using the test-retest method, the correlation coefficient value was .8252. This also indicated a high reliability of the content test instrument. Interrater reliability verifies the instrument stability and is based on one observation to examine the correlation of respondents' answers or judgments (Cronbach, 1970; Stevens, 2002). To measure the internal consistency of the attitudinal survey questions, Cronbach's alpha was used. Studies showed that Cronbach's alpha is considered acceptable when it is larger than .70 (Nunnally, & Bernstein, 1994; Zhao & Kanda, 2000); however, Oppenheim (1992) suggested that reliability is better when Cronbach's alpha, the correlation coefficient, is greater than .80. The results in the attitudinal survey showed an alpha coefficient value of .8936.

Validity

Validity, according to McMillan (1996), is "the degree to which an instrument measures what it says and it measures or purports to measure" (p. 118). The two kinds of validity examined in this study were face validity and content validity.

Face validity, according to Gall, Gall, and Borg (2003), is a causal judgment to determine whether a test contains the subject matter it plans

to estimate. Questions from the content test were valid for this criterion since they are the same exercises from the textbook selected by three participating schools. Questions from the attitudinal survey also met this criterion since they were sent to a graduate research class to determine the face validity. Content validity represents an instrument containing the measurement of a precise subject matter covered during the teaching process (Charles & Mertler, 2002; Nunnally, & Bernstein, 1994). In the content test, questions were derived from the textbook without changing the word usage to maintain content validity. The attitudinal survey was sent to five panel members to obtain their professional judgments. An instrument should be able to clarify the consistency of responses; or in other words, the "consciousness" of participants (Labaw, 1980, p. 66). The first and the fourth questions in the attitudinal survey were reverse worded to ensure valid information in the attitudinal survey. All negatively worded questions in this survey were coded opposite from the positive questions.

Results and Analysis

Research Question One

To measure academic achievement, students in the whole brain instructional group in School A (62.70) and B (66.37) performed better than students in the conventional instructional group. However, student in the whole brain instructional group in School C (77.83) performed less than students in the conventional instructional group (see Table 1).

To further analyze the discrepancy stated above, ANOVA analysis was presented in Table 2. The results demonstrated that there was no statistically significant main effect of method, $F_{(1, 2)} = 0.441$, $p > .05$, or school, $F_{(2, 2)} = 13.434$, $p > .05$. However, a significant interaction existed between school and method, $F_{(2, 242)} = 4.71$, $p < .05$. A Bonferroni post hoc test indicated that a

Table 1. Students' achievement scores as the first content posttest by instructional method and school

| | Instructional Method | | | | | |
| | Whole Brain Instruction | | | Conventional Instruction | | |
School	n	M	SD	n	M	SD
A	53	62.70	11.88	55	55.06	10.93
B	38	66.37	9.28	26	66.54	12.17
C	35	76.43	9.32	41	77.83	10.81
Total	126	67.62	11.85	122	65.16	14.96

Note. M = mean score of the first content posttest.

Table 2. Analysis of variance for treatment effect on achievement scores

Source of Variation	df	MS	F	p
Method	1	238.26	.44	.57
Error 1	2	540.51		
School	2	02.65	13.43	.07
Error 2	2	551.03		
Method by School	2	551.03	4.71	.01*
Error 3	242	117.00		

Note. School refers to Schools A, B, and C. Method refers to the whole brain instruction and conventional instruction method.
*p <.05.

statistically significant difference existed between the conventional and whole brain groups in the content test in school A (p =.001) but not in schools B or C (p = 1.00 for both schools) (see Table 3).

Based aforementioned information, in this study, method or school along does not have a significant impact. However, when considered the interaction between method and school, a statistically significant difference was found.

Therefore, students' academic performance will improve when considering both school and method factors.

Research Question Two

The second research question was also addressed by using ANOVA to analyze student attitudes in the survey instrument results. This scale consisted

Table 3. Students' achievement scores using analysis of variances with bonferroni correction

School	Whole Brain Instruction	Conventional Instruction	t	Uncorrected 1-tail p-value	Corrected 1-tail p-value
	M	M			
A	62.70	55.06	3.671	.000	.001*
B	66.37	66.54	-0.062	.475	1.000
C	76.43	77.83	-0.562	.287	1.000

Note. M = mean score of the first content posttest.
*p <.05.

Table 4. Students' attitude scores by instructional method and school

| School | Instructional Method | | | | | |
| | Whole Brain Instruction | | | Conventional Instruction | | |
	n	M	SD	n	M	SD
A	53	2.93	.28	55	2.99	.28
B	38	3.14	.37	26	2.74	.36
C	35	3.06	.34	41	2.98	.25
Total	126	3.03	.33	122	2.93	.30

Note. M = mean score of the attitudinal survey. Judgments were made on 4-point Likert scales.

of 24 items and asked respondents to rate their learning attitudes (from 1 "strongly disagree" to 4 "strongly agree") toward such topics as the teaching method, learning environment, and the accounting subject itself. Reverse worded questions were reverse coded, and then the average of all 24 items was calculated. While Schools B and C showed a treatment effect, only in the case of School B was the treatment effect significant. The mean scores and standard deviations of the three schools are presented in Table 4.

The result of the ANOVA in Table 5 demonstrated that there was no statistically significant main effect of school, $F (2, 2) = .137, p > .05$, or method, $F (1, 2) = 1.142, p > .05$. However, there was a significant interaction between method and school, $F (2, 242) = 10.644, p < .05$.

A Bonferroni post hoc test indicated that there was a statistically significant difference between

the conventional instruction and whole brain instruction as reflected by the average attitudinal scores in school B ($p < .05$) but not in schools A ($p > .05$) or C ($p > .05$) for both schools (see Table 6).

Based aforementioned information, in this study, method or school along does not have a significant impact. However, when considered the interaction between method and school, a statistically significant difference was found. Therefore, students have better learning attitudes when considering both school and method factors.

Research Question Three

To determine whether there was a significant difference in learning retention in the control group, content posttest two (the same test as posttest one) was administered, and a repeated measures

Table 5. Analysis of variance for treatment effect on attitude scores

Source of Variation	df	MS	F	p
School	2	.14	.14	.88
Error 1	2	1.01		
Method	1	1.13	1.14	.40
Error 2	2	.99		
Method by School	2	1.01	10.64	.00*
Error 3	242	.10		

Note. School refers to Schools A, B, and C. Method refers to the whole brain instruction and conventional instruction method.
*p < .05

Table 6. Analysis of variances with bonferroni correction of learning attitudes

	Whole Brain Instruction	Conventional Instruction	t	Uncorrected 1-tail p-value	Corrected 1-tail p-value
School	M	M			
A	2.93	2.99	-0.978	.165	.494
B	3.14	2.74	5.023	.000	.000*
C	3.06	2.98	1.142	.127	.382

Note. M = mean score of the 4-point Likert attitudinal survey.
*p <.05.

Table 7. Student achievement posttest one and two with conventional instruction method

	Posttest One			Posttest Two		
School	n	M	SD	n	M	SD
A	55	55.06	10.93	55	60.40	10.12
B	26	66.54	12.17	26	65.40	12.12
C	41	77.83	10.81	41	75.85	10.04
Total	122	65.16	14.96	122	66.58	12.51

Note. M = mean score of the content posttest

ANOVA was performed. Since the three-way interaction (of school, method and retention) was significant, Bonferroni corrected post hoc tests were performed for all pairwise comparisons of interest. Table 7 provides means and standard deviations for both tests in the conventional instruction group.

Among three schools in the control group, only School A performed better in the second posttest while Schools B and C scored lower in the second posttest. A Bonferroni correction further determined there was a statistically significant increase (p <.05) in School A regarding learning retention. However, in Schools B and C, there was no sta-

tistically significant change (p = 1.00 for School B and p =.408 for School C) (see Table 8).

Means and standard deviations for two posttests for the whole brain instructional group are listed in Table 9. Three schools within the whole brain instructional group performed better in posttest two then posttest one as reflected by mean difference shown in Table 10. With the adjustment of Bonferroni corrected post hoc tests, it indicated that there were statistically significant increases.

With the adjustment of Bonferroni post hoc tests, there were statistically significant differences in learning retention in School A (p <.05),

Table 8. Analysis of variances with bonferroni correction of learning retention with conventional instruction

School	Mean Difference	t	Uncorrected 1-tail p-value	Corrected 1-tail p-value
A	5.35	-3.628	.001	.002*
B	-1.14	0.623	.501	1.000
C	-1.98	1.522	.136	.408

*p <.05

Table 9. Student achievement posttest one and two with whole brain instruction method

School	Posttest One			Posttest Two		
	n	M	SD	n	M	SD
A	53	62.70	11.88	53	66.60	12.13
B	38	66.37	9.28	38	70.16	11.18
C	35	76.43	9.32	35	80.63	6.88
Total	126	67.62	11.85	126	71.57	12.05

Note. M = mean score of the content posttest

Table 10. Analysis of Variances with Bonferroni Correction of Learning Retention with Whole Brain Instruction Method

School	Mean Difference	T	Uncorrected 1-tail p-value	Corrected 1-tail p-value
A	3.91	-2.716	.009	.027*
B	3.79	-2.549	.015	.045*
C	4.20	-3.429	.002	.005*

*$p < .05$

School B ($p < .05$), and School C ($p < .05$) (see Table 10).

To determine whether there was a significant difference in learning retention in the treatment group, content posttest two, the same test as the first posttest, was administered. Table 11 illustrates repeated measures ANOVA results as reflected by different teaching methods when comparing posttest one and two. Significant differences occurred in retention, $F(1, 242) = 12.91$, $p < .05$, interaction between retention and school, $F(2,$ 242) = 3.90, $p < .05$, interaction between retention and method, $F(1, 242) = 6.85$, $p < .05$, as well as interaction among retention, school, and method, $F(2, 242) = 4.19$, $p < .05$. Since the three-way interaction (of school, method and posttests) was significant, Bonferroni corrected post hoc tests were performed for all pairwise comparisons.

To further determine whether students of different scoring levels were impacted by whole brain instruction, students were assigned to high, median, or low scoring levels based their first

Table 11. Analysis of variance for treatment effect on retention scores for both whole brain and conventional instruction

Source of Variation	df	MS	F	p
Retention	1	612.04	12.91	.00*
Retention by School	2	184.95	3.90	.02*
Retention by Method	1	324.66	6.85	.01*
Retention by School by Method	2	198.39	4.19	.02*
Error	242	47.40		

Note. Retention refers to the difference between content posttest one and two. School refers to Schools A, B, and C. Method refers to the whole brain instruction and conventional instruction method.
*$p < .05$

Table 12. Distribution of student numbers by school, teaching method and scoring level

	Scoring Level						Total
	High		Median		Low		
	n	Percentage	n	Percentage	n	Percentage	
Whole Brain Instruction							
School A	9	4%	21	8%	23	9%	53
School B	8	3%	20	8%	10	4%	38
School C	23	9%	10	4%	2	1%	35
Conventional Instruction							
School A	2	1%	12	5%	41	17%	55
School B	7	3%	10	4%	9	4%	26
School C	31	12%	7	3%	3	1%	41
Total	80	32%	80	32%	88	36%	248

content posttest. Students who scored in the first 33% of all participants were placed in the high scoring level, students who scored in the bottom 34% were placed as the low scoring level, and students who scored between were placed in the median scoring level. Therefore, students who scored at 74 or higher were placed in the high scoring level, those scoring between 62 and 73 were placed in the median scoring level, and those scoring 61 or below were placed in the low scoring level. Table 12 illustrates student number distribution and percentage based on teaching method, school, and scoring level. (see Table 13)

To determine whether students in different scoring levels and teaching methods perform differently on their content posttest two, A Bonferroni post hoc correction was used. As Table 14 indicates, students from whole brain instruction performed better in their second posttests across all scoring levels. However, students from conventional instruction performed worse in their second posttests only except for low scoring level. In other words, in the whole brain instruction group, students in high scoring level performed better in their second posttests but not there was no statistically significant difference. Students in the median and low scoring levels

performed significantly better in their second posttests.

However, results were not consistent in the conventional instruction group. Students in the high scoring level performed statistically worse in their second posttests. Students in the median scoring performed worse in their second posttests, but there was no statistically significance. Students in the low scoring level performed statistically significant better in their second posttests.

CONCLUSION

Based on the results of this study, it is inclusive to articulate whether whole brain instruction along does significantly impact student academic achievement. In this study, when considering method and school factors results would appear to support this. Academic achievement is composed of multifaceted factors, such as parental support, social economic status, or student comprehension ability, and could affect this result.

Based on the results stated before, students tend to like whole brain instruction. Students from two classes from the treatment group had positive learning attitudes while students, from the remaining four classes possessed negative

Table 13. Analysis of variance for total effect of learning retention

Source of Variation	df	MS	F	p
School	2	233.96	3.173	.044*
Method	1	368.59	4.999	.026*
Level	2	9045.81	122.689	.000*
School by Method	2	13.80	0.187	.829
School by Level	4	9.88	0.134	.970
Method by Level	2	33.68	0.457	.634
School by Method by Level	4	7.95	0.108	.980
Error 1	230			
Retention	1	8.84	8.838	.003*
Retention by School	2	2.10	2.102	.124
Retention by Method	1	6.89	6.891	.009*
Retention by Level	2	10.56	10.564	.000*
Retention by School by Method	2	.43	0.430	.651
Retention by School by Level	4	1.30	1.297	.272
Retention by Method by Level	2	.70	0.700	.498
Retention by School by Method by Level	4	.17	0.165	.956
Error 2	230			

Note. Retention refers to the difference between posttest one and two. School refers to Schools A, B, and C. Method refers to the whole brain instruction and conventional instruction. Level refers to the high scoring, median scoring, and low scoring.

*p <.05

Table 14. Analysis of variances with bonferroni correction of learning retention by scoring level and teaching method

	Posttest One	Posttest Two	Mean Difference	t	Uncorrected 1-tail p-value	Corrected 1-tail p-value
	M	M				
Whole Brain Instruction						
High	80.43	80.95	.52	-0.5184	.607	1.000
Median	68.00	72.18	4.18	-3.3662	.001	.009*
Low	52.43	59.97	7.54	-4.0407	.000	.002*
Conventional Instruction						
High	82.23	77.73	-4.50	3.4671	.001	.008*
Median	67.79	65.66	-2.13	1.1704	.252	1.000
Low	50.83	58.68	7.85	-6.0802	.000	.000*

Note. M = mean score of the content test.

*p <.05

attitudes toward learning. As noted, teaching is a complex process that is composed of many aspects, such as teachers, course material, school schedules, and students. The way the teacher presents information may encompass factors such as personal characteristics, communication skills, teaching styles as well as student responses. It is worthwhile to conduct further research about this topic.

Significant increases in learning retention were found across all three classes in the whole brain instruction. This consistent result evidenced that students regardless from private or public school types or with different academic backgrounds retain content knowledge into their long-term memory. Whole brain instruction includes providing diverse learning opportunities and enriched learning environments to help learners to obtain information in meaningful and multiple manners. This can help students to recall this information later. However, conventional instruction had a significant influence on student learning retention in one class, but not the other two.

In addition, when considering another variable, scoring level, different aspects were perceived. The high scoring students in the treatment group did not demonstrate a significant difference in learning retention; however, those in the control group decreased significantly in their learning retention. The median scoring level students in the treatment group performed significantly better in learning retention, while their counterparts in the control group showed no difference. The low scoring level students in the treatment and the control groups both performed significantly better in their learning retention. Both methods might equally contribute to this consequence.

Further Studies Recommendations

Future research possibilities and recommendations for replication of this study are stated as follows. First, people tend to present information in a way that meets their comfort zones and teachers may tend to fall back to their old ways of teaching. Even two surveys were given to participating teachers to investigate how well they carried out whole brain lessons. However, a video tape or audio recording of each teacher in every class would provide direct and qualitative information and would be beneficial in a future study of this type.

Second, this study was done in an introductory accounting course with 10th grade students. Replication of this study with an intermediate or advanced course would allow one to examine how similar the results would be. Third, this study investigated whether whole brain instruction would positively affect accounting education. It would be interesting to investigate how student academic achievement, attitudes, and retention are affected in other subject areas (English literacy, mathematics or history).

A larger group of students using whole brain instruction for a longer period of time is recommended for a future study. For example, employing more population by using one semester of treatment instead of four weeks, as in this study, might reveal a different effect whole brain instruction. To investigate whether demographics affect the results, a further study should be conducted to include information, such as gender, social economic status, and learning style. Moreover, the major issue in the e-learning environment is lack of student to student interaction. It is interested to examine whether the intervention of whole brain instruction can solve this problem and help to improve student academic achievement, attitudes, and retention.

REFERENCES

Abu, R. B., & Flowers, J. (1997). The effects of cooperative learning methods on achievement, retention, and attitudes of home economic students in North Carolina. *Journal of Vocational and Technical Education, 13*(2), 16–22.

Accounting Education Change Commission. (1990). Objective of education for accountants: Position statement number one. *Issues in Accounting Education, 5*(2), 307–312.

Accounting Education Change Commission. (1992). The first course in accounting: Position statement no. two. *Issues in Accounting Education, 7*(2), 249–251.

Albrecht, W. S., & Sack, R. J. (2000). *Accounting education: Charting the course through a perilous future.* Sarasota, FL: American Accounting Association.

American Accounting Association. Committee on the Future Structure, Content, and Scope of Accounting Education (the Bedford Committee). (1986). Future accounting education: Preparing for the expanding profession. *Issues in Accounting Education, 1*(1), 168–195.

Appell, C. J. (1991). *The effects of the 4MAT system of instruction on academic achievement and attitude in the elementary music classroom.* Unpublished doctoral dissertation, University of Oregon, Columbia.

Atkinson, R. C., & Shiffrin, R. M. (1971). The control of short-term memory. *Scientific American, 225,* 82–90. doi:10.1038/scientificamerican0871-82

Ausubel, D. P. (1968). *Educational Psychology: A cognitive view.* New York: Holt, Rinehart & Winston.

Bar-On, R. (2000). Emotional and social intelligence: Insights from the emotional quotient inventory. In Bar-On, R., & Parker, J. D. A. (Eds.), *The handbook of emotional intelligence* (pp. 363–388). San Francisco: Jossey-Bass.

Becktold, T. H. (2001). Brain based instruction in correctional settings: Strategies for teachers. *Journal of Correctional Education, 52*(3), 95–97.

Bennett, E. L., Diamond, M. C., Krech, D., & Rosenweig, M. R. (1964). Chemical and anatomical plasticity of brain. *Science, 146,* 610–619. doi:10.1126/science.146.3644.610

Black, J. E., Isaacs, K. R., Anderson, B. J., Alcantara, A. A., & Greenough, W. T. (1990). Learning causes synapogenesis, where motor activity causes angiogenesis, in cerebellar cortex of adult rats. *Neurobiology, 87,* 5568–5572.

Boone, H. N., & Newcomb, L. H. (1990). Effects of approach to teaching on student achievement, retention and attitude. *Journal of Agricultural Education, 31*(4), 9–14. doi:10.5032/jae.1990.04009

Borkowski, S. C., & Welsh, M. J. (1996). 4MAT/formatting the accounting curriculum. *Accounting Educators'. Journal, 8*(2), 67–90.

Bowers, P. S. (1987). *The effect of the 4MAT system on achievement and attitudes in science.* Unpublished doctoral dissertation, University of North Carolina at Chapel Hill, Columbia.

Bransford, J. D., Brown, A. L., & Cocking, R. R. (1999). *How people learn: Brain, mind, experience, and school.* Washington, DC: National Academy Press.

Bruer, J. T. (1998). Brain science, brain fiction. *Educational Leadership, 56*(3), 14–18.

Bruer, J. T. (1999). In search of ... brain-based education. *Phi Delta Kappan, 80*(9), 648–657.

Bruner, J. S. (1961). The act of discovery. *Harvard Educational Review, 31,* 21–32.

Charles, C. M., & Mertler, C. A. (2002). *Introduction to Educational Research.* Boston: Allyn & Bacon.

Chen, W. (2002). *An empirical study of the impact of the implication of information technology integrated instruction on learning effective and the establishment of teaching platform: In the case of senior high school accounting principle course.* Unpublished master's thesis, Feng Chia University, Taichung, Taiwan.

Chuang, C. (2001). *Comparing constructive approach and traditional approach in teaching accounting in the senior commercial vocational school.* Unpublished master's thesis, National Changhua University of Education, Changhua, Taiwan

Cronbach, L. J. (1970). *Essentials of psychological testing* (3rd ed.). New York: Author.

Dwyer, B. M. (2002). Training strategies for the twenty-first century: Using recent research on learning to enhance training. *Innovations in Education and Teaching International, 39*(4), 265–270. doi:10.1080/13558000210161115

Erlauer, L. (2003). *The brain-compatible classroom.* Alexandria, VA: Association for Supervision and Curriculum Development.

Francis, M. C., Mulder, T. C., & Stark, J. S. (1995). *Intentional learning: A process for learning to learn in the accounting curriculum.* Sarasota, FL: American Accounting Association.

Freire, P. (2000). *Pedagogy of the oppressed* (Ramos, M. B., Trans.). New York: Continuum. (Original work published 1968)

Gagné, R. M. (1985). *The conditions of learning and theory of instruction* (4th ed.). Orlando, FL: Holt, Rinehart & Winston.

Gagné, R. M., & Briggs, L. J. (1979). *Principles of instructional design* (2nd ed.). New York: Holt, Rinehart & Winston.

Gall, M. D., Gall, J. P., & Borg, W. R. (2003). *Educational research* (7th ed.). Boston: Pearson Education.

Genesee, F. (2000). *Brain research: Implications for second language learning.* (Report No. EDO-FL-00-12). Washington, DC: Center for Research on Education. (ERIC Document Reproduction Service No. ED447727)

Getz, C. M. (2003). *Application of brain-based learning theory for community college developmental English students: A case study.* Unpublished doctoral dissertation, Colorado State University, Columbia.

Greenleaf, R. K. (2003). Motion and emotion in student learning. *Education Digest, 69*(1), 37–42.

Jacobs, B., & Scheibel, A. B. (1993). A quantitative dendritic analysis of Wernicke's area in humans. *The Journal of Comparative Neurology, 327*(1), 83–96. doi:10.1002/cne.903270107

Jensen, E. (2000). *Brain-based learning* (Rev. ed.). San Diego, CA: The Brain Store.

Jensen, E. (2005). *Teaching with the brain in mind.* Alexandria, VA: Association for Supervision and Curriculum Development.

Jones, E. (1979). Business education in public and private schools. In Wakin, B. B., & Petitjean, C. F. (Eds.), *Alternative learning styles in business education* (pp. 1–8). Reston, VA: National Business Education Association.

Jorgensen, C. E. (1979). Teaching and learning by means of achievement levels or competencies. In Wakin, B. B., & Petitjean, C. F. (Eds.), *Alternative learning styles in business education* (pp. 196–206). Reston, VA: National Business Education Association.

Jorgenson, O. (2003). Brain scam? Why educator should be careful about embracing "brain research". *The Educational Forum, 67*(4), 364–369. doi:10.1080/00131720308984585

Kaplan, L. S. (1998). Using the 4MAT instructional model for effective leadership. *NASSP Bulletin, 82*(599), 83–92. doi:10.1177/019263659808259912

Karni, A., Meyer, G., Jezzard, P., Adams, M. M., Turner, R., & Ungerleider, L. G. (1995). Functional MRI evidence for adult motor cortex plasticity during motor skill learning. *Nature, 377*(14), 155–158.

Kelly, C. (1990). Using 4MAT in law school. *Educational Leadership, 48*(2), 40–41.

Kitchens, A. N., Barber, W. D., & Barber, D. B. (1991). Left brain/right brain theory: Implications for developmental math instruction. *Review of Research in Education, 8*(3), 3–6.

Labaw, P. J. (1980). *Advanced questionnaire design.* Cambridge, MA: Abt Books.

Lefrancois, G. R. (1999). *Psychology for teaching* (10th ed.). Belmont, CA: Wadsworth/Thomson Learning.

Lindquist, T. M. (1995). Traditional versus contemporary goals and methods in accounting education: Bridging the gap with cooperative learning. *Journal of Education for Business, 70*(5), 278–284. doi:10.1080/08832323.1995.10117764

Loo, R. (2002). A meta-analytic examination of Kolb's learning style preferences among business majors. *Journal of Education for Business, 77*(5), 252–256. doi:10.1080/08832320209599673

Magnuson, J. (2002). Middle school family and consumer sciences: Brain-based education from theory to practice. *Journal of Family and Consumer Sciences, 94*(1), 45–47.

Mayer, R. E. (1996). Learners as information processor: Legacies and limitations of educational psychology's second metaphor. *Educational Psychologist, 31*(4), 151–161. doi:10.1207/s15326985ep3103&4_1

McCarthy, B. (1985). What 4MAT training teachers us about staff development. *Educational Leadership, 42*, 61–68.

McCarthy, B. (2000). *About teaching: 4MAT in the classroom.* Chicago: About Learning.

McInerney, V., McInerney, D. M., & Marsh, H. W. (1997). Effects of metacognitive strategy training with a cooperative group learning within a cooperative group learning context on computer achievement and anxiety: An aptitude-treatment interaction study. *Journal of Educational Psychology, 89*(4), 686–695. doi:10.1037/0022-0663.89.4.686

McMillan, J. H. (1996). *Educational research: Fundamentals for the consumer* (2nd ed.). New York: HarperCollins.

Nunnally, J. C., & Bernstein, I. H. (1994). *Psychometric theory* (3rd ed.). New York: McGraw-Hill.

Nunnelley, J. C., Whaley, J., Mull, R., & Hott, G. (2003). Brain compatible secondary schools: The visionary principal's role. *NASSP Bulletin, 87*(637), 48–59. doi:10.1177/019263650308763705

O'Neil, J. (1990). Making sense of style. *Educational Leadership, 48*(2), 4–9.

Oppenheim, A. N. (1992). *Questionnaire design, interviewing and attitude measurement.* London: Continuum.

Ravenscroft, S. P., Buckless, F. A., McCombs, G. B., & Zuckerman, G. J. (1995). Incentives in student team learning: An experiment in cooperative group learning. *Issues in Accounting Education, 10*(1), 97–109.

Rosenzweig, M. R., Love, W., & Bennett, E. L. (1968). Effects of a few hours a day of enriched experience on brain chemistry and brain weights. *Physiology & Behavior, 3*, 819–825. doi:10.1016/0031-9384(68)90161-3

Sanders, B. (2001). *The supply of accounting graduates and the demand for public accounting recruits-2001.* New York: American Institute of Certified Public Accountants.

Sousa, D. A. (2001). *How the brain learns* (2nd ed.). Thousand Oaks, CA: Sage.

Sparapani, E. F. (1998). Encouraging thinking in high school and middle school: Constraints and possibilities. *Clearing House (Menasha, Wis.)*, *71*(5),274–276.doi:10.1080/00098659809602722

Sperry, R. W. (1975). Left brain-right brain. *Saturday Review*, 30–33.

Springer, S. P., & Deutsch, G. (1998). *Left brain, right brain: Perspectives from cognitive neuroscience* (5th ed.). New York: W. H. Freeman.

Stevens, J. (2002). *Applied multivariate statistics for the social sciences*. Mahwah, NJ: Lawrence Erlbaum Associates.

Stronge, J. H. (2002). *Qualities of effective teachers*. Alexandria, VA: Association for Supervision and Curriculum Development.

Taiwan Ministry of Education. (2008). *Decade analysis report for educational development.* Retrieve August 20, 2008, from ttp://140.111.34.54/statistics/content.aspx?site_content_sn=8169

Vaughn, V. F. (1991). *A comparison of the 4MAT system of instruction with two enrichment units based on Bloom's taxonomy with gifted third-grader in a pull-out program.* Unpublished doctoral dissertation, Purdue University, Columbia.

Wang, H. F., Sheu, L. D., & Chen, M. C. (2008). An empirical study of college student's learning in accounting knowledge: The application of teaching model for conceptual change. *Journal of Education Studies*, *42*(1), 79–96.

Weber, P., & Weber, F. (1990). Using 4MAT to improve student presentations. *Educational Leadership*, *48*(2), 41–46.

Wilkerson, R. M., & White, K. P. (1988). Effects of the 4MAT system of instruction on students' achievement, retention, and attitudes. *The Elementary School Journal*, *88*(4), 357–368. doi:10.1086/461544

Wittrock, M. C. (1990). Generative teaching of comprehension. *The Elementary School Journal*, *92*, 345–376.

Yang, M. (2001). *The investigation of current accounting education in commercial senior high schools and the fundamental competence cultivation of graduates from commercial senior high schools.* Unpublished master's thesis, National Changhua University of Education, Changhua, Taiwan.

Zhao, H., & Kanda, K. (2000). Translation and validation of the standard Chinese version of the EORTC QLQ-C30. *Quality of Life Research, 9,* 129–137. doi:10.1023/A:1008981520920

This work was previously published in International Journal of Distance Education Technologies, Volume 7, Issue 3, edited by Qun Jin, pp. 63-84, copyright 2009 by IGI Publishing (an imprint of IGI Global).

Chapter 17
Using S-P Chart and Bloom Taxonomy to Develop Intelligent Formative Assessment Tools

Wen-Chih Chang
Chung Hua University, Taiwan

Hsuan-Che Yang
TungNan University, Taiwan

Timothy K. Shih
Asia University, Taiwan

Louis R. Chao
Tamkang University, Taiwan

ABSTRACT

E-learning provides a convenient and efficient way for learning. Formative assessment not only guides student in instruction and learning, diagnose skill or knowledge gaps, but also measures progress and evaluation. An efficient and convenient e-learning formative assessment system is the key character for e-learning. However, most e-learning systems didn't provide methods for assessing learners' abilities but true-score mode. In this article, Sato's Student-Problem Chart (SP Chart) is applied to integrate with our proposed on-line assessment system. Teachers are able to analyze each learner easily and efficiently. In addition, the Bloom Taxonomy of Educational Objective supports each item in our assessment management system during the authoring time. In our proposed system, it provides groups of function for student, teacher, and system administrator. According to the SP Chart analysis and Bloom taxonomy of items, we can divide all items into four types, and students into six types. With these types of diagnosis analysis chart, teacher can modify or delete the items which are not proper. With diagnosis analysis chart of students, teachers can realize learners' learning situation easily and efficiently.

DOI: 10.4018/978-1-60960-539-1.ch017

INTRODUCTION

Assessment is the process to measure and analyze students' performance and learning skill. Assessment is also able to give feedback both to the teacher and student in how to improve their future performance. Assessment can be denoted as the central part in learning and mental development. Robert Glaser (1962) first constructed an "Instructional System" which is composed of instructional goals, entering behavior, instructional procedures, and performance assessments. Instructors set instructional goals and apply appropriate teaching and learning activities for students. With the result and analysis of assessment, instructors can revise the related teaching strategies and change the learning materials to help the students to overcome the obstacles. Many studies concentrate on providing assessment system to test and to verify their point of views. Olly Gotel, Christelle Scharff and Andrew Wildenberg (2008) also combined with innovative pedagogical approach, which is based on students contributing programming problems to an open source web-based system that is used for student practice and instructor assessment of assignments. This requires students to construct comprehensive unit tests that can assure both the usability and accuracy of their work prior to deployment. Wang (2007) demonstrated a well designed on-line assessment system and strategy makes students achieve better learning effectiveness.

Ebel and Frisbie (1991) observed that the terms "formative" were introduced by Scriven (1967) to describe the various roles of evaluation in curriculum development and instruction. Formative assessment is one of the assessment methods. It monitors the instructional process and determines whether learning is taking place as planned. Formative assessment assists learner learning, diagnoses learning knowledge gap, evaluates learning performance and measures teaching progress. Teachers could modify the teaching techniques and tutoring strategies, and determine what knowledge concept needs more teaching or more exercises. After a period of time, teachers can collect the assessment result to make some adjustments for future performance. Formative assessment not only guides student instruction and learning, diagnoses skill or knowledge gaps, but also measures progress and evaluate instruction. Teachers apply formative assessment to decide what concepts require more teaching and what teaching techniques require modification. Over time, educators use results to evaluate instruction strategies, curriculum and teachers, and make adjustments for better student performance.

The learning cycle used in these lesson plans follows Bybee's (1997) five steps of Engagement, Exploration, Explanation, Elaboration, and Evaluation. As in any cycle, there's really no end to the process. After the elaboration ends, the engagement of the next learning cycle begins. Evaluation is not the last step. Evaluation occurs in all four parts of the learning cycle. The description of each part of the learning cycle draws extensively from our previous works (Lin, Nigel H., Chang W.C., Shih T. K., & Keh H.C., 2005; Chang W.C., Hsu H.H., Shih T. K., & Wang C.C., 2005).

Black and William (1996; 1998) define assessment broadly to include all activities that teachers and students undertake to get information that can be used diagnostically to alter teaching and learning. Under this definition, assessment encompasses teacher observation, classroom discussion, and analysis of student work, including homework and tests. Assessments becomes formative when the information is used to adapt teaching and learning to meet student needs. Assessment focuses on the gap between students performance and instruction goal. Formative assessment focused on the information gathered must be used to adapt the teaching or the learning to meet the needs of the learner. However, formative assessment feedback is difficult for teachers to provide, because they always face large numbers of students, lengthy pieces of work, or practical constraints such as time and workload (Buchanan, 1998; 2000). Efficient and convenient e-learning formative assessment system is the key character for e-learning. Learners study in e-learning environment lack adaptive feedback and formative assessment, except synchronous learning provides real-time interaction. However it cost a lot time and money for arranging the teachers or tutors in e-learning. To support formative assessment in e-learning is necessary.

In this study, we mainly use a tool called the S-P Chart (Student-Problem Chart) integrated in our proposed on-line assessment system. Teachers are able to analyze learners with it easily and efficiently. There are two main purposes in our study. First, teachers can measure and understand learners' further learning performances with caution index for course for students (CS) provided in S-P Chart. Second, teachers are able to observe items quality with caution index for problems (CP) provided in S-P Chart with this integrated system. In addition, learning resources or test items should be classified to facilitate the analysis. The Bloom Taxonomy of Educational Objective (Bloom, Englehart, Furst, Hill, & Krathwohl, 1956) is commonly used for categorizing cognitive domains. In our research, we also integrate the revised Bloom taxonomy (Anderson, & Krathwohl, 2001) to assist categorizing our test items. After the assessments were held, teachers are not only able to evaluate the learners' ability, but also to point out the deficiency of learners in the assessments.

The rest sessions of this article are briefly summarized as follows. The related work section describes Sato's S-P Chart analysis and the Bloom Taxonomy of Educational Objective; some related studies are discussed as well. After the related work section, the system structure and system

flow chart are presented, Following is the main method of our system, it delineates how to integrate S-P Chart to diagnose students and estimate their learning abilities. An assist system is discussed in proposed system section. Then the discussion session comes after. Finally, a brief conclusion and future work is drawn.

RELATED WORK

A good assessment not only supplies suggestions for instructors to edit their learning material but also supports learners to comprehend the knowledge they misunderstood. Therefore, finding the relationship between the learner, the course, and the exam is important. Some research focused on these issues and they are listed in the following.

The Student-Problem Chart (S-P Chart) is proposed by a Japanese scholar Takahiro Sato in '70s (Sato, 1975). The S-P Chart is a graphical analysis tool to represent the relationship between students and the response situations of answering some problems by these students. The main purpose of the S-P Chart is to obtain the diagnosis materials of each student when they study. Teachers can provide better study counseling to each student according to these analyzed materials. There are numbered indices used in S-P chart. Including disparity index, homogeneity index, caution index for student (CS), and caution index for problem (CP). With these indices, teachers are able to diagnose students' learning conditions, instructive achievement, and problem quality (Sato, 1980; 1985). In our research, we use caution index for problems (CP) and students (CS) to analyze the test items (problem) and students. These indices can be used for judging whether students or problems have any unusual phenomenon when the assessment was made. New coefficient formulas can modify by these two attention coefficients as shown below (Yu, 2002).

Caution Index for Problems (CP)

$$CP_j = 1 - \frac{\sum_{i=1}^{N}(y_{ij})(y_i) - (y_j)(\mu)}{\sum_{i=1}^{y_i} y_i - (y_j)(\mu)} = \frac{\sum_{i=1}^{y_i}(1-y_{ij})(y_i) - \sum_{i=y_j+1}^{N}(y_{ij})(y_i)}{\sum_{i=1}^{y_i} y_i - (y_j)(\mu)}$$

$$= \frac{\left[\begin{array}{l}\text{The sum of students' scores}\\\text{when their answer is "0"}\\\text{that test item "j" is above}\\\text{the P curve}\end{array}\right] - \left[\begin{array}{l}\text{The sum of students' scores}\\\text{when their answer is "1"}\\\text{that test item "j" is below}\\\text{the P curve}\end{array}\right]}{\left[\begin{array}{l}\text{The sum of all students'}\\\text{total scores}\\\text{that test item "j"}\\\text{is above the P curve}\end{array}\right] - \left[\begin{array}{l}\text{The number of}\\\text{correct responses}\\\text{for all of test-takers}\\\text{for test item "j"}\end{array}\right] \times \left[\begin{array}{l}\text{The average score}\\\text{of the students}\end{array}\right]}$$

Caution Index for Students (CS)

$$CS_i = 1 - \frac{\sum_{j=1}^{n}(y_{ij})(y_j) - (y_i)(\mu')}{\sum_{j=1}^{y_i} y_j - (y_j)(\mu')} = \frac{\sum_{j=1}^{y_i}(1-y_{ij})(y_j) - \sum_{j=y_i+1}^{n}(y_{ij})(y_j)}{\sum_{j=1}^{y_i} y_j - (y_i)(\mu')}$$

$$= \frac{\left[\begin{array}{l}\text{The number of correct responses}\\\text{for all test items}\\\text{when their answer is "0"}\\\text{that student "i" is left}\\\text{the S curve}\end{array}\right] - \left[\begin{array}{l}\text{The number of correct responses}\\\text{for all test items}\\\text{when their answer is "1"}\\\text{that student "i" is right}\\\text{the S curve}\end{array}\right]}{\left[\begin{array}{l}\text{The sum of correct}\\\text{responses for all}\\\text{test items that}\\\text{student "i" is left}\\\text{the S curve}\end{array}\right] - \left[\begin{array}{l}\text{The number of correct}\\\text{responses of student i}\\\text{on all of the test item}\end{array}\right] \times \left[\begin{array}{l}\text{The average number}\\\text{of correct responses}\\\text{for all test items}\end{array}\right]}$$

Kazuo Yamanoi (2007) used Microsoft Excel to implement the SP chart. The tool is useful and user-friendly. It can draw the S-curve and the C-curve easily. However the results are analyzed by human, not by computer. Dai, Cheng, Sung, & Ho (2005) discovered some significant things: (1) the class-based analysis unit of the S-P chart; (2) the diagnosis of students' learning outcome in regards to S-P chart; (3) the diagnosis of test item quality according to S-P chart; (4) the forecast of students' placement; (5)facilitation to the analysis and testing the test quality of the related subjects test bank; (6) an blend tool to construct the web-based test. Chen, Lai, & Liu (2005) incorporated the response time, the difficulty index, and the discriminatory index of each test item into an S-P model during the analysis.

To improve further the SP chart, Shih et al. (2003) developed the Student-Problem-Course (SPC) table to analyze the relations among student, problem, and course in three dimensions. Integrating the SP chart and course, the SPC table provides three domains, course-problem, student-problem and course-student. The SP domain is the same as the SP chart method. The SP chart records the relationship between learners and questions in an exam. In the CP domain, instructors are able to know the relationship between the course and the question of an exam. The SC domain presents the relationship between the learner and the course. Chang et al. (2005) proposed an assessment metadata model which integrates assessment and SCORM for e-Learning operations. With support from assessment metadata, the authors can incorporate measured aspects of the following list into the metadata description at the question cognition level, the item difficulty index, the item discrimination index, the questionnaire style, and the question style. The assessment analysis model provides analytical suggestions for individual questions, summary of test results, and cognition analysis. Lin et al. (2005) applied influence diagram method to analyze the learning progress. The authors combined SCORM (Sharable Content Object Reference Model) specification with design of the course diagram. The courseware can be generated automatically with the distance learning specifications. The instructor can receive prompt feedback from students. The item analysis provides information about the reliability and validity of test items and learner performance. Item Analysis has two purposes (Brown, 1971): First, to identify defective test items and secondly, to pinpoint the learning materials (content) the learners have and have not mastered, particularly what skills they lack and what material still causes them difficulty. Item Analysis is performed by comparing the proportion of learners who pass a test item in contrasting criterion groups. That is, for each question on a test, how many learners with the highest test scores (U) answered the question correctly or incorrectly compared with the learners who had the lowest test scores (L). The upper (U) and lower (L) criterion groups are selected from the extremes of the distribution. The use of very extreme groups, say the upper and lower 10 percent, would result in a sharper differentiation, but it would reduce the reliability of the results because of the small number of cases utilized. In a normal distribution, the optimum point at which these two conditions balance out is 27 percent H(Kelly, 1939).

The Taxonomy of Educational Objectives, often called Bloom's Taxonomy, is a classification of the different objectives and skills that educators set for students. The taxonomy was proposed in 1956 by Benjamin Bloom, an educational psychologist at the University of Chicago. In 1956, Bloom created the six cognition levels from the simple recall or recognition of facts. From easy to complex, the six levels are knowledge, comprehension, application, analysis, synthesis and evaluation. The sequence of six levels is also list through more complex and more abstract mental levels. Learner has to learn the front level (ex. knowledge) before later level (ex. comprehension). Learner who does not understand lower level (ex. knowledge) cannot forward to higher level (ex. comprehension). In 2001, Anderson et al. (2001) proposed a revised version of cognition level which is composed of cognitive process dimension and knowledge dimension. The cognitive process dimension emphasizes on how to assist learner's knowledge of retention and transfer. The knowledge dimension focuses on inform teachers how to teach. Knowledge dimension involves factual knowledge, conceptual knowledge, procedural knowledge and meta-cognitive knowledge. Cognitive process dimension includes remember, understand, apply, analyze, evaluate and create. (Airasian, & Maranda, 2002).

SYSTEM ARCHITECTURE

Our proposed system contains three main functions for students, teachers and system administrators. As Figure 1 show, the functions for students are 1) Grade Search, 2) On-line Assessment and 3) Individual Information Transaction. The functions for Teachers are 1) Item Design, 2) S-P Chart and Bloom Analysis and 3) Scores Management. With these functions, teachers are able to diagnosis learners and to evaluate learning objects after the assessment.

Process Flow

About the flow of our running process, we can divide it in ten steps.

1. Course Establish/Transaction: At the beginning, administrators create courses and register all users' information.
2. Update/Add Test Item: Teachers edit test items. Update or add test items.
3. On-line Assessment: Students attend the assessment with browser.
4. System corrects each test sheet when assessments were done: When students finish the assessment, the system will correct each item in the assessment.
5. Mark the correct answers of each wrong answer: When system finish correcting test items, system will also mark the correct answers.
6. Make Bloom Analysis Results for each student: When all items are corrected and right answers are marked, system will provide Bloom analysis result for each student.
7. Save Bloom Analysis Results: Bloom analysis results will be saved in the database.
8. Generate S-P Chart: S-P Chart analysis will be generated.
9. Save S-P Chart: Save the S-P Chart analysis results in the database.

Figure 1. System architecture

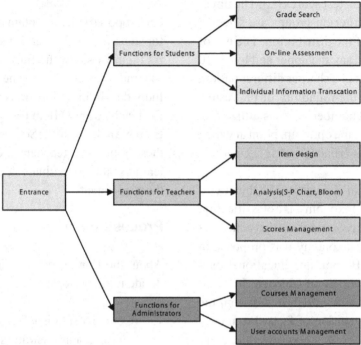

10. Students and Teachers can retrieve the analysis results of S-P Chart and Bloom

In the final step, students and teachers can search both S-P Chart and Bloom analysis results as well. For students, they want to know their learning ability. For teachers, they can observe students' learning ability and items' qualities.

Main Method of Our System

As mentioned, we use caution index for student and caution index for problem to estimate learning result and item quality. We arrange them with two charts shown as Figure 2 and Figure 3.

• Diagnosis analysis chart of Test Items:
• Zone A: In zone A, all items have well discrimination. With these items, system can distinguish students who have well academic achievement or not.

• Zone B: In zone B, all items have high difficulty and proper for distinguishing the students who have high academic achievement.
• Zone A': In zone A', items have impure element in the question structure which includes stem and choices. The test items need modify the stem or the improper choices.
• Zone B': Items in zone B' are seriously bad and have much impure elements. That means the items need to be modified immediately.
• Diagnosis analysis chart of Students:
• Type A: When students locate in this area, they have steady learning behavior and have excellent performance.
• Type B: When students located in this area, that means students' learning behavior is stable but not good enough, and they need work harder.

Figure 2. Diagnosis analysis chart of Test Items

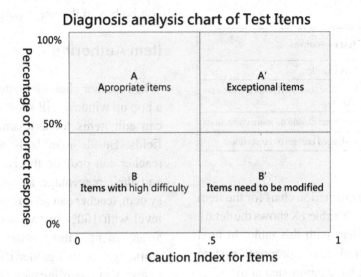

- Type C: Students not study enough and their performance is poor. They need study much harder.
- Type A': The students who locate in this area study hard and have good performance. But they might make some mistakes with carelessness.
- Type B': When students locate in this area, they won't have well preparation for the assessment and attend the assessment with carelessness.
- Type C': Students in this area never read the book. (Table 1)

When teacher want to setup an assessment, it's a better way to make sure that the item is proper or not. A good item can make a well judgment for students' performance. Ebel and Frisbie

Figure 3. Diagnosis analysis chart of Students

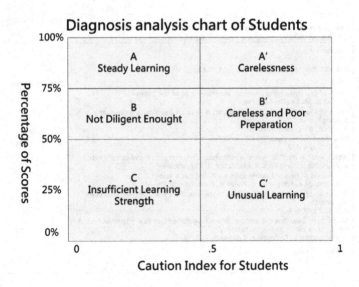

Table 1. The evaluation standard chart of item discrimination index

Item discrimination index	Test assessment
Over 0.40	Very excellent
0.30~0.39	Excellent, but maybe need some corrections
0.20~0.29	Good, but should do more corrections
Below 0.19	Bad, need erasure or corrections

(1991) provided the evaluation chart for the item discrimination index. XTable 1X shows the detail. Teachers can pick item with this table. In next session, we will introduce our proposed system supporting what we have mentioned above.

PROPOSED SYSTEM

We propose an on-line assessment system supporting item and assessment authoring and S-P Cart analysis function and Bloom cognition level setting. In Figure 4, teacher can hold assessments and edit test items. Teacher can switch to other assessment by selecting other selection in the combo box in the upper part.

Item Authoring

When teacher click the button behind each item, a pop up window will show as Figure 5. Teacher can edit items for assessment by filling some fields. Beside item body and correct answer, teacher can provide the Bloom cognition level and their percentage as well. In our proposed system, teacher can set only one Bloom cognition level with 100% or two levels with proportion arrangement. After teacher finish the authoring work, system will gather Bloom information of assessment according witch item inside automatically. As shown in Figure 6, teachers can realize the distribution of Bloom cognition level in the assessment immediately.

Diagnostic and Analysis

One of the special features in our proposed system is diagnostic and analysis. We diagnose students' learning results with caution index for student and diagnosis analysis chart. We also analyze

Figure 4. Assessment design

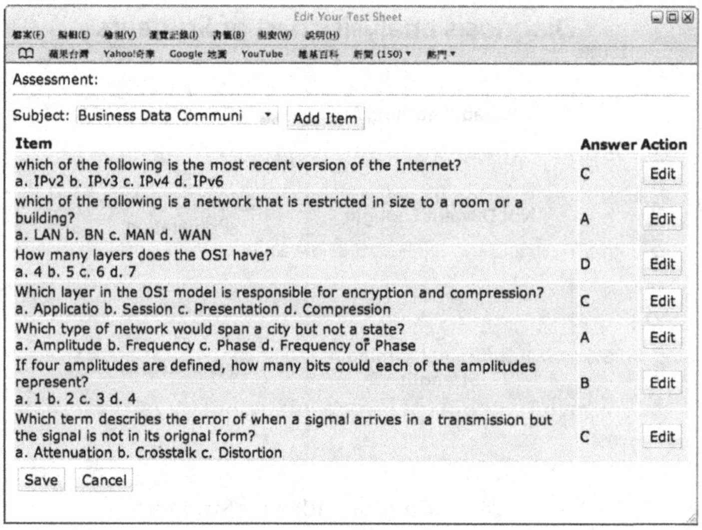

Figure 5. Creating test item

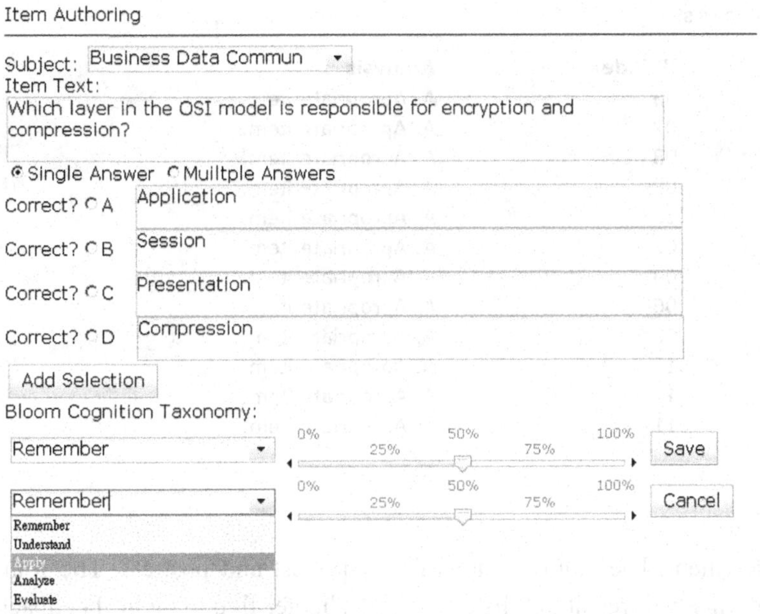

Item Authoring
_____

Subject: Business Data Commun ▼
Item Text:
Which layer in the OSI model is responsible for encryption and compression?

⦿ Single Answer ○ Muiltple Answers

Correct? ○ A   Application

Correct? ○ B   Session

Correct? ○ C   Presentation

Correct? ○ D   Compression

[Add Selection]

Bloom Cognition Taxonomy:

| Remember ▼ | 0%   50%   100% | [Save] |
| | 25%   75% | |

| Remember | 0%   50%   100% | [Cancel] |
| | 25%   75% | |
Remember
Understand
Apply
Analyze
Evaluate

items' attribute with caution index for items and diagnosis analysis chart. It provides an efficient way to evaluate the qualities of items and students.

Test item diagnostic and analysis is shown in Figure 7. The left hand side shows the items in assessment, the CP index and the item type. Right hand side shows the test item classification according to the test item caution index.

The student diagnostic and analysis is shown in Figure 8. The left hand side shows the students

Figure 6. Assessment attribute with Bloom classification

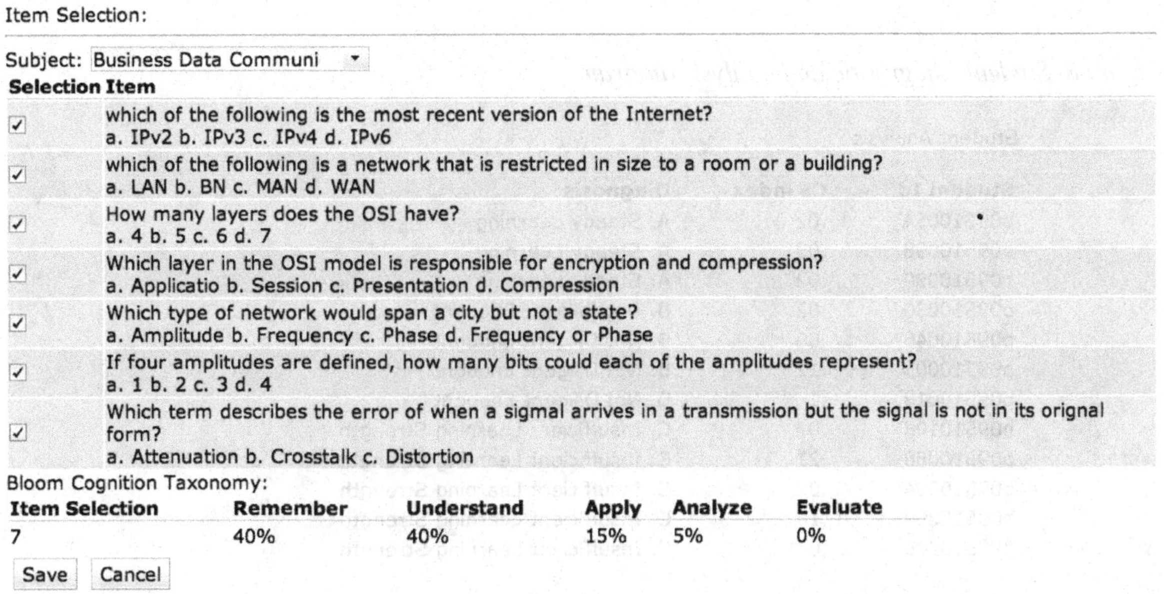

Item Selection:
_____

Subject: Business Data Communi ▼

Selection Item

✓	which of the following is the most recent version of the Internet? a. IPv2 b. IPv3 c. IPv4 d. IPv6
✓	which of the following is a network that is restricted in size to a room or a building? a. LAN b. BN c. MAN d. WAN
✓	How many layers does the OSI have? a. 4 b. 5 c. 6 d. 7
✓	Which layer in the OSI model is responsible for encryption and compression? a. Applicatio b. Session c. Presentation d. Compression
✓	Which type of network would span a city but not a state? a. Amplitude b. Frequency c. Phase d. Frequency or Phase
✓	If four amplitudes are defined, how many bits could each of the amplitudes represent? a. 1 b. 2 c. 3 d. 4
✓	Which term describes the error of when a sigmal arrives in a transmission but the signal is not in its orignal form? a. Attenuation b. Crosstalk c. Distortion

Bloom Cognition Taxonomy:

Item Selection	Remember	Understand	Apply	Analyze	Evaluate
7	40%	40%	15%	5%	0%

[Save] [Cancel]

Figure 7. Test item diagnostic and analysis diagram

Item Analysis

item	CP index	Analysis
29	.05	A. Apropriate item.
20	.07	A. Apropriate item.
30	.08	A. Apropriate item.
14	.08	A. Apropriate item.
7	.13	A. Apropriate item.
28	.07	A. Apropriate item.
26	.08	A. Apropriate item.
17	.06	A. Apropriate item.
18	.08	A. Apropriate item.
24	.1	A. Apropriate item.
22	.1	A. Apropriate item.
21	.11	A. Apropriate item.

who attend the assessment. The caution index of student and student's analysis results are listed as well. Right hand side shows the student classification according to the caution index of student.

DISCUSSION

Our experiment subject was the sophomore. The course name was the business data communication. The course content was about the network. In this course, we used four chapters which had pretest and posttest. The four chapters include chapter five to eight. Feedback information was came from the incorrect answers that each student to respond in pretest. It had the section and book page in feedback information. The main goal was help each student received the correct concepts easily. (Figure 9)

We received the detailed information for every student. Most of class B students had done better than class A. In the table, the scope of S-P curve that in Figure 10 was bigger than Figure 9. At the final exam we gave a simple questionnaire for

Figure 8. Students diagnostic and analysis diagram

Student Analysis

Student Id	CS index	Diagnosis
b09510054	.02	A. Steady Learning
b09510098	.03	A. Steady Learning
b09510090	.02	A. Steady Learning
b09510030	.02	B. Not Diligent Enought
b09510046	.06	B. Not Diligent Enought
b09510005	.11	B. Not Diligent Enought
b09510018	.1	B. Not Diligent Enought
b09510108	.07	C. Insufficient Learning Strength
b09510088	.21	C. Insufficient Learning Strength
b09510004	.07	C. Insufficient Learning Strength
b09510204	.16	C. Insufficient Learning Strength
b09510206	.07	C. Insufficient Learning Strength

Figure 9. S-P table to Class A-the P curve -- the S curve

	1	14	4	2	3	15	6	8	9	13	5	10	11	7	12	
2	1	1	1	1	1	1	1	1	1	1	1	1	1	0	1	14
3	1	1	1	1	1	1	1	1	1	1	1	1	1	0	1	14
1	1	1	1	1	1	1	0	1	1	1	1	1	1	1	0	13
16	1	1	1	1	1	1	1	1	1	1	1	1	1	0	0	13
29	1	1	1	1	1	1	0	1	1	1	1	1	1	0	1	13
30	1	1	1	1	1	1	1	1	0	1	1	1	1	0	1	13
4	1	1	1	1	1	1	1	1	1	0	1	0	1	0	1	12
19	1	1	1	1	1	1	1	1	1	0	1	0	0	0	1	12
21	1	1	1	1	1	1	1	0	1	0	1	1	1	1	0	12
34	1	1	1	1	0	1	1	1	1	1	0	0	1	1	1	12
24	1	1	1	1	1	1	1	0	0	1	1	1	1	0	0	11
10	1	1	1	1	1	1	1	1	1	0	1	0	0	0	0	10
14	1	1	1	1	1	1	1	1	1	0	1	0	0	0	0	10
39	1	1	1	1	1	1	1	1	0	1	1	1	0	0	0	10
12	1	1	1	1	0	1	1	1	1	1	0	0	0	0	0	9
18	1	1	1	1	1	1	1	0	1	0	0	0	1	0	0	9
27	1	1	0	1	1	1	1	1	1	0	1	1	0	0	0	9
31	1	1	1	1	1	1	1	1	1	0	1	0	0	0	0	9
5	1	1	1	1	1	0	1	0	0	0	1	0	1	0	0	8
11	1	1	0	1	1	1	0	1	1	0	0	1	0	0	1	8
13	1	1	1	1	1	1	0	1	0	1	0	0	0	0	0	8
17	1	1	1	1	1	1	0	1	0	1	0	0	0	0	0	8
9	1	0	1	0	0	1	0	0	0	0	1	1	1	1	0	7
23	1	1	0	1	1	1	0	1	0	0	1	0	0	0	0	7
26	1	1	0	1	0	0	0	0	0	0	0	1	1	1	1	7
28	1	1	0	0	0	1	0	1	0	0	0	1	1	1	0	7
38	1	1	1	1	0	0	0	0	1	1	0	0	0	0	0	7
40	1	1	1	0	0	0	1	1	1	0	0	0	0	1	0	7
33	1	0	1	0	1	1	0	1	0	1	0	0	0	0	0	6
37	1	1	1	0	1	0	0	0	1	0	0	0	1	0	0	6
7	1	0	1	0	0	0	0	1	0	1	0	0	0	1	0	5
20	1	1	1	0	0	1	0	0	0	0	0	1	0	0	0	5
25	1	0	0	0	0	1	0	0	1	0	0	0	1	1	0	5
8	1	0	0	0	0	0	0	1	0	0	0	1	1	0	0	4
15	1	1	0	0	0	0	0	1	0	0	0	1	0	0	0	4
22	1	0	0	1	1	0	0	0	0	0	0	0	1	0	0	4
35	1	0	0	0	0	0	1	0	1	1	0	0	0	0	0	4
6	1	0	0	0	0	0	0	1	0	0	0	1	0	0	0	3
32	0	0	0	0	0	0	1	0	0	0	0	0	0	0	0	1
36	0	0	0	0	0	0	0	0	0	0	0	0	0	0	0	0
	38	29	28	26	26	25	23	23	20	19	18	16	16	10	9	

Figure 10. S-P table to Class B-the P curve -- the S curve

	15	1	9	14	12	13	4	8	3	6	7	5	2	10	11	
2	1	1	1	1	1	1	1	1	1	1	1	1	1	1	1	15
23	1	1	1	1	1	1	1	1	1	1	1	1	1	1	1	15
29	1	1	1	1	1	1	1	1	1	1	1	1	1	1	1	15
3	1	1	1	1	1	1	1	1	1	1	0	1	1	1	1	14
10	1	1	1	1	1	1	1	1	1	1	1	1	0	1	1	14
20	1	1	1	1	1	1	1	1	1	1	1	1	0	1	1	14
21	1	1	1	1	1	1	1	1	1	1	1	1	0	1	1	14
24	1	1	0	1	1	1	1	1	1	1	1	1	1	1	1	14
30	1	1	1	1	1	1	1	0	1	1	1	1	1	1	1	14
32	1	1	1	1	1	1	1	1	0	1	1	1	1	1	1	14
33	1	1	1	1	1	1	1	1	1	1	1	1	0	1	1	14
5	1	1	1	1	0	1	1	1	1	1	1	1	1	0	1	13
13	1	1	1	1	1	1	0	1	1	1	1	1	1	0	1	13
16	1	1	0	1	1	1	0	1	1	1	1	1	1	1	1	13
19	1	1	1	1	1	1	1	1	1	1	0	0	1	1	1	13
25	1	1	1	1	1	1	1	1	1	1	0	1	1	0	1	13
26	1	1	1	1	1	1	1	1	0	1	1	0	1	1	1	13
34	1	1	1	1	1	1	1	1	0	1	1	1	1	0	1	13
40	1	1	1	1	1	0	1	1	1	1	1	1	1	1	0	13
4	1	1	1	1	1	1	1	0	1	1	0	1	0	1	0	12
9	1	1	1	1	1	1	1	1	1	0	1	0	0	0	1	12
15	1	1	1	1	1	1	1	1	1	0	1	0	0	1	1	12
17	1	1	1	1	1	0	1	0	1	1	1	1	1	0	1	12
35	1	1	1	1	1	1	1	1	0	0	1	0	1	0	1	11
6	1	1	1	1	0	1	1	0	1	0	1	1	0	1	0	10
22	1	1	1	1	1	0	1	0	1	1	0	1	1	0	0	10
1	1	1	1	1	0	0	1	0	0	1	1	1	0	1	1	9
8	1	0	1	1	1	1	1	1	0	0	0	0	0	0	1	9
12	1	1	1	1	1	0	1	0	1	0	1	0	1	1	0	9
14	1	1	0	1	1	1	0	1	0	0	1	1	1	0	0	9
18	1	1	1	1	0	1	1	0	1	0	0	0	1	1	0	9
27	1	1	1	1	1	1	1	0	1	0	0	1	1	0	0	9
28	1	1	1	1	1	1	1	0	1	0	1	0	0	0	1	9
31	1	1	1	0	0	1	0	1	1	1	0	1	1	0	0	9
38	1	1	1	1	1	1	0	1	1	1	0	0	0	0	0	9
7	1	1	1	0	0	1	1	0	1	0	1	0	0	1	0	8
11	1	1	1	1	1	1	1	0	0	0	0	0	1	0	0	8
39	1	1	0	1	0	0	1	1	1	1	1	0	0	0	0	8
37	1	0	1	0	0	1	0	1	0	1	0	0	0	0	0	5
36	1	1	0	0	0	0	0	0	0	0	0	0	0	0	1	3
	40	38	35	34	33	33	30	30	29	28	27	26	24	23	23	

students. It inquired for the suggestion to students who got the feedback after every exam. The detailed contents to four questions under line:

Did you feel the feedback for each student helped review the course after the exam?

Did you feel the feedback enhanced the concept for each chapter?

Did you feel the feedback helped to know the misunderstand part in each chapter?

Did you feel the feedback helped the course very much?

All of the result appeared in Table 2. Most students (80.43%) felt the feedback helped them review the course. Furthermore, 73.91% agreed or strongly agreed with feedback enhanced their concept. 91.30% know their misunderstand part depend on the information too much. A few of students thought the information no use to them. And too crowded exam would make preparation not enough.

In order to define the disparity index of the S curve and P curve, Sato proposed a formula to calculate it. After we discussed the disparity index, we have some suggestions about this formula. We compared Sato's original work and our proposed idea for minor modification. In order to discuss this formula easily, we take an ideal example which includes the sum of the questions are 30~40 and the students are 30~60. If the curve of the student-problem chart can be fit in the targeted area (See Figure 11) which is surrounded by the two dotted lines, then we called it is perfect curve. When S curve and P curve are overlay, it will become only one curve. Our method can provide immediate response for the teachers and detect the original curve is perfect cure or not. We made five rules as following.

$$D^* = \frac{C}{4N_n \bar{P}(1-P)D_B(M)}$$

D*: Disparity Index
C: The number of '1' and '0' which are circumvented by the S curve and P curve.
N: The number of the students.
n: The number of the problems.

$$\bar{P}: \bar{P} = \frac{\sum_{i=1}^{N} X_i}{N_n}, \text{ Xi is the score of each student.}$$

M: $M = G[\sqrt{N_n} + 0.5]$

Rule 1: If C > 0, Then $D^* = \dfrac{C}{4N_n \bar{P}(1-P)D_B(M)}$

Rule 2: If C < 0, Then D* < 0, Contradiction.

Rule 3: If C = 0, N = 0, n = 0, $\bar{P}$ = 0, M = 0, Then Meaningless (Insignificance).

Rule 4: If S curve and P curve are settled in the surrounding area by dotted lines. There are two dotted lines have $10\%\sqrt{X^2 + Y^2}$ away from the diagonal - Perfect Curve, Y: Sum of Problems, X: Sum of Students

Rule 5: If S curve and P curve are not settled in the surrounding area by dotted lines - Imperfect Curve.

Rule 4 and Rule 5 are listed because the original formula proposed by Sato has some mistakes. We made some examples to show our advantages.

Table 2. Student questionnaire for feedback

item	SD(%)	D(%)	N(%)	A(%)	SA(%)
(1)	0	0	19.57%	58.70%	21.74%
(2)	0	4.35%	21.74%	50%	23.91%
(3)	0	0	8.70%	52.17%	39.13%
(4)	0	0	19.57%	45.65%	34.78%

(SD: Strongly Disagree, D: Disagree, N: Neutral, A: Agree, SA: Strongly Agree)

Figure 11. The target area for ideal curve

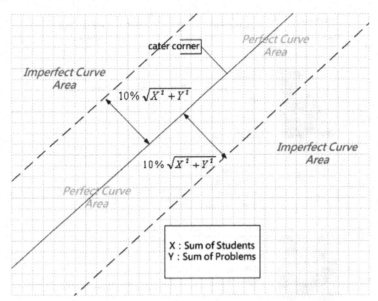

CONCLUSION

Assessment helps teachers to plan and conduct future instruction. The exam is not only a score record but also guidance for students toward improving their own performances. For the teachers, the assessment result motivates and shapes learning and instruction. Teachers use formative assessment, effective teachers often monitor and modify instructional plans based on their students' educational progress and needs. Intelligent assessment technologies supports web based learning environment to provide students adaptive learning suggestions, give teachers hints to modify learning content and estimate the individual learner's ability to assist them maximize learning performance.

In this article, the methodology of estimating learning situation is discussed. We use Sato's Student-Problem Chart to diagnose students' learning conditions with assessments they attended. We also provide an on-line assist system for assessment. According to the S-P Chart analysis and the Bloom taxonomy of items, we can divide all items in four types, and divide all students in six types. With these four types of diagnosis analysis

chart of items, teacher can modify or delete the items which are not proper. With these six types of diagnosis analysis chart of students, teachers can realize learners' situation. For improving our system, we could build an on-line learning management system to support the learning content provided. For experiment, we analyze the pretest and posttest of one class for the experimental group and control group. We find out the learning abilities variation to apply individual learning in e-learning environment. These experiment results provide us a valuable example for the learning management system or tutoring system construction in the future. (Figure 12)

ACKNOWLEDGMENT

We would like to thank two of our master students, Chih-Huang Hsu and Tsung-Pu Lee. They led the project team which is organized by Xiao-Jun Luo, Hsien-Tang Shih, Chen-Te Lin and Chien-Yu Chen. Without their support, the system can't work. For the perfect curve simulation program, we would like to thank Nick C. Tang. This study

Figure 12. Comparison of Sato's ideal curve and our proposed idea

Analysis Figures	Description	Sato's method	Our method
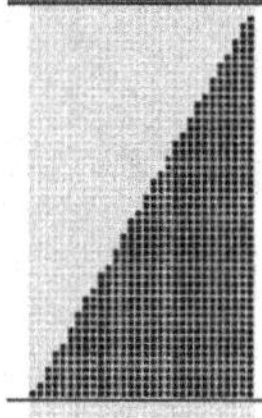	50students, 30problems, perfect curve	Perfect curve	Perfect curve
	50students, 30problems, all students answer correct	Perfect curve	Imperfect curve
	50students, 30problems, all students answer wrong	Perfect curve	Imperfect curve
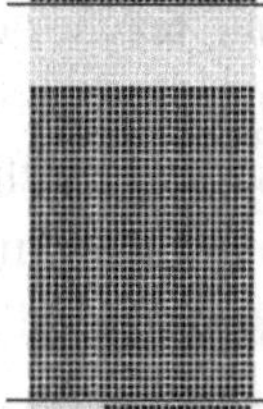	50students, 30problems, only 10 students answer correct	Perfect curve	Imperfect curve
	50students, 30problems, all students answer correct with 10 questions	Perfect curve	Imperfect curve

is supported in part by the National Science Council of the Republic of China under contract numbers NSC 96-2520-S-216-001 and NSC 96-2524-S-032-001.

REFERENCES

Airasian, P. W., & Maranda, H. (2002). The role of assessment in the revised Bloom's Taxonomy. *Theory into Practice, 41*(4), 349–354. doi:10.1207/s15430421tip4104_8

Anderson, W., & Krathwohl, D. R. (2001). A taxonomy for learning teaching and assessing: A revision of Bloom's educational objectives. New York, NY: Longman.

Black, P., & William, D. (1998). Inside the black box: Raising standards through classroom assessment. *Phi Delta Kappan, 80*(2), 139-148. (Available online: Hhttp://www.pdkintl.org/kappan/kbla9810.htmH.)

Bloom, B., Englehart, M., Furst, E., Hill, W., & Krathwohl, D. (1956). Taxonomy of Educational Objectives. In *Handbook I: The Cognitive Domain* New York: Longmans Green.

Brown, F. G. (1971). *Measurement and Evaluation*. Itasca, Illinois: F.E. Peacock.

Buchanan, T. (1998). Using the World Wide Web for formative assessment. *Journal of Educational Technology Systems*, *27*, 71–79. doi:10.2190/167K-BQHU-UGGF-HX75

Buchanan, T. (2000). The efficacy of a World Wide Web mediated formative assessment. *Journal of Computer Assisted Learning*, *16*, 193–200. doi:10.1046/j.1365-2729.2000.00132.x

Bybee, R. W. (1997). Achieving scientific literacy: From purposes to practices. Portsmouth, NH: Heinemann.

Chang, W. C., Hsu, H. H., Shih, T. K., & Wang, C. C. (2005). Enhancing SCORM metadata for assessment authoring in e-Learning. *Journal of Computer Assisted Learning*, *20*(4), 305–316. doi:10.1111/j.1365-2729.2004.00091.x

Chen, D. J., Lai, A. F., & Liu, I. C. (2005). The Design and Implementation of a Diagnostic Test System Based on the Enhanced S-P Model. *Journal of Information Science and Engineering*, *21*, 1007–1030.

Dai, C. Y., Cheng, J. K., Sung, J. K., & Ho, C. P. (2005). An Applied Model of SP Chart in the Technological and Vocational Schools Entrance Examination, Redesigning Pedagogy: Research, Policy, Practice. *International Conference on Education*. Singapore: Nanyang Technological University.

Ebel, R. L., & Frisbie, D. A. (1991). Essentials of educational measurement (5th ed.). Englewood Cliffs, NJ: Prentice-Hall.

Glaser, R. (1962). Psychology and instructional technology. In R. Glaser (Ed.), *Training, research and education*. Pittsburgh: University of Pittsburgh Press.

Kazuo, Y. (2007). *The preparation of the S-P Table*. Hhttp://www.kasei.ac.jp/cs/Yamanoi/Program/sphyo/index-e.htmlH [Last access July 11th, 2007]

Kelly, T. L. (1939). The Selection of Upper and Lower Groups for the Validation of Test Items. *Journal of Educational Psychology*, *30*, 17–24. doi:10.1037/h0057123

Lin, N. H., Chang, W. C., Shih, T. K., & Keh, H. C. (2005). Courseware Development Using Influence Diagram Supporting e-Learning Specification. *Journal of Information Science and Engineering*, *21*(5), 985–1005.

Olly, G., Scharff, C., & Wildenberg, A. (2008). Teaching software quality assurance by encouraging student contributions to an open source web-based system for the assessment of programming assignments. *Proceedings of the 13th annual conference on Innovation and technology in computer science education* (pp. 214-218).

Sato, T. (1975). The Construction and Interpretation of the S-P Table – Instructional Analysis and Learning Diagnosis. Tokyo, Japan: Meiji Tosho.

Sato, T. (1980). The S-P Chart and the Caution Index. [&C Systems Research Laboratories, Nippon Electric Co., Ltd., Tokyo, Japan.]. *NEC Educational Information Bulletin*, *80-1*, C.

Sato, T. (1985). Introduction to S-P Curve Theory Analysis and Evaluation. Tokyo, Japan: Meiji Tosho. (in Japanese).

Scriven, M. (1967). The methodology of evaluation. In R. Tyler (Ed.), *Perspectives of Curriculum Evaluation* (pp. 39–83). AERA Monograph Series on Curriculum Evaluation (no. 1). Skokie, IL: Rand McNally.

Shih, T. K., Lin, N. H., & Chang, H. P. (2003). An Intelligent E-Learning System with Authoring and Assessment Mechanism. *Proceeding of the 17th International Conference on Advanced Information Networking and Applications* (pp.782-787).

Wang, T. H. (2007). What strategies are effective for formative assessment in an e-learning environment? *Journal of Computer Assisted Learning, 23*, 171–186. doi:10.1111/j.1365-2729.2006.00211.x

William, D., & Black, P. (1996). Meanings and consequences: a basis for distinguishing formative and summative functions of assessment? *British Educational Research Journal, 22*, 537–548. doi:10.1080/0141192960220502

Yu, M. N. (2002). *Educational Assessment and Evaluation* (2nd ed.). Taiwan: The Profile of Psychological Publishing Co., Ltd.

Chapter 18
A Study of English Mobile Learning Applications at National Chengchi University

Pei-Chun Che
National Chengchi University, Taiwan

Han-Yi Lin
National Chengchi University, Taiwan

Hung-Chin Jang
National Chengchi University, Taiwan

Yao-Nan Lien
National Chengchi University, Taiwan

Tzu-Chieh Tsai
National Chengchi University, Taiwan

ABSTRACT

The pervasive popularity of the Internet in the past decade has changed the way many students live and learn, in part, because modern technology has made it possible for learners to access Real-Time Multimedia information on the Internet, or research any topic of interest to them from virtually any computer anywhere in the world. Students can also receive immediate feedback from their peers and/ or their teachers when involved in collaborative projects. As a result, teachers of all disciplines need to incorporate the Internet and the concept of mobile learning into today's classrooms to take advantage of this technology. This research investigated the response of English majors to a mobile learning platform (NCCU-MLP) developed at National Chengchi University (NCCU) in which they were involved as participants. The goal of the NCCU-MLP is to improve the students' English ability as well as to update the teachers' understanding of how to use the technology. The purpose of this research was to investigate the responses of students to a mobile learning environment. The research involved 18 participants in a pilot study and 37 participants in a follow-up study who participated in a group activity involving mobile learning activities. The students were asked to complete the activity following which they completed a

DOI: 10.4018/978-1-60960-539-1.ch018

brief survey of their response to the mobile learning activity. The findings indicate a positive response from the participants regarding the content and procedures involved in the activity. Technical support for the project was found to need enhancement for future projects of this nature.

BACKGROUND

The pervasive popularity of the Internet in the past decade has changed the way people process information. It has also changed the way many students live and learn (Prensky, 2001; Wagner, E. D. & Wilson, P. (2005). Learning has evolved from the traditional teacher-centered classroom to a more collaborative student-centered classroom, and to mobile learning wherein students have direct interaction with the teachers, their peers, and even the world via the Internet. Technology has taken learning to the next level of innovation. With the installment of WiFi (Wireless Fidelity) or IEEE 802.11 WLAN (Wireless Local Area Network), it is possible for learners to access Real-Time Multimedia information on the Internet. Students with a mobile device such as a PDA, or a notebook computer, can access the information they wish to know and learn from virtually any location in the world at anytime of the day or night. In that sense, learning has become mobile. Facing a group of students who grew up with the Internet, "digital natives" as researchers have called these students, teachers of all disciplines need to incorporate the Internet and the concept of mobile learning into today's classrooms (Prensky, 2001). In addition, since more than 70% of the information on the Internet is in English, English has become the most commonly used language for people around the world to access information and to communicate. As a result of these circumstances, how to improve the students' English ability is another challenge that teachers face today.

Being one of the campuses that celebrates a WiFi environment, National Chengchi University provides its teachers and students with a "mobile learning" context. However, how to encourage students to take advantages of this environment to improve their English is a question that has remained unanswered. After a series of discussions, a proposal was made by the authors to combine the traditional approaches to learning and the latest technology to the English learning activities where students participate in groups to test the feasibility of incorporating mobile learning into a college level English class. NCCU, being the top rated internationalized university in Taiwan, postulated that both local students and international students on campus should be able to take advantage of this "mobile learning" context.

This article is divided into three main parts. The review of the evolution of learning in the past decades, the theory of mobile learning, and the significance of its application in learning is discussed first. In this section, the gap found in the literature review will also be discussed. In the second section, the design of the group activity and the technical support will be described in detail. The last section will focus on the discussion of the results of the study, its limitations, and future possibilities.

LITERATURE REVIEW

To receive an education, schools are no longer the only option for students. In fact, a student can take courses tailored to one's needs at any time and any place today. Such is the nature of distance learning (d-learning), where students and the instructors are separated by time and/or distance (Georgiev, T., Georgieva, E. & Smrikarov, A., 2004). D-learning offers numerous advantages, especially for those who need flexibility in their life, such as learners with restricted mobility, an irregular work schedule, or family responsibilities. In addition to having freedom in time and location, d-learning is also student-centered. Not only do learners choose their materials in some cases, they also proceed at their own pace and intensity in some cases (USjournal.com, LLC). Students are not the only beneficiary of distance learning; institutions also increase revenue by delivering education to distance learning students since the class size increases while overhead stays the same in some cases (Valentine, 2002).

Though distance learning is often thought to be a new form of education, it actually has a history of over 100 years. As early as the 19th century, efforts were made to promote adult education beyond university campuses using correspondence type courses where interaction takes place through the postal system. With technological improvements, more and more mediums have become available to serve as educational tools. During the World Wars, the concept of serving education through radio was developed when broadcasting licenses were granted to many higher educational institutions by the U.S. government. Though the concept never matured, it prompted research in other possible mediums, such as educational television in the mid 20th century. A few decades later, in the 1970s and 1980s, cable and satellite television and videotapes were used as delivery tool for distance learning courses (Nasseh, B., 1997; Valentine, D., 2002).

With the advancements of technology in the 1980s, the electronic learning (e-learning) era reigned. It compensated for a major defect in distance learning, the lack of face-to-face learning. It became possible for teachers to instruct a class in another country, and have real-time discussions with their students. By using the three major didactic uses of technology, satellites, videoconferencing, and the World Wide Web, learners were able to interact with their instructors and other learners. However, in the e-learning environment, the equipment decided where learning would take place. The cables and wires restricted the movement of the students as seen in Figure 1.

As technology advanced to its wireless phase at the end of the 20th century, devices such as cell phones and laptop computers were incorporated with wireless communications (e.g. Wi-Fi) and technologies (e.g., 3G) allowing learning to become interactive, taking place at anytime and

Figure 1. The e-learning environment (Keegan, D., 2000)

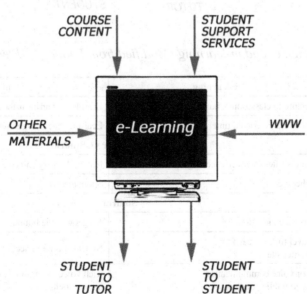

anywhere (Georgiev, T., Georgieva, E. & Smrikarov, A., 2004). Nevertheless, the term "mobile learning" (m-learning) has different definitions depending on the viewpoint one takes. From a more technological perspective, Quinn (2000) views m-learning as learning made possible through mobile devices. In line with that definition is O'Malley, et al (2003), where m-learning is seen as "[a]ny sort of learning that happens when the learner is not at a fixed, predetermined location, or learning that happens when the learner takes advantage of the learning opportunities offered by mobile technologies." Sharples (2005), on the other hand, takes a more construc-

tivist view of m-learning; he believes that mobile technology increases the amount of communication and interaction in learning. This research project will adopt the m-learning definition by Sharples, Taylor, & Vavoula (2005), which is "the processes of coming to know through conversations across multiple contexts amongst people and personal interactive technologies." (Figure 2)

M-learning significantly improves the education environment in e-learning, as seen in Table 1 (Laouris & Eteokleous, 2005). From the pedagogical perspective, m-learning allows more types of instruction and gives student flexibility in their

Figure 2. The m-learning environment (Keegan, 2000)

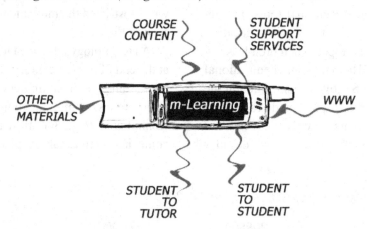

Table 1. Differences between e- and m-learning (Modified from Laouris & Eteokleous, 2005)

	e-learning	m-learning
Pedagogical differences	Lecture in classrooms, home, or in Internet labs	Learning occurring in the field or while mobile (Anywhere)
	Lecture at restricted time	Learning occurring at non-restricted time (Anytime)
Communication differences	**Teacher vs. Student**	
	Time-shifted (delayed checking of e-mails or web)	Instant delivery and check of e-mail or Instant Messages
	Scheduled	Spontaneous
	Student vs. Student	
	Restricted location	No geographic boundaries
	Travel time to reach to Internet site	No travel time to access WLAN
	Poor voice communication due to public courtesy	Rich voice communication due to reduced inhibitions in open field

environment. When learners communicate with the teacher and other fellow students, m-learning is instantaneous, spontaneous, and not restricted by time or geographical locations.

Today's students are different from their predecessors; these students are the first generation growing up in a ubiquitous computer environment. Prensky (2001) labels them as digital natives who are born in the digital era and fluent with the use of technology. Digital natives carry out many daily activities online, such as chatting with their friends via instant messaging, meeting new people on virtual communities, and doing their shopping online. With wireless technology combined with portable gadgets, students can conduct these activities anytime and anywhere. Students nowadays are characterized as those who are accustomed to on-demand information, multitasking, preferring visuals to texts, and constantly networking (Prensky, 2001; Valentine, 2002). As most instructors are born before the digital era, they never experienced what their students went through. The instructors will encounter problems applying conventional methods that worked for them in the past to this new breed of students. Prensky (2001) urges instructors to communicate in the style of the students to bridge the gap between them.

Mobile learning is the answer to the students' needs because of its numerous advantages. First, learning for students is no longer restricted in terms of physical space or time; rather, they are able to engage in nomadic learning. At any time or place, students can easily access learning materials of their choice. Teachers are able to conduct lessons outside of the classroom into the students' surroundings. The learning then becomes more contextual, and personal, rather than hierarchical and lecture-recited (Naismith, Lonsdale, Vavoula, & Sharples (2005). Furthermore, students make better use of their time because of mobile learning. They receive formal learning experiences (e.g., taking a class, attending a workshop) with informal learning experiences (e.g., on a school

bus). Students could be using their time more efficiently.

Secondly, the ubiquity of wireless devices and services allows mobile learning to be easily integrated into peoples' lives. By the end of first quarter of 2006 in Taiwan, there were 22.51 million cell phone numbers in use, and about 1.91 million people who subscribed to mobile Internet services, allowing them to be connected to the web using their cell phones. Moreover, the popularity of WiFi in Taiwan has increased annually (see Figure 3). Lastly, the prices of personal digital gadgets continue to decrease as time passes, making them more affordable to the public. Hence, they provide more opportunity for people to have access to mobile learning (Wagner & Wilson, 2005).

Taiwan has a large population of Internet users. The nation's population totaled 22.75 million as of October, 2005 and more than 65% use Internet services as seen in Figure 3. The number of Internet users has steadily grown over the last 4 years, as shown in the July, 2006 Taiwan Network Information Center (TWNIC) summary report of Internet broadband usage. In just a few years, a growth of 60%, or 6 million users, used Internet services. More impressively, approximately one out of five Internet users used wireless Internet services as of 2006, and the number of wireless customers continues to climb annually (see Figure 4). The number of wireless Internet users has doubled, from 1.5 million to 3 million people in just two years, from July 2003 to July 2005. An additional half a million used the service in the next year, from July 2005 to July 2006. We can expect the number of wireless Internet users to continue to increase as the government of Taiwan actively promotes the wireless services.

THEORETICAL UNDERPINNINGS

Learning with mobile technology can be examined using an adapted version of Engeström's (1987) expansive activity model, which originated

Figure 3. Growth of Internet users in Taiwan from 2003-2006

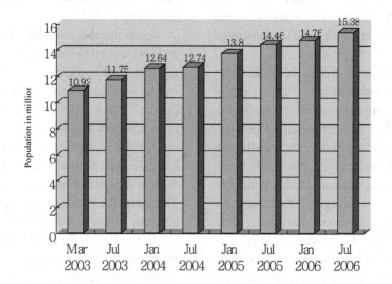

from activity theory. The theory was developed from sociocultural theory, founded by Vygotsky, Leont'ev, and Lauria in the 1920s and 1930s, but was only internationalized half a century later, in the 1980s and 1990s (Engeström, 1999). The basic tenet of sociocultural theory is that the human mind is mediated and relies on tools and labor activity to establish indirect relationship among themselves and the world (Lantolf, 2000). The tools may be symbolic, such as language, or physical, like computers. Activity theory is an extended theory developed from sociocultural theory, focusing on Vygotsky's claim that "human behaviors results from the integration of socially and culturally constructed forms of mediation into human activity" (As quoted in Jin, Wu, Liao, & Liao, 2003, p. 8).

Engeström (1999) illustrates how activity theory applies to education in his expansive activity model (see Figure 5). To achieve the final

Figure 4. Growth of wireless Internet users in Taiwan from 2003-2006

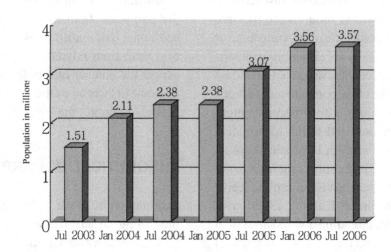

Figure 5. Engestrom's expansive activity model (Engestrom, 1987)

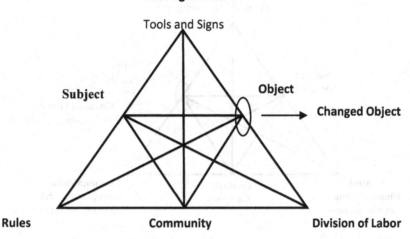

outcome of learning, may it be one's well being, or success, the premise is to produce objects, in this case, knowledge. The subject, or the learner, engages in activity in order to obtain the object (knowledge). During the process, the learner uses artifacts, or mediating instruments, which includes both tools and signs (e.g., language, learning resources), to conduct the activity. Another element that mediates activity is the community, which is composed of individuals or the group involved. The subjects may share responsibility of achieving the objective with the community, realized through the division of labor. Finally, the community may establish rules referring to the regulations and norms that restrict actions and interactions of the subjects (Engeström, 1987).

A modified Sharples et al. (2005) model of mobile learning explained that using the activity theory will serve as the framework for this study. The mediating artifacts refer to the mobile learning technology, which the subjects, in this case the students, mediate in their learning activity. Control refers to issues regarding human-computer interaction, such as rules indicating acceptable behaviors (e.g., network etiquette) in operating mobile devices students must adhere to during learning. The students will conduct the activities in various buildings on campus, the context they will be exploring. During the activity, students will communicate with their peers, and also interact with their laptops to gather information. Finally, students' knowledge and skills should be improved and revised upon completion of these activities. By integrating mobile technology with learning, an optimal learning environment that caters to needs of today's students is provided. Figure 6 is an illustration of this modified model.

RELEVANT MOBILE LEARNING STUDIES

Tate Modern Multimedia Tour

In 2002, the Tate Modern Museum in the UK launched a multimedia guide for visitors to learn more about the art of its galleries (Tate Modern and Antenna Audio Ltd.). A 3-month pilot project studied how visitors evaluated the guide. Visitors used PDAs that provided them with more contextual information of the artwork on display via different media, such as still images, audio clips, and videos. Visitors could use the interactive screen to select the media desired, and play games and

Figure 6. Modifided Sharples et al. activity theory model of mobile learning [21]

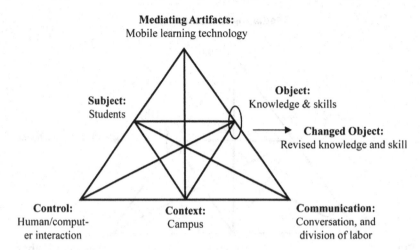

quizzes about the work. The wireless network in the project is location sensitive, meaning correct information is sent to the visitors at the right time and place. As a central server stores all the information, the content sent to the PDA is limitless in continent and easily updated. Some 825 visitors participated in the pilot study, and questionnaires and focus groups were used to gather feedback.

The results showed that the visitors enjoyed the tour, spending an average of 55 minutes on the tour, and 70% of the participants commented that they had spent longer in the museum than expected, and a similar percentage said the tour had improved the quality of their visit. Multi-tasking

and multi-tracking of different media (e.g. looking between screen and artwork) was not a problem for the users. However, they did not tolerate long messages and blank screens. Using PDAs to enhance learning is demonstrated in Tate Modern Museum's media guide. The photos in Figure 7 are from Tate Modern, 2002.

A mobile butterfly-watching learning system (Chen, Kao, Yu, & Sheu, 2004) was developed for 4th-grade Taiwanese elementary students to learn about local butterfly species. The experimental group was divided into teams of two, and each team received a PDA with a LAN card and a digital camera. The teacher used a notebook

Figure 7. Butterfly-Watching System

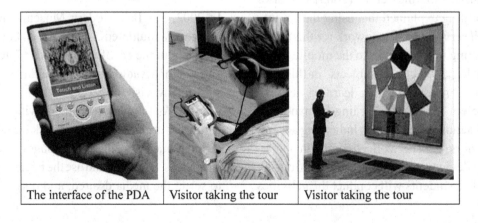

with a wireless LAN card system that acts as the server, containing a database of the butterflies in Taiwan. The students visited a butterfly farm six times. The first step of the procedure is self-selection, where students take pictures of butterflies. Second, in the self- determination step, students transfer the photo to the database to find possible matches. Next, in the self-modification step, students modify their previous search to arrive at the final decision. The last step is for students to record their findings and their learning process in their journals, and then the teacher sends her comments to the students on their PDAs. The experimental group was compared with a control group, who used a butterfly textbook instead of a mobile system. To evaluate the learning effects of mobile system implemented, multiple-choice questions on a butterflies' key features were administered before and after the trial. Results showed that the experimental group did better than the control group in identifying key features. The following photos of the mobile system are taken from Chen, Kao, Yu, & Sheu (2004). (Figure 8)

A study was conducted by Thornton & Houser (2004) in Japan to see how university students' acquired English vocabulary using SMS. Forty-four students received 100-word text messages three times a day, for a period of two weeks. Each week the students studied five vocabulary words

used in context and reviewed them periodically. The medium of learning vocabulary through the cell phone was then compared with Internet and paper-based materials. In the first experiment, a within-in subject, counter-balance design was used. One group of students received a 10 word vocabulary set from their cell phones while the second group logged onto the instructor's website to retrieve the same material. After two weeks, the groups switched the media and the experiment ran for another two weeks. The results from pre-tests and posttests revealed that mobile text messaging showed an improvement over using the Internet method. In the second experiment, one group of students learned vocabulary via SMS while the other received vocabulary on paper. The same tests were run, and the results revealed that students who studied by mobile text messaging did significantly better than the other groups.

Gap Found in the Literature Review

In the domain of mobile learning, most studies are conducted in science education with few studies conducted related to language learning and teaching. In Taiwan, the studies focused mainly on elementary education. Numerous studies implement mobile gadgets such as tablet PCs and PDAs in elementary schools to see how effective these devices are for students' motivation and learning.

Figure 8. Short Message Service (SMS)

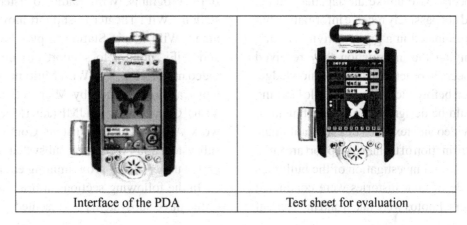

| Interface of the PDA | Test sheet for evaluation |

Content of the studies included aquatic life (Kao, 2006; Tsai, 2004, & Wu, 2006), botany (Ling, 2004) and bird-watching (Su, 2003). The results from these studies indicate positive results for motivation, though in some cases, the effectiveness is not more significant than conventional methods. There are a lack of studies in the area of integrating foreign language education and mobile learning, especially in higher education. Hence, the purpose of this study was to address the issue with the hope to explore the students' response to mobile learning with the future possibility of incorporating mobile learning in university classrooms.

Technical Support and Activity Design

Before designing an English learning activity that could be used by NCCU students on campus, the first question to be answered was "What should or can students learn on campus using mobile devices?" The answer, after discussion, was the history and the stories of some old buildings on campus. By adopting the activity model proposed by Sharples et al. (2005), students learned the knowledge in a context with a group of peers using English and a mobile device as the tool when participating in this activity. Unlike the Japanese study discussed above, English in this activity was not just the goal of learning, but also a tool to learn new knowledge, and a tool for communication with peers. Also unlike the Japanese study, students did not passively receive information but actively participated in a group activity sharing and exchanging the information they received with their peers in order to learn new knowledge.

However, before such a group mobile learning activity could be designed, the establishment of the audio, video and text files of these buildings, and the confirmation of technical support are vital. As a result, a field investigation of the buildings and the study of their histories were conducted by the authors. Photos were taken and the content

of the introduction were recorded in digital files. A series of experiments were conducted as well to ensure the "friendliness" of the campus. In the following sections, the experiments conducted and the decisions made on the technology side and the detailed design of the group activity are discussed.

TECHNICAL SUPPORT

NCCU-Mobile Learning Platform (NCCU-MLP)

In order to investigate the feasibility of mobile learning on campus, the activity designed needed to be able to foster group work, peer communication, and Internet access while subjects walked around campus. Thus, a NCCU-mobile learning platform (NCCU-MLP) was implemented to meet these needs. This platform consisted of three main subsystems which included an Instant Communication subsystem, a Positioning subsystem, and a WiFi Multimedia subsystem as shown in Figure 9.

The Instant Communication subsystem had an Instant Message and Push-to-Talk to exchange text messages and voice message among a group of participants. The Positioning subsystem was used to determine the locations of the users through surrounding WiFi access points (APs). NCCU-MLP has to dynamically detect the user location first then access the right learning materials. The WiFi Mutimedia subsystem has WiFi TV to play IPTV programs, WiFi Radio to listen to radio stations, WiFi Theater to support movies on demand, WiFi Music Station to play local music, and WiFi Monitor to support on site real-time video monitoring. The WiFi Multimedia subsystem was programmed by Microsoft Embedded Visual C++ 4.0 and Java JMF (Java Media Framework API). Both the Instant Communication subsystem and Positioning subsystem were integrated under a Java programming environment.

In the following sections, a brief description of the three subsystems is presented.

Figure 9. NCCU-mobile learning platform

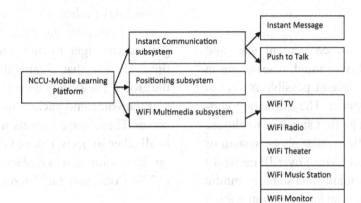

INSTANT COMMUNICATION SUBSYSTEM

Characteristics of Group Communication

As stated earlier, in order to test the feasibility of mobile learning on campus, the activity designed must be able to foster group work and peer communication on the move. In other words, a wireless instant group communication system becomes a very important part of a mobile learning environment. Generally speaking, a mobile group communication system must be inexpensive in cost, convenient in use, and comprehensible in quality.

Before discussing what might be the most appropriate system to be adopted for this study, it is important to understand the demands of an instant group communication. The demands are as follows:

- The system must be able to manage the group membership, including adding, removing, and authorizing group members;
- A user must be able to initiate a "talk" to all members in one touch (it is not desirable to have callers to call all members one by one);

- A user must be able to broadcast his/her "talk" to all other members;
- The communications must be able to proceed in full or half duplex conversation mode. (In full duplex mode, any user can talk to all others at any time, while in half duplex mode, only one user can talk to all others at a time);
- The communication delay time MED (the time latency from the speaker's mouth to the listeners' ears) must be controlled within a reasonable limit. (The maximum allowable MED is yet to be determined);
- The consumed network bandwidth must be kept as low as possible;
- And users must be able to communicate with others in writing or drawing.

Though the last characteristic is essential in a mobile learning system, as the participants in this study may need to communicate to each other by writing or drawing to assist voice communications, it is not the priority of this section to discuss the use of "White Board" in this study. Voice communication will be the main focus here.

Selection of Communication Technology

With inexpensive cost, convenient use, and comprehensible quality in mind, researchers in this study evaluated several possible means to be used in this subsystem. The evaluation consisted of two steps. The first step was to choose to use either the public cellular phone system or an Internet-Based VoIP (Voice over IP network) system. With its high quality and stability, public cellular phone system is an ideal communication system to meet this study's need. However, it is simply too expensive to use. Thus, the VoIP over WLAN was chosen for this study, although it has a lower reliability and quality (long MED delay, large jitter, and high packet loss rate).

The second step was to choose to use either half-duplex or full-duplex conversation mode. Full-duplex conversation mode, also named "Conference Call," is a better conversation mode in a high bandwidth and high quality communication system. On the other hand, VoIP over WLAN has a limited network bandwidth and a lower quality in delivering voice streams. Thus, it can only support a very limited number of simultaneous users with what is called "double talk" problem. However, half-duplex conversation mode, which has a popular name, "Push-to-Talk" (PTT), consumes less network bandwidth such that it can support more simultaneous users. Furthermore, it allows only one user to talk at a time such that it can tolerate much longer MED delay to avoid the double-talk problem. Therefore, PTT was chosen to be implemented on the NCCU-MLP system.

Subsystem Design and Implementation

As a result, the PTT was implemented in Java programming language and was an integral part of the NCCU-MLP System. A group management system was deployed in a server located in the Mobile Communication Lab. The server also performed the re-broadcast function. Participants in this study pushed a button on the NCCU-MLP system to acquire the right to talk. The server granted the right to only one participant at a time. The one that obtains the right can talk to the group. The system used G.711 Codec to convert the voice into packets and send them to the server. These voice packets were then broadcast to all other subjects. (Since G.711 consumes 64k bps bandwidth, it was replaced by either iLBC or G.729a Codec to reduce bandwidth consumption.)

Positioning Subsystem

The most popular positioning systems are GPS (Global Positioning System), infrared, ultrasonic, and RF (Radio Frequency). Among them, RF suited this study for the following reasons. First, since the activity was conducted indoors, GPS failed to meet the need. Second, infrared or ultrasonic positioning usually needs more receivers installed for good coverage, and thus is not cost-effective. Third, PDAs or small laptops equipped with mobile users are embedded with WiFi which uses RF to connect to AP (Access Point) to access Internet, and can penetrate walls and thus have better coverage than infrared systems. As a result, using a RF-based positioning system was the most promising and convenient for this study.

RADAR and its Limitations

Among all RF-based works, RADAR and its variations are probably the most famous and popular ones (Bahl, & Padmanabhan, 2000; Krumm, & Platt, 2003). RADAR refers to a positioning system which requires a construction of a RM (Radio Map) by measuring RF SS (Signal Strength) for every grid point of any given space before it can be used. The biggest disadvantage of the process of constructing RM, known as calibration, is that it is time consuming because in order to achieve accuracy, more calibration data in the RM is

Figure 10. Accuracy of reducing calibration effort

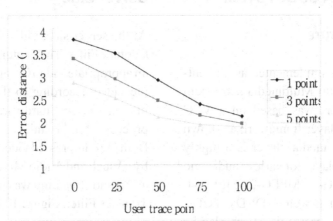

required to be measured manually to fight the otherwise fading channel.

With this limitation in mind, RADAR would not be ideal for this study. In the following section, a modified RF-based positioning subsystem was proposed to maintain the accuracy while reducing calibration efforts.

Modified RF-Based Positioning Subsystem Design and Implementation

In order to achieve acceptable accuracy while reducing the time and man-power investment in the positioning subsystem, the following measures were taken. First, instead of measuring SS for many points manually, a few points, one, three or five, in any given space was measured in the offline calibration phase. After these points were measured, researchers, then, carried the WiFi device to walk around this space and pause 3-5

seconds at random spots for the system to collect data. Third, after this process, the system automatically "learned" or traced the best possible path using HMM (Hidden Markov Model) and the wireless channel propagation model in order to complete the RM necessary for the positioning system to function.

In this study, a space with a dimension of 11X52 meters was used for testing. With one, three, and five calibration points measured prior random trace points were learned, Figure 10 below demonstrates how our modified positioning subsystem increased accuracy with the increase of "learned" trace points.

Compared with RADAR and its modification Microsoft positioning system, the proposed modified positioning subsystem adopted in this study performs the best with the least time investment as shown in Table 2.

Table 2. Comparison of different positioning systems

	Our Modified Subsystem	RADAR [1]	Microsoft [2]
Mean error distance (m)	2.89	1.92	9.19
Reduced calibration effort percentage	99%	0%	90%

WIFI MULTIMEDIA SUBSYSTEM

System Architecture

The NCCU-MLP was implemented as a client-server model. The WiFi Multimedia subsystem (except WiFi Monitor) was based on a VLC (VideoLAN) media player framework as shown in Figure 11. A VLC media player is a highly portable multimedia player for various audio and video formats (MPEG-1, MPEG-2, MPEG-4, DivX, mp3, ogg, etc.) as well as DVDs, VCDs, and various streaming protocols. It can also be used as a server to stream in unicast or multicast in IPv4 or IPv6 on a high-bandwidth network.

Server Side

At the server side, video is captured by a Video Capture Filter. The capture filter will then select an appropriate Video Compress Filter to compress the video according to the bandwidth of information flow and hardware equipment. All those processes for the audio are done in a similar way. Both the compressed video and audio were mixed by a Video and Audio Mixed Filter. Finally, video and audio streaming was sent through a Network Transfer Filter. Figure 12 illustrates the process.

Figure 11. VLC media player framework (http://www.videolan.org/vlc)

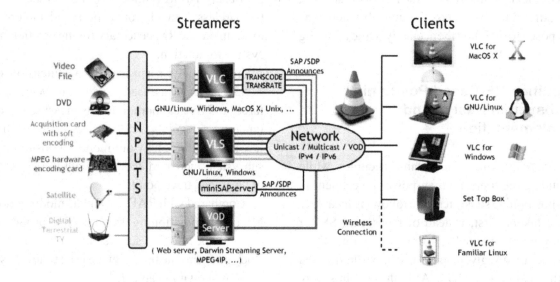

Figure 12. Media process at the server side

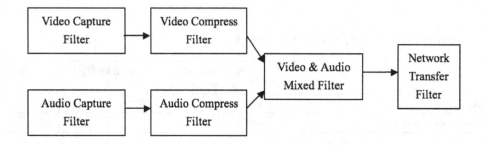

Figure 13. Media process at the client side

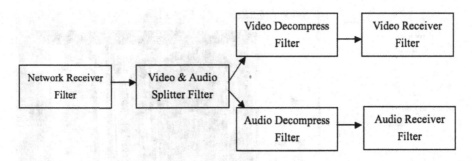

Client Side

The client retrieves the information flow through WiFi, and separates this flow into video and audio through the Splitter Filter. Both the split video and audio are sent to the Video Decompress Filter and Audio Decompress Filter, respectively. The decompressed video is received by Video Receiver Filter, and audio by the Audio Receiver Filter. Output devices can be any kind of monitors and speakers. Figure 13 illustrates this process.

Figure 14 and Figure 15 show the main page of the NCCU-MLP. On the left side, there are "Talk to Others," "Video," "Media," and "Ques-

tions" buttons. The logo of our system displays on the right side. When pressing the "Talk to Others" button, the participants of this study will be prompted a small window of two parts to the left side of the original window. The window above is for Push to Talk, the window below is for Instant Message. Before the participants talk or write to others, they should select a group of persons from the contact list. The "Push to Talk" button and the "Stop to Talk" button are used to start and end the talk session, respectively. Once the button of "Push to Talk" is pressed, the participant's voice will be sent to each person in the group. When using Instant Message, the partici-

Figure 14. The main page of NCCU-MLP

Figure 15. The "Talk-to-Others" and tour navigation video of NCCU-MLP

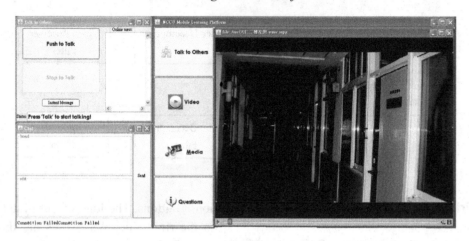

pants only need to type messages and press the "Send" button. When pressing the "Video" button, the participants will be prompted with a tour navigation video. One of the videos will be intelligently selected according to the locations the participants are on campus. As long as the mobile learning device is on, the participants' locations will be dynamically tracked by the Positioning Subsystem. When they press the "Media" button, the participants can access all multimedia services, such as WiFi TV, WiFi Radio, WiFi Theater, WiFi Music Station and WiFi Monitor. Pressing the "Questions" button will bring subjects to the learning assessment system.

ACTIVITY DESIGN

With the above technical support, the mobile learning activity was designed as follows:

Sample

A total of 18 students from one English Honors Program freshman class were chosen as the participants of the pilot study. Another group of 37 students from two English Honors Program classes were chosen as the participants of the main study. The students' average English proficiency is high

as their Joint College Entrance Exam English score ranked them as the top 1% among all freshman students. In the pilot study, students were divided into 5 groups of 4 or 5; while in the main study, due to the limited amount of mobile devices, two sessions of the main study were conducted. Again, students in each session were divided into 5 groups of 4 or 5. Each group was assigned to one of the five buildings on campus to fulfill several tasks designed by the research team.

Activity Development

The activity was a timed activity. Subjects were given 50 minutes to finish answering five questions regarding the campus historical buildings. At the end of the 50 minutes, the participants were required to submit answers to these questions on line to the researchers. With the technical support, Tablet PC was chosen as the mobile learning device.

In accordance with the features of these five buildings, researchers designed five questions for each building. In order to foster group and peer communication on the move, the questions were categorized into three types. They were "compare and contrast," "current events," "on-site interviews," and "important dates, numbers or figures." Compare and contrast questions required the participants to compare and contrast information with other groups. For example, subjects needed to exchange information in order to answer which building is the oldest on campus. Current event or on-site interviews emphasized the mobility in this activity. For example, the participants were required to find out one professor's teaching schedule for the semester. Important dates, numbers or figures, on the other hand, expected participants to collect information from different floors in the building to answer questions like the total amount of labs in that building.

Most importantly of all, among the five questions that were given the participants who were assigned to a certain building, only one question was related to that building. The rest of the four questions were questions for the other buildings. With this design, subjects were forced to do constant communication using the mobile device while walking up and down the building they are assigned.

Additionally, an online questionnaire in relation to content, procedure, technical support and mechanism was designed and used to verify the effectiveness of the group activity and students' motivation.

Procedure

With the consent of the participants, the pilot study was conducted on June 8, 2007 and the main study on December 13 and 14, 2007. After the participants were divided into 4 or 5-person groups and assigned to five different buildings on campus with Tablet PCs at hand, a 20-minute orientation concerning the steps, tools and equipments used was given. Participants were asked to learn the history of the building they were assigned using the NCCU-MLP presented on their Tablet PCs. Then, within the following 50 minutes, each group was asked to communicate with other group members using Push-To-Talk, whiteboard, and other technology supported by the PC. In the meantime, through learning and

sharing information concerning the building, the participants were asked to download a worksheet containing questions related to different buildings, give answers to the questions and then submit them via the mobile device to the server. At the end of the activity, the participants were asked to fill out an online questionnaire to verify the content, feasibility, user-friendliness, and mobility of the developed materials. The participants every communication during the activity was recorded and transcribed for evaluation and study. A quantitative analysis was applied to the online questionnaires.

A brief of the study result and its limitations will be discussed in the last section below.

RESULTS, LIMITATIONS AND FUTURE POSSIBILITIES

To assess the effectiveness of this group activity, improve students' motivation for language learning and assist in developing a model for m-learning in universities, an online questionnaire in relation to content, technical support, procedure and mechanism was designed. The participants in both the pilot and the main study completed this questionnaire. Many technological flaws were improved and debugged after the pilot study and the analysis of questionnaire result.

Results

In this section, only the results of the main study are discussed. In this survey, 30 respondents from two classes out of 37 participants ranked their degree of satisfaction concerning the criteria mentioned and further provided additional information for this learning experience by responding to 4 open-ended questions. The followings are the four charts illustrating the outcome of the online questionnaire.

Figure 16 shows an overall evaluation in terms of 3 criteria concerning content, technical support, and procedure. The chart indicates that the results

Figure 16. Overall response to content, procedure, and technical support of this activity

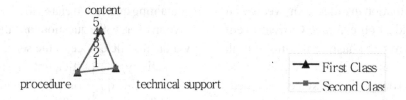

of these 2 classes are consistent with each other. They had a close rapport with the use of content and the implementation of the procedure, but ranked technical support lower than the other 2 criteria.

Figure 17, Figure 18, and Figure 19 show the analyses of these 3 criteria respectively. Figure

17, focusing on content indicates the participants considered the material design and interaction among groups rich and English subtitles essential. Over half of students agreed that the questions designed in the activity can enrich communication in teams and enrich the collaboration through

Figure 17. The analysis of content

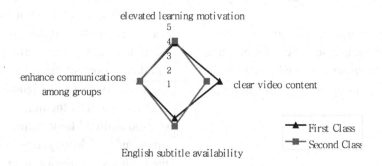

Figure 18. The analysis of technical support

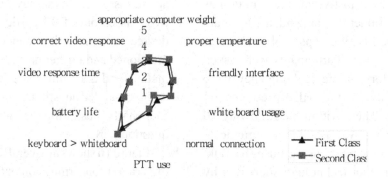

Figure 19. The analysis of procedure

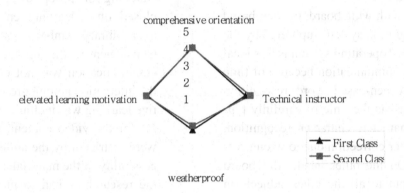

discussions with others at a distance. Furthermore, 21 students would like to consult English subtitles when replaying the video clips, while 4 students did not consider it essential. However, they had different views on if the video clips were explained clearly. Twenty-three students agreed the oral descriptions of the video clips were of such clarity, while 4 students remained neutral, and 3 disagreed with this item.

Figure 18 illustrates that students needed more technical support from some improvements in the mobile devices themselves, the interface, the use of whiteboard, and mobile network connection. The limitations of technical support will be further discussed.

Figure 19 indicates that the participants were satisfied with the procedure of this group activity in relation to the inclusion of some technical instructors and a comprehensive orientation, except for the inconvenience and a certain lack of mobile device effective performance caused by the unpredictable weather condition. Approximately 26 students indicated that technical assistants played an important role in implementing this activity. Also, approximately 21 respondents were pleased with the comprehensive orientation given at the beginning of the activity.

In general, these 4 figures illustrate that students showed great interest in using this innovative learning method; however, they felt a bit frustrated and overwhelmed when the technology was not so supportive and helpful.

In the following section, weaknesses in the activity and future possibilities for such activities are discussed in more detail.

Weaknesses

Mobile computing and communication systems are in general more vulnerable than those on fixed networks, such as a PC. The followings are the limitations found in the experiments:

- Battery life is limited so that it is difficult for NCCU-MLP to support any long activity over two hours.

- The transmission quality of a wireless radio signal is highly dependent on the weather conditions, especially on rainy days. As a consequence, the stability of a mobile network connection is lower than fixed networks. The design of a mobile learning environment must take this into consideration.

- The software system in a mobile computing environment is much more complicated than that on fixed networks. Thus, it needs more effort to make the software system robust.

- Compared with whiteboard, the pen-based word recognition system supported by the Windows XP operating system is less ideal for group communication because of time concern. A pen-based word recognition system consists the time of carefully typing the character, character recognition, and character correction due to wrong recognition. On the other hand, whiteboard reflects input to all the other subjects in terms of image. There is no time wasted in both recognition and correction.

- Compared with a voice communication tool, like PTT, a whiteboard is even less ideal for group communication. First, people are used to talking rather than writing. Second, voice communication is much faster than that of hand-writing. Third, whiteboard is a groupware. Images from different ends can easily be mixed up and then reflected to each end. In other words, whiteboard fails to transmit images correctly and clearly.

- In some special environment such as a library, the use of voice communication will be limited. This may hurt the efficiency of collaborative learning. A simple earphone, wired, or wireless, will easily solve the problem.

- Users prefer full-duplex conversation mode to half-duplex mode. However, it remains a great technical challenge to offer group voice communication in full-duplex conversational mode under limited bandwidth.

- In order to achieve high accuracy in a positioning system, the more AP in any given space are better.

With regards to the activity design and content, the followings are some weaknesses that were found:

- In this activity, whether during video-watching or group discussion, any enclosed quiet learning environment such as a library, embarrassed our students. Consequently, the limited use of voice communication was not encouraging and the interaction among groups in collaborative learning was inefficient.

- As for the video content, the researchers were restricted by the authenticity and accessibility of the materials. In other words, the researchers had to make great effort to find motivating, informative authentic material on campus. They also had to help students apply new knowledge and skills, and integrate these into the learners' world to make learning effective. As a result, students complained about the content of these video clips as not exciting and intriguing enough.

- The students relied on their technical assistants mainly because there was considerable anxiety among them about high-tech use. It may prove that students need a certain amount of related prior learning and training.

Future Possibilities

The followings are the future plans for the development of a better (or more powerful) group communication system:

- Making both the group communication and positioning systems more robust;

- Porting the system to the newer WiMAX wireless communication system;

- Porting the system to light-weighted, small-size, powerful UMPC (Ultra Mobile PC) platform

- Installing formative evaluation to track learner's improvement over time.

Again, with regards to the activity design and content, the followings are some future possibilities:

- Improving and enriching the quality and quantity of the content to enhance learning and motivation as some students suggested the creative use of interesting anecdotes about the buildings to add interest and liveliness to the group activity, while others showed interest in learning more about other buildings and areas on campus.
- Redesigning a competition game like "Treasure Hunting" to elevate learning interest.

CONCLUSION

In conclusion, the participants found the m-learning environments enjoyable and creative. In addition, m-learning provides flexibilities, practicality, and usability for various learning styles. However, as the questionnaire illustrated, students depend heavily on technical assistants to execute the activity. In other words, even many students are digital natives, prior learning and training seem necessary for m-learning activity implementation. Last, for teachers and researchers, the challenge remains in how to design and develop relevant and interesting learning environments based on sound pedagogical principles to foster the use of mobile learning devices.

REFERENCES

Bahl, P., & Padmanabhan, V. N. (2000, March). RADAR: An In-Building RF-based User Location and Tracking System. *IEEE INFOCOM, 2,* 775–784.

Chai, X., & Yang, Q. (2005). Reducing the calibration Effort for Location Estimation Using Unlabeled Samples. *3rd IEEE International Conference on Pervasive Computing and Communications (PerCom'05)* (pp. 95-104).

Chen, Y. S., Kao, T. C., Yu, G. J., & Sheu, J. P. (2004). A mobile butterfly-watching learning system for supporting independent learning. *2nd IEEE International Workshop on Wireless and Mobile Technologies in Education* (pp. 11-18). JungLi, Taiwan.

Engeström, Y. (1987). *Learning by expanding: An activity-theoretical approach to developmental research.* Helsinki, Finland: Orienta-Konsultit Oy. Retrieved Nov. 14, 2008 from http://communication.ucsd.edu/LCHC/MCA/Paper/Engestrom/expanding/toc.htm.

Engeström, Y. (1999). Activity theory and individual and social transformation. In Y. Engeström, R. Miettinen & R.-L. Punamäki (Eds.), *Perspectives on Activity Theory* (pp. 19-38). Cambridge: Cambridge University Press.

Georgiev, T., Georgieva, E., & Smrikarov, A. (2004). M-Learning - A New Stage of E-Learning, From d-Learning, to e-Learning, to m-Learning. *International Conference on Computer Systems and Technologies - CompSysTech'2004.* Retrieved July 28, 2006 from http://ecet.ecs.ru.acad.bg/cst04/Docs/sIV/428.pdf.

Jang, H. C., Wang, Y. X., & Chen, C. W. (2006). Implementation of Mobile Multimedia Applications Service Platform on Windows Mobile 2003/2005. *Multimedia and Networking Systems Conference.* Taiwan, I-Shou University.

Jin, M. H., Wu, E. H. K., Liao, Y. B., & Liao, H. C. (2003, December). 802.11-based Positioning System for Context Aware Applications. *IEEE GLOBECOM, 2,* 929–933.

Jin, M. H., Wu, E. H. K., Wang, Y. T., & Hsu, C. H. (2004). An 802.11-based Positioning System for Indoor Applications. *ACTA Press Proceeding, 422.*

Kao, C. L. (2006). *The Study of Using Mobile Learning Device to Assist Elementary School Students to Study Aquatics at Campus' Eco-education Garden.* Unpublished Master's Thesis, Taipei Municipal University of Education.

Keegan, D. (2000). From d-Learning, to e-Learning, to m-Learning. *40th anniversary celebrations of Shanghai TV University.* Retrieved July 28, 2006 from http://www.nettskolen.com/forskning/From%20d%20learning.doc.

Krumm, J., & Platt, J. C. (2003). Minimizing calibration effort for an indoor 802.11 device location measurement system. Tech. Rep. No. Retrieved Nov. 7, 2007 from MSR-TR-2003-82, Microsoft, ftp://ftp.research.microsoft.com/pub/tr/tr-2003-82.pdf.

Lantolf, J. P. (2000). Introducing sociocultural theory. In J. P. Lantolf (Ed.), *Sociocultural theory and second language learning.* Oxford: Oxford University Press.

Laouris, Y., & Eteokleous, N. (2005). We need an educationally relevant definition of mobile learning. *mLearn, 2005.* Retrieved August 20, 2006 from http://www.mlearn.org.za/CD/papers/Laouris%20&%20Eteokleous.pdf.

Ling, F. T. (2004). *A Study on Mobile Learning Device Applied to the Nature Science Class in Elementary School.* Unpublished Master's Thesis. Taipei Municipal University of Education.

Mobile and wireless Internet (2005). *Foreseeing Innovative New Digiservices.* Retrieved August 20, 2006 from http://www.find.org.tw/eng/news.asp?msgid=222&subjectid=10&pos=1.

Mobile phone subscribers Q1 (2006). *Foreseeing Innovative New Digiservices.* Retrieved Aug. 20, 2006 from http://www.find.org.tw/eng/news.asp?msgid=249&subjectid=13&pos=1.

Naismith, L., Lonsdale, P., Vavoula, G., & Sharples, M. (2005). Literature Review in Mobile Technologies and Learning. *Futurelab Series,* Report 11. Retrieved Aug. 20, 2006 from http://www.futurelab.org.uk/download/pdfs/research/lit_reviews/futurelab_review_11.pdf

Nasseh, B. (1997). *A Brief History of Distance Education.* Retrieved August 20, 2006 from http://www.seniornet.org/edu/art/history.html.

O'Malley, C., et al. (2003). Guidelines for Teaching/Learning/Tutoring in a Mobile Environment. Retrieved July 28, 2006 from http://www.mobilearn.org/download/results/guidelines.pdf.

Prensky, M. (2001). Digital natives, digital immigrants. *On the Horizon, 9*(5), 1–2. Retrieved Aug. 20, 2006 from http://www.marcprensky.com/writing/Prensky%20-%20Digital%20Natives,%20Digital%20Immigrants%20-%20Part1.pdf

Quinn, C. (2000). mLearning: Mobile, Wireless, In-Your-Pocket Learning. *LiNE Zine.* Retrieved Aug. 20, 2006 from http://www.linezine.com/2.1/features/cqmmwiyp.htm.

Sharples, M. (2005, April). *Learning as conversation: Transforming education in the mobile age.* Paper presented at Conference on Seeing, Understanding, Learning in the Mobile Age. Budapest, Hungary. Retrieved Aug. 20, 2006 from http://www.eee.bham.ac.uk/sharplem/Papers/Theory%20of%20learning%20Budapest.pdf.

Sharples, M., Taylor, J., & Vavoula, G. (2005). A Theory of Learning for the Mobile Age. In R. Andrews (Ed.), *The Handbook of Elearning Research.* London. Retrieved Aug. 20, 2006 from http://www.nottingham.ac.uk/lsri/msh/Papers/Theory%20of%20Mobile%20Learning.pdf.

Su, L. H. (2003). *The Wireless Technology into the Outdoor Activities of Bird Watching for Observation and Reflection in the Mobile Learning Situation-the Team of Experts to Adapt to Try and to Become Mature in the Using Up-to-date Wireless Technology.* Unpublished Master's Thesis, Taipei Municipal University of Education.

Tate Modern and Antenna Audio Ltd. Tate Modern multimedia tour pilots 2002-2003. Retrieved Aug. 20, 2006 from http://www.tate.org.uk/modern/multimediatour/phase1_keyfindings.pdf.

Thornton, P., & Houser, C. (2004). Using mobile phones in English education in Japan. *Journal of Computer Assisted Learning, 21,* 217–228. doi:10.1111/j.1365-2729.2005.00129.x

Tsai, I. H. (2004). *A Study of the Development of Courseware for Mobile Learning and Students' Learning Effectiveness in Primary Education: Using Wetland Crabs as an Example.* Unpublished Master's Thesis, National Tsing Hua University.

Tsai, T. C., & Li, C. L. (2006, October). Reducing Calibration Effort for WLAN Location System using Segment Technique with Autocorrelation. *IEEE First International Conference on Communications and Networking in China (China-com2006),* Beijing, China.

USjournal.com. LLC. The advantages of distance learning. *US Journal of Academics.* Retrieved Aug. 20, 2006 from http://www.usjournal.com/en/students/help/distancelearning.html.

Valentine, D. (2002). Distance Learning: Promises, Problems, and Possibilities. *Online Journal of Distance Learning Administration, 5(3).* Retrieved Aug. 20, 2006 from http://www.westga.edu/~distance/ojdla/fall53/valentine53.html.

Wagner, E. D., & Wilson, P. (2005, December). Disconnected: Why learning professionals need to care about mobile learning. *T+D. American Society for Training and Development* (pp. 40–43).

Wu, W.-H. (2006). *Applications of Learning Cycle Based Mobile Learning to Enhance Primary School Students' Learning about Aquatics.* Unpublished Master's Thesis, Taipei Municipal University of Education.

This work was previously published in International Journal of Distance Education Technologies, Volume 7, Issue 4, edited by Qun Jin, pp. 38-60, copyright 2009 by IGI Publishing (an imprint of IGI Global).

Chapter 19
E–Learning Practice and Experience at Waseda E–School:
Japan's First Undergraduate Degree-Awarding Online Program

Shoji Nishimura
Waseda University, Japan

Douglass J. Scott
Waseda University, Japan

Shogo Kato
Tokyo Woman's Christian University, Japan

ABSTRACT

In 2003, the School of Human Sciences, Waseda University (Japan), established the e-School, Japan's first complete undergraduate program enabling students to earn their bachelor degrees solely through e-learning. Supported by the widespread availability of high-speed Internet connections, it has become possible to economically transmit videotaped lectures with an image quality close to that of television across Japan and throughout the world. In addition, lecture contents are transmitted with an image quality that allows students to easily read what is written on the blackboard. Waseda's e-School has many features that contribute to its success, among these are the coupling of online and on-campus courses enhancing students educational experiences. In addition, online classes are relatively small—most are capped at 30 students—and new classes are created to respond to students' needs and interests. This chapter outlines the e-School's history, curriculum, administration, and management learning system. Various data are presented for the first four years of the e-School's operation (2003-2006), when the newly-created program was under the Ministry of Education's mandatory supervision period.

DOI: 10.4018/978-1-60960-539-1.ch019

1. INTRODUCTION

Waseda University, one of Japan's oldest private universities, started to issue "Waseda Kogiroku" ("transcripts of lectures") for off-campus students in 1886, only four years after the University was founded. Waseda Kogiroku continued to be issued until 1957 and was ultimately distributed to a total of 2.7 million students. Such students include many distinguished leading researchers and scholars in Waseda University and Japan, such as Soukichi Tsuda, the famous historian specializing in Japanese and Chinese intellectual histories. Waseda Kogiroku, along with the "itinerant lectures" given in various regions in Japan, deserve special mention in the history of lifelong education in Japan.

Since 1949, Waseda University was engaged in providing continuing education by its School of Political Science and Economics II (closed in 1973), the School of Law II (closed in 1973), the School of Letters, Arts and Sciences II, the School of Commerce II (closed in 1973), and the School of Science and Engineering II (closed in 1968), all of which were evening courses, as well as the School of Social Sciences established in 1966 (classes were offered both in the daytime and evenings). However, these courses were offered oncampus and the University had no correspondence courses as a university under the post-war system. The advent of widely-available Interent connections was to greatly change the University's educational delivery options.

In the United States, e-learning on the Internet was actively introduced by higher education institutions since the middle of the 1990's. In particular, with regard to distance education, the University of Phoenix introduced e-learning in a successful manner (Sperling 2000, Yoshida 2002). Japan's entrance into Internet-based education was slower to start, ideed, Japanese law didn't allow universities to offer Internet-based education until 2001. Amendments to the standards for the establishment of universities by the Ministry of Education, Culture, Sports, Science and Technology in March 2001 specified that "a class utilizing the Internet" (i.e. a kind of e-learning) could be recognized as one form of "a class conducted by using media (remote teaching)." This allowed universities' correspondence courses to use the Internet as the primary means of delivering course content for all credits required for graduation (i.e. 124 credits) (Shimizu 2002).

Changes in access to high-speed Internet connections also contributed to the development of Internet-based education in Japan. According to the Ministry of Public Management, Home Affairs, Posts and Telecommunications Japan, as of the end of March 2003, the accumulated number of subscribers of broadband Internet connections amounted to approximately 6.9 million (DSL: 6,589,867, FTTH: 305,387) (Economic Research Office, General Policy Division, Information and Communications Policy Bureau, Ministry of Public Management, Home Affairs, Posts and Telecommunications, Japan 2004). The spread of broadband Internet connections made it easier to deliver dynamic picture images in high quality to the average home.

Various Japanese universities have conducted Internet-based educational programs. In Japan, national universities were given independent status in April, 2004, and these universities have become eager to highlight their school's assets, which has created increasing interest in e-learning and distance learning (Shimizu 2004). Some universities, such as Yashima Gakuen University, Japan Cyber University, Nihon University Graduate School, Shinshu University, and Nagaoka University of Technology, have started to offer e-learning-based curricula coordinated by each school. Yashima Gakuen University is a correspondence university established in April 2004. The students can graduate by using the Internet without the need to study on campus. The program's characteristic learning method is multiple simultaneous communications known as Media Schooling (Asai 2005). Japan Cyber University was established in 2006. Nihon

University Graduate School of Social and Cultural Studies was the first correspondence graduate school in Japan. Nihon University Graduate School of Social and Cultural Studies was established in 1999. Shinshu University, Graduate School of Science and Technology on the Internet (SUGSI) was established in 2002, and the undergraduate course on the Internet (Shinshu University, School on the Internet; SUSI) was established in 2004. In particular, the Internet Graduate School of Shinshu University allows students to complete their master courses solely by taking classes over the Internet (Fuwa et al. 2004, Ueno 2004).

While other Japanese college programs offered Internet-based education, Waseda University was the first to offer a complete undergraduate degree program using the Internet. Through the activities carried out by the Digital Campus Consortium established in 1999 and the active use of on-demand lectures that were started mainly by Waseda's School of Letters, Arts and Sciences in 2001 (lecture delivery using on-demand streaming), Waseda University had already accumulated various know-how regarding classes utilizing the Internet and had established infrastructure such as a transmission system (Matsuoka 2001). These programs helped establish Waseda's e-School degree program which was the first university in Japan to establish correspondence courses enabling undergraduate students to graduate solely by taking classes utilizing the Internet.

This online undergraduate degree program was developed by the faculty of the School of Human Sciences (established in 1987, an appropriate choice given the School's emphasis on a wide variety of social concerns. The School of Human Sciences was established, in part, concerns that humanity had been impaired by a number of social problems as it moved toward the 21st century. Waseda University advocated the broad study of human sciences with the lofty goals of alleviating such a situation, restore humanity, and help cultivate people who can be engaged academically

in education and research with respect to every kind of issue regarding humankind. Initially, with the goal of solving various problems with modern society and establishing a sustainable society, the School of Human Sciences pursued education and research focused on comprehensive and academic perspectives as approaches that are different from deepening each segmented field of science. Later, the rapid change in the world and Japan society particularly in the last 10 years brought a significant change to the contents of the education and research at the School of Human Sciences of Waseda University. The School of Human Sciences, then, was reorganized in 2003 into three new departments that were developed based on the results of the education and research accumulated so far and set new targets for education and research. Specifically, the School of Human Sciences decided to address "environment," "health and welfare" and "information," to better address the urgent issues of the 21st century.

It is considered that generally every member of society is conscious of problems in the environment, health and welfare, and information. When compared with students without work experience, people who are employed or supporting a family are considered to be more conscious of such problems more deeply and urgently due to various experiences they have accumulated in the real world. On the other hand, these working people often had limited opportunities to learn ways to challenge such problems. The spread of broadband access to the Internet through ADSL and the amendments made to the standards for establishment of universities enabled such people to acquire their bachelor degrees by attending classes from home in their spare time.

Under these circumstances, it has become possible to provide a place for learning about the academic and technical approaches to working adults and other members of the society who are highly conscious about problems regarding the environment, health and welfare, and information. This article describes the correspondence courses of the School of Human Sciences, Waseda University (generally called "e-School of the School of Human Sciences, Waseda University"; hereinafter referred to as "e-School"), the first ever university correspondence courses in Japan established in April, 2003, enabling students to acquire their bachelor degrees solely by taking classes on the Internet. It also reports on the actual achievement in two years, and discusses e-learning as an educational method.

This paper will focus on the first four years of operation, from the induction of the first class to their graduation four years later. The following sections of this paper outlines the e-School's curricula, management structure, and system, and reports on the current status of the courses by analyzing the results of a questionnaire survey conducted after one year from their establishment and the state of credits registered and earned by students.

2. ORGANIZATION STRUCTURE

2.1. Faculty Organization and Administrative Structure

The e-School was launched in April, 2003, at the same time of the reorganization of the School of Human Sciences and the integration of full-time faculties; all of the full-time faculty members (69 at that time) teach classes for both e-School and on-campus courses. The burden on faculty members was adjusted to balance the classes for correspondence courses and on-campus courses, and the number of classes assigned to each faculty is almost the same as the average number of classes assigned to each faculty member overall at Waseda University (90 minutes per class, 7 classes per week, for one academic year). In addition, from among the full-time faculty members, an Associate Dean of Academic Affairs and an Associate

Dean of Student Affairs are assigned as executive members of the School of Human Sciences and they are engaged in the operation of the School.

With regard to the administrative work, the creation of lecture contents and the system's operation, aside from the two full-time staff members in charge of the e-School, are managed by professionals staff dispatched by a company funded by Waseda University (hereinafter referred to as the "University's affiliated company") as these tasks require know-how that is different from the on-campus courses. Creation of lecture contents, management and operation of the lecture delivery system, and Learning Management System (LMS), training of mentors (discussed below), personnel management, and publicity activities are mainly performed by such personnel.

For creating lecture contents, two directors, two camera operators, one editor, and one person in charge of copyright aquisition (including license acquisition for third parties' literary works) work on a regular basis in an studio on the Tokorozawa Campus of Waseda University where the School of Human Sciences is located. The lecture delivery system and Learning Management System (LMS) are operated by three staff members of the University in charge of these systems in cooperation with staff members of the company that established the server and is hosting the same. In addition, three other staff members assist with clerical work.

2.2. Academic Coaches

University faculty are assisted in their teaching of the e-School's courses by "Academic Coaches." The position of instructor under former university correspondence courses was reinterpreted as "Academic Coach" so that it matches the system of the e-School that focuses on classes utilizing the Internet. During the semester, in cooperation with the professor of record, Academic Coaches act as contact people to receive and answer questions posted by the students on the Bulletin Board

System (BBS) or sent by e-mail as well as taking the role of mentors to provide other learning assistance, instruction, and advice. Academic Coaches are required to respond to questions from students within 48 hours, however, inquiries are usually within the same day in most cases.

Every semester, all people assuming positions as Academic Coaches get together for a one-day training session on the overall picture of the e-School, curriculum, coaching on the Internet, and how to utilize LMS, among others. Then, they take a two-week online training course using the training lecture contents placed on the actual system in a manner that is similar to actual class management. These training programs and recruitment are handled by the University's affiliated company under the supervision of the School of Human Sciences.

Ideally, Academic Coaches are researchers in a field closely related to the field of the professor of record, so most Coaches are Doctoral students in Waseda University (with the recommendation and approval of their academic advisor). In the future, as the e-School becomes more widely recognized, we plan to recruit people for the position and manage Academic Coaches as part of a human resource bank. As of December 2006 (the end of the Ministry of Education's mandatory four year supervisory period), 138 people have registered as Academic Coaches, of which 55 people belong to the Graduate School of Human Sciences of Waseda University, 37 people belong to other graduate schools of Waseda University, 22 people belong to graduate schools of other universities, and 24 people are housewives who have complete graduate schools or are active professionals in fields that are close to the subject. From among these registrants, the Academic Coaches in charge are chosen for each subject/class after interviews with the faculty members in charge of the subject/class for each semester in consideration of the class schedule and the number of classes to be opened.

3. CURRICULUM

3.1. Allocation of Subjects

The e-School's curriculum is essentially the same as the curriculum for on-campus courses, and requires the same number of credits (124) for graduation. One of the features of the School of Human Sciences' curriculum (both e-School and on-campus) is that students are allowed to freely choose subjects regardless of whether they are offered by the department in which the students have enrolled (an unusual situation in Japan) and all courses pass count towards graduation. With regard to research methods and senior thesiss research courses, students can also take subjects taught by faculty members that belong to departments other than their own. However, as the maximum number of students for these subjects is limited, where the number of students wishing to take such subjects exceeds the maximum, students belonging to the same department as the professor will have priority. With regard to specialized lecture subjects, there is no enrollment limit and classes are opened in accordance with the number of students wishing to take them.

The number of subjects allocated for on-campus courses is 457, and 341 for the e-School. The reason for this differences is that there are time schedule and class size restrictions for the on-campus curriculum. In contrast, e-School students can register for subjects without being affected by the time schedule and class size, so fewer courses need to be available to accommodate full registration by all students.

The number of courses allocated for the e-School was determined based on an admission limit of 300 students. As the e-School allows students to take courses across departments, the following is a simplified estimation for the School as a whole. 69 courses are offered in the categories of Seminar I, II and Graduation Thesis Research, wherein one subject is taken by 4.3 students on average. The enrollment limit for each subject in the category of Research Methods is 20, and 59 courses are offered in this category (these courses alternate through half being offered during one year and the remaining courses being offered the following year). Students are required to take 2 courses from this subject category by the time of their graduation. The capacity for providing enough space is indicated by the calculation: 300 (students) * 2 (courses) / 59 (courses) = 10.2. In addition, the number of specialized lecture courses is 98 and students are required to take at least 98 credits (49 courses) by the time of their graduation. Based on the calculation of 300 (students) * 49 (courses) / 98 (courses) = 150, we have judged that where the enrollment limit per class is 30, we can secure the capacity by offering five classes per each subject on average.

The features of the allocation of courses are shared by both on-campus courses and correspondence courses: Students do not need to distinguish between the department to which they belong and other departments in selecting the subjects they take. In extreme cases, students can graduate by taking only subjects offered by other departments.

However, with regard to research methodology courses, seminars and senior thesis research, there are enrollment limits for such course (research methodology is about 20 students, seminars and senior thesiss research is about 10 students).

It was necessary to establish the curriculum for the e-School to respond to the needs of students based on the assumption of having various types of students with a wide variety of backgrounds. One of those changes was a subject selection step that is different from students in on-campus courses, most of whom graduate in four years. We introduced the concept of "levels" as a substitute for the concept of grades under on-campus courses. There are four levels and each level corresponds to the relevant year under on-campus courses, but, in order to advance to the upper level, students need to have earned a prescribed number of credits in the subject categories as designated by the current level. The definition of "levels" for e-School is shown in Table 1.

While on-campus courses require students to learn two foreign languages (8 credits in total) that are freely chosen by each student from Ger-

Table 1. Definition of e-School's "levels"

Level 1
The required subjects of Level 1 are: Statistics I, II (2 credits for each) English IA, IIA, IB, and IIB (one credit for each) and specialized subjects (13 courses, 26 credits). Upon earning sufficient credits for these courses (34 credits in total), students are allowed to take courses included in Level 2.

Level 2
The required subjects of Level 2 are: Research Methods (2 subjects, 8 credits) and specialized subjects (13 courses, 26 credits). Upon earning sufficient credits for these courses (34 credits in total), students are allowed to take courses included in Level 3.

Level 3
The required subjects of Level 3 are: Seminars (2 subjects, 8 credits) and specialized subjects (10 subjects, 20 credits). Upon earning sufficient credits for these courses (28 credits in total), students are allowed to take courses included in Level 4.

Level 4
The required subjects of Level 4 are: Senior Thesis Research (8 credits) and specialized subjects (10 subjects, 20 credits).

| Note: Upon earning all credits for Levels 1-4 (124 credits in total), students will be eligible to graduate. |

man, French, Chinese, Spanish and English, the e-School only requires that the students take English courses (4 credits). The methods for experiments, surveys, and research (subject group), which are the elective, required subjects (2 subjects, 8 credits), are allocated over the first to third grades under on-campus courses, but are allocated to Level 2, which corresponds to the second grade, for the e-School courses.

3.2. Method of Conducting Classes

A class in the e-School mainly includes lectures and assignments given by faculty and discussions through the BBS. As this system is based on interaction among the faculty, Academic Coach and students, it is necessary for students to actively participate in the class. Classes with regard to specific subjects are conducted as below:

(1) English Education

The only required foreign language course in the e-School is English. For the English subjects, 4 credits (2 subjects) need to be taken in Level 1.

Classes are conducted by an outside language school company, and the students' performance is evaluated by the faculty group in charge of English in the School of Human Sciences. Under the learning system provided by the language school company, native English speakers living all over the world serve as tutors and provide each student with reading/writing training by e-mail and listening/speaking training by telephone. All tutors are professional English teachers with a Master's degree.

(2) Statistics

For statistics, 4 credits (2 classes) need to be taken in Level 1. Statistics are learned in Level 1 as the core methodology for experiments, tests and surveys and as basic literacy for understanding and processing quantitative or qualitative data.

The subject is taught by using PSI (Personalized System of Instruction) (Kogo 2003) designed for online learning, and each question is separately answered by instructors online, through which it aims for students to be actively involved in learning the subject completely.

(3) Specialized Lecture Subjects

Each specialized lecture class is taught for a half-year period and earns 2 credits. The total number of subjects is 98 (see Table 2). These courses are in the form of lectures which are allocated to each department. The volume of a lecture equivalent to one class under on-campus courses is divided into several segments of about 15 minutes (the length of a lecture for one week is 60 to 90 minutes) and new lecture contents are delivered weekly. Lecture contents are accompanied by a Bulletin Board System (BBS), an assignment submission system, and a handout distribution system. Classes are formed for each subject on a 30-students-per-class basis. An Academic Coach is assigned to each class to coordinate BBS discussions and to give instructions to reports submitted by students. The Department of Human Informatics and Cognitive Sciences has slightly more subjects than other departments because it has a teacher-training course (information study for high school students).

(4) Research Methods

Courses for students to learn basic research methodology are categorized in one subject group called "methods for experiments, surveys and research" which include preparatory training for seminars and writing senior theses. Each subject belonging to this group is taught for a half-year and provides 4 credits. Level 2 requires 2 classes to be taken. Methods for experiments, surveys and research have 59 courses in total, and half of them are offered once every two years and the other half are offered in the alternate years.

Table 2. List of Specialized lecture subjects

Department of Human Behavior and Environment Sciences	Department of Health Sciences and Social Welfare	Department of Human Informatics and Cognitive Sciences
Archaeology	Behavior Therapy	Basic Psychology
Architectural Ergonomics	Bioethics	Cognitive Psychology
Behavioral Development	Cognitive Behavior Theory	Cognitive Technology
Communication	Cognitive Behavior Therapy	Communication Network
Constitution	Cytology and Histology	Database
Country Hills Conservation	Developmental Biology	Distance Learning
Cultural Anthropology	Ergonomics	Educational Media Science
Developmental Psychology	Health Administration Medicine	Educational Method for Informatics I
Ecological Anthropology	Health and Welfare Industrial Technology	Educational Method for Informatics II
Ecological Science	Health Sciences and Promotion	Educational Psychology
Egyptian Civilization	Human Science of Lifestyle Related Disease	Guidance and Career Counseling
Environment Management Planning	Immunology	Human Information Processing
Environmental Information Science	Infectious Disease	Information and Man
Environmental Psychology	Introduction to Social Work Methodology I	Information and Profession
Environmental Sociology	Physiology	Information of Colors
French Culture	Psychology	Information Society and Information Ethics
Geosphere-Biosphere System	Psychosomatic Medicine	Instructional Design
German Society and Culture	Public Assistance	Intercultural Communication
Intercultural Education	School Counseling	Introduction to Computer Systems
Life Course Theory	Social Security I	Introduction to Teaching
Motivation Theory	Social Security I	Introduction to the Information System
Professional Sociology	Social Welfare System	Learning and Media
Psychology of Space	Social Work for the Aged I	Mathematics for Information Processing
Pyramid Civilization	Social Work for the Aged II	Measurement and Evaluation of Education
Regional/Global Environment	Special Activities	Mechanical Analysis of Sports Motion
Safety and Disaster Prevention	Sports Practice I	Multimedia
Seminar on Topical Subjects	Sports Practice II	Principles of Education I
Social Development	Therapeutic Recreation	Principles of Education II
Structure and Functions of the Brain	Welfare for the Disabled I	Programming I
	Welfare for the Disabled II	Programming II
		Response to Harsh Environment
		Safety and Human Factors
		Sensational Information Processing
		Sports Practice III
		Teaching Practice I
		Teaching Practice II
		Teaching-Learning Process
		The Developing Adult
		Web Design

From among these courses, students are required to choose 2 in Level 2.

In these classes, not only the methodology for each research field is studied, but also basic knowledge of the underlying theory is acquired. Limiting the number of students per class to 20 at maximum, these classes focus on discussions through BBS and the learning of research methods by working on surveys and assignments. Each class has an Academic Coach. Delivery of lectures, submission of assignments, etc., are all conducted online. However, with regard to subjects that include experiments using equipment or that are required to be conducted face-to-face, such intensive schooling is conducted using the university's Tokorozawa Campus, Oiwake Seminar House, etc. In such cases, the number of days for face-to-face schooling is limited to the minimum (about 2 days) and the required class hours are secured mainly through online classes.

(5) Seminars I, II

The curriculum includes seminars in order to promote the determination by students of subject of their senior thesis research, the understanding of the current status of research in the research field as preferred by each student, and the effective implementation of research. Seminar are more than just small courses taken by upper-division students. Seminars at Waseda University are year-long courses that allow third year students to work intensively with one professor on a particular theme. After finishing their third-year seminar, fourth year students continue to work with their professor to write a senior thesis, a key graduation requirement for students in the School of Human Sciences. For seminar subjects, seminar I (half-year period, 4 credits) and seminar II (half-year period, 4 credits) are required to be taken in Level 3. The seminars have 69 subjects for seminar I and II respectively, which are assigned to all faculties each year. The methods of conducting the classes are the same as for the methods for experiments, surveys and research. Basically, one faculty member takes care of 2 or 3 students wherein individual instructions are given which link to the bachelor's research of each student.

(6) Senior Thesis Research

As mentioned previously, a senior thesis is a key graduation requirement. Senior thesis research is a full-year subject earning 8 credits. Like seminars, the number of courses for senior thesis research is 69. The instructions for students' research are given by telephone and e-mail as well as through the video meeting system using the Internet.

3.3. Educational Considerations

In the e-School, in order to provide a strong motivation and more detailed instructions than those provided in face-to-face classes, class size is kept to 30 students on average (specialized lecture subjects) and one Academic Coach is assigned to each class. Where many students wish to take a certain subject, it is handled by increasing the number of classes not by increasing the number of students in a class. Class size is kept to 30 students because it was found that, based on the on-demand classes offered by Waseda University for the past three years (dozens of courses), the number of students that can be easily taken care of by one Academic Coach was 30. Based on the facts that, in the United States, the most advanced nation in online classes, online learning is easily discontinued unless there is strong motivation and that the dropout rate in correspondence courses is historically high (Priluck 2004), our e-School adopted the basic concept of promoting individual treatment and mutual learning between students: Academic Coaches provide mentoring mainly focusing on academic aspects.

In addition, in order to help students keep their motivation and to alleviate the sense of isolation, a BBS is utilized for communication not only between students and faculties but also among students to serve as a ground for interaction with faculties, other students and alumni. Furthermore, homerooms (30 students per homeroom at maximum) are established and a full-time faculty member is assigned to each such homeroom. An Academic Coach is also assigned to each homeroom to serve as a contact person for providing various types of support to students.

Additionally, student support, such as use of facilities including libraries, awarding of scholarships, and assistance to extracurricular activities, is provided to the extent possible.

4. CLASSES

4.1. E-Learning Based on a "Campus" Model

Traditional e-learning mainly uses self-learning materials (contents) based on the instructional design in high-quality finished form, and the focus is placed on independent learning by the learner rather than instruction by the teacher. This can be termed e-learning in the "desktop" model wherein learners study by opening "text books" at their desk. The features of this desktop e-learning model are:

(i)   Teaching materials (contents) in high-quality finished form;
(ii) High degree of freedom with respect to study time (learners can learn at their own pace), and
(iii) Communication with faculty is supplementary (mainly for questions where it exists at all).

In contrast, e-learning that models a campus situation includes a virtual environment that includes:

(i)   Blackboard/platform (moving image contents).

(ii) Classroom (communication between faculty and students as well as among students through BBS, etc.).
(iii) Faculty room (Learning Management System).

This is called "campus model" e-learning here. The features of this model are:

(i)   Teaching materials are prepared on the premise that communication between faculty and students exists (contents are not designed for independent use).
(ii) Reasonable degree of freedom with respect to study time (students are bound by semesters and required to study on a weekly basis.
(iii) Communication with instructors is essential.

The desktop model is highly effective for acquiring specific skills, such as in-company training, as learners can proceed with study at their own pace. On the other hand, in a Japanese university curriculum, learners are required to take about 10 courses per semester in order to graduate in 4 years and learners need to take courses in a well-planned manner. Where general learners need to learn many subjects systematically, it is considered that they can pick up their study pace more easily and can learn more effectively with the campus model of e-learning which emulates the traditional on-campus educational situation and to which learners are accustomed. In addition, under this model, learners are given some sort of assignment for each course every week and learners can maintain the pace naturally by working on the assignment by the deadline. Furthermore, the campus model is desirable for Waseda's e-School as its curriculum has many subjects that are near-equivalents to on-campus courses.

4.2. Lecture Contents

As the e-School shares the curriculum with on-campus courses, basically lecture contents can be

Figure 1. A snapshot from a lecture shown in the resolution actually transmitted to students

created by filming and editing classroom lessons. However, lectures are also filmed in a special studio for various reasons such as problems in arranging a camera crew.

Regardless of whether filming is conducted in the classroom or in a studio, lectures are filmed by the same professional camera crew and then edited and encoded for use with Real Media at 400 x 300 pixels resolution and at 15 frames/second. Figure 1, which is one frame of the lecture contents in the resolution actually transmitted, shows that the screen image is sufficient to allow students to read what is written on the blackboard. In addition, the bandwidth to be used by streaming is 384 Kpbs. Traditional e-learning contents used a norrower bandwidth (56 kbps), and in order to work within this limitation, materials needed to be treated as still images. Bceause of this restriction, it was necessary to integrate the images and audio of the faculty members and computerized teaching materials by using an authoring system which was a large obstacle in creating e-learning contents that simulated a classroom setting. Larger bandwidth allowances enable e-School coures contents to replicate the activities and contents used in the classroom or studio, anything that can be filmed by

a video camera such as the lecturer, blackboards, OHP and images projected on the screen.

Once the lecture contents have been video taped, they must be processed and uploaded to the servers. Originally this process took days or weeks to complete, but as the production staff become more experienced, contents can now be published on the day after the lecture was filmed. This speedy processing increases the faculty members flexibility in amending or replacing online contents. It also provides the online students with the most up-to-date information available to on-campus students. This quick production and delivery system is one of Waseda's e-School's key elements. Although one-day processing is possible, most courses are completed in one academic year for use in the following academic year. However, for subjects that address current topics, the filming is conducted flexibly to suit speedy delivery.

Japanese on-campus courses tend to meet for 90 minutes once each week (one key exception is the seminar course described above). As part of the e-School's lecture processing, lecture contents corresponding to one day's lesson within an on-campus courses is divided into several files of about 15 minutes each which are placed on the server. The reasons behind such division of segments include

- short lengths of about 15 minutes help to reduce the need for rebuffering if there is a network problem,
- lecturers can more easily redo selected portions of a lecture, and
- it helps reduce student fatigue by giving them a break every 15 minutes similar to a TV program.

4.3 Questionnaire Survey to Evaluate Classes

A questionnaire survey regarding the e-School's classes was conducted for each course at the end of each semester during the 2003-04 academic year. The questionnaire survey system on the e-School Website was used allowing the respondents to respond voluntarily on an anonymous basis. The total number of responses was 661 out of a potential number of 1,123 students for the spring semester and 569 out of 1,094 for the fall semester, indicating response rates of 58.8% and 52.0% respectively.

In addition to items regarding the quality of lecture contents, the survey included various items such as the BBS (43 items). Some of the characteristic survey items and answers included were, "Is the course generally well-planned?" and "Overall, was the course helpful?" For the first question (course is well-planned), the mean score was 5.7 out of a high score of 7. The second question (course is helpful) also averaged a score of 5.7 out of 7. Thus, both questions received highly positive responses which was the tendency for the survey overall.

In order to check if there was any difference in the lecture contents filmed in the classrooms and those filmed in the studio, the data was analyzed in detail. Although 36 courses were offered in 2003 (the first year of operation), 25 subjects were covered by this analysis, excluding subjects that used Web materials only and that had both classroom-filmed lectures and studio-filmed lectures. The items that were analyzed included four items as shown in Table 3. Eight classes were filmed in classrooms (total number of responses was 270) and seventeen classes were filmed in the studio (total number of responses was 653).

The median values and mode values shown in Table 2 indicate that all four items covered by the analysis received a positive evaluation with scores of 4 through 6 out of 7. In addition, with regard to the comprehension of subjects, given the survey results that both classroom-filmed and studio-filmed lectures scored a mode value of 6, it is considered that the lecture contents were satisfactory for students to comprehend the subject matter.

In order to check if there was any difference in quality between classroom-filmed contents and studio-filmed contents, the two groups of lecture contents were examined based on the Mann-Whitney U test. As a result, a significant difference was recognized only with respect to the image quality at the 5% level. It is considered that where a lecture is filmed in a classroom with students present, due to the restrictions on the location of the camera and lighting, the image quality of the film tends to be lower than lecture contents filmed in a studio. On the other hand, no difference was indicated with regard to sound. The reason for this is attributed to the fact that the faculty members wear the same type of wireless pin microphone on the chest both in the classroom filming and studio filming.

For each questionnaire item, respondents were asked to answer by indicating any one score out of scores of 1-7, wherein the former answer in the brackets corresponds to score 1 and the latter correspond to score 7. X(Y)/Z in the table indicates the values of median value(X), quartile value(Y),

Table 3. Analysis of the results of questionnaire survey on lecture contents evaluation

Questionnaire items	Classroom	Studio	p-value
Could you comprehend the subject? (I could not – I could)	5(2)/6	6(1)/6	0.1672
Image quality (bad – good)	4(2)/4	5(2)/4	0.0309
Sound (bad – good)	5(2)/4	5(3)/4	0.8352
As your impression on the whole, was the lecture interesting? (Boring – Interesting)	6(2)/7	6(2)/7	0.9987

Figure 2. System Configurations

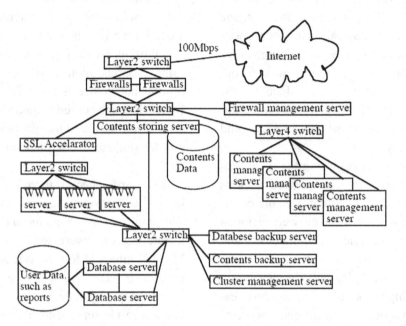

and mode value (Z), respectively, and p-values are based on the Mann-Whitney U test.

With regard to the image quality, it was demonstrated that lecture contents filmed in classrooms have a slightly lower image quality than lecture contents filmed in a studio. On the other hand, with regard to the comprehension of a subject and the impression of the lecture as a whole, no significant difference was recognized between the classroom-filmed lectures and studio-filmed lectures. Based on these analyses, it is considered that the lecture contents of our e-School are of the quality needed for learning, although there is room for improvement with regard to lecture contents filmed in classrooms, in particular.

5. DELIVERY SYSTEM AND LEARNING MANAGEMENT SYSTEM (LMS)

5.1. Server Hardware

As the server hardware of the e-School system not only stores lecture contents but also records stu-

dents' online activities, the hardware is configured by placing importance on stability and security. The hardware is designed in such a manner that the devices are basically duplicated and the entry is protected by firewalls (see Figure 2). In addition, in order to deliver streaming contents of 384 kbps without any delay, the bandwidth for connection to the Internet backbone is 100 Mbps which has proven to be more than sufficient to handle daily traffic: A test with 300 people accessing the system at the same time was conducted and favorable results were obtained.

Actual loads were analyzed during the first and second academic years to confirm that the system was operating as designed. Access records from the middle of April 2004 to the middle of May 2004—a period just after the start of classes having a relatively high amount of traffic—were examined and showed that the number of access attempts peaked at 77 per hour (April 25, 2004, 22:00-23:00), and no processing delays were experienced during that time period. In addition, the bandwidth used for streaming peaked at 10.78 Mbps throughout 2004. Therefore, even if the number of students doubles four years after es-

Figure 3. Front page screen

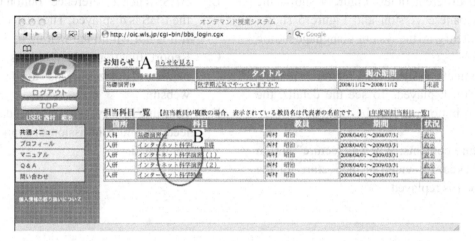

tablishment of the e-School, the bandwidth is sufficient to cope with it. Indeed, the e-School's system operation has been uninterrupted since its creation.

5.2 LMS

The LMS used in the e-School is unique to Waseda University and is called the On-demand Internet Class (OIC). The OIC has functions that are equipped with general LMS, including lecture contents references, handout distribution, attendance management, report submissions, quizzes, Bulletin Board System (BBS), learning history management and questionnaires. The OIC is described in greater detail below.

(1) Front Page of the On-Demand Lecture System

Figure 3 shows the screen that appears after login. The screen shows the menu shared by the whole system (on left, under the OIC logo), information and a list of registered subjects, etc.

A.   Information: indicates important information from faculty members in charge or system administrators. In order to ensure all pieces

of information have been checked, any unread information is marked "unread."

1.   When the title is clicked, the details of the information are displayed.
2.   The details of the information may be sent to the e-mail address registered as profile information if it is so arranged by the author of the information.
3.   The front page displays unread information only. To check all pieces of information within the posting period, "See all information" option needs to be clicked.

B.   List of registered subjects: subjects for which the student is registered are listed. By clicking the name of a subject, a screen to take a class (list of lectures) is displayed. From this screen, students can refer to assignments and the syllabus, use the BBS, confirm and submit report assignments, answer questionnaires and work on quizzes.

(2) Weekly Course Content Page

For each subject, the class contents are organized on a week-by-week basis. The lecture contents to be delivered for the week are about 60 to 90 minutes in total length. Each week's contents are divided into several chapters, enabling students to view at different times. Figure 4 shows the original Japanese version and Figure 5 shows similar content with the system's language setting on "English."

Assignments: assignments, reference materials, etc., are displayed. To see the details, the "reference" button needs to be clicked.

A. Lecture contents: When a "lecture" button is clicked, the video of the lecture for the chapter is replayed.

B. BBS: When a "reference" button is clicked, the BBS is displayed. The BBS can be read if it is not within the writing period.

C. Report functions, etc.: reports, questionnaires and quizzes are also dealt with on the website.

D. Learning history: status of attendance at the lectures and submission of reports can be confirmed.

Figure 4.Weekly course content screen shot

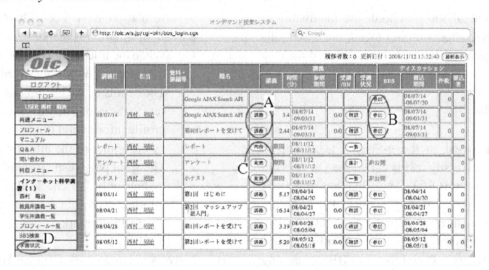

Figure 5. Weekly course content screen shot in English

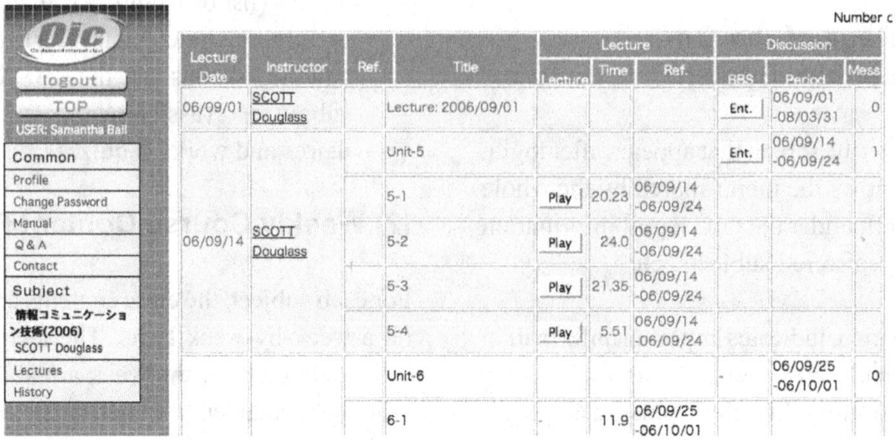

6. STUDENTS

6.1. Selection

Student application and admissions processes are different for the e-School and the on-campus academic programs. e-School applicant screening is conducted based on a statement of purpose 3,000 Japanese characters and a study plan of 1,000 words submitted by each applicant. Then, in the second stage of selection, face-to-face interviews are conducted. The ratio of successful applicants is shown in Table 3.

6.2. Student Enrollment

The number of students enrolled in 2003 was 169 in total consisting of 40 for the Department of Human Behavior and Environment Science, 85 for the Department of Health Science and Social Welfare, and 44 for the Department of Human Informatics and Cognitive Sciences, of which 164 were on the register as of April 2004 and 152 were on the register as of February 2005. This indicates that about 10% of the total students enrolled have

left school for some reason. In 2004, the number enrolled was 143 in total consisting of 35 for the Department of Human Behavior and Environment Science, 64 for the Department of Health Science and Social Welfare, and 44 for the Department of Human Informatics and Cognitive Sciences, of which 140 were on the register as of February 2005 with 3 students having left the school. The total number of students on the registry was 567 in 2006.

6.3. Area of Residence, Age, and Occupation

According to the results of a survey conducted in the spring of 2004, 80% of the students on the registry lived in the Kanto region (in and around the city of Tokyo) with 108 out of 292 living in Tokyo itself. However, students from nearly all of Japanese 47 prefectures were enrolled, although in most cases by only a couple of students. All e-School students are Japanese, but some of them lived and studied in other countries. Students who currently live aboard include: 1 in Morocco, 1 in England, 1 in the United States and 1 in Australia.

Table 3. Acceptance ratios for the three departments

Year	Human Behavior & Environmental Science	Health Science & Social Welfare	Human Informatics & Cognitive Sciences
2003	1:1.33	1:1.22	1:1.38
2004	1:1.38	1:1.36	1:1.32
2005	1:1.71	1:1.48	1:1.51
2006	1:1.57	1:1.26	1:1.42

Table 4. Enrollment data for the three departments

Year	Human Behavior & Environmental Science	Health Science & Social Welfare	Human Informatics & Cognitive Sciences	Total Enrollment
2003	40	85	44	169
2004	35	64	44	143
2005	44	83	41	168
2006	34	79	30	143

About 62% of the total students were 30 years old or older at the time of their enrollment and about 80% of them were employed. The male-female ratio is almost 1:1. It is notable that about 27% of the students on the registry have already graduated from a four-year university.

6.4. Questionnaire on Learning Conditions

In the beginning of July 2003, a questionnaire survey of the students was conducted with regard to the number of courses for which they had registered and the length of time they had spent for studying. The number of respondents was 83 out of the 164 total students on the registry at that time. The most common answer was nine courses, the second most common was 10 followed by eight. This number of courses is roughly equal to the total courses taken by on-campus students.

Regarding the day of the week on which they study, there is not much difference according to the day of the week except that slightly more time is spent for studying on the weekends. The peak time for their study was between 22:00~24:00 probably because many students are employed. In addition, regarding the hours spent studying per day, the most common answer was between two and three hours with the next most common response being between three and four hours.

From the above results, it was found that typical students of the e-School study an average of one or two classes for two to three hours everyday including Saturdays and Sundays.

We analyzed the volume of outgoing video lecture signals from the e-School servers for two weeks in October, 2004. The total volume of traffics for the two week period was 3.95 Tbits. The total number of course hours (i.e. total students * enrolled classes) was about 2,039, so the amount of the packets received per student per course was about 1.94 Gbits during the two week period. In one week, one student had received approximately 970Mbits. The bitrate of the streaming video was 385Kbps, so one students watched video lecture clips for about 42 minutes (2,536 seconds) per course per week. The average weekly lecture for e-School courses is about one hour so on average students were watching somewhat less than a full lecture each week.

A breakdown of the network traffic is provided for weekends (Figure 6) and weekdays (Figure 7).

We analyzed the record of the volume of outgoing video lecture signals from the e-School servers for two weekends in October, 2004 (i.e. October 16, 17 and 23, 24) as shown in Figure 5a. The figure shows that the heaviest access was during the evenings starting at 9:00 p.m. (2100 hours in the Figure).

Figure 6. Transmission volume of lecture videos—Weekends

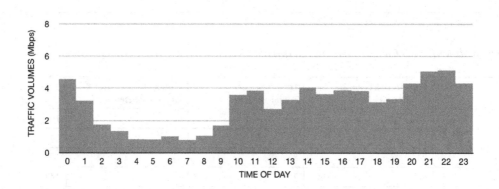

Figure 7. Transmission volume of lecture videos—Weekdays

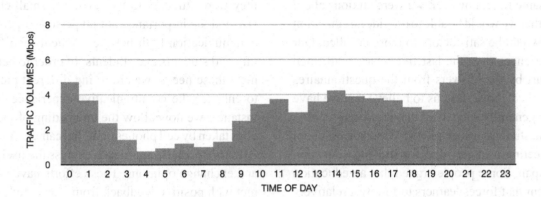

Figure 5b shows the volume of outgoing video lecture signals during the weekdays for the two-week sample period in October, 2004. The figure shows that the heaviest access was during the evenings starting at 9:00 p.m. the same as on the weekends, however, total access was higher than on the weekends.

6.5. State of Registration

The average number of credits earned by e-School students was similar to those earned by on-campus students. From among the new entrants in 2003, the number of students who registered for subjects in both the spring semester and autumn semester was 150. The total number of credits for which they registered was 5,514 credits (about 36.8 credits per 1 student). On the other hand, the total number of credits acquired in the same period was 4,484 credits (about 29.9 credits per 1 student). This means that the ratio of acquired credits to registered credits was 81%. In addition, 82 students, which accounts for about 55% of the total students, acquired 30 credits or more in 1 year. From among students who enrolled in 2003, 53 students (about 31% of the total enrollment) graduated in four years and the accumulated rate of graduation is 57% by the end of March 2010. From among those who graduated in March 2007,

20 people advanced to graduate school (mainly the Graduate School of Human Sciences of Waseda University). For comparison purposes, students who entered on-campus courses in 2003, the number of students in the registry was 745 and the number of total credits registered was 26,481 credits (about 35.5 credits per student), of which 21,995 credits were acquired (about 29.5 credits per student). This ratio of acquired credits to registered credits is almost the same as the ratio for the e-School courses. In addition, from among the 646 new entrants in 1999, 512 (about 79%) graduated in four years although this data refers to a previous course.

7. DISCUSSION AND CONCLUSION

With the improved information infrastructure and changes to relevant educational laws, the environment was conducive to creating Japan's first undergraduate degree-awarding e-learning course. We were hopeful that our on-campus curriculum (which focuses on the environment, health and welfare, and information) would appeal to working adults and other members of society as these topics are currently of great interest. Through this new online learning environment, Waseda University would be able to offer new opportunities for lifelong learning in the era of the Internet. At the same time, however, we were anxious about whether we would be able to provide an education that would be satisfactory to those enrolled. Our experiences over the last five years, confirmed in part by the answers from the questionnaires described above, lead us to believe that we have been generally successful in our efforts. As 82% of the students are employed Waseda's e-School is meeting a larger need for lifelong education in Japan. Some people argued that an education system that forces learners to follow a relatively strict schedule (i.e. not self-paced learning) is not suitable for lifelong education targeting working adults. However, many students of our program in their 30's and 40's and at their working prime manage to work and study at the same time.

The e-School enables students to graduate without taking on-campus schooling and we stressed this point as a feature. However, in our experience, many students want to visit the campus and meet with their classmates and instructors if they have a chance. This is inferred by the fact that, in 2003, about 60% of the students on the registry took physical education classes that required attending intensive, two-day, on-campus classes held on the weekends. Intensively conducted for two days (Saturday and Sunday) after taking online lectures and completing physical exercise assignments for about 10 weeks for the teacher-training course. 30 students in a teacher certification course were asked why they came all the way to attend on-campus schooling, many students replied that they wanted to meet their friends with whom they normally communicate only on the BBS. In addition, many students stated that the education system of the e-School is perfect for those who want to come to school and learn every day if possible but cannot do so due to their occupation and who seek a learning style that is similar to on-campus courses.

This interest in distance learning coupled with a desire for more personal contact is an ongoing challenge for the e-School faculty. It seems that many students joined the e-School because they were attracted to the relatively small class size and the importance put on person-to-person communication both between students and faculty and students and students. In order to better meet these needs, we are trying different media to enhance the communicative experience. For instance, we now allow the upoloading of video clips taken by cell phones or digital cameras to the BBS (up to 1MB) in order to express themselves and exchange opinions. These efforts have been met with positive feedback from many students. In another example, seminars with one teacher taking care of one or two students, we plan to utilize not only e-mails and BBS but also video chat and telephone. Of course, we continue to work to improve the lecture contents, but at the same time, we need to provide a communication means for more personal exchanges.

The acquisition of credits by students in correspondence the e-School courses is the same level as students in on-campus courses. It is true that the rate of graduation in four years under the e-School courses, at 31%, falls short of the graduation rate under on-campus courses but is remarkably high for university correspondence courses (the rate climbes to 43% when 19 students who graduated in September 2007 are included). We hope to see the graduation rate in six years exceed 70%. We interviewed many students on various occasions and found that generally, students have a strong sense of purpose for learning in the e-School and they are all hard workers. Typical the e-School students study from around 21:00 to around 24:00 after work and dinner at home, and study on weekends intensively to make up for any delay during weekdays. It is true that, for one course, it takes about 90 minutes to view the lecture contents (many students take notes) plus about 1 hour to work on the quizzes and reporting assignments which are given to students each time in standard classes. As the average student takes nine classes, they must make considerable effort just to keep up. In addition, it is notable that the quality of their reports submitted on various occasions is very high when compared with that of students in on-campus courses. We assume that it is probably because students are not just viewing lecture contents passively, but also actively exchanging opinions and deepening their ideas on the BBS, etc.

So long as the high degree of satisfaction felt by students as reflected in the results of the questionnaire survey as well as the state of the acquisition of credits and learning conditions are examined, the current status of the e-School is favorable. As the e-School has not yet reached the end of its first four years from its establishment, we cannot determine that the the e-School has been a success. However, given the situation of the last two years, we think the e-School is on the right track, and we are sure that it will turn out to be a success as it has such excellent students as stated above.

ACKNOWLEDGMENT

The authors would like to thank the e-School staff who have supported the operation of e-School, the Academic Coaches who have made great efforts in managing classes, and to the faculty members who have worked hard to create the highest-level course contents possible. We also want to thank our students: As educators, we feel very fortunate to meet such excellent students as you.

REFERENCES

Asai, K. (2005). Yashimagakuendaigaku ni okeru e-learning sisutemu no genjou to kadai [The Current Situation and Issues of e-Learning System at Yashima Gakuen University] *Media research, 1*(2), 59-71. (in Japanese)

(2004). *Economic Research Office, General Policy Division, Information and Communications Policy Bureau, Ministry of Public Management, Home Affairs, Posts and Telecommunications.* Japan: WHITE PAPER Information and Communications in Japan.

Fuwa, Y., Kunimune, H., Niimura, M., Wasaki, K., Shidama, Y., & Nakamura, Y. (2004). Shinshu-daigaku Internet Daigakuin no Genjyo to Shorai-Keikaku [Current Status and Future Plan of the Graduate School on the Internet, Shinshu University] [in Japanese]. *Media Research, 1,* 11–18.

Kogo, C. (2003). Daigaku ni Okeru Web Base Kobetsu-ka Kyojyu Shisutemu [Conducting Classes through Web-based Personalized System of Instruction (PSI) in Universities] [in Japanese]. *Annual Journal of Educational Psychology, 42,* 182–192.

Matsuoka, I. (2001). *Dejitaru Kyanpasu* [Digital Campus]. Tokyo: Toyo Keizai Inc.(in Japanese)

Randi, P. (2004). Web-Assisted Courses for Business Education: An Examination of Two Sections of Principles of Marketing. *Journal of Marketing Education, 26,* 161–173. doi:10.1177/0273475304265635

Shimizu, Y. (2002). e-Learning wo Sasaeru Seisaku to Kongo no Tembo [Polices to Support e-Learning and Foresight Thereof] [in Japanese]. *Information Processing, 43,* 421–426.

Shimizu, Y. (2004). Koto-Kyoiku ni okeru e-Learning no Shien to Kyoiku Kontentsu no Kyoyu [Support by e-Learning in Higher Education and Sharing of Educational Contents]. *Media research 1,* 1-10. (in Japanese)

Sperling, J. (2000). *Rebel with a Cause: The Entrepreneur Who Created the University of Phoenix and the For-Profit Revolution in Higher Education.* New York: John Wiley & Sons.

Ueno, M. (2004). Kompakuto na e-Learning Keiei [Small Scaled e-Learning Management]. *Articles Compiled for* the *29th National Conference of* the *Japanese Society for Information and Systems in Education*, 125-126. (in Japanese)

Yoshida, A. (2002). Koto-Kyoiku ni okeru e-Learning - Virtual University no Tojyo [e-Learning in Higher Education - the Advent of Virtual Reality] [in Japanese]. *Information Processing*, *43*, 407–413.

Compilation of References

A. D. L. (2006). *SCORM 2004 3rd Edition, Sharable Content Object Reference Model*. Advanced Distributed Learning.

Abbas, Z., Umer, M., Odeh, M., McClatchey, R., Ali, A., & Ahmad, F. (2005). A Semantic Grid-based E-Learning Framework (SELF). *Proceedings of the 5th IEEE/ACM International Symposium on Cluster Computing and the Grid*, (pp. 11-18). Cardiff, UK.

Abu, R. B., & Flowers, J. (1997). The effects of cooperative learning methods on achievement, retention, and attitudes of home economic students in North Carolina. *Journal of Vocational and Technical Education, 13*(2), 16–22.

Accounting Education Change Commission. (1990). Objective of education for accountants: Position statement number one. *Issues in Accounting Education, 5*(2), 307–312.

Accounting Education Change Commission. (1992). The first course in accounting: Position statement no. two. *Issues in Accounting Education, 7*(2), 249–251.

ADL SCORM. (2004). Advanced Distributed Learning (ADL) SCORM 2004 Specification, from http://www.adlnet.org.

ADL. (2007). Advanced Distributed Learning, Sharable Content Object Reference Model (SCORM®) 2004 3rd Edition. Retrieved December 20, 2007, from http://www.adl.org

Advanced Distributed Learning (ADL). (2004). Sharable Content Object Reference Model (SCORM) 2004 2nd Edition Overview. Retrieved from http://www.adlnet.org/.

Aglets. (n.d.). Retrieved from http://aglets.sourceforge.net/

Ailamaki, A., DeWitt, D. J., Hill, M. D., & Skounakis, M. (2001). Weaving Relations for Cache Performance. In Proceedings of VLDB conference.

Airasian, P. W., & Maranda, H. (2002). The role of assessment in the revised Bloom's Taxonomy. *Theory into Practice, 41*(4), 349–354. doi:10.1207/s15430421tip4104_8

Albrecht, W. S., & Sack, R. J. (2000). *Accounting education: Charting the course through a perilous future*. Sarasota, FL: American Accounting Association.

Allal, L., & Ducrey, G. P. (2000). Assessment of – or in – the zone of proximal development. *Learning and Instruction, 10*, 137–152. doi:10.1016/S0959-4752(99)00025-0

Altera (n.d.). Retrieved from http://www.altera.com/

Altinel, M., Bornhövd, C., Krishnamurthy, S., Mohan, C., Pirahesh, H., & Reinwald, B. (2003). Cache Tables: Paving the Way for an Adaptive Database Cache. In Proceedings of VLDB conference.

American Accounting Association. Committee on the Future Structure, Content, and Scope of Accounting Education (the Bedford Committee). (1986). Future accounting education: Preparing for the expanding profession. *Issues in Accounting Education, 1*(1), 168–195.

Amorim, R. R., Lama, M., Sánchez, E., Riera, A., & Vila, X. A. (2006). A Learning Design Ontology based on the IMS Specification. *Journal of Educational Technology & Society, 9*(1), 38–57.

Anderson, W., & Krathwohl, D. R. (2001). *A taxonomy for learning teaching and assessing: A revision of Bloom's educational objectives*. New York, NY: Longman.

Antonietti, A., & Giorgetti, M. (1997). The Verbalizer-Visualizer Questionnaire: A review 1. *Perceptual and Motor Skills, 86*(1), 227–239.

Apkarian, J., & Dawes, A. (2000). Interactive control education with virtual presence on the web. *Proceedings of the 2000 American Control Conference (ACC)* (Vol. 6, pp. 3985-3990). Chicago, IL: American Automatic Control Council.

Appell, C. J. (1991). *The effects of the 4MAT system of instruction on academic achievement and attitude in the elementary music classroom.* Unpublished doctoral dissertation, University of Oregon, Columbia.

Asai, K. (2005). Yashimagakuendaigaku ni okeru e-learning sisutemu no genjou to kadai [The Current Situation and Issues of e-Learning System at Yashima Gakuen University] *Media research, 1*(2), 59-71. (in Japanese)

Atkinson, R. C., & Shiffrin, R. M. (1971). The control of short-term memory. *Scientific American, 225,* 82–90. doi:10.1038/scientificamerican0871-82

Ausubel, D. P. (1968). *Educational Psychology: A cognitive view.* New York: Holt, Rinehart & Winston.

Baddeley, A. D. (1986). *Working Memory.* New York, NY: Oxford University Press.

Bahl, P., & Padmanabhan, V. N. (2000, March). RADAR: An In-Building RF-based User Location and Tracking System. *IEEE INFOCOM, 2,* 775–784.

Bajraktarevic, N., Hall, W., & Fullick, P. (2003). *ILASH: Incorporating Learning Strategies in Hypermedia.* Paper presented at the Fourteenth Conference on Hypertext and Hypermedia.

Baker, F. B. (1992). *Item Response Theory: Parameter estimation techniques.* NY: Marcel Dekker Inc.

Baldoni, M., Baroglio, C., Patti, V., & Torasso, L. (2004). *Reasoning about learning object metadata for adapting SCORM courseware.* Paper presented at the EAW'04.

Baldoni, M., Baroglio, C., Brunkhorst, I., Henze, N., Marengo, E., & Patti, V. (2006). A Personalization Service for Curriculum Planning. In proceedings of *14th Workshop on Adaptivity and User Modeling in Interactive Systems,* Hildesheim.

Baldoni, M., Baroglio, C., Patti, V., & Torasso, L. (2002). Using a rational agent in an adaptive web-based tutoring system. In proceedings of the *Workshop on Adaptive Systems for Web-Based Education, 2nd Int. Conf. on Adaptive Hypermedia and Adaptive Web-based Systems, pages 43-55,* Malaga, Spain.

Bardossy, A., & Duckstein, L. (1995). *Fuzzy Rule-Based Modeling with Applications to Geophysical, Biological, and Engineering Systems.* Boca Raton, USA: CRC Press.

Barneva, R., Brimkov, V., & Kanev, K. (2009). Combining Ubiquitous Direction-Sensitive Digitizing with a Multimedia Electronic Dictionary for Enhanced Understanding. *International Journal of Imaging Systems and Technology, 2*(19), 39–49. doi:10.1002/ima.20189

Bar-On, R. (2000). Emotional and social intelligence: Insights from the emotional quotient inventory. In Bar-On, R., & Parker, J. D. A. (Eds.), *The handbook of emotional intelligence* (pp. 363–388). San Francisco: Jossey-Bass.

Barrett, E., & Lally, V. (1999). Gender differences in an on-line learning environment. *Journal of Computer Assisted Learning, 15*(1), 48–60. doi:10.1046/j.1365-2729.1999.151075.x

Becktold, T. H. (2001). Brain based instruction in correctional settings: Strategies for teachers. *Journal of Correctional Education, 52*(3), 95–97.

Bejar, I. I., Lawless, R. R., Morley, M. E., & Wagner, M. E. (2003). A Feasibility Study of On-the-Fly Item Generation in Adaptive Testing. In R.E. Bennett & J. Revuelta (Eds.), *The Journal of Technology, Learning, and Assessment, 2*(3), 3-29.

Ben, L., & Haas, Z. J. (2003, October). Predictive Distance-Based Mobility Management for Multidimensional PCS Networks. *IEEE/ACM Transactions on Networking, 11*(5).

Benmohamed, H., Lelevé, A., & Prévot, P. (2005). Generic Framework for Remote Laboratory Integration. In *Proceedings of the 6th International Conference on Information Technology Based Higher Education and Training* (pp. T2B-11-T2B-16), Santo Domingo, Dominican Republic.

Bennett, E. L., Diamond, M. C., Krech, D., & Rosenweig, M. R. (1964). Chemical and anatomical plasticity of brain. *Science, 146,* 610–619. doi:10.1126/science.146.3644.610

Berchtold, S., & Kriegel, H. (1997). S3: Similarity search in CAD database systems. *Proc. SIGMOD*, 564–567.

Berk, R. A., & Griesemer, H. A. (1976). Software Review: ITEMAN: An Item Analysis Program for Tests, Questionnaires, and Scales. *Educational and Psychological Measurement*, *36*(1), 189–191. doi:10.1177/001316447603600122

Bermejo, S. (2005). Cooperative Electronic Learning in Virtual Laboratories Through Forums. *IEEE Transactions on Education*, *48*(1), 140–149. doi:10.1109/TE.2004.837045

Bersin., & Associates. (2004). *Study: Learning Management Systems 2004*. Bersin & Associates, http://www.bersin.com/

Black, J. E., Isaacs, K. R., Anderson, B. J., Alcantara, A. A., & Greenough, W. T. (1990). Learning causes synapogenesis, where motor activity causes angiogenesis, in cerebellar cortex of adult rats. *Neurobiology*, *87*, 5568–5572.

Black, P., & William, D. (1998). Inside the black box: Raising standards through classroom assessment. *Phi Delta Kappan, 80*(2), 139-148. (Available online: Hhttp://www.pdkintl.org/kappan/kbla9810.htmH.)

Blackboard (2008). Available at http://www.blackboard.com.

Blackboard. (2007). http://www.blackboard.com/us/index.aspx.

Blessing, S. B., & Anderson, J. R. (1996). How people learn to skip steps. *Journal of Experimental Psychology. Learning, Memory, and Cognition*, *22*, 576–598. doi:10.1037/0278-7393.22.3.576

Bloom, B. S. (1968). Mastery learning. *Evaluation Comment*, *1*, 1–16.

Bloom, B., Englehart, M., Furst, E., Hill, W., & Krathwohl, D. (1956). Taxonomy of Educational Objectives. In *Handbook I: The Cognitive Domain* New York: Longmans Green.

Bonk, J. (2008). Motivational Strategies. Retrieved January 14, 2008, from http://www.indiana.edu/~bobweb/mt_web.html

Boone, H. N., & Newcomb, L. H. (1990). Effects of approach to teaching on student achievement, retention and attitude. *Journal of Agricultural Education*, *31*(4), 9–14. doi:10.5032/jae.1990.04009

Borcoci, E., et al. (2010). *A Novel Architecture for Multimedia Distribution Based on Content-Aware Networking*. 2010 Third International Conference on Communication Theory, Reliability, and Quality of Service (CTRQ), 162-168.

Borkowski, S. C., & Welsh, M. J. (1996). 4MAT/formatting the accounting curriculum. *Accounting Educators'. Journal*, *8*(2), 67–90.

Botsios, S., Georgiou, D., & Safouris, N. (2008). Contributions to AEHS via on-line Learning Style Estimation. *Journal of Educational Technology & Society*, *11*(2).

Bottoni, P., Kanev, K., & Mirenkov, N. (2010). *Distributed and Context-focused Discussion on Augmented Documents and Objects*. In Proceedings of the 9th Int. Conf. on the Design of Cooperative Systems, pp.50-59.

Bowers, P. S. (1987). *The effect of the 4MAT system on achievement and attitudes in science*. Unpublished doctoral dissertation, University of North Carolina at Chapel Hill, Columbia.

Brachman, R. J., Khabaza, T., Kloesgen, W., Pieatetsky-Shapiro, G., & Simoudis, E. (1996). Mining Business Databases. *Communications of the ACM*, *39*(11), 42–48. doi:10.1145/240455.240468

Bradley, R. S., Barry, R. G., & Kiladis, G. (1982). *Climatic fluctuations of the western United States during the period of instrumental records. Final report to the National Science Foundation*. Amherst: University of Massachussets.

Bransford, J. D., Brown, A. L., & Cocking, R. R. (1999). *How people learn: Brain, mind, experience, and school*. Washington, DC: National Academy Press.

Brine, J., Kanev, K., Turk, D., & Orr, T. (2007). Cloze Information Gap Tasks with Print-Based Digital Content Interfaces. In Proc. of the 7th IEEE International Conference on Advanced Learning Technologies (ICALT'07), pp. 318-319.

Brine, J., Turk, D., & Kanev, K. (2006). *Supporting Reading Jigsaws with Print-based Digital Content Interfaces*. Paper presented at JALTCALL'06 International Conference.

Brown, E., Cristea, A., Stewart, C., & Brailsford, T. (2005). Patterns in authoring of adaptive educational hypermedia: A taxonomy of learning styles. *Educational Technology and Society, 8*(3), 77–90.

Brown, T. H. (2005). Towards a Model for m-Learning in Africa. *International Journal on E-Learning, 4*(3), 299–315.

Brown, E. J., & Brailsford, T. (2004). *Integration of learning style theory in an adaptive educational hypermedia (AEH) system*. Paper presented at the ALT-C Conference.

Brown, F. G. (1971). *Measurement and Evaluation*. Itasca, Illinois: F.E. Peacock.

Brown, J. C., Frishkoff, G. A., & Eskenazi, M. (2005). Automatic Question Generation for Vocabulary Assessment. *Proceedings of the conference on Human Language Technology and Empirical Methods in Natural Language Processing* (pp 819-826).

Bruer, J. T. (1998). Brain science, brain fiction. *Educational Leadership, 56*(3), 14–18.

Bruer, J. T. (1999). In search of … brain-based education. *Phi Delta Kappan, 80*(9), 648–657.

Bruner, J. S. (1961). The act of discovery. *Harvard Educational Review, 31*, 21–32.

Brusilovsky, P. (1996). Methods and techniques of adaptive hypermedia. *User Modeling and User-Adapted Interaction, 6*(2-3), 87–129. doi:10.1007/BF00143964

Brusilovsky, P. (2003). Adaptive navigation support in educational hypermedia: The role of student knowledge level and the case for meta-adaptation. *British Journal of Educational Technology, 34*(4), 487–497. doi:10.1111/1467-8535.00345

Brusilovsky, P., & Pyelo, C. (2003). Adaptive and Intelligent Web-based Educational Systems. *International Journal of Artificial Intelligence in Education, 13*(2-4), 159–172.

Brusilovsky, P., & Rizzo, R. (2002). Map-based horizontal navigation in educational hypertext. *Journal of Digital Information, 3*(1).

Brusilovsky, P., & Vassileva, J. (2003). Course sequencing techniques for large-scale web-based education. *International Journal of Continuing Engineering Education and Lifelong Learning, 13*(1-2), 75–94.

Brusilovsky, P. (2003). Adaptive navigation support in educational hypermedia: The role of student knowledge level and the case for meta-adaptation. *British Journal of Educational Technology, 34*(4), 487–497. doi:10.1111/1467-8535.00345

Brusilovsky, P. (1998). Methods and Techniques of Adaptive Hypermedia. P. Brusilovsky, A. Kobsa, J. Vassileva (Ed.), *Journal of User Modeling and User-Adapted Interaction 6 (2-3), Special Issue on Adaptive Hypertext and Hypermedia,* 87-129.

Brusilovsky, P. (2001). Adaptive hypermedia. *User Modelling and User-Adapted Interaction, 11*(1-2).

Brusilovsky, P. (2003). Developing Adaptive Educational Hypermedia Systems: From Design Models to Authoring Tools. Murray, T., Blessing S., & Ainsworth, S. (Ed.), *Authoring Tools for Advanced Technology Learning Environments: Toward cost-effective adaptive, interactive, and intelligent educational software,* (pp. 377-409). Norwood, Ablex.

Brusilovsky, P. (2004). Adaptive Educational Hypermedia: From generation to generation. *Proc. Fourth Hellenic Con. Information and Communication Technologies in Education (*pp 19-33).

Brusilovsky, P., & Millan, E. (2007). User Models for Adaptive Hypermedia and Adaptive Educational Systems. In P. Brusilovsky, A. Kobsa, & W. Nejdl (Eds.), *The Adaptive Web* (Vol. 4321, pp. 3-53). Berlin Heidelberg: Springer-Verlag.

Brusilovsky, P., & Miller, P. (2001). Course Delivery Systems for the Virtual University. In T. Della Senta & T. Tschang (Eds.), *Access to Knowledge: New Information Technologies and the Emergence of the Virtual University* (pp. 167-206). Amsterdam: Elsevier Science.

Buchanan, T. (1998). Using the World Wide Web for formative assessment. *Journal of Educational Technology Systems*, *27*, 71–79. doi:10.2190/167K-BQHU-UGGF-HX75

Buchanan, T. (2000). The efficacy of a World Wide Web mediated formative assessment. *Journal of Computer Assisted Learning*, *16*, 193–200. doi:10.1046/j.1365-2729.2000.00132.x

Bybee, R. W. (1997). Achieving scientific literacy: From purposes to practices. Portsmouth, NH: Heinemann.

Cabral, L., & Domingue, J. (2005). Mediation of Semantic Web Services in IRS-III. In Proceeding of the *Workshop on Mediation in Semantic Web Services in conjunction with the 3rd International Conference on Service Oriented Computing*, Amsterdam, The Netherlands.

Cabral, L., Domingue, J., Galizia, S., Gugliotta, A., Norton, B., Tanasescu, V., & Pedrinaci, C. (2006). IRS-III: A Broker for Semantic Web Services based Applications. In roceedings of the *5ʰ International Semantic Web Conference (ISWC 2006)*, Athens, USA.

Cabri, G., Leonardi, L., & Zambonelli, F. (2000). MARS: A Programmable Coordination Architecture for Mobile Agents. *IEEE Internet Computing*, *4*(4), 26–35. doi:10.1109/4236.865084

Camp, G., Paas, F., Rikers, R., & van Merriënboer, J. J. G. (2001). Dynamic problem selection in air traffic control training: a comparison between performance, mental effort and mental efficiency. *Computers in Human Behavior*, *17*, 575–595. doi:10.1016/S0747-5632(01)00028-0

Carmona, C., & Cionejo, R. (2004). A Learner Model in a Distributed Environment. P. De Bra, W. Nejdl (Ed.)., *Third Int'l Conf. Adaptive Hypermedia and Adaptive Web-Based Systems (AH'04), Lecture Notes in Computer Science*, vol. 3137, (pp. 353-359). Berlin, Springer Verlag.

Carver, C. A. Jr, Howard, R. A., & Lane, W. D. (1999). Enhancing student learning through hypermedia courseware and incorporation of student learning styles. *IEEE Transactions on Education*, *42*(1), 33–38. doi:10.1109/13.746332

Chai, X., & Yang, Q. (2005). Reducing the calibration Effort for Location Estimation Using Unlabeled Samples. *3ʳᵈ IEEE International Conference on Pervasive Computing and Communications (PerCom'05)* (pp. 95-104).

Chang, S. K., Arndt, T., Levialdi, S., Liu, A. C., Ma, J., Shih, T., & Tortora, G. (2000). Macro University A Framework for a Federation of Virtual Universities. *International Journal of Computer Processing of Oriental Languages*, *13*(3), 205–221. doi:10.1142/S0219427900000168

Chang, W. C., Hsu, H. H., Shih, T. K., & Wang, C. C. (2005). Enhancing SCORM metadata for assessment authoring in e-Learning. *Journal of Computer Assisted Learning*, *20*(4), 305–316. doi:10.1111/j.1365-2729.2004.00091.x

Charles, C. M., & Mertler, C. A. (2002). *Introduction to Educational Research*. Boston: Allyn & Bacon.

Chen, C. M., Liu, C. Y., & Chang, M. H. (2006). Personalized curriculum sequencing utilizing modified item response theory for web-based instruction. *Expert Systems with Applications*, *30*(2), 378–396. doi:10.1016/j.eswa.2005.07.029

Chen, J. N., Huang, Y. M., & Chu, W. C. C. (2005). Applying dynamic fuzzy petri net to web learning system. *Interactive Learning Environments*, *13*(3). doi:10.1080/10494820500382810

Chen, D., Tian, X., Shen, Y., & Ouhyoung, M. (2003). *On Visual Similarity Based 3D Model Retrieval*. Proc. Eurographics.

Chen, D. J., Lai, A. F., & Liu, I. C. (2005). The Design and Implementation of a Diagnostic Test System Based on the Enhanced S-P Model. *Journal of Information Science and Engineering*, *21*, 1007–1030.

Chen, C. M., Duh, L. J., & Liu, C. Y. (2004). A Personalized Courseware Recommendation System Based on Fuzzy Item Response Theory. *Proceedings of the IEEE International Conference on e-Technology, e-Commerce and e-Service*, Taipei, Taiwan (pp. 305—308).

Chen, C.-Y., Liou, H.-C., & Chang, J. S. (2006). FAST: an automatic generation system for grammar tests. *Proceedings of the COLING/ACL on Interactive Presentation Sessions* (pp 1-4).

Chen, W. (2002). *An empirical study of the impact of the implication of information technology integrated instruction on learning effective and the establishment of teaching platform: In the case of senior high school accounting principle course.* Unpublished master's thesis, Feng Chia University, Taichung, Taiwan.

Chen, Y. S., Kao, T. C., Yu, G. J., & Sheu, J. P. (2004). A mobile butterfly-watching learning system for supporting independent learning. *2nd IEEE International Workshop on Wireless and Mobile Technologies in Education* (pp. 11-18). JungLi, Taiwan.

Chesire, M., Wolman, A., Voelker, G. M., & Levy, H. M. (2001). Measurement and Analysis of a Streaming-Media Workload. In Proceedings of the USENIX Symposium on ITS. (Best paper award).

Chiueh, T. (1994). Content-Based Image Indexing. Proc. VLDB, 582–593.

Chou, C. (2003). Incidences and correlates of Internet anxiety among high school teachers in Taiwan. *Computers in Human Behavior, 19*(6), 731–749. doi:10.1016/S0747-5632(03)00010-4

Chrobak, M., Larmore, L. L., Regingold, N., & Westbrook, J. (1997). Page Migration Algorithms Using Work Functions. *Journal of Algorithms, 24*(1), 124–157. doi:10.1006/jagm.1996.0853

Chuang, C. (2001). *Comparing constructive approach and traditional approach in teaching accounting in the senior commercial vocational school.* Unpublished master's thesis, National Changhua University of Education, Changhua, Taiwan

Civanlar, M. R., & Trussel, H. J. (1986). Constructing membership functions using statistical data. *Fuzzy Sets and Systems, 18*, 1–14. doi:10.1016/0165-0114(86)90024-2

Claroline. (2007). http://www.claroline.net/.

Coalition, O. W. L.-S. (2004). *OWL-S 1.1 release.* from http://www.daml.org/services/owl-s/1.1/

Collis, B., & Strijker, A. (2004). Technology and Human Issues in Reusing Learning Objects. *Journal of Interactive Media in Education,* 2004(4). Special Issue on the Educational Semantic Web, from www-jime.open.ac.uk/2004/4.

Conati, C. (2002). Probabilistic assessment of user's emotions in educational games. *Applied Artificial Intelligence, 16*(7-8), 555–575. doi:10.1080/08839510290030390

Concepcion, A. I., Ruan, J., & Samson, R. R. (2002). SPIDER: A Multi-agent Architecture for Internet Distributed Computing System. In *Proceedings of the ISCA 15th International Conference on Parallel and Distributed Computing Systems* (pp. 147-152), Louisville, KY, USA.

Conklin, J. (1987). Hypertext: An Introduction and Survey. IEEE. *Computer, 20*(9), 17–41. doi:10.1109/MC.1987.1663693

Conlan, O., Wade, V., Gargan, M., Hockemeyer, C., & Albert, D. (2002). An architecture for integrating adaptive hypermedia services with open learning environments. P. Barker and S. Rebelsky, eds., *Proc. ED-MEDIA'2002 - World Conf. Educational Multimedia, Hypermedia and Telecommunications,* (pp. 344-350). Denver, CO, AACE.

Costagliola, G., Ferrucci, F., Fuccella, V., & Oliveto, R. (2007). eWorkbook: a Computer Aided Assessment System. *International Journal of Distance Education Technologies, 5*(3), 24–41. doi:10.4018/jdet.2007070103

Costagliola, G., et al. (2007). *A Web-Based E-Testing System Supporting Test Quality Improvement.* Proceedings of the 6th International Conference on Web-based Learning, pp.190-197

Cronbach, L. J. (1970). *Essentials of psychological testing* (3rd ed.). New York: Author.

Cui, G., Chen, F., Chen, H., & Li, S. (2004). OntoEdu: A Case Study of Ontology-Based Education Grid System for e-Learning. *Global Chinese Journal of Computers in Education, 2*(2), 59–72.

Curtis, D. D. (2001). Exploring Collaborative Online Learning. [JALN]. *Journal of Asynchronous Learning Networks, 5*(1), 21–34.

Dai, C. Y., Cheng, J. K., Sung, J. K., & Ho, C. P. (2005). An Applied Model of SP Chart in the Technological and Vocational Schools Entrance Examination, Redesigning Pedagogy: Research, Policy, Practice. *International Conference on Education.* Singapore: Nanyang Technological University.

Davidovic, A., Warren, J., & Trichina, E. (2003). Learning benefits of structural example-based adaptive tutoring systems. *IEEE Transactions on Education, 46*(2), 241–251. doi:10.1109/TE.2002.808240

Davis, F. D. (1989). Perceived Usefulness, Perceived Ease of Use, and User Acceptance of Information Technology. *Management Information Systems Quarterly, 13*(3), 319–340. doi:10.2307/249008

De Bruijn, J., Lausen, H., Krummenacher, R., Polleres, A., Predoiu, L., Kifer, M., & Fensel, D. (2005). *Web service Modeling Language (WSML).* Final Draft, from http://www.wsmo.org/TR/d16/d16.1/v0.21/20051005/

Deugo, D., & Weiss, M. (1999). A Case for Mobile Agent Patterns. In *Proceedings of the Mobile Agents in the Context of Competition and Cooperation (MAC3) Workshop Notes* (pp. 19-22), Seattle, WA, USA.

DiBello, L., Stout, W., & Roussos, L. (1995). Unified cognitive/psychometric diagnostic assessment likelihood-based classification techniques. In Nichols, P. D., Chipman, S. F., & Brennan, R. L. (Eds.), *Cognitively Diagnostic Assessment* (pp. 361–389). Hillsdale, NJ: Lawrence Erlbaum Associates.

DiBello, L., Stout, W., & Hartz, S. (2000). *On identificability of parameters in the unified model for cognitive diagnosis.* Proceeding of the Annual Meeting of Psychometric Society, Vancouver, Canada.

Dietze, S., Gugliotta, A., & Domingue, J. (2007a). *Using Semantic Web Services to enable Context-Adaptive Learning Designs. Special Issue on IMS Learning Design and Adaptation of Journal of Interactive Media in Education.* JIME.

Dietze, S., Gugliotta, A., & Domingue, J. (2007b). Context-aware Process Support through automatic Discovery and Invocation of Semantic Web Services. In proceedings of *IEEE International Conference on Service-Oriented Computing and Applications (SOCA'07),* Newport Beach, California.

Dijkstra, E. W. (1959). A note on two problems in connection with graphs. *Numer Math, 1,* 269–271. doi:10.1007/BF01386390

Dimakis, N., Polymenakos, L., & Soldatos, J. (2006). *Enhancing Learning Experiences Through Context-aware Collaborative Services: Software Architecture and Prototype System.* In Proc. of the 4th IEEE Int. Workshop on Wireless, Mobile and Ubiquitous Technology in Education (ICHIT'06).

Dimitracopoulou, A. (2005). Designing collaborative learning systems: Current trends & future research agenda. In Koschmann, T., Suthers, D., & Chan, T. W. (Eds.), *Proceedings of Computer Supported Collaborative Learning 2005: The next 10 years!* (pp. 115–124). Mahwah, NJ: Lawrence Erlbaum. doi:10.3115/1149293.1149309

Domingue, J., Galizia, S., & Cabral, L. (2005). Choreography in IRS-III- Coping with Heterogeneous Interaction Patterns in Web services. In Proceedings of *4th International Semantic Web Conference,* Galway, Ireland.

Dow, C. R., Li, Y. H., & Bai, J. Y. (2006). A Virtual Laboratory for Digital Signal Processing. *International Journal of Distance Education Technologies, 4*(2), 31–43. doi:10.4018/jdet.2006040103

Dow, C. R., Lin, C. M., & Chen, S. S. (2002). The Development of a Virtual Digital Circuit Laboratory Using VDSL. *The Journal of Chinese Institute of Electrical Engineering, 9*(3), 251–257.

Dow, C. R., Lin, C. Y., Shen, C. C., Lin, J. H., & Chen, S. C. (2002). A Virtual Laboratory for Macro Universities Using Mobile Agent Techniques. *The International Journal of Computer Processing of Oriental Languages, 15*(1), 1–18. doi:10.1142/S0219427902000509

Dunn, R., & Dunn, K. (1992). *Teaching elementary students through their individual learning styles.* Boston: Allyn and Bacon.

Duval, E. (2003). 1484.12.1 *IEEE Standard for learning Object Metadata,* IEEE Learning Technology Standards Committee, from http://ltsc.ieee.org/wg12/

Dwyer, N., & Suthers, D. D. (2006). Consistent Practices in Artifact-mediated Collaboration. *International Journal of Computer-Supported Collaborative Learning, 1*(4), 481–511. doi:10.1007/s11412-006-9001-1

Dwyer, B. M. (2002). Training strategies for the twenty-first century: Using recent research on learning to enhance training. *Innovations in Education and Teaching International, 39*(4), 265–270. doi:10.1080/13558000210161115

Ebel, R. L., & Frisbie, D. A. (1991). Essentials of educational measurement (5th ed.). Englewood Cliffs, NJ: Prentice-Hall.

ECMAScript. (2008). Standard ECMA-262, ECMAScript Language Specification, available at http://www.ecma-international.org /publications/files/ECMA-ST/Ecma-262.pdf.

Edys, S. (2009). Quellmalz James W. Pellegrino. Technology and Testing. *Science, 323*(2), 75–79.

Eklund, J., & Zeilenger, R. (1996). Navigating the Web: Possibilities and Practicalities for Adaptive Navigation Support. *Proc. Ausweb96: The Second Australian World-Wide Web Conference* (pp. 73-80), Southern Cross University Press.

Elad, M., Tal, A., & Ar, S. (2001). Content Based Retrieval of VRML Objects - An Iterative and Interactive Approach. Proc. EG Multimedia, 97–108.

Ellis, A. (2001). *Student-centred Collaborative Learning via Face-to-face and Asynchronous Online Communication: What's the Difference?* In Proc. of the 18th Annual Conference of the Australian Society for Computers in Learning in Tertiary Education (ASCILITE'01), pp. 169-177.

Engeström, Y. (1987). *Learning by expanding: An activity-theoretical approach to developmental research.* Helsinki, Finland: Orienta-Konsultit Oy. Retrieved Nov. 14, 2008 from http://communication.ucsd.edu/LCHC/MCA/Paper/Engestrom/expanding/toc.htm.

Engeström, Y. (1999). Activity theory and individual and social transformation. In Y. Engeström, R. Miettinen & R.-L. Punamäki (Eds.), *Perspectives on Activity Theory* (pp. 19-38). Cambridge: Cambridge University Press.

Erlauer, L. (2003). *The brain-compatible classroom.* Alexandria, VA: Association for Supervision and Curriculum Development.

Eshet, Y., Klemes, J., & Henderson, L. (2000). Under the microscope: Factors influencing student outcomes in a computer integrated classroom. *Journal of Computers in Mathematics and Science Teaching, 19*(3), 211–236.

Esquembre, F. (2002). Computers in physics education. *Computer Physics Communications, 147,* 13–18. doi:10.1016/S0010-4655(02)00197-2

Exarchos, T. P., Tsipouras, M. G., Exarchos, C. P., Papaloukas, C., Fotiadis, D. I., & Michalis, L. K. (2007). A methodology for the automated creation of fuzzy expert systems for ischaemic and arrhythmic beat classification based on a set of rules obtained by a decision tree. *Artificial Intelligence in Medicine, 40*(3), 187–200. doi:10.1016/j.artmed.2007.04.001

Exel, M., Gentil, S., Michau, F., & Rey, D. (2000). Simulation workshop and remote laboratory: Two web-based training approaches for control. *Proceedings of the 2000 American Control Conference (ACC)* (vol. 5, pp. 3468-3472). Chicage, IL: American Automatic Control Council.

FCL. (1997): Fuzzy Control Prog. Committee Draft CD 1.0 (Rel. 19 Jan 97), http://www.fuzzytech.com/binaries/ieccd1.pdf.

Felder, R. M., & Silverman, L. K. (1988). Learning and teaching styles in engineering education. *English Education, 78*(7), 674–681.

Fensel, D., Lausen, H., Polleres, A., de Bruijn, J., Stollberg, M., Roman, D., & Domingue, J. (2006). *Enabling Semantic Web Services – The Web service Modelling Ontology.* Springer.

Ferscha, A., Holzmann, C., & Oppl, S. (2004). *Context Awareness for Group Interaction Support.* In Proc. of the Second Int. Workshop on Mobility Management & Wireless Access Protocols (MobiWac'04), pp. 88-97.

Foster, I., Kesselman, C., Nick, J. M., & Tuecke, S. (2002). *The Physiology of the Grid.* Retrieved from http://www.globus.org/research/papers/ogsa.pdf.

Foundation for Intelligent Physical Agents (FIPA). (2002). *FIPA Device Ontology Specification.* Retrieved from http://www.fipa.org/specs/fipa00091/XC00091C.pdf.

Francis, M. C., Mulder, T. C., & Stark, J. S. (1995). *Intentional learning: A process for learning to learn in the accounting curriculum.* Sarasota, FL: American Accounting Association.

Freire, P. (2000). *Pedagogy of the oppressed* (Ramos, M. B., Trans.). New York: Continuum. (Original work published 1968)

Fu, A., Chan, P., Cheung, Y., & Moon, Y. (2000). Dynamic VP-Tree Indexing for N-Nearest Neighbor Search Given Pair-Wise Distances. VLDB Journal.

Funkhouser, T., Min, P., Kazhdan, M., Chen, J., Halderman, A., Dobkin, D., & Jacobs, D. (2003). A Search Engine for 3D Models. *ACM Transactions on Graphics, 22*(1), 83–105. doi:10.1145/588272.588279

Funkhouser, T., Kazhdan, M., Shilane, P., Min, P., Kiefer, W., Tal, A., et al. (2004). Modeling by Example. Proc. ACM SIGGRAPH.

Future Internet Engineering Project. (2010). *Future Internet Engineering Project Working Raports*. Retrieved from http://www.iip.net.pl

Fuwa, Y., Kunimune, H., Niimura, M., Wasaki, K., Shidama, Y., & Nakamura, Y. (2004). Shinshu-daigaku Internet Daigakuin no Genjyo to Shorai-Keikaku [Current Status and Future Plan of the Graduate School on the Internet, Shinshu University] [in Japanese]. *Media Research, 1*, 11–18.

Gagne, R. M., Briggs, L. J., & Wager, W. W. (1992). *Principles of instructional design* (4th ed.). Orlando: Harcourt Brace Jovanovich College Publishers.

Gagné, R. M. (1985). *The conditions of learning and theory of instruction* (4th ed.). Orlando, FL: Holt, Rinehart & Winston.

Gagné, R. M., & Briggs, L. J. (1979). *Principles of instructional design* (2nd ed.). New York: Holt, Rinehart & Winston.

Gal, A., & Eckstein, J. (2001). Managing Periodically Updated Data in Relational Databases: A Stochastic Modeling Approach. *Journal of the ACM, 48*(6), 1141–1183. doi:10.1145/504794.504797

Gall, M. D., Gall, J. P., & Borg, W. R. (2003). *Educational research* (7th ed.). Boston: Pearson Education.

Gallardo, T., Guerrero, L. A., Collazos, C., Pino, J. A., & Ochoa, S. (2003). *Supporting JIGSAW-type Collaborative Learning*. In Proc. of the 36th Hawaii International Conference on System Sciences (HICSS'03).

Gamson, Z. F. (1994). Collaborative Learning Comes of Age. *Change, 26*(5), 44–49.

Gangemi, A., & Mika, P. (2003). Understanding the Semantic Web through Descriptions and Situations. In Meersman, R., Tari, Z., and et al. (Eds), *On The Move Federated Conferences (OTM'03)*, LNCS. Springer Verlag.

Gangemi, A., Guarino, N., Masolo, C., Oltramari, A., & Schneider, L. (2002). Sweetening Ontologies with DOLCE. In A. Gómez-Pérez, V. Richard Benjamins (Eds.) *Knowledge Engineering and Knowledge Management. Ontologies and the Semantic Web: 13th International Conference, EKAW 2002*, Siguenza, Spain.

Ganter, B., & Wille, R. (1999). *Formal Concept Analysis. Mathematical Foundations*. Springer.

Genesee, F. (2000). *Brain research: Implications for second language learning*. (Report No. EDO-FL-00-12). Washington, DC: Center for Research on Education. (ERIC Document Reproduction Service No. ED447727)

George, L., & Gerald, M. J. (1996). A class of mobile motion prediction algorithms for wireless mobile computing and communications. *Mobile Networks and Applications, 1*, 113–121. doi:10.1007/BF01193332

Georgiev, T., Georgieva, E., & Smrikarov, A. (2004). M-Learning - A New Stage of E-Learning, From d-Learning, to e-Learning, to m-Learning. *International Conference on Computer Systems and Technologies - CompSysTech'2004*. Retrieved July 28, 2006 from http://ecet.ecs.ru.acad.bg/cst04/Docs/sIV/428.pdf.

Getz, C. M. (2003). *Application of brain-based learning theory for community college developmental English students: A case study*. Unpublished doctoral dissertation, Colorado State University, Columbia.

Gierl, M. J., Leighton, J. P., & Hunka, S. M. (2000). Exploring the logic of Tatsuoka's Rule-Space Model for test development and analysis. *Educational Measurement: Issues and Practice*, 34–44.

Gierl, M. J., & Ackerman, T. (1996). Software Review: XCALIBRE — Marginal Maximum-Likelihood Estimation Program, Windows Version 1.10. *Applied Psychological Measurement, 20*(3), 303–307. doi:10.1177/014662169602000312

Gierłowski, K., & Gierszewski, T. (2004). *Analysis of Network Infrastructure and QoS Requirements for Modern Remote Learning Systems*. Proceedings of the 15th International Conference on Systems Science Wroclaw, September 2004, Oficyna Wydawnicza Politechniki Wrocławskiej, Wroclaw.

Gierłowski, K., & Nowicki, K. (2002). *Simulation of Network Systems in Education*. Proceedings of the XXIVth Autumn International Colloquium Advanced Simulation of Systems(pp. 213-218), Krnov, September 2002, MARQ, Ostrava.

Gierłowski, K., et al. (2003). *Didaktische simulationsmodelle für E-learning in der IK-ausbildung*. Proceedings of 7th Workshop Multimedia für Bildung und Wirtschaft, pp. 77-82, Ilmenau, Septamber 2003, Tech. Univ. Ilmenau, Ilmenau.

Gladney, H. M. (1989). Data Replicas in Distributed Information Services. *ACM TODS*, *14*(1), 75–97. doi:10.1145/62032.62035

Glaser, R. (1962). Psychology and instructional technology. In R. Glaser (Ed.), *Training, research and education*. Pittsburgh: University of Pittsburgh Press.

Global, I. M. S. (2003). *IMS Learning Design Specification*, from http://www.imsglobal.org

Gomez, F. J., Cervera, M., & Martinez, J. (2000). A World Wide Web Based Architecture for the Implementation of a Virtual Laboratory. In *Proceedings of the 26th Euromicro Conference, 2* 56-61. Maastricht, The Netherlands.

Google Documentation. (2007). Retrieved from http://www.google.com/

Graf, S., & Kinshuk (2007). *Considering Cognitive Traits and Learning Styles to Open Web-Based Learning to a Larger Student Community*. Paper presented at the International Conference on Information and Communication Technology and Accessibility.

Greenleaf, R. K. (2003). Motion and emotion in student learning. *Education Digest*, *69*(1), 37–42.

Gressard, C. P., & Loyd, B. H. (1985). Age and staff development experience with computers as factors affecting teacher attributes toward computers. *School Science and Mathematics*, *85*(3), 203–209. doi:10.1111/j.1949-8594.1985.tb09613.x

Gruber, T. R. (1995). Toward principles for the design of ontologies used for knowledge sharing. *International Journal of Human-Computer Studies*, *43*(4-5), 907–928. doi:10.1006/ijhc.1995.1081

Gutl, C., Pivec, M., Trummer, C., Garcia-Barrios, V. M., Modritscher, F., Pripfl, J., et al. (2005). AdeLE (Adaptive e-Learning with EyeTracking): Theoretical Background, System Architecture and Application Scenarios. *European Journal of Open, Distance and E-Learning (EURODL)*.

Guzdial, M., Kolodner, J., Hmelo, C., Narayanan, H., Carlson, D., & Rappin, N. (1996). Computer support for learning through complex problem solving. *Communications of the ACM*, *39*(4), 43–45. doi:10.1145/227210.227600

Hadwin, A. F., Gress, C. L. Z., & Page, J. (2006). *Towards Standards for Reporting Research: A Review of the Literature on Computer-Supported Collaborative Learning*. In Proc. of the Sixth Int. Conf. on Advanced Learning Technologies (ICALT'06).

Hambleton, R. K., & Swaminathan, H. (1985). *Item Response Theory: Principles and Applications*. Boston: Klumer-Nijhoff publishing.

Harasim, L. (1999). A framework for online learning: The virtual-U. *Computer*, *32*(9), 44–49. doi:10.1109/2.789750

Harger, R. O. (1996). Teaching in a computer classroom with a hyperlinked, interactive book. *IEEE Transactions on Education*, *39*, 327–335. doi:10.1109/13.538755

Heinssen, R. K. J., Glass, C. R., & Knight, L. A. (1987). Assessing computer anxiety: development and validation of the Computer Anxiety Rating Scale. *Computers in Human Behavior*, *3*(1), 49–59. doi:10.1016/0747-5632(87)90010-0

Heit, E. (2000). Properties of inductive reasoning. *Psychonomic Bulletin & Review*, *7*(4), 569–592.

Henson, R., & Douglas, J. (2005). Test construction for cognitive diagnosis. *Applied Psychological Measurement*, *29*(4), 262–277. doi:10.1177/0146621604272623

Henze, N. (2006). Personalized E-Learning in the Semantic Web. Extended version of 4. [iJET]. *International Journal of Emerging Technologies in Learning*, *1*(1).

Henze, N., Dolog, P., & Nejdl, W. (2004). Reasoning and Ontologies for Personalized E-Learning. *Journal of Educational Technology & Society*, *7*(4).

Herremans, A. (1995). Studies #02 New Training Technologies. UNESCO Paris and ILO International Training Centre.

Hibernate (2008), available at http://www.hibernate.org.

Hilaga, M., & Shinagawa, Y. Kohmura, & T., Kunii, T (2001): Topology Matching for Fully Automatic Similarity Estimation of 3D Shapes. Proc. ACM SIGGRAPH.

Ho, R. G., & Yen, Y. C. (2005). Design and Evaluation of an XML-Based Platform-Independent Computerized Adaptive TestingSystem. *IEEE Transactions on Education*, *48*(2), 230–237. doi:10.1109/TE.2004.837035

Hoi, K. S. (1990). *Principles of Test Theories*. Hillsdale, NJ: Lawrence Erlbaum Associates.

Honey, P., & Mumford, A. (2000). *The Learning Styles Helper's Guide*. Maidenhead: Peter Honey Publications.

Hoshino, A., & Nakagawa, H. (2007). A Cloze Test Authoring System and Its Automation. *Proceedings of 6th International Conference on Web-Based Learning* (pp. 174- 181).

Hsieh, C. T., Shih, T. K., Chang, W. C., & Ko, W. C. (2003). Feedback and Analysis from Assessment Metadata in E-learning. *Proceedings of the 17th International Conference on Advanced Information Networking and Applications*, Xi'an, China, (pp. 155—158).

Hsu, P. S., Chang, T. J., & Wu, M. H. (2009). A new diagnostic mechanism of instruction: A dynamic, real-time and non-interference quantitative measurement technique for adaptive e-learning. *International Journal of Distance Education Technologies*, *7*(3), 85–96. doi:10.4018/jdet.2009070105

Huang, H. P., & Lu, C. H. (2003). Java-based distance learning environment for electronic instruments. *IEEE Transactions on Education*, *46*(1), 88–94. doi:10.1109/TE.2002.808271

Huang, M. J., Huang, H. S., & Chen, M. Y. (2007). Constructing a personalized e-learning system based on genetic algorithm and case-based reasoning approach. *Expert Systems with Applications*, *33*, 551–564. doi:10.1016/j.eswa.2006.05.019

Hung, J. C., Lin, L. J., Chang, W. C., Shih, T. K., Hsu, H. H., Chang, H. B., et al. (2004). A Cognition Assessment Authoring System for E-Learning. *Proceedings of the 24th Int. Conf. on Distributed Computing Systems Workshops* (pp. 262—267).

Hwang, G. H., Chen, J. M., Hwang, G. J., & Chu, H. C. (2006). A time scale-oriented approach for building medical expert systems. *Expert Systems with Applications*, *31*(2), 299–308. doi:10.1016/j.eswa.2005.09.050

I. M. S. (2001). *IMS Learner Information Packaging Information Model Specification*. Instructional Management Systems.

IA. (2008). *Item Analysis*. Available at http://www.washington.edu/oea/pdfs/resources/item_analysis.pdf.

IEEE Standards Library. (2007). IEEE 802.11-2007, Wireless LAN Medium Access Control (MAC) and Physical Layer (PHY) Specifications for Wireless Local Area Networks (WLANs), June 2007.

IEEE Standards Library. (2007). IEEE 802.15.1-2002, Wireless Medium Access Control (MAC) and Physical Layer (PHY) Specifications for Wireless Personal Area Networks (WPANs), June 2002.

IETF. http://www.ietf.org/rfc/rfc1321.txt

Integrity (2008). Integrity - Item analysis and collusion detection tools. http://integrity.castlerockresearch.com/

Jacobs, B., & Scheibel, A. B. (1993). A quantitative dendritic analysis of Wernicke's area in humans. *The Journal of Comparative Neurology*, *327*(1), 83–96. doi:10.1002/cne.903270107

Jang, H. C., Wang, Y. X., & Chen, C. W. (2006). Implementation of Mobile Multimedia Applications Service Platform on Windows Mobile 2003/2005. *Multimedia and Networking Systems Conference*. Taiwan, I-Shou University.

Jenkins, T. (2001). The Motivation of Students of Programming. *Proc. Integrating Technology into Computer Science Education Conf. (ITiCSE '01)* (pp. 53-56).

Jensen, E. (2000). *Brain-based learning* (Rev. ed.). San Diego, CA: The Brain Store.

Jensen, E. (2005). *Teaching with the brain in mind*. Alexandria, VA: Association for Supervision and Curriculum Development.

Jesukiewicz, P., et al. (2006). *ADL Initiative Status and ADL Co-Lab Network*. Academic ADL CoLab archives, http://www.academiccolab.org/

jFuzzyLogic (2008): Open Source Fuzzy Logic (Java). Available at http://jfuzzylogic.sourceforge.net/html/index.html.

Jiang, G., Lan, J., & Zhuang, X. (2001). Distance Learning Technologies and an Interactive Multimedia Educational System. In *Proceedings of the IEEE International Conference on Advanced Learning Technologies* (pp. 405-408), Madison, WI, USA.

Jin, M. H., Wu, E. H. K., Liao, Y. B., & Liao, H. C. (2003, December). 802.11-based Positioning System for Context Aware Applications. *IEEE GLOBECOM, 2*, 929–933.

Jin, M. H., Wu, E. H. K., Wang, Y. T., & Hsu, C. H. (2004). An 802.11-based Positioning System for Indoor Applications. *ACTA Press Proceeding, 422.*

Jin, S. D., Bestavros, A., & Iyengar, A. (2002). Accelerating Internet Streaming Media Delivery using Network-Aware Partial Caching. In Proceedings of ICDCS conference.

Johansen, D., & Lauvset, K. (2002). An Extensible Software Architecture for Mobile Components. In *Proceedings of the 9th Annual IEEE International Conference and Workshop on the Engineering of Computer-based Systems* (pp. 231-237), Lund, Sweden.

Johnson, D. W., & Johnson, R. T. (1996). Cooperation and the Use of Technology. In Jonassen, D. H. (Ed.), *Handbook of Research for Educational Communications and Technology*. New York: Simon and Schuster.

Joint US/EU ad hoc Agent Markup Language Committee (2004), *OWL-S 1.1 Release*, from http://www.daml.org/services/owl-s/1.1/

Jonassen, D. H., & Wang, S. (1993). Acquiring structural knowledge from semantically structured hypertext. *Journal of Computer-Based Instruction, 20*(1), 1–8.

Jonassen, D. H., & Grabowski, B. L. (1993). *Handbook of individual differences: Learning and instruction*. Hillsdale, New Jersey: Lawrence Erlbaum Associates.

Jones, E. (1979). Business education in public and private schools. In Wakin, B. B., & Petitjean, C. F. (Eds.), *Alternative learning styles in business education* (pp. 1–8). Reston, VA: National Business Education Association.

Jorgensen, C. E. (1979). Teaching and learning by means of achievement levels or competencies. In Wakin, B. B., & Petitjean, C. F. (Eds.), *Alternative learning styles in business education* (pp. 196–206). Reston, VA: National Business Education Association.

Jorgenson, O. (2003). Brain scam? Why educator should be careful about embracing "brain research". *The Educational Forum, 67*(4), 364–369. doi:10.1080/00131720308984585

Jou, M. (2005). Development of an e-Learning System for Teaching Machining Technology. In *Proceedings of the 2005 International Conference on Active Media Technology* (pp. 347-352), Takamatsu, Japan.

Junge, T. F., & Schmid, C. (2000). Web-based remote experimentation using a laboratory-scale optical tracker. *Proceedings of the 2000 American Control Conference (ACC)* (vol.4, pp. 2951-2954). Chicago, Illinois: American Automatic Control Council.

Kalyuga, S. (2007). Expertise reversal effect and its implications for learner-tailored instruction. *Educational Psychology Review, 19*, 509–539. doi:10.1007/s10648-007-9054-3

Kalyuga, S., Ayres, P., Chandler, P., & Sweller, J. (2003). The expertise reversal effect. *Educational Psychology, 38*, 23–31. doi:10.1207/S15326985EP3801_4

Kalyuga, S., Chandler, P., & Sweller, J. (2000). Incorporating learning experience into the design of multimedia instruction. *Journal of Educational Psychology, 92*(1), 126–136. doi:10.1037/0022-0663.92.1.126

Kalyuga, S., Renkl, A., & Paas, F. (2010). Facilitating flexible problem solving: A cognitive load perspective. *Educational Psychology Review, 22*, 175–186. doi:10.1007/s10648-010-9132-9

Kalyuga, S., & Sweller, J. (2004). Measuring knowledge to optimize cognitive load factors during instruction. *Journal of Educational Psychology, 96*, 558–568. doi:10.1037/0022-0663.96.3.558

Kalyuga, S., & Sweller, J. (2005). Rapid dynamic assessment of expertise to improve the efficiency of adaptive e-learning. *Educational Technology Research and Development, 53*(3), 83–93. doi:10.1007/BF02504800

Kanev, K. (2008). Tangible Interfaces for Interactive Multimedia Presentations. *Int. Journal of Mobile Information Systems: Special Issue on Information Assurance and Advanced Human-Computer Interfaces*, 3(4), 183–193.

Kanev, K., Barneva, R., Brimkov, V., & Kaneva, D. (2009-2010). Interactive Printouts Integrating Multilingual Multimedia and Sign Language Electronic Resources. *Journal of Educational Technology Systems*, 2(38), 123–143. doi:10.2190/ET.38.2.e

Kanev, K., Gnatyuk, P., & Gnatyuk, V. (in press). Laser marking in digital encoding of surfaces. *Advanced Materials Research*.

Kanev, K., & Kimura, S. (2005). *Digital Information Carrier. Patent Registration No 3635374*. Japan Patent Office.

Kanev, K., & Kimura, S. (2006). Direct Point-and-Click Functionality for Printed Materials. *The Journal of Three Dimensional Images*, 20(2), 51–59.

Kanev, K., & Orr, T. (2006). Enhancing Paper Documents with Direct Access to Multimedia for an Intelligent Support of Reading. In *Proc. of the IEEE Conference on the Convergence of Technology and Professional Communication (IPCC'06)*, pp.84-91.

Kanev, K., Morishima, Y., & Watanabe, K. (2008). Surface Code Readers for Image Based Human-Computer Interfaces. In *Proceedings of the Eleventh Int. Conf. on Humans and Computers HC'08*, pp. 57-62.

Kangasharju, J., Roberts, J., & Ross, K. W. (2002, March). Object replication strategies in content distribution networks. *Computer Communications*, 25(5), 376–378. doi:10.1016/S0140-3664(01)00409-1

Kao, C. L. (2006). *The Study of Using Mobile Learning Device to Assist Elementary School Students to Study Aquatics at Campus' Eco-education Garden*. Unpublished Master's Thesis, Taipei Municipal University of Education.

Kaplan, L. S. (1998). Using the 4MAT instructional model for effective leadership. *NASSP Bulletin*, 82(599), 83–92. doi:10.1177/019263659808259912

Karampiperis, P., Lin, T., & Sampson, D. G., & Kinshuk. (2006). Adaptive cognitive-based selection of learning objects. *Innovations in Education and Teaching International*, 43(2), 121–135. doi:10.1080/14703290600650392

Karampiperis, P., & Sampson, D. (2005). Adaptive learning resources sequencing in educational hypermedia systems. *Educational Technology and Society*, 8(4), 128–147.

Karni, A., Meyer, G., Jezzard, P., Adams, M. M., Turner, R., & Ungerleider, L. G. (1995). Functional MRI evidence for adult motor cortex plasticity during motor skill learning. *Nature*, 377(14), 155–158.

Karsenti, T. (1999). Student Motivation and Distance Education on the Web: Love at First Sight? *Proc. Fifth Int'l Conf. Web-Based Learning* (pp. 119-134).

Kastenmüller, G., Kriegel, H., & Seidl, T. (1998). Similarity Search in 3D Protein Databases. Proc. German Conf. on Bioinformatics.

Kavcic, A. (2000). The Role of User Models in Adaptive Hypermedia Systems. *Proc. Tenth Mediterranean Electrotechnical Conf*erence, Lemesos, Cyprus

Kazanidis, I., & Satratzemi, M. (2007). Adaptivity in a SCORM compliant Adaptive Educational Hypermedia System. *Proc. Sixth International Conference Web-based Learning (ICWL'2007), LNCS 4823*, Springer.

Kazhdan, M., Funkhouser, T., & Rusinkiewicz, S. (2003). Rotation Invariant Spherical Harmonic Representation of 3D Shape Descriptors. Proc. Symp. on Geometry Processing.

Kazhdan, M., Funkhouser, T., & Rusinkiewicz, S. (2004). Shape Matching and Anisotropy. Proc. ACM SIGGRAPH.

Kazuo, Y. (2007). *The preparation of the S-P Table*. Hhttp://www.kasei.ac.jp/cs/Yamanoi/Program/sphyo/index-e.htmlH [Last access July 11th, 2007]

Keegan, D. (2000). From d-Learning, to e-Learning, to m-Learning. *40th anniversary celebrations of Shanghai TV University*. Retrieved July 28, 2006 from http://www.nettskolen.com/forskning/From%20d%20learning.doc.

Keim, D. (1999). Efficient Geometry-based Similarity Search of 3D Spatial Databases. Proc. SIGMOD, 419–430.

Kelly, C. (1990). Using 4MAT in law school. *Educational Leadership*, 48(2), 40–41.

Kelly, T. L. (1939). The Selection of Upper and Lower Groups for the Validation of Test Items. *Journal of Educational Psychology*, 30, 17–24. doi:10.1037/h0057123

Khuller, S., Kim, Y. A., & Wan, Y. C. (2003). Algorithms for Data Migration with Cloning. In Proceedings of PODS conference.

Kiefer, J. C. (1987). *Introduction to statistical inference.* Springer-Verlag.

Kienzle, J., & Romanovsky, A. (2002). A Framework Based on Design Patterns for Providing Persistence in Object-oriented Programming Languages. *IEE Software Engineering Journal, 149*, 77–85. doi:10.1049/ip-sen:20020465

Kindley, R. (2002). The Power of Simulation-based e-Learning. *The e-Learning Developers' Journal*, https://www.elearningguild.com/showfile.cfm?id=95.

Kinshuk, & Lin, T. (2004). Cognitive profiling towards formal adaptive technologies in web-based learning communities. *International Journal of Web Based Communities, 1*(1), 103-108.

Kitchens, A. N., Barber, W. D., & Barber, D. B. (1991). Left brain/right brain theory: Implications for developmental math instruction. *Review of Research in Education, 8*(3), 3–6.

Klemm, R. P. (1999). WebCompanion: A Friendly Client-Side Web Prefetching Agent. *IEEE TKDE, 11*(4), 577–594.

Klyne, G., Reynolds, F., Woodrow, C., Ohto, H., Hjelm, J., Butler, M. H., & Tran, L. (2003). Composite *Capability/Preference Profiles (CC/PP): Structure and Vocabularies.* http://www.w3.org/TR/2003/WD-CCPP-struct-vocab-20030325/.

Knight, C., Gašević, D., & Richards, G. (2006). An Ontology-Based Framework for Bridging Learning Design and Learning Content. *Journal of Educational Technology & Society, 9*(1), 23–37.

Kobayashi, H., Yu, S. Z., & Mark, B. L. (2000). An integrated mobility and traffic model for resource allocation in wireless networks. In Proceedings of the Third ACM International Workshop on Wireless Mobile Multimedia (pp. 39-47).

Kogo, C. (2003). Daigaku ni Okeru Web Base Kobetsu-ka Kyojyu Shisutemu [Conducting Classes through Web-based Personalized System of Instruction (PSI) in Universities] [in Japanese]. *Annual Journal of Educational Psychology, 42*, 182–192.

Kolb, D. A. (1984). *Experimental learning: Experience as the source of learning and development.* Jersey: Prentice Hall.

Kolb, D. A. (1999). *Learning Style Inventory - version 3: Technical Specifications*: TRG Hay/McBer, Training Resources Group.

Kolman, B., Busby, R. C., & Ross, S. (1996). *Discrete Mathematical Structures* (p. 261). Upper Saddle River, NJ: Prentice Hall.

Komiya, T., Ohsida, H., & Takizawa, M. (2002). Mobile Agent Model for Distributed Objects Systems. In *Proceedings of the 5th IEEE International Symposium on Object-Oriented Real-Time Distributed Computing* (pp. 62-69), Washington, DC, USA.

Kossmann, D., Franklin, M. J., & Drasch, G. (2000). Cache Investment: Integrating Query Optimization and Distributed Data Placement. *ACM TODS, 25*(4), 517–558. doi:10.1145/377674.377677

Krumm, J., & Platt, J. C. (2003). Minimizing calibration effort for an indoor 802.11 device location measurement system. Tech. Rep. No. Retrieved Nov. 7, 2007 from MSR-TR-2003-82, Microsoft, ftp://ftp.research.microsoft.com/pub/tr/tr-2003-82.pdf.

Labaw, P. J. (1980). *Advanced questionnaire design.* Cambridge, MA: Abt Books.

Lantolf, J. P. (2000). Introducing sociocultural theory. In J. P. Lantolf (Ed.), *Sociocultural theory and second language learning.* Oxford: Oxford University Press.

Laouris, Y., & Eteokleous, N. (2005). We need an educationally relevant definition of mobile learning. *mLearn, 2005.* Retrieved August 20, 2006 from http://www.mlearn.org.za/CD/papers/Laouris%20&%20Eteokleous.pdf.

Lee, P. M., & Sullivan, W. G. (1996). Developing and implementing interactive multimedia in education. *IEEE Transactions on Education, 39*(3), 430–435. doi:10.1109/13.538769

Lefrancois, G. R. (1999). *Psychology for teaching* (10th ed.). Belmont, CA: Wadsworth/Thomson Learning.

Leighton, J. P., Gierl, M. J., & Hunka, S. M. (2004). The attribute hierarchy method for cognitive assessment: A variation on Tatsuoka's Rule Space approach. *Journal of Educational Measurement, 41*(3), 205–237. doi:10.1111/j.1745-3984.2004.tb01163.x

Leighton, J. P., & Gierl, M. J. (2007a). Why cognitive diagnostic assessment? In Leighton, J. P., & Gierl, M. J. (Eds.), *Cognitive Diagnostic Assessment for Education: Theory and Applications* (pp. 3–18). Boston, MA: Cambridge University Press. doi:10.1017/CBO9780511611186.001

Lemaire, P. (1999). *Psychologie Cognitive*. Bruxelles: De Boeck Universite.

Lertap (2008). Lertap 5! http://www.lertap.curtin.edu.au/

Lew, M., Sebe, N., Djeraba, C., & Jain, R. (2006). Content-based Multimedia Information Retrieval: State-of-the-art and Challenges. *ACM Trans. on Multimedia Computing, Communication, and Applications, 2*(1), 1–19. doi:10.1145/1126004.1126005

Li, F., & Lau, R. (2004). A Progressive Content Distribution Framework in Supporting Web-Based Learning. Proc. ICWL, 75–82.

Liaw, S. S., Huang, H. M., & Chen, G. D. (2007). Surveying instructor and learner attitudes toward e-learning. *Computers & Education, 49*(4), 1066–1080. doi:10.1016/j.compedu.2006.01.001

Lim, E. J., Park, S. H., Hong, H. O., & Chung, K. D. (2001). A Proxy Caching Scheme for Continuous Media Streams on the Internet. In Proceedings of ICIN conference.

Lin, H., & Ding, S. (2007). An Exploration and Realization of Computerized Adaptive Testing with Cognitive Diagnosis. *Acta Psychologica Sinica, 39*(4), 747–753.

Lin, N. H., Chang, W. C., Shih, T. K., & Keh, H. C. (2005). Courseware Development Using Influence Diagram Supporting e-Learning Specification. *Journal of Information Science and Engineering, 21*(5), 985–1005.

Lin, T. (2003). *Cognitive Trait Model for Persistent and Fine-Tuned Student Modelling in Adaptive Virtual Learning Environments.* Massey University, Palmerston North, New Zealand.

Lindquist, T. M. (1995). Traditional versus contemporary goals and methods in accounting education: Bridging the gap with cooperative learning. *Journal of Education for Business, 70*(5), 278–284. doi:10.1080/08832323.1995.10117764

Ling, F. T. (2004). *A Study on Mobile Learning Device Applied to the Nature Science Class in Elementary School.* Unpublished Master's Thesis. Taipei Municipal University of Education.

Loo, R. (2002). A meta-analytic examination of Kolb's learning style preferences among business majors. *Journal of Education for Business, 77*(5), 252–256. doi:10.1080/08832320209599673

Loukoupoulos, T., & Ahmad, I. (2000). Static and Adaptive Data Replication Algorithms for Fast Information Access in Large Distributed Systems. In Proceedings of ICDCS conference.

Magnuson, J. (2002). Middle school family and consumer sciences: Brain-based education from theory to practice. *Journal of Family and Consumer Sciences, 94*(1), 45–47.

Mahmood, M. A., & Swanberg, D. L. (2001). Factors affecting information technology usage: a meta-analysis of the empirical literature. *Journal of Organizational Computing, 11*, 107–130. doi:10.1207/S15327744JOCE1102_02

Mamdani, E. H., & Assilian, S. (1999). An experiment in Linguistic Synthesis with a Fuzzy Logic Controller. *International Journal of Human-Computer Studies, 51*(2), 135–147. doi:10.1006/ijhc.1973.0303

Manasse, M. S., McGeoch, L. A., & Sleator, D. D. (1990). Competitive Algorithms for Server Problems. *Journal of Algorithms, 11*(2), 208–230. doi:10.1016/0196-6774(90)90003-W

Marcoulides, G. A. (1988). The relationship between computer anxiety and computer achievement. *Journal of Educational Computing Research, 4*(2), 151–158. doi:10.2190/J5N4-24HK-567V-AT6E

Marcy, W. M., & Hagler, M. O. (1996). Implementation issues in SIMPLE learning environments. *IEEE Transactions on Education, 39*(3), 423–429. doi:10.1109/13.538768

Martin, E., & Paredes, P. (2004). Using Learning Styles for Dynamic Group Formation in Adaptive Collaborative Hypermedia Systems. Paper presented at *AHCW'04 held in conjunction with the International Conference on Web Engineering (ICWE'04)*.

Massey (2007). The Relationship Between the Popularity of Questions and Their Difficulty Level in Examinations Which Allow a Choice of Question. *Occasional Publication of The Test Dev. and Res. Unit*, Cambridge.

MATLAB. (n.d.). Retrieved from http://www.mathworks.com/

Matsuda, N., Kanev, K., Hirashima, T., & Taki, H. (2009). Ontology-based Annotations for Test Interpretation and Scoring. In *Proceedings of the 12th Int. Conf. on Humans and Computers HC'09*, pp.118-122.

Matsuoka, I. (2001). *Dejitaru Kyanpasu* [Digital Campus]. Tokyo: Toyo Keizai Inc.(in Japanese)

Mayer, R. E. (1996). Learners as information processor: Legacies and limitations of educational psychology's second metaphor. *Educational Psychologist*, *31*(4), 151–161. doi:10.1207/s15326985ep3103&4_1

McCarthy, B. (1985). What 4MAT training teachers us about staff development. *Educational Leadership*, *42*, 61–68.

McCarthy, B. (2000). *About teaching: 4MAT in the classroom*. Chicago: About Learning.

McGlohen, M. K. (2004). *The application of cognitive diagnosis and computerized adaptive testing to a large-scale assessment*. Unpublished doctoral thesis, University of Texas at Austin.

McGuinness, D. L., & Harmelen, F. v. (2004). *OWL Web Ontology Language Overview*. Retrieved from http://www.w3.org/TR/2004/REC-owl-features-20040210/.

McInerney, V., McInerney, D. M., & Marsh, H. W. (1997). Effects of metacognitive strategy training with a cooperative group learning within a cooperative group learning context on computer achievement and anxiety: An aptitude-treatment interaction study. *Journal of Educational Psychology*, *89*(4), 686–695. doi:10.1037/0022-0663.89.4.686

McMillan, J. H. (1996). *Educational research: Fundamentals for the consumer* (2nd ed.). New York: HarperCollins.

MEAP. (2007). State of Michigan – Department of Education. *Design and Validity of the MEAP Test*. Available at http://www.michigan.gov/mde/0,1607,7-140-22709_31168-94522--,00.html.

Meier, A., Spada, H., & Rummel, N. (2007). A Rating Scheme for Assessing the Quality of Computer-supported Collaboration Processes. *International Journal of Computer-Supported Collaborative Learning*, *2*(1), 63–86. doi:10.1007/s11412-006-9005-x

Miettinen, M., Kurhila, J., & Tirri, H. (2005). On the Prospects of Intelligent Collaborative E-learning Systems. In *Proc. of the 12th International Conference on Artificial Intelligence in Education (AIED'05)*, pp. 483-490.

Mika, P., Oberle, D., Gangemi, A., & Sabou, M. (2004). Foundations for Service Ontologies: Aligning OWL-S to DOLCE, In proceedings of the *13th International Conference on World Wide Web*.

Miller, G. A. (1956). The magic number seven, plus or minus two: Some limits on our capacity for processing information. *Psychological Review*, *63*(2), 81–96. doi:10.1037/h0043158

Milosevic, D. (2006). Designing Lesson Content in Adaptive Learning Environments. *International Journal of Emerging Technologies in Learning*, *1*(2).

Milosevic, D., Brkovic, M., Debevc, M., & Krneta, R. (2007). Adaptive Learning by Using SCOs Metadata. *Interdisciplinary Journal of Knowledge and Learning Objects*, *3*, 163–174.

Mitkov, R., & Ha, L. A. (2003). Computer-Aided Generation of Multiple-Choice Tests. *Proceedings of the HLT-NAACL 03 workshop on Building educational applications using natural language processing - Volume 2* (pp. 17-22).

Mobile and wireless Internet (2005). *Foreseeing Innovative New Digiservices*. Retrieved August 20, 2006 from http://www.find.org.tw/eng/news.asp?msgid=222&subjectid=10&pos=1.

Mobile phone subscribers Q1 (2006). *Foreseeing Innovative New Digiservices*. Retrieved Aug. 20, 2006 from http://www.find.org.tw/eng/news.asp?msgid=249&subjectid=13&pos=1.

Momoh, J., Srinivasan, D., Tomsovic, K., & Baer, D. (2000). Expert Systems Applications. In Tomsovic, K., & Chov, M. Y. (Eds.), *Tutorial on Fuzzy Logic Applications in Power Systems*.

Monova–Zheleva, M. (2005). Adaptive Learning in Web-based Educational Environments. *Journal Cybernetics and Information Technologies*, 5(1).

Montgomery, C. (2002). Role of Dynamic Group Therapy in Psychiatry. *Advances in Psychiatric Treatment*, 8, 34–41. doi:10.1192/apt.8.1.34

Moodle (2008). Available at http://moodle.org.

Moodle Course Management System Documentation. (2010). Retrieved from http://moodle.org/

Moodle. (2007). http://moodle.org/.

Moore, A., Brailsford, T. J., & Stewart, C. D. (2001). *Personally tailored teaching in WHURLE using conditional transclusion*. Paper presented at the Proceedings of the ACM Conference on Hypertext.

Morales, R. (2003). The VIBORA project. G. Richards, eds, *Proc. World Conf. E-Learning in Corporate, Government, Healthcare, and Higher Education* (pp. 2341-2344).

Motta, E. (1998). An Overview of the OCML Modelling Language, In proceedings of the *8th Workshop on Methods and Languages*.

Mousavi, S. Y., Low, R., & Sweller, J. (1995). Reducing cognitive load by mixing auditory and visual presentation modes. *Journal of Educational Psychology*, 87(2), 319–334. doi:10.1037/0022-0663.87.2.319

Murray, T., Shen, T., Piemonte, J., Condit, C., & Tibedau, J. (2000). Adaptivity for conceptual and narrative flow in hyperbooks: The Metalink system. *Adaptive Hypermedia and Adaptive Web-based system. Lecture Notes in Computer Science*, 1892, 155–166. doi:10.1007/3-540-44595-1_15

Muzak, G., Cavrak, I., & Zagar, M. (2000). The Virtual Laboratory Project. In *Proceedings of the 22nd Internal Conference on Information Technology Interfaces* (pp. 241-246), Zagreb, Croatia.

Naismith, L., Lonsdale, P., Vavoula, G., & Sharples, M. (2005). Literature Review in Mobile Technologies and Learning. *Futurelab Series*, Report 11. Retrieved Aug. 20, 2006 from http://www.futurelab.org.uk/download/pdfs/research/lit_reviews/futurelab_review_11.pdf

Najjar, J., Klerkx, J., Vuorikari, R., & Duval, E. (2005). Finding appropriate learning objects: An empirical evaluation, *Lecture Notes in Computer Science (including subseries Lecture Notes in Artificial Intelligence and Lecture Notes in Bioinformatics)* (Vol. 3652 LNCS, pp. 323-335).

Nam, C. S., & Smith-Jackson, T. L. (2007). Web-Based Learning Environment: A Theory-Based Design Process for Development and Evaluation. *Journal of Information Technology Education*, 6, 23–43.

Nash, S. S. (2005). Learning Objects, Learning Object Repositories, and Learning Theory: Preliminary Best Practices for Online Courses. *Interdisciplinary Journal of Knowledge and Learning Objects*, 1, 217–228.

Nasseh, B. (1997). *A Brief History of Distance Education*. Retrieved August 20, 2006 from http://www.seniornet.org/edu/art/history.html.

Nilsson, N. J. (1998). *Artificial Intelligence: A New Synthesis*. San Francisco, CA: Morgan Kaufmann.

Novotni, M., & Klein, R. (2003). 3D Zernike Descriptors for Content Based Shape Retrieval. Proc. ACM Symp. on Solid Modeling and Applications.

Nowicki, K., & Gierłowski, K. (2004). *Implementation of Didactic Simulation Models in Open Source and SCORM Compliant LMS Systems*. Proceedings of XXVIth International Autumn Colloquium, Advanced Simulation of Systems, pp. 161-166, Sv Hostyn, September 2004, MARQ, Ostrava

Nunnally, J. C., & Bernstein, I. H. (1994). *Psychometric theory* (3rd ed.). New York: McGraw-Hill.

Nunnelley, J. C., Whaley, J., Mull, R., & Hott, G. (2003). Brain compatible secondary schools: The visionary principal's role. *NASSP Bulletin*, 87(637), 48–59. doi:10.1177/019263650308763705

O'Neil, J. (1990). Making sense of style. *Educational Leadership*, 48(2), 4–9.

Oakley, B. (1996). A virtual classroom approach to teaching circuit analysis. *IEEE Transactions on Education, 39,* 287–296. doi:10.1109/13.538749

Oestereich, B. (2002). *Developing Software with UML: Object-Oriented Analysis and Design in Practice.* Addison-Wesley.

Ogata, H., & Yano, Y. (1998). Knowledge Awareness: Bridging Learners in a Collaborative Learning Environment. *Int. Journal of Educational Telecommunications, 2/3*(4), 219–236.

Ogata, H., & Yano, Y. (2003). How Ubiquitous Computing can Support Language Learning. *Proceedings of the First International Conference on Knowledge Economy and Development of Science and Technology (KEST 2003),* (pp. 1-6). Honjo City, Japan.

Ohbuchi, R., Nakazawa, M., & Takei, T. (2003). Retrieving 3D Shapes Based On Their Appearance. Proc. ACM SIGMM Workshop on Multimedia Information Retrieval.

Okada, A., Tarumi, H., & Kambayashi, Y. (2000). Real-Time Quiz Functions for Dynamic Group Guidance in Distance Learning Systems. In *Proc. of the First International Conference on Web Information Systems Engineering (WISE'00),* pp.188-195.

Oliveira, J. M. P. d. (2002). *Adaptation Architecture for Adaptive Educational Hypermedia Systems.* Paper presented at the World Conference on E-Learning in Corporate, Government, Healthcare, and Higher Education 2002.

Olly, G., Scharff, C., & Wildenberg, A. (2008). Teaching software quality assurance by encouraging student contributions to an open source web-based system for the assessment of programming assignments. *Proceedings of the 13th annual conference on Innovation and technology in computer science education* (pp. 214-218).

O'Malley, C., et al. (2003). Guidelines for Teaching/Learning/Tutoring in a Mobile Environment. Retrieved July 28, 2006 from http://www.mobilearn.org/download/results/guidelines.pdf.

Oppenheim, A. N. (1992). *Questionnaire design, interviewing and attitude measurement.* London: Continuum.

Osada, R., Funkhouser, T., Chazelle, B., & Dobkin, D. (2001). Matching 3D Models with Shape Distributions. Proc. Int'l Conf. on Shape Modeling and Applications, 154–166.

Paas, F., & van Merriënboer, J. J. G. (1993). The efficiency of instructional conditions: an approach to combine mental effort and performance measure. *Human Factors, 35,* 737–743.

Paas, F., & van Merriënboer, J. J. G. (1994). Instructional control of cognitive load in the training of complex cognitive tasks. *Educational Psychology Review, 6,* 51–71. doi:10.1007/BF02213420

Paknikar, S., Kankanhalli, M., Ramakrishnan, K. R., Srinivasan, S. H., & Ngoh, L. H. (2000). A Caching and Streaming Framework for Multimedia. In Proceedings of ACM MM conference.

Pantic, M., Zwitserloot, R., & Grootjans, R. J. (2005). Teaching Introductory Artificial Intelligence Using a Simple Agent Framework. *IEEE Transactions on Education, 48*(3), 382–390. doi:10.1109/TE.2004.842906

Papadimitriou, C. H. (1994). *Computational complexity.* Addison-Wesley.

Papanikolaou, K. A., Mabbott, A., Bull, S., & Grigoriadou, M. (2006). Designing learner-controlled educational interactions based on learning/cognitive style and learner behaviour. *Interacting with Computers, 18*(3), 356–384. doi:10.1016/j.intcom.2005.11.003

Perdikeas, M. K., Chatzipapadopoulos, F. G., Venieris, I. S., & Marino, G. (1999). Mobile Agent Standards and Available Platforms. *Computer Networks Journal, 31*(19), 1999–2016. doi:10.1016/S1389-1286(99)00076-6

Poindexter, S. E., & Heck, B. S. (1999). Using the web in your courses: What can you do? What should you do? *IEEE Control Systems Magazine, 19*(1), 83–92. doi:10.1109/37.745773

Prensky, M. (2001). Digital natives, digital immigrants. *On the Horizon, 9*(5), 1–2. Retrieved Aug. 20, 2006 from http://www.marcprensky.com/writing/Prensky%20-%20Digital%20Natives,%20Digital%20Immigrants%20-%20Part1.pdf

Prentzas, D., & Hatziligeroudis, I. (2001). Adaptive Educational Hypermedia: Principles and Services. *Proc. First Panhellenic Conf. Open and Distance Learning*, Greece. (in Greek).

Prentzas, D., Hatziligeroudis, I., Koutsogiannis, K., & Rigou, M. (2001). The architecture of a Web-based Intelligent Tutoring System for the Instruction of New Informatic's Technologies. *Proc. First Panhellenic Conf. Open and Distance Learning*. Patra, Greece (in Greek).

Pressley, M., & McCormick, C. B. (1995). *Advanced Educational Psychology for Educators, Researchers, and Policymakers*. New York: Harper Collins.

Protégé. (2007). http://protege.stanford.edu/.

QTI Public Draft Specification Version 2. (2008). Retrieved from http://www.imsproject.org/question/

Questionmark (2008). Available at http://www.questionmark.com.

Quinn, C. (2000). mLearning: Mobile, Wireless, In-Your-Pocket Learning. *LiNE Zine*. Retrieved Aug. 20, 2006 from http://www.linezine.com/2.1/features/cqmmwiyp.htm.

RacerPro. (2007). http://www.racer-systems.com/.

Ramakrishnan, V., Zhuang, Y., Hu, S. Y., Chen, J. P., Ko, C. C., Chen, B. M., et al. (2000). Development of a web-based control experiment for a coupled tank apparatus. *Proceedings of the 2000 American Control Conference (ACC)* (vol. 6, pp. 4409-4413). Chicago, Illinois: American Automatic Control Council.

Ramanathan, R. (2001). A note on the use of the analytic hierarchy process for environmental impact assessment. *Journal of Environmental Management*, *63*, 27–35. doi:10.1006/jema.2001.0455

Randi, P. (2004). Web-Assisted Courses for Business Education: An Examination of Two Sections of Principles of Marketing. *Journal of Marketing Education*, *26*, 161–173. doi:10.1177/0273475304265635

RASCAL. (2008). RASCAL - Rasch Analysis Program. http://www.assess.com/xcart/product.php?productid=253&cat=29&page=1

Ravenscroft, S. P., Buckless, F. A., McCombs, G. B., & Zuckerman, G. J. (1995). Incentives in student team learning: An experiment in cooperative group learning. *Issues in Accounting Education*, *10*(1), 97–109.

Rehak, D., & Mason, R. (2003). Keeping the learning in learning objects. In A. Littlejohn (Ed.), *Reusing Educational Resources for Networked Learning*. London: Kogan.

Rey-Lopez, M., Fernadez-Vilas, A., Diaz-Redondo, R. P., Pazos-Arias, J. J., & Bermejo-Munoz, J. (2006). Extending SCORM to create adaptive courses. *Lecture Notes in Computer Science (including subseries Lecture Notes in Artificial Intelligence and Lecture Notes in Bioinformatics)*, *4227 LNCS*, 679-684.

Rezaei, A. R., & Katz, L. (2004). Evaluation of the reliability and validity of the cognitive styles analysis. *Personality and Individual Differences*, *36*(6), 1317–1327. doi:10.1016/S0191-8869(03)00219-8

Riding, R., & Cheema, I. (1991). Cognitive styles - An overview and integration. *Educational Psychology*, *11*(3-4), 193–215. doi:10.1080/0144341910110301

Riding, R., & Rayner, S. (1998). *Cognitive Styles and Learning Strategies*. London: David Fulton Publishers.

Ringwood, J. V., & Galvin, G. (2002). Computer-aided learning in artificial neural networks. *IEEE Transactions on Education*, *45*(4), 380–387. doi:10.1109/TE.2002.804401

Rogers, Y., Price, S., Randell, C., Fraser, D. S., Weal, M., & Fitzpatrick, G. (2005). Interaction design and children: Ubi-learning Integrates Indoor and Outdoor Experiences. *Communications of the ACM*, *48*(1), 55–59. doi:10.1145/1039539.1039570

Roiger, R. J., & Geatz, M. W. (2007). *Introduzione al Data Mining*. McGraw-Hill. (in Italian)

Rosenblatt, M. (1974). Random processes. Springer-Verlag. RTSTP. http://www.rtsp.org/

Rosenzweig, M. R., Love, W., & Bennett, E. L. (1968). Effects of a few hours a day of enriched experience on brain chemistry and brain weights. *Physiology & Behavior*, *3*, 819–825. doi:10.1016/0031-9384(68)90161-3

Rowe, J., Razdan, A., Collins, D., & Panchanathan, S. (2001). A 3D Digital Library System: Capture, Analysis, Query, and Display. Proc. Int'l Conf. on Digital Libraries.

Rubner, Y., Tomasi, C., & Guibas, L. (2000). The Earth Mover's Distance as a Metric for Image Retrieval. *International Journal of Computer Vision, 40*(2), 99–121. doi:10.1023/A:1026543900054

Rumetshofer, H., & Wo, W. (2003). XML-based adaptation framework for psychological-driven E-learning systems. *Educational Technology and Society, 6*(4), 18–29.

Saaty, T. L. (1977). A scaling method for priorities in hierarchical structures. *Journal of Mathematical Psychology, 15*(3), 234–281. doi:10.1016/0022-2496(77)90033-5

Saaty, T. L. (1980). *The Analytic Hierarchy Process: Planning Setting Priorities, Resource Allocation* (p. 20). New York, NY: McGraw-Hill Press.

Sadler-Smith, E. (2001). The relationship between learning style and cognitive style. *Personality and Individual Differences, 30*(4), 609–616. doi:10.1016/S0191-8869(00)00059-3

Sakai Project. (2007). http://www.sakaiproject.org/.

Sakai: Collaboration and Learning Environment for Education Documentation. (2010). Retrieved from http://sakaiproject.org/

Salden, R. J. C. M., Paas, F., Broers, N. J., & van Merriënboer, J. J. G. (2004). Mental effort and performance as determinants for the dynamic selection of learning tasks in air traffic control training. *Instructional Science, 32*(1-2), 153–172. doi:10.1023/B:TRUC.0000021814.03996.ff

Salden, R. J. C. M., Paas, F., & van Merriënboer, J. J. G. (2006). A comparison of approaches to learning task selection in the training of complex cognitive skills. *Computers in Human Behavior, 22*(3), 321–333. doi:10.1016/j.chb.2004.06.003

Sampson, D., Karagiannidis, C., & Cardinali, F. (2002). An architecture for web-based e-learning promoting re-usable adaptive educational e-content. *Educational Technology and Society, 5*(4), 27–37.

Sanders, B. (2001). *The supply of accounting graduates and the demand for public accounting recruits-2001.* New York: American Institute of Certified Public Accountants.

Sato, T. (1980). The S-P Chart and the Caution Index. [&C Systems Research Laboratories, Nippon Electric Co., Ltd., Tokyo, Japan.]. *NEC Educational Information Bulletin, 80-1,* C.

Sato, T. (1975). The Construction and Interpretation of the S-P Table – Instructional Analysis and Learning Diagnosis. Tokyo, Japan: Meiji Tosho.

Sato, T. (1985). Introduction to S-P Curve Theory Analysis and Evaluation. Tokyo, Japan: Meiji Tosho. (in Japanese).

Scardamalia, M., Bereiter, C., McLean, R. S., Swallow, J., & Woodruff, E. (1989). Computer Supported Intentional Learning Environments. *Journal of Educational Computing Research, 5*(1), 51–68.

Schelfthout, K., Coninx, T., Helleboogh, A., Holvoet, T., Steegmans, E., & Weyns, D. (2002). Agent Implementation Patterns. In *Proceedings of the OOPSLA 2002 Workshop on Agent-Oriented Methodologies* (pp. 119-130), Seattle, WA, USA.

Schiper, A. (2006). Dynamic Group Communication. *Distributed Computing, 18*(6), 359–374. doi:10.1007/s00446-005-0129-4

Schmidt, A. (2005). *Bridging the Gap Between E-Learning and Knowledge Management with Context-Aware Corporate Learning (Extended Version), In proceedings of Professional Knowledge Management (WM 2005).* Springer.

Schmidt, A., & Winterhalter, C. (2004). User Context Aware Delivery of E-Learning Material: Approach and Architecture [JUCS]. *Journal of Universal Computer Science, 10*(1).

SCORM. 2004 3rd Edition Documentation. (2007). Advanced Distributed Learning Initiative. Retrieved from http://www.adlnet.gov/

Scriven, M. (1967). The methodology of evaluation. In R. Tyler (Ed.), *Perspectives of Curriculum Evaluation* (pp. 39–83). AERA Monograph Series on Curriculum Evaluation (no. 1). Skokie, IL: Rand McNally.

Sears, A. L., & Watkins, S. E. (1996). A multimedia manual on the world wide web for telecommunications equipment. *IEEE Transactions on Education, 39,* 342–348. doi:10.1109/13.538757

Sharples, M. (2005, April). *Learning as conversation: Transforming education in the mobile age.* Paper presented at Conference on Seeing, Understanding, Learning in the Mobile Age. Budapest, Hungary. Retrieved Aug. 20, 2006 from http://www.eee.bham.ac.uk/sharplem/Papers/Theory%20of%20learning%20Budapest.pdf.

Sharples, M., Taylor, J., & Vavoula, G. (2005). A Theory of Learning for the Mobile Age. In R. Andrews (Ed.), *The Handbook of Elearning Research.* London. Retrieved Aug. 20, 2006 from http://www.nottingham.ac.uk/lsri/msh/Papers/Theory%20of%20Mobile%20Learning.pdf.

Shen, B., Lee, S. J., & Basu, S. (2003). Performance Evaluation of Transcoding-Enabled Streaming Media Caching System. In Proceedings of MDM conference.

Shih, T. K., Lin, N. H., & Chang, H. P. (2003). An Intelligent E-Learning System with Authoring and Assessment Mechanism. *Proceeding of the17th International Conference on Advanced Information Networking and Applications* (pp.782-787).

Shilane, P., & Min, P. Kazhdan, & M., Funkhouser, T. (2004). The Princeton Shape Benchmark. Proc. Int'l Conf. on Shape Modeling and Applications.

Shimizu, Y. (2002). e-Learning wo Sasaeru Seisaku to Kongo no Tembo [Polices to Support e-Learning and Foresight Thereof] [in J apanese]. *Information Processing, 43,* 421–426.

Shimizu, Y. (2004). Koto-Kyoiku ni okeru e-Learning no Shien to Kyoiku Kontentsu no Kyoyu [Support by e-Learning in Higher Education and Sharing of Educational Contents]. *Media research* 1, 1-10. (in Japanese)

Shladover, S. E. (1992). The California PATH Program of IVHS Research and Its Approach to Vehicle-Highway Automation. In Proceedings of the ACM Symposium on IV.

Shor, M. H. (2000). Remote-access engineering educational laboratories: Who, what, when, where, why and how? *Proceedings of the 2000 American Control Conference (ACC)* (vol. 4, pp. 2949-2950). Chicago, Illinois: American Automatic Control Council.

Shuqun, Y., Shuliang, D., & Qiulin, D. (2010). The Incremental Augment Algorithm of *Qr* matrix. *Transactions of Nanjing University of Aeronautics and Astronautics, 27*(2), 183–189.

Silva, L. M., Soares, G., Martins, P., Batista, V., & Santos, L. (2000). Comparing the Performance of Mobile Agent System: A Study of Benchmarking. *Computer Communications, 23*(8), 769–778. doi:10.1016/S0140-3664(99)00237-6

Simon, B. Dolog., P., Miklós, Z., Olmedilla, D. and Sintek, M. (2004). Conceptualising Smart Spaces for Learning. *Journal of Interactive Media in Education.* 2004(9), from http://www-jime.open.ac.uk/2004/9

Smith, S., & Woody, P. (2000). Interactive Effect of Multimedia Instruction and Learning Styles. *Teaching of Psychology, 27*(3), 220–223. doi:10.1207/S15328023TOP2703_10

Sousa, D. A. (2001). *How the brain learns* (2nd ed.). Thousand Oaks, CA: Sage.

Sparapani, E. F. (1998). Encouraging thinking in high school and middle school: Constraints and possibilities. *Clearing House (Menasha, Wis.), 71*(5), 274–276. doi:10.1080/00098659809602722

Specht, M., & Oppermann, R. (1998). ACE - adaptive courseware environment. *New Review of Hypermedia and Multimedia, 4,* 141–161. doi:10.1080/13614569808914699

Specht, M., & Kobsa, A. (1999). *Interaction of domain expertise and interface design in adaptive educational hypermedia.* Paper presented at the Proceedings of Second Workshop on Adaptive Systems and User Modeling on the World Wide Web.

Sperling, J. (2000). *Rebel with a Cause: The Entrepreneur Who Created the University of Phoenix and the For-Profit Revolution in Higher Education.* New York: John Wiley & Sons.

Sperry, R. W. (1975). Left brain-right brain. *Saturday Review,* 30–33.

Springer, S. P., & Deutsch, G. (1998). *Left brain, right brain: Perspectives from cognitive neuroscience* (5th ed.). New York: W. H. Freeman.

Sreenivasan, R., Levine, W. S., & Rubloff, G. W. (2000). Some dynamic-simulator-based control education modules. *Proceedings of the 2000 American Control Conference (ACC)* (vol. 5, pp. 3458-3462). Chicago, Illinois: American Automatic Control Council.

Stage, C. (1999). A Comparison Between Item Analysis Based on Item Response Theory and Classical Test Theory. A *Study of the SweSAT Subtest READ*. Available at http://www. umu. se/ edmeas/ publikationer/ pdf/ enr3098sec.pdf.

Sternberg, R. J., & Zhang, L. F. (2001). Perspectives on Thinking, Learning, and Cognitive Styles. *The Educational Psychology Series*, 276.

Stevens, J. (2002). *Applied multivariate statistics for the social sciences*. Mahwah, NJ: Lawrence Erlbaum Associates.

Stronge, J. H. (2002). *Qualities of effective teachers*. Alexandria, VA: Association for Supervision and Curriculum Development.

Struts (2008), The Apache Struts Web Application Framework, http://struts.apache.org

Su, L. H. (2003). *The Wireless Technology into the Outdoor Activities of Bird Watching for Observation and Reflection in the Mobile Learning Situation-the Team of Experts to Adapt to Try and to Become Mature in the Using Up-to-date Wireless Technology*. Unpublished Master's Thesis, Taipei Municipal University of Education.

Sudmann, N. P., & Johansen, D. (2001). Supporting Mobile Agent Applications Using Wrappers. In *Proceedings of the 12nd International Workshop on Database and Expert Systems Applications* (pp. 689-695), Munich, Germany.

Sun, K. T. (2000). An Effective Item Selection Method for Educational Measurement. *Proceedings of the International Workshop on Advanced Learning Technologies* (pp. 105—106).

Sundar, H., Silver, D., Gagvani, N., & Dickinson, S. (2003). Skeleton Based Shape Matching and Retrieval. Proc. Int'l Conf. on Shape Modeling and Applications.

Suwu, W., & Das, A. (2001). An Agent System Architecture for E-commerce. In *Proceedings of the 12nd International Workshop on Database and Expert Systems Applications* (pp. 715-726), Munich, Germany.

Sweller, J. (2003). Evolution of human cognitive architecture. *Psychology of Learning and Motivation, 43*, 215–266. doi:10.1016/S0079-7421(03)01015-6

Sweller, J., Mawer, R., & Ward, M. (1983). Development of expertise in mathematical problem solving. *Journal of Experimental Psychology. General, 112*, 639–661. doi:10.1037/0096-3445.112.4.639

Sweller, J., van Merriënboer, J. J. G., & Paas, F. (1998). Cognitive architecture and instructional design. *Educational Psychology Review, 10*(3), 251–285. doi:10.1023/A:1022193728205

Taiwan Ministry of Education. (2008). *Decade analysis report for educational development.* Retrieve August 20, 2008, from ttp://140.111.34.54/statistics/content. aspx?site_content_sn=8169

Tal, A., & Zuckerberger, E. (2004). Mesh Retrieval by Components. Technical Report, Faculty of Electrical Engineering, Technion, CCIT–475.

Tam, G., & Lau, R. (2007)... *Deformable Model Retrieval Based on Topological and Geometric Signatures, IEEE Trans. on Visualization and Computer Graphics, 13*(3), 470–482.

Tangelder, J., & Veltkamp, R. (2003). Polyhedral Model Retrieval Using Weighted Point Sets. Proc. Int'l Conf. on Shape Modeling and Applications, 119–129.

Tarpin-Bernard, F., & Habieb-Mammar, H. (2005). Modeling elementary cognitive abilities for adaptive hypermedia presentation. *User Modeling and User-Adapted Interaction, 15*(5), 459–495. doi:10.1007/s11257-005-2529-3

Tate Modern and Antenna Audio Ltd. Tate Modern multimedia tour pilots 2002-2003. Retrieved Aug. 20, 2006 from http://www.tate.org.uk/modern/multimediatour/ phase1_keyfindings.pdf.

Tatsuoka, K. K. (1983). Rule Space: An approach for dealing with misconceptions based on item response theory. *Journal of Educational Measurement, 20*(4), 345–354. doi:10.1111/j.1745-3984.1983.tb00212.x

Tatsuoka, K. K. (1991). *Boolean algebra applied to determination of universal set of knowledge states. RR-91-44-ONR* [R]. Princeton, NJ: ETS.

Tatsuoka, K. K., & Tatsuoka, M. M. (1997). Computerized cognitive diagnostic adaptive testing: effect on remedial instruction as empirical validation. *Journal of Educational Measurement, 34*(1), 3–20. doi:10.1111/j.1745-3984.1997.tb00504.x

Tatsuoka, K. K. (1995). Architecture of knowledge structure and cognitive diagnosis: A statistical pattern recognition and classification approach. In Nichols, P. D., Chipman, S. F., & Brennan, R. L. (Eds.), *Cognitively Diagnostic Assessment* (pp. 327–361). Hillsdale, NJ: Lawrence Erlbaum Associates.

Tessmer, M. (1993). *Planning and Conducting Formative Evaluations: Improving the Quality of Education and Training*. London: Kogan Page.

Thomas, R., Gilbert, H., & Mazziotto, G. (1988, September). Influence of the movement of mobile station on the performance of the radio cellular network. In Proc. of 3rdNordic Seminar, Copenhagen.

Thornton, P., & Houser, C. (2004). Using mobile phones in English education in Japan. *Journal of Computer Assisted Learning*, *21*, 217–228. doi:10.1111/j.1365-2729.2005.00129.x

Todman, J., & Day, K. (2006). Computer anxiety: the role of psychological gender. *Computers in Human Behavior*, *22*(5), 856–869. doi:10.1016/j.chb.2004.03.009

Triantafillou, E., Pomportsis, A., Demetriadis, S., & Georgiadou, E. (2004). The value of adaptivity based on cognitive style: An empirical study. *British Journal of Educational Technology*, *35*(1), 95–106. doi:10.1111/j.1467-8535.2004.00371.x

Tsai, I. H. (2004). *A Study of the Development of Courseware for Mobile Learning and Students' Learning Effectiveness in Primary Education: Using Wetland Crabs as an Example*. Unpublished Master's Thesis, National Tsing Hua University.

Tsai, P. J., Hwang, G. J., & Tseng, J. C. R. (July, 2004). *I-Designer: a Computer-Assisted System for Conducting Information Technology Applied Instructions.* Paper presented at The Eighth Pacific-Asia Conference on Information Systems (PACIS 2004), Shanghai, China.

Tsai, T. C., & Li, C. L. (2006, October). Reducing Calibration Effort for WLAN Location System using Segment Technique with Autocorrelation. *IEEE First International Conference on Communications and Networking in China (Chinacom2006)*, Beijing, China.

Tsinakos, A., & Margaritis, K. G. (2001). See Yourself IMprove (SYIM) Implementing an educational environment for the provision of personalized distance education services and the formulation of student models. *Proc. World Conf. of the Web Society (WebNet 2001)*.

Turk, D., Brine, J., & Kanev, K. (2006). *Social Reading Activities Using Print-Based Digital Content Interfaces*. In Proc. of the 2nd IASTED International Conference on Education and Technology (ICET'06), pp. 51-55.

Turner, S. G. (1998). *A Case Study Using Scenario-Based Design Tools and Techniques in the Formative Evaluation Stage of Instructional Design: Prototype Evaluation and Redesign of a Web-Enhanced Course Interface*. Doctoral dissertation, Virginia Polytechnic Institute and State University, Virginia

Tzeng, H. W., & Tien, C. M. (2000). Design of a Virtual Laboratory for Teaching Electric Machinery. In [), Nashville, TN, USA.]. *Proceedings of the IEEE International Conference on Systems, Man, and Cybernetics*, *2*, 971–976.

U.S. House of Representatives. (2001). *Text of No Child Left Behind Act*. Cheng, Y., & Cheng, H. (2007). *The modified maximum global discrimination index method for cognitive diagnostic CAT*. In D. Weiss (Ed.), Proceedings of the 2007 GMAC Computerized Adaptive Testing Conference. Cheng, Y. (2008). *Computerized Adaptive Testing-New Developments and Applications*. Unpublished doctoral thesis, University of Illinois at Urbana-Champaign.

Ueno, M. (2004). Kompakuto na e-Learning Keiei [Small Scaled e-Learning Management]. *Articles Compiled for the 29th National Conference of the Japanese Society for Information and Systems in Education*, 125-126. (in Japanese)

USjournal.com. LLC. The advantages of distance learning. *US Journal of Academics*. Retrieved Aug. 20, 2006 from http://www.usjournal.com/en/students/help/distancelearning.html.

Valentine, D. (2002). Distance Learning: Promises, Problems, and Possibilities. *Online Journal of Distance Learning Administration, 5(3)*. Retrieved Aug. 20, 2006 from http://www.westga.edu/~distance/ojdla/fall53/valentine53.html.

Van Gerven, P. W. M., Paas, F., van Merriënboer, J. J. G., & Schmidt, H. G. (2004). Memory load and the cognitive papillary response in aging. *Psychophysiology, 41*, 167–174. doi:10.1111/j.1469-8986.2003.00148.x

Van Merriënboer, J. J. G., & Sweller, J. (2005). Cognitive load theory and complex learning: recent developments and future directions. *Educational Psychology Review, 17*(2), 147–177. doi:10.1007/s10648-005-3951-0

Vargas, L. G. (1990). An overview of the analytic hierarchy process and its application. *European Journal of Operational Research, 48*(1), 2–8. doi:10.1016/0377-2217(90)90056-H

Vaughn, V. F. (1991). *A comparison of the 4MAT system of instruction with two enrichment units based on Bloom's taxonomy with gifted third-grader in a pull-out program.* Unpublished doctoral dissertation, Purdue University, Columbia.

Venkatesh, V., & Davis, F. D. (2000). A theoretical extension of the technology acceptance model: four longitudinal studies. *Management Science, 46*(2), 186–204. doi:10.1287/mnsc.46.2.186.11926

Vranic, D., & Saupe, D. (2001). 3D Shape Descriptor Based on 3D Fourier Transform. Proc. ECMCS, 271–274.

Wagner, E. D., & Wilson, P. (2005, December). Disconnected: Why learning professionals need to care about mobile learning. *T+D. American Society for Training and Development* (pp. 40–43).

Wang, H. F., Sheu, L. D., & Chen, M. C. (2008). An empirical study of college student's learning in accounting knowledge: The application of teaching model for conceptual change. *Journal of Education Studies, 42*(1), 79–96.

Wang, T. H. (2007). What strategies are effective for formative assessment in an e-learning environment? *Journal of Computer Assisted Learning, 23*, 171–186. doi:10.1111/j.1365-2729.2006.00211.x

Wang, B., Sen, S., Adler, M., & Towsley, D. (2002). Optimal Proxy Cache Allocation for Efficient Streaming Media Distribution. In Proceedings of INFOCOM conference.

Wang, W., Hao, T., & Liu, W. (2007). Automatic Question Generation for Learning Generation in Medicine. *Proceedings of 6th International Conference on Web-Based Learning* (pp. 198-203).

Wang, Y. (2002). Dispatching Multiple Mobile Agents in Parallel for Visiting E-shops. In *Proceedings of the 3rd International Conference on Mobile Data Management* (pp. 61-68), Amsterdam, The Netherlands.

Wang, Z. J., Kumar, M., Das, S. K., & Shen, H. P. (2003). Investigation of Cache Maintenance Strategies for Multicell Environments. In Proceedings of MDM conference.

Watson, J., Ahmed, P. K., & Hardaker, G. (2007). Creating domain independent adaptive e-learning systems using the sharable content object reference model. *Campus-Wide Information Systems, 24*(1), 45–71. doi:10.1108/10650740710726482

WebCT. (2007). http://www.webct.com/.

Weber, P., & Weber, F. (1990). Using 4MAT to improve student presentations. *Educational Leadership, 48*(2), 41–46.

Weber, G. (1999). Adaptive learning systems in the World Wide Web. *Proc. Seventh Int'l Con. User Modeling* (pp. 371-377).

Wilkerson, R. M., & White, K. P. (1988). Effects of the 4MAT system of instruction on students' achievement, retention, and attitudes. *The Elementary School Journal, 88*(4), 357–368. doi:10.1086/461544

Will, W. M., Andersson, R., & Streith, K. O. (2005). Examining user acceptance of computer technology: an empirical study of student teachers. *Journal of Computer Assisted Learning, 21*(6), 387–395. doi:10.1111/j.1365-2729.2005.00145.x

William, D., & Black, P. (1996). Meanings and consequences: a basis for distinguishing formative and summative functions of assessment? *British Educational Research Journal, 22*, 537–548. doi:10.1080/0141192960220502

Williams, S. M., & Kline, D. B. (1994). An object-oriented graphical approach for teaching electric machinery analysis. *IEEE Transactions on Power Systems, 9*(2), 585–588. doi:10.1109/59.317686

Winters, T., & Payne, T. (2005). What Do Students Know? An Outcomes Based Assessment System. *Proceedings of the 2005 international workshop on Computing education research* (pp. 165-172).

Witkin, H. A., Moore, C. A., Goodenough, D. R., & Cox, P. W. (1977). Field-dependent and field-independent cognitive styles and their educational implications. *Review of Educational Research*, *47*(1), 1–64.

Wittrock, M. C. (1990). Generative teaching of comprehension. *The Elementary School Journal*, *92*, 345–376.

Wolf, C. (2003). *iWeaver: Towards 'Learning Style'-based e-Learning in Computer Science Education*. Paper presented at the Proceedings of the Fifth Australasian Computing Education Conference on Computing Education 2003.

Wood, S. L. (1996). A new approach to interactive tutorial software for engineering education. *IEEE Transactions on Education*, *39*(3), 399–408. doi:10.1109/13.538765

Woodford, K., & Bancroft, P. (2005). Multiple Choice Items Not Considered Harmful. *Proceedings of 7th Australian Conference on Computing Education* (pp. 109—116).

World Wide Web Consortium. W3C (2001). *WSDL: Web services Description Language (WSDL) 1.1*, from http://www.w3.org/TR/2001/NOTE-wsdl-20010315

World Wide Web Consortium. W3C (2003a). *Simple Object Access Protocol (SOAP)*, Version 1.2 Part 0: Primer, from http://www.w3.org/TR/soap12-part0/

World Wide Web Consortium. W3C (2003b). *Universal Description, Discovery and Integration: UDDI Spec Technical Committee Specification v. 3.0*, from http://uddi.org/pubs/uddi-v3.0.1-20031014.htm

WSMO Working Group. (2004). D2v1.0: Web service Modeling Ontology (WSMO). WSMO Working Draft, from http://www.wsmo.org/2004/d2/v1.0/

Wu, K. L., Yu, P. S., & Wolf, J. L. (2001). Segment-Based Proxy Caching of Multimedia Streams. In Proceedings of WWW conference.

Wu, W.-H. (2006). *Applications of Learning Cycle Based Mobile Learning to Enhance Primary School Students' Learning about Aquatics*. Unpublished Master's Thesis, Taipei Municipal University of Education.

Xuemin, S., Mark, J. W., & Jun, Y. (2000). User mobility profile prediction: An adaptive fuzzy inference approach. *Wireless Networks*, *6*, 363–374. doi:10.1023/A:1019166304306

Yang, S., Ding, S., Cai, S., & Ding, Q. (2008). An Algorithm of Constructing Concept Lattices for CAT with Cognitive Diagnosis. *Knowledge-Based Systems*, *21*(8), 852–855. doi:10.1016/j.knosys.2008.03.056

Yang, M. (2001). *The investigation of current accounting education in commercial senior high schools and the fundamental competence cultivation of graduates from commercial senior high schools*. Unpublished master's thesis, National Changhua University of Education, Changhua, Taiwan.

Yoshida, A. (2002). Koto-Kyoiku ni okeru e-Learning - Virtual University no Tojyo [e-Learning in Higher Education - the Advent of Virtual Reality] [in Japanese]. *Information Processing*, *43*, 407–413.

Yu, J. (2001). The analysis on different cognitive trait items with Item Response Theory. *Journal of Nanjing Normal University (. Social Sciences*, *1*, 99–103.

Yu, C. H. (2005). A Simple Guide to the Item Response Theory (IRT) http://seamonkey.ed.asu.edu/~alex/computer/sas/IRT.pdf

Yu, C. H., & Wong, J. W. (2003). Using SAS for classical item analysis and option analysis. *Proceedings of 2003 Western Users of SAS Software Conference*. http://www.lexjansen.com/wuss/2003/DataAnalysis/c-using_sas_for_classical_item_analysis.pdf

Yu, M. N. (2002). *Educational Assessment and Evaluation* (2nd ed.). Taiwan: The Profile of Psychological Publishing Co., Ltd.

Yu, M., Atmosukarto, I., Leow, W., Huang, Z., & Xu, R. (2003). 3D Model Retrieval with Morphing-based Geometric and Topological Feature Maps. Proc. IEEE CVPR.

Zadeh, L. A. (1977). *Fuzzy Sets and Their Applications to Pattern Classification and Clustering*. River Edge, NJ, USA: World Scientific Publishing Co. Inc.

Zhang, B., & Zhang, L. (1992). *Theory and Applications of Problem Solving*. North-Holland.

Zhao, H., & Kanda, K. (2000). Translation and validation of the standard Chinese version of the EORTC QLQ-C30. *Quality of Life Research*, *9*, 129–137. doi:10.1023/A:1008981520920

Zhou, G., Wang, J. T. L., & Ng, P. A. (1996). Curriculum knowledge representation and manipulation in knowledge-based tutoring systems. *IEEE Transactions on Knowledge and Data Engineering, 8*(5), 679–689. doi:10.1109/69.542023

Zhou, J., Li, Q., Xu, D., Chen, Y., & Xiao, T. (2005). Fuzzy Rule-based Integrated System Multi-indicators Economic Performance Evaluation and Decision Making Support Framework. *Proceedings of International Conference on Computational Intelligence for Modelling, Control and Automation/ International Conference on Intelligent Agents, Web Technologies and Internet Commerce* (pp. 714-720).

About the Contributors

Qun Jin is a professor of networked information systems in the Department of Human Informatics and Cognitive Sciences, Faculty of Human Sciences, Waseda University (Japan). He has been engaged extensively in research works on computer science, information systems, and social and human informatics. His recent research interests include e-learning, human-computer interaction, human-centric ubiquitous services computing, information retrieval and recommendation, and computing for well-being. He seeks to exploit the rich interdependence between theory and practice in his works with interdisciplinary and integrated approaches. For additional information about Dr. Jin visit www.f.waseda.jp/jin/.

* * *

Sotirios Botsios was born in 1981. BSc and Master. Aristotle University of Thessaloniki (AUTh), Greece. Polytechnics School, Chemical Engineering Department. PhD cand. Democritus University of Thrace (DUTh), Polytechnics School, Computer and Electrical Engineering Department. Professor Assistant as PhD cand (2007-2008) on Statistics and Differential Equations. In his first steps of his academic career he participated with full and short papers in international scientific conferences and published articles in Chemical Engineering and E-Learning scientific journals. Research interests: 1. Adaptive Hypermedia, 2. Standards of Learning Objects Metadata, 3. Adaptive retrieval of Learning Objects, 4. Learning Style diagnosis, 5. virtual-co-learner agents.

Te-Jeng Chang is currently a Ph.D. candidate in the Department of Industry Education at the National Taiwan Normal University (NTNU) in Taiwan. His research interests include dynamic assessment technology, cognitive load, learning diagnostic techniques, adaptive e-learning, organizational learning and innovation. He received the Master of Science degree in mechanical engineering from the University of Michigan, USA. Since 1990, he has been worked in mechanical manufacturing industry more than 18 years. Prior to entering NTNU as a Ph.D. student, he has been the executive operation officer for several global enterprises. The practical experiences in both applying e-learning for human resources training and constructing organizational learning environment and system enlighten him on attending Ph.D. program in industry education and devoting effort in related researching. His recent researches were focus on dynamic quantitative assessment techniques, learning progressive diagnosis, and intrinsic motivation in innovation.

Wen-Chih Chang received the B.S.B., M.S., and Ph.D. degrees from the Department of Computer Science and Information Engineering of Tamkang University in 1999, 2001 and 2005. From 2001 to 2005, he focused on SCORM and e-learning at MINELAB. His research interests include mobile agent, distance learning, cooperative learning, petri net, web technology and e-learning specifications (ADL SCORM, IMS SS and IMS QTI). He is an assistant professor in Department of Information Management, Taiwan.

Louis R. Chao received B.S. and M.S. degrees from National Taiwan University, Taiwan in 1965 and 1968, respectively, and the Ph.D. degree from Duke University, U.S.A., in 1971, all in electrical engineering. Since 1972, he had served as Head of Computer Science, Dean of Engineering, Vice President, President, and Chair Professor of Tamkang University, Taiwan. He is also the founding member of e-Learning Society of Taiwan and the International Journal of Information and Management Sciences. His interests include system science, computer-aided learning and digital communication systems.

Pei-Chun Che received her BA in English from National Chengchi University, Taiwan, MA in Linguistics from Indiana University, Bloomington, U.S.A., and Ph.D. in Rhetoric & Linguistics from Indiana University of Pennsylvania, U.S.A. She served as the Executive Secretary of Committee of Research and International Cooperation, the Director of Language Center, President's Special Assistant of National Chengchi Unviersity. Currently, she is an associate professor in Language Center, National Chengchi University, the Chair of Department of Applied English, Kainan University, the Editor in Chief of Taoyuan Journal of Applied English, and has been on the IADIS Mobile Learning international conference committee since 2006. Dr. Che's research areas include curriculum design, cross-cultural communication, ESP/EAP, and mobile learning.

Sheng-Chang Chen was born in 1979. He received the B.S. and M.S. degrees in information engineering from Feng Chia University, Taiwan, in 2001 and 2002, respectively. He is currently a candidate for the Ph.D. degree in the Department of Information Engineering and Computer Science, Feng Chia University, Taiwan. His research interests include mobile computing, ad-hoc wireless networks, and fault tolerance techniques.

Huey-Wen Chou is currently a professor of the Department of Information Management at National Central University in Taiwan. Her articles can be found in such professional journals as Computers & Education, Computers in Human Behavior, International Journal of Information Management among others.

Chien-Chih Chou is a Principal Engineer in Advanced Control & Systems Inc., Taiwan. He received his B.S. degree in Electrical Engineering from National Chinyi Institute of Technology, and a M.S. degree in Information Management from Chung Yuan Christian University. His current research interests include process control, software engineering, and grid Computing.

Hui-Chun Chu is a PhD candidate of the Department of Information and Learning Technology at National University of Tainan in Taiwan, Republic of China. She received her Master degree in Information Management Department from National Chi-Nan University, Taiwan. Her research interests include e-learning, information technology-applied instructions, Computer-assisted diagnosis of learning problems and knowledge engineering.

Gennaro Costagliola received the laurea degree in computer science from the Università degli Studi di Salerno, Fisciano, Italy, in 1987. Following four years postgraduate studies, starting in 1999, at the University of Pittsburgh, he joined the Faculty of Science, Università degli Studi di Salerno, where in 2001, he reached the position of professor of computer science in the Dipartimento di Matematica ed Informatica. His research interests include Web systems and e-learning and the theory, implementation, and applications of visual languages. He is a member of the IEEE, the IEEE Computer Society, and the ACM.

Stefan Dietze has studied Business Information Systems at the University of Cooperative Education, Heidenheim (Germany) and received his Diploma Degree as well as a BA (hons) in 2001. Afterwards he did a Dr. rer. nat. (PhD) in Computer Science at the Potsdam University, what was finished in 2004. Whereas studying, he already worked for several IT service providers and took a fulltime position as research associate at the Fraunhofer Institute for Software and Systems Engineering (Berlin, Germany) while doing his PhD research from 2001 till 2004. Currently he is a research fellow at the Knowledge Media Institute of the Open University (Milton Keynes, UK) in the area of Semantic Web Services.

Shuliang Ding is professor of computer science and technology and a member of the Centre of Statistical Measurement for Education and Psychology at the Jiangxi Normal University. His major is mathematical statistics. His specialization is Item Response Theory and its applications, in particular the test equating, test construction, parameter estimation and computerized adaptive testing. Professor Ding's current research is focused on cognitive diagnosis, including Q matrix theory, construction test for cognitive diagnosis, development of the new methods for cognitive diagnosis, and combination of computerized adaptive testing with cognitive diagnosis. He is a member of National Council on Measurement in Education of China. His research is funded by the National Natural Science foundation of China.

John Domingue is the Deputy Director of the Knowledge Media Institute at The Open University, UK. He has published over 100 refereed articles in the areas of Semantic Web Services, Semantic Web, Ontologies and Human Computer Interaction. Up until last year he was the Scientific Director of DIP an EU Integrated Project (IP) on Semantic Web Services which involved 17 partners and had a budget of 16M Euros. Also last year he chaired the European Semantic Web Conference. Currently he is the Scientific Director of SUPER, another EU IP which unites Semantic Web Services and Business Process Modeling. Dr Domingue also currently sits on the Steering Committee for the European Semantic Conference Series, is a co-Chair of the WSMO working group and a co-Chair of the OASIS Semantic Execution Environment Technical committee.

Chyi-Ren Dow was born in 1962. He received the B.S. and M.S. degrees in information engineering from National Chiao Tung University, Taiwan, in 1984 and 1988, respectively, and the M.S. and Ph.D. degrees in computer science from the University of Pittsburgh, USA, in 1992 and 1994, respectively. Currently, he is a Professor in the Department of Information Engineering and Computer Science, Feng

Chia University, Taiwan. His research interests include mobile computing, ad-hoc wireless networks, agent techniques, fault tolerance, and learning technology.

Vittorio Fuccella received the laurea (cum laude) and PhD degrees in computer science from the University of Salerno, Fisciano, Italy, in 2003 and 2007, respectively. He is currently a research fellow in computer science in the Dipartimento di Matematica ed Informatica, Universita` degli Studi di Salerno. He won the Best Paper Award at ICWL '07. His research interests include Web engineering, Web technologies, data mining, and e-learning.

K. Gierłowski Received his M.Sc. degree in electronics and telecommunications from the Faculty of Electronics, Gdańsk University of Technology (GUT), Poland, in 2002. The faculty is also his current place of employ as a researcher and instructor. He is author or co-author of more than 30 scientific papers and designer of many production-grade network systems. He has received best paper award for article "Analysis of Network Infrastructure and QoS Requirements for Modern Remote Learning Systems" (XVth International Conference on Systems Science, 2004). His scientific and research interests include e-learning systems, wireless local and metropolitan area networks, complex wireless network architectures, network/application security and distributed computing.

Dimitrios Georgiou was born in 1948. BSc. AUTh Mathematics Department, PhD. DUTh Postdoc, UCBerceley. Visiting Scholar at UC, Davis (1980-1982). Visiting Professor URI (1989-92). Associate Professor, School of Engineering DUTh since 1991. Instructor of several undergraduate and postgraduate courses he also teaches vocational courses to Hellenic Power Corporation, Center for Productivity and Development, Training School for High School Teachers, Hellenic Air Force e.a. He published six text books. Research interests: 1) Qualitative behaviour of solutions of ODE, Difference Equations, and PDEs, 4) Numerical Methods for Boundary Value Problems, 5) Intelligent Tutoring Systems. 6) Computer Networks. Research Papers published in Several Scientific Journals and conference. Member of IEEE Computer Society, AACE, AMS, ECMI e.a. Referee for the Journal of Mathematical Analysis and its Applications and other journals in mathematics and educational technology.

Alessio Gugliotta has studied Computer Science at the University of Udine (Italy) and received his Master's Degree in March 2002, cum laude, followed by a Ph.D. in Computer Science at the University of Udine, in March 2006. Since January 2006, he has a position of Research Fellow in the topic of Semantic Web Services at the Knowledge Media Institute of the Open University (Milton Keynes, UK). His current research is focused on Service Oriented Computing, Knowledge Representation and Semantic Web Services, and their application within multiple domains such as e-Government and e-Learning.

Aiguo He received the M.E. and Ph.D degrees from Nagoya University, Japan in 1985 and 1988, respectively. Now he is an assistant professor at the Department of Computer Software, University of Aizu, Japan. He currently is working on distant education, computer science education, software engineering, computer vision, software visulization and computer network. He is a member of IEEE, IEICE, IEEJ and IPSJ.

Jung-Lung Hsu is currently a doctoral candidate of the Department of Information Management at National Central University in Taiwan. His research interests include e-learning, cyber psychology, behavior science in information technology, and virtual group dynamics. His articles have published in such professional journals as Computers & Education, Journal of Educational Technology and Society, Journal of Educational Computing Research among others.

Fu-Wei Hsu received the B. S. and M. S. degrees in information engineering and computer science from Feng Chia University, Taiwan, in 1998 and 2003, respectively. His research interests include personal communications, mobile computing, learning technologies, and network agents. He is currently a software engineer on 2G/3G mobile phone solution in Sunplus mMobile Inc.

Jason C. Hung is an Assistant Professor of Department of Information Technology, the Overseas Chinese Institute of Technology, Taiwan, R.O.C. His research interests include Multimedia Computing and Networking, Distance Learning, E-Commerce, and Agent Technology. Dr. Hung received his BS and MS degrees in Computer Science and Information Engineering from Tamkang University, in 1996 and 1998, respectively. He also received his Ph.D. in Computer Science and Information Engineering from Tamkang University in 2001. Dr. Hung participated in many international academic activities, including the organization of many international conferences. He is the founder and Workshop chair of International Workshop on Mobile Systems, E-commerce, and Agent Technology. He is also the Associate Editor of the International Journal of Distance Education Technologies, published by Idea Group Publishing, USA.

Gwo-Jen Hwang is currently a professor of the Department of Information and Learning Technology, as well as Dean of the College of Science and Engineering, at National University of Tainan in Taiwan, Republic of China. Dr. Hwang received his PhD degree from the Department of Computer Science and Information Engineering at National Chiao Tung University in Taiwan. His research interests include e-learning, computer-assisted testing, expert systems and mobile computing. Dr. Hwang has published 250 papers, including more than 80 papers in professional journals. Owing to the good reputation in academic research, Dr Hwang has received the 2007 outstanding research award from the National Science Council of Taiwan.

Pi-Shan Hsu is currently an associate professor of human resource development at Ching Kuo Institute of Management and Health in Taiwan. Her research interests include dynamic assessment technology, learning diagnostic techniques, adaptive e-learning, and Creativity. She received Ph.D. in the Department of Industry Education at the National Taiwan Normal University (NTNU) and the Master of Art degree in teacher education from the Eastern Michigan State University, USA. She has been a teacher more than 17 years. Her practical teaching experiences enhance her research work both in profundity and widely broad scope. In the period of her research, she has led several research teams of the national projects from National Science Council which focuses on creativity scales and assessment, mental operation process of technological creativity, innovation, curriculum development for adaptive e-learning and learning diagnostic technique development. She received the best achievement of vocational education from Taiwan government because of her significant contribution in vocational education in past decades.

Howard Leung is currently an Assistant Professor in the Department of Computer Science at City University of Hong Kong. He received the B.Eng. degree in Electrical Engineering from McGill University, Canada, in 1998, the M.Sc. degree and the Ph.D. degree in Electrical and Computer Engineering from Carnegie Mellon University in 1999 and 2003 respectively. Howard's current research projects include 3D Human Motion Analysis, Intelligent Tools for Chinese Handwriting Education, Chinese Calligraphic Image Analysis and Automatic Content Adaptation for PDA Viewing of E-Comics.Howard has also been actively involved in various professional activities. He is currently a member of the Multimedia Systems & Applications Technical Committee (MSATC) which is a subsidiary organization of the IEEE Circuits and Systems (IEEE-CAS) Society. He is also a member of the IEEE Signal Processing Society. He is the Treasurer of the Hong Kong Web Society and the Treasurer of the ACM Hong Kong Chapter.

Qing Li received the BEng from the Hunan University, Changsha, China, and his MSc and PhD degrees from the University of Southern California, Los Angeles, USA, all from Computer Science. He is concurrently a Chair Professor of the Zhejiang Normal University and a Professor at the Dept of Computer Science, City University of Hong Kong. Meanwhile, he is also a Guest Professor of the University of Science and Technology of China (USTC), an Adjunct Professor of the Hunan University (Changsha, China), and a Guest Professor (Software Technology) of the Zhejiang University (Hangzhou, China). Prof. Li's research areas range from data modeling, multimedia indexing and retrieval, workflow and Web services, to data warehousing/mining and e-learning; he has published over 260 papers in these areas on refereed international journals. He is actively involved in the research community by serving as an associate or guest editor for several technical journals, and as an organizer/co-organizer of numerous international conferences.

Cheng-Min Lin was born in 1964. He received the B.S. and M.S. degrees in electronic engineering from National Taiwan University of Science and Technology, Taipei, Taiwan, in 1989 and 1991, respectively, and the Ph.D. degree in Department of Information Engineering and Computer Science, Feng-Chia University, Taichung, Taiwan. Currently, he is an Associate Professor in the Department of Computer and Communication Engineering and Graduate Institute of Electrical Engineering and Computer Science, Nan Kai University of Technology. His research interests include mobile computing, distributed systems, and embedded systems. Dr. Lin is a member of the IEICE and the IEEE Computer Society.

Hung-Chin Jang received his BS in Applied Mathematics from National Chengchi University, Taiwan, in 1984, MS in Mathematics, Statistics, & Computer Science, and Ph.D. in Electrical Engineering & Computer Science from University of Illinois at Chicago, U.S.A., in 1988 and 1992, respectively. He was an associate professor in Applied Mathematics, the Chair of Department of Computer Science, National Chengchi University. Currently, he is an associate professor in Computer Science, and the Chair of Mater Program in Computer Science for Professional Education, the Director of Mobile Computing and Communication Lab., National Chengchi University, His current research interests include WLAN, Vehicular Ad Hoc Network (VANET), WiMAX, mobile communication systems, and mobile learning.

Kamen Kanev received the M.S. degree in mathematics and the Ph.D. degree in computer science, both from Sofia University, Sofia, Bulgaria in 1984 and 1989, respectively. He is a Professor with the Research Institute of Electronics, Graduate School of Informatics, and Graduate School of Science and Technology, Shizuoka University, Hamamatsu, Japan, where he teaches and supervises students majoring in computer and information science. His main research interests are in interactive computer graphics, user interfaces and surface based interactions, and in vision information processing. On this and related topics he has authored and coauthored more than 80 scientific journal and conference papers and patents. Dr. Kanev is a member of the IEEE, the Association of Computing Machinery (ACM), and the Asia-Pacific Society for Computers in Education (APSCE).

Shogo Kato is a lecturer in Department of Communication, Tokyo Woman's Christian University in Japan and a part-time instructor in the Faculty of Economics, Dokkyo University in Japan. He earned a Ph.D. from Tokyo Institute of Technology in 2005. His general research interests include educational technology; the application of behavior science, psychology, and information and communication technology (ICT) to educational scenes. Dr. Kato is particularly interested in the emotional aspects in virtual community, such as net bullying.

Ioannis Kazanidis received his MS degree in computing from the University of Coventry in 2003 and he is a PhD candidate at the Department of Applied Informatics, University of Macedonia. Currently, he is working as lab cooperator at the Technological Institute of Kavala. His research interests include adaptive educational systems, knowledge representation and computer-human interaction. He has published two papers in proceedings of conferences.

Shigeo Kimura received the M.S. and the Ph.D. degrees in Mechanical Engineering, both from University of Colorado, Boulder, Colorado, USA in 1980 and 1983, respectively. He is a Professor with Institute of Nature and Environmental Technology, and the Department of Mechanical Systems Engineering, Kanazawa University, Kanazawa, Japan, where he teaches fluid mechanics and heat transfer. His main research interests are in transport processes due to environmental fluid motions. On this and related topics he has authored and coauthored more than 100 scientific journal and conference papers and patents. Dr. Kimura is a member of the Japan Society of Mechanical Engineers (JSME) and the American Society of Mechanical Engineers (ASME).

Rynson W.H. Lau received a first class honors B.Sc. degree in Computer Systems Engineering from the University of Kent and a Ph.D. degree in Computer Science from the University of Cambridge. He has been on the faculty of University of Durham, City University of Hong Kong, and The Hong Kong Polytechnic University. He is currently with City University of Hong Kong. Rynson Lau serves on the Editorial Board of *Computer Animation and Virtual Worlds*. He has served as the Guest Editor of a number of journal special issues, including *ACM Trans. on Internet Technology, IEEE Trans. on Multimedia, IEEE Trans. on Visualization and Computer Graphics, Presence*, and *IEEE Computer Graphics & Applications*. He has also served in the conference committee of a number of conferences, including Program Co-chair of *ACM VRST 2004, ICAT 2006, ICEC 2007*, and Conference Co-chair of *ACM VRST 2005, CASA 2005, ICWL 2007, IDET 2008*.

Li-Tze Lee is an Assistant Professor in the Department of Accounting Information at the Overseas Chinese Institute of Technology at Taiwan, R.O.C. She received her Ed. D. in Human Resource Training and Development from Idaho State University (ISU) in 2005. Dr. Lee is an active licensed Certified

Public Accountant (CPA) of Idaho State Board of Accountancy. She is also a member of Institute of Internal Auditors (IIA)-Taiwan Chapter since 2007. In 2008, she received a grant from Taiwan Bureau of the Employment and Vocational Training as a principal executive to conduct an accounting and information learning project. Her research interests include accounting education, teaching strategies and corporate governance.

Frederick Li received both a BA (Hons.) degree and an MPhil. degree from The Hong Kong Polytechnic University, and a Ph.D. degree from the City University of Hong Kong. He is currently a Lecturer (Assistant Professor) at the University of Durham. Prior to the current appointment, he taught at The Hong Kong Polytechnic University. Before that, he was the project manger of a Hong Kong Government Innovation and Technology Fund. Frederick also serves as an Associate Editor of International Journal of Distance Education Technologies on Communications Technologies (Distributed and Collaborative Learning). He has served as the Guest Editor of two journal special issues of International Journal of Distance Education Technologies. In addition, he has served in the committee of ACM VRST 2004-2008, CASA 2005, and ICWL 2005, 2007-2008, and as a Program Co-chair of ICWL 2007-2008 and IDET 2008.

Yi-Hsung Li was born in 1979. He received the B. S. and M. S. degrees in information engineering and computer science from Feng Chia University, Taiwan, in 2001 and 2003, respectively. He is currently a candidate for the Ph.D. degree in the Department of Information Engineering and Computer Science, Feng Chia University, Taiwan. His research interests include personal communications, mobile computing, learning technologies, and network agents.

Ching-Jung Liao is an Assistant Professor in Department of Information Management at Chung Yuan Christian University, Taiwan. He received his B.S. and M.S. degrees in Computer Science and Biomedical Engineering from Chung Yuan Christian University, respectively, and a Ph.D. of Information Engineering and Computer Science from Feng Chia University. He has been a guest scientist in the Institute of Informatics of Technical University of Munich, Germany. His current research interests include grid computing, Rich Internet Applications, and E-Learning.

Yao-Nan Lien has been a professor of the Department of Computer Science at the National Chengchi University since 1995. He was the Chairman of the department from 1996 to 1999 and the Dean of the College of Science from 2000-2003. He received his BS from National Cheng Kung University in 1979, and his MS and PhD degrees from Purdue University in 1981 and 1986, all in Electrical Engineering. He was an assistant professor of Computer and Information Science at the Ohio State University from 1986 to 1989 and a Member of Technical Staff at AT&T Bell Laboratories from 1989 to 1993. From 1993 to 1995, he joined the Computer and Communication Research Laboratories, Industrial Technology Research Institute being the Deputy Director of the Computer Software Technology Division. His research interests include mobile computing, communication networks, and database systems. He can be reached via email at lien@cs.nccu.edu.tw.

Han-Yi Lin has worked for Foreign Language Center of National Chengchi University since 1990, serving as the coordinator of Mandarin Studies Program, the coordinator of Teaching and Research Section of Language Center, and as a co-editor of the 2nd National Conference on College English. She received her BA in English from National Chengchi University, Taiwan, and MA in Media Technology for TEFL from University of Newcastle upon Tyne, Newcastle, U.K. Currently, she is an Instructor in Foreign Language Center of National Chengchi University and has been the coordinator of Extension Program of the Center since 2008. Her interests and research areas include materials/curriculum design, self-access learning, ESP/EAP, and CALL (Computer-assisted Language Learning).

Shoji Nishimura is a professor at Waseda University, Tokyo, Japan. His current research interests include educational technology, especially education and the Internet. He received his bachelor's degree in mathmatics from Waseda Univercity and MSc in applied physics from Waseda University. In 1991, he joined the Advance Research Center, INES Corporation as a senior researcher. Then, he joined the School of Human Sciences, Waseda University, as an assistant professor in 1997. Currently, he is a professor in Faculty of Human Sciences, Waseda University. He is a member of Japan Society for Educational Technology, Japanese Society for Information and Systems in Education, and Information Processing Society of Japan.

K. Nowicki received his M.Sc. and Ph.D. degrees in electronics and telecommunications from the Faculty of Electronics, Gdańsk University of Technology (GUT), Poland, in 1979 and 1988, respectively. Ph.D. Krzysztof Nowicki is author or co-author of more than 100 scientific papers and author and co-author of four books, e.g. "LAN, MAN, WAN – Computer Networks and Communication Protocols" (- 1st ed. 1998 - 2nd - ed. 2000), "Wired and Wireless LANs", issued in 2002 (both books were awarded the Ministry of National Education Prize, in 1999 and 2003; respectively), "Protocol IPv6" (2002) and "Ethernet-Networks (2006). His scientific and research interests include network architectures, analysis of communication systems, analysis of e-learning systems.

Maya Satratzemi received the BS degree in math from the Aristotle University of Thessaloniki in 1980, and the PhD degree in informatics -algorithmic graph theory from the University of Macedonia in 1991. She is a professor at the Department of Applied Informatics, University of Macedonia. Her main research interests lie in the area of algorithms, programming languages, algorithmic graph theory, educational software, and didactics of informatics. She has published over than 25 papers in journals and 60 papers in proceedings of conference.

Douglass Scott is a professor at Waseda University, School of Human Sciences, Human Informatics and Cognitive Sciences Department. Dr. Scott's research interests include gender and intercultural differences in the use of communication technologies, especially concerning mobile telephone email. His current research projects include emotional transfer in Japanese young people's text messages and the comparative study of Japanese, Chinese and American young people's use of communication technologies.

Timothy K. Shih is a professor of the Department of Computer Science at National Taipei University of Education, Taiwan. He is a Fellow of the Institution of Engineering and Technology, UK. As a senior member of IEEE and ACM, Dr. Shih joined the Educational Activities Board of the Computer Society. His current research interests include Multimedia Computing and Distance Learning. Dr. Shih is an associate editor of the ACM Transactions on Internet Technology and the IEEE Transactions on Learning Technologies. He was also an associate editor of the IEEE Transactions on Multimedia.

Gary K.L. Tam received a first-class honors B.Eng. degree in Computer Science from the Hong Kong University of Science and Technology in 2002. In the same year, he was selected as one of the 23 Youth Telecom Ambassadors in the Event of "ITU Telecom Asia 2002 Youth Forum" in Hong Kong. In 2004, He received an MPhil degree from City University of Hong Kong. After graduation, he worked as an instructor in the Department of Computer Science of the same university for about two years. He is currently a PhD student at the University of Durham, England. His research mainly focuses on computer graphics and geometry processing.

Pei-Jin Tsai is a Ph.D. student of the Department of Computer Science and Information Engineering at National Chiao Tung University in Taiwan. Her research interests include e-learning and information technology-applied instructions.

Tzu-Chieh Tsai received his BS and MS degrees both in Electrical Engineering from National Taiwan University in 1988, and from University of Southern California in 1991, respectively. He got his PhD degree in Computer Science at UCLA in 1996. During 2005/08~2008/07, he was the Chair of Department of Computer Science at National Chengchi University, Taipei, Taiwan. He is currently an associate professor and is leading a "Mobile Computing and Network Communications Lab". His current research interests include WLAN & QoS, IEEE 802.11e, 802.11s (Wireless Mesh Network), 802.16(WiMAX), Intelligent Transport System, Vehicular Ad hoc Network, Location-Based Service, Mobile Learning, Digital Smart Home, P2P Steaming, and Wireless Sensor Network.

Shuqun Yang is associate professor of computer science and technology at Fujian Normal University. She received the B.S. degree (June, 1991) and M.S. degree (June, 2003) from Jiangxi Normal University in china, and PhD degree (May, 2009) in Nanjing university of Aeronautics and Astronautics in China. Her major is computer application technology. Her specialization is formal concept analysis and item response theory, in particular cognitive diagnosis and computerized adaptive testing. Professor Yang's current research is focused on Q matrix theory, and combination of computerized adaptive testing with cognitive diagnosis. Her research is funded by national natural science foundation of china.

Tzu-Chi Yang is a graduate student of the Department of Information Management at National Chi-Nan University in Taiwan. His research interests include information technology-applied instructions, mobile learning, ubiquitous learning and computer assisted learning.

Jin Tan David Yang is a Professor in Teaching Mandarin as Second language (TMSL) at Ming Chuan University, Taipei Taiwan. He received his B.S. at National Chung Hsiung University in Taiwan and M.S. degrees in Computer Science at State University of New York at Buffalo, USA and a Ph.D. of Computer in Education at University of Oregon in 1993. He was Co-Chair of ICALT 2005 (5th IEEE *International Conference on Advanced Learning Technologies)* held in Kaohsiung, Taiwan. His current research interests include e-Learning and ontological engineering.

Hsuan-Che Yang received B.S., M.S. and Ph.D. degree from Department of Computer Science and Information Engineering (CSIE) at Tamkang University, Taiwan in 1996, 2005 and 2008. He is currently an adjunct assistant professor in the Department of Educational Technology at Tamkang University. His research interests include Distance Learning, Computerize Assessment, Intelligent Tutoring System and ubiquitous computing.

Jianmin Zhao is a PhD supervisor and full Professor of the Zhejiang Normal University where he concurrently serves as the Dean of the College of Mathematics, Physics and Information Engineering. He is the Principal Investigator for numerous research and applied research projects, many of which have been awarded by the Provincial government and State government. His research interests include pattern recognition and image processing, agent-oriented requirements engineering, business intelligence and data mining, sensor networks and e-learning.

Xinzhong Zhu received the BSc from the Beijing University of Science and Technology, and his MSc degree from the National Defense University of Technology, China, both from Computer Science. He is currently an Associate Professor of the Zhejiang Normal University where he joined as a faculty member since 1998. He has served in numerous capacities and actively participated in over 40 (applied) research projects. His research interests include pattern recognition and image processing, business intelligence and data mining, multimedia indexing and management, personalized e-learning and user modeling.

Index

Symbols

3D applications 105
3D databases 105
3D deformable models 105, 108
3D engines 105
3D geometry 104, 105, 106, 107, 112
3D graphics 104
3D modeling tools 105
3D models 104, 106, 107, 108
3D training systems 105
4MAT 261, 262, 265, 268, 269, 279, 280, 281, 282
4MAT teaching model 261, 262, 265, 268, 269

A

ability estimation stage 164
academic achievement 261, 264, 265, 270, 271, 276, 278, 279
academic high schools 265
academic performance 262, 265, 272
access points (APs) 308
Accounting Education Change Commission (AECC) 262, 263
Adaptation Module (AM) 175, 176, 178, 180, 181, 188
Adaptive Educational Hypermedia Systems (AEHS) 173, 174, 176, 177, 179, 181, 186, 187, 188
adaptive e-learning 70, 83
adaptive hypermedia system (AHS) 174, 175, 176
adaptive learning 191, 192, 193, 194, 198, 210, 295

B

Advanced Distributed Learning (ADL) 71, 72, 115, 116, 117, 126, 128, 129, 130, 132, 134, 135, 173, 177, 178, 188
algebraic problems 141, 142
Analytic Hierarchy Process (AHP) 35, 36, 37, 39, 40
animation 104, 105
antecedent conditions 215
applied representations 2
assessment 283, 284, 285, 286, 287, 289, 290, 291, 292, 295, 296, 297, 298
asynchronous support systems 233
Asynchronous Transfer Mode (ATM) 46, 54
attribute hierarchy 151, 153, 154, 155, 157, 158, 159, 160, 161, 163, 165, 166, 168, 169, 170
Attribute Hierarchy Method (AHM) 151, 153, 154, 158
automatic grading mechanisms 46, 55
Average Service Delay (ASD) 91, 92, 100

B

Backbone Traffic Reduction Ratio (BTRR) 92
Based on Rule Space Model (RSM) 151, 153, 154, 169
Best-First (BF) 95
Blackboard 192, 211, 214, 227, 229, 322, 332
Bloom Taxonomy of Educational Objective 283, 285
brain processing preferences 261, 262, 268
Brokered Goals (BG) 123, 124, 127, 128, 129, 130, 131
browsing count 70, 80
browsing time 70, 80